PERSONALITY
Second Edition

Photo by Paula Christensen

ABOUT THE AUTHOR

Christopher Peterson attended the University of Illinois as a National Merit Scholar, graduating with a major in psychology and a minor in mathematics. Then he enrolled in the social/personality graduate program at the University of Colorado, Boulder. He received his Ph.D. in 1976.

His first teaching positions were in New York, first at Kirkland College, which was followed shortly by a position at Hamilton College. Wishing to expand what he knew about psychology, Chris went in 1979 to the University of Pennsylvania for postdoctoral respecialization in clinical psychology and experimental psychopathology.

In 1981, he moved to Virginia Polytechnic Institute to teach, and in 1986 he took a position at the University of Michigan, where he currently is professor of psychology, affiliated with the Clinical Psychology and Personality Graduate Programs.

Chris is an award-winning teacher. One of his courses was recently voted by students as "the outstanding university course" at the University of Michigan.

In addition to *Personality,* he has written an introductory psychology textbook and is in the process of writing an abnormal psychology textbook. With W. A. Scott and D. W. Osgood, he wrote *Cognitive Structure.* With L. M. Bossio, he wrote *Health and Optimism.*

His research interests include personality influences on achievement, depression, and physical well-being. Chris has been on the editorial boards of *Journal of Abnormal Psychology, Journal of Personality and Social Psychology,* and *Psychological Bulletin.* He is a member of the American Psychological Association Media Referral Service.

PERSONALITY
Second Edition

Christopher Peterson
University of Michigan

Harcourt Brace Jovanovich College Publishers

Fort Worth Philadelphia San Diego New York Orlando Austin San Antonio
Toronto Montreal London Sydney Tokyo

To my brother's family: Kathleen, David, Christopher, and Mary Kate.

Acquisitions Editor: Philip Curson
Manuscript Editor: Kay Kaylor
Production Editor: Jennifer Johnson
Text Designer: Cheryl Solheid
Cover Designer: Melinda Huff
Art Editor: Karen DeLeo
Production Managers: Lynne Bush and Alison Howell

Library of Congress Catalog Number: 91-76556

ISBN: 0-15-569600-9

Printed in the United States of America

Copyrights and Acknowledgments and Illustration Credits appear on pages 583–585, which constitute a continuation of the copyright page.

One of the important realizations of this century is that each of us sees the world from a particular perspective. Numerous assumptions, both acknowledged and unacknowledged, filter our observations, shape our conclusions, and direct our activities. Thomas Kuhn introduced the term *paradigm* to describe such perspectives as they exist within the sciences. Kuhn and others persuasively argue that even "objective" observation is theory-laden.

Unlike the physical sciences, where a single perspective dominates at any given time, the social sciences usually have several perspectives flourishing simultaneously. Individual social scientists adopt one of these views and pose their questions accordingly. What constitutes an adequate theory? How should research be conducted? What applications are sensible? Within a particular group of social scientists, answers to these questions are consensual and coherent. Across different groups, we sometimes see indifference, disagreement, or even outright hostility.

Some theorists debate whether the social sciences can be described in terms of overarching paradigms, but I found the possibility so compelling that I used the notion of paradigm to organize the first edition of *Personality*. I continue to do so in the second edition. As I view the field today, the psychology of personality is captured by four major paradigms: the psychodynamic, the humanistic, the trait, and the cognitive-behavioral. Within each are three major concerns: theory, research, and application. Permutations of paradigms and relevant concerns comprise the core chapters of *Personality,* Second Edition.

What makes up the rest of the book? I begin with a three-chapter introduction that addresses matters cutting across the major paradigms: the meaning of personality, the history of personality psychology, and the notion of paradigm itself. Chapters 4 through 13 present the paradigms. Finally, in Chapter 14, I reflect briefly on the field of personality psychology.

How does *Personality,* Second Edition, differ from other textbooks? Two types of personality textbooks exist. The first models itself after the traditional Calvin S. Hall and Gardner Lindzey book, which describes in successive chapters the major personality theorists. The second and more recent type focuses on research topics currently of interest to personality psychologists.

In using paradigms as the means of organization, *Personality,* Second Edition, accomplishes what these other textbooks do not. It allows us to have it both ways: theory and research in the same package. This textbook does not force instructors to choose between a book that stresses theory and a book that stresses research. Theory and research both matter, and once the field of personality psychology is organized in terms of its dominant paradigms, the relationship between them becomes clear.

In contrast to the "theorists" textbooks, *Personality,* Second Edition, clearly demonstrates the coherence of personality psychology. There is a reason Freud and Adler and Jung seem to be saying similar things. It's because they often are! I don't devote separate chapters to theorists who can be sensibly placed within the same paradigm. And in contrast to "research" textbooks, *Personality* better shows the diversity of personality psychology. The field as a whole is not defined by a monolithic view of the scientific method. Researchers within the psychodynamic, humanistic, trait, and cognitive-behavioral paradigms work from drastically different assumptions, which I've tried to make clear.

A further dividend of using paradigms to organize *Personality,* Second Edition, is that I could cover the range of applications that make the field so intriguing. Readers will find not just the standard discussions of how personality pertains to childrearing and psychopathology. They also will find discussions of advertising, cognitive maps, criminality, education, Esalen, health promotion, personnel selection, political polls, psychohistory, surrealism, and television programming, among other topics. I locate none of these discussions in "boxes" because I think they are more than mere tickles. Applications are an integral part of personality psychology, yet most other textbooks find no easy way to describe them. *Personality* does so by integrating applications with theory and research.

How does the second edition differ from the first? Based on suggestions from instructors and students who used the first edition, I made three organizational changes. The first was to start my discussion of the paradigms more quickly. So the beginning chapters have been streamlined. The second change was to discuss the humanistic paradigm in its own right, rather than scattering its topics across the other paradigms. The third change was to recognize that the field of personality psychology has changed in the last few years to such an extent that a cognitive-behavioral paradigm has now coalesced. In the first edition, I talked separately about cognitive theories and learning theories; here the discussion is combined.

I have updated material throughout the entire book. Of the approximately eleven hundred references in *Personality,* four hundred twenty-five are new to this edition. New topics include criticisms of Freud's handling of his seduction hypothesis, object relations, existential theories, phenomenological theories, the human potential movement, circumplex approaches, evolutionary and genetic approaches to personality, the Big Five, social intelligence, and the influence of personality on physical well-being.

I obviously approached the writing of this book as a teacher (this is, after all, a textbook), but I also wore the hats of the clinician, the researcher, and the writer. I tried to strike a balance between the abstract and the concrete. I wanted to be engaging—entertaining as well as enlightening. Some users of the first edition found my sense of humor distracting, so I reined it in a bit in the second edition. But I still believe that playful humor and serious purpose need not trip over one another.

Several people were kind enough to review the first edition and make suggestions about how to proceed with this second edition. I'd like to thank the following:

- David M. Buss, University of Michigan
- Keith Davis, University of South Carolina
- David Funder, University of California, Riverside
- Carolin Keutzer, University of Oregon
- Walter R. Stevens, Professor Emeritus of Psychology, San Diego State University
- J. Kevin Thompson, University of South Florida

I appreciate the time and energy they devoted to their reviews.

The folks at Harcourt Brace Jovanovich were consistently enthusiastic about this project, and I enjoyed working with each of them. My editors included Marcus Boggs, Rick Roehrich, Cynthia Sheridan, Phil Curson, and Eve Howard. Karen DeLeo put together the art package. Cheryl Solheid designed the page layout, and Melinda Huff designed the cover. Lynne Bush and Alison Howell supervised production. Eleanor Garner helped secure permissions. Kay Kaylor and Jennifer Johnson deserve particular thanks for their outstanding work on the manuscript in its various stages, and for their good cheer throughout.

Finally, let me acknowledge my special gratitude to Lisa M. Bossio. "My friend in California" helped me with the second edition the same way she did with the first edition, by working hard and being intelligent, by seeing the trees as well as the forest, and by never settling for anything less than the best we could do. Thanks, Lisa, as usual.

Christopher Peterson

LIST OF CHAPTERS

CONTENTS

PERSONALITY
Second Edition

WHAT IS PERSONALITY?

"She has a good personality."
"He has no personality."
"He doesn't have much personality."
"He has too much personality."
"She is a personality."
"It's just her personality."
"She has her mother's personality."
"He and I have a personality conflict."

These opening quotes are all statements about personality that I have heard people say recently. You've probably heard or said similar things yourself, and you might decide from these statements that *personality* has no simple or single meaning. We understand what each conveys, but we have trouble seeing what is common to all of their meanings. Personality psychologists have the same difficulty, only more so, which brings me to the purpose of this book: to discuss personality and how psychologists attempt to understand it.

THE FAMILY RESEMBLANCE OF PERSONALITY

One way to understand the meaning of a complex concept like personality is to consider all the ways it is used in everyday conversation. The juxtaposition of different uses suggests what the term means. Personality may not have a precise definition, but it can be characterized by the set of attributes that tend to cut across the various ways people make use of the term.

This approach to definition has come to be known as the **family resemblance approach** (Wittgenstein, 1953). The term comes from a once-popular procedure of superimposing photographs of individuals from the same family. Characteristics like a jutting jaw or curly hair possessed by many family members were exaggerated in the composite picture, while other characteristics, possessed by only a few family members, were blurred and lost. The resulting picture was a summary of how the family looked, so to speak, but not an exact facsimile of how any one family member looked. Still, it was usually apparent that two individuals belonged to the same family because they possessed some characteristics in common.

Family resemblance approach: A strategy for defining a concept that identifies the attributes common to many (but not necessarily all) examples of the concept.

Although no two of these family members exactly resemble each other, we can readily see that some characteristics tend to be shared. Different uses of personality evidence a similar family resemblance.

Let's arrive at an understanding of the family resemblance of personality by examining this chapter's opening quotes. What cuts across these particular uses of *personality?*

She has a good personality. Most simply, this statement is a positive evaluation. You like something about this woman, and it is not her looks, her possessions, her connections, or her status. Rather, something about her makes you feel good: her way of acting, her beliefs, style, flair, or character, the "way" she has about her, quirks, kinks, virtues and vices, and what she brings to a situation that someone else does not. You enjoy being with this woman, and would clone her if possible, since others would probably enjoy being with her as well.

He has no personality. Again, this statement is an evaluation, but a negative one. You do not like this guy. You don't dislike him either, unless you happen to be trapped in an elevator or a two-person office with him for forty hours a week. Dislike is an active emotion, and someone with no personality arouses no emotions. This man has nothing that stamps him as different from others: no passion, character, strange hobby, or peculiar ability, and no desire to be anything except there. He neither likes nor dislikes the New York Giants. He can take or leave Chinese food, Spike Lee, and video games. He has no strange but endearing pet, no mismatched socks, no bumper stickers on his car. This man just is—like a piece of furniture.

He doesn't have much personality. Here's an ambivalent evaluation, but it's not too ambivalent, because the additional message tucked between the lines is quite positive: "But he doesn't need much personality; he's got something else going for him." You tend to like this man, not for who he is, but for what accompanies him. Here we see that personality is not everything associated with a person.

He has too much personality. You believe that this person is overbearingly himself, making every situation his own, even if he doesn't pay the rent. This is someone who expands to fill every enclosure, even if it is someone else's wedding, surprise party, or funeral. If he is a vegetarian, then don't eat lunch with him unless you want to feast on spinach salad. If he smokes cigarettes, have the nurse disconnect your oxygen when he visits you in the hospital. And if he doesn't smoke, don't accompany him to Winston-Salem, North Carolina, because he may get the War Between the States started up again. He's a damn Yankee, an ugly American, and a wild and crazy guy. Everyone should have some personality, but they should know when to leave it in the holster.

She is a personality. According to Andy Warhol, in the future everyone will be famous for fifteen minutes. Then it will be someone else's turn. Until such a time, though, some people are celebrities and others are not. *People* magazine and *The National Enquirer* write about celebrities so noncelebrities can read about them. And the most notable type of celebrity is the personality. Roseanne Barr, Donald Trump, Madonna, and Bill Cosby are celebrities who are also personalities, since they are famous in part for being themselves. They are important, not just for what they do but for how they do it. In this sense, a personality is an individual who plays a role in our culture in such a way that the role becomes identified with what the personality brings to the role.

It's just her personality. You are offering an excuse, attempting to explain why a woman did something that was annoying or offensive. Her personality is blamed for the action, and the woman herself is excused, since she doesn't have much control over the sort of person she is. We expect people of a given sort to do those things that people of their sort do. Crude people shock our sensibilities, shy people tiptoe around us, and crazy people defy our understanding. When their actions impinge on us, we may get upset, but we don't take it personally. Their personality may be accorded a role independent of their intentions, and it's only an accident that we happen to be in the path of such a personality. Anyone else in the situation would have been treated the same way.

She has her mother's personality. Many statements about personality point to distinguishing characteristics, what makes each of us different in some way. But personality is also used to make comparisons among people, pointing to commonalities and similarities. For most of us, it is second nature to catalogue how people remind us of others we have known. They may have similar mannerisms. When she laughs, she may shake her hair just like her mother does. And maybe they have similar temperaments. She cries easily over sad movies just like her mother does. The similarity may even be global—the entire personality. If you are a member of a large family, you have played an endless game your entire life with other members of your family:

> Well, you may have Aunt Gloria's pretty blue eyes, but you also have Daddy's stubbornness. I'd rather be me. No blue eyes but also no stubbornness. Plus, I'm glad I have Mommy's way with children and animals. You're just a doofus like Cousin Ichabod.

He and I have a personality conflict. Here, you are explaining why you don't get along with this man. Further, you are also predicting that you two will never get along, unless one of you changes who you are. Personalities are sometimes regarded as inherently incompatible, conflicting with each other regardless of how each person acts. Personality conflicts may erupt over the most trivial instance: how to arrange the office furniture, what television channel to watch, which ingredients should be ordered for the pizza. We believe that certain types of people simply do not mix well, like oil and water, and that bad feelings will ensue for all involved, including bystanders, when these natural enemies come into contact.

Personality Attributes

Personality: Psychological characteristics of the individual that tend to be general, characteristic, enduring, integrated, and functional.

These uses of personality help capture its family resemblance. What pertinent attributes do they suggest? **Personality** is something that is a property of the individual: psychological in nature; general in its manifestation; characteristic of the individual; enduring over time; integrated with itself and with other aspects of the individual; and related to how the individual functions in the world, or fails to function.

Personality As a Property of the Individual

Personality usually refers to something a person has, does, or is; it is attached to a specific person. We do not refer to personality apart from people. When we attribute personality to other entities, like groups, nations, animals, or machines, we imply that these entities are like people, not that people are like them. Personality is also usually brought to a situation and taken away from it. When we speak of personality, we mean a quality that transcends the momentary demands and pressures of a particular time and place.

Personality As Psychological

As we have seen, personality is rarely used to describe the material attributes, possessions, and status of a person. Personality usually refers to the person, to his or her behavior—thoughts, actions, and feelings. Accordingly, personality is the province of the psychologist, not the biologist, economist, or historian.

Personality As General

Not every aspect of a person's psychological makeup is typically classified as personality. Most uses of personality point to general properties of a person—thoughts, actions, and feelings painted with a broad brush. And it usually refers to pervasive properties of an individual, those evident in a variety of domains. Personality is not how you cut your toenails, unless that is also how you cut your fingernails, trim your moustache, mow your lawn, trim your steak, cut your losses, sever your romances, and purge your computer files. In this sense, personality describes the whole person, not just the fine print.

Personality As Characteristic   Personality is frequently used to describe properties of an individual that distinguish him or her from others. When we call someone aggressive or introverted or energetic, we mean that the person is exceedingly so, more than others. In this sense, personality denotes a person's psychological signature or fingerprint. Psychologists sometimes call the study of personality the field of individual differences, meaning the ways people differ from each other.

Personality As Enduring   As we have seen, we use personality to point to lasting properties of the individual. A headache is not considered part of someone's personality, unless it is a chronic migraine. Bad moods, fleeting thoughts, temporary fatigue, or broken arms are also not classed as part of personality. Personality may of course change throughout one's life, and it may even do so suddenly. However, we generally reserve the term for the relatively enduring characteristics of a person; when they do change, we expect them to do so quite gradually or in response to a profound event.

Personality As Integrated   Personality is also frequently used to mean what is unitary about the person. In other words, one's *self* is an excellent example of personality, since most of us regard our self as singular. We acknowledge facets of who we are, and we are vaguely aware of inconsistencies among our thoughts, actions, and feelings. However, we believe that a singular self lurks behind our various facets and integrates the surface inconsistencies. We commonly ask others to explain who they really are, and we often want to reveal to them who we really are. This "who" is the integrated aspect of personality.

Personality As Functional or Dysfunctional   Finally, personality sometimes means the way people get along in the world. Do we survive in good fashion? Then we have a healthy or strong personality. Do we seem destined to join the dodo? Then we have a disordered or weak personality. We frequently use personality characteristics to explain how and why we are happy or sad, successful or failing, fully functional or just getting by. We have to be careful not to treat a description of health as its explanation, that is, to invoke a happy personality to explain happiness, when our only evidence for a happy personality is the observed happiness. Nevertheless, personality is often defined as the source of a person's success or failure at life.

In sum, we can define personality by using a family of pertinent attributes. None of these attributes is necessary or sufficient to call something personality. However, we do expect each instance of personality to possess at least some of these attributes, and we expect some instances to at least somewhat resemble others.

"*Might I point out, sir, that that one goes particularly well with your tie?*"

SOURCE: Drawing by Gahan Wilson; © 1982 The New Yorker Magazine, Inc.

A GOOD EXAMPLE OF PERSONALITY: TRAITS

Are there any particularly good examples of personality? A good example would be one that possesses most of the pertinent attributes just identified: psychological properties of a person that are also general, characteristic, enduring, integrated, and functional. Personality **traits** seem to fit the bill nicely, because these by definition are *pervasive* ways people differ from one another.

In the personality psychology courses I teach, I ask my students on the first day of class to write a one-page essay to describe "whatever is general, characteristic, enduring, integrated, and functional" about themselves. I do this mainly as an informal exercise to get them to think about what we mean by personality. Based on my reading of hundreds if not thousands of these essays, I believe that most of my students most of the time describe these aspects of themselves with personality traits.

Trait: A pervasive characteristic of an individual.

Here is an example of one of these essays:

The most important thing about me is my friends and how we treat each other. We never let each other down. If they need anything, then I drop whatever I am doing, and I'm always there. And they're just as loyal to me as I am to them. People are real important to me; I'm a social person, and I need to be around others.

My friends and I have a lot of fun together. I have a crazy sense of humor, and I'm always doing things to make people laugh, like hiding their notebooks for school or pretending to be someone else on the telephone. Most of the time, at least, my friends get a kick out of what I do.

When I'm by myself, I like to play my guitar or listen to my tapes. I've always been a fan of rock-and-roll. In high school, I used to play in a band. I haven't hooked up with one here yet, but I will. And I must have almost a thousand different cassettes. I never get tired of listening to them. But I don't have a Walkman. I always go out with other people, and those things are rude when you're with others.

What else? It may not seem like it, but I'm pretty close with my family, and that's a strength for me. I can always turn to them for support and encouragement. If school is tough, or if I get worried about my future, I know that my family will be there.

When I was growing up, my parents and I never had any of those big fights like other families did. We talk about most things, and even now when I'm away at school, we talk on the phone a couple of times a week. I really respect my father. He had to sacrifice a lot to raise the family, and I never heard him complain about it once. And the same with mom—she had wanted to go to college, but there wasn't enough money, so she never went. But she never has complained about that, and I respect her for it.

The writer has assigned to himself a number of traits: sociability, loyalty, humor, musical ability, and respect for his parents. These traits are psychological properties. They are general: note that he has used words like "never" and "always" to describe the way he acts. The assigned traits are also characteristic because they set him apart from others. Sometimes this is implied, as with his "crazy sense of humor." Sometimes this is explicitly stated, as with his extreme closeness to his family. His traits are enduring; he has traced several of them to early in his life. Also, they are integrated. They belong together. After describing himself as a wild and crazy guy who is close to his friends, the writer felt obliged to point out that his good relationship with his parents might seem a bit inconsistent with his other characteristics, but that it really wasn't. Finally, the traits he described are importantly related to how he gets along in the world—with other people, with his schoolwork, and with his future plans.

The Variety of Traits

In 1936, Gordon Allport and Henry Odbert published the results of a massive undertaking. They read through the entire 1925 *Webster's New International Dictionary,* approximately 400,000 entries, and extracted all the words that describe personality. They found 17,953 such terms. That's about 4.5 percent of the total English vocabulary! These words range from the esoteric to the mundane, but the point is that we have an incredible variety of ways to describe people in terms of their traits.

But Do Traits Exist?

Granted the extensive vocabulary we have available to us to describe these good examples of personality, you may find it surprising that some contemporary personality psychologists have been skeptical about the existence of traits. Just because we have words doesn't mean we can apply them to things in the real world. People may not think, act, or feel in general, characteristic, and enduring ways. Perhaps we can point to nothing in their behavior in assigning a personality trait. As you will see, the possibility that people cannot be described in terms of personality traits has been an overriding issue in personality psychology.

Every time we ascribe a personality trait to someone, we assume this person will show at least some consistency across situations. This assumption is embodied in each of the 17,953 trait terms that Allport and Odbert identified. Someone who is *bold* is expected to act in a bold fashion in a variety of settings. *Friendly* folks are expected to be frequently so. But in 1968, Stanford psychologist Walter Mischel surveyed the personality research literature to see if people indeed acted consistently in different situations. It was an extreme blow to common sense and to personality psychology when he concluded that there was little evidence for cross-situational consistency in people's thoughts, actions, and feelings. Children who acted dishonestly in one situation did not necessarily act dishonestly in a different situation. Adults who respected authority in one setting, such as the army, did not always respect authority in another setting, such as the workplace.

What's going on here? If personality traits aren't really reflected in the real world, then why do trait terms exist? According to Mischel, the popularity of trait terms may in part result from a cognitive illusion—a trick of the mind, so to speak. When we watch a person doing something, we assume the action originates from within, caused by a pervasive trait. We neglect to consider the possibility that we are observing a product of the situation the person happens to be in.

Consider, for example, Stanley Milgram's (1963) experiments on destructive obedience. In these studies, research subjects were asked to deliver what seemed to be exceedingly painful electric shocks to another person. Despite the protests of this person, who actually was an actor in cahoots with the experimenter, approximately 60 percent of the research subjects complied, a surprisingly high figure.

The important point of these studies is that situational demands (in this case a psychology experimenter urging a research subject to continue with the experiment) may have a tremendous effect on what people do, regardless of who they are. These experiments have been repeated frequently enough so that we know it is the situational demand that is mostly responsible for the compliance.

When I explain this point to my students, I tell them, "Odds are you'd do exactly the same thing in that situation." But some of them insist something was really wrong with Milgram's research subjects. "They were spineless, sadistic, or confused. That's why they complied with the request. The situation was not the cause of their behavior." These students are making an error, just as you would if you ever asked, "What's a nice person like you doing in a place like this?" That's because the answer is, "The same thing you're doing, because that's what everybody does in places like this."

Are we always guilty of such errors when we talk about personality? Are the characteristics of people that *seem* to be general, characteristic, enduring, functional, and integrated nothing but mistaken perceptions on our part, which vanish when researchers take a hard look at the evidence? We will take up these questions in later chapters, but let me note here that traits have survived this controversy. However, what has resulted is a more sophisticated view of traits in particular and personality in general. This after all is the purpose of scientific inquiry, examining hypotheses—for example, about the nature of personality—in light of relevant evidence.

THE PSYCHOLOGY OF PERSONALITY

Personality psychology, quite obviously, is the field within psychology that studies personality. Granted our complex characterization of personality itself, you might expect that personality psychology is similarly complex. And you would be correct. Indeed, within this field we can distinguish different approaches that focus on one or another of the pertinent attributes comprising the family resemblance of personality. I will in this section sketch two particularly disparate activities of personality psychologists, one concerned with the "general" aspect of personality and the other with its "characteristic" aspect. My intent is to illustrate the range of topics that fall within personality psychology.

Models of Human Nature

Most fields of psychology are concerned with parts of people and aspects of their behavior: particular sensations, perceptions, habits, beliefs, attitudes, and so on. Personality psychology is different, because it often takes as its subject matter the person as a whole. For this reason, many personality psychologists grapple with big questions about human nature, which we can identify as the "general" aspect of personality. Theorists have proposed numerous models or metaphors in an attempt to specify the essence of being a person.

The use of models has been common throughout the history of science. The early Greeks believed the earth was held aloft by a giant who stood on the back of a turtle. I suspect they did not literally believe a large man was squeezing the planet. They did not fear, for instance, that he would lose his grip on Italy and crush Egypt as he juggled the earth or that federal regulations would require him to wear a hard hat and allow him to take frequent coffee breaks. Rather, the vision of Atlas and his heroic task was a metaphor for understanding the world and its secure place in the physical universe.

A **model** is a simple version of a more complex phenomenon. It includes characteristics of the actual phenomenon that are essential in defining it, leaving out less important ones. If you built model cars when you were little, you knew even then that a model was not an exact copy. It was "realistic" not because it reproduced the literal Ford Edsel, but because it included some of the details that comprised your prototype of a car.

When personality psychologists propose a model of human nature, some metaphor for understanding why people behave, we also should not take these models literally. What is important is whether a model aids our understanding of personality, not whether it exactly replicates people in the real world. From our previous analysis of personality, we have good reason to believe there is no single essence to being human. Any attempt to specify such an essence is never going to be 100 percent successful, regardless of the metaphor. Still, some metaphors for human nature resemble our various behaviors enough to often ring true. Let us consider some of them.

In some ways, people can be understood as animals.

People As Animals   Darwinian ideas have influenced all branches of psychology, including personality psychology. Perhaps the most basic of these ideas is that human beings are members of the animal kingdom, in some ways best understood as animals. Throughout the twentieth century, this model of people as animals has been quite popular.

Sigmund Freud's personality theory, which we'll examine in detail later, proposes that one key to understanding human beings lies in recognizing their sexual and aggressive instincts—biologically based drives that demand satisfaction. Although society may coerce a person into expressing these instincts indirectly, they are always present, close to the surface, and waiting to erupt, like David Banner turning into the Incredible Hulk.

People As Energy Systems   Another popular metaphor likens people to energy systems. Again, Sigmund Freud championed this idea, proposing that human functioning involves the transformation of psychological energy, what he called *libido*. Like real energy, libido obeys the laws of thermodynamics: It can be neither created nor destroyed, and once present, demands to be used.

Freud believed that if one's psychological energy is used for one purpose, then it cannot be used for another. Only so much libido is available, and emotional problems are literally exhausting. They are like bad investments, tying up your psychological assets and precluding their more productive use.

People As White Rats   Psychologists and everyday people sometimes joke that psychology is the scientific investigation of what the white rat *(Rattus norwegicus)* and the college sophomore *(Homo sophomorus)* have in common. They refer mainly to white rats being used in laboratory experiments concerned with learning. However, they also refer to the tendency to view human beings as if they were white rats. Although this metaphor is not usually acknowledged, it has nonetheless played an important role in psychology as a model of human nature.

What are the essential characteristics of a white rat? If you are squeamish, when you think of white rats, visions occur and recur of beady red eyes and naked tails. If you are dispassionate, you see them as domesticated animals living under highly confined and controlled conditions. They follow a life of routine and are keenly responsive to rewards and punishments—Purina Rat Chow and electric shock. Think of them as the consummate hedonists, pursuing pleasure and avoiding pain.

People As Machines   Most psychologists are materialists, believing that, ultimately, human action will be fully explained by referring to chemical and physical forces. This materialistic assumption can be reflected in a model of people as machines—systems of physical parts related by simple cause-and-effect processes.

Also, a psychologist who believes people are like machines is committed to the view that our understanding of the complex aspects of the machine must be grounded in an understanding of the more basic aspects. This means that psychological aspects of the person, such as personality, are best understood after an introduction to the biological aspects.

Field: A self-regulating system where changes in one part affect all other parts.

People As Fields

You may be less familiar with what scientists mean by a **field,** so I'll start by contrasting a field with a machine. Machines are systems of parts where changes in a given part only influence a small number of other parts, those that are physically connected. In contrast, a field is a system of parts where changes in one part influence all other parts. Compare a lawn mower with a waterbed. The lawn mower is composed of a number of parts attached to each other by nuts and bolts. If you run over a large stone that bends the blades of the mower, you have broken blades and perhaps a twisted axle. The handle, the wheels, and the grass-catcher are undisturbed by the accident.

What happens, though, if this same stone is propelled by the lawn-mover blades through your bedroom window, where it hits your waterbed? It doesn't hit the bed hard enough to break it, thank goodness, but it arrives with some velocity. In contrast to the lawn mower, where few parts were affected by the stone, the entire waterbed responds. The bed pushes up everywhere that the stone doesn't hit. Once the stone rebounds, the bed again responds as a whole. It sloshes up and down, and if someone were on it, he too would slosh up and down. The point is that the entire waterbed is responsive to changes in each of its parts.

Some psychologists feel that people should be described in field terms instead of mechanistic terms. Remember, personality often refers to what is integrated about an individual. Machines have no overall unity, no guiding principle. They are simply a set of parts. In contrast, fields are unified. They are defined by the interrelation of their parts, and there is a wholeness to them.

Another characteristic of fields that makes this model attractive to personality psychologists is their self-regulation. Recall your waterbed. It was sloshing around when we left it, but it has now restored itself to its prior condition. It has returned to an equilibrium. Similarly, magnetic fields, gravitational fields, and ecosystems return to their original states: *homeostasis.* Unlike machines, fields can survive dramatic disturbances like a forest fire. Fields heal themselves. Machines do not.

People As Information Processors

With the advent of the computer age, a new metaphor was developed to understand human nature: people as computers. This model attributes properties of both machines *and* fields to people. From the middle 1960s through the present, psychologists have explored the limits of this metaphor. Does the essence of a person lie in her ability to process information according to rules and strategies?

One reason for the popularity of this metaphor is that computers are sufficiently complex to do justice to the complexity we attribute to people. Most of the models I am discussing in this section are simplistic; this model is not. A second reason for its popularity is the ease in assimilating it to ways of thinking already established within psychology. Thus, information or data readily correspond to stimuli in the environment. Output is analogous to behavior. Hardware has its counterpart in the neurons and organs that comprise our

We like Mr. Spock because he is a thoroughly rational processor of information; we love him when his human side surfaces.

physical body, while software is akin to what we learn—attitudes, opinions, beliefs, values, and so on.

People As Scientists   A metaphor of human nature similar to the computer model is one that likens people to scientists. George Kelly (1955) forcefully stated this model in his *personal constructs* theory, which I'll discuss in some detail later. Kelly argues that everyday people are engaged in much the same business as the scientist—trying to understand the world. They represent this understanding in terms of theories about the world, and they undertake various tests of their theories.

Sometimes the tests confirm one of their theories, and the theory is regarded with confidence: "I knew he was a schmuck all along. I gave him a chance to do something nice, and he just acted in the same old selfish way!" Other times the tests prove a theory wrong: "Well, my first impression was a mistake. I didn't think she could handle the job I gave her, but she did it twice as well as anybody else ever has!"

The person-as-scientist metaphor has been popular in contemporary psychology for the same reasons the computer metaphor has been popular. Both characterize people as rational and orderly, making sense of environmental information. Both suggest new ways of looking at seemingly irrational actions and intervening to change them.

People As Actors   "All the world's a stage, and all the men and women merely players." If Shakespeare's well-known expression is true, then some personality psychologists are drama critics. This popular metaphor of human nature, the actor model, proposes that the essence of a person lies in the roles he or she plays.

The term **role** is borrowed directly from the theater. When we apply it to a person's everyday life, we suggest that behavior is due to parts or positions assigned by society and not by the person playing the role. Viewing people as actors does not mean regarding them as shams or fakes. Rather, it means everything we do is the result of one or more roles. No person is behind all of these roles; instead, the person is the sum of the roles played.

When we contrast the actor metaphor with other models of human nature, we see that it lends itself poorly to the purposes of psychology. It is primarily a sociological account. Society provides the roles, not the individual. People differ in the manner they play a role, but the actor metaphor leaves little room for improvisation. Perhaps this metaphor would be more useful if it were combined with another model. It could explain the public part of personality, while an additional metaphor could explain what is private or personal about personality.

People As Pilots Finally, the pilot model is a metaphor that could be combined with the actor model. It is an explicit attempt to understand what lies behind the roles we play. In this view, a person is the ghost in the machine of the body—the pilot of the airplane. Have you ever asked someone who he or she *really* is? You were asking for the identity of the pilot, for an acknowledgment and description of what personality psychologists call the **self.**

People often pursue goals. I presume you are attending college in order to graduate, in order to obtain a certain sort of job, in order to live a certain style of life, in order to be happy, maybe even to gain wisdom. What allows you to pursue these goals? Machines have no destinations; neither do fields, animals, or computers. Something has to be added to these models to account for the purposive nature of behavior. That something is often identified as the self.

It is difficult to define or characterize the self in such a way that psychologists can use it in their theories and research. Despite our awareness of a self within us, it is not a real thing. It has no location, no height, no weight. If we are aware of a self, then what in us is having this awareness? Can the self be aware of the self, as if it is looking in a mirror?

Similarly, if we do things that protect our self from slights, then what is doing the protecting? Can the self protect itself without being aware it is doing so? Finally, if the self is the pilot of our aircraft, who pilots the self? Does the concept of the self merely push the problem of explanation back one step, acknowledging the need for explanation without accomplishing it?

Some of the problems with the notion of the self are avoided if the self is regarded not as a literal thing but as a metaphor, a hypothetical entity that proves useful in explaining the integrated and purposive aspects of a person. Like any metaphor, the pilot model only applies up to a point.

In sum, one of the important activities of personality psychologists is to explore models of human nature. They present us not with a single view, but rather with multiple possibilities. While no single model is likely to capture all that is meant by personality, if put together, they paint the family portrait of our species.

Is an integrated view possible—the personality psychology equivalent of a medley of greatest hits? Yes, but the suggestion for a model that partakes of all models should not be made glibly. After all, a given model has cohered in the way it has for a reason, and some models are largely incompatible with others. We don't play cops-and-robbers with bows and arrows; we don't serve Chinese vegetables over Spanish rice—and we don't combine a model of people as wild animals with a model of them as information processors.

However, an integrated model could be developed in one of two ways. First, it could specify which people are best described by which model. Some individuals are indeed like scientists, while other individuals are more like actors, or white rats, or machines. One way to integrate the various models proposed by personality theorists is to regard them as a system of pigeonholes: a given individual can be classified in one of the categories.

"Yes, they're all fools, gentlemen... But the question remains, 'What KIND of fools are they?' "

SOURCE: "The Far Side" cartoon by Gary Larson is reproduced by permission of Chronicle Features, San Francisco.

Second, an integrated model could specify which *aspects* of people are best described by which model. Each model applies to all people, but only to some aspect of them. The person-as-scientist metaphor could be invoked to explain how people cope with problems. The person-as-wild-animal metaphor, in contrast, could explain how people express their biological needs. And so on.

Individual Differences

Many personality psychologists are interested in the "characteristic" aspect of personality. How are people consistently like themselves and different from others? These personality psychologists focus on describing, measuring, and finally explaining **individual differences**—the myriad of ways people are different. We've already mentioned traits, and you will see in subsequent chapters such psychological notions as temperaments, types, factors, styles, habits, skills, motives, and values. All of these are variables, attempts to depict what is unique about an individual. You will also encounter an equally imposing variety of tests and measures that try to assess individual differences.

Because of its complexity, the psychology of individual differences is an academic field in itself. For now, let me identify several topics that particularly interest psychologists who work with individual differences.

Origins   The *nature versus nurture* controversy—whether a characteristic results from genetic inheritance (nature) or environmental influence (nurture)—occurs repeatedly in the field of individual differences. This is not an idle academic controversy, since important policy decisions hang in the balance.

Suppose intelligence, like hair color or eye color, is passed on through the genes. Then society would not be so concerned with assuring equal opportunity in education. Intelligent adults, identified by their prominent positions in society, would have intelligent children, who are then accorded the best education. If intelligence is a biological matter, then the status quo need not change. If anything, steps should be taken so only the privileged are accorded future privilege.

On the other hand, suppose intelligence is mainly the result of your early experiences with learning. Then intelligence is created by providing a stimulating home environment where books are available, the television set is turned to "Sesame Street" instead of "All-Star Wrestling," and family members value education. If so, then equal opportunity in education should be a pressing societal concern, both morally and practically.

The nature versus nurture controversy rarely has a simple answer. It certainly does not have a simple one-or-the-other answer with regard to intelligence. I'm sure you're aware of the arguments surrounding this particular version of the issue. Nature versus nurture was partly at the root of the Supreme Court decision regarding segregation, and it has surfaced again in the current furor over busing, open admissions, affirmative action, and so on.

Adaptation   Although researchers can readily establish a link between high intelligence and good grades in school, they are usually not satisfied with just

---

Individual differences: All the ways people differ from one another.

describing this relationship. They also want to know how it is brought about. Intelligence does not leap off an IQ test onto a report card. What transpires in-between? In an attempt to understand this link, some psychologists have broken intelligence into components and studied how comprehension, retention, and recall of abstract information lead to better academic performance.

Similarly, consider *psychopathy,* a personality characteristic associated with grossly inappropriate actions toward others. The classic psychopath lies, cheats, and steals. Since punishment appears ineffective in dissuading the psychopath, Pritchard (1837) dubbed this characteristic "moral insanity" to convey the psychopath's seeming lack of a conscience and insensitivity to rebuke. Why such unsavory actions?

Schachter and Latané (1964) suggest that psychopathy is associated with a failure to be physiologically aroused by the threat of punishment. Try to appreciate that our conscience—our moral self—probably arises from early experiences of our parents punishing us for minor transgressions, like pulling the cat's tail. Freud and others have theorized that most children learn to anticipate punishment for certain deeds and thus refrain because they experience anxiety at the mere thought—except the future psychopaths, who seem incapable of such learning. As a result, they fail to develop a conscience, and the rapacious behavior that comprises their problem (and ours) results.

Measurement   Personality psychologists are concerned with individual differences not just in the abstract but also in the concrete. What is the best way to measure how people differ? How can we go about placing them along a personality dimension, as high or low or somewhere in-between?

A concept crucial to personality assessment is the **reliability** of an assessment procedure—its *ability to assign an individual the same score on different occasions.* You hope, for instance, your speedometer is reliable: if you discover on Tuesday that driving to school at 37 miles per hour is sufficient for you to find a parking place 30 minutes after your alarm clock goes off, you want the same thing to be true on Thursday.

A second crucial concept is the **validity** of an assessment procedure—its *ability to measure what it purports to measure.* Again, you hope your speedometer is valid: if you drive at 55 miles per hour through a speed trap on an interstate highway, you want the 55 on your speedometer to be the same 55 that appears on the digital readout of the state trooper's radar machine. (You also want both to correspond to the speed of a car that can traverse a measured mile in one minute and six seconds.)

Although everyone recognizes that perfect reliability and perfect validity are ideal standards impossible to achieve, there is considerable and legitimate controversy about how good is good enough. How reliable should a test be before it can be used? How valid should it be? The line is fuzzy, and it shifts depending on the particular purpose of the test.

To answer such questions, personality psychologists rely on information depicted by **correlation coefficients.** You may already have encountered these in a statistics course. Their importance to personality assessment cannot be exaggerated.

Reliability: The degree to which a psychological measure consistently provides the same result.

Validity: The degree to which a psychological measure indeed measures what it purports to measure.

Correlation coefficient: A statistic reflecting the degree to which two variables are associated with one another. A *positive correlation* means that increases in one variable are associated with increases in another; an *independent* (or *zero*) *correlation* means that two variables are unrelated; a *negative correlation* means that increases in one variable are associated with decreases in another.

To those of you unfamiliar with correlation coefficients, here is a brief introduction, starting with the notion of correlation. Correlation refers to the association between two characteristics. So if we measured the height and weight of everyone in your class, we might be interested in how these two variables go together. We could graph them as shown at the left of Figure 1–1. On the whole, height and weight are associated because increases in one usually involve increases in the other. This is what is meant by a *positive correlation*.

Let's introduce two other characteristics of you and your fellow students. We can assess how much money each of you has in your pockets and the length of hair on your head. Again, we can graph the relationship between these two variables (see the middle of Figure 1–1). This time, we find that spare change and hair length do not go with each other at all. The two variables are *independent* of each other, showing a *zero correlation*.

Finally, let's assess everyone's social-security number and ask everyone how many times they've been in New York City. (A background fact: social-security numbers are assigned geographically and get bigger from East to West.) If we graph the relationship, we see an association occurs (right of Figure 1–1). The higher the social-security number, the less frequently one has been in New York City, and vice versa. This is called a *negative correlation*.

Now you have a feel for correlation. A correlation coefficient is a mathematical expression of the degree to which two variables are associated. High correlations reflect strong associations. In other words, if the points on a graph fall tightly along a straight line, a high correlation coefficient results. If they do not fall along a line too well, we have a low correlation.

Correlation coefficients range from −1.00 (a perfect negative association between two variables) through 0.00 (no association at all) to a +1.00 (a perfect positive association). When correlation coefficients take on these particular values, no one has difficulty interpreting the association between the variables involved—they either go together perfectly or not at all. In practice, however, correlation coefficients take on intermediate values, and considerable debate ensues about what to make of these intermediate correlations.

How strongly should two characteristics be associated before we attach importance to their correlation? This question lies at the heart of the debate over

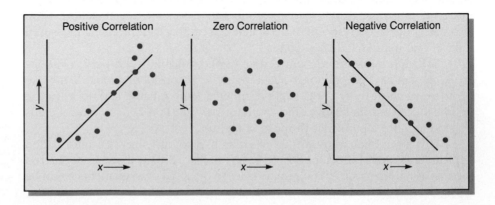

**FIGURE 1–1
Examples of
Correlation
Coefficients**

the consistency or inconsistency of personality. More generally, researchers must address this question every time they try to ascertain the reliability or validity of a personality measure.

The most intuitive way to gauge the reliability of a psychological test is to give it to the same group of individuals on two occasions. Do they receive the same scores each time? If so, then the measure has **test-retest reliability.** But it may be impractical to test people twice. Or because people have already taken the test, it may render the second testing suspect. Consider the last midterm examination you took. If your instructor wanted to show that her midterm examination was reliable, she probably would not let you take it twice. Presumably, everybody would score higher the second time.

A more common way to investigate the reliability of a test is to employ one that has several different items, each attempting to measure the same thing, like your knowledge of European history. If you answer one item correctly or incorrectly, is the same true for the other items? If so, then the test has **internal reliability,** or **consistency.** Most personality tests use multiple items so their internal reliability can be calculated. The more items employed to measure the dimension of concern, the more likely the extraneous determinants of scores will cancel out.

The validity of a personality test is more difficult to ascertain than its reliability, because of the problems in making concrete what a test is trying to measure. As I have emphasized, the abstract notions used in personality theories differ from what people do in the real world. The goal of personality assessment is to describe people's actual behavior in terms of abstract personality dimensions, and this endeavor isn't always a simple one.

It would be simple to judge a personality test's validity if an unambiguous measure of the real characteristic under study is used. The degree to which the personality test yields scores that correlate with this measure would be its validity. However, most personality characteristics do not have a single and true manifestation against which a test can be calibrated. Remember, personality and personality characteristics tend not to have necessary and sufficient conditions. Complex concepts are difficult to measure, and the measures—once created— are problematic to evaluate.

Theorists have devised many ways of ascertaining the validity of personality assessment techniques. Table 1–1 describes some of the different types of validity that personality psychologists use to judge measures of individual differences.

Test-retest reliability: The degree to which a psychological measure provides the same result on repeated occasions.

Internal reliability (consistency): The degree to which different items on a psychological test provide the same results.

IMPLICATIONS OF PERSONALITY'S COMPLEXITY

The family resemblance approach to defining personality is a powerful tool. It helps us understand the complex notion of personality in terms of the attributes that cut across the disparate ways *personality* is used. And it helps bring order to the field of personality psychology, the complexity of which parallels the

TABLE 1–1
Types of Validity

face validity Whether the test looks like it measures what it is supposed to measure; for example, exit interviews at polling places *seem* to be a reasonable way to ascertain how people voted.

content validity Whether the assessment technique contains a representative sample for the behavior of interest; for example, secretarial tests usually ask applicants to type a letter.

criterion validity How well a test predicts the particular behavior being studied; for example, intelligence tests often predict someone's grades in school.

known-group validity Whether the test distinguishes between two groups known to differ with respect to the characteristic under study; for example, people in prison score higher than the general population on a test measuring the degree to which someone feels that important outcomes are outside of their personal control (Rotter, 1966).

construct validity Whether scores on the test relate to scores of another test attempting to measure a theoretically-related dimension; for example, a test of verbal creativity relates as expected to the extent of one's vocabulary.

complexity of personality itself. Let's conclude this introductory chapter by considering some further implications of this approach to defining personality.

Why It Is Difficult to Define Personality Precisely

It is not just the term *personality* that resists precise definition. The same holds true for specific personality terms. Consider any of a number of trait names, such as *timid, independent, anxious,* or *energetic.* Each of these is used in a variety of senses, and probably no critical elements cut across all of these senses. Like the general term *personality,* the specific terms that we select to describe personality are captured by a family resemblance, a set of pertinent attributes, with no single attribute being necessary or sufficient.

Why Some Characteristics of a Person Are Ambiguously Classified As Part of Personality

I have stated that personality traits are good examples of what we mean by personality. But there are also poor examples, aspects of a person that seem to be somewhat part of her personality and somewhat not. The family resemblance idea with its set of attributes helps resolve this ambiguity. Borderline instances of personality characteristics are precisely that: characteristics that possess some of the pertinent attributes comprising the family resemblance of personality, but not many. Whether we regard them as part of personality or not depends on our purpose.

Attitude is a poor example of a personality characteristic, possessing only some of the pertinent elements. Social psychologists usually employ attitudes to predict and explain prejudiced behavior. Let's look at Gordon Allport's definition of attitude:

> A mental and neural state of readiness to respond, organized through experience and exerting a directive and dynamic influence on behavior. (1968a, p. 63)

Defined in this way, an attitude is a psychological property of an individual, an evaluation that dictates behavior. It follows that we all differ with respect to our attitudes: I may hate reruns of "I Love Lucy" while you love them, and a third person may be indifferent. An attitude is therefore characteristic of all people. It is also functional or dysfunctional, since it channels how a person interacts with the world.

But when we compare attitudes to personality traits, we usually regard the former as less general, less enduring, and less integrated. In other words, when we speak of attitudes, we usually treat them as less central than personality traits in defining who a person is. But exceptions occur. Someone who has an extreme attitude is apt to be importantly characterized by it. If a member of the Ku Klux Klan, for instance, were to be described as merely someone with a negative attitude toward religious and ethnic minorities, this description wouldn't really capture him very well. His personality certainly includes this negative attitude, and we would expect it to be generally apparent, long-lasting, and related to much of what he thinks, does, and feels. For some people at least, attitudes are an important part of their personality, while for other people, they are not.

Physical characteristics also fall along the edge of what we mean by personality. Our physical appearance—general, characteristic, and enduring—is certainly part of our personal identity. I have never been in someone's house or apartment without seeing at least one mirror. Hair color, skin color, height, and weight distinguish us from others, and we all have strong opinions about our best and worst features (not to mention those of others).

Perhaps to our dismay, research by social psychologists shows that the way a person looks can be overwhelmingly important in determining how others react. Doors open or close, people smile or frown, dates are made or broken, all in accord with physical characteristics. Clearly, physical characteristics are seen as functional or dysfunctional.

However, in everyday conversation, we usually don't consider physical characteristics as part of personality, since they are physical properties of the individual rather than psychological ones. This may be erroneous, though, because the idea of family resemblances suggests that the physical realm and the psychological realm may overlap. And people can exercise considerable control over their appearance. They color their hair, tattoo their skin, and pierce their ears. They restrict calories and take laxatives to become emaciated, or they lift weights and ingest steroids to become muscle-bound. And people adorn themselves in various costumes: bangles and beads, leather and lace, Lacoste shirts and Top-siders. So when does the physical start to become the psychological?

In a series of interesting studies, McGuire and McGuire (1981) asked young people to respond in their own words to questions like "Tell us about yourself," much as I have done with college students in my personality psychology classes. These researchers were concerned with the most salient aspects of this "spontaneous self-concept." They found that physical character-istics figure predominantly in the self-concepts of children. So, in one study, height was spontaneously mentioned by 19 percent of the sample, weight by 11 percent, hair color by 14 percent, and eye color by 11 percent.

McGuire and McGuire were even able to predict which kids would or would not mention a given physical characteristic in their spontaneous self-concept by taking into account how distinctive the characteristic was within the child's classroom. Children who were taller or shorter than their peers were more likely to include height in their descriptions than were children of average height. Children who were heavier or lighter than their peers were more likely to mention weight than were the other children. And so on. Physical characteristics define who we are to the degree that they stamp us as different from those around us. For some people with certain physical characteristics in certain situations, physical characteristics are part of personality.

Another instance of an ambiguous personality characteristic is ethnicity or race (Scarr, 1988). Most everyday people and personality psychologists do not consider either as part of personality, maybe because it seems prejudiced to suggest that racial or ethnic groups differ in personality. Nevertheless, an individual's racial or ethnic group possesses some of the attributes of personality. Group membership is a property of the individual that is usually general, enduring, integrated, and functional. Is it psychological? Well, to the degree we can speak of ethnic identity or racial consciousness, of course ethnicity and race are psychological.

But are these characteristics part of personality? According to the family resemblance idea, they sometimes are and sometimes are not. It depends in part on how characteristic they are. If someone is the only black in an otherwise white classroom, or the only Jew in an otherwise Roman Catholic town, or the only Vietnamese in in an otherwise Hispanic neighborhood, then ethnicity or race are clearly instances of personality. In a segregated society, ethnicity and race are not part of personality. But in the complex world where most of us live, they are ambiguously characteristics of personality.

Finally, gender is another ambiguous personality characteristic. It is a property of the individual that is usually general, enduring, integrated, and functional. Although we regard maleness or femaleness as biological, they are probably more psychological than anything else. Gender is sometimes part of personality, and sometimes not. In an all-girl school, being female is irrelevant. And, the fact that the current president of the United States is a male is of no interest to anyone trying to contrast his personality with those of his predecessors.

When I use the term personality, I am applying it to both good and ambiguous examples. Both importantly define who a person is, and both possess at least some of the attributes that comprise the family resemblance of personality: that is, characteristics that are general, characteristic, and so on.

Why the Field of Personality Psychology Is Diverse and Diffuse

In a typical day, two personality psychologists may have little to do with each other's work. They may be interested in different questions, employ different research methods, study different samples of people, and publish their findings in different journals. If they teach courses, they might use different textbooks, and they certainly choose different lecture topics. At the same time, however, these two personality psychologists can and do speak to each other. They have enough in common that they cannot afford to ignore each other's work. Even if personality psychology is a smorgasbord, it is still served on the same table.

The reason for the considerable but not total diversity of personality psychology is the diversity of instances of personality. Different fields have developed different approaches to examine, respectively, those instances that are general, those that are characteristic, those that are enduring, and so on.

Why the Field of Personality Psychology Embraces a Variety of Theoretical Perspectives

We use theories to predict and explain occurrences in the real world. Since personality is applied to so many different instances in the real world, which bear only a family resemblance, personality psychology must employ a variety of theories. Although it's a tempting goal, no theorist has been able to develop an all-inclusive theory of personality. Granted, the way I have defined personality, no theorist is likely to do so in the future, since the topic is not unitary. As a student, you may be dismayed by the variety of theoretical perspectives, and you may assume that personality psychologists are incapable of agreeing on things. However, I think the real reason for the field's diversity is its subject matter.

Any given theory does a particularly good job explaining some aspects of personality while doing a particularly poor job at others. Think of a theory as an explicitly stated game, and you can see why it works well in some domains of the real world and not so well in others. Numerous games can be played with bats and balls, but if we were limited to this equipment, baseball would be one of the most sensible. If we had only rackets and shuttlecocks at our disposal, baseball would be an unwieldy "theory" to apply, and we had best search for a different game. If we are fortunate, we'll come across badminton.

The same is true within the field of personality psychology. We should try to match up the theory with that part of the real world it best fits. I'll describe a number of personality theories in the remainder of this book, and in each case, part of my description will entail a sketch of where it fits and where it doesn't. Freud's theory of personality, for example, does a good job of explaining our dark and passionate side, but it doesn't have much to say about how we learn to do long division.

Why the Field of Personality Psychology Employs a Variety of Research Methods

Because the different instances of personality are diverse, they can't be studied in the same way. We have already seen that no single operational definition captures the whole of personality. Similarly, no single research approach is always appropriate for the study of personality. Sometimes personality psychologists work in experimental laboratories, studying people or even rats. Sometimes they spend half a lifetime talking to the same individual about her dreams, fears, and fantasies. Sometimes they pass out questionnaires to half of a campus, half of a town, or half of the world. The research method they choose depends on what they want to know about whatever aspect of personality interests them.

Why the Findings of Personality Psychology Have Been Applied to Such an Array of Topics

Many personality psychologists have applied what they know about personality to the real world. Psychotherapists, for instance, attempt to help people solve their problems so they can get along better with themselves and others. Other personality psychologists choose to work in schools, trying to predict which students will do well or poorly in which courses. Still other personality psychologists work for private businesses, attempting to make products like Cheerios, Cabbage Patch Dolls, or Chryslers look more attractive to the consumer. Others devote time to basketball players, helping them make free throws; to defense lawyers, helping them select lenient jurors; or to interior decorators, helping them choose appropriate colors and textures.

I will describe a number of the applications of personality psychology. They are diverse, but no more diverse than the meanings of personality. Although these applications bear a family resemblance to each other, they never perfectly overlap. Successful marketing does not involve the same ingredients as successful psychotherapy. Both involve the creative application of theories and findings from personality psychology, but the particular theory and the particular findings usually differ from application to application.

Why Prediction and, Ultimately, Explanation Are Bound

One of the important topics in personality psychology is measurement—how to assess an individual's personality category, how to ascertain the manner in which an individual functions. Once measurement is complete, psychologists employ the scores to predict future behavior—instances of thinking, acting, and feeling. To the disappointment of many, predictions are far from perfect. Usually, measurement-based forecasts improve upon the randomness of mere chance, but not to the degree that we should feel dazzled (or threatened).

One reason for these very real boundaries on prediction is compelled by the family resemblance idea. Prediction is based on a theory, but it is applied to the real world of concrete particulars. In the course of measurement, different instances are classed together, and it is inevitable that this classification is sometimes erroneous, since measurement treats particulars as identical when they are not. The upper limit to one's accuracy in predicting future behavior cannot be 100 percent. It will always be lower. Explanation is also bounded. We cannot give a full theoretical account of what occurs in the real world, because the real world will always bear an imperfect relationship to our theories.

SUMMARY

This chapter discusses what is meant by the term *personality*. I first considered ways *personality* is used in everyday conversation. Personality proves to be a complex concept, used in a variety of senses and characterized by a set of attributes. Taken together, these attributes define what we mean by personality: psychological aspects of an individual that are general, characteristic, enduring, integrated, and functional.

A good example of personality defined in this way are personality traits, which abound in the English language. A trait embodies the entire set of attributes of personality that comprise the family resemblance approach. However, the actual existence of traits has been questioned, in that people do not always act consistently in different settings. This controversy has led researchers to a more sophisticated view of traits in particular and personality in general.

This book concerns itself with the psychology of personality, a field as diverse and complex as the term *personality* itself. Depending on the aspects of personality in which different psychologists are interested, their activities may take on quite different forms.

For instance, personality psychologists may propose models (or metaphors) of human nature that attempt to specify some essence that lies at the core of being human. In other words, these metaphors are used to understand what people think, do, and feel. Among the metaphors that have been popular within personality psychology are those that liken people to animals, energy systems, white rats, machines, fields, computers, scientists, actors, and pilots.

A quite different activity of personality psychologists is the attempt to understand how people are consistently like themselves yet different from others. Psychologists here try to identify, measure, and explain individual differences. Several issues crosscut their activity. What is the origin of a particular individual difference? How is a given characteristic related to good or poor functioning in the world? How can we measure individual differences?

In sum, personality psychology is concerned with the concrete individual, describing and explaining personality against the background of the social world. It is a practical field. And in keeping with the complexity of personality, personality psychology houses its share of theoretical controversies.

THE HISTORY OF PERSONALITY PSYCHOLOGY

Personality psychology was born in the twentieth century, the offspring of such ancestors as experimental psychology, psychiatry, and the psychological testing tradition. These ancestors in turn resulted from a productive nineteenth-century marriage between philosophy and science. In this chapter, I will describe the three immediate ancestors of personality psychology, and then sketch the field's history throughout the twentieth century.

I want to give you a historical perspective on personality psychology to place it in a social context. Then perhaps I can dispel the mistaken notion you may have that scientific theories simply appear out of thin air. Newton did not invent physics just because an apple fell on his head. Scientific theories emerge from a particular cultural and intellectual setting. To describe this interdependence of scientific theory and the real world where the theorist lives, historians have introduced two concepts.

Zeitgeist is a German word that translates as "spirit of the times," conveying the notion that scientific ideas reflect the given time when they are proposed. The history of science is filled with examples of simultaneous discoveries, each making the point that discoveries come from someplace. When the raw ingredients for a theory are present and when the time is right, then the discoveries appear. For instance, Charles Darwin proposed the theory of evolution at about the same time as Alfred Russell Wallace did, in 1859.

Zeitgeist: The intellectual spirit of a particular historical era.

Ortgeist is another German word, which translates as "spirit of the place"—scientific theories reflect the given place where they are proposed. Thus, explanations from different cultures have a characteristic stamp on them. Personality psychology originated in several nations, and the spirit of each nation is still evident. The German approach to psychology emphasizes the mind, possibly because the German language allows the expression of great subtleties among mental states. Influenced by evolutionary theory, the English approach stresses classification. Thus, the testing tradition first appeared in England. An emphasis on emotion and irrationality characterizes a French

Ortgeist: The intellectual spirit of a particular place.

approach, creating great breakthroughs in how to conceive psychopathology. And, finally, the American approach is pragmatic: What's the consequence? What works? And so what? Applied psychology is a characteristically American endeavor.

The history of personality psychology is also the history of personality psychologists. A handful of creative and charismatic theorists created the field. Their work reflected who they were, and who they were was a product of a given time and place. Sigmund Freud may have created psychoanalytic theory, but it was Victorian Europe that created Sigmund Freud.

IMMEDIATE ANCESTOR 1: EXPERIMENTAL PSYCHOLOGY

E. G. Boring wrote the definitive history of experimental psychology in 1950. He placed the origin of this field in Europe during the 1800s, when different scientific and philosophical trends came together to form the Zeitgeist from which psychology emerged. Most historians point specifically to the establishment of Wilhelm Wundt's experimental psychology laboratory in 1879 at the University of Leipzig as the culmination of these trends and the beginning of experimental psychology. Soon after, psychology branched into different approaches, and from each stemmed a particular way of regarding personality.

The Psychology of Wundt: What Are the Elements of Consciousness?

Ideas and discoveries emerge from a social and cultural context, but they do not automatically appear without the talents of a particular individual. In experimental psychology, this individual was Wilhelm Wundt, a German who lived from 1832 to 1920, a period that spanned great cultural and scientific change. As a young man, Wundt studied and specialized in physiology. He taught at several universities and in 1875 was appointed professor of philosophy at the University of Leipzig. Then in 1879, he received permission to establish a laboratory for his experiments, and the Psychologische Institut was founded, as a single room.

Why is Wundt considered the first experimental psychologist? Unlike his intellectual predecessors who might be given this title, Wundt considered himself a psychologist. He discarded earlier definitions of psychology as too philosophical and instead defined the field as the science of consciousness, regarding experimentation as the beginning point (Wertheimer, 1979).

The goal of Wundt's psychology, now called **structuralism,** was to understand experience as it is immediately given to the individual. Following the examples of chemistry and physics, he tried to specify the basic elements of experience, using techniques pioneered in the investigations of physiology and sensation. Wundt felt that once the basic elements of consciousness had been identified, the exact manner in which they combined to form complex mental

Structuralism: The general approach within psychology concerned with specifying the elements of consciousness.

phenomena could be ascertained. The elements of consciousness were discovered through a form of observation called **introspection,** a literal "in-looking" where the research subject observed his immediate experience and discovered the constituent units, presumably different types of sensations and feelings.

Wundt's structuralism flourished for decades. As we will see, though, its details were controversial, and ultimately structuralism passed on, leaving little direct influence on personality psychology. However, it did mark the beginning of experimental psychology, paving the way for other approaches that directly influenced personality psychology.

Why was Wundt's system controversial? In a nutshell, structuralism attempted to discover via introspection the mental elements of the normal, adult European male. As such, it was a static and abstract endeavor, with no relevance to pragmatic concerns. Further, the method of introspection proved less objective than the structuralists believed.

Three major alternatives to structuralism developed in response to the different shortcomings of Wundt's approach. **Gestalt psychology** took issue with the assumption that mental elements were fundamental, proposing instead that relationships were the basis of mental phenomena. **Functionalism** took issue with the static character of structuralism, suggesting that the consequences of mental activity were more important than its elements. This approach concerned itself with individual differences, extending psychology to include animals, children, the mad, and so on. In short, functionalism was applied psychology. Finally, **behaviorism** took issue with the technique of introspection, branding it subjective and unreliable. More profoundly, behaviorism also disagreed with Wundt's definition of psychology as the study of consciousness, decreeing instead that psychology's subject matter was observable behavior. Let's now look in detail at each of these alternatives.

Gestalt Psychology: Relationships Are Fundamental

Max Wertheimer, a German psychologist, created Gestalt psychology following his discovery of the *phi phenomenon:* the illusion of apparent movement that all of us experience if we sit still in a train next to another train that begins to move. We have the momentary experience that our train has moved, when in actuality the experience was illusory, caused by the movement of the other train. Do you see how the phi phenomenon challenged the assumption that conscious experience can be understood by breaking it into constituent elements? Nothing in the person's constituent sensations corresponds to the experience of the train moving. So, immediate experience cannot be created from the building blocks of individual sensations.

The German word **gestalt** means *whole,* or *pattern,* or *configuration;* thus, the basic stance of gestalt psychology is that immediate experience itself is patterned. The whole (of experience) is not equal to the sum of its parts (sensations). Gestalt psychology contends that structuralism's interest in supposedly "immediate" experience is itself an error, a profound mistake that misdirects psychology's attention to parts rather than wholes.

A melody exemplifies the notion of a gestalt. One can play a tune at the left end of a piano keyboard, where the notes are deep. Then one can scoot up to the right end and play the same tune, where the notes are high. Assuming one's fingers do not slip, the tunes are recognizable as the identical melody, even though none of the notes are the same. Why? Because the pattern—the gestalt—is fundamental.

The first gestalt psychologists—Max Wertheimer, Kurt Koffka, and Wolfgang Kohler—were concerned with such psychological processes as perception, learning, and thinking. They stressed the importance of relationships and interpreted psychological phenomena as fields, as interdependent with their context. In the process of perception, irregularities and asymmetries are smoothed out. Percepts seek **good gestalts,** examples of the self-regulating nature of a field and its inherent movement toward homeostasis.

Good gestalt: A psychologically fundamental organization.

The gestalt approach was influential, and other psychologists applied its basic tenets to a variety of topics: psychopathology, group processes, and personality. Kurt Lewin is the giant figure among those applying gestalt ideas to complex human behavior. His 1935 book *A Dynamic Theory of Personality* examined the person in field terms, paying particular interest to self-regulating processes. Lewin termed the psychological field in which behavior occurred the **life space,** and studied how the equilibrium of the life space was restored following a disturbance. He posited psychological forces called *vectors* that worked to establish a good gestalt in the life space.

Life space: According to Kurt Lewin, the psychological field in which behavior occurs.

In 1932, Lewin came to the United States, where he taught at Stanford and Cornell Universities, the University of Iowa, and MIT, attracting scores of students who have gone on to make their own mark in social and personality psychology. All share several Lewinian emphases. First is a concern with the concrete person in the concrete situation. Lewin disagreed with generalizations like these:

> He is psychotic because of his heredity.
> The rigidity of his problem-solving behavior is due to his ethnocentrism.
> Friends work better together than do strangers.
> A highly cohesive group will be more productive than a less cohesive group.
>   (Deutsch, 1968, p. 418)

These statements pull apart the person and the situation. In contrast, Lewin believed that psychology should address particulars, and particulars involved individual people in immediate situations. As you have seen, this idea still thrives in contemporary personality psychology.

A second Lewinian emphasis is a recognition of the importance of reality as it is perceived. Behavior occurs within a psychological field, not a physical one. When people behave, they do so according to what is psychologically real for them, and psychological reality may include ghosts and demons, or the military-industrial complex, or the necessity for getting straight A's. Clearly, psychological reality varies from individual to individual, and the personality psychologist must see the world as his or her research subject sees it.

Finally, a third emphasis is Lewin's belief that psychology can and should be used to solve social problems. He advocated action research: the explicit blurring of pure and applied investigation. How can effective leadership styles be cultivated? How can prejudice be eliminated? How can marital conflict be resolved?

In sum, gestalt psychology has influenced contemporary personality psychology in several ways. First, it is an early example of a field theory, an increasingly popular way of explaining personality. Second, in its emphasis on relationships and good gestalts, gestalt psychology provides a framework for regarding the unity and integrity of personality. Third, gestalt psychology, particularly the work of Lewin, led personality psychologists to attend to the particular manner in which the individual sees reality. The numerous cognitive theories in contemporary personality psychology attest to the importance of this emphasis.

Functionalism: The Mind in Use

Just as gestalt psychology reacted against an aspect of Wundt's structuralism, so, too, did *functionalism*. In this case, functionalism was concerned not with the structure of the mind, as was Wundt's psychology, but instead with its function. The structuralists asked *what* and *how;* the functionalists asked *why.*

Functionalism can be traced to Darwinian thought, and in particular to how the Englishman Herbert Spencer applied it to human action in the late 1800s. Sir Francis Galton, whose contribution to the testing tradition will be discussed later in this chapter, can also be described as a functionalist. However, functionalism was primarily an American endeavor, and its story starts with two important figures, William James of Harvard University and John Dewey of the University of Chicago and Columbia University.

William James was the first American psychologist. The brother of novelist Henry James, William completed a Harvard medical degree in 1869 and stayed on to teach physiology and later philosophy. In 1890, he published his two-volume *Principles of Psychology,* a brilliant textbook that touches on a variety of topics: habit, emotion, will, memory, consciousness, and so on. This book paved the way for a functional psychology, one that emphasizes the mind meeting the demands of everyday living. James argued that memory is not an abstract and general property of the mind, but rather a task-specific skill used in particular activities with particular consequences.

James founded the first psychology laboratory in the United States, but he was never much of an experimentalist. Instead, he taught a number of men and women who went on to perform important psychology experiments. And the students who first learned about psychology through his textbook are beyond count.

In his later years, James turned his attention from psychology per se to matters of philosophy, where he is well-known for his contributions to **pragmatism,** the only wholly American philosophy. Pragmatism stresses the relativity of knowledge and the necessity for evaluating knowledge in terms of its applications. Again, James professed a functional point of view.

Pragmatism: An approach to philosophy that stresses practical consequences.

The other significant figure in the history of functionalism is John Dewey, who won fame not just as a psychologist, but also as a philosopher and educational theorist. After appointments at the Universities of Michigan and

Minnesota, Dewey went to the new University of Chicago in 1894, where he founded the Laboratory School, also known as the Dewey School, as a natural setting in which to test his ideas about education. After ten years at Chicago, he went to Columbia where he was associated with the famous Teachers College.

Like James, Dewey influenced psychology not just by his particular contributions but also by his general attitude of pragmatism. He was a champion of progress, of experiment, of use, and of innovation. He opposed what he saw as artificial categories imposed on thought and action by the structuralists and others. His most influential paper, "The Reflex Arc Concept in Psychology," attacks the familiar stimulus-response dichotomy (Dewey, 1896). Dewey believed no stimulus can occur without a response, no response without a stimulus. Speaking of them as if they were separate entities misses the important point that human activity is a whole, a means of coordinating the person with the world.

He cites an example of a child who burns his finger by touching a lighted candle. One might say that being burned was the stimulus, and pulling the finger away was the response. Dewey objects to this description because it makes it seem that the child's action involved two steps: burning his finger and pulling it away. Instead, according to Dewy, these steps are the same action, one best understood in terms of its result: stopping the pain.

The influence of Dewey on the form of American education is still felt. His approach of learning by doing reflects his belief that the developing child is active and curious. Education should neither drill information into a passive observer nor let the child run rampant through the halls and the curriculum. Instead, education should encourage the child's natural tendencies through guided opportunities that put these lessons into practice.

This manner of education embodies the functional approach by emphasizing not the formal properties and contents of the mind so much as the consequences of the mind when used. Dewey believed in habit and felt that virtue and intelligence followed from habits of fair-mindedness, objectivity, imagination, and courage. Dewey himself was a social critic, an advocate of democracy and academic freedom.

Functionalists made important inroads into what we now recognize as personality psychology. In keeping with Darwinian thought, they examined all manner of populations, not just adult European males. They also maintained the Darwinian emphasis on fitness, examining individual differences in thought and action. For instance, Robert Woodworth (1918) emphasized the role of motivation, particularly drives. A person's actions could be understood in terms of what drove them, and different individuals have different drives—hence, different personalities.

Functionalism stimulated a number of applied psychologies still around today: child psychology, educational psychology, abnormal psychology, industrial psychology, animal psychology, cross-cultural psychology, psychology of women, and so on. But as a discrete approach to psychology, functionalism rather quickly gave way to behaviorism, which is as much a descendant of functionalism as a reaction against structuralism. But the legacy of functionalism is still with psychology and particularly with personality psychology. First, functionalism forced psychology to attend to action, stressing that action should be understood in terms of its consequences. Second, functionalism leads to the contemporary interest in adaptation. And third, functionalism—along with the testing tradition—stimulated interest in individual differences, one of the characteristic concerns of personality psychology.

Behaviorism: An Emphasis on Overt Actions

The final reaction to Wundt's structuralism was *behaviorism,* which objected not just to the use of introspection to discover the elements of consciousness but also to the very definition of psychology as the study of consciousness. Instead, according to John B. Watson, the first behaviorist, psychology should study observable behavior.

Watson was an animal psychologist and, at first, a functionalist. As I have mentioned, the functionalists saw the study of animals as legitimate for psychology, since Darwin stressed the continuity between animals and people. At the turn of the century, animal psychology was concerned with the minds of animals. Not surprisingly though, this field was just as concerned with what animals did, interpreting their behavior in terms of *tropisms,* reflexive movements toward or away from objects in the environment.

The time was right for John Watson to take these ideas one step further and apply them to people. While at Johns Hopkins University in 1913, he published his famous paper "Psychology As the Behaviorist Views It," laying out his criticisms of psychology and proposing his solutions to the problems. More

John Watson, the first behaviorist, is shown here— wearing a Santa Claus mask—with Rosalie Rayner and the infant Little Albert.

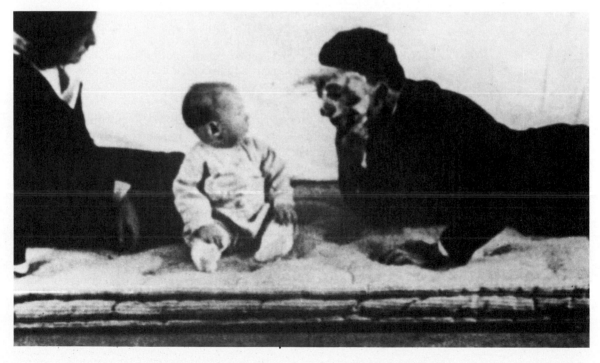

basically, he criticized introspection as the structuralists employed it. According to Watson, the major problem with this supposedly objective research technique was that different observers saw different things when they peered within their minds. So, consciousness was an inappropriate subject matter for psychology, one that should not be studied. Instead, psychology should deal with observable behavior.

Consciousness has since returned to a respectable position within psychology, along with more acceptable ways of investigating it, but it was lost for quite a while in the wake of Watson's arguments. In the meantime, Watson made a positive contribution to the field as well. He proposed that *conditioning,* as described by the Russian physiologist Ivan Pavlov, should be the cornerstone of his new *objective psychology* of animal and human behavior. In **classical conditioning,** one learns through experience to associate two stimuli. Reflexes originally elicited by the one stimulus come to be elicited by the other as well.

> **Classical conditioning: A form of learning where two stimuli come to be associated with one another.**

In a famous study with an infant known as Little Albert, Watson and Rayner (1920) demonstrated that fear of furry animals could be brought about by clanging a metal bar with a hammer when Little Albert viewed a white rat. Though just a demonstration, this example of a conditioned fear has become important to psychology, particularly to behaviorism, suggesting that psychopathology, in this case a phobia, might be brought about by mundane processes of learning.

If phobias can be learned, then so, too, can more productive ways of behaving. Watson's emphasis on conditioning led to an optimism about what psychology could accomplish, an optimism that still characterizes behavioral approaches to psychology:

> Give me a dozen healthy infants, well-formed, and my own specified world to bring them up in, and I'll guarantee to take any one at random and train him to become any type of specialist I might select—doctor, lawyer, artist, merchant, chief, and, yes, even beggar-man and thief, regardless of his talents, penchants, tendencies, activities, vocations and race of his ancestors. (Watson, 1930, p. 65)

America at the turn of the century responded well to this promise of a better world through conditioning theory, and Watson's influence spread as he further extended his ideas to people. Other behaviorists soon followed his example.

> **Operant conditioning: A form of learning where behaviors come to be associated with their consequences.**

Some emphasized Pavlov's classical conditioning approach, while others made use of **operant conditioning,** where one learns through experience the consequences of particular behaviors. This type of learning was first called the Law of Effect by Edward Lee Thorndike (1911), a Columbia functionalist who studied at Harvard with William James. Thorndike devised puzzle-boxes from which cats and other animals could escape if they performed some response like clawing at a rope. Thorndike showed that such learning proceeded slowly as the animal learned through trial-and-error which responses led to good outcomes (escape) and which did not.

Although behaviorism has certainly influenced personality psychology, a noticeable tension exists between the two. Much of what is meant by personality cannot be explained well by behaviorism. Rather than focusing on the individual, behaviorism focuses on the environment. Rather than looking at someone's general characteristics, behaviorism concerns itself with highly specific habits. Although able to explain individual differences in terms of different histories of conditioning, behaviorism regards individual differences as arbitrary and easily subject to modification. Similarly, rather than expecting behavior to endure, behaviorism views it as transient, under the sway of the particular rewards and punishments in the immediate environment.

However, behaviorism does a spectacular job of explaining what is functional or dysfunctional about behavior, and one of the success stories of modern psychology is **behavior modification,** the application of learning theory to therapy. For a number of problems, behavior modification is the treatment of choice. To Watson's catalogue of doctor, lawyer, beggar-man, and thief can be added another type of person made possible by conditioning: the individual free of needless worry and fear.

Behavior modification: The application of learning theory to therapy.

Thus, behaviorism has left its mark on contemporary personality psychology in several ways. First, it legitimized the application of theories and findings from the animal learning laboratory to people. Second, it elevated the experimental method to the most respected position among the research techniques of psychologists, an occurrence that has not always served personality psychology well. Third, and most important, behaviorism and its distrust of superfluous explanation have helped curb the occasionally extravagant and muddled theories sometimes invoked to explain personality.

IMMEDIATE ANCESTOR 2: PSYCHIATRY

Modern medicine appeared on the scene about the same time as experimental psychology. Although the medical profession has been practiced since the time of the early Greeks, the 1800s marked the most important medical breakthrough to date: the germ model of disease was formulated. Today, we are so familiar with this model that it is a bit sobering to realize that the world had printing presses, steam engines, soccer, bicycles, and *The New York Times* before it had the idea that germs caused illness.

As summarized by Maher and Maher (1979), the germ model consists of five related assumptions:

1. For each disease a specific germ exists.
2. Successful identification of the germ depends on careful description and classification of the clinical syndrome of the disease.
3. The germ is necessary and sufficient for the disease.
4. Any treatment that removes or prevents the germ from entering the body will cure the disease.
5. Immunization to the disease results from prior infection with small intensities of the germ.

The germ model was soon elaborated to propose that illness also resulted from defects in the body or from injuries to the body.

The Medical Model: From Physical Illness to Psychopathology

Medical model: The theory that diseases—including psychological difficulties—are caused by physical problems: germs, injuries, or defects.

Taken together, these views that illness results from germs, from defects, or from injuries are termed the **medical model.** As Bursten (1979) observes, the medical model assumes that illness is a biologically based dysfunction that the patient does not choose. When employed in psychiatry, the medical model means, "whenever you see mental illness, look to biology for the significant etiological data" (p. 662).

The medical model was brought about by some of the same trends that influenced experimental psychology. Although the histories of these two fields diverged considerably until personality psychology reunited them in the twentieth century, they have in common an intellectual ancestor, the theory of evolution. That experimental psychology took one path while modern medicine took another is largely due to the differing demands of the university versus the clinic.

Stimulated by discoveries about the nervous system, the entirely new medical field of neurology developed between 1840 and 1900.

> The advent of the specialty of neurology raised the "nervous" patient to a status that demanded and received dignified recognition. Symptoms attributable to the brain and the spine standing upon an objective footing were subject to therapeutic enterprise. With increasing accent on nervous symptoms, hitherto impatiently dealt with by physicians, or treated by hypnotists or faith-healers, came a new series of descriptive terms. . . . As medical men gladly relinquished their troublesome hysterics, neurologists accepted the burden. (Bromberg, 1959, p. 151)

In short fashion, neurology merged with the primitive psychiatry then in practice, and by the turn of the century, researchers were attempting to find the basis of mental disorders like senility, epilepsy, general paresis, and mania within defects of the nervous system. Sigmund Freud's original medical training was in neurology, and much of psychoanalytic theory can be viewed as a straightforward translation of neurological concepts into the realm of mind and behavior (Sulloway, 1979).

The medical model represented a unifying perspective on disease, allowing physicians to share a common viewpoint on the causes of various illnesses and how to prevent and treat them. This perspective was extended to supposed diseases of the nervous system, and in the 1800s medicine began to treat a whole new class of patients, folks we now recognize as suffering from psychological problems. The physicians who treated these "mental" patients increasingly recognized the importance of psychological factors, but they continued to use the vocabulary and perspective of the medical model in their explanations and treatments.

Freud's theory of abnormality formed the basis for his theory of personality, one that is couched in the language of the medical model, even though early in his career Freud abandoned his attempts to find specific neurological equivalents of the processes he hypothesized.

Of great importance in psychoanalytic theory is the mental conflict, which plays the role of a metaphorical germ. It rests within the person, producing a host of observable symptoms for him. The analyst must work backward from these symptoms to discover the particular conflict at work. More often than not, the conflict was implanted early in life, where it attacked a vulnerable part of the mind. Problems are cured by removing the conflict through any of a number of techniques. These problems can be prevented, however, by metaphorical immunization—exposing the ego to small frustrations and difficulties that thereby strengthen it.

The Emergence of Modern Psychiatry: Mesmer to Charcot to Janet to Freud

In contrast to experimental psychology, which originated mainly in Germany and England, psychiatry's important roots lie in France. The French were more attuned to the subject matter of psychiatry: abnormality, irrationality, emotion, and the unconscious. In fact, French medicine stressed the clinical study of the patient, making French hospitals and asylums for the mentally ill among the most advanced in the world. They provided a setting for research and the training of psychiatrists. However, because the reality of the clinic forced attention on the specific problems of the individual, the theories developed to explain these problems embraced of necessity the entire person. They were personality theories in the modern sense of the term.

Among the patients who attracted the attention of French psychiatrists were women suffering from **hysteria,** an inexplicable paralysis of some part of the body accompanied by a host of other symptoms:

Hysteria: The form of psychopathology characterized by the failure of a body part or system, with no physical cause.

> She had been ill for some months. . . . She had paralysis of the right arm, both legs were paralyzed, and she could move only the fingers of her left hand. She was unable to feed herself, and she was barely able to turn her head because of what appeared to be a paralyzed neck muscle. She complained of visual difficulty, so that she could neither write nor read. . . .
>
> Bertha spoke in half or broken sentences and complained that "black snakes" and "death's heads" were present in the room . . . most of the time Bertha did not appear to hear what was being said to her. She appeared very weak and sickly and refused to eat any food that was given to her. (Rosenbaum, 1984, p. 2)

Since the time of Hippocrates, hysteria was thought to be a disease peculiar only to women, the result of a wandering uterus, which had become dislodged and had traveled through the body, causing the symptoms that comprise the disorder. The thinkers of the 1800s mostly viewed hysteria in physical terms, quite literally applying the medical model.

One such figure was Franz Anton Mesmer, who lived from 1734 to 1815 and is best known for developing the technique of **mesmerism,** now called hypnotism. Mesmer was a Viennese physician who used magnets to treat various

Mesmerism: The techniques used by Mesmer for inducing a hypnotic state.

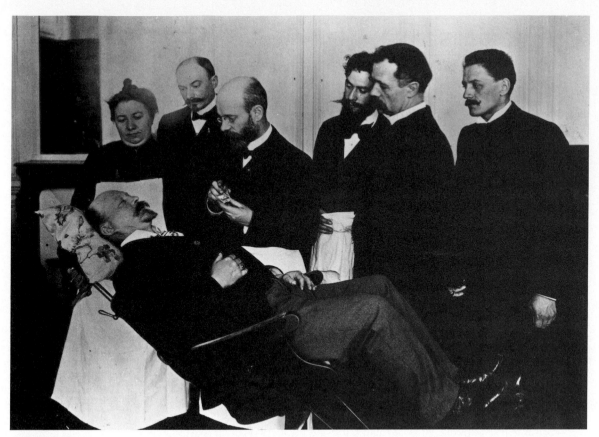

Hypnosis was widely used in the nineteenth century.

illnesses, including hysteria. He held that living beings were influenced by *animal magnetism,* a fluid that fills the universe. (Perfume and cologne advertisements still adhere to this belief in modified form; animal magnetism now resides in a spray bottle, available for a modest price.) An imbalance of animal magnetism resulted in illness, and cures involved redistributing the fluid.

Magnets were one way to achieve this redistribution, but eventually Mesmer relied only on his own being, dressing in a magician's robe and inducing a state of hypnosis. Although Mesmer's techniques seemed to be effective, his therapy aroused great opposition, probably because of its resemblance to magic and its trappings of quackery. In 1778 he moved to Paris, where he continued to cure hysterics and attract great public attention. Again, he was discredited, this time in 1784 by a scientific commission that included Benjamin Franklin.

Still, hypnosis techniques survived Mesmer's decline and fall, becoming a tool for French psychiatrists. One well-known user of hypnosis was Jean Martin Charcot (1825–1893), a Parisian physician who established the famous Salpêtrière neurological clinic in the middle of the nineteenth century. Charcot made the important observation that the symptoms of hysteria corresponded to the expectations of the patient and not to what was known about the nervous system. For instance, cases of glove paralysis, a type of hysteria where all feeling is lost in the hand from the wrist down, were seen as anatomically impossible, because nerves aren't distributed that way in the hand. Nevertheless, Charcot adhered to a physical interpretation of hysteria and its treatment by hypnosis.

Charcot's famous student, Pierre Janet, who lived from 1859 to 1947 (spanning Darwin and Hiroshima, if you care to marvel at what some individuals have seen), proposed a psychological interpretation of hysteria. Janet suggested that the problem resulted from personality splitting, with consciousness concentrating in one part and retracting from the other. Hypnosis restored the balance.

The most important student of the French approach to psychiatry was the young Sigmund Freud, who spent 1885 in Paris learning the techniques of hypnosis. Upon Freud's return home to Vienna, he began work with Joseph Breuer, an older physician who specialized in the psychological treatment of hysteria. From this early work, psychoanalysis was born, bringing to an end my brief account of the early history of psychiatry.

In sum, psychiatry has influenced personality psychology in several ways. First, it introduced the medical model to the field, a perspective on problems and how to treat them that is still the benchmark against which other approaches are measured. Second, psychiatry is concerned with clinical phenomena, concrete individuals with concrete problems of adaptation; much of personality psychology focuses on the abnormal case, and several of the most influential personality theorists have been clinicians.

IMMEDIATE ANCESTOR 3: PSYCHOLOGICAL TESTING

The **psychological testing** tradition is the story of particular tests of individual differences, the statistical procedures developed to interpret them, and their applications. When psychological testing began, the tests measured intelligence and ability. These tests subsequently influenced personality psychology by providing a model for assessing individual differences. The giant figures in the story of psychological testing include Sir Francis Galton in England (who originated psychological testing), James McKeen Cattell in the United States (who popularized testing), and Alfred Binet in France (who provided the first great success of testing with his IQ measure).

Some of the main characters in the history of psychological testing also played important roles in the history of experimental psychology. However, the two fields are distinct in that mainstream experimental psychology was concerned with basic psychological processes in the average adult, while psychological testing was concerned with individual differences. Consequently, like functionalism, psychological testing was extended to a variety of populations, often for practical purposes. What was regarded as error by experimental psychologists was of substantive importance to psychological testers.

Psychological testing: The use of psychological tests to describe individual differences.

Francis Galton: Mental Testing

The psychological testing tradition begins with the Englishman Sir Francis Galton, a cousin of Darwin who lived from 1822 to 1911. One of Galton's best-known works is the book *Hereditary Genius* (1869), a biographical study of the tendency of genius to run in families. Galton quantified the degree of genius and assumed it was distributed in the general population according to a bell-shaped curve. Like eggs, movies, or restaurants, geniuses were rated *A, B, C,* and so on through *X,* with *A* meaning "just above average" and *X* meaning "one in a million." Genius (or intelligence) determined eminence in science, literature, and so on.

Other important books by Galton included *English Men of Science* (1874) and *Natural Inheritance* (1889). In 1876 Galton published a paper on twins and how resemblances between them might be used to disentangle the effects of nature and nurture, terms first introduced in his paper. What has become known as the *twin method* is now a standard research procedure for investigating the role of genetics in personality and intelligence.

Mental test: A brief procedure for assessing an individual's mental abilities through observation of performance.

Galton invented the **mental test,** a procedure characterized by its brevity and emphasis on performance. In contrast to the elaborate techniques of experimental psychology, the mental test does not attempt to reveal everything about mental functioning, but rather tries to show individual differences in the consequences of functioning (Boring, 1950). Galton developed several tests for measuring imagery, pitch, visual judgment, muscular sense, reaction time, and so on. Many of these tests are still part of standard laboratory procedures in psychology.

Galton believed that intelligence could be measured with simple tests of sensory capacities, such as the ability to discriminate among tones or weights. Such tests proved of little value, but they influenced the course of psychological testing until Alfred Binet showed that intelligence was better measured with tests reflecting complex mental operations (Freeman, 1962).

Personality questionnaire: A written measure of a personality characteristic.

Galton also introduced the earliest version of the **personality questionnaire** (Freeman, 1926). To measure vividness of mental imagery, he asked people to report what they remembered their breakfast to have looked like that morning. From such descriptions, a researcher could quantify the vividness of an individual's visual imagery.

Fully a century ago, Galton laid out the basic assumptions for the study of individual differences and the assessment of personality. Further, he believed that individual differences had a biological basis, determined by evolution and perhaps amenable to enlightened manipulation by modern science. In 1883, he even proposed a field called **eugenics** to "improve the race" by encouraging intelligent selection.

Eugenics: Approach to improving the human species through selective breeding.

As you might imagine, eugenics was and is controversial. It assumes a biological basis to eminence and achievement that is hardly as well-established as Galton believed. In *Hereditary Genius,* for instance, insufficient attention was given to the very real possibility that the sons of famous fathers have greater opportunities than do other people. Their "genius" may reflect these opportunities and nothing more.

Finally, Galton (1888) contributed the concept of correlation, discussed in Chapter 1. He sought a way to quantify the strength of relations between variables (the link between fathers' genius and that of their sons, for example), since some pairs show a stronger relationship than do others. The index of *co-relation* was thus developed, soon to be rechristened the correlation coefficient.

James McKeen Cattell: Psychological Testing

James McKeen Cattell was a student of William Wundt. Indeed, the American Cattell was Wundt's first research assistant. As the story goes, Cattell brashly introduced himself to Wundt, "Herr Professor, you need an assistant, and I will be your assistant" (Boring, 1950, p. 324)! And indeed he was. But despite his central role in Wundt's experimental laboratory, Cattell was always more of a functionalist than a structuralist. He was interested in individual differences in reaction time, which led him to a concern with psychological testing, the term Cattell himself coined.

Cattell taught at the University of Pennsylvania, then Bryn Mawr College, then briefly at Cambridge University where he met Galton, again at Pennsylvania, and finally at Columbia, where he stayed the longest, from 1891 to 1917. Even after his dismissal from Columbia because of his pacifism in the face of World War I, Cattell remained active in psychology, leaving his mark in a number of ways.

Cattell maintained his interest in individual differences and their measurement throughout his career. In 1890, he published one of the first test batteries, which included ostensible measures of intelligence and personality. Like Galton, Cattell assumed that tests of simple reactions would give information about more complex processes. As I said earlier, this assumption has since been abandoned by mental testers, who now favor complex tests, often those with content validity. Also like Galton, Cattell was interested in eminence. He started the series *American Men of Science,* a ranking of men in the scientific professions with stars after the names of the most distinguished.

But Cattell's importance to the psychological testing tradition goes far beyond his specific contributions. He was a tireless advocate of psychology, particularly its study of individual differences. He edited numerous psychology journals, served on national committees for the American Psychological Association, and was active in the Psychological Corporation, an organization that made psychological services available to industry and the general public (Boring, 1950). Indeed, the Psychological Corporation is still one of the primary sources for psychological tests.

According to Boring (1950), Cattell was in the right place at the right time. Because he was in tune with the American Zeitgeist, people listened to him, and he was able to shape American psychology in fundamental ways:

Cattell's psychology is, however, something more than mental tests and reaction times and statistical methods and the resultant objective judgments that are not introspections. . . . It is motivated by a desire to determine how well men can do in this or that situation. . . . It is important to realize the significance of the movement, because it, almost more than any other school, has been typical of the American trend. (pp. 539–540)

Alfred Binet: Intelligence Testing

The tests that Galton and Cattell employed came from the laboratories of experimental psychologists. But, as already mentioned, these tests did not prove useful in predicting the achievement outcomes that psychological testers were interested in. At best, they found modest correlations between scores on sensory and motor tests and academic performance (Freeman, 1926). Because the tests were intended to measure intelligence, and because intelligence is presumably reflected in academic performance, something was amiss.

Alfred Binet solved the problem. Instead of borrowing simple tasks from experimental psychology to test intelligence, Binet devised measures that tapped the higher mental functions—memory, imagery, attention, comprehension, and so on. And they proved useful in predicting academic achievement, so much so that tests like the SAT and the ACT still embody the belief that achievement is best predicted from performing complex tasks.

At about the turn of the century, Binet was commissioned by the minister of public instruction in France to develop a procedure for separating dull children from those having difficulty at school for nonintellectual reasons. Modern intelligence tests were thus born, as Binet (in collaboration first with Victor Henri and then with Theodore Simon) devised tests with complex tasks like the following:

CHILDREN OF EIGHT YEARS

I. Compares Two Remembered Objects. This is a valuable test because it does not depend in the least on instruction, and brings into play the natural good sense of the subject. It consists in investigating whether the subject can, in thinking of two objects, distinguish a difference between them. . . .

II. Counts from 20 to 0. This is partly a test of school knowledge; one must have learned to count to be able to reverse the process. . . .

III. Indicates Omissions in Pictures. Four pictures are shown successively . . . in one an eye is lacking, in one the nose, in one the mouth, in one the arms. The child is asked each time: "What is missing in this picture?" (Binet & Simon, 1913)

Similar tasks were given to children of different ages, and scoring is relative to other children of the same age.

Binet introduced a number of ideas still important in psychological testing. First, test items were kept or deleted in accordance with what has become the known-group validity procedure, described in the last chapter. The very best and the very worst students were selected from a classroom and given a variety of potential test items. Only those questions where the best outscored the worst students were retained for the test.

Second, Binet introduced the idea of scoring intelligence tests on a relative basis. The term *mental age* refers to the average performance by a child of a particular age. A mental age of six corresponds to the average score of a six-year-old child. Mental age may or may not correspond to chronological age, a fact that led to William Stern's (1904) suggestion that intelligence be represented as the quotient of mental age and chronological age. So, IQ is just shorthand for *intelligence quotient*.

Third, Binet recognized that the bottom line for such tests was the degree to which they served their intended purpose. Galton and Cattell's tests were developed and administered for quite some time before their limited usefulness was recognized. In contrast, Binet's tests proved useful from the start in identifying intellectually deficient students.

Several revisions of Binet's measures were made before he died in 1911. Since that time, his tests have been translated into a number of languages, and the revisions continue. In 1912, Lewis Terman at Stanford developed an English-language version of the test that still exists as the Stanford-Binet (see Terman & Childs, 1912).

World War I provided the impetus for group-administered intelligence tests. Because modern war had become so complicated, it was desirable to separate bright from dull soldiers. Intelligence tests seemed a good way to accomplish this purpose, but up to this time, they had only been administered

World War I recruits were among the first to "sit through" intelligence testing.

individually. The necessity of testing some 2 million American recruits demanded another procedure. So psychologists developed the Army Alpha Examination, a pencil-and-paper test that could be taken by large groups of individuals at the same time. Army Alpha was the forerunner of the group testing to which all of us have been subjected.

By the 1920s, the limitations of intelligence testing had come to be recognized. That the Stanford-Binet and the Army Alpha were culture-bound became apparent. They favored native speakers of English and those from a bookish or verbal environment (Boring, 1950). Plus, the assumption that intelligence was some unitary and fixed characteristic of the individual was also challenged. Special abilities and talents unrelated to general intelligence were documented, and more specific aptitude tests were developed to measure these.

Throughout the twentieth century, psychologists have suggested culture-fair tests: measures of intelligence unbiased by a person's particular social and educational background. So far, none of these tests have proven satisfactory, probably because their goal is impossible. Culture-fair tests are based on the doubtful assumption that one can speak of adaptation (intelligence) apart from a particular setting. Most intelligence tests are validated against the criterion of academic performance, and this criterion clearly favors certain cultural and social backgrounds over others. That poor people and minorities sometimes score badly on standard intelligence tests says more about bias in academic institutions than anything else.

Intelligence testing has influenced personality testing by providing an example of how an individual difference can be reliably measured and used to predict subsequent behavior. However, the success of intelligence testing stems from the unambiguous criterion (school grades) against which they have been continually validated. This criterion is typically the behavior to be predicted. In contrast, personality tests are validated against an ambiguous criterion, and the behavior they attempt to predict may be different than this criterion. No wonder personality tests have sometimes been unsuccessful.

The Emergence of Personality Testing

Intelligence tests dominated early psychological testing, but personality tests followed closely on their heels, using the procedures exemplified by measures of intelligence. For instance, in 1919, Eleanor Morgan, Helen K. Mull, and Margaret W. Washburn described a measure of cheerfulness versus depression validated by the known-groups method. The researchers presented subjects with a list of 50 words on each of five successive days. For each word, the subject thought of some experience that was then classified as either pleasant or unpleasant. Later, subjects were asked to remember the words in the lists and were given a score reflecting the proportion of pleasant to unpleasant words they recalled. These scores were compared to reports by friends on whether the subjects were generally optimistic or pessimistic. As you might expect, cheerful (optimistic) subjects recalled a greater proportion of pleasant words than the depressed (pessimistic) subjects, who showed the opposite pattern (see Bower, 1981).

Also early in the century, at the request of General John Pershing, Robert Woodworth created the first personality measures that asked subjects to describe their own personality, the Personal Data Sheet, which was used with army recruits in World War I and published in 1919. The Personal Data Sheet attempted to identify men who were unfit for military service because of personality maladjustment. Individuals were asked to respond to such questions as

- Does the sight of blood make you sick or dizzy?
- Do you sometimes wish that you had never been born?
- Are you happy most of the time?
- Do people find fault with you much?

A person who gave a sufficient number of undesirable answers was then interviewed. Because the Personal Data Sheet attempted to assess a variety of personality characteristics, it is also the first example of a personality inventory, foreshadowing such later tests as the MMPI.

Other early personality measures included tests of temperament (Downey, 1923), emotion (Pressey, 1921), moral judgment (Fernald, 1912), aesthetic sensitivity (Thorndike, 1916), and so on. Each measure regarded some aspect of personality as an individual difference and assigned scores to subjects reflecting how much of the aspect they possessed. Methods included self-report questionnaires, ratings by observers, word-association tasks, and analyses of behaviors such as handwriting.

More and more tests of personality appeared as the result of attempts to measure the individual differences suggested by an ever-increasing number of personality theories. Psychoanalytic theory inspired measures of individual differences in needs and drives, and Gestalt theory gave rise to measures of individual differences in tendencies to tolerate uncertainty and ambiguity. In other cases, personality measures appeared in response to practical demands. Just as World War I led to group intelligence testing, the more settings applied psychologists worked in, the more measures of individual differences they devised in response to the practical questions posed in these settings (Freeman, 1926).

When should children enter school? Once there, are they performing up to their ability? Which applicants should be chosen for professional school? For what job is a person best suited? What abilities are needed to perform a particular task? Who commits crime? Which individuals should be allowed to immigrate to the United States?

To date, the clinic has been the most important setting for applied psychologists. In the early days of clinical psychology, psychologists did not do psychotherapy. Rather, clinical psychologists administered psychological tests to patients under the care of psychiatrists (Korchin, 1983). These tests were used to diagnose particular problems, to understand their causes, to recommend treatments, and to forecast outcomes. (World War II created an urgent demand for more therapists, a need filled by clinical psychologists, but that is a different story.)

**Projective test:
A personality test
that presents individ-
uals with ambiguous
stimuli onto which
they "project" their
personality char-
acteristics as they
respond.**

Chief among the tests administered to mental patients by clinical psychologists are **projective tests,** so named because they present ambiguous stimuli that allows subjects to project their personality in responding to them. The best-known projective measure is Hermann Rorschach's Inkblot Tests:

> The subject is given one plate after the other and asked, "What might this be?" He holds the plate in his hand and may turn it about as much as he likes. The subject is free to hold the plate near his eyes or as far away as he chooses. . . . An attempt is made to get at least one answer to every plate, though suggestion in any form is, of course, avoided. . . .
>
> The test has proven to be of diagnostic value. In normals it makes possible differential diagnosis of personality; in patients, the diagnosis of illness. Furthermore, it presents an intelligence test almost completely independent of previous knowledge, memory, practice, and degree of education. It is possible by means of the test to draw conclusions concerning many affective relationships. The test has the advantage of almost unlimited applicability making possible without further data comparison of the results in the most heterogeneous subjects. (1942, pp. 14–18)

The popularity of the Inkblot Test stems from its compatibility with psychoanalytic theory, which holds that an individual's underlying needs and drives affect all spheres of functioning. The basic premise of the Rorschach Inkblot Test is that individual responses reveal personality characteristics as readily as do dreams, free associations, and slips of the tongue.

Another well-known projective test is the Thematic Apperception Test, developed by Christiana D. Morgan and Henry Murray at the Harvard Psychological Clinic in 1935. The TAT, as it is known, presents subjects with ambiguous pictures. The subject tells a story about the characters in the picture. She tells any sort of story she wants, so long as it has a beginning, middle, and end. Again, the individual reveals her personality by projecting it on the pictures she sees. Murray and his colleagues were particularly interested in individual differences in needs, such as the need for achievement or the need for recognition, and they devised ways to score these needs from TAT stories.

The Minnesota Multiphasic Personality Inventory (MMPI) is yet another wisely used clinical test. Starke R. Hathaway and J. C. McKinley (1943) created this test during World War II by presenting a number of statements to individuals with known psychiatric diagnoses. They determined the pattern of responses associated with a particular diagnosis, just as Binet determined which of his test items accompanied good versus poor academic achievement. The MMPI is widely used to make initial diagnoses of emotional difficulty. Further, because it measures a number of ways people can differ from each other, it is considered an **inventory:** a collection of personality measures that attempts to be exhaustive, if not exhausting. The MMPI has also been extensively used with normal subjects.

**Inventory: A collec-
tion of personality
tests that attempts to
be exhaustive.**

The personality testing field thrives today, with new discoveries in statistics and the technological revolution of computers allowing ever-sophisticated attempts to measure individual differences and predict subsequent functioning. Despite this sophistication, personality testing still suffers from validity problems. Of special concern is that the criterion of a particular test is ambiguous, because the individual difference of concern usually bears no simple relation to a particular aspect of the world.

PERSONALITY PSYCHOLOGY DURING THE LAST SIXTY YEARS

When did modern personality psychology first appear? I have described its three immediate ancestors—experimental psychology, psychiatry, and psychological testing—but the field has no specific date of birth. As various researchers and theorists began to weave together the ideas, methods, and applications provided by these ancestors, personality psychology began in many ways at many times. But, as we look backward, we see that something significant was taking place in the early decades of the twentieth century.

Once established, personality psychology followed a course that parallels the history of psychology in general (Wertheimer, 1979). First, in the 1930s and 1940s, great schools promoted by charismatic theorists flourished. Next, in the 1950s, came a breakdown of these schools and the creation of a second generation of theories more closely linked to research findings. Then, in the 1960s, personality psychology suffered several crises of confidence and began a period of intensive self-scrutiny that continued into the 1970s. Finally, we see today a new era in personality psychology, one marked by creativity and growth in which personality psychologists are responding to the years of self-criticism. Today, personality psychology has surmounted past crises while remaining true to the earlier vision of a scientific account of individual lives.

Great Schools (1930–1950)

When he first proposed his theories at the turn of the century, Freud was controversial and unpopular. However, by the 1930s his ideas had gained acceptance and respect, and Freud was recognized as a towering intellectual figure. A school of psychoanalytic thought had developed around him, one with notable advocates and dissenters. Psychoanalytic theory during the 1930s was extended by Freud and others in agreement with his position, as well as by the neoFreudians, theorists who emphasized the role of the environment to a greater degree than did the orthodox Freudians.

At the same time, other schools of thought proposing general theories of personality flourished. Carl Jung (1924) and Alfred Adler (1927), who had broken with Freud some time earlier, elaborated their *psychodynamic* theories, attracting many followers. Henry Murray (1938) of TAT fame published *Explorations in Personality,* describing a personality theory based on motivation. He called his approach **personology** to emphasize his interest in understanding the individual person.

Gordon Allport of Harvard also made numerous contributions to personality psychology during the 1930s. He reported his *Studies in Expressive*

Personology: Murray's term for personality psychology, stressing that the field should be concerned with the person.

Movement (Allport & Vernon, 1933), an investigation into the consistency of behavioral styles, and published a still-used questionnaire that measures values (Allport & Vernon, 1931). Most important, *Personality: A Psychological Interpretation* (1937) contained Allport's argument that personality psychology must recognize and study the uniqueness of the individual person. Personality psychology thus stands apart from all other sciences, which are concerned with the general case. This was the first phrasing of a debate still alive today over whether personality psychology entails understanding the unique or the general.

Other personality schools reflected Gestalt orientations. Kurt Lewin (1935) and Kurt Goldstein (1939) applied gestalt ideas to personality. Goldstein coined the term **self-actualization,** the idea that people have a drive to fulfill their inner potential, to seek the good gestalt inherent in their personality. Self-actualization became a central aspect of later theories in **humanistic psychology,** an approach to psychology that emphasizes people's inherent goodness, healthiness, and growth. Also, Murray and Allport used gestalt ideas in their personality theories, emphasizing that people must be understood as coherent wholes, not in terms of disconnected parts.

Other personality theories of this era were William Sheldon's (1940) *constitutional approach,* a theory of personality based on physique, and Gardner Murphy's (1947) *biosocial approach,* an integration of biological and cultural determinants. Edward C. Tolman (1932) at University of California, Berkeley, B.F. Skinner (1938) at Harvard, and Clark L. Hull (1943) at Yale University offered influential views about behaviorism. And what else? Lewin and Murray introduced experimentation to the study of personality. And the first textbooks in personality psychology appeared, written by Ross Stagner (1936) and Gordon Allport (1937).

This was an exciting era in personality psychology: Bold theories were proposed by bold theorists; students debated their pros and cons; and pioneering applications of personality psychology were made in the classroom, the workplace, and the clinic. Although disagreement characterized the field, so, too, did great expectations. The use of scientific psychology to answer questions about human nature promised much.

Nevitt Sanford was one participant in this age of great schools, a student at Harvard in the 1930s and a faculty member at Berkeley in the 1940s. He writes of this time:

> The most important expectation was that all hands should have intellectual interests. When scholars said to one another, "That's interesting," the reference, almost always, was to ideas, theoretical issues, or research findings that had significance within a theoretical framework.
>
> As to *what* a person was interested in, there was a great diversity, and broad tolerance for the diversity. The spirit of William James walked abroad. People remembered with what satisfaction he had said, after successfully recruiting a philosophical opponent, that now *all* points of view were represented in his department.
>
> Given this value for diversity, which was based on the conviction that no pathway to the truth should be neglected, professors and students had to learn how

Self-actualization: The drive to realize one's inner potential.

Humanistic psychology: The general approach to psychology concerned with people's inherent goodness, healthiness, and growth.

to differ; they had to familiarize themselves with their opponents' positions and accord them respect, while forthrightly expressing their own views. (1976, p. 757)

The spirit of the time and the university allowed grand theories of personality to be proposed. But as universities became more specialized, professors and students no longer devoted time and energy to such activities. Instead, research (gathering and publishing data) became more important than theory (proposing general accounts of human nature). Nevertheless, personality psychology continued to attract more than its share of brilliant contributors.

Second Generation Theories (1950–1960)

During the 1950s, important empirical research gave rise to a second generation of personality theories. Each of these theories flowed from one of the grand approaches of the preceding decades, but they were more tied to research findings and somewhat more narrow in scope.

One well-known study resulted in *The Authoritarian Personality* (Adorno, Frenkel-Brunswik, Levinson, & Sanford, 1950), an attempt to understand the

What is the appeal of dictators like Hitler?

phenomenon of European fascism. What was the appeal of such dictators as Mussolini and Hitler? Why had their message been so popular? Why did six million die in concentration camps?

Susceptibility to fascism was explained with an individual difference called **authoritarianism,** comprised of rigid conventionality, submission to authority, prejudice, and preoccupation with dominance and submission, coupled with an exaggerated concern with sexual matters (Dillehay, 1978). The authors of *The Authoritarian Personality* used psychoanalytic and gestalt ideas to explain how certain forms of child-rearing produced the rigid and intolerant authoritarian.

Another important line of personality research beginning in the 1950s was David McClelland's (1961, 1965, 1971) investigations of **achievement motivation.** Starting with the TAT, McClelland refined techniques for scoring individual differences in the motive to achieve. Applying his techniques to all sorts of material—folk stories, Greek vases, even Dick-and-Jane readers—he was able to predict the subsequent success or failure of individuals, as well as societies!

Raymond B. Cattell (1950) and Hans J. Eysenck (1952b) used sophisticated statistical techniques to discern patterns in how people responded to diverse personality measures. They regarded the patterns they discovered as basic dimensions of personality, and each proposed his own theory to interpret these. In both cases, they relied on learning theory.

John Dollard and Neal E. Miller (1950) also applied learning theory to personality, particularly to the way individuals resolved conflicts. We now sprinkle our ordinary conversations with the phrase *approach-avoidance conflict,* first introduced by Dollard and Miller.

A number of important personality theories were also proposed by psychotherapists moving beyond their original psychoanalytic training. Erik Erikson (1950) extended psychoanalytic theory to include development across the entire life span. At Ohio State University, Julian B. Rotter (1954) articulated his *social learning theory,* which casts principles of learning in field terms and assigns central importance to an individual's expectations about the world. Another Ohio State professor, George Kelly (1955), drew on his years of clinical practice to write his two-volume *Psychology of Personal Constructs,* a theory of personality based on the person-as-scientist metaphor. Carl R. Rogers published *Client-Centered Therapy* in 1951, in which he presented his *self theory of personality and psychotherapy.* According to Rogers, a positive perception of the self is needed for health and happiness: Abnormality results from low self-regard; psychotherapy tries to boost it.

Cross-cultural psychology took form as John Whiting and Irving Child (1953) began to use data from various cultures to test explicit hypotheses. Of particular interest were psychoanalytic predictions relating child-rearing practices to adult personality types. Correlations were computed not on the scores of individuals but on the scores of entire societies. For instance, high rates of alcohol use in a society are associated with strong pressures on children to achieve (Child, 1968).

Authoritarianism: An individual difference reflecting the degree to which one is rigidly conventional, submissive to authority, and prejudiced.

Achievement motivation: The need or drive to excel in situations characterized by a standard of excellence.

In addition to new personality theories, this era also saw the intensive investigation of specific individual differences measured by particular personality tests. These variables usually originated in some general theory of personality; but in keeping with the increasing specialization of psychology, they often took on a life of their own as the focus of circumscribed research. Herman A. Witkin and his colleagues (1954) studied field dependence and independence; Donn Byrne (1961) investigated repression; Julian Rotter (1966) looked at locus of control, and so on.

Self-Criticism, Doubt, and Crisis (1960–1980)

The 1960s and 1970s were times of turmoil and doubt, in society as a whole as well as in personality psychology. Perhaps the self-criticism reflected some aspect of the Zeitgeist, a realization that the American Dream did not always come true, that science did not hold all the answers to human problems, that the old maps did not describe the new territories.

Psychological testing was criticized as a tool of the establishment, a way to rationalize prejudice and preserve the status quo. It had been recognized for years that intelligence tests were culture-bound, but the 1960s brought recommendations that tests therefore be abandoned, and consumer advocate groups instituted lawsuits to bring this about.

Related skepticism surfaced about the wisdom of researchers relying on personality questionnaires. Some feared that personality psychology was becoming the scientific study of questionnaire completion. And questionnaire completion itself might reflect merely a collection of response biases, such as tendencies to answer in socially acceptable ways, to answer extremely (or moderately), even to lie and conceal. "Where's the person in personality research?" asked Rae Carlson (1971) in a well-known review of questionnaire studies.

Psychotherapy was branded ineffective, as critics such as Hans Eysenck (1952a) marshaled evidence that it did not work. More profoundly, other critics led by Thomas Szasz (1961) attacked the very notion of mental illness, calling it a myth. Perhaps the medical model had nothing to say about problems in living; perhaps the personality theories that embody the medical model, in part or whole, were irrelevant to understanding why people think, feel, and act as they do.

Humanists took issue with the overly mechanistic theories that dominated psychology. Influential approaches like psychoanalysis and behaviorism were seen as relegating people to the role of passive victims, pulled and pushed about by internal drives or external stimuli. Inspired by existential thought, humanistic psychologists called for a psychology broad enough to incorporate what they deemed critical to being human: experience, freedom, choice, meaning, and will. Traditional personality theories were seen as lacking, and psychotherapies based on these theories were branded inevitable failures.

Stanford psychologist Walter Mischel struck the most telling blow in his 1968 book *Personality and Assessment*. As he describes in the preface to this important work, he began with an attempt to write a textbook on personality psychology "to survey six or seven equally viable alternative theoretical approaches to personality and to examine the implications of each for personality assessment, psychotherapy, and research" (p. vii). In the course of his library research, though, something unsettling occurred. Mischel concluded from the studies he read that one of the basic assumptions of personality psychology—that people act consistently across situations—was contradicted by the facts.

As noted in Chapter 1, *Personality and Assessment* turned into a presentation of these facts and the far-reaching conclusion that people could not be described sensibly in terms of pervasive personality traits. Instead, personality was better understood in terms of the situation in which the person was found, a position fully consistent with the social-learning orientation Mischel espoused. Of course, a situational account of personality is really not personality psychology. Mischel's critique of personality traits therefore went far beyond traits per se and struck at the entire field. To some, the conclusion from *Personality and Assessment* was that personality psychology was dead (cf. McAdams, 1990).

Contemporary Personality Psychology (1980–)

Was personality psychology really dead? Mischel's (1968) book at first attracted heavy and widespread criticism. The basic data on which he relied, his strategy of selecting studies, the inferences he made from them, and his social-learning alternative to traditional personality psychology were all attacked. However, once the smoke cleared, the book's contributions were recognized, and theorists and researchers began to accommodate them to the field. In 1983, Stephen West wrote:

> From the vantage point of 15 years, it appears that Mischel's *Personality and Assessment* has provided a valuable corrective for the field of personality. It helped precipitate a much needed critical reexamination of the field out of which has emerged a number of genuine contributions and a generally more cautious and precise approach to the prediction of behavior. . . . Personality research has achieved considerable vitality and a number of researchers are actively addressing these important issues. Far from being a moribund field as some earlier critics maintained, personality has emerged from its crisis period to become one of the most exciting areas of research in psychology. (p. 283)

Today, far from being regarded as the individual who did away with personality psychology, Mischel is regarded as one of the field's most important contributors. He shook things up, and as they settled, they were put together in new and exciting ways (Buss & Cantor, 1989).

Assessment is now approached with more sophistication (West, 1986). The complex nature of personality has been recognized, so questionnaires are now validated against a number of behaviors instead of a single criterion (Epstein, 1980). Highly specific personality measures are more successful in predicting relevant outcomes than highly general measures (Jaccard, 1974). New techniques for combining the results of different studies—called **meta-analysis**—have uncovered relationships not otherwise obvious. For instance, meta-analysis suggests that psychotherapy is effective after all (Smith & Glass, 1977), so millions of psychotherapists can breathe easily (and so can their clients).

Another reaction to Mischel's book is *interactionism,* a rediscovery of Lewin's dictum that behavior is the joint product of the person and the situation (Bowers, 1973; Ekehammar, 1974; Endler & Magnusson, 1976a, 1976b). From this view, personality traits per se do not explain what a person thinks, says, or does. Neither do situational factors. We must consider the concrete person in the concrete situation.

Daryl Bem and Andrea Allen (1974) similarly resurrected one of Gordon Allport's ideas: that people differ in terms of traits best used to describe them. Because a trait, by definition, is shown only when a person acts consistently, then it follows that some traits only apply to some people, not all people. Said another way, different people have different traits. These researchers demonstrated that impressive consistency in behaviors reflecting a trait like conscientiousness does indeed exist for folks nominating themselves as consistent, but not for others.

New ways to study individual lives with *psychobiography* and *psychohistory* appeared (McAdams & Ochberg, 1988), and longitudinal studies found impressive coherence in personality over decades (West & Graziano, 1989). Henry Murray's (1938) vision of a scientific personology again took form.

In the last decade, personality psychology has become increasingly cognitive. In his 1968 review, Mischel did find evidence for consistency of certain cognitive characteristics. Kelly's (1955) *personal construct theory* is now more popular than ever, as are newer formulations like Albert Bandura's (1986) *self-efficacy theory* that regard personality as the way people think about themselves and the world. Mischel (1986) calls these cognitive characteristics **person variables** to distinguish them from traits, but they still refer to individual differences that are general and enduring.

As personality psychology has become more cognitive, it has also begun to emphasize more what people actually do (Cantor, 1990). *Personality* refers not just to characteristics people possess but also to how they go about their behavior: thinking, feeling, and acting. Although John Watson and other early behaviorists might have disapproved, contemporary personality theorists combine cognitive ideas with notions from learning to such a degree that we can sensibly speak of a cognitive-behavioral approach to personality (e.g., Bandura, 1986; Cantor & Kihlstrom, 1987).

Yet another noteworthy aspect of contemporary personality psychology is renewed interest in the biological underpinnings of personality (Buss, 1990). Recent research findings imply that personality characteristics may have a genetic basis (Tellegen et al., 1988). Other lines of investigation attempt to unravel the physiological pathways by which personality is related to good and bad physical health (Suls & Rittenhouse, 1987).

Sociobiology: An extension of evolutionary ideas to complex behavior.

Related to this interest in biology is the recent application of ideas from **sociobiology** to the basic concerns of personality psychology (Buss, 1991). Sociobiology is an extension of evolutionary theory to complex behavior (Wilson, 1975). From this vantage, one asks about the evolutionary significance of personality. Has our species somehow profited because of individual differences? And if so, just how has that taken place? Sociobiological discussions of personality are provocative *and* controversial, because they suggest that important human differences, like those between men and women, may have their basis in evolutionary history.

To conclude this chapter, the complexity of personality psychology reflects not just its subject matter but also its diverse ancestry. The contemporary personality psychologist must master many skills, from designing a laboratory experiment to interviewing a patient to computing a correlation coefficient to understanding the prehistory of the human species. Most importantly, today's personality psychologist must integrate these skills into the scientific understanding of what is general, characteristic, enduring, and functional about the individual person.

SUMMARY

Personality psychology started to take form in the 1800s with the emergence in Europe and the United States of experimental psychology, psychiatry, and psychological testing. These fields were the immediate ancestors of personality psychology as we now know it. In this chapter, I described the histories of these ancestors.

In 1879, Wilhelm Wundt founded the first experimental psychology laboratory. His approach to psychology, now called structuralism, has since passed into disfavor, but it stimulated vigorous opposition in the form of alternative approaches that still influence psychology, including approaches to personality. Gestalt psychology was an approach with the patterns inherent in experience. Functionalism stressed mind-in-use; its focus on the consequences of behavior gave rise to applied psychology. Finally, behaviorism called for a study of what was observable—overt behavior rather than subjective experience—and thus popularized theories of learning.

Psychiatry resulted from the application of the medical model to problems in living. According to this approach, illness and disease result from malfunctions of the body, so perhaps psychological difficulties are similarly produced. Jean Charcot and Pierre Janet studied hysteria and devised ways to treat it. The young Sigmund Freud, studying in France, became interested in hysteria as well, and his attempts to understand it resulted in psychoanalytic theory, a metaphorical neurology of the mind.

The testing tradition started in England with the work of Darwin's cousin, Sir Francis Galton, who was interested in intelligence and interpreted it in evolutionary terms. He invented psychological tests and pioneered statistical techniques to interpret their results. Psychological testing was given further boosts by James McKeen Cattell in the United States and Alfred Binet in France. Tests of personality characteristics followed the example of intelligence tests.

Personality psychology as a discrete field first cohered in the 1930s in the work of charismatic theorists like Freud, Gordon Allport, Henry Murray, and Kurt Lewin, who proposed general theories of personality. Additional theories appeared through the 1950s in conjunction with a variety of studies and applications. In the 1960s, personality psychology began a period of intensive self-criticism highlighted by Walter Mischel's 1968 critique of personality traits as useless fictions. Personality psychology emerged successfully from this period by developing new approaches to theory and research. Today, personality psychology is a thriving endeavor.

PARADIGMS OF PERSONALITY PSYCHOLOGY

*S*ome activities are highly prescribed; by consensus, there is one and only one way to go about them. Making a hamburger at McDonald's, filling out a loan application, and performing long division are invariably done the same way by almost all people. In contrast, other activities are quite loosely prescribed. Again by consensus, there are dozens of ways to go about them. Shopping for groceries, packing a suitcase, and decorating an apartment are done in different ways by almost all people. So, activities can be classified along a dimension of uniformity versus idiosyncrasy.

So, too, can we classify the sciences. In some cases, scientists agree about the best way to propose a theory, conduct a study, and apply the results. In other cases, they disagree. Theory, research, and application are almost a matter of taste. Where does personality psychology fall along this continuum?

As I see the field, it's someplace in the middle. Agreement is neither high nor low regarding the best way to go about it. More than one perspective in personality psychology exists, but not an infinity of them. Indeed, the number is quite small—four to be exact, and they are the subject of the remainder of this book. In this chapter, I will present an overview of the important concerns of the following personality perspectives with regard to theory, research, and application:

■ The **psychodynamic paradigm.** This perspective began in Freud's psychoanalytic theory and stresses unconscious motives and the interplay between people's thoughts and feelings.
■ The **humanistic paradigm.** This perspective stresses people's conscious experience and will, along with their drive to fully realize their inner potential.
■ The **trait paradigm.** This perspective assumes people are defined by stable and pervasive individual differences, often of a biological nature.

Psychodynamic paradigm: A general approach to personality that stresses unconscious motives and the interplay between people's thoughts and feelings.

Humanistic paradigm: A general approach to personality that stresses people's conscious experience and will, along with their drive to realize their potential.

Trait paradigm: A general approach to personality that describes people in terms of stable and pervasive individual differences.

Cognitive-behavioral paradigm: A general approach to personality that stresses people's thoughts and beliefs, as well as learning.

■ The **cognitive-behavioral paradigm.** This is the most recent perspective to take form, from the combination of theories that stress people's thoughts and beliefs on the one hand and learning on the other.

SCIENTIFIC PARADIGMS: WEBS OF BELIEF

Paradigm: A scientific worldview.

I have referred to each perspective as a **paradigm.** This term has various meanings, captured by such synonyms as *procedure, framework,* and *approach* applied in the broadest sense to a science.

> "Scientific paradigm" . . . refers to the total complex of a science. It includes the language, theories, conceptual schemas, methods, and limits of the science. It determines which aspects of the world the scientist studies and the kinds of explanations he considers. Most important, it includes the way the scientist sees the data, laws, and theories of his science. (McCain & Segal, 1973, p. 81)

In other words, a scientific paradigm is a *worldview,* a set of related assumptions and values the scientist uses while going about scientific activities.

Philosophers W. V. Quine and J. S. Ullian (1978) describe the interrelatedness of any system of beliefs, including scientific paradigms, as a web. Particular beliefs are woven together with other beliefs, and we judge a given fact in terms of how well it fits within the entire web of belief. Some beliefs are more central than others, because they bear upon a large number of other beliefs. We are reluctant to give these up because doing so would entail an overhaul of our entire system:

> When our system of beliefs supports our expectation of some event and that event does not occur, we have the problem of selecting certain of our interlocking beliefs for revision. This is what happens when an experiment is made to check a scientific theory and the result is not what the theory predicted. The scientist then has to revise his theory somehow; he must drop some one or another, at least, of the beliefs which together implied the false prediction. (Quine & Ullian, 1978, p. 20)

The scientific paradigm tells one which beliefs are to be revised in the face of contrary evidence. The paradigm itself is rarely changed. It is where you stand to paint the floor. You can't very well paint the same place on which you are standing.

Thomas Kuhn (1970), a historian of science, uses the notion of scientific paradigm to explain change. According to Kuhn, science does not evolve slowly and surely. Instead, it changes in leaps and bounds, in what he calls *paradigm shifts,* as if the channel selector on your television set were suddenly spun. Kuhn describes these rapid changes as *revolutions,* since they entail the replacement of one paradigm with another.

Most of the time, scientists work within a given paradigm, conducting research, making slight corrections in theory, and so on. The basic paradigm is unaffected by these activities, which Kuhn calls *ordinary science.* But it may happen that anomalous findings occur, or that theoretical contradictions surface. Kuhn believes the science then enters a *crisis state.* Problematic findings or deductions are either ignored or swept away, or a new paradigm emerges to accommodate them. Scientific revolutions are rare, but when a new paradigm wins out, profound changes take place, just as you would find in the aftermath of a political revolution.

You might compare the process of scientific revolution described by Kuhn to the more familiar phenomenon of religious conversion. Perhaps a friend or family member (or even you) has made a dramatic change in the way religion (or politics or sexuality) is regarded. Whether this involved taking on new beliefs, discarding old ones, or both, the conversion was a radical change in perspective. All thought, actions, and feelings were affected. A paradigm shift occurred, no doubt precipitated by some event or belief that could not be accommodated within the old way of thinking.

Kuhn based his theory of scientific change on the physical sciences, using physics as his primary example. The Copernican paradigm gave way to the Newtonian paradigm, which in turn gave way to the new physics of Einstein (for a readable history of this process, see Zukav, 1979). Kuhn hesitates to extend his ideas to the social sciences, which he considers *pre-paradigmatic.*

In other words, the social sciences—including psychology—have not matured to the point where a single paradigm dominates scientific activity. I have to agree with Kuhn on this point, because as noted I see at least four major perspectives regarding proper science within personality psychology alone. However, I think Kuhn's ideas are still quite useful in the social sciences, because they help make sense of what otherwise seems a hodgepodge of theories, methods, and applications.

It is not an accident that personality psychologists who favor a particular theory also favor a particular research method, nor is it an accident that they make only certain applications of their ideas. The activities of personality psychologists are clustered together, and these clusters seem pretty much what Kuhn calls paradigms.

At the same time, they are not exactly what he means by a paradigm because several of them exist at the same time, overlapping in some ways (but not in others). Consider Kuhn's paradigm a prototype of the way science is conducted, and consider the personality paradigms that I will discuss here as less-than-perfect examples of this prototype.

Paradigm shifts occur among the perspectives of personality psychology, as well. These may not always supplant earlier perspectives, but they arise in response to anomalies, and they represent a profoundly different way to regard personality. When Freud introduced the idea of childhood sexuality, he did so to explain some puzzling aspects of hysteria. Personality psychology has not been the same since. And hysteria has all but vanished! Ideas are powerful.

Why are there only four paradigms of personality psychology? If a paradigm is a point of view, there surely can be more than four of them. Hypothetically, I'm sure this is the case. But the history of personality psychology provided only so many raw ingredients to combine into points of view about how to conduct personality psychology.

Additionally, remember that personality psychology tries to explain personality. Personality psychology has only so many paradigms because there are only so many ways to explain what is general, characteristic, enduring, and functional about an individual.

PERSONALITY PARADIGMS: DIFFERENT STRATEGIES OF EXPLANATION

The personality paradigms to be discussed in this book provide explanations that differ not only in details but in overall thrust. Have you ever considered how something can be explained in altogether different ways? Let's take the question "Why did you leave the room?" It requires an explanation, but many are possible:

"I left the room because it was too hot."
"I left the room because I wanted to."
"I left the room because I wasn't interested in what was being said."
"I left the room because I'm not the sort of person who can sit still too long."
"I left the room because it was time to leave."
"I left the room because I was angry."
"I left the room because I was thirsty."
"I left the room because my business there was through."
"Why did I leave the room? You really should ask why I stayed as long as I did."

These all might be perfectly reasonable explanations in response to the question, but they answer it in different ways. One explanation points to a characteristic of personality ("I'm not the sort of person who can sit still . . ."), and another to a cause in the situation ("It was hot . . ."). Yet another points to a developmental factor ("It was time . . .") or to an interaction between the person and the situation ("My business was through . . ."). And still another "explanation" may even be the denial that anything needs to be explained.

To the degree that the different personality paradigms stress one mode of explanation rather than another, they are attempting to do different things (Johnson, Germer, Efran, & Overton, 1988). If one paradigm has something reasonable to say about personality, we cannot automatically assume the other paradigms do not.

In past decades, quite a debate raged in psychology about the relative contribution of person characteristics versus situational characteristics in explaining behavior. Each side produced data showing that behavior can be well-accounted for by properties of the person or the situation, and then concluded that the other side must be wrong. This debate is now recognized as being at cross-purposes (Nisbett & Ross, 1991). The argument overlooked the point that the different sides endorsed different types of explanations that prove to be complementary. Indeed, the cognitive-behavioral paradigm has become a productive perspective precisely because it goes beyond this particular debate to emphasize both the person and the situation.

Given that the different paradigms of personality represent different strategies of explanation, let us characterize each paradigm a bit more fully.

Psychodynamic Paradigm

The psychodynamic paradigm began in Freud's psychoanalytic theory, which emerged from psychiatry. Psychiatry in turn resulted from the application of the medical model to problems in living. Throughout much of this historical process, theorists used biological explanations (Sulloway, 1979). For example, Freud emphasized instinctive drives and described development as the unfolding of an inherent nature while the individual passes through stages defined by the part of the body that provides gratification.

Theorists who follow in Freud's footsteps tend to downplay his strong biological emphasis, stressing instead the social determinants of personality. They concern themselves with unconscious motives and the interplay between one's thoughts and feelings, and this approach therefore continues to address psychological dynamics. Behavior is seen as complexly determined. Because a distinction is made between what can be seen on the surface and what lies beneath, meaning and symbolism take on central importance.

Research within the psychodynamic tradition has often used the case-study method, intensive examinations of a single individual over time. Case studies are derived from medical records, which in turn are similar to the early descriptions of naturalists. What better way to understand the unfolding of our inner nature than to describe this process as it occurs to an individual in a natural habitat?

Many applications stemming from the psychodynamic perspective try to reroute an individual's energy. Psychoanalytic therapy aims at freeing the energy devoted to neurotic symptoms. If and when this happens, it becomes available for other—presumably healthier—purposes. Other applications try to find outlets for people's sexual and aggressive drives. Your college no doubt has an extensive intramural program. Part of the rationale for sports is to cultivate sportsmanship and the like, but the rest of the rationale is to divert your not-so-nice instincts into harmless outlets. No one ever got pregnant from a "high five."

Still other applications take off from the premise that overt behavior bears a richly symbolic relationship to what lies hidden within human nature. According to psychodynamic theorists, cultural products—art, literature, music, religion, even graffiti and television commercials—reflect our incessant need to satisfy inner drives. Some artists, such as Salvador Dali, have self-consciously used this theory to help them choose symbols in their works.

Humanistic Paradigm

Self-actualization: The individual's drive to realize an inner potential.

The humanistic paradigm is a coalition of related intellectual traditions, all concerned with basic questions abut what it means to be a person. In general, *humanists* propose that the needs and values of human beings take precedence over the material world. People must be accorded special characteristics: consciousness, rationality, and most notably the need to achieve their potential, striving for inner goals via the process of **self-actualization.** The humanistic paradigm also embraces ideas from existentialism and phenomenology. As you would imagine, *existentialists* stress the primacy of human existence and experience. To understand someone, it is necessary to do so subjectively, from the inside out, taking into account his or her unique perspective. People are seen as products of their choices. Along these same lines, *phenomenologists* attempt to describe someone's conscious experience in terms meaningful to that individual.

This paradigm stands apart from other approaches to personality because many of its advocates criticize "scientific" psychology, charging that a concern with mechanical causes and effects misses what is truly important about people (Maslow, 1966). Sometimes this criticism shows itself as indifference or even hostility toward conventional research. At the same time, some individuals within the humanistic tradition are concerned with conventional scientific pursuits. For example, case studies are sometimes conducted by humanistic psychologists because they allow the individuality of a person to be captured (e.g., Laing, 1959).

Two of the best-known theorists in this tradition are Abraham Maslow (1970) and Carl Rogers (1961), both of whom were greatly concerned with the process by which people attempt to fulfill their potential. Maslow contributed to psychology the notion that people's motives can be described in terms of a hierarchy. Basic needs like food and water must be satisfied before higher needs like self-actualization can be pursued.

Along these lines, Rogers described how one's interactions with others can thwart or facilitate self-actualization. He even devised his own approach to therapy—client-centered therapy—based on these ideas. It is one of the major applications of the humanistic paradigm. Existential thinkers such as Viktor Frankl (1975) have also added to the repertoire of psychotherapists by devising techniques that lead clients to consider basic questions about the meaning of existence.

Trait Paradigm

The trait paradigm describes people in terms of broad and presumably invariant characteristics. In Chapter 2, we saw how this paradigm developed from functionalism and the psychological testing tradition. The ultimate origin of the trait paradigm is therefore in evolutionary theory. We should not be surprised that trait theorists, whatever particular traits they may study, assume that these individual differences are critical in determining our adaptation.

Research within the trait paradigm centers on personality tests, usually questionnaires. Large numbers of subjects are studied at a given time to obtain considerable variation in characteristics. Success or failure at adaptation is also measured in this research, and correlations between the individual difference and the measure of adaptation are computed. Of relatively minor concern within the trait paradigm is change, because traits—by definition—are thought not to vary.

Accordingly, applications of the trait approach try to describe and predict how individuals behave more than they try to change people. The goal of psychological testing in the workplace, the school, and the clinic is to tell it like it is, under the assumption that how it is, is how it will be. *Amelioration* consists of matching the person to the right setting. Placement in a job, a school, or a therapy program is a typical application within the trait paradigm.

Cognitive-Behavioral Paradigm

The cognitive-behavioral paradigm views people in terms of their characteristic thoughts and beliefs. People presumably think in order to predict and control events in the world. Their goal is to achieve pleasure while avoiding or escaping pain. Said another way, the cognitive-behavioral paradigm assumes people are thinking hedonists . . . or hedonistic thinkers, if you prefer.

As mentioned earlier, this approach to personality has taken form rather recently. One ingredient was cognitive theories growing out of the gestalt psychology tradition, theories that regard perception as the joint product of the world (stimuli) and the perceiver (tendencies to seek good gestalts). The other ingredient was social learning theories that stress the social environment and how people think about it as the most critical determinants of what they learn to do. Cognitive and social learning theories both emphasize the importance of thinking about the world, so their recent combination is a sensible one.

As for research, the cognitive-behavioral paradigm uses various approaches borrowed from its immediate ancestors. Cognitive theories encourage researchers to rely on an individual's self-report, under the assumption that the best way to understand reality as it is perceived is to ask the person who perceives it. Often these perceptions are assessed with a questionnaire, and sometimes they are measured with an interview. Occasionally, they are inferred from the way someone acts: "Because she gave up at the task, she probably believes it has no solution."

Social learning theories lead researchers to observe how people actually behave in particular situations. Because of their interest in situational influences on behavior, researchers may use experiments where they manipulate factors in the environment to see how behavior is affected. Albert Bandura, for example, is a social learning theorist well-known for his investigations of how children are influenced by seeing someone else act in an aggressive fashion (Bandura, Ross, & Ross, 1963). If circumstances are arranged so that this other person—termed a model—meets with rewards for acting aggressively, then children are more apt to follow the model's example.

Within the cognitive-behavioral paradigm, applications try to facilitate the fit between individuals and the world. This can be done either by encouraging persons to change the way they see things or by changing the world itself. Often, both goals are pursued at the same time. Therapy for depression, for example, helps persons to think better of themselves while also advising them to seek out friends who will confirm this belief (Beck, Rush, Shaw, & Emery, 1979).

THEORY IN PERSONALITY PSYCHOLOGY

Theories are sets of conventions created by theorists; these conventions involve assumptions about the real world, interrelations among these assumptions, and explicit definitions (or *operationalizations*) about how one moves from observations about the world to theoretical assumptions (Hall & Lindzey, 1970, pp. 10–12). Whether theories are strictly true or false is not a reasonable criterion by which to judge them. Instead, theories are useful or not, and any particular theory must be regarded as tentative, to be used until a better theory—for the purpose at hand—comes along. And what are the purposes of a personality theory? As I discussed in the last chapter, on the history of personality psychology, the field has served various masters. Let me enumerate some of the more important of these.

A Personality Theory Must Account for Known Facts   We know a lot about personality: general, characteristic, enduring, and functional aspects of a person. A personality theory must speak to what we know. I sometimes suggest to my students that they start to read the *Washington Post* or the *Chicago Tribune* from front to back and attempt to explain each fact they encounter from the perspective of some psychological theory. When they get stuck on some particular fact, they should stop and note the page number. This is a quantitative measure of how well the theory accounts for miscellaneous facts.

Personality theories almost always get students a lot further in this task than do other psychological theories. What can a theory of memory do for the reader of the *Post* or the *Tribune?* In the days of Watergate, it could explain—after a fashion—the lapses of recall that made headlines. But most of the time, theories of memory don't explain too many facts in the paper. How about a theory of psychophysiology? It depends on the particular news stories. Say someone climbed a tower and shot at passersby. Maybe this madman had a brain tumor.

In contrast, theories of personality explain the headlines in Section A: politics, war, murder, and arson; they account for the human-interest topics in Section B: Ann Landers, popular adventure movies, exercise books by celebrities, another craze from California; they explain the business facts in Section C: interest rates up, building rates down, Christmas spending steady; they help us account for facts in the sports pages of Section D, and so on.

Why are theories of personality so general? Unlike other psychological theories, personality theories apply to people, not to parts of people. As you saw in Chapter 1, most things people do fall under the heading of personality. Personality theories must be applicable to the whole spectrum of human activities. And these theories often originated in the attempt to explain abnormal behavior. Why do the symptoms of hysteria co-occur? Why do alcoholics drink to the point of violent illness? Why do depressed people kill themselves? A personality theory must be able to explain a lot.

As if this were not enough, the theory is expected to work in a simple fashion. Brevity of explanation, or **parsimony,** is one of the virtues to which a theory aspires. Consider this saying among doctors attempting a diagnosis: "When you hear hoofbeats, think horses, not zebras." They remind themselves to attempt explanation in a mundane fashion before reaching for an exotic account.

Parsimony: Brevity; simplicity.

John Watson's behaviorism was so popular in psychology because it promised to account for all sorts of facts with a few simple principles of learning. Of course, there is often a tradeoff between the scope of a theory and its simplicity, and some argue that comprehensiveness and efficiency require an inevitable compromise (Thorngate, 1976). Psychoanalysis is the most comprehensive personality theory; it is also the most complex.

A Personality Theory Must Generate New Facts   Scientists do more than look backwards to rationalize what has already happened. Important as postdiction may be, the true test of any scientific theory is prediction. Can the theory tell the future? Can it specify what will happen granted the fulfillment of certain conditions? All personality theories involve a number of assumptions about how to predict future thoughts, feelings, and actions. The most general forecast relies on *psychological inertia:* past behavior predicts future behavior. Most personality theories make this prediction, although we have already seen that it is far from universally true. More precise predictions specify when the past is continuous with the future and when it is not.

Personality psychology research allows a test of how well a particular theory can predict the future. Will the new facts gathered in research (data) be accommodated within the theory? Different theories emphasize different sorts of data, but in each case, the theory is explicit about how it is supported or denied by new facts.

A Personality Theory Must Be Useful to the Practitioner   Personality psychology is pragmatic, and theories must not wilt outside the ivory tower. Can they be used by personality psychologists who work in clinics, schools, or industries to make concrete decisions about specific individuals? If personality theories were used only to account for esoteric facts or to adjudicate hair-splitting debates, considerable latitude could be exercised in choosing among theories.

However, applications of personality psychology bear critically on the lives of individuals and on the course of society. A personality theory must be explicit about assessment procedures. Are psychological tests reliable and valid? Anyone who wants to go to college, medical school, or law school should care about the answers to these questions. So should anyone who seeks help from a psychotherapist. Applications of personality psychology affect your life, and you should hope that reasonable theories dictate them.

Most personality theories are also explicit about development and change. How and why do they occur? Can they be facilitated by parents, teachers, or other responsible adults? Can they be thwarted by poverty, ignorance, or prejudice? Can they be corrected by therapy or other social interventions? A personality theory needs to answer these questions.

Within these general guidelines, personality theories show considerable variability. Even theories classified within the same paradigm differ. What are the individual differences among personality theories? Consider that every personality theory has to provide an answer to the following questions.

What Aspect of Personality Is Explained?

Personality refers to a variety of human activities. Although most personality theories attempt to be general, each invariably does a better job explaining some of the things meant by personality than it does explaining other things. George Kelly (1955) calls this aspect of a theory its *range of convenience*. In other words, to what behaviors is it most applicable? These comprise the theory's range of convenience. To what behaviors is the theory awkward or irrelevant? These fall outside the range.

In the era of the great schools of psychological thought, theories mostly had wide ranges of convenience. They aspired to be general theories of behavior, and most therefore accounted for personality as a special case of general behavior. In recent years, psychology has moved away from general theories to more circumscribed explanations. Only in personality psychology do we still find theories attempting broad applicability.

However, even among personality theories, variation in the range of convenience occurs. Not surprisingly, most cognitive-behavioral theories best explain conscious thoughts and beliefs, whereas emotions fall outside their range. Some writers call emotions *hot cognition* to distinguish them from the cool, calm, and collected thought best explained by the typical theory (Abelson, 1963).

One of the most impressive things about psychodynamic theory is the range of topics it can explain. Indeed, almost all things human admit to explanation within this paradigm: jokes, Marilyn Monroe, art, music, Richard Nixon, religion, slips of the tongue, the Goodyear Blimp, leaders, followers, Prince, masochism, fear of flying, cigarette smoking, love, hate, and ambivalence.

But the broad range of convenience possessed by the psychodynamic paradigm does not automatically lend it preferred status. Indeed, this paradigm is often criticized because it achieves breadth at the cost of simplicity. Mundane behaviors that are quite easily explained by more circumscribed theories are attacked with the same complexity that psychodynamic theory brings to bear on diffuse and unusual behaviors.

In sum, the different personality paradigms have different ranges of convenience. Each paradigm does a better or worse job explaining specific aspects of personality. Once again, we see why we must evaluate personality theories in light of particular goals and purposes.

What Units Are Employed?

Gordon Allport (1961) regards this as the most fundamental question for personality psychology. Let us examine what he means by a *unit* in personality theory:

> Man's nature, like all of nature, is composed of relatively stable structures. The success of psychological science, therefore, as of any science, depends in part upon its ability to identify the significant units of which its assigned portion of the cosmos is composed. Without its table of elements chemistry could not exist. Where would physics be without its quanta, or biology without the cell? All science is analytic, and *analysis* means "to loosen or unbind". . . .
>
> It is often said that personality is "far behind" other sciences because psychology cannot discover its fundamental units. . . . Something must account for the *recurrences* and *stabilities* in personal behavior. Although we admit that units cannot exist in a "pure state" . . . , still we do find that personality is relatively stable over time and in different situational fields. How can we account for this fact unless we search for some sort of structures? (pp. 311–312)

Units therefore explain the recurrence and stability of personality.

The history of personality psychology could well be told in terms of the rise and fall of different units of explanation. Humors, faculties, instincts, drives, needs, values, sentiments, temperaments, traits, habits, and factors have all had their champions as the best way to describe and explain personality. But none of these units have won general acceptance.

Perhaps the problem in finding the basic units of personality lies in the multiplicity of candidates and their variation in complexity and generality. Contrast the narrow habit with the general trait. Even more global units of description include the "fundamental project" of existential thought and the "life-style" of common vernacular. Why do so many units of personality exist? I think it is because we can sensibly describe personality in terms of them all, with no description more fundamental than any other.

The purpose at hand usually dictates the choice of units. Each of the personality paradigms therefore has a set of theoretical terms (units) to describe and explain what people do, and they range from general to specific. The psychodynamic paradigm proposes instincts and drives as units of personality, but also involves specific defense mechanisms and character types. The humanistic model makes use of notions such as choice, will, and responsibility to describe the human condition, as well as someone's specific actions. The trait paradigm describes and explains with personal dispositions that vary in their specificity. Finally, the cognitive-behavioral paradigm relies on thoughts and behaviors, which range from specific beliefs and habits to general styles of interacting with the world.

What Model of Human Nature Is Assumed?

Remember the models of human nature I described in Chapter 1? Articulating such metaphors is a common activity of personality psychologists. A particular paradigm relies on one or more of these metaphors, using them to help predict and understand what people actually do.

The psychodynamic paradigm uses a host of related biological metaphors (e.g., people as animals, people as energy systems), whereas the humanistic paradigm sometimes likens people to actors. The cognitive-behavioral paradigm is fond of altogether different metaphors (e.g., people as white rats, fields, computers, or scientists). The trait paradigm uses the largest array of metaphors, each in keeping with the particular trait of interest.

As you can see, a model of human nature explicitly states what people are like. Jut as importantly, a model implicitly conveys a statement about what is irrelevant to human nature. Models preclude as well as include, and thus serve the paradigm in its role as a filter or template for the personality psychologist.

What Stance Is Taken on Fundamental Issues?

What basic issues separate the personality paradigms (Wertheimer, 1972)? First, to varying degrees the paradigms regard people either as masters of their fate or as victims. Said another way, each paradigm addresses the control people have over their thoughts, actions, and feelings. The psychodynamic and trait paradigms accord much less purposiveness to people than does the humanistic paradigm. Only in this latter approach to personality is personal choice given serious consideration. The cognitive-behavioral paradigm straddles the issue. To the degree thoughts are emphasized, a theorist may speak of people as being conscious agents— masters of their fate, if you will. To the degree behaviors are emphasized, a theorist may consider people as simply creatures of habit— victims of their own psychological makeup.

Second, the paradigms differ in their view of people as good versus evil. Although a given personality theory usually won't employ such straightforward moral language, these evaluations are often implied. So, the psychodynamic paradigm paints a dark picture of human nature. People have inherently selfish motives, held in check by a coercive society. The trait paradigm characterizes people as amoral, playing out the cards dealt to them by fate. The cognitive-behavioral paradigm, as already emphasized, sees people as hedonists and thus again as amoral. Finally, the humanistic model regards people as inherently well-intentioned.

Third, the paradigms differ in whether they emphasize the mind or the body. Explanations tend to be phrased in either mental or physical terms. The psychodynamic paradigm, for instance, explains mental events, but often does so with the metaphor of neurology. As you will see in the next chapter, Freud's (1950) "project for a scientific psychology" was a bold attempt to explain the mind solely in terms of the body. Although unfinished, this project stamped the psychodynamic paradigm with the materialism that still characterizes it. Similarly, the trait paradigm, derived from evolutionary thought, favors a physical explanation. Allport (1961) described traits as neurologically based, and today's trait theories look for a genetic basis to these characteristics. In contrast, the humanistic paradigm explicitly disavows physical explanations, focusing solely on the mental. Again, we find the cognitive-behavioral paradigm straddling this issue, relying on both mental and physical explanations.

Fourth, personality paradigms differ in their orientation toward subjectivity versus objectivity. What is the best way to understand someone, from the inside or the outside? Both the psychodynamic and the humanistic paradigms opt for the "inside" view, under the assumption that psychological reality is not the same thing as physical reality. Different people live in different worlds defined by their varying needs, drives, goals, and choices. The cognitive-behavioral paradigm also favors a look from the inside, with the qualification that what is to be found on the inside often bears a resemblance to what is found on the outside. Finally, the trait paradigm takes pretty much an "outside" view. Psychological tests were not developed to reveal the processes involved in our performance. Instead, the pragmatic emphasis was on the observable consequences of these hidden processes, the actual test performance.

Fifth, personality paradigms explain behavior with factors either in the past or in the immediate present. This then-now distinction is of course one of relative emphasis, but both the psychodynamic and trait paradigms lean toward the then and away from the now. Psychodynamic theories trace current actions to early childhood experiences, and some versions of this approach assume personality is fixed by adolescence, a chilling thought for those of us who were creeps in high school. Trait theorists also regard adult dispositions as originating in childhood, or even in the moment of conception. The humanistic and cognitive-behavioral paradigms, in contrast, take more of a nonhistorical view of behavior. What a person does is determined by current events. If someone runs from a burning building, it might simply be because the building is hot; information about the person's past life adds little here.

Sixth, the paradigms of personality psychology take different positions with respect to the **nature versus nurture controversy** (described in Chapter 1): whether behavior is due to inherent biological characteristics (nature) or to learning and socialization (nurture). The trait paradigm clearly embraces the "nature" end of this debate, whereas the humanistic and the cognitive-behavioral paradigms opt for the "nurture" end. The psychodynamic paradigm often works both sides of the street. For example, in explaining the obsessions of a patient known as the Rat Man (because of his preoccupation with rats), Freud (1909b) enumerated experiential factors that produced the patient's problems, as well as a biological predisposition that allowed the environmental events to do damage in the first place.

Nature versus nurture controversy: The debate that centers on whether behavior reflects innate causes (nature) or environmental causes (nurture).

Finally, the different personality paradigms vary in terms of their simplicity versus complexity. How many principles are suggested? How many terms are introduced? What range of behaviors is explained? The psychodynamic paradigm is the most complex. (Some of my students complain that psychologists tend to oversimplify things—except Freud, who makes them seem more complicated than they really are.) Trait theories and humanistic theories are much more simple. Cognitive-behavioral approaches vary, at times proposing but a single principle governing personality, such as a drive toward consistency, and at other times suggesting many more.

There are no right or wrong answers to these issues. However, realize that the paradigms take a position with respect to each, and that these are consonant with the rest of the paradigm—theoretically, methodologically, and practically. Additionally, they help place the four paradigms in their historical and intellectual context, linking them to like-minded movements in science and philosophy and distinguishing them from ideological opponents.

If you read the Dr. Dolittle books when you were young, you might recall the pushmi-pullyu, a fanciful animal that was a gazelle on each end (see Figure 3–1). Every time this creature walked forward, it also walked backward. And vice versa. The two parts of the pushmi-pullyu are in obvious conflict, but neither would have much of an existence without the other. I think of the fundamental issues of personality psychology in the same way. Each stance needs the opposite to make any sense. More generally, each paradigm needs the other paradigms as well. This might mean that personality psychology will not be dominated by a single paradigm until basic questions about human nature are answered.

What Is the Relationship of Theory and Research?

In the ideal of science, theory and research are symbiotic—one uses a theory to make a prediction about the world and then conducts research to check one's

FIGURE 3–1
Dr. Dolittle's Pushmi-Pullyu

" 'Lord save us!' cried the duck. 'How does it make up its mind?' "
SOURCE: From Lofting, H. (1968). *Doctor Dolittle: A treasury.* London: Jonathan Cape, p. 27.

prediction against the facts. If the facts confirm the prediction, then the theory remains as is. If the facts contradict the prediction, then the theory is changed to accommodate them.

This ideal somewhat captures the business of science, but it overlooks the role of paradigms in determining whether research findings are "true" facts or not. As Kuhn (1970) argues, theories are not changed simply by facts. Indeed, their fundamentals are rarely changed at all. They flourish, and then they die, replaced by another theory.

In Kuhn's view of science, research and theory can have relationships other than simple calibration. In some cases, research dominates theory. The facts are of more interest to scientists than their abstract meaning. Description precedes explanation. Theory is cursory, perhaps just a summary of findings or a restating of observed relationships. Trait "theory" sometimes has this character.

In other cases, theory is more important than research. Explanation precedes description, coloring it to such a degree that research doesn't test theory as much as it illustrates it. A common criticism of Freudian theory is that it is nonfalsifiable. The theory provides such a powerful explanation for all sorts of facts that nothing can ever count against it. In the humanistic paradigm, theory dominates. Indeed, as already mentioned, some humanistic theorists are quite disinterested in research. The cognitive-behavioral paradigm sometimes has research dominating, sometimes theory.

I've sketched extreme variations of the relationship between theory and research. But research never proceeds in complete independence of theory. Otherwise, the facts of the Manhattan phone book would be considered scientific data, and that's not so. And never does theory exist oblivious to the facts. Otherwise, any ideology would be considered a scientific theory, and that's not so either. Though the extremes don't exist, they define a real continuum along which the paradigms may be placed.

What Is the Relationship of Theory and Application?

A final question that each personality paradigm needs to answer regards the proper relationship of theory and application. On the simplest level, applied personality psychology simply takes a theory and extrapolates to the real world to accomplish a particular purpose. However, nothing is ever so simple, and practitioners must look to their paradigm for guidance in how to regard an application, not just in how to go about it.

The applied psychologist may take on different roles, and the various paradigms regard some as more legitimate than others. The most fundamental distinction comes from the question of who the applied psychologist serves: the individual, the group, or the society? Consider the case of a convicted criminal ordered by the court to start psychotherapy. You are the therapist. Who are you trying to make happy? You answer may be a glib, "I'm trying to make the client happy by helping him fit into society, which will also be happy. And then I'll be happy." But when the situation is made concrete, your answer is seen as empty as "Have a nice day" uttered on "The Day After." Suppose your client is a child molester. Suppose he is a champion of religious freedom. Suppose he is a public drunk. Suppose he is a murderer whose victim was a would-be mugger. Who are you trying to make happy?

A personality theory will not contain all that is needed to answer questions about proper roles for the applied psychologist. However, it often steers the practitioner in one direction or another. Remember the fundamental issues? Many are related to those classic political positions of liberal versus conservative. If a theory assumes the goodness of people, subjectivity, choice, and so on, it leads to a liberal perspective in that problems are viewed as solvable. The status quo should be changed so people can be happy within it. In contrast, if a theory assumes the opposite, it leads to a more conservative approach. Problems are inherent, and so people should be changed to fit the status quo.

By and large, the psychodynamic and trait paradigms involve conservative applications. According to Freud (1930), people may be doomed to accept an unhappy compromise between their instinctive drives and the dictates of a repressive society. Therapy, therefore, should help the individual adjust. Similarly, those who administer psychological tests use them to match people to the world, not vice versa. The cognitive-behavioral paradigm may also give rise to conservative applications, if intervention is directed at the individual. But if intervention is directed at the world, then the cognitive-behavioral paradigm gives rise to liberal applications. Finally, the humanistic paradigm is necessarily liberal, because it is based on the premise that people matter most, certainly more than institutions.

METHOD IN PERSONALITY PSYCHOLOGY

In personality psychology, method varies as much as theory. Although certain methodological concerns cut across the paradigms, each has its favored research strategy. Any strategy has inherent strengths and weaknesses and is better suited for some purposes than others. A researcher makes his or her choice of a method of investigation according to the broader perspective of a personality paradigm.

Crosscutting Research Issues

Regardless of the paradigm in which one works, one must address issues common to all personality research: operationalization; reliability and generality; validity; emphasis on pure versus applied research; and nomothetic versus idiographic goals. Additionally, one must decide how tightly or loosely to bind research and theory.

Operationalization   In Chapter 1, I mentioned the need to measure, or *operationalize,* a personality characteristic. Let me repeat some of the points I made. First, operationalizations are absolutely necessary for science. Without explicit rules about what facts in the real world correspond to what assumptions in the scientific theory, the whole scientific endeavor comes to a halt. Second, at the same time, operationalizations are imperfect translations of reality into theory. Particularly in the case of personality, where terms do not have necessary and sufficient conditions, measures of concepts are imprecise. Third, it follows that operationalizations are not the same thing as the concepts they purport to measure. Intelligence is not the same thing as an IQ score, despite a casual way of speaking that equates them. Whenever a personality researcher makes conclusions about intelligence, or authoritarianism, or whatever, you should fill in what has not been specifically stated: intelligence as I have operationalized it, authoritarianism as I have operationalized it, and so on.

Research within each of the different personality paradigms needs to be explicit about operationalization. The basis for going from facts to theory, or from theory to facts, should be clear so the research can be evaluated by the careful consumer. Psychoanalysis has sometimes been criticized because the links between constructs and observations are numerous, tenuous, and unstable. This makes research difficult, but it need not preclude investigations. As you will see, the psychodynamic researcher often uses case studies because they provide rich information and allow these links to be disentangled.

The trait paradigm is the most straightforward in terms of its operationalizations, but this can be a misleading impression. Questionnaires in which research subjects choose "like me" or "unlike me" are objective in that the researcher can easily and reliably score them, but objectivity in scoring is not the same as precision and simplicity in operationalization. An objective questionnaire may or may not be a good measure.

Finally, the cognitive-behavioral paradigm also uses straightforward operationalizations, assessing thoughts and beliefs by asking people to report them. But remember John Watson's distrust of introspection. Some of this legitimate skepticism spills over onto contemporary operationalizations that rely on self-report. Respondents may distort, lie, or simply not know the answer.

Most insidiously, respondents may sincerely answer questions even though they don't know the answer. In an article entitled "Telling More Than We Can Know," Richard Nisbett and Timothy Wilson (1977) argue that subjects in a psychological investigation will hazard an answer to any question asked, even questions that make no sense. For instance, subjects will report why they like their roommate, or why they prefer pretzels over potato chips, or why they have a Mohawk haircut and a pierced nose. Nisbett and Wilson caution that such attributed causes should not be confused with the "real" causes of these behaviors, since folks may not really know why they do these things. What they report may provide a clue, but the report is not the same thing as the real motive. This is just another way of saying that measures are not theoretical constructs. Motivation exists in a psychological theory, not on the tip of a research subject's pen or tongue.

For reasons like these, researchers in the cognitive-behavioral paradigm also devise experiments where people are called on to *show* their thoughts and beliefs in action. Researchers give subjects memory and decision-making tasks, for example, and then make inferences about their cognitions on the basis of how they respond. And when the interest centers on the environmental influences on our behavior, once again experiments are the obvious choice of a researcher.

Why do people conform? Directly asking them may not be the best way of answering this question.

Reliability: The degree to which measures repeatedly give the same answers.

Generality: The degree to which investigations give broadly applicable conclusions.

Reliability and Generality As I described in Chapter 1, **reliability** is the degree to which measures repeatedly give the same answer. **Generality** is the degree to which investigations repeatedly give the same conclusion. Lack of reliability and generality undercut a science, and psychology has had its share of false alarms: exciting findings that could not be replicated (Greenwald, 1976).

For instance, at one time it seemed that functions of the autonomic nervous system—involuntary responses like dilation of blood vessels—could be controlled with biofeedback (Miller, 1969). The prospect that people could cure difficulties like hypertension by learning to regulate their bodies was discounted by subsequent investigations unable to repeat the original results (Miller & Dworkin, 1974).

Confidence in results increases with their reliability, and reliability increases with the number of observed facts that count toward results. Thus, questionnaires with many items yield more reliable scores for individual differences than do questionnaires with few items (Epstein, 1980). Remember Mischel's (1968) conclusion that behavior is inconsistent across different situations? This conclusion has in turn been criticized for relying on studies assessing but one action per situation. In contrast, if many behaviors reflecting the same personality trait are assessed in the various situations, then cross-situational consistency is apt to increase above the low levels Mischel (1968) reports, since behavior has been estimated more reliably (Epstein, 1983b).

Reliable measures are a necessary precondition for generality of findings. Further, generality is served by increasing the number of research participants, as well as the number of independent investigations of the same question. Studies with many research subjects yield more reliable results than do studies with few subjects. Studies repeated several times yield more general conclusions than studies conducted once. Let me distinguish two sorts of replications: *exact replications,* where the procedure of a study is exactly repeated in a second study, and *conceptual replications,* where different operationalizations of the same theoretical concepts are employed in separate studies.

Research within the personality paradigms differs in terms of reliability and generality. Psychodynamic and humanistic research typically study a small number of individuals in great depth. Because so many observations are made, reliability is great. However, generality is poor.

Trait research typically investigates a greater number of individuals in less depth. Generality is satisfactory, but not necessarily reliability. A given questionnaire is usually reliable in the sense of high internal consistency, because it contains many items. However, attempts to operationalize the same trait with different questionnaires have sometimes been disastrous; different measures may not correlate at all (see, for example, Scott, Osgood, & Peterson, 1979).

Cognitive-behavioral research also studies a large number of research participants in the same investigation, strengthening generality of the results. But self-report measures of thoughts and beliefs do not always contain multiple items, so their reliabilities are unknown. Like trait research, attempts to show convergence of different measures of presumably similar cognitive characteristics have sometimes been unsuccessful (Goldstein & Blackman, 1978).

Validity My discussion of reliability and generality spills over into a discussion of validity, because the distinctions among them are vague. Measures must be reliable in order to be valid (see Table 1–1). The generality of results across different samples and different procedures argues for their **validity**—that the research is indeed concerned with what is purports to be.

Most of the forms of validity are easy to understand and judge: face validity, content validity, criterion validity, and known-group validity. The exception, however, is construct validity, because it relies on the theoretical framework in which the measure is regarded (Hogan & Nicholson, 1988). Consider a measure of creativity and its correlation with the verbal test of the SAT. Does a substantial relationship count toward construct validity? Well, yes and no; it depends on whether your theory holds creativity to be related to vocabulary.

Attempts to demonstrate construct validity thus reflect as much on theory as they do on research. Accumulated evidence for construct validity is sometimes described as a net, because validity is metaphorically snared by the entire set of pertinent evidence (Cronbach & Meehl, 1955). Like Quine and Ullian's (1978) web of belief, construct validity does not rest on any single strand of evidence.

Validity: The degree to which measures reflect what is intended.

How do the various personality paradigms regard construct validity? The psychodynamic paradigm holds that a particular fact bears on numerous theoretical concepts. Construct validity may therefore be difficult to establish. However, the psychodynamic paradigm is also explicit that each and every fact must bear on each and every theoretical concept. Psychoanalysts do not attribute odd findings to error.

The trait paradigm relies on vast amounts of data, presented as correlations, to establish construct validity of measures. As already noted, this paradigm is open to criticism for over-reliance on a single method. Despite what seems to be a richly woven net of evidence, it all depends on a critical thread. One pull and the construct validity may unravel.

Authoritarianism: An individual difference reflecting the extent to which someone is rigidly conventional and submissive to authority.

Consider the personality trait of **authoritarianism,** defined as the degree to which someone is rigidly conventional and submissive to authority (Adorno, Frenkel-Brunswik, Levinson, & Sanford, 1950). Authoritarianism is often measured with a questionnaire called the *F-Scale* (the "F" stands for fascism), which asks respondents whether they agree with a number of statements reflecting an authoritarian stance. The F-scale was used in innumerable investigations before it was realized that a high score, supposedly indicating a high degree of authoritarianism, might simply reflect someone's tendency to agree with statements regardless of their content (Cohn, 1956). The intent of the F-scale is of course to measure the more specific beliefs endorsed by Fascists. Subsequent research suggests that the F-scale measures both general acquiescence and specific fascism (Goldstein & Blackman, 1978).

Confound: A factor other than the intended one that affects a measure or result.

A factor other than the intended one that affects a measure or result is called a **confound.** Is an obtained relationship between two variables like popularity and good grades produced by a third variable like cheerfulness that causes both? If so, then the popularity-grade correlation is confounded by cheerfulness, and a researcher must be careful not to attribute good grades to popularity or popularity to good grades. Research in the trait paradigm is not uniquely susceptible to confounds. As I describe empirical investigations throughout the book, one of my standard exercises will be to consider possible third variables that might confound the results.

Let me make it clear that confounds are not simply nuisances. They interfere with a researcher's original intent, to be sure, but they can also clarify the meanings of concepts and even extend them in unanticipated directions. Part of the business of research is to follow the lead of your data, and the identification and examination of confounds can be among the most profitable of these leads. For example, a subject's tendency to agree with statements regardless of their content—at first a confound—is now seen as an individual difference in its own right (cf. Cronbach, 1946).

For the humanistic and cognitive-behavioral paradigms, the biggest threat to validity stems from problems with self-report. Is a research participant sincere when reporting on a belief or idea? If sincere, is she or he accurate? A related difficulty is demonstrating theoretical claims that patterns of thought precede outcomes of interest. If measures of both are taken at the same time, one cannot justifiably conclude that thought precedes outcome.

Do not despair from my discussion of validity that personality research is fatally flawed. Problems of validity occur in all sciences, and what helps the personality researcher solve them is the pragmatic stamp on all four paradigms. Research always comes back to the real world, back to an application, back to the attempt to say something meaningful about function and dysfunction. The contact made with concrete individuals in concrete situations is always sobering and helps researchers judge what is good or bad (valid or invalid) about their investigations. If it don't work, it ain't valid! In contrast to other psychology fields, where statistical significance of results is the bottom line, personality psychology additionally looks to practical significance.

Pure versus Applied Research   Within personality psychology, the line is fuzzy between investigations of theory per se and investigations of the real world. In all four paradigms, theory is about the real world, and so research is often conducted there.

However, it is my sense that cognitive-behavioral research relies most on ivory-tower investigations of college students, whereas psychodynamic and humanistic research relies least on these. Trait research varies, sometimes administering batteries of questionnaires to captives from Introductory Psychology and sometimes not. The more applied the research, the more imprecise it becomes. At the same time, the more applied, the more general. A researcher has to make a difficult choice in deciding where to divide the continuum of pure versus applied personality research.

Nomothetic versus Idiographic Goals   A final issue that personality researchers address is whether investigations should result in general conclusions applicable to all people or in specific conclusions applicable only to some individuals. When personality psychology speaks about people per se, it is described as **nomothetic;** when concerned with the unique individual, it is termed **idiographic.** These ideals are extremes, and most researchers attempt a combination of the two. Still, a relative emphasis can usually be discerned.

Nomothetic research: Investigations concerned with people per se.

Although psychodynamic research often studies but one individual at a time, the goal is nomothetic. Psychodynamic theories intend to be generally applicable accounts of behavior. At the same time, conclusions should apply to each and every individual, not just to the average Joe or Josephine.

Idiographic research: Investigations concerned with the unique individual.

Because of its concern with statistical prediction, trait research is largely nomothetic (Eysenck, 1954), even though trait theorist Gordon Allport (1937) first phrased the nomothetic-idiographic distinction, making a case for the idiographic goal. Recently, renewed calls have arisen within the paradigm for a greater concern with the individual and his or her unique developmental history (for example, see Rosenzweig, 1986; Silverstein, 1988).

The cognitive-behavioral paradigm is generally sympathetic to idiographic conceptions and research, but like much sympathy, it lies more in word than deed. Research tools relying on self-report are equipped to capture the unique constellation of a person's thoughts and beliefs (Kelly, 1955). Behaviorist research as popularized by B. F. Skinner (1938) often looks at how single subjects respond to environmental stimuli. However, these strategies have not been used frequently in cognitive-behavioral research. Instead, nomothetic conclusions are usually advanced.

It is in the humanistic paradigm that we find idiographic goals most fully realized. The concern of this paradigm on the individual's experience requires a constant focus on the specific person. "Experience" always belongs to a given individual; it can only be understood from his or her vantage. And this demands idiographic investigation.

Binding Research and Theory   Although personality research never proceeds without a theoretical rationale, there is wide latitude with regard to how tight a leash theory holds on research. Does the paradigm frown on innovative methods? Does it encourage exploratory investigations, studies where specific hypotheses have not yet been formulated? Does the paradigm respond quickly, sluggishly, or not at all to seemingly anomalous results?

In short, what is the relationship of research to theory? Many of these questions complement those discussed earlier in this chapter about the relationship of theory to research. Researchers must decide the degree to which research versus theory will lead. They must decide how closely to bind the two together.

Psychoanalytic theory developed from Freud's clinical observations, and he repeatedly revised his ideas in response to these observations. Thus, Freud himself was not rigid about the relationship of research to theory. Subsequent workers within the psychodynamic paradigm have become more dogmatic, however, so appropriate research activities are highly prescribed by the theory, which has been accorded a much-more-than-tentative status.

> Instead of leading in the development of new concepts, as was true during the early part of the century, psychoanalysis has entrenched itself behind concepts that it is largely prepared to defend rather than lay on the line for scholarly scrutiny. (Fisher & Greenberg, 1977, p. 7)

(In this regard, it is interesting to note Freud's reported comment, "Moi, je ne suis pas un Freudiste." [I myself am not a Freudian.])

I have already pointed out that those who work within the humanistic paradigm may be indifferent—even hostile—to conventional psychological research. For this reason, some regard the humanistic approach as more of a point of view about human nature than an actual scientific paradigm. I have been calling it a paradigm because it seems to posses many of the pertinent attributes. Nonetheless, this approach to personality is quite different from psychodynamic, trait, and cognitive-behavioral approaches, in large part because its theory and research are not at all tightly connected.

In the trait paradigm, exploratory research is common, because the computer revolution has made it possible to sift through the incredible amounts of data gathered in the course of trait research. Researchers nickname this kind of exploration sifting, snooping, fishing, skimming, data massaging, even data mugging! Most of these terms are pejorative, because the procedure can uncover "results" simply by chance. On the other hand, all trait researchers explore their data somewhat independently of their theory, hoping to uncover an intriguing finding that might be parlayed into a theory.

For instance, schizophrenic patients from lower-class families are more apt to be born during the winter months than their counterparts from the middle class (Meer, 1984). What does this mean? Perhaps lower-class mothers have a nutrient-poor diet during the winter, lacking fresh fruits and vegetables. Perhaps brain development during the last trimester of pregnancy has something to do with schizophrenia. Or perhaps not. Future research will tell, but my point is that this interesting fact was probably uncovered in the course of exploring some large set of data, in particular, by correlating month-of-birth with psychiatric diagnosis.

Research in the cognitive-behavioral paradigm is bound somewhat tightly to theory in terms of the questions investigated, but not so tightly with respect to particular methods. Personality researchers interested in thoughts and beliefs are mindful of the difficulties of self-report and devote considerable attention to the development of more valid procedures. Of current interest are research procedures developed within experimental psychology to study perception, memory, and cognition. Personality psychologists are borrowing these procedures and adapting them to the study of personality (Taylor & Fiske, 1982).

Research Strategies

Our discussion of personality research has been pretty abstract so far. Although the issues I've discussed are critical, they only come into play when an actual investigation is conducted. And the most important consideration in conducting an actual investigation is which strategy of research will be followed. In general, three alternatives are available—case studies, correlational studies, and experiments. Pros and cons exist for each strategy, and researchers make their choices within the context of the personality paradigm they're operating under.

Case Studies A **case study** is "the presentation and interpretation of detailed information about a single subject: whether an event, a culture, or . . . an individual life" (Runyan, 1982, p. 121). Usually, the case study coheres around a particular problem that its subject suffers, and the goal of this method is to understand this problem and devise a solution. Case studies have been critical in the development of psychodynamic theory and clinical thinking in general. As the most obvious way to study individual lives, they have seen considerable use as a research strategy in personality psychology (White, 1966).

Case study: The intensive investigation of a single subject.

At the same time, case studies are the most controversial research strategy employed to investigate personality. Some researchers dismiss them entirely as nonscientific, useful perhaps for suggesting ideas to be investigated in appropriate ways, but so plagued by threats to reliability and validity that they cannot yield scientific data (Campbell & Stanley, 1966).

One way to resolve these polar opinions about the usefulness of case studies is to distinguish between their in-principle shortcomings and the avoidable shortcomings that occur as some employ them. This distinction shows the case study strategy to be a properly scientific strategy, although not a perfect approach (since none exist).

What are the in-principle difficulties in studying only one individual? First, in an intensive study, some information is secondhand or retrospective, perhaps distorted in the process. Second, because a case study is just one shot, it is difficult to separate factors critical for subsequent outcomes from irrelevant factors that just happen to be there. Third, even if valid conclusions are drawn about the individual under study, they are best limited only to this individual; generality is severely bound.

These shortcomings can be illustrated in a brief case study of the playwright Eugene O'Neill. You probably know of O'Neill (1888–1953) as the author of such plays as *Long Day's Journey into Night, Mourning Becomes Electra,* and *The Iceman Cometh.* You may not know that he was also a ferocious alcoholic, even during his most productive period as a writer.

Psychiatrist Donald Goodwin (1971) attempted to make sense of O'Neill's alcoholism. To do so, he relied on several biographies of O'Neill. He also examined O'Neill's plays, which most critics regard as thinly disguised versions of his own life.

According to Goodwin, the push to abuse alcohol was present from the very beginning of O'Neill's life. He came from an Irish-American family, and both his father and older brother were heavy drinkers. As an infant he was quieted with whiskey. He began to drink in earnest as an adolescent and developed a particular taste for absinthe, a form of alcohol now outlawed because of its extreme toxicity. O'Neill's drinking was periodic; he would go on binges that lasted several days, often with his brother as a drinking companion.

Goodwin suggested that O'Neill drank in part because his family drank. Goodwin also emphasized the role that alcohol played in the Irish-American culture of O'Neill's era. Alcohol was widely endorsed as a cure for physical and emotional ailments. It was considered a substitute for sex as well as a solution for a broken heart. It was also a social lubricant. Not to drink with another man was an insult. Finally, drunkenness was widely tolerated in this culture, even regarded with open amusement.

Goodwin concluded that these broad explanations in terms of O'Neill's family and culture tell us why he drank in the first place, but they fail to account for the extent of his drinking. More specific causes had to exist, so he suggested that O'Neill was guilt-ridden, blaming himself because his mother was a narcotics addict. His birth was an extremely painful one. (He reportedly weighted eleven pounds.) To help in his delivery, the attending physician prescribed morphine to Mrs. O'Neill, and she thereafter became an addict. Perhaps the son later drank to excess because he felt responsible for his mother's plight and wished to forget about it.

Perhaps there is yet another reason why O'Neill was an alcoholic. His father was a traveling actor whose family often accompanied him. So the young O'Neill grew up as a transient, feeling that he never really belonged. He was reportedly shy and insecure—except when he drank. Then he became talkative and gregarious.

Finally, Goodwin speculated that O'Neill abused alcohol because of various emotional problems, including lifelong phobias and depression. Perhaps intoxication rescued him, however temporarily, from states of fear and despair.

There is an interesting postscript to the alcoholism of Eugene O'Neill. He eventually stopped drinking at the age of 37, following the death of his brother and a brief session of psychoanalytic therapy. O'Neill had previously resisted therapy because he was afraid it would destroy his creativity. This did not happen, although sobriety slowed down his productivity. To be more exact, he continued to write at a fast pace once sober, but he became ever more reluctant to consider any particular play complete. Goodwin noted that O'Neill's previous drinking binges provided a rhythm to his life and thus signposts that works were done. Without his binges, O'Neill's writing life was insufficiently interrupted.

This case study is certainly a fascinating one, and many of Goodwin's interpretations seem compelling. But let us put aside these reactions for the time being and take a skeptical look at the in-principle difficulties with this research strategy.

First, Goodwin did not meet with O'Neill. He relied instead on written documents. Even if Goodwin had been able to interview his subject directly, he would still have needed to rely on retrospective reports about past incidents, such as O'Neill being given whiskey as an infant.

Second, it seems critical to Goodwin's interpretation that O'Neill's mother was a morphine addict, but how could Goodwin know this wasn't simply an unfortunate coincidence? Perhaps he would have become an alcoholic even if his mother did not use narcotics. Similarly, Goodwin emphasized the role played by O'Neill's alcoholic older brother, but again there is no way to know for certain that O'Neill's habits would have been any different if he had a sober brother, or no brother at all.

Third, suppose O'Neill indeed was an alcoholic because of the factors Goodwin specified. Can the same formula be used to explain the alcoholism of people in general or even other famous writers, like F. Scott Fitzgerald or Ernest Hemingway? We have no way of knowing, so our conclusions are probably best limited to Eugene O'Neill, who may or may not have been a typical alcoholic.

Are these shortcomings sufficient to void the use of case studies in personality research? Contemporary opinion says no, that they are analogous to problems with reliability and validity that potentially threaten any strategy of investigation. The task of the researcher is to minimize these threats so firm conclusions result. Case studies should be judged as good or bad on an individual basis because this judgment *can* be made.

Runyan (1981) proposed a number of questions to be asked about conclusions made from case studies:

1. Are they logically sound?
2. Are they comprehensive, accounting for all of the available information?
3. Do they survive attempts to prove them wrong?

4. Are they consistent with all of the available evidence?
5. Are they consistent with what is known about people in general?
6. Are they more credible than alternative conclusions?

(Note that these questions could be asked about conclusions from any study of personality, regardless of the strategy of investigation.)

The researcher who uses a case-study strategy must operationalize concepts and must ascertain their reliability and validity. This probably involves independent confirmation of secondhand and retrospective information, not an impossible undertaking. Conclusions must be evaluated against alternatives, and confounds must be ruled out. Finally, the criterion of parsimony must be applied. Is the alcoholism of Eugene O'Neill more easily explained in terms of unconscious motives or in terms of mundane principles of learning?

The issue of generality remains a real one that researchers must confront. Freud is well-known for his case studies, and he argued that conclusions had to be established on the basis of repeated cases (cf. Rosenwald, 1988). Those cases Freud published seem intended as illustrations. Nonetheless, when a theory— like psychoanalysis—aspires to be generally applicable, even a single case study can carry considerable weight if it disproves one of its predictions.

Let me turn to the virtues of the case-study method. First, as just explained, case studies can serve as existence proofs or disproofs, challenges to theories that say this or that can never be, or that they always are. The well-known studies of chimpanzee language are, after all, case studies, because a single ape is studied at one time (Premack, 1971). But the importance of these case studies is incredible since they challenge long-established beliefs about the uniqueness of language to human beings.

Second, case studies are the only way rare phenomena can be investigated. Personality psychology in particular is often concerned with abnormality, and some instances of abnormality are so rare as to be encountered only once or twice in the lifetime of a researcher. You may be aware of C. H. Thigpen and H. Cleckley's description of a multiple personality, the well-known individual of *The Three Faces of Eve* (1957). No personality psychologist wishes to dismiss these descriptions as nonscientific just because they are only based on one research subject (or on three).

Third, case studies provide the rich detail conspicuously lacking from other research strategies. If one's research goal is to study the complexity of an individual's personality, then case studies are the strategy of choice. They are well-suited for psychodynamic research, which intends a careful description of the development of personality within a social context. Detail is needed for such a description, under the assumption that facts are related to theoretical constructs in diverse and diffuse ways. Only the intensive approach of a case study allows these tenuous links to be specified.

Correlational Studies The second major research strategy of personality psychologists is the correlational approach. This strategy measures pertinent variables and calculates correlations reflecting the degree of association among these variables. It is the basic research strategy of personality psychologists

Joanne Woodward starred in The Three Faces of Eve, *based on the celebrated case study of a woman with a multiple personality.*

interested in how people are characteristically themselves and different than others (Cronbach, 1957).

Nevertheless, this research strategy is problematic for two related reasons. First, if it is deployed to answer questions about the sequence of two factors, it may lead to erroneous conclusions if both factors are measured at the same time. Correlational research is sometimes used to answer questions about causes, but the identified "cause" may not precede the "effect" under study.

For instance, schizophrenia is sometimes attributed to disordered patterns of communication within the family (see, for example, Bateson, Jackson, Haley, & Weakland, 1956; Laing, 1959; and Lidz, 1975). One way this hypothesis could be tested is for the researcher to visit the homes of a number of individuals, some with diagnosed schizophrenia and some without. She could sit quietly in the corner and watch while the family members interacted, noting whether they encourage each other to doubt their own experiences. A count of exchanges like this could be made:

Father: Have you chosen your college courses yet?
  Son: Yes, I've thought about taking biology, calculus, and English, then maybe something else.
Father: That sounds pretty difficult. Are you sure you can handle it?

Son: Gee, I think so. Anyway, those are courses that I have to take to go pre-med.

Father: You know you're going to get overwhelmed by those courses. You get so carried away.

Son: Maybe I should postpone taking calculus. I could take photography. I understand the college has a great introductory course in that.

Father: How can we afford to buy you a camera? You must think I'm made out of money. You're going to college to make something of yourself, not to snap pictures.

Son: But Dad . . .

Mother: Now, son, you listen to your father. You know he loves you and wants what's best.

Father: The most important thing is for you to be happy. Whatever you want is fine with me.

In this conversation, both Mother and Father seem to deny what has been communicated to their son. He is criticized first as a marginal student and then as a frivolous one; the summary of these criticisms, however, is that he is loved and can do what he wishes.

(Do not be too upset if this conversation is typical of your dinner table, because it may not be disordered communication at all. Your family members may recognize these exchanges as fussing on the part of a father who is reluctant to see his son grow up and leave home. As long as everyone recognizes your father's motives, then communication is perfectly clear. The schizophrenia researcher is, however, interested in the case where the dynamics of the conversation are obscure and only the surface meanings are recognized. In this case, the son is apt to feel like a tennis ball going back and forth, back and forth, after which he is told everybody left their rackets at home.)

If the researcher visits one hundred homes and stays at each for an hour, she will have a set of scores to correlate with the diagnosis of schizophrenia (1) or not (0). Suppose she finds that the two variables are substantially correlated, so that schizophrenics tend to come from families with a great deal of disordered communication, while nonschizophrenics do not. What can be concluded? The researcher may be tempted to believe that disordered communication leads to schizophrenia. Her data are after all consistent with this conclusion.

However, cause and effect may be entangled here because of the correlational research strategy (Mischler & Waxler, 1968). No one established that disordered communication preceded schizophrenia, as it must if it is to be considered a cause. Perhaps the schizophrenic family member preceded the disordered communication, perhaps even causing it by frustrating, disappointing, or confusing the parents. The researcher cannot distinguish between this possibility and the first one she considered.

Besides its insensitivity to the sequence of variables, the correlational research strategy has another shortcoming: possible confounding by third variables. Consider again the example of disordered communication and schizophrenia. The researcher must hesitate not only in assigning one of these factors a causal role but also in concluding that they bear any direct relationship at all. Some theorists believe that schizophrenia is biologically based and that it may be genetically transmitted. Suppose that the "gene" for schizophrenia causes disordered communication in some family members and full-blown schizophrenia in others. If so, then the same correlation is expected, except in this case it is because of an underlying variable. (The actual cause of schizophrenia remains as elusive as this extended example suggests.)

All personality researchers recognize these in-principle difficulties with the correlational research strategy. Why then do they continue to employ it? Like the case study method, the correlational method also possesses several virtues, so the choice to use it reflects a decision that the benefits outweigh the shortcomings.

One benefit of the correlational research strategy is that it allows prediction, often with great accuracy. One variable may be highly related to a second variable, whether or not it is a cause. If a researcher wishes to predict this second variable, then it may be irrelevant that the causal relationship is unclear. Perhaps you are familiar with the highly successful attempts by lawyers to choose sympathetic jurors for a given case. These rely on the correlational strategy. The community from which jurors are drawn is canvassed, and with correlations it is established that citizens who favor acquittal also tend to read certain magazines but not others, say *Rolling Stone* instead of *Soldier of Fortune*. In screening jurors, then the lawyer can ask about magazine preferences and in effect be asking about attitudes toward acquittal. Reading preference may not directly cause these attitudes, but knowledge of it makes for an accurate prediction.

Another benefit of the correlational strategy is that it allows the relationships among variables to be characterized numerically. In contrast to the case study method, the correlational strategy yields conclusions about the relative strength or weakness of associations. Personality psychologists use this research strategy to discover types of people. What characteristics frequently go together?

Fisher and Greenberg (1977) summarized a number of studies investigating Freud's (1908a) proposed anal character type, an individual who is excessively orderly, greedy, and obstinate. In a number of studies, operationalizations of individual differences with respect to these three characteristics indeed correlate with each other, as proposed. No attempt is made to point to one factor as the cause of another, or even to specify the sequence in which these characteristics might appear. Researchers who work within the trait paradigm usually favor the correlational strategy, which is well-suited for categorization.

Still, causal questions are frequently of interest to personality researchers. For this reason, correlational researchers have refined their basic strategy so causal conclusions can be drawn. The simplest refinement is to use a longitudinal design. If factors at Time One correlate with factors at Time Two, then one can certainly rule out the possibility that the latter variables cause the former. Causes do not work backwards in time. With a longitudinal design, researchers therefore eliminate one alternative to the causal explanation they favor. This strategy lies at the basis of *epidemiology research,* which correlates variables of interest with possible outcomes known to follow them in time. Smoking cigarettes is correlated with heart disease. But the circulation difficulties suffered by a 60-year-old cannot reach backwards in time to cause the 15-year-old adolescent to sneak a smoke in the school bathroom. If the two are directly related, then smoking has to be the cause, since it precedes heart disease.

More sophisticated attempts to use the correlational strategy for conclusions about causes are called experiments of nature or **quasi-experiments** (Campbell & Stanley, 1966). These strategies use various control groups to rule out possible third variables. True experiments eliminate third variables explicitly by randomly assigning research participants to various groups where the experiment imposes different events on them. Quasi-experimentation arose within educational settings where true experimentation was unwieldy or impossible.

Here is an example of a quasi-experiment. A few years ago, I completed an investigation of "burnout" among counselors at a camp for multi-handicapped individuals. Such counseling can be emotionally taxing, and the counselor may end up tired, depressed, and disillusioned. The Department of Recreation at Virginia Polytechnic Institute and State University runs a brief camp for the multi-handicapped, using undergraduate students as the counselors. The counselors spend the first eight weeks of a school term in a classroom, learning about counseling. Then they spend a week at the camp putting what they have learned into practice with handicapped campers.

I wished to see if the counselors would experience burnout, so I devised a self-report questionnaire measuring the feelings that accompany burnout and administered it to the 120 counselors during the first week of class and again right after the week-long camp. Scores were quite a bit higher the second time. The counselors were burned out.

However, I could not conclude that counseling per se was the culprit. Maybe all undergraduate students get tired and depressed as the school term progresses. In fact, this seems quite plausible. I couldn't definitely attribute the increase in burnout to what happened at camp. I had anticipated this difficulty, however, and had administered the questionnaire at the same times to another groups of students who did not participate in the camp. Although these students showed some increase in bad feelings from Time One to Time Two, the magnitude of increase was nowhere near that of the counselors.

With these data available, I could conclude more confidently that counseling produces burnout. If you are reading this carefully, you see that my conclusion should still be tentative. Other "third" variables might be present. Maybe students who are likely to sign up to be counselors are also likely to feel emotional fatigue as the school term goes on, regardless of what happens. The week-long camp may have been irrelevant in producing burnout. I could not rule out this possibility, but I think you see how other controls might be introduced to do so. Suppose only half of the 120 volunteers actually went to

Quasi-experiment: A research strategy in which correlational data are treated as if they were obtained through experimentation.

camp and only these showed burnout. This fact would further strengthen my causal conclusion.

In recent years, researchers who use correlational methods have introduced a host of sophisticated statistical procedures that discern the influences across time among variables they have measured. These procedures as a whole are referred to as **causal modeling,** because the intent of those who use them is to use correlational data to draw conclusions about causes and effects. Causal modeling can never prove that one factor causes another, because the analyzed data remain correlational and potentially confounded by third variables. Nonetheless, causal modeling reduces the ambiguity that usually accompanies causal conclusions from these kind of data (cf. Judd, Jessor, & Donovan, 1986).

Causal modeling: Statistical procedures for drawing causal conclusions from correlational data.

Experiments   The third major research strategy for personality psychologists is the experiment. Experiments have been favored within psychology since the

"For crying out loud, gentlemen! That's us! Someone's installed the one-way mirror in backward!"

SOURCE: "The Far Side" cartoon by Gary Larson is reproduced by permission of Chronicle Features, San Francisco.

time of Wilhelm Wundt and John Watson because of their notable ability to isolate causes. Many important psychological questions ask about causes and effects, and the experiment is the best way to go about answering them.

The researcher's control over which research participants experience which events defines an experiment, and the very language used to describe experiments conveys the importance of this control. Research participants are called subjects because they are "subject to" whatever the researcher imposes on them. Experimental groups are given different manipulations called independent variables. Dependent variables are measured, so termed because they "depend on" the manipulation.

In the ideal experiment, everything is held constant except the relevant independent variable. Research subjects are randomly assigned to different treatment conditions, which has the effect of canceling out extraneous factors that the subjects may bring with them to the experiment. In my study of camp counselors and burnout, I did not control who was a counselor and who was not; therefore, I could not definitely attribute the observed burnout to the experience of the camp, as I had wished to do. Instead, burnout may have been due to uncontrolled individual differences like sensitivity that distinguished counselors from noncounselors. In a true experiment, this alternative would not be a viable one because the process of *randomization* cancels out such third variables.

Experiments are usually conducted in laboratories where control over extraneous factors is easier to exercise. However, laboratory settings are neither necessary nor sufficient for experimentation. Instead, what is important is the researcher's control, and this may be exercised in nonlaboratory settings. (These are called *field studies,* because the very first experiments of this nature were agricultural investigations literally conducted in fields.)

To take a more contemporary example, let's say that some psychologists want to know the best way to arrange the controls on a power lawn mower. They create several different configurations and randomly assign research participants to the different mowers and let them mow lawns. The researchers determine which arrangement of controls results in the fastest motion, the least confusion, the fewest accidents, the most fun, and so on. A conclusion can then be drawn that ignores the people pushing the mower, because their characteristics are canceled out by randomization.

The primary strength of experimentation also involves its primary weakness, at least for personality psychology. Because experiments allow the researcher to look beyond the characteristics of research subjects to identify situational causes, they are also insensitive to individual differences. As you saw in Chapter 1, such differences often define personality, and experimentation of necessity precludes their investigation. For this reason, experimentation has never dominated personality research to the degree it has other psychology fields.

For the personality psychologist, a second shortcoming of the experimental research strategy is that it confines study to reactions by subjects. Part of what is meant by personality is what a person spontaneously does. Folks do more than just respond to stimuli in the environment. Indeed, the concept of self-actualization suggests that people may even push against the environment, transcending it by resisting its potential causes.

Cognitive-behavioral theories of personality are concerned with the give and take between people and their social context, what Albert Bandura (1978) calls *reciprocal determinism*. If the person and the environment indeed affect each other, then experiments make this process impossible to study. Experimenters, for instance, do not allow subjects to determine the nature of the experimental treatment. If they did, control would be relinquished, and an experiment would no longer exist.

Experimentation in personality psychology has several other shortcomings. It may be impractical, for reasons of time or money, to study certain questions experimentally. If you are interested in the effects of different forms of childrearing on how well an individual adjusts to retirement, you could conceivably proceed with an experiment. However, few researchers would wish to wait 65 years or more to assess the dependent variable.

Similarly, it may be impossible to study other questions experimentally. If you are interested in gender differences on achievement, you cannot randomly assign some subjects to be males and other subjects to be females. Your independent variable walks into the laboratory, so to speak, making a true experiment impossible.

Also, it may be unethical to investigate certain questions experimentally, even though it would be simple to do so. Personality psychology is often concerned with adjustment and maladjustment, and many theories propose potential causes of this disorder or that. One would not wish to impose these possible causes on randomly assigned subjects to see if depression, anxiety, failure, or hatred results. One might be right!

In all these cases, the researcher may opt for a case-study strategy or a correlational strategy. Problems of logistics, logic, and ethics may thereby be minimized. However, if the central question is causal, then strong conclusions are also minimized.

Finally experiments are not always successful in isolating operative causes. They suffer the same problems of reliability and validity that plague all research strategies. Operationalizations are not always good ones. Experimental manipulations may be confounded by third variables. An experiment is no guarantee of good research.

Consider the well-known laboratory experiment by Stanley Milgram (1963) mentioned in Chapter 1. Milgram studied the willingness of subjects to administer presumable painful electric shocks to another person. Whether factors like the proximity of the victim to the research subject influenced the magnitude of shocks was studied experimentally by manipulating these factors.

Milgram (1963) viewed his experiment as a study of obedience, operationalized by the magnitude of shocks administered. Is this a good operationalization? It probably is, but Milgram (1974) felt obliged to argue against its interpretation as a measure of aggression. Aggression is hardly the same thing as obedience, but it might have a similar effect on this particular measure.

In an intriguing argument, Donald Mixon (1971) made the point that Milgram's experiment may have measured trust instead of obedience: trust on the part of the subject that the experimenter knew what he was doing, that the supposed victim would be all right. My point here is that operational-izations should always be scrutinized, regardless of the research strategy that employs them.

Experiments may be particularly liable to certain confounds called **experimental artifacts** (Rosenthal & Rosnow, 1969). Once a subject finds himself in an experiment, it may profoundly affect the way he responds. The subject, for instance, may experience *evaluation apprehension,* the fear that the experimenter is judging his mental health or competence (Rosenberg, 1965). "Gee, if I say that I don't like that guy, I'll seem antisocial. But if I say that I do like him, maybe that'll look like I'm superficial. I don't even know him." Whatever the subject decides to do, it will probably not reflect only the processes of interest to the experimenter.

Subtle and unintended cues from the experimenter may also bias results if subjects pick up on these and act in response to them. *Experimenter bias* has been documented in a variety of experimental settings, including some used in personality psychology (Rosenthal, 1966). The sensitivity of subjects to *demand characteristics* in the experiment that "demand" certain behavior is also well-known (Orne, 1962). The essential idea is that the relationship between an experimenter and a subject is a social one. As human beings, researchers may inadvertently communicate an expectation regarding the experiment's hypoth-esis. Also as human beings, research subjects may sense this expectation and act in accordance with it.

The artificiality of experiments in sometimes cited as a shortcoming, but I think this is misplaced criticism. What makes an experiment powerful is its simplicity. Only by holding constant as many extraneous factors as possible can an experiment be used to isolate a cause, and artificiality is the price to be paid. The researcher willingly chooses causal conclusions over rich detail about natural occurrences, and these conclusions are made on an individual basis. Artificiality per se is not a shortcoming of experimentation.

Another misplaced criticism of experimentation singles out the difficulty of generalizing from the typical experimental subjects: college sophomores recruited from Introductory Psychology classes. Certainly, college sophomores are different from some other groups, but there is no reason to believe they are particularly unique. In other words, generalization from college students is no more and no less difficult than generalization from any other group that personality psychologists study. Whether generalization from one sample to another is warranted must be ascertained on an individual basis. Again, undergraduate samples per se are not a shortcoming of experimentation.

How are experiments most sensibly used in personality psychology? They have three major purposes. First, like case studies, experiments may be used as proofs or disproofs. In fact, they may be even more suited for this purpose than case studies, because the experimenter can play an active role in bringing about an informative demonstration. One of the important aspects of Milgram's (1963) experiment is that situational factors may override personality traits, which were also measured. This flies in the face of common intuition, and as such, it is a valuable fact.

Second, experiments may serve the related role of providing evidence for arguments about plausible (or implausible) determinants of some behavior. Because of difficulties in generalizing from the special circumstances of the psychology experiment, the researcher can never conclude from an experiment what is universal. However, the researcher can conclude what is possible. Granted that the causes of personality are perhaps innumerable, such a conclusion may be the strongest to which a personality researcher aspires.

Third, experiments can be used to compare the relative influence of different factors on the particular behavior of interest. Some factors exert a demonstrable influence on what we do, but the magnitude of this influence is slight. Other factors, in contrast, are overwhelming in their influence. Most personality theories, at least by implication, take a stance concerning the more versus the less robust causes of behavior, and experiments allow these predictions to be tested. The person-versus-situation controversy described earlier in the chapter (p. 63) was resolved in large part by studies that explicitly played these two sources of potential influence off against one another. It eventually became clear to investigators that neither type of influence was consistently stronger than the other. So they concluded that both mattered.

APPLICATION IN PERSONALITY PSYCHOLOGY

In his famous presidential address to the American Psychological Association, George Miller (1969) exhorted psychologists to "give psychology away," to contribute to society the substantive knowledge they possessed. Personality psychologists were giving away their knowledge long before Miller's speech. Indeed, applications of "personality" predated any formal recognition of the field itself.

From the beginning, proponents of the psychological testing tradition and functionalists in general applied their ideas. Psychoanalysts and other personality psychologists concerned with abnormality applied their ideas in the clinic and in the hospital, diagnosing and treating failures of adaptation. And I showed you in Chapter 2 how Robert Woodworth helped during World War I by designing assessment procedures. Henry Murray and others did the same for the Office of Strategic Services (1948) during World War II. Contemporary personality psychologists advise the government how to prevent terrorism, resist brainwashing, and treat released hostages.

What is the difference between applied psychology and just regular psychology? As you might imagine, the distinction can blur, particularly for personality psychology, an inherently pragmatic endeavor. Anne Anastasi (1979) concludes that "applied psychology does not differ in any fundamental way from the rest of psychology" (p. 6). According to her, the distinction mainly corresponds to whether the research question is phrased in theoretical or practical language: "Is the investigation concerned with the nature of learning or with the most effective method for training airplane pilots?" (p. 9). This is also a statement of the difference between basic versus applied research.

In other words, the distinction roughly corresponds to whether or not a research finding challenges a theory. Compare physics with engineering. If a building collapses, one does not doubt the principles of statics (and dynamics!) that were used to design its foundation. Instead, one doubts the implementation of these principles. In plain language, your lawyer will contact the building's engineer, not the physicist with whom the engineer studies.

Similarly, applied psychological research is less likely to produce facts that call theory into question than is basic research. For example, Geller (1983) attempts to encourage the use of seat belts through various rewards like cash, prizes, and praise, a clear application of Edward Thorndike's Law of Effect. If the efforts prove unsuccessful, Geller does not question the theory that rewards lead to increases in the rewarded behavior. Instead, he believes that the right reward has not been used.

However, this distinction cannot be pushed too far because all theories somewhat resist contrary evidence. That is the nature of a scientific paradigm. So, how I will identify applied personality psychology in this book is simply by psychologists who happen to work outside of academia, providing a specific service.

Fields of Applied Personality Psychology

Applied personality psychologists possess highly technical skills, and their day-to-day activities may seem far removed from those of their academic counterparts. However, every personality psychologist works within a paradigm, and the major personality paradigms have each given rise to particular applications that fall within the paradigm's range of convenience. Let me discuss the major fields of applied psychology (Anastasi, 1979) and comment on how the personality paradigms have made their impact felt.

Industrial Psychology   The term *applied psychology* is often used in a narrower sense than I am using it: to refer to applications in business and industry. As early as 1913, Hugo Munsterberg defined this field, which thrives today in the form of personnel selection and classification. These applications of personality mainly involve the trait paradigm and its research procedures for assessing individual differences in job-related interest, ability, and performance (Dunnette, 1976).

Organizational Psychology   The closely related field of organizational psychology is concerned with the behavior of individuals within complex organizations, usually an industrial setting but sometimes schools, hospitals, sports teams, and the military. Organizational psychologists try to balance the demands of organizational effectiveness with worker satisfaction. These psychologists often adopt a field perspective, emphasizing the interdependence of the individual and the organization (Hackman, Lawler, & Porter, 1977). As such, they apply ideas from the cognitive-behavioral paradigm, particularly those of Kurt Lewin (1951) and his followers.

Engineering Psychology   Also known as *human factors,* this field of applied psychology is concerned with optimizing work methods, equipment, and the

*Even sports
teams employ
psychologists
to help athletes
cope with stress.*

work environment (McCormick, 1976). For the most part, engineering psychology draws on traditional experimental psychology and its findings regarding sensation, perception, and motor behavior. However, some engineering psychologists also apply theories and research from the personality paradigms. Their focus may be on individual differences in susceptibility to fatigue, boredom, accidents, and so on; if so, then they borrow ideas from the trait paradigm. Or their focus may be on the degree to which the work environment satisfies the needs of the worker. Finally, engineering psychology presupposes a particular model of human nature, and all aspects of the field reflect the assumed model (Argyris, 1969). The different personality paradigms are consulted to help articulate these assumptions.

Environmental Psychology   This field concerns itself with the relationships between people and their physical environment. Such topics as personal space, territoriality, privacy, crowding, and noise pollution may be studied by environmental psychologists, who are called on to solve the problems associated with them (Altman, 1975). Although they focus on the physical environment, environmental psychologists find cognitive notions useful in understanding how the physical world impacts on the individual. For instance, crowding has negative effects to the degree that a person perceives little control over it (Schmidt & Keating, 1979).

Consumer Psychology   Beginning with studies of advertising (Scott, 1908), consumer psychology has grown to encompass the entire relationship between the producer of products or services and the consumer (Jacoby, 1976). All four personality paradigms give rise to applications within this field. The psychodynamic and humanistic paradigms are used to conceive consumer needs and how best to meet them. For example, the controversial technique of subliminal advertising stems from the Freudian notion that people's motives may be aroused without their awareness. Correlational research techniques from the trait paradigm are employed in consumer surveys and the targeting of certain ads to certain segments of the population. The cognitive-behavioral paradigm provides models of decision making that may underlie product choice.

Clinical Psychology   The most familiar form of applied psychology is clinical psychology. The typical clinical psychologist is called on to perform two major duties: assess problems in living and treat these problems. Both involve the application of personality psychology. Assessment means psychological testing, and intellectual and personality tests are administered. Treatment means psychotherapy, and psychodynamic, humanistic, and cognitive-behavioral interventions are popular.

Counseling Psychology   This field bears a strong resemblance to clinical psychology. The counseling psychologist performs the same tasks as the clinical psychologist, with the major difference residing in the client with whom they work. Clinicians usually help profoundly troubled people change in basic ways, so they are no longer depressed, anxious, or crazy. Counselors usually help less-troubled people muster already-existing skills to solve particular problems. Counselors often work in schools, where they help students choose a course of study or decide on a career. Or they may work in other settings, where they help people adjust to difficulties encountered with work, marriage, retirement, illness, or injury. Client-centered therapy is particularly popular among counselors.

Educational Psychology   Psychology has always been involved with education. The entire psychological testing tradition received its original impetus from the need to ascertain the intellectual abilities of students. To this day, educational psychologists design and administer tests. I'm sure you have taken the Scholastic Aptitude Test, a product of the Educational Testing Service in Princeton, New Jersey. Other activities of educational psychologists include teacher training and the development of instructional techniques. These activities are based on theories and findings of personality psychology, and depending on the particular paradigm employed, they take radically different forms.

Community Psychology   This field of applied psychology subsumes many of the fields already described. It plays a role within psychology analogous to that of public health within medicine. Community psychologists attempt to prevent psychological difficulties by intervening at the level of the community. Like organizational psychologists, they adhere to a field of orientation and emphasize the interrelation between people and their social context. Prevention of problems involves interventions that enhance well-being, such as prenatal care, sheltered workshops, community mental health centers, hot lines, and job training. These interventions embody the field theory assumptions that the different aspects of personality are entwined, and that strengthening of some results in strengthening of others.

Health Psychology   It has long been believed that psychological factors play a role in the origin and treatment of disease. The field of applied psychology that studies these factors is health psychology, and it draws heavily on all the personality paradigms. Psychosomatic medicine may employ psychoanalytic theory to interpret symptoms such as hypertension, constipation, asthma, and peptic ulcers in terms of underlying conflicts (Alexander, 1950). The trait paradigm provides methods to help identify individuals at risk for certain diseases because of their lifestyle. For instance, coronary problems have been linked to an individual difference called the *Type A personality,* comprised of excessive time urgency, competitiveness, and hostility (Glass, 1977). At present, proponents of the cognitive-behavioral paradigm are examining the role played by thoughts and beliefs in mediating the effects of stressful life events on susceptibility to infectious disease (Peterson & Bossio, 1991). Popular books on health and its promotion, such as those by Norman Cousins (1981b, 1989) and Bernie Siegel (1986, 1989), use ideas borrowed from the humanistic tradition to argue that someone's will to survive can be the most important determinant of good health.

Aesthetics and Criticism   Psychologists have also been concerned with how and why people find pleasure in art, music, and literature. The person who produces beauty and the person who appreciates the beauty have been investigated from the perspective of all four personality paradigms. Of interest to personality psychologists has been how best to interpret and perhaps to cultivate aesthetic ability and sensitivity. Psychodynamic theorists emphasize unconscious drives and how they are expressed in creative products. Trait psychologists look to individual differences in skills and preferences. Humanists regard art as an important avenue for fulfillment. Workers within the cognitive-behavioral paradigm follow the lead of gestalt psychology in emphasizing the "good" relationships among the components of an aesthetic product. Like problem solving, aesthetic appreciation can be taught by encouraging attention to the whole. A related application of personality psychology is by art and literary critics, who find the psychodynamic perspective particularly useful in under-standing creative works. Ernest Jones (1910) interpreted Hamlet in terms of Freudian theory, for instance, in one of the most famous of such applications.

Psychohistory   This field uses psychological theories to illuminate historical figures and events. Although all historians and biographers make implicit assumptions about psychology, the psychohistorian uses psychology explicitly. For the most part, psychohistory is tied to the psychodynamic paradigm. Sigmund Freud pioneered this field with his studies of Leonardo da Vinci

(1910), Fyoder Dostoyevski (1928), and Moses (1939). Erik Erikson further developed psychohistory by applying psychoanalytic theory to such individuals as Adolf Hitler (1950), Martin Luther (1958), George Bernard Shaw (1968), Mahatma Gandhi (1969), Thomas Jefferson (1974), and others. The similarities between life histories and case histories are emphasized by psychohistorians, and the criteria used to judge a good case history are also used to evaluate psychohistory (Runyan, 1982). Recently, the potential pertinence of the other three personality paradigms to historical interpretation has received considerable attention (e.g., Runyan, 1988).

BOUNDARY CONDITIONS: WHEN PERSONALITY PSYCHOLOGY FAILS

Despite the numerous applications of personality psychology, limitations do exist. Not all topics are profitably explained in psychological terms. In some cases but not in others, a phenomenon falls within the *range of convenience* of psychology. A psychological explanation may be unwieldy, awkward, or simply wrong. Personality psychologists are called on to explain a variety of social ills and perhaps to suggest solutions. And while their efforts make sense in some cases, it is important for applied workers to recognize that nonpsychological factors sometimes swamp personality characteristics in determining a social problem.

Remember the inferential error I described in Chapter 1—explaining everything people do in terms of pervasive personality traits. This extends to social problems as well. We may believe poverty exists because poor people are lazy or ignorant, crime exists because criminals are violent or irresponsible, prejudice exists because bigots are misinformed or hateful. On examination, though, we learn that larger factors play a role in many social problems.

For instance, the women's movement is struggling not just against sexist attitudes (a psychological factor) but also against economic factors (women are paid less than men for doing the same job), historical factors (women are infrequently groomed for political office), religious factors (women are not allowed to play a full role in many major religions), and so on. The issues of central concern to the women's movement do not simply involve personality characteristics of women and men.

Emergent property: A characteristic of a complex system not present in any of its parts.

Sociologists call such larger factors **emergent properties,** because they do not reflect individuals but arise only from human collectivities. As the gestalt psychologists emphasized, the whole may not be the same as its parts. This is true not just for perception but also for groups of people. Sometimes the group, and in particular what ails the group, may have little to do with the personalities of the group members.

The idea of institutional racism shows how an emergent property works. This idea implies that an organization has rules or procedures that in effect discriminate against people of a particular race, even though no individual in the organization is prejudiced. Consider this standard policy: "Last hired, first fired." In times of cutback, the most recently hired employees are let go. This seems pretty reasonable, doesn't it? But suppose the most recently hired employees are black, while the more senior employees are all white. What happens now in times of cutback? Something has to give, and whether it is the new or the old employees, discrimination occurs. This dilemma has no easy solution, but the cause of the problem has nothing to do with the personalities involved. If a solution is to be found, it will not involve changing personalities.

The applied personality psychologist must exercise caution in deploying skills. They may prove irrelevant to the need at hand. My work as a clinical psychologist in a Veterans Administration Medical Center convinced me that psychological disorder may involve too few jobs and too little money as much as faulty learning, irrational beliefs, or inner conflicts.

The application of personality psychology seems an attractive way to solve social problems. First, Americans greatly emphasize the individual. The American Dream, rugged individualism, Yankee ingenuity, and the Me Generation all reflect the belief that the individual is paramount. However, this belief is sometimes unwieldy. Second, interventions against personality are easier than interventions against society. They cost less in time and money, and they are more palatable politically. However, they may not work.

Where does this leave personality psychologists? I'm not recommending that they become sociologists, economists, politicians, engineers, or revolutionaries. Rather, I'm saying that they must acknowledge the role of emergent properties in the domains where they work. These nonpsychological factors determine the boundary conditions of applied personality psychology. Indeed, all four personality paradigms recognize these conditions, although they differ in how they are regarded.

The orthodox psychoanalytic position treats society as coercive, in conflict with people's instinctive drives, but a given against which it is futile to struggle (Freud, 1930). More contemporary versions of psychoanalytic theory suggest that society can indeed change as technology provides new ways of living, so they present a more optimistic vision (Brown, 1959; Marcuse, 1962). In either case, emergent properties are clearly in sight.

Although their language can be quite different, humanistic psychologists regard society in much the same way as psychodynamic theorists—as possibly harmful. People's inner potential can be thwarted by a coercive or indifferent social order. Some humanists are optimists, though, and believe the world can be changed for the better. Others are more skeptical. In any case, the existence and importance of emergent properties are explicitly acknowledged.

Workers within the trait paradigm usually assess and diagnose difficulties in adaptation. Because society provides the criteria for judging adaptation, society is often regarded as fixed. Interventions are conservative and directed at the individual. Sometimes they are not undertaken at all, since the individual's nature is attributed to his biology. Not coincidentally, few forms of psychotherapy have originated within the trait paradigm, because personality is seen as static. But like the psychodynamic paradigm, the trait paradigm recognizes the importance of nonpsychological factors in social problems.

Finally, the cognitive-behavioral paradigm acknowledges emergent properties but may ignore them in focusing on the individual's beliefs and habits. Theory emphasizes that one's ideas are a joint product of the person and the world, but applications sometimes overemphasize the freedom a person may exercise in viewing the world. The following are considered irrational beliefs in the sense that strict adherence to them may result in disappointment and depression (Jones, 1968):

> It is important to me that others approve of me.
> Everyone needs someone to depend on for help and advice.
> Too many evil persons escape the punishment they deserve.
> It is almost impossible to overcome the influences of the past.

However, isn't it also the case that these so-called irrational beliefs are a pretty good mirror of the social world in which we all live?

At any rate, the four paradigms of personality psychology give rise to characteristic applications. An applied psychologist's chosen paradigm dictates the problems considered worthy of attention, the methods to be used in solving them, and the standards for judging these solutions. The paradigm also determines the boundary conditions of an application and how these should be regarded.

SUMMARY

A scientific paradigm is the worldview of a scientist. It encompasses preferred theories, methods, and applications, and it is consistent within itself. Contemporary personality psychology has four major paradigms: the psychodynamic paradigm, the humanistic paradigm, the trait paradigm, and the cognitive-behavioral paradigm.

Each paradigm in personality psychology has its own strategy of explanation that is regarded as most satisfactory. The psychodynamic paradigm stresses unconscious motives and the interplay between people's thoughts and feelings. The humanistic paradigm emphasizes people's conscious experience and their drive to realize their inner potential in a process referred to as self-actualization. The trait paradigm approaches personality in terms of people's stable and pervasive individual differences; often these are regarded as biologically based. Finally, the cognitive-behavioral paradigm concerns itself with people's thoughts and habits. The give and take between a person and the world receives particular emphasis within this paradigm.

All personality paradigms must account for known facts, generate new findings, and be useful to the practitioner. At the same time, these theories show considerable diversity with respect to which aspects of personality they explain, the units they employ, the models of human nature they assume, the stances on philosophical issues they take, and the relationships between theory and research and between theory and application they endorse.

Methods in personality psychology must grapple with operationalization of constructs, reliability, generality, and validity of results, with emphasis on pure versus applied research, and with adoption of nomothetic versus idiographic goals. Another decision to make is whether to bind research and theory loosely or tightly.

Three research strategies are employed in personality psychology: the case study, the correlational study, and the experiment. Each has its own strengths and weaknesses, and no research strategy best suits all purposes. The researcher's paradigm dictates the preferred approach for a given purpose.

Applications of personality psychology take a variety of forms and again are shaped by the particular paradigm from which they spring. Different fields of applied personality exist, and I briefly described each of them. Every application of personality psychology is bounded by nonpsychological factors that importantly determine phenomena of concern. Applied personality psychologists must be attentive to the factors that fall outside their paradigms.

In sum, the most important idea in this chapter is that each of the four major approaches to personality psychology is coherent. Theory, research, and application are mutually consistent. The choice of theory leads a psychologist to a particular method—and vice versa. Certain applications are easier within some paradigms than others.

PSYCHODYNAMIC PARADIGM: THEORY

By far the best-known explanations of personality are those proposed by Sigmund Freud and his followers. Psychoanalysis originated in a medical context, from the attempts of nineteenth-century psychiatrists to explain the puzzling aspects of hysteria and other emotional difficulties. Taken together, these explanations comprise the theory of the psychodynamic paradigm. Among the important models of human nature adopted by psychodynamic theorists is one that likens people to complex energy systems. These explanations account for personality by describing the process by which this energy is transformed and eventually discharged.

Noteworthy in psychodynamic explanation is the assumption that particular behaviors are **over-determined,** brought about by numerous causes operating simultaneously. Even the most trivial of actions reflect complex processes. A satisfactory explanation within this paradigm is one that specifies all the pertinent influences. So, slips of the tongue—Freudian slips, as they have come to be called—are treated not as accidents but rather as lawfully determined actions, products of unconscious motives.

Over-determined behavior: The psychodynamic assumption that each behavior has numerous causes.

Psychodynamic theory is different than other personality theories, so much so that many psychologists approach it with caution. Indeed, some believe that a psychodynamic explanation is not a psychological theory at all, and that the writings of Freud are best relegated to bookshelves devoted to literature or philosophy. What lies behind these negative opinions?

For one thing, psychodynamic explanation is heavily weighted in favor of *postdiction,* explaining what has already happened. In contrast, other psychological theories attempt *prediction,* explaining what will happen.

Furthermore, psychodynamic explanation is not quantitative. Although these theories are often phrased in ways that would seem to lend themselves well to quantitative expression, Freud and his followers did not take the step toward quantification. As a result, psychodynamic theories do not easily meet the requirements for correlational and experimental research. This is why they are dismissed in some quarters as "literary."

And psychodynamic explanation is not systematized. Freud himself wrote extensively over a 50-year period, constantly revising, discarding, and extending his theories. He never presented a definitive statement of his psychoanalytic theory. Further, Freud stimulated numerous other personality theorists to propose theories similar to his own. As you know, all of these theories make up the psychodynamic paradigm. It can be quite difficult to sort them all out.

Finally, as already noted, psychodynamic explanation assumes that behavior is over-determined. The most mundane aspect of personality is shaped by various forces, and all of these forces must be specified in a satisfactory account. This assumption is diametrically opposed to the principle of parsimony honored by most psychological theorists. Where other theories of personality strive for simplicity, psychodynamic explanation allows for complexity.

Compounding these difficulties is the fact that psychodynamic theories serve different purposes. Sometimes they are intended as an account of personality. Other times they comprise a general view of psychology. And still other times, psychodynamic theories focus on explaining why people have psychological problems and how these might be treated. In an ironic sense, the very success of this paradigm hampers our full understanding of it, because it has become so broad.

In describing psychodynamic theory, my strategy is to emphasize the ways important ideas originated and developed. The presentation is therefore chronological. Several individuals figure prominently. First is Sigmund Freud, whose theory stresses the sexual instinct and its inherent conflict with the demands of society. Freud's theory is termed **psychoanalysis.** Next are Alfred Adler and Carl Jung, associates of Freud who followed him at first but later broke away to propose their own psychodynamic theories emphasizing other forces. Then come the **neoFreudians,** a group of theorists who in many ways followed in Freud's footsteps but differed by stressing the social nature of personality. Last are the contemporary **object relations theorists,** who focus on how people think about themselves and important others in their lives. I conclude this chapter by describing David Rapaport's (1959) systematic summary of psychodynamic theorizing.

Psychoanalysis: Freud's psychodynamic theory.

NeoFreudians: psychodynamic theorists who emphasize the importance of the social environment more than biological instincts.

Object relations theorists: Psychodynamic theorists who focus on how people think about themselves and others.

THE FAMILY RESEMBLANCE OF PSYCHODYNAMIC EXPLANATIONS

The various psychodynamic theories of these individuals differ in important ways, but they share a family resemblance justifying their inclusion in a single chapter. First, many psychodynamic theories embody an energy model. People are thought to possess a fixed amount of psychic energy, termed **libido.** Behavior is driven by this energy in accordance with a psychological version of the laws of thermodynamics.

Second, many psychodynamic theories have a biological emphasis. They tend to emphasize motivation and are phrased in terms of drives and instincts.

Libido: Psychic energy.

Although the neoFreudians expand emphasis to include social determinants of behavior, they still speak of these social factors in terms of needs that require satisfaction.

Third, many psychodynamic theories have been influenced by Darwin's account of evolution through natural selection. This influence is reflected in a concern with function and dysfunction, with the consequences of past struggles and how they were resolved.

Fourth, many psychodynamic theories propose a conflict between the individual and society. The theories differ with regard to the exact nature of the conflict and its inevitability. Freud (1930), for instance, sees the conflict as an unavoidable one between sexual needs and societal restrictions. The neoFreudian Erich Fromm (1941), in contrast, proposes that the conflict between individuals and their society results from alienation: separation of people from the natural world and from each other. With profound societal change, this conflict can be avoided.

Fifth, many psychodynamic theories propose that people experience inner conflicts. This emphasis clarifies the one just discussed. In the course of socialization, people internalize what society deems right and wrong. When individuals feel the urge to act out sexual or aggressive impulses, it is not just the external world that keeps them in check but their own consciences as well. According to many psychodynamic theories, inner conflicts are never fully resolved, so all people are characterized by at least some degree of ambivalence.

Sixth, most psychodynamic theorists adopt a developmental perspective (Loevinger, 1976). In keeping with their biological emphasis, they attempt to understand present behavior in terms of the past. How did we get here from there? What path was traveled? A number of psychodynamic theories describe development in terms of stages: discrete periods through which people pass in a fixed sequence. One's mode of functioning differs across these stages.

Seventh, most psychodynamic theories have been proposed by individuals actively engaged in clinical work, usually in the role of a medical doctor. Their explanations of personality rest on facts about people with profound problems.

Eighth, most psychodynamic theories propose a single guiding principle that describes the course of development and represents the most satisfactory adjustment of a person to society. This principle can be regarded as the criterion of a healthy personality. According to Jung, for example, a healthy person integrates, bringing together disparate aspects of the self into a coherent whole.

SIGMUND FREUD: FOUNDING FATHER

The most important psychodynamic figure is of course Sigmund Freud (1856–1939), the Viennese neurologist who created psychoanalysis and guided it for 50 years. Although skepticism first greeted Freud's theories, and controversy has always surrounded them, Freud is regarded as one of the towering intellectual figures of all times. In terms of impact, he can be classified with Confucius, Plato, Copernicus, Darwin, Marx, and Einstein (Gay, 1988).

Sigmund Freud poses for the sculptor O. Newman in September 1931.

Sigmund Freud was born into a lower-middle-class family in what is now Czechoslovakia. He was the first child of his parents, although his father—20 years older than his mother—had two sons from a previous marriage. When Freud was four years old, the family moved to Vienna, where he lived for the next eight decades.

The realities of anti-Semitism led him to one of the few careers open to a Viennese Jew in the 1870s: medicine. During medical school, Freud was greatly influenced by Ernest Brucke, one of his instructors who was a well-known physiologist. Brucke promoted the idea that people were dynamic energy systems obeying the laws of the physical universe. Freud took these lessons seriously and later applied them to his psychoanalytic theory to such a degree that it is sometimes regarded as a neurology of the mind (Sulloway, 1979).

In school, Freud investigated adult and fetal brains, concluding that early structures formed the basis for later ones. We can see how Freud in his later work translated this idea from the neurological realm to that of the mind. Psychoanalytic theory proposes that the infant's manner of thinking and feeling—termed **primary process**—persists into adulthood, where it forms the foundation for another type of mental activity—termed **secondary process.**

Primary-process thinking is dominated by wishes and impulses. It disregards constraints of time, space, and logic. According to Freud, primary

Primary process: Thinking dominated by wishes and impulses.

Secondary process: Thinking characterized by logic and rationality.

process embodies the **pleasure principle.** In contrast, secondary-process thinking is oriented to the demands of the real world, operating according to the **reality principle.** Primary process is regarded as more basic and fundamental than secondary process. In unguarded moments, those occasioned by dreams, fevers, fears, or lusts, the infantile shows through undisguised: "I want my MTV!"

To return to Freud's personal life: In 1881, he received his medical degree and began private practice in neurology with Joseph Breuer, a somewhat older physician and physiologist who had also studied with Brucke. Breuer treated cases of hysteria with the technique of **catharsis,** the so-called talking cure. If a hysterical patient could be induced under hypnosis to talk about earlier events, a full expression of the emotions accompanying these events sometimes occurred, bringing an end to the hysterical symptoms.

Breuer and Freud (1895) interpreted hysteria, hypnosis, and catharsis in terms of energy transformations. Following Brucke's teachings, they assumed that people possessed a given amount of energy. Hysterical symptoms resulted from a tying up of this energy in unexpressed emotions. Hypnosis allowed an avenue to be opened to these emotions, and catharsis was their expression.

However, limitations of hypnosis soon became apparent. Not all patients could be hypnotized, so Freud came up with the technique of **free association** as a substitute. Patients were encouraged to say anything that came to mind, and the resulting pattern of associations often led to repressed memories: emotional conflicts long hidden from awareness.

They also discovered **transference:** patients transferred emotions from prior relationships to the relationship with the therapist—that is, the female patients of Breuer and Freud fell in love with them. Breuer was so disturbed by transference that he left the treatment of hysterics to Freud, who went on with the work alone.

The Seduction Hypothesis

In 1896, Freud delivered a paper before a Viennese meeting of neurologists and psychiatrists in which he proposed that every case of hysteria was preceded by a sexual experience in early childhood. Each female patient whom he had treated for hysteria reported a traumatic sexual event, usually an older male relative forcing his attention on her. The language of Freud's era termed this seduction; we now call it sexual abuse. Freud was convinced that these reports were valid because his patients described them with such reluctance and emotional difficulty.

Shortly after he delivered the paper with this striking thesis, Freud decided he was wrong. He became convinced that most (if not all) of these early sexual assaults did not in actuality occur. When patients reported them, what they were really doing was recounting their fantasies. In other words, as young children they wanted some sort of sexual contact. They could not make a clear distinction between what they desired and what actually happened, and so as time passed, they misremembered.

Freud's recanting of his original seduction theory had far-ranging consequences for his subsequent theorizing. Most basically, he shifted the

Pleasure principle: According to Freud, the principle by which primary-process thinking operates.

Reality principle: According to Freud, the principle by which secondary-process thinking operates.

Catharsis: The outpouring of emotion that follows expression of an unconscious conflict.

Free association: A technique for investigating the unconscious that asks the individual to associate one idea with another without censorship.

Transference: The tendency of an individual in therapy to transfer emotions from past relationships to the present relationship with the therapist.

emphasis away from external reality and onto someone's inner life. For understanding the causes of someone's problems, actual trauma became less important than imagined trauma. For understanding the nature of one's personality, the interplay of factors within the mind became more important than the interplay between oneself and the world.

Suppose Freud was right in the first place about the role of early sexual trauma in the genesis of hysteria? Jeffrey Masson (1984) pursued this argument in his controversial book *The Assault on Truth*. Masson believes that child sexual abuse was indeed widespread during Freud's era. He suggests that Freud lacked the courage to follow through on his initial discovery, because of the indignation and disbelief that greeted it. By giving up the seduction theory, Freud thereby made his work more acceptable to the general public as well as to the scientific community.

The damage done, according to Masson, is that orthodox psychoanalytic therapists to this very day follow Freud's lead and ignore the possibility that actual trauma may be responsible for psychological problems. Indeed, reports of sexual abuse are not simply disregarded but interpreted as desires. This is insidious, to say the least.

Masson's arguments are disturbing yet important, because the psychoanalytic emphasis on inner reality permeates much of contemporary psychotherapy (Masson, 1988). One of the bitter discoveries within recent years is that the physical and sexual abuse of children is rampant (e.g., MacFarlane & Waterman, 1986). We have no reason to think practices were all that different during Freud's era. Whether or not Freud intentionally revised his theory out of cowardice, as Masson charges, is perhaps not nearly as important as the plausibility of the original theory.

The Motivated Unconscious

Conscious: Thoughts and feelings currently in awareness.

Preconscious: Thoughts and feelings not currently in awareness but able to be brought into it.

Unconscious: Thoughts and feelings not able to be brought into awareness because they are threatening.

Topographical theory: Freud's division of the mind into the conscious, preconscious, and unconscious.

For whatever reasons, Freud at the turn of the century began to explore the implications of fantasy. He rapidly published books on dreams (1900), slips of the tongue (1901b), humor (1905b), and sexuality (1905c). All of these works assumed the existence of motives unavailable to a person's conscious mind that determine behavior. That an idea could be unconscious yet still affect conscious experience and behavior was Freud's germinal observation, leading him to develop his psychoanalytic theory. And because the notion of the unconscious is such an important idea, we'll examine it in some detail.

According to Freud, the mind has three parts: the **conscious,** the **preconscious,** and the **unconscious.** What we are aware of at a given moment is the conscious. What we can voluntarily call into consciousness is the preconscious. What we cannot become aware of is the unconscious. This division of the mind into three parts is called Freud's **topographical theory.**

In proposing the unconscious, Freud is not merely saying that people are sometimes unaware of what they are doing and why they are doing it. Occasional unawareness is an everyday fact incorporated into all psychological theories of the mind. Attention to one aspect of the world is simultaneously lack of attention (unawareness) to some other aspect, and the process of learning to do anything involves routinizing the activity, turning it into a habit and making it something of which we are unaware. Consider these activities: playing the piano, swinging a baseball bat, driving a car, tying a shoelace, delivering a speech, or dancing. You do not consciously direct or monitor these behaviors while performing them. In this sense, the assumption of the unconscious is not at all controversial.

What is controversial about Freud's proposal is his belief that the unconscious is motivated. According to Freud, the mental contents and processes of which we are unaware are kept unconscious because they are threatening or upsetting. Freud is not concerned with how we tie shoelaces. Instead, he is concerned with why we fail to remember the name of our first lover, with why a hysteric does not know when his symptoms began, with why a surgeon cannot describe when she first became interested in medicine.

To keep material unconscious requires an expenditure of psychic energy. If a great deal of material is to be kept unconscious, then so much energy is devoted to this end that the psychological equivalent of the energy crisis ensues. This crisis is termed a **neurosis:**

> In a neurosis . . . the (conscious mind) drew back, as it were, after the first shock of its conflict with the objectionable impulse; it debarred the impulse from access to consciousness and to direct motor discharge, but at the same time the impulse retained its full charge of energy . . . it was obviously a primary mechanism of defense. (Freud, 1925, pp. 29–30)

Freud called this process *repression* and regarded it as the foundation of all neuroses.

The motivated unconscious figures prominently in Freud's theory of dreams (1900) and humor (1905b). In both cases, ideas and impulses unacceptable to the conscious mind are actively kept in the unconscious. This material is usually threatening because of its sexual or aggressive content. However, the libido invested in the unacceptable material seeks discharge. And because direct release would be too overwhelming to the individual, indirect satisfaction occurs. In both dreams and humor, expression of sexual and aggressive instincts is disguised.

The Interpretation of Dreams (1900) is regarded as one of Freud's most impressive works. In it, he grapples with an age-old concern: the meaning of dreams. Dream interpretation has always failed because dreams so often seem meaningless: jumbled, inconsistent, elusive. Freud's insight was to regard the chaos of dreams as their defining characteristic—the meaning is hidden behind their surface content. Indeed, the purpose of the surface content is to disguise the meaning, which in most cases Freud felt was a *wish*.

Sometimes the wishful nature of a dream is clear, as when you dream that a lost friend or lover reappears in your life. But other times the wish is obscure, because its blatant statement would be unacceptable. You may be extremely angry with your brother, for instance, so much so that you would like to kill him. But if you dreamed about murdering your brother, your conscious mind would probably be so upset that you would awaken. So instead you dream that some disaster befalls him: he is hit by a car, shot by a sniper, fired from his job. Your aggressive impulse is satisfied, and your conscious mind is not ruffled. Most importantly, your sleep is undisturbed.

The dreamer has various techniques available for disguising unacceptable impulses so sleep is preserved. Among the chief techniques of what Freud calls the *dreamwork* are condensation, displacement, and symbolism. In *condensation,* the dreamer combines different impressions and experiences. One of my frequent dreams is of me walking through a building, the successive rooms and halls of which are from all the various places I went to school. And sometimes in my dreams I speak with a person who is both my brother and my father.

Displacement occurs when emotional significance is transferred from its actual source to another. As an example, Freud describes examination dreams, common among students, in which the dreamer becomes lost on the way to take a test for a course. According to Freud, that course is not one where the student is having difficulty; fear of failing has been displaced from some other course.

In *symbolism,* "the dream-thoughts . . . are not clothed in the prosaic language usually embodied by our thoughts, but are . . . represented . . . by means of similes and metaphors, in images resembling those of poetic speech" (Freud, 1901a, p. 659). Since dreams are mostly visual, pictorial symbols figure prominently. We are all familiar with the idea that long, pointed objects like the Washington Monument, link sausages, baseball bats, and Corvettes may symbolize male genitals. However, Freud does not believe in universal symbols. Riding a horse may symbolize sexual intercourse, but not necessarily.

Humor and Its Relation to the Unconscious (1905b) similarly analyzes humor. In fact, Freud began this book in the course of writing his book on dreams, sparked by the observation that many dreams had the form of jokes, using techniques of condensation, displacement, and symbolism. Further, jokes often disguise sexual or aggressive wishes that would shock our sensibilities if directly expressed.

In the course of doing research with children, a psychologist friend of mine was told the following riddle:

Child: "What's pink, goes in hard and dry, and comes out soft and wet?"

Adult (with trepidation):   "I'm not sure . . ."

Child: "Bubble gum!"

The riddle is funny, and the interaction between the child and my friend is even funnier. On both levels, we are allowed to express our interest and expertise in sexual matters without seeming crass. A frequent technique of jokes is to put the punchline in the mouth of a child or a fool. They innocently say what our conscious mind will not allow us to say.

Freud termed such jokes *tendentious* since they have a tendency or purpose: to satisfy indirectly our unacceptable impulses. Jokes work because their techniques obscure these impulses. A failed joke is often one where the impulse is too blatant, just as a nightmare from which you awake is a failed dream because the impulse became too much for the dreamwork to disguise.

Consider practical jokes. They rarely strike their victim as funny, since, from his or her point of view, the hostility inherent in them is obvious. "I was only joking" accompanies apologies too frequently for us to doubt that Freud captures something important about humor. Or consider dirty jokes. Freud observes that they are often told within earshot of an unwilling victim, one to whom the jokers are sexually attracted. The joke conveys the impulse, engages the target in a sexual encounter, and protects the jokers from rebuke, all at the same time!

In *The Psychopathology of Everyday Life* (1901b), Freud catalogued the way the unconscious makes itself known through slips of the tongue or the pen. Several years ago, I was being interviewed for a position teaching at a prestigious university. One of the faculty members who was evaluating me had his office lined with photographs of movie stars inscribed with personal greetings. "Oh, yes," said I, "Alan Alda. He's one of my biggest fans." The man interviewing me did not let on that he had heard me exchange the subject and object of the sentence. Regardless, it was an embarrassing slip. From Freud's perspective, however, my error was not without meaning. I was trying to aggrandize myself and had doubts that anything I had to say would be of interest to someone who was friends with the stars. Oh well, I wasn't offered the job. I hope Alan Alda still likes me.

SOURCE: *Never Eat Anything Bigger Than Your Head & Other Drawings,* published by Workman Publishing Company. Copyright © 1976 by B. Kliban. Used with permission.

Freud's generalization of ideas gleaned from his work with hysterics to such everyday behaviors as dreams, jokes, and slips of the tongue created psychoanalysis:

> [It] was no longer a subsidiary science in the field of psychopathology, it was rather the foundation of a new and deeper science of the mind which would be equally indispensable for the understanding of the normal. (Freud, 1925, p. 47)

In short, psychoanalysis had become a personality theory.

Childhood Sexuality and the Oedipus Complex

Of Freud's early works, none were more controversial than his essays on childhood sexuality. We've already discussed how the notion of sexual fantasies during childhood emerged from Freud's therapy with hysterical patients. Freud's next step was to propose that such fantasies were not unusual but instead characterized the mental life of all children. Tsk tsk! People do not like to hear that children have a sexual life. Perhaps childhood sexuality seems so bizarre because we think Freud is saying that children are sexual in the same sense adults are sexual. This is not what the concept means. Obviously, children and adults are different.

What Freud proposes is that both have a sexual instinct, a drive that demands satisfaction. Where many people would suggest that one's sex drive appears for the first time during puberty, proponents of childhood sexuality argue that it is present all along:

> The sexual function . . . has to pass through a long and complicated process of development before it becomes what we are familiar with as the normal sexual life of the adult. (Freud, 1925, p. 35)

Psychosexual development: Freud's theory of development. Children pass through stages defined by the part of their body that provides sexual gratification.

The process through which the child's sexuality passes is termed **psychosexual development,** and as I have already mentioned, Freud views this development in terms of stages. As they grow up, children pass through different stages defined by the part of the body that is sensitive to sexual stimulation. The child is thought to pass through these stages in an invariant sequence.

Oral stage: The first stage of psychosexual development, where gratification centers on nursing and feeding.

First is the **oral stage,** so named because the child's mouth provides basic gratification: sucking, eating, biting, cooing, crying, and so on. Any of you familiar with infants know that the mouth is the vehicle for becoming acquainted with the world. New parents learn quickly that Junior will put anything and everything in his mouth that will fit.

Anal stage: The second stage of psychosexual development, where gratification centers on the retention and elimination of feces.

Next is the **anal stage,** which occurs after weaning has been accomplished and reflects the role of the anus in providing pleasure. The young child derives sexual gratification in two ways: eliminating feces and retaining them. Again, new parents learn quickly that Junior engages in both activities with equal skill. Pediatricians have become rich answering phone calls from frantic parents who cannot understand what Junior is doing (or not doing, as the case may be).

During the anal stage, the child encounters strong societal demands in the form of toilet training. Retention and elimination of feces, heretofore uninhibited activities, now must reflect realities of time and place.

Then the **phallic stage** occurs. Libido is concentrated in the genitals, and children derive pleasure from touching their genitals, playing doctor, and asking questions about storks and the like. Yet again, new parents may despair over Junior's activities in the phallic stage. However, at about the age of five, children pass into what Freud calls a **latency period,** a time marked by repression of sexual impulses and a curbing of oral, anal, and phallic activities that provide pleasure.

The child emerges from latency with the onset of puberty, passing into the **genital stage.** According to Freud, this is the last psychosexual stage, that of mature sexuality, in which pleasure is provided through the genitals in the course of heterosexual activity. Although great changes occur from adolescence to old age, Freud believed that sexuality stayed the same, set in the pattern established early in life.

A question might have occurred to you while reading about these stages: Why does the child pass through them? Why doesn't Junior just stay where life is simple and comfortable, with pleasure readily available and frustrations rare? The answer to this question lies in the biological nature of Freud's approach. According to psychoanalytic theory, children unfold their inherent nature. This process can be thwarted or encouraged, but its essence is a biological given. It's in the nature of people to pass through the psychosexual stages, whether they want to or not. Oak trees cannot stay twigs, cats cannot stay kittens, and people cannot stay in the oral stage.

Nevertheless, people pass through the stages with varying success. The way individuals traverse the psychosexual stages puts a characteristic stamp on their adult personalities. Gratifications may occur too easily. Alternatively, they may be frustrated. Consider the oral stage. Children may be weaned too quickly. Or they may be overindulged. Although the child passes into the anal stage and beyond, an investment of libido is left behind, unavailable for future activities.

If too much libidinal energy is tied up in a past stage, then **fixation** occurs. The person is metaphorically stuck at that stage, and its concerns continue to color his or her personality. As an adult, the individual thus fixated is said to display a corresponding **character type.**

The **oral character** is one who makes incessant use of his or her mouth: eating, drinking, talking, smoking cigarettes, ingesting drugs. If you borrow a pen from such a character, you'll end up wiping it off, because it will be sticky, and kissing someone fixated at the oral stage is apt to be exciting, in both good and bad ways.

Karl Abraham (1927) subdivided the oral stage into *oral eroticism* (sucking and eating) and *oral sadism* (biting and chewing). Fixation at the oral eroticism stage results in persons who are cheerful, optimistic, and dependent, who expect the world to take care of them and react by overeating or overdrinking if this fails to occur. Fixation at the oral sadism stage results in persons who are cynical, pessimistic, and mean, who will "bite your head off" and "chew you out" if you cross them.

Phallic stage: The third stage of psychosexual development, where gratification centers on the manipulation of one's genitals.

Latency period: The temporary cessation of sexual gratification during psychosexual development.

Genital stage: The final stage of psychosexual development, where gratification centers on intercourse with a partner of the opposite sex.

Fixation: The tying up of energy at a particular stage of psychosexual development.

Character type: A personality type thought to result from fixation at a particular stage of psychosexual development.

Oral character: A character type concerned with activities of the mouth.

Fixation at the anal stage results in the **anal character** type, which takes one of two forms reflecting the two basic strategies available to the child who has difficulty meeting demands for toilet training: *anal compulsive* and *anal expulsive*. With the first strategy, the child may respond by retaining feces altogether. Not only is this intrinsically pleasurable, but it also allows the child to punish the parents for their difficult-to-meet demands. "Okay, I'll show you just how full of crap somebody can be." The anal compulsive character is therefore a person who is excessively neat and orderly. Such a person cannot tolerate a mess, washes the dinner dishes before the meal is served, puts slipcovers on couches, and, of course, cleans the house thoroughly before the maid arrives.

The second strategy of the child coping unsuccessfully at the anal stage is to respond by expelling feces at the worse possible times—for example, right after the diaper has been changed, when the family is on a crowded train, or when the toilet is broken. Again, this strategy is intrinsically pleasurable as well as an attack against one's parents: "Okay, I'll shit all over you then."

So the anal expulsive character is at times stubborn and stingy, at other times wasteful and messy. The chaos created by this individual punishes those who make what are seen as unreasonable demands. All teachers who ask students to type papers are periodically tortured by anal expulsive students. I've been given typed papers so grimy and filthy that I'm afraid to handle them, and I've read a number of papers typed with what must be the very first ribbon ever made.

Fixation at the phallic stage results in the **phallic character** type, an individual whose sexual impulses are excessively oriented toward the self. According to psychoanalytic theorist Wilhelm Reich (1933), fixation at the phallic

stage is produced by too little or too much genital contact. The individual becomes narcissistic, preoccupied with himself or herself. Traits of the phallic character include arrogance, vanity, confidence, and aggressiveness.

The macho man of contemporary society typifies the phallic character. He needs to stand out in a group, to be the center of attention. His sexuality is exaggerated with overwhelming cologne, gold chains, and an open shirt. He may lift weights and develop his body to such an extent that his profile takes on a phallic form: rigid, upright, and bulging with veins. At the same time, his sexuality has no social reference. It doesn't connet with a romantic partner. The macho man prowls through bars alone, dancing with himself.

Insofar as adult personality is concerned, the most critical events occur during the phallic stage. According to Freud, the young child, with libido newly centered in the genitals, experiences a severe conflict: a wish to possess the parent of the opposite sex and a desire to do away with the parent of the same sex. This conflict is termed the **Oedipus complex,** after the Greek drama in which the main character unknowingly acted out this scenario by killing his father and marrying his mother.

Freud felt the Oedipus complex is a universal fact of human development, brought about by the concentration of libido in the genitals. The child's love for the parent becomes sexually colored, and jealousy of the other parent results. The particular manner in which the child resolves this conflict shapes adult personality.

Here are some of the factors entering into the Oedipus complex. First, the child fears the retaliation of the same-sex parent. Second, the child feels guilty about these ill wishes. Third, the child typically resolves the Oedipus complex symbolically, by identifying with the same-sex parent and thereby indirectly possessing the opposite-sex parent. Freud called this process **defensive identification** and regarded it as the means by which children acquire the behaviors, attitudes, and interests that characterize them as adults. Little boys become their fathers, and little girls become their mothers, presumably as a way out of the romantic triangle they experience at an early age. And then they have their own children, and the drama is played out again.

The most important distinction affecting the course of the Oedipal conflict and its resolution is whether the child is a boy or a girl. The process for boys is more straightforward than for girls. In keeping with the sexual theme of the Oedipus complex, boys fear that their fathers will retaliate by castrating them. **Castration anxiety** results, which in turn leads to repression of the boy's sexual desire for his mother and identification with his father. "My father can beat up your father," says one toddler to another, perhaps reflecting the more primal thought, "because my father can cut off my parts!"

What makes things more complicated for girls is that just like boys, their first object of love is Mother. When the phallic stage is entered, their genital curiosity leads to the observation that boys have penises and they do not. The little girl concludes that she once had a penis and that it was cut off. Her mother probably had something to do with it, since she has no penis either. Annoyance with Mother then leads to increased affection for Father, tinged with sexuality as well as envy. After all, Dad still has his penis.

Oedipus complex: According to Freud, the wish of a young child to possess the parent of the opposite sex sexually and to do away with the parent of the same sex.

Defensive identification: According to Freud, the process by which the child comes to identify with the same-sex parent.

Castration anxiety: According to Freud, a young boy's fear that his father will castrate him.

Penis envy: According to Freud, a young girl's wish to have a penis.

Freud proposed that girls experience **penis envy,** the desire to have male genitals. Little girls wish to have sex with their father and bear him children as a way to deal with their penis envy. The child born from this incestuous union is equated with a penis. It eventually occurs to little girls that marrying Father is impractical, helped along by the fear of Mother's wrath. Identification with Mother therefore occurs, along with repression of all sexual desire for Father. However, this resolution does not occur as clearly as with boys, since little girls do not experience a fear as strong as castration anxiety. (Castration has presumably already occurred.) So, they do not have the same motivation to resolve the conflict represented by the Oedipus complex. And according to Freud, females do not resolve it as well as males do.

Everyone would agree with Freud that children are biological beings, that they pass through stages as they develop, with attention centering around different parts of their body. Everyone would agree that conflict and anxiety are no strangers to children. "But," you might ask, "why call this sexual? *Sexual* is X-rated, for adults only. So why confuse things by explaining the facts in terms of childhood sexuality?"

Quite simply, the evidence available to Freud led him to describe development in sexual terms. His clinical work invariably pointed to sexual factors in childhood that created conflicts and became repressed. His observation of children showed that they often were greatly concerned with the hows and whys of the body, particularly the genitals, and his reading of mythology and literature revealed the theme of incest to be present in all cultures.

Furthermore, the childhood sexuality allows a variety of behaviors to be explained by reference to a biological function: *pleasure.* The means in which pleasure is achieved changes, bowing to the demands of the immediate environment, but the basic instinct is present in all people, from birth to death. Freud felt that the notion of infant sexuality is not at all strange. Rather, it is the opposite belief, what he called *the agreeable legend of the asexuality of childhood,* that should be regarded with astonishment.

In the early part of the twentieth century, as Freud's writings became known throughout Europe, he attracted several able disciples, notably Alfred Adler and Carl Jung. Both men were later to break with him over the primacy he assigned to sexual motives. But, while the departure of Adler and Jung wounded Freud, he saw their disagreement as stemming from an intolerance of the truth about sexuality and its overriding importance in human personality.

The Structural Theory

The pattern of Freud's life was soon set. He extended his ideas to both normal and abnormal behavior, until the entire range of human activity fell under his theoretical umbrella. In particular, the Oedipus complex provided a far-reaching explanation for a variety of behaviors: creativity, religion, the origin of society. Most generally, psychoanalysis allowed the symbolic aspects of human activity to be explained.

Freud and his followers to this day have applied the psychoanalytic perspective to a broad spectrum of human products, from fairy tales to graffiti, from the books of the Bible to MTV, from sadism to masochism, and from the lives of saints to the lives of the rest of us. Human behavior is inherently symbolic, and most psychology theories cannot grapple well with the numerous levels on which behavior has meaning. In contrast, psychoanalytic theory, with its assumption of over-determined behavior and its rich vocabulary for describing people's motives, is comfortable on all of these levels. As I stressed in Chapter 3, psychoanalysis can often explain exactly those topics that other psychological theories cannot.

In his later life, Freud revised psychoanalytic theory by supplanting the topographical theory of the mind (its division into the conscious, preconscious, and unconscious) with what is now known as the **structural theory,** which posits three interacting psychological structures. What motivated him to propose the structural theory? Several inconsistencies arose in Freud's distinction between the unconscious and the conscious that he needed to resolve (Fancher, 1973).

Structural theory: Freud's division of the mind into the id, ego, and superego.

In his earlier writings, Freud had characterized the unconscious in different ways. On the one hand, the unconscious was defined as whatever is not conscious or able to be made conscious. On the other hand, the unconscious was defined in terms of the pleasure principle, operating without regard to the constraints of reality.

In many cases, these different characterizations of the unconscious peacefully coexist. What is not conscious disregards time, space, and logic, and vice versa. In other cases, however, contradiction occurs. Some of the material that is kept unconscious because it is threatening is organized, consistent, and pertinent to the real world. A number of the dreams described by Freud in *The Interpretation of Dreams* disguise wishes that do not conform to the pleasure principle. Fantasies that lurk behind dreams and neurotic symptoms may be grounded in reality and highly elaborate. The Oedipal conflict is a good example of an unconscious wish that is somewhat sensitive to reality, in particular, the revenge of the same-sex parent.

Another difficulty with dividing the mind into unconscious, preconscious, and conscious parts centers on where to locate the *censor* of the threatening thoughts. The censor cannot be in our conscious or preconscious mind, because we are not aware that we are unaware of certain impulses. We are simply unaware. At the same time, the censor cannot be in our unconscious mind either; that would require the unconscious to be sensitive to what would upset the conscious mind, that is, to operate by the reality principle. By definition, the unconscious doesn't work that way.

Freud found a way out of these difficulties by slicing the mental apparatus in another way. He proposed that the mind was composed of three interacting systems or structures: the *id,* the *ego,* and the *superego.* These structures are not to be confused with the earlier divisions into unconscious, conscious, and preconscious. They are different metaphors for the mind, methods of organization rather than places. With his new metaphor, Freud could resolve the contraditions inherent in the previous one.

The crucial aspect of the new metaphor is the **ego,** the part of the mind that is reality-oriented and therefore makes use of secondary process. However,

Ego: According to Freud, the mental structure that is oriented to reality and mediates conflicts between the id and superego.

the ego is not necessarily conscious, unconscious, or preconscious. All three are represented in the ego, depending on its particular function. In resisting threatening impulses, the ego operates unconsciously. In other activities, the ego operates consciously.

Id: According to Freud, the mental structure that is the source of instincts and impulses.

The part of the mind that makes use of primary process is the **id,** literally the "it" in German. The id is unconscious and undifferentiated, the source of instincts and impulses. At birth, a child's mind is exclusively id. The infant is out of time and space, lost in bliss. Only through interactions with the world does the ego develop, to help the child satisfy his or her needs without running afoul of reality, as represented by the demands and dangers of the world beyond the cradle. Freud thus maintains the developmental emphasis of his theory. With age, the child becomes increasingly adapted to the real world. The ego is the vehicle that makes this adaptation possible. At the same time, the id is always close at hand, waiting to erupt at any opportunity.

It seemed to Freud, though, that the developing person was not solely a bundle of passions held in check by a pragmatic ego. Sometimes people act in outright opposition to both selfish need and common sense. Sometimes people act morally or justly, sacrificing instinctive and practical considerations for what was good and right. People return wallets that they find, even with hundreds of dollars in them. Soldiers on a battlefield may give up their lives so their fellows will survive. The id and ego cannot make these sacrifices.

Superego: According to Freud, the mental structure that embodies the moral sense.

Freud posited another mental structure to do so: the **superego,** the moral sense of a person. The superego doesn't appear until late childhood, developing from the Oedipal conflict and its resolution. As the child identifies with the same-sex parent and represses his or her own impulses, the values of that parent are incorporated. The resentment toward the parent is now displaced against the self, and our all-too-familiar guilty conscience appears as the tool of the superego.

The three structures of the mind constantly interact, negotiating the ways libidinal energy is to be utilized. People have a tendency to reify these structures, treating them as literal things within one's mind. Indeed, Freud's discussions of the structural theory are so vivid that we are tempted to regard the id, ego, and superego as little people, with the id yelling, "Go for it," the superego proclaiming, "Over my dead body," and the ego hedging, "Well, maybe when I know you better." Needless to say, these psychological structures are neither little people nor literal things. According to psychoanalytic theory, all three structures influence everything we do, with their particular blend stamping each of us with our characteristic personality.

Defense Mechanisms and Ego Psychology

Defense mechanisms: Strategies that protect the conscious mind from threatening thoughts and feelings.

The ego must adjucate the inherent conflict between instincts and morality. Freud devoted great attention to how the ego accomplished this job. He proposed that the ego has at its disposal techniques of compromise called **defense mechanisms.** Freud's description of these techniques ranks among his most stunning achievements.

One can discern many of the defense mechanisms in prior writings: in the Bible, in Aesop's fables, and in Shakespeare's plays. However, Freud was the one who brought them together and explained them in the same way. Many of the theoretical terms he introduced to explain defense mechanisms are now part of our everyday speech.

Common to all defense mechanisms is a compromise between wishes and reality. Further, their operation is for the most part unconscious. Like dreams and jokes, defense mechanisms allow wishes and impulses to be satisfied indirectly, without ruffling the conscious mind and without bringing about retaliation from an outraged world.

Here are some of the defense mechanisms described by Freud:

- **Repression** occurs when a dangerous memory is forced from consciousness, as might happen if a person is responsible for a horrible accident where someone else gets killed. The details of the accident may not be remembered.

    Repression: Defense mechanism in which someone keeps a dangerous memory from consciousness.

- **Projection** is the attribution of one's own unacceptable impulses and characteristics to someone else. You periodically read of a zealous citizen who has led battles against pornography but has then been arrested for propositioning someone in the restroom of a department store. His public criticism of sexual "perverts" may be a projection of the repugnance he feels for his own sexual drive.

    Projection: Defense mechanism in which someone attributes his or her own unacceptable characteristics to someone else.

- **Reaction formation** is the replacement of one impulse with its opposite, hiding love with hate or hate with love. In elementary school (and beyond), little boys are apt to splash mud on the little girls they find attractive. And little girls are apt to find some boys more creepy than others, those who are not at all creepy. You must know couples whose relationship started with instant dislike.

    Reaction formation: Defense mechanism in which someone replaces an impulse with its opposite.

- **Regression** occurs when a person retreats to an earlier way of acting. An individual walks down the up escalator of the psychosexual stages until a comfortable place is found, one where she or he had earlier coped with no difficulty. Regression is acting like a child in the face of demands that cannot be met. I chew my fingernails on an airplane because I am very anxious about flying.

    Regression: Defense mechanism in which someone acts in a more primitive way in the face of stress.

- **Sublimation** is the channeling of instinctive impulses into activities that are socially valued. A surgeon might be redirecting aggressive impulses by putting people under the knife. A clinical psychologist might be satisfying sexual needs by listening in on other people's marital problems. According to psychoanalytic thought, everyone has underlying instincts. Individuals who sublimate are to be respected, since their use of these instincts is the most generally helpful.

    Sublimation: Defense mechanism in which someone channels instinctive impulses into socially valued activities.

Of all of Freud's original concepts, none have been elaborated by other thinkers better than the notion of defense mechanism. From this extension a new branch of psychoanalysis was born, known as **ego psychology,** which goes beyond the conflict-ridden model of the mind proposed by Freud.

Ego psychology: A version of psychoanalysis that stresses the role of the ego in normal adaptation.

According to the ego psychologists, the ego does more than simply react to the demands of the id. Its techniques are more than just defensive. Instead, the ego is involved in normal adaptation and is responsible for health, growth, and creativity. Among the important ego psychologists are Freud's daughter Anna Freud (1937), Heinz Hartmann (1939), and Ernest Kris (1952).

So far in my discussion, I have implied that some defenses are quite healthy. It might even be a mistake to call them a defense, since that has connotations of weakness. So some theorists prefer to call defense mechanisms *coping techniques,* with some leading to good adaptation and some not.

Psychiatrist George Vaillant (1971) gives us one of the most complete taxonomies of defense mechanisms (see Table 4–1). In keeping with the ideas of ego psychology, he calls them *ego mechanisms* and arranges them in a hierarchy from immature to mature. According to Vaillant, people use characteristic ego mechanisms, so they differ with respect to the maturity of their personality. Mature individuals are expected to show superior adaptation in a variety of domains.

TABLE 4–1
Ego Mechanisms

Maturity Level	*General Characterization*	*Examples*
1. Narcissistic	Strategies that alter a person's perception of reality	Delusion Denial Distortion
2. Immature	Strategies that reduce a person's distress—associated with threat of intimacy or its loss	Acting out Falling ill Fantasy Passive-aggressive behavior Projection
3. Neurotic	Strategies that change a person's private feelings or expression of instincts	Displacement Dissociation Intellectualization Reaction formation Repression
4. Mature	Strategies that integrate a person's conscience and feelings	Altruism Anticipation Humor Sublimation Suppression

SOURCE: From Vaillant, 1971.

The Death Instinct

Toward the end of his life, Freud made a second major change in his psychoanalytic theory. This change involved his view of instincts. In his early writings, Freud emphasized the libido, under which he categorized the instinct for self-preservation and the instinct for sexual gratification. Taken together, these are called the **life instinct** or *Eros,* after the Greek god of love. However, evidence from Freud's clinical work caused him to question his assumption that all instincts serve life (Fancher, 1973).

Freud found that some of his patients acted in therapy just as they acted out of it: neurotically. So what? Although the tendency to repeat past actions does not seem at odds with common sense, if those past actions are injurious, their repetition contradicts Freud's assumption of a dominant instinct directed toward preservation of self and species.

A contemporary example of the **compulsion to repeat** is the *post-traumatic stress disorder* that occurs among some Vietnam veterans. Years after a traumatic event, individuals may continue to relive its painful details. They experience anxiety during the day and bad dreams during the night, all centered around an event that occurred years ago. The life instinct cannot explain post-traumatic stress disorder.

In *Beyond the Pleasure Principle* Freud (1920) revised his theory of the instincts, positing an instinct the worked against Eros. The **death instinct,** or *Thanatos* (after the Greek god of death) as some call it, "*is an urge inherent in organic life to restore an earlier state of things* . . . it is a kind of organic elasticity . . . the expression of the inertia inherent in organic life*" (Freud, 1920, p. 36, Freud's italics). What is now living was once nonliving, and the death instinct pushes the individual back to this earlier state. The compulsion to repeat is one manifestation of the death instinct.

Like the life instinct, the death instinct may be "satisfied" in various ways. If directed inward, it may be evident in masochism, thrill-seeking, or suicide, including slow deaths like alcoholism and drug addiction. If directed outward, it may show up as sadism, aggression, or hostility, all of the profound and trivial ways people can be mean to each other.

The death instinct has not been generally accepted, even among those who otherwise embrace psychoanalytic theory. It seems at odds with the more general biological principles on which Freud based his ideas. How could a death instinct prove helpful in meeting the challenges of the environment? How could it evolve?

Despite considerable resistance to the specifics of his ideas, acclaim came to Freud within his lifetime. So, too, did popular attention, which may or may not have appealed to him. He was even offered a job writing an advice column for the lovelorn in *Cosmopolitan.*

At the same time, Freud suffered his share of disappointments, and some believe his idea of the death instinct stemmed from his own despair. As I have mentioned, many of Freud's earlier followers struck off on their own, severing personal as well as professional relationships with him. Due perhaps to his incessant smoking of cigars, Freud developed cancer of the mouth and jaw. He

---

Life instinct: Freud's idea that people have an inherent drive for self-preservation and sexual gratification.

Compulsion to repeat: According to Freud, the tendency of a person to repeat painful experiences.

Death instinct: Freud's idea that people have an inherent drive for destruction and death.

had part of his palate surgically removed, and thus he had great trouble speaking. In all, he had 33 operations and was in constant pain. To add to his troubles, the rise of Nazism in Europe was a special horror. At the very end of his life, he was forced to flee Vienna and take refuge in London, where he died in 1939.

ALFRED ADLER: STRIVING FOR SUPERIORITY

One of the first followers of Freud, Alfred Adler (1870–1937) was a Viennese physician born the second son in a well-to-do family. Adler remembered his childhood as unhappy, because he was unfavorably compared to his older brother, a reportedly model child whose attractiveness and physical prowess Adler felt incapable of matching.

He received his medical degree in 1895 from the University of Vienna, specializing in ophthalmology and later practicing general medicine. In one of his earliest papers (1907), Adler examined the issue of *organ inferiority.* It was well-known to medicine that disease often attacked weaker organs of the body, but Adler additionally observed that disease was not the inevitable consequence of a weak organ. Under some circumstances, the body may compensate for this weakness and develop a strength.

In making this general point, Adler drew on psychological examples as well as biological ones. History and literature provided him with apt illustrations of how inferiority could be turned to superiority under favorable environmental conditions. Teddy Roosevelt was a weakling as a child, but developed into a hearty and robust adult. He started our National Park Service, coined the term "rugged individualism," and popularized the slogan "Speak softly but carry a big stick." (He also inspired the teddy bear, which is irrelevant in the present context, but an interesting fact, nonetheless.)

In 1910, Adler furthered his ideas by proposing that organ inadequacy leads to subjective feelings of inferiority. These feelings impel the attempt at compensation in the domain of inferiority. He introduced the concept of **masculine protest,** claiming that inordinate strength and power are compensations for feelings of being unmanly. The macho man of contemporary society can thus be viewed as one who sees himself sexually and socially inadequate, protesting excessively against his perceived inferiority with displays of exaggerated manliness.

Masculine protest: According to Adler, inordinate strength and power exercised to compensate for feelings of being unmanly.

Striving to compensate for inferiority is seen not in just the occasional person, but in everyone, because children universally feel small and dependent compared to adults. Inferiority is a natural part of development, and striving to compensate for it is an inevitable drive. However, when overcompensation is taken to an extreme, pathology results. Adler coined the term **inferiority complex** to describe what happens when individuals organize their entire life styles around perceived inadequacies and mistakes. They no longer attempt to compensate for shortcomings but rather wallow in them.

Inferiority complex: The organization of one's life around perceived inadequacies and mistakes.

Adler's ideas about people's tendencies to compensate for real or perceived defects led him to introduce the more general notion of **striving for superiority.** This encompasses an individual's continuous attempt to be ever more competent at the activities of life. Striving for superiority resembles self-actualization as emphasized by humanistic theorists, although it can take on different forms. For the healthy individual, it shows itself in socially useful ways. For the unhealthy individual, the same drive may lead an individual to a search for prestige, notoriety, and domination over others.

During the early years of the twentieth century, when Adler's ideas were taking shape, he came into contact with Freud. Although the details of their first meeting are not clear, it is known that they attended the same weekly discussion as early as 1902. However, a break between these two important theorists was imminent, and it occurred over the primacy Freud assigned to sexuality. While Adler acknowledged that sexual conflicts were often significant, and that feelings of inferiority could result from inadequate sexual development, he felt that people's problems stemmed from a variety of social sources, not just sexual conflicts. So, while Freud argued that women feel inferior because they lack male genitals, Adler looked to women's interactions with society to find the source of their perceived inferiority—not to their anatomy.

At about this time, Adler read Hans Vaihinger's (1911) book, *The Psychology of "As If,"* which proposed that people live in accordance with fictional goals they set for themselves. These goals may or may not be real, but when people treat them as real, they become psychologically significant and determine thoughts, actions, and feelings. Vaihinger's ideas greatly influenced Adler because they provided a way to argue against Freud's strict determinism. According to Adler, then, people are motivated more by their future goals than by their past experiences, an explanation now called *teleology.* People are usually not aware of their goals, argued Adler, and goals are therefore the key contents of the unconscious, guiding their striving for superiority.

Another important concept Adler (1927) introduced is **social interest.** According to this idea, people are inherently concerned with the welfare of others. Social interest is what lies behind empathy and altruism. He originally regarded it as a force that opposed striving for superiority, preventing people from being ruthlessly selfish. However, Adler later entwined the two, proposing that the enhancement of social interest was the most important goal toward which people strived (Ansbacher, 1980). In contrast to Freud, who believed that individuals and society are in conflict, Adler believed that the relationship between people and their larger world is in principle harmonious. Indeed, human nature as he conceived it entails an intrinsic concern for others.

Adler (1927) is also responsible for the attention given to a child's place within a family. He felt one's birth order influenced treatment by others and eventually determined one's personality. The eldest child is the first to be the center of attention, only to be dethroned time and again with the birth of each subsequent brother or sister. As a result, the eldest child is thought to understand power and authority better than the later children in the family. The eldest child can compete with younger siblings for parental approval only by acting maturely. She or he may be thrust into the role of teacher or caregiver.

Striving for superiority: According to Adler, the individual's continuous attempt to be ever more competent at the activities of life.

Social interest: According to Adler, people's inherent concern with the welfare of others.

The second child in a family sees the eldest child as a rival to be overcome. As a result, the child may set unrealistically high goals:

> Through his childhood he has a pacemaker. A typical second child is easy to recognize. He behaves as if he were in a race, is under full steam all of the time, and trains continually to surpass his older brother and conquer him. The Bible gives us many marvelous psychological hints, and the typical second child is beautifully portrayed in the story of Jacob. (Adler, 1931, p. 148)

If you recall, Jacob and Esau were the highly competitive sons of Isaac. Jacob (the second child) induced Esau to sell his birthright to him for a meal of bread and lentils, surely an extreme reaction to sibling jealousy! In contrast, if the eldest is supportive, the second child will develop in a healthy fashion. Otherwise, resentful, the second child will develop in an insecure way.

The youngest child in a family is often spoiled and pampered. Because there are several older siblings, this child may follow a variety of examples. Hand-me-down clothes may not be desirable, but hand-me-down roles are. So the youngest child may be flexible and diverse. As the baby, he or she receives support and protection from all, while at the same time feeling particularly inferior. A good friend of mine is the youngest in a family of four. A while back, she remarked to me that just once in her life she would like to hear someone compare one of her older sisters to her rather than vice versa. According to Adler, this is a common complaint among the youngest in a family.

After World War I, Adler played a dominant role in the establishment of child-guidance clinics in Vienna's school system. His ideas about parent-child relationships were extended to teacher-student relationships, and he came to have a lasting effect on educational theory and practice. School disobedience was seen as an attempt to achieve superiority, and disobedient children were to be encouraged to seek more productive means of achieving their goals.

In 1926, Adler visited the United States for the first time, and he accepted appointments at Columbia University and later at Long Island College of Medicine. He made the United States his permanent home in 1934, but in 1937 died of a heart attack suffered during a strenuous European lecture tour.

How should Adler be remembered? In terms of his contribution to the psychodynamic paradigm, his notion that people are social beings rather than sexual ones is his most notable achievement (Hall & Lindzey, 1978). This characterization paved the way for later theorizing in which the social nature of men and women is accorded fundamental status. The theorists who proposed this view are called neoFreudians, in recognition of their debt to Sigmund Freud. NeoAlderians might be a better term, however, because their ideas are more directly foreshadowed by Adler.

CARL GUSTAV JUNG: THE COLLECTIVE UNCONSCIOUS

Another early associate of Freud, the Swiss physician Carl Jung (1875–1961) broke with Freud to found his own school of psychodynamic thought. By all reports, Jung was originally Freud's favorite associate. He was a man of

Carl Jung was a brilliant individual, but his place in psychology is still not clear.

staggering knowledge and intelligence, groomed by Freud to be his successor as the leader of the psychoanalytic movement. By the same token, Jung greatly admired Freud and throughout his life acknowledged the importance of Freud's ideas. The eventual break between the two men was painful on both sides.

Jung was born in Kesswyl, Switzerland, the son of a pastor. He grew up in Basel, where he entered the university intending to become a philologist and archaeologist. However, he soon became interested in the natural sciences and then in medicine. After receiving his medical degree from the University of Basel, he took a position in 1900 at a Zurich mental hospital.

Investigations of word associations were among Jung's first inquiries. He prepared a list of 100 words and presented it to normal individuals as well as to psychiatric patients. "Answer as quickly as possible with the first word that occurs to your mind." Response time was calculated with a stop watch. Jung also measured the individual's breathing and perspiring during the word-association task.

Although previous researchers like Francis Galton and James McKeen Cattell had studied word associations, their concern was with what they revealed about intelligence. Jung was instead concerned with what word associations said about emotions. He found that some individuals took a particularly long time to respond to certain words and also showed increased signs of arousal. They might repeat the stimulus word several times, as if unable to think of any response at all. In such cases, the word was usually associated with some topic of emotional significance, providing Jung a clue to begin his clinical inquiry.

Sometimes the patient was quite aware of why he or she had an emotional response to the word. But other times the patient seemed unable to recognize its emotional significance, despite the reaction it provoked. Jung regarded the latter case as evidence of an unconscious **complex,** an aspect of mental functioning split off from the rest of the mind. Complexes arise because of emotional trauma or conflict; they cannot coexist with the rest of the mind.

Complex: A cluster of unconscious ideas that function autonomously from the rest of personality.

Jung was also concerned with the possible causes of schizophrenia. He was struck by the fantasies and delusions of psychotic patients. They seemed to resemble the myths and beliefs of far-flung cultures. Jung was so impressed by these parallels that he believed the contents of schizophrenic thought transcended the patients' personal experience and reflected ideas and feelings common to the entire human race. These universal beliefs resided in the **collective** or **racial unconscious,** to Jung a more important aspect of personality than Freud's so-called personal unconscious.

Collective (racial) unconscious: According to Jung, memories and tendencies inherited from our ancestors.

Like Freud, then, Jung was grappling with the unconscious. With his word-association test, Jung had a way to gauge the influence of unconscious emotions on behavior that paralleled Freud's methods of free association and dream analysis. But where Freud entered psychiatry through clinical work with hysterics, Jung did so through work with much more troubled individuals. And while Freud brought knowledge about the nervous system to bear on personality, Jung drew on philosophy, religion, and anthropology.

Jung was initially attracted to Freud's ideas on reading *The Interpretation of Dreams.* This book, with its emphasis on dream symbolism, contained many ideas that agreed with Jung's observations. In 1907, Jung published *The Psychology of Dementia Praecox,* a monograph applying Freud's ideas to psychotic patients. He drew parallels between the disintegrated word associations of schizophrenics and the dreams of hysterics. Both became meaningful when one peered beneath their surface. The apparent emotional flatness of the schizophrenic was attributed to repression.

In 1906 Freud and Jung began a correspondence, and in 1907 they met for the first time and began to work closely together. Freud sensed in Jung the ideal spokesperson for psychoanalytic thought. Freud was keenly aware that in some quarters his ideas were dismissed simply because he was a Jew. Jung was a Gentile—indeed, the son of a pastor—and therefore an ideal associate for Freud. On Jung's tongue, psychoanalytic ideas might reach a broader audience.

In many ways, Freud was right about Carl Jung. He would extend psychoanalytic ideas in creative directions, he would win followers and students, and he would reach a worldwide audience. However, Jung did not do so as Sigmund Freud's protégé. The break started as early as 1911 and was clearly evident in Jung's 1912 book, *Symbols of Transformation.* Jung accepted the existence of psychic energy—libido—but felt that it manifested itself in numerous ways, such as religion and power. Jung also felt that people should be viewed not just in terms of past causes but also in terms of future goals and aspirations. Like Adler, Jung favored teleological explanations: People strive toward fulfillment and unity. In 1912 Freud and Jung ceased their personal correspondence.

Jung became greatly interested in the interpretation of dreams and began to view them not as disguised wishes but as attempts to solve current problems. To explore the significance of symbols, Jung undertook field expeditions to study the minds and myths of preliterate individuals, traveling in the 1920s to Africa (to study Kenyans) and to the Southwest of the United States (to study Pueblo Indians). Jung was impressed with the apparent universality of certain psychological symbols and he strengthened his belief in the collective unconscious—the storehouse of these symbols.

His theory of **archetypes** took form. According to Jung, by virtue of being born into the human race, we inherit not just physical characteristics but also mental and emotional predispositions. Chief among these are archetypes, determinants of how we experience and interpret significant events. Because of archetypes, all people think, feel, and act similarly when confronted with similar situations. Archetypes can explain the tendency of symbols, myths, and beliefs to appear across different cultures, the tendency of even the most mundane of us to act out in our own lives the stories of Cain and Abel, Romeo and Juliet, and so forth.

Consider the archetype of the **shadow**— our darker self. The image of an immoral, passionate, and evil figure lurks in many legends. Satan, Dracula, Mr. Hyde, Charlie Manson, Darth Vader, and J. R. Ewing bear a strong family resemblance to each other. The shadow represents what is inferior, primitive, and unadapted about ourselves. We locate the shadow outside, in nooks and crannies, in those sorts of places where nice people don't go, but the actual location of the shadow is within ourselves.

On a physical level, archetypes are at odds with what we know about biological inheritance. But from a metaphysical perspective, the idea of archetypes makes some sense. If we accept the premise of evolution, we conclude that the mind as well as the body has evolved. This means that psychological continuity should occur across species, and some forms of continuity are indeed obvious. The Law of Effect (operant conditioning) applies alike to people and planaria, dogs and cats, aardvarks and zebras. It makes sense in evolutionary terms that living things avoid pain and seek out pleasure. For the most part, these tendencies ensure survival. Granted that we live in a social world and that our ancestors evolved within a social world, it is possible that certain tendencies to get along with other people were also favored by natural selection.

Archetypes may therefore be regarded as social tendencies with survival value. For example, the **anima** is the feminine aspect of a man's personality, while the **animus** is the masculine aspect of a woman's personality. The anima and animus help us understand and anticipate the opposite sex. When we fall in love with another person, our idealizations of "man" and "woman" also become involved, and the affair recreates all past loves. We overlook flaws, minor and major, and we disregard mundane reality. Like Adam and Eve, we become the first people in the world. And like Adam and Eve, we populate the earth, at least to the extent of raising 2.3 children, a dog, and a cat.

So, archetypes are tendencies: structures or forms. They are not a specific content. In my earlier example of the shadow, I was careful not to say that J. R. Ewing of "Dallas" *is* the shadow. Rather, he *represents* the shadow, fleshed out with the details of Texas and American culture. J. R. unabashedly indulges himself in liquor, women, and power. He wheels and deals, but he never seems

Archetypes: According to Jung, inherited tendencies to pattern experiences in particular ways.

Shadow: The archetype that embodies what is inferior and evil about ourselves.

Anima: The archetype that embodies the female aspects of a male.

Animus: The archetype that embodies the male aspects of a female.

to work. He appeals to us because he is a case study of what is inferior in ourselves, and we of course live in the same society he does. By scrutinizing J. R., we scrutinize ourselves, and we may come to integrate the shadow into the rest of our personality. In another time and place, the shadow would still be apparent but in different trappings.

Self: The archetype that embodies one's striving for unity among the different components of personality.

One of the most important archetypes identified by Jung is the **self,** a person's striving for unity among the various components of personality. This archetype is often symbolized as a *mandala,* or magic circle (see Figure 4–1). Mandala symbolism appears in all cultures and represents completeness and balance to Jung (Wilhelm & Jung, 1931). The self only appears late in life, if at all, since the different parts of personality must first develop themselves before they can be integrated into a coherent whole. Jung himself fashioned numerous mandala drawings, and contemporary art therapy may be traced to his belief that such drawings make our journey to unity a concrete one.

Attitudes: According to Jung, general approaches to the world—extraversion and introversion.

What are the disparate aspects of personality that individuals strive to integrate throughout life? Jung provides a complicated answer. People are described both in terms of **attitudes,** which refer to general orientations to the world, as well as in terms of **functions,** which refer to basic psychological processes. For given people, particular attitudes and orientations are dominant in their conscious lives. However, other attitudes and orientations are present in their unconscious. Throughout a person's development, she or he attempts to bring the conscious and unconscious into balance.

Functions: According to Jung, basic psychological processes—feeling, thinking, sensing, and intuiting.

Two basic attitudes exist, according to Jung. **Extraversion** is someone's attention to the outer, objective world, whereas **introversion** is attention to the inner, subjective world (Jung, 1924). These notions have entered our everyday language, and we often describe an outgoing and gregarious individual as extraverted and a shy and retiring individual as introverted. But remember Jung's theoretical point; the person who meets our eye as an extravert also has an introverted side, and vice versa.

Extraversion: General orientation to the outer, objective world.

Introversion: General orientation to the inner, subjective world.

Jung names four functions, arranged in two pairs—**feeling** versus **thinking** and **sensing** versus **intuiting.** For a given person, one function in each pair is dominant, expressing itself at the expense of the other. I see a mundane example of the four functions every Christmas when I visit with the family of my brother's "in-laws." Several grandchildren are in the family, and the grandparents usually give the kids identical presents. The reactions differ markedly. On receiving a portable tape player, one child exclaims, "It's beautiful" (feeling); another child says, "Oh, a tape player" (sensing); yet another child takes it apart and explains the wiring to us (thinking); and finally another child breathlessly whispers, "My oh my, I just knew I'd get this for a present. I had a dream I would" (intuiting).

Feeling: According to Jung, the basic function characterized by emotions.

Thinking: According to Jung, the basic function characterized by thoughts.

Again remember the complexity of Jung's view. The nondominant functions still exist in someone's unconscious, from where they exert an influence.

Sensing: According to Jung, the basic function characterized by sensations.

As you can see, attitudes and functions represent a personality typology, one that is, however, more complicated than the typical typology, because all attitudes and functions are present in all people, although in differing degrees. A person's particular type is not fixed, because the self pushes toward balance among the attitudes and functions.

Intuiting: According to Jung, the basic function characterized by intuitions.

FIGURE 4–1
*Mandala
Symbolism*

*To Jung, the
"magic circle"
symbolizes a
person's quest for
unity among the
different parts of
personality. Left:
from Tibet. Right:
by a European
patient.*

In his later life, Jung continued to extend his ideas. He cultivated an interest in the occult, in flying saucers, in spiritualism—not as a believer but as a psychologist (Hall & Nordby, 1973). He felt that such subjects revealed the collective unconscious. Although continuing to live in Switzerland, he traveled and lectured widely, receiving honorary degrees at Harvard and Oxford Universities. He was the subject of several stories in *Time* magazine, and an interview with him appeared in an early issue of *Psychology Today.* He even appeared on television, and several interviews with him were filmed, so perhaps your instructor can arrange to have one of these shown. Jung died in 1961 at the age of 85.

His place in psychology is still not clear. Several contributions are obvious: the use of word-association tests to identify emotions, the notion of a complex, and the theory of psychological types. His theories about art, literature, religion, and mythology have been influential as well.

NEOFREUDIANS: A SOCIAL EMPHASIS

Many of the psychodynamic theorists who came after Freud share an emphasis on the social determinants of personality. Better informed by sociological and anthropological research than their predecessors, these neoFreudian theorists refashioned psychoanalytic thought to better fit new discoveries in the social sciences (Hall & Lindzey, 1978). At the same time, they placed less emphasis on biology, instincts, and sexuality. Accordingly, the neoFreudians believe the human condition can be modified, and social criticism is an integral part of their theorizing (Brown, 1964). Karen Horney, Erich Fromm, and Erik Homburger Erikson are among the major neoFreudians.

Karen Horney

Karen Horney (1885–1952) was born in Hamburg, Germany. She attended medical school in Berlin and was trained as a psychoanalyst. Horney's first interest was in female personality. As you saw earlier in this chapter, Freud's view of women was not positive, and Horney disagreed with his pronouncements regarding women, in particular with his idea of penis envy. More generally, Horney disagreed with the entire Oedipal conflict and with Freud's emphasis on sexuality.

Horney interprets the Oedipal conflict not in terms of sex and aggression but in terms of anxiety and insecurity. Her primary concept is **basic anxiety:** feelings of isolation and helplessness caused by disturbed relationships between people (Hall & Lindzey, 1970). Basic anxiety originates in childhood, if the child's needs are not met by the parents, if intimidation occurs, or if strict prohibitions are enforced. The child responds to basic anxiety with different strategies, among them the jealousy, dependency, and ambivalence that Freud labels the Oedipal conflict.

Children who experience basic anxiety attempt to make their lives more tolerable. To use Horney's term, they search for safety. The particular avenue they choose reflects the nature of the basic anxiety they experience. For example, someone who feels helpless may reach out for assistance from others. Someone who feels isolated may exaggerate aloofness and dissociate completely from others. Someone who feels under attack may beat others to the punch and become hostile and aggressive.

The problem with these reactions is that they are one-sided, and the individual who habitually uses but one way of relating to others is necessarily incomplete. The search for safety has taken on such importance that new vulnerabilities will probably emerge. Individuals will most likely have a shaky sense of self and little trust in their own spontaneous feelings.

These reactions to basic anxiety become an important element in an individual's personality, and Horney (1945) identifies a number of such reactions she calls **neurotic needs:** incessant striving for affection and approval, for power, for prestige, for achievement, for perfection, and so on. Because these needs are insatiable, they lead to conflicts. Notice that these derivative needs are similar to the ones Freud, Adler, and Jung regard as primary. Horney's version of psychoanalytic theory therefore makes the bold attempt to subsume its other versions.

Horney (1937) attributes much of neurosis to the person's particular culture. So, contemporary American life makes contradictory demands on the individual. Many of these pertain to our treatment of others. Can we love our

Basic anxiety: Feelings of isolation and helplessness caused by disturbed relationships with other people.

Neurotic needs: According to Horney, maladaptive reactions to basic anxiety.

neighbor and at the same time be into winning? Can we regard all people as equal and at the same time believe income is the sole measure of worth? Can we oppose nuclear weapons and at the same time favor the right to abortion? (Or vice versa?)

Horney is optimistic that conflicts can be prevented or resolved. If the child is raised by parents who provide security and love, then the child's basic anxiety never becomes overpowering. If society can be changed to minimize its contradictions, then many forms of neurosis can be headed off at the pass.

Today, Horney is best remembered for her careful examination of women from a psychodynamic perspective. Traditional psychoanalytic theory proposes that women are inherently submissive and dependent, even masochistic. Horney found such pronouncements unsatisfactory (Kelman, 1966). They simply did not fit the facts. She believed the behavior of women was more persuasively explained in terms of culturally enforced patterns, and it was here that she was ahead of her time. Furthermore, once we view women's behavior in cultural terms, we can do the same with men's behavior.

Erich Fromm

Erich Fromm (1900–1980) was also born in Germany, in Frankfurt. Unlike the theorists so far discussed, he was not a medical doctor. Instead, he studied psychology and sociology, receiving his doctorate in 1922. Fromm then pursued psychoanalytic training. He came to the United States in the 1930s, where he taught at a number of universities and psychoanalytic institutes. In 1976, he moved to Switzerland, where he died.

Fromm is primarily a social critic and theorist. His most direct contribution to personality psychology is a typology of character resulting from his analysis of contemporary society. In his theorizing, Fromm was as much influenced by Karl Marx as by Sigmund Freud, and like other twentieth-century writers, attempts a synthesis of the two, a plausible undertaking because both emphasize conflicts and their resolution. Following Freud, Fromm is concerned with neurosis. Following Marx, Fromm attributes neurosis to *alienation:* the estrangement of people from the products of their labor.

In *Escape from Freedom,* Fromm (1941) argues that only people can be alienated. Indeed, the potential for feeling alone defines our species. This means that a strictly biological interpretation of personality—one that emphasizes what people and animals share—will fail to capture our essence.

Throughout history, different forms of society have developed in an attempt to reduce alienation. Feudalism, capitalism, fascism, socialism, and communism all promise to provide the means for people to unite with each other and gain security (Hall & Lindzey, 1970). They do not necessarily promise freedom, but according to Fromm, freedom is not always attractive. It brings with it a greater potential for isolation. For this reason, totalitarian political movements like Nazism have some appeal: They provide a way to escape the alienation freedom brings.

People's most basic needs have nothing to do with sexual and aggressive instincts. Instead, Fromm (1955) describes our needs in terms of the unique aspects of human existence. So, we have needs to become interdependent with others, to be creative, to be part of the world, to be a unique person, and to understand the world. These needs are not provided by society. Instead, they are inherent in people—the product of evolution. They only become evident in the context of a particular society. Personality is the product of the way a given culture allows a person to manifest and satisfy his or her needs.

Consider the back-to-nature movement popular in segments of the United States. Individuals who favor environmental causes, health food, exercise, and a "small is beautiful" philosophy are attempting to satisfy the basic needs of existence. To become interdependent, they form a food cooperative, buying food in bulk and distributing it among the members. To become creative, they seek out new ways of making do with less. To be part of the world, they study ecology and backpack out whatever they have backpacked in. To be a unique person, they put their own stamp on a particular mix of granola. To have a coherent way of understanding the world, they interact with like-minded individuals and discuss their philosophy.

Fromm (1947) identifies several character types prevalent in today's society that represent the interaction of basic needs with the opportunities allowing their expression in a materialistic, capitalistic society such as our own:

- *Receptive character types* believe that all good things come from without. They are dependent and passive, incapable of seeing the relationship between what they do and what the world provides. They are what you might call wimps.
- *Exploitative character types* take what they want from others by force or by guile. They do not produce things by their own efforts but by using others. They are what you might call rip-offs.
- *Hoarding character types* withdraw from the external world, keeping what they produce for themselves. They are aloof, selfish, and suspicious Scrooges who only want to be left alone.
- *Marketing character types* are buyers and sellers of personality. They are interested in maintaining appearances, with making themselves attractive. When marketing types speak of keeping their options open, they don't mean stocks and bonds but themselves. Marketing types have no real concern for others, regarding them only as a potential source for a line on their resumes. Let the buyer beware!
- *Necrophilous character types,* described more recently by Fromm (1973), are attracted to everything dead. They are fascinated with sickness, decay, and destruction. They worship power and technology, seeing violence as the solution to all problems. They have transformed what is living into something dead. Fromm attributes nuclear proliferation to people with this character type. They are sickies.
- *Biophilous character types* are the only healthy ones identified by Fromm. They love life and are genuinely concerned with others. They are not alienated. They are together, with themselves and with others.

Fromm argues that societies are sick to the degree that they produce sick people. Certainly, he criticizes contemporary American society, pointing to its flaws and the human toll. At the same time, though, Fromm (1968) believes reform is possible. Society must be reworked to provide everyone a meaningful and responsible role that involves performing attractive and enjoyable work.

Erik Homburger Erikson

In some ways, Erik Erikson (born in 1902) is an ego psychologist, emphasizing the active role of the person in coping with the demands of the world. And in other ways, he is a neoFreudian, emphasizing the social determinants of personality. Erikson prefers to call himself a postFreudian, supplementing the theories of Freud without replacing them.

Erikson was born in Frankfurt, Germany, to Danish parents. Before his birth, his father abandoned his mother, so Erikson never knew him. His mother subsequently married Theodor Homburger. Young Erik was not told the truth about his heritage until he was an adolescent, which precipitated an identity crisis. As an adult, he changed his surname from Homburger to Erikson. In his later theories, Erikson assigns great importance to the establishment of an identity.

After graduating from high school, he traveled about Europe attempting to settle on a career. At age 25, he was offered a job teaching at a nursery school. Through this work he met Anna Freud, who was engaged in the psychoanalytic study of young children. Erikson was then introduced to Sigmund Freud and became a student of psychoanalysis. (At one point, he was Freud's chauffeur.) In 1933 he completed psychoanalytic training.

Erikson came to the United States in the same year and settled in Boston, where he became affiliated with Harvard. He continued to work with children, observing the course of their development. He then moved to California and studied children of the Yurok Indian tribe. His anthropological observations led him to a social view of development, because Freud's psychosexual theory proved limited.

In 1950 Erikson presented his own theory of development in *Childhood and Society,* his major contribution to personality psychology. His theory is similar to Freud's theory of psychosexual development in that it proposes stages to be traversed in an invariant sequence. However, it differs importantly by regarding people as inherently social beings. The defining characteristic of each **psychosocial stage** is the social conflict to be resolved. Further, these stages encompass the entire lifespan of the individual—from birth to death.

Erikson identifies eight different stages (see Table 4–2), explaining each in terms of the conflict to be resolved and the virtue that results from its satisfactory resolution. Passage through the stages is not automatic. Although people have the inborn potential to move through them, the environment can help or hinder them. *Ritualizations* are socially provided aids to help resolve a conflict. *Ritualisms* are ritualizations that have become counterproductive and rigid, subverting their original purpose.

Psychosocial stage: According to Erikson, a stage of development characterized by a particular social conflict that must be resolved.

TABLE 4-2
Erikson's Psychosocial Stages

Stage	Conflict	Virtue
1. Oral-sensory	Trust versus Mistrust	Hope
2. Muscular-anal	Autonomy versus Doubt	Will
3. Locomotor-genital	Initiative versus Guilt	Purpose
4. Latency	Industry versus Inferiority	Competence
5. Puberty and Adolescence	Identity versus Role Diffusion	Fidelity
6. Young Adulthood	Intimacy versus Isolation	Love
7. Adulthood	Generativity versus Stagnation	Care
8. Maturity	Integrity versus Despair	Wisdom

SOURCE: Based on Erikson, 1950.

Let's consider several of the latter stages in Erikson's theory. Most of you have probably just emerged from stage five and the task of establishing an identity. Who shall I be: doctor, lawyer, beggar, or thief? Out of *role confusion* comes *identity crisis;* from its resolution comes *identity* and the accompanying virtue of *fidelity,* the ability to sustain loyalties.

Now many of you are young adults in stage six. The major psychosocial conflict you presently face is *intimacy* versus *isolation.* Can you unite your newly created identity with that of another person? Can you get the help you need to make it through the night, through the weekend, through the rest of your life? If you can, you develop the virtue of *love,* defined by Erikson as mutuality of devotion, caring for each other as you care for yourselves.

Are you familiar with "The Gift of the Magi," the short story by O. Henry? A young couple with absolutely no money face the coming Christmas holiday. They desperately want to buy each other a fitting present. She has beautiful long hair in which she takes great pride, so he wishes to buy her tortoise-shell combs for her hair. He has a beautiful gold watch in which he takes great pride, so she wishes to buy him a chain for the watch.

Each is faced with a dilemma. She solves it by selling her hair to a wig-maker; with the money she gets, she buys a watch chain. At the same time, he solves the problem by selling his watch to a pawnbroker; with the money he gets, he buys tortoise-shell combs. They surprise each other on Christmas Eve. If you think this is a sad story or a funny one, then you have yet to resolve Erikson's stage six. Gifts need not be what one person gives to another, but what the two share in common.

Society attempts to help young people find a partner. Opportunities are provided by schools, churches, and other institutions in the form of dances and parties. Advice is given in magazines and newspapers. Food for thought is provided in the lyrics of popular songs. In general young adulthood involves a host of affiliative activities. When these ritualizations lose their purpose the ritualism is *elitism,* marked by exclusive groups where who is *not* a member is more important than who is a member.

Eventually we grow old. According to Erikson, maturity presents us with a conflict between *integrity* and *despair*. Does life have meaning? Are we satisfied with the way we have lived? Integrity is present to the degree that previous conflicts have been satisfactorily resolved. In old age, individuals may develop the virtue of *wisdom,* regarded by Erikson (1964) as a "detached concern with life itself in the face of death" (p. 133).

The ritualizations of old age involve all of the ways someone can respect and accept others who are different but integrated in their own way. I always enjoy walking through parks in the spring and seeing old men sitting together in silent enjoyment of each other. They may be black or white, rich or poor, but they respect each other, perhaps in ways that were impossible in their youth. The ritualism of old age is *sapientism,* the pretense of wisdom, marked by endless sentences beginning with, "When I was your age."

Erikson is also well-known for using his psychosocial theory to explain the lives of historical figures: Adolf Hitler (1950), Martin Luther (1958), George Bernard Shaw (1968), Mahatma Gandhi (1969), Thomas Jefferson (1974) and others. In so doing, he articulated principles of interpretation that have become central to the field of psychohistory. Most generally, to understand the person, one must understand the historical and social context in which he or she lived. You cannot rip a person's life from its time and place.

Erikson has had a great influence on personality psychology. In particular, his lifespan theory of development has helped psychologists take a broader (should I say longer?) view of personality. This view of personality development now predominates, even among those who do not endorse psychodynamic theory. Erikson returned to Harvard in 1960, and from there he retired in 1970.

With old age may come increased respect for and acceptance of others.

OBJECT RELATIONS THEORISTS: THINKING ABOUT SELF AND OTHERS

Object relations theory: Psychodynamic theory concerned with people's relations with one another and how they think about these relations.

The most recent development in psychodynamic theory is the perspective known as **object relations theory.** A number of theorists have contributed to this approach and they are far from agreeing on all points (Greenberg & Mitchell, 1983). Nonetheless, we can characterize this theory as concerned with people's relations with one another and in particular how they think about these relations. "Object" is a broad term that refers not only to inanimate things but also to people. It is deliberately chosen to remind us that other people are often the objects of our drives. So when we think about them, our thoughts can be highly emotional and ambivalent, with important aspects hidden deep in our unconscious minds.

Object relations theory began when psychodynamic clinicians started to do therapy with certain individuals who seemed incapable of maintaining intimate relationships with other people (Fairbairn, 1952; Guntrip, 1971; Winnicott, 1971). These individuals were erratic and emotional. In particular, the way they thought about the other people in their lives was bizarre. They attributed exaggerated characteristics to them, both good and bad. They frequently flip-flopped in their characterizations. And they saw the world as filled with danger. These beliefs, called **object representations,** led them to act in maladaptive ways (Kernberg, 1975; Kohut, 1966).

Object representations: According to object relations theory, the particular ways people think about others.

In trying to make sense of such object representations, theorists found themselves drawn to the early childhood of their clients. They often discovered actual trauma and deprivation (e.g., Herman, Perry, & van der Kolk, 1989). Like all children, those raised in harsh and inconsistent ways internalize the world to which they are exposed. They form their sense of self from the way they are treated by others. If parents are inconsistent, then the child will see the world as if through a kaleidoscope. If parents are capricious and cruel, then the child's very identity will be fragmented. These ways of thinking are carried into adulthood.

As already explained, traditional psychoanalytic theory places great emphasis on events surrounding the Oedipus complex. Object relations theory, in contrast, concerns itself with earlier events in a child's life, particularly the nature of the emotional attachment between infants and their mothers (Bowlby, 1969). To the degree these attachments are disrupted, so, too, are object relations.

Contemporary object relations theorists debate several issues (Westen, 1990). All entail the attempt to conceptualize the links between their approach and Freud's psychoanalytic theory. For example, how are object relations connected to instinctive drives? Some theorists side with Freud and regard people as inherently pleasure-seeking; relations with others are simply a means to this end. Other theorists follow the lead of Adler and neoFreudians to hypothesize that people are more concerned with relating to others than with pleasure per se. The important implication of this debate is how pathological we judge disturbed object relations to be. Relatedly, goals and strategies of therapy take different directions depending on one's conception of which is more basic: drives versus social relations.

Another concern is how object relations pertain to the structural model of the mind as proposed by Freud. Are object representations components of the id, the ego, or the superego? "Cognition" is regarded by psychoanalytic theorists as an ego function, so in this sense, object representations should be aligned with the ego. But the origins of object relations stretch back to infancy, when only one's id is thought to exist, so in this sense, object relations should be aligned with the id. Finally, the object relations of profoundly disturbed individuals are laden with oughts and shoulds, the hallmark of the superego.

Perhaps object relations theorists should be less concerned with the pertinence of their approach to Freud's psychoanalysis and more concerned with how it pertains to the relatively more recent psychodynamic theorizing of the neoFreudians. Theorists such as Harry Stack Sullivan (1947) and Melanie Klein (1948), contemporaries of the neoFreudians, more clearly foreshadow today's object relations theory than did Freud.

RAPAPORT'S SYSTEMIZATION OF PSYCHODYNAMIC THEORIZING

I want to conclude this chapter with a systemization of psychodynamic theorizing by David Rapaport (1959). Rapaport is one of the most profound of psychodynamic scholars, and among his chief accomplishments is the following description of psychodynamic thought. In studying the work of Freud, Adler, Jung, and others, Rapaport discerned a number of different perspectives. When juxtaposed, these perspectives result in a composite psychodynamic theory of personality. And while no given theorist endorses all of the perspectives identified by Rapaport, they are not incompatible points of view.

Indeed, I prefer to think of Rapaport's systemization as an exhaustive catalogue of the factors that comprise an overdetermined explanation of behavior. A fully satisfactory psychodynamic explanation partakes of each perspective. If one or more perspectives is left out of an explanation, then the explanation may be deficient. This will be clear in the next chapter, when I describe Freud's famous case studies. In each instance, you will see how Freud weaves together these multiple perspectives to capture the complexity of each subject.

1. The subject matter of psychodynamic theory is behavior. In using this perspective, one runs the risk of getting lost in the theoretical constructs—left to drift amid the ids and other intriguing hypotheticals. However, remember that they are explanations, a means to an end. The end is what people actually do.

2. Behavior is integrated and indivisible. A risk in using psychodynamic explanation is the temptation to use different theoretical constructs to explain different behaviors. So, one might regard some action as due to the superego or some other action as due to primary process. This is not careful use of these ideas, and it is at odds with the idea of overdetermined behavior. All actions reflect all hypothesized determinants. A particular construct refers to a particular component of behavior—not to an entire action.

3. No behavior stands in isolation. This perspective repeats one of the pertinent attributes of personality that emerged from the analysis in Chapter 1: All behavior reflects the integrated personality. In giving a psychodynamic explanation of some behavior, one must be sure the explanation fits with the rest of what is known about the person.

4. All behavior is part of a genetic (developmental) series. According to this perspective, present behavior can be understood only by studying its antecedents. The typical psychodynamic interest in early childhood reflects this perspective.

5. The crucial determinants of behavior are unconscious. Further, the unconscious is motivated. Psychodynamic theory regards people as unaware of the important contents of their mind, and they are unaware because these contents are upsetting to them.

6. All behavior is ultimately determined by drives. Although controversy over the exact nature and number of these drives exists, theorists regard drives as the ultimate determinants of behavior. It is important here to realize that ultimately does not mean immediately. Sometimes the drives behind a person's actions are far removed. Consider the example of sublimation.

7. All behavior is regulated by psychological energy. The drives provide the energy, and the energy obeys laws of conservation. Like physical energy, psychological energy can neither be created not destroyed. Once present, it can only be transformed. Individuals must do something with their libidinal energy.

8. All behavior has structural determinants. As you recall, these determinants refer to the division of mental processes into id, ego, and superego.

9. All behavior is determined by reality. By reality, Rapaport (1959) means external stimuli. Here he is recognizing the important role within psychodynamic thought of ego psychology.

10. All behavior is socially determined. And to follow up the previous perspective, the last point of view specified by Rapaport (1959) states that social reality is the most important reality. This of course is the thrust provided by the neoFreudians and the object relations theorists.

SUMMARY

The subject matter of this chapter was psychodynamic theory, the product of such individuals as Sigmund Freud, Alfred Adler, Carl Jung, Karen Horney, Erich Fromm, Erik Homburger Erikson, and the object relations theorists. To introduce psychodynamic theory, I first described some of the difficulties in mastering this way of explaining personality. It tends to account for what has already happened—not what will happen. It is not quantitative. It is not systemized. It assumes that behavior has numerous determinants. Then I sketched the family resemblance of the theories proposed by psychodynamic thinkers. These theories tend to embody an energy model, to have a biological emphasis, to have been influenced by Darwin, to propose a conflict between the individual and society, to adopt a developmental perspective, to have emerged from clinical work, and to endorse a single principle describing the course of development.

The bulk of the chapter described the development of the major psychodynamic theories. Freud's theory was described in the most detail. The other theories were then covered, with notations of when and how they diverged from Freud's version of psychodynamic theory. For the most part, the other psychodynamic theorists disagree with Freud's emphasis on the sexual drive as primary and with the corresponding biological nature of his theory. Instead, they pay much more attention to the social determinants of personality.

To conclude this chapter, I described Rapaport's (1959) systemization of psychodynamic theorizing. Rapaport identified ten points of view that capture the whole of psychodynamic explanation. Taken together, these points of view may be regarded as the various factors needed to fully satisfy such an explanation.

PSYCHODYNAMIC PARADIGM: RESEARCH

As controversial as psychodynamic theory is, psychodynamic research is even more controversial, at least when viewed from the perspective of traditional psychological investigations. After reading Chapter 4, you can understand why. The standard laboratory experiment cannot always be used to investigate psychodynamic theory. Experiments typically proceed by holding all factors but one constant and then manipulating that factor to see its effects on a so-called dependent measure. Experiments are ideally suited for investigating simple cause-and-effect relationships. However, psychodynamic theory does not consist of simple causal hypotheses. Instead, it consists of a variety of propositions at different levels of abstraction. Further, it assumes that behavior is overdetermined, that behaviors depend not on one factor but on many. Further yet, the critical determinants lie beneath the surface and therefore are difficult to manipulate—except indirectly.

It is therefore not surprising to encounter harsh indictments of psychodynamic theory in terms of its suitability for empirical tests:

> [Psychodynamic] theories were in a different class. They were simply non-testable, irrefutable. There was no conceivable human behavior which could contradict them. This does not mean that Freud and Adler were not seeing things correctly. . . . But it does mean that these "clinical observations," which analysts naively believe confirm their theory, cannot do this more than the daily confirmation which astrologers find in their practice. (Popper, 1959, p. 37)

> Freud's theory is hard to test . . . in part because his constructs are ambiguous and hard to quantify. The terms often are loose and metaphoric and convey different meanings in different contexts. Clear, observable referents for them are rarely specified. . . . Bluntly, some of these concepts do not offer the possibility of ever being disconfirmed by research. (Mischel, 1971, p. 44)

Should the chapter end right here? No, I think not. If psychodynamic theorists are sometimes guilty of overstating the scientific case for their approach, then critics are equally guilty of understating it. In this chapter, I will describe how psychodynamic theory can be regarded so it may be tested against the evidence. I will then describe some of its important tests. Finally, I will conclude the chapter with a revision of Rapaport's (1959) "composite" psychodynamic theory (pp. 137–138) to reflect research findings to date.

CAN PSYCHODYNAMIC THEORIES BE TESTED?

Two related themes run through the criticism of this theory with respect to research. To begin with, constructs are regarded as ambiguous and difficult to measure. Further, predictions are regarded as impossible to disconfirm.

What about these criticisms? The ambiguity of psychodynamic constructs refers to the multiplicity of thoughts, actions, and feelings that may (or may not) reflect their presence or absence. This is sometimes referred to as the phenotype-genotype problem, a term borrowed from the field of genetics to convey the complex relationship between surface appearances (phenotypes) and underlying causes (genotypes). Brown eyes, for example, may be the result of several different combinations of genes. Looking only at someone's brown eyes, we are uncertain just what combination of genes he or she happens to possess.

Similarly, in psychodynamic theory, a person's behavior does not always bear a simple relationship to its underlying determinants. Someone may smoke cigarettes because she has a death wish, because she is identifying with her mother who smokes, because she is experiencing penis envy, because of all these factors, or because of none of them; she may simply enjoy smoking. Of course this is complicated, but does it mean that psychodynamic theory is nonscientific?

Not unless we conclude that genetics is nonscientific as well. When we see persons with brown eyes, we don't see their genotype. Geneticists do not shrug their shoulders when faced with a brown-eyed phenotype. They merely proceed to gather more information. What color eyes do the parents have? How about the children? Further information often allows a good inference about underlying genotype.

The researcher investigating psychodynamic theory must similarly regard the relationship between overt behavior and underlying determinants as potentially ambiguous—yet not capricious. To disentangle these links, the researcher must gather information above and beyond the particular behavior she wants to explain.

She can draw on several strategies. First, she may obtain a wealth of detail about an individual's life. This is the case-study method, and one can use it to judge the adequacy of a psychodynamic explanation by seeing how coherently it ties *all* the details of the case together. Second, she may obtain information about a large number of different individuals who have or have not behaved in the way under study. This is the correlational research strategy. One can use it to judge a psychodynamic explanation by seeing how closely the explanation corresponds to generalizations about the behavior of concern. Third, she may obtain information about the behavior of interest in different conditions she controls. This is the experimental research strategy, and one can use it to evaluate psychodynamic explanations by seeing if they correctly predict the occurrence or nonoccurrence of behaviors under specified circumstances. As applied to psychodynamic research, the bottom line for each strategy is to narrow the range of uncertainty in making inferences. Information is the only way to accomplish this.

The second common criticism of psychodynamic theory with regard to research is that its predictions are impossible to prove wrong. Nothing ever counts against this kind of explanation. So, for example, suppose we are looking for evidence of the Oedipus conflict. Junior acts in a hostile way toward his father and in a loving way toward his mother. This pattern reflects the essence of Freud's ideas. Or, suppose Junior acts in a loving way toward his father and in a hostile way toward his mother. If this reflects reaction formation, then it is also consistent with the Oedipal conflict.

Does Junior do anything that cannot be stretched to fit Freud's theory? Probably not, if our goal is to make isolated aspects of Junior's behavior fit the Oedipal mold, but this is not the point of research. Instead, we want to evaluate a theory in light of evidence gathered in such a way that the theory has a chance to be correct as well as incorrect.

Consider the two examples. According to this theory, the first should appear before the second. Junior should act lovingly toward his mother before he cools to her. He should act hostilely toward his father before he disguises his resentment, and Junior's switch in overt behavior should be triggered by a real or imagined rebuke from his father.

The research supports Freud's theory to the degree that information about Junior corresponds to this line of events. The research disconfirms the theory to the degree that the facts are at odds with this scenario. If the researcher uses a case study approach, studying in great detail the life of one particular Junior, she should look for evidence about the sequencing of his feelings toward his mother and father. If she employs a correlational strategy, obtaining information on 100 Juniors, she should look at the correlation between the age of the child and his feelings toward his parents. If she chooses experimentation, manipulating the circumstances under which different Juniors inhibit anger toward authority figures, she should look at the degree of inhibition under conditions of rebuke versus no rebuke. And so on. Psychodynamic theory can be proven wrong if the researcher does more than look at a single behavior under a single circumstance.

On the other hand, aspects of psychodynamic theory cannot easily be proven or disproven. These are the bedrock aspects of the paradigm, and the testable theory sits on these assumptions, called **metapsychological propositions.** These are assumptions that go beyond data, such as the notion of psychic energy. I'm not sure it is possible to prove or disprove the existence of libido. One simply assumes people are energy systems and proceeds from there. Such bedrock assumptions also exist in everyday life, where they are called our *natural attitude:* unquestioned beliefs about the way the world is. One's natural attitude might include the notions that people are good (or bad), that miracles

Metapsychological proposition: A theoretical assumption that cannot be tested by research.

occur, that plants understand what is said to them, that anyone can grow up to be president, a rock star, or a millionaire.

Clinical proposition: A theoretical assumption that can be tested by research.

The testable aspects of psychodynamic theory are called **clinical propositions,** because they can be checked against the actual behavior of patients in therapy. For instance, the psychodynamic explanation of depression proposes that individuals prone to this disorder have experienced loss of love from a significant other early in life. This proposition can be tested. Indeed, it proves true for some but not all depressives (see, for example, Lloyd, 1980).

Lloyd Silverman (1976) regards the clinical propositions of psychodynamic theory as more important than the metapsychological propositions. He argues that since they cannot be tested against evidence, the metapsychological propositions are nonessential and can be discarded. But in keeping with the idea of scientific paradigms described in Chapter 3, I disagree with his line of reasoning here. The metapsychological propositions provide the background against which the clinical propositions make sense. They hold psychodynamic theory together, just as our natural attitude holds our experience of everyday reality together.

At the same time, I find the distinction between metapsychological and clinical propositions quite useful in regarding research. Investigations can only test the clinical propositions. If the majority are supported, one has faith in the bedrock assumptions. If the majority are not supported, one suspects that the metapsychological assumptions are poor ones.

So, the testing of psychodynamic theory against evidence requires a distinction between what is amenable to test and what is immune. This distinction is not always clear, however. Metapsychological assumptions and clinical hypotheses are endpoints of a continuum along which actual theoretical propositions fall. In this chapter, I will focus on the aspects of psychodynamic research more or less close to the ideal of clinical hypotheses.

CASE STUDIES

Because Freud's name is almost synonymous with the case study method, you may be surprised to learn that Freud published few of them—about half a dozen in detail (Brody, 1970; Goshen, 1952). The ethics at his time prevented clinicians from disclosing details from cases. Because the assumption of over-determined behavior makes details important, it is difficult to present case studies as tests of psychodynamic theory without revealing the identity of their subject. Nevertheless, what separates science from other ways of knowing is that its basic evidence is public.

Freud's Cases: The Original Data of Psychoanalysis

When Freud published a case study, he tried to make a theoretical point. I want to describe some of these studies and the points they make. Remember, these case studies, despite dealing with patients who suffered with serious problems, were published by Freud to test critical aspects of psychoanalytic theory.

The Case of Anna O.   This first of the famous psychoanalytic cases was actually seen by Joseph Breuer, Freud's early collaborator (Breuer & Freud, 1895). Anna O. was an extremely intelligent young woman who showed a variety of hysterical symptoms. With Anna O.'s active collaboration, Breuer discovered catharsis. When Anna O. recalled memories long hidden, she experienced an emotional relief, and her hysterical symptoms subsided. For example, at one time in her illness, Anna O. could not drink water, despite thirst. Under hypnosis, she described a childhood incident where she had seen a dog drink from a glass, a scene that disgusted her. But once she had described the incident, she was able to drink water without difficulty. Anna O. referred to this procedure as *chimney sweeping.*

Anna O.'s real name was Bertha Pappenheim, and she later became famous as Germany's first social worker. Contemporary opinion suggests that she may have been more responsible for developing catharsis than Breuer (Rosenbaum, 1984). Perhaps subsequent histories of psychoanalysis will accord her the greater recognition she seems to deserve. Regardless, the case of Anna O. is important because it marked the discovery of catharsis as a treatment for hysteria. That catharsis worked in the way it did, alleviating hysterical symptoms by bringing forgotten memories to light, points to critical psychodynamic notions like the unconscious, psychic energy, and traumatic childhood events.

The Case of Little Hans   One of Freud's (1909a) well-known case studies was of a young boy known to history as Little Hans. Hans was the son of two of Freud's associates, and he was greatly afraid of horses. Specifically, he feared a horse would bite him. Freud himself never met with Hans, but he formulated an explanation for the boy's fear through conversations with his parents.

Little Hans was almost five years old, exactly the age when the Oedipal conflict is thought to emerge in full force. As such, Freud interpreted Hans's fear of horses in Oedipal terms. If you recall, this conflict shows itself in two related ways.

First, the child is sexually drawn to the parent of the opposite sex. No one doubted that Little Hans enjoyed being with his mother and having her cuddle with him. Is it reasonable to interpret this as a sexual desire? Perhaps, because on at least one occasion reported by Freud, Hans asked his mother to touch his penis. "It would be great fun," urged Hans.

Second, the child feels hostility toward the parent of the same sex, but also experiences fear. Here is where the aversion to horses enters the picture, because Freud felt that the little boy had displaced his fear of his father onto horses. Hans had reportedly noticed that horses had large penises—as presumably did his father—which highlighted his own vulnerability to castration. Also, he was particularly afraid of horses wearing blinkers, perhaps because his father wore eyeglasses.

Little Hans eventually overcame his fear of horses. It is believed he grew up to be the story director of the New York Metropolitan Opera (Silverman, 1980). This case study is important because it was Freud's first attempt to document the Oedipal dynamics he had hypothesized. Freud never did clinical work with children, so Little Hans represented a rare opportunity for him to test his theory.

The Case of the Rat Man   Another well-known case study by Freud (1909b) is that of a young man suffering from an obsessive fear of rats. In particular, the Rat Man—as he has come to be known—experienced recurring thoughts that a horrible torture would befall those close to him. His father's or his fiancée's naked bottom would be strapped over a metal pot containing a hungry rat. The rat would then do a typical rat thing: burrow into the area of least resistance.

The Rat Man suffered from other problems as well. Although his father was dead, he would not recognize it. And he experienced a number of internal prohibitions forbidding him to engage in certain acts for fear that disastrous consequences would befall him or someone close to him. For instance, the Rat Man was extremely fond of his niece Ella. He thought that if he made love with someone, then something bad would happen to Ella.

By now you should understand that Freud looks to the troubled individual's childhood to find the roots of the problem. In the early life of the Rat Man, critical events were unearthed. First, his sexual life began early, at about four or five, when his governess allowed him to touch her genitals. Second, he experienced a strong urge to see women naked. Third, he had been punished by his father for masturbation.

His strong sexual urges coupled with the equally strong fear of future punishment for indulging in them led to hatred of his father. At the same time, the Rat Man loved his father and felt guilty about his hatred. This conflict resulted in his various symptoms. The rat torture reflected anger toward his father and fiancée. Not recognizing the death of his father stemmed from guilt about wishing his father would die. And so on. Freud describes his therapy with the Rat Man as successful, bringing unconscious material to light and liberating the patient from its burden.

This case is important because it includes a detailed discussion by Freud on obsessions. To Freud, recurring thoughts an individual cannot control reflect underlying struggles. The manifest content of the obsession symbolizes what is unconscious, as do dreams and jokes, so the psychoanalyst may use it as a clue to understand the obsessive patient.

Figure 5–1 diagrams one of the Rat Man's obsessive thoughts: "If I have intercourse, then my niece will die." This seemingly irrational belief made more sense once Freud traced the Rat Man's train of thought through the unconscious. Obsessions result from a process called *distortion by omission*. As you can see in the figure, the Rat Man omits from his conscious mind the thoughts that distress him.

The Case of Schreber   Freud (1911) never met Daniel Paul Schreber. Instead, the material for this case study came from an autobiography written by Schreber, a German judge of some note, following his recovery from two psychotic episodes marked by delusions of persecution. Schreber was paranoid to such a degree that everyday life became impossible and institutionalization was necessary.

In an early phase of his difficulties, Schreber felt that his physician, Dr. Flechsig, intended to harm him. In a later phase, Schreber believed that God wanted to harm him. For instance, God usually arranged for someone to occupy

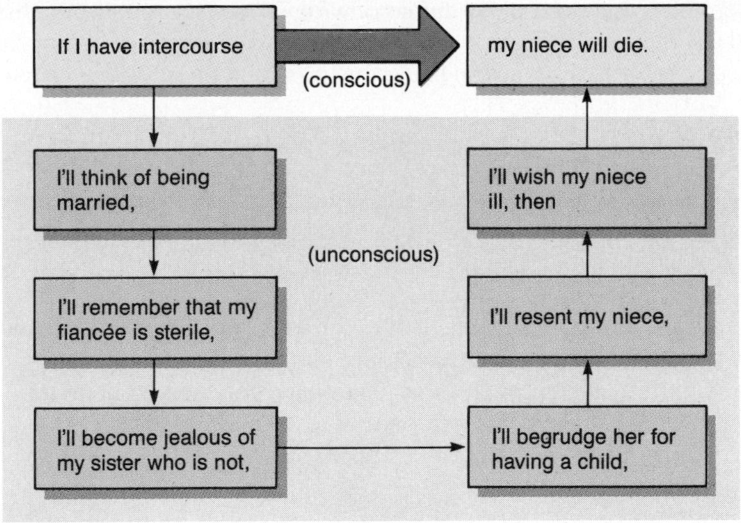

FIGURE 5–1 Distortion by Omission

If I have intercourse → (conscious) → my niece will die.

(unconscious)

I'll think of being married, | I'll wish my niece ill, then

I'll remember that my fiancée is sterile, | I'll resent my niece,

I'll become jealous of my sister who is not, → I'll begrudge her for having a child,

SOURCE: From Freud, 1909.

a bathroom when Schreber needed to use the facilities. Additionally, Schreber held a number of unusual beliefs about bowel movements and their relationship to God. In his most severe state, Schreber believed God intended a special purpose for him: Schreber would be the bride of God and the mother of a new race of immortal beings who would populate the earth. To prepare Schreber for his role, God would turn him into a woman.

Freud felt that Schreber's paranoia was a defense against unacceptable impulses. Specifically, Schreber was afraid of homosexual urges. Working from Schreber's statements about his childhood, Freud proposed that the young Schreber was extremely ambivalent about his father, both respecting and fearing him. The senior Schreber was a physician and writer well-known for his views on how to raise children—the Dr. Spock of his era—except he advocated such harsh practices as forcibly restraining children so they could not masturbate (see Chapter 6).

As a youngster, Schreber's fear of castration was so overwhelming that his sexual interest turned away from women altogether. Although on the outside Schreber showed no signs of homosexuality, Freud proposed that Schreber was indeed a homosexual with respect to his unconscious fantasy life. To guard against these unconscious fantasies ("I am attracted to this man"), Schreber turned them around ("I hate this man because he persecutes me").

Because the homosexual urges persisted despite this defense, Schreber made them more palatable by substituting God for Flechsig (who had in the first place been a substitute for Schreber's father). In this way, he could entertain his homosexual fantasies without shame, because emasculation for the purpose of marrying God could hardly be a disgrace. Needless to say, such a "solution" to unacceptable impulses doesn't work particularly well.

The case of Schreber is important in psychodynamic thought for several reasons. First, it extended this way of thinking to extremely troubled individuals, underscoring it as a personality theory of wide scope. Second, for the first time, it stated a controversial position: paranoia stems from repressed homosexuality. I'll describe the research investigating this possibility in the next chapter.

The Case of Dora Dora was a young woman suffering from many of the symptoms of hysteria: migraine headaches, fits of nervous coughing, loss of her voice, poor appetite. Conventional treatments failed to relieve her of her symptoms, and her family referred her to Freud (1905a) for treatment.

Information about Dora's parents and their relationship with another couple, Herr and Frau K., fills the case study. Dora's parents did not get along well with each other. Apparently, Dora's father had a long-standing affair with Frau K., of whom Dora was quite resentful. At the same time, Dora was courted by Herr K., whose attentions she seemed to have encouraged up to a point. But when he propositioned her, Dora became extremely angry and slapped him. She informed her father of the matter, and all sorts of troubles ensued, with Herr K. denying the proposition altogether.

Freud interpreted Dora's hysterical symptoms in terms of her repressed sexuality. As a child, she loved her father and resented her mother, playing out the role assigned to a young girl by the Oedipal conflict. As a young woman, she continued to love her father, although now the love was repressed. It reappeared, though, in her resentment of Frau K., because her father had chosen Frau K. as his lover. Further, it appeared in her encouragement of Herr K., who represented her father.

This case is noteworthy because Dora abruptly terminated therapy, taking Freud by surprise. In retrospect, he decided she was fleeing him just as she had fled from Herr K.: because she loved Freud and yet was angry at him. Dora's termination occasioned a fuller understanding of transference—the tendency of patients in therapy to transfer feelings from past relationships to the current relationship with the therapist. According to this line of thinking, Dora loved Freud not for himself but because he reminded her of other men in her life. She took revenge for the same reason. Her compulsion to repeat painful past actions inspired Freud to posit the death instinct (Chapter 4).

Evaluation What are we to make of these case studies? Psychodynamic theory would not exist as it does without the facts provided by them. Recall the inherent difficulties with case studies: Information may be distorted; causality may be difficult to infer; and generality to other individuals may be suspect.

Each of Freud's case studies may be criticized on each of these grounds, especially that of distorted information. Not only must we accept the patient's reports of events as accurate, but we must also accept the psychoanalyst's reports as faithful. It is unreasonable to think Freud or any therapist is unaffected by human lapses in memory or biases induced by expectation.

Let's turn our attention to the question of whether Freud correctly identified causality. Here at least some of the case studies are on firmer ground, because Freud went about identifying causes by looking for patterns in what the patients did: consistencies across time and situation. To the degree the same pattern shows up repeatedly, a cause is indicated. So, Anna O. invariably showed relief from her hysterical symptoms after talking about her problems. This occurred a number of times, leading to the conclusion that this talking was indeed a cure.

In other case studies, Freud infers causality from much more flimsy information. The fact that Dora terminated therapy is thought to be caused by a transference neurosis, but again, evidence for this is insufficient. Maybe she stopped seeing Freud for a more mundane reason. The Little Hans case has been severely criticized over the years as relying on quite tenuous evidence. Reported by Freud in the original case study, although without special emphasis, is the fact the child had been frightened one day by an actual incident involving a horse. This experience preceded his general avoidance of horses and might therefore represent classical conditioning (Wolpe & Rachman, 1960). Perhaps Little Hans was simply afraid of horses in their own right.

What about generality? Some of Freud's case studies served the purpose of existence proofs (like Dora), so this criterion is not always relevant. But other case studies are intended to show what is universally true (like Anna O.), so the question of generality is sometimes pertinent. Freud intended most of his case studies as illustrations, and he often tells the reader that his psychoanalysis of other patients is consistent with what he reports. This is problematic, raising again questions about the fidelity of Freud's information. If a case study is to be used to establish what is generally true about personality, it is essential to report replications in full detail.

To these difficulties another can be added. Although these case studies support psychoanalytic theory in general, they do not easily allow a choice among the particular theories advanced by Freud, Jung, Adler, or whomever (Farrell, 1981). Despite Freud's assertion that these cases provide unique support for his version of psychoanalysis, any of the cases can be interpreted to support any of the different theories. Schreber can be seen as attempting integration among the (extremely) disparate parts of his personality. Dora can be seen as struggling with basic insecurity. And so on.

To summarize, Freud's case studies were important sources of psychodynamic ideas. However, the actual evidence on which the case studies are based—the raw data, so to speak—was gathered in an unscientific manner. Further, the cases do not allow a choice among the different versions of psychodynamic theory. All in all, these cases strike me as borderline instances of research, a mix of strengths and weaknesses.

However, do not feel dismayed by the less-than-satisfactory scientific status of Freud's case studies. They were conducted almost a century ago. I have discussed them in detail not because they are the final word on psychodynamic thinking but because they are quite literally the first. Personality research is now much more sophisticated than when Freud pioneered the case study approach. Psychodynamic investigations, capitalizing on this increasing sophistication, have also flourished. But not all current investigations have abandoned the case study approach. After all, case studies are uniquely appropriate for testing psychoanalytic ideas. The problem with the typical case study has been mainly in its implementation. But in the last 20 years, researchers have developed better ways of conducting and reporting case studies than did Freud.

Refinement 1: The Symptom-Context Method

Symptom-context method: A research method for studying phenomena (symptoms) as they naturally occur (in context) during psychotherapy.

Psychologist Lester Luborsky (1970) pioneered a refinement of the case study approach that he calls the **symptom-context method.** His method exploits the now widespread practice of tape-recording psychotherapy sessions, which represents not only a technical advance but also changes in how the privacy of case-study subjects is regarded. (Anonymity, rather than complete confidentiality, is now the rule.) The resulting tape is a permanent record of events transpiring in therapy. With the tape available, problems with the therapist's recall are avoided. Luborsky has been interested in a patient's symptoms as they appear in the course of a psychotherapy session. So problems with the patient's recall are avoided as well.

Working from the tape, the researcher determines when a given symptom does or does not occur. This determination can be checked by other researchers, and its reliability thereby ascertained. Then the researcher characterizes the context in which the symptom appears (or not). What topics were discussed? How did the patient express feelings? What did the therapist do? Again, this can be checked by others and is scientific in a way that Freud's original case studies are not.

To test psychodynamic hypotheses linking characteristics of the context to the occurrence of symptoms, the researcher typically assesses context characteristics from four different points in the therapy session: prior to a segment where the symptom under study appears; after such a segment; prior to a segment where the symptom does not occur; and after such a segment. Information from such a research design allows the researcher to conclude whether a given context characteristic indeed precedes a particular symptom.

Do you see how this conclusion can be made? Suppose the hypothesis being tested proposes that incestuous thoughts lead to anxiety attacks. We can operationally define an anxiety attack in terms of shallow, rapid breathing. (Of course, there is more to anxiety than rate of respiration, but remember that no operationalization ever perfectly measures a construct.)

We have hundreds of psychotherapy sessions with a particular patient on tape. We fast-forward the tapes until we hear sounds of hyperventilation. Suppose we find 10 such incidents. We run the tape back three minutes before the anxiety attack (as we have defined it) occurs, and we note whether or not the patient is discussing sexual feelings about his mother. We then run the tape forward three minutes past the anxiety attack, and again we note whether the patient is expressing sexual desire for his mother. We then choose 10 incidents at random from all those where hyperventilation does not occur, and we note the topics of the patient's conversation before and after these comparison incidents. Do they mention sexual feelings about Mother?

What will we see in these data if the Oedipal hypothesis is correct? Quite simply: The greatest mention of incestuous thoughts will precede the anxiety attacks. Further, the least mention should follow the attacks, because the anxiety presumably marks the repression of the incestuous feelings. Finally, little evidence of Oedipal thoughts will occur in the comparison segments (see Figure 5–2). Other patterns of data will not support the hypothesis.

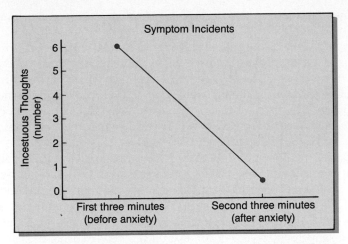

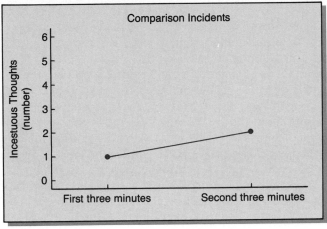

SOURCE: From Luborsky, 1970.

FIGURE 5–2
Example of
Symptom-Context
Method

Note that the data provided by the symptom-context method are correlational in nature. Although they are often used to draw conclusions about causes, these conclusions may be derailed by confounds. Research using this method must carefully examine possible third variables. For example, suppose incidents containing symptoms tend to come from therapy sessions conducted at a particular time of the year, whereas incidents without symptoms tend to be drawn from sessions conducted at other times. This introduces the possibility that various seasons and everything associated with them—such as colds, allergies, summer vacations, or income-tax deadlines—both give rise to symptoms and their apparent contexts.

Luborsky (1964) first used the symptom-context method to study sudden forgetting: coming up blank in the middle of a sentence. This is akin to a *parapraxis,* a slip of the memory rather than the tongue. According to psychodynamic theory, momentary forgetting occurs when the topic being discussed threatens the individual. In a study of a single patient, Luborsky found that themes of rejection and feelings of helplessness preceded episodes of sudden forgetting, but not comparison episodes.

Luborsky has also used the symptom-context method to study such symptoms as asthma attacks, stomach pains, migraine headaches, and *petit mal* seizures. For each individual, a theme of conflict preceded the symptom of concern. Common across the individuals studied, a sense of helplessness in the face of the conflict characterizes the context in which the symptom occurs. On the whole, these data are consistent with psychodynamic theory (Luborsky, 1970; Luborsky, Sackeim, & Christoph, 1979).

What are the limitations of the symptom-context method? First, the rate of a given symptom in therapy may be low. Some symptoms may not occur at all during a session. Second, the symptom as it occurs in the therapy session may not match the symptom as it appears at other times in the patient's life. Third, the provided data are correlational (linking symptoms to context), so causality can only be tentatively inferred. Fourth, even if the determinants of symptoms are correctly identified, one is limited to immediate causes. More distant determinants, including many of interest to psychodynamic theory, cannot be investigated with this technique. Fifth, to date the symptom-context method has been used mainly with therapy audiotapes.

On the other hand, the symptom-context method is precise and public. Within its limitations, it is reliable and valid. The method can obviously be used with therapy videotapes, so nonverbal symptoms and contexts are thereby accessible. I imagine it can be extended outside of therapy as well. Now that people are videotaping important events like births and weddings as readily as they once snapped Polaroids of these special times, the symptom-context method can be used to study personality in a variety of settings.

Along these same lines, my colleagues and I studied the sorts of statements Lyndon Johnson made during his press conferences in the era of the Vietnam War (Zullow, Oettingen, Peterson, & Seligman, 1988). When Johnson made particularly optimistic statements during a press conference, he was apt the following week to embark on a risky course of action, such as escalating the war. When he made less optimistic statements, he was apt the next week to be cautious and passive in the implementation of his foreign policy.

Refinement 2: The Core Conflictual Relationship Theme Method

Luborsky has also created a method for analyzing therapy transcripts in order to study transference (e.g., Luborsky & Crits-Christoph, 1988, 1989). The idea that patients in psychotherapy express attitudes and behaviors derived from earlier relationships is one of the most important psychodynamic concepts (Freud, 1912). But if the only support for transference is the therapist's intuition on the matter, you can see why this is unsatisfactory. Unintentional bias can influence the therapist, affecting what is remembered from the therapy sessions and how this is interpreted.

As we have seen for the symptom-context method, tape recordings of therapy sessions make available a public and objective record of what transpires.

TABLE 5–1
The Core Conflictual Relationship Theme Method (an example)

Condensed Episode	*Coding*
This guy tried to dominate conversation. . . . It irritated me. . . . I repressed everything and just sank back . . . brooding . . . pissed off. . . . I had fantasies of putting him down.	Wish: to assert self Response of patient: becomes angry, withdrawn Response of other: dominates
Cop comes up and tells her to sit right. . . . They stood up to him. . . . I got really anxious. . . . I would have automatically obeyed.	Wish: to assert self Response of patient: becomes anxious, passive Response of other: dominates

SOURCE: Condensed from Luborsky, 1984, Appendix 4.

So, Luborsky's **core conflictual relationship theme method** (**CCRT**) starts with transcripts of one or more sessions of therapy. Independent judges read a transcript, paying particular attention to the way the patient describes episodes involving other people. (Such narrative episodes are as common in psychotherapy as in everyday conversation!) For each episode, the judge identifies these three components:

Core conflictual relationship theme method (CCRT): A research method for studying transference in psychotherapy by analyzing the themes under discussion.

1. The patient's main wishes, needs, or intentions toward the other person
2. The response of the other person
3. The response of the patient

Table 5–1 gives a brief example of how these components are identified. Different judges usually agree highly in identifying specific wishes and responses (Luborsky, Crits-Christoph, & Mellon, 1986).

The researcher codes at least 10 episodes, then calculates the specific answer that occurs most frequently for each component. Taken together, these answers constitute the patient's core conflict: the theme that characterizes transference. According to Freud, most patients have one such theme, and Luborsky's method confirms this claim. The same theme shows up in 80 percent of the episodes described by a given patient (Luborsky, Crits-Christoph, & Mellon, 1986). Further, different patients have different core conflicts, and these are stable over the course of year-long therapy.

What is the relationship of the core conflict to the way the patient relates to the therapist? This after all is the crux of the transference concept. When the core conflict derived from episodes involving people other than the therapist is compared to the core conflict derived from episodes involving only the therapist, they are essentially the same (Luborsky, Crits-Christoph, & Mellon, 1986). This is an important finding, because it confirms Freud's original proposition that patients think about and act toward their therapist as they think about and act toward other people in their lives.

Luborsky and his colleagues have also found that a patient's core conflict becomes less pervasive with successful psychotherapy. In other words, as patients begin to solve the problems that brought them to therapy in the first place, they become less likely to interpret their interactions with others in the same terms. Different wishes and different responses come to characterize different relationships. Again, this is an important finding, supporting the psychodynamic claim that a patient must "work through" transference in order for therapy to be successful. Working through transference simply means the patients no longer conduct their lives according to old patterns.

The CCRT has drawbacks. It is a laborious procedure. Further, it requires highly trained judges, usually individuals conversant with psychodynamic theory. And the shared expertise of the judges may introduce a subtle bias in the procedure, creating agreement and confirmation for the wrong reason. For instance, suppose a patient mentions feeling sad in an episode. Unwitting application of the psychodynamic formula may lead the judges to infer that the patient wishes to be nurtured and that the other person is failing to do so. Agreement is high, but this is misleading. The only objective fact was the patient's sadness. Finally, the CCRT is only useful if the patient is articulate. This is often the case in psychodynamic therapy, but the generality of the CCRT may thereby be limited.

Despite these problems, of which Luborsky is aware, the CCRT is still a powerful refinement of the case-study method. By formalizing the clinician's intuition, it allows transference to be studied more objectively than was possible in Freud's era. And findings to date support psychodynamic claims regarding transference and its central role in psychotherapy.

Refinement 3: The Natural History Method

Natural history method: A research approach where the lives of people are described in great detail over a significant period of time.

Psychiatrist George Vaillant (1977, 1983) has made extensive use of yet another refinement of the case-study approach, one that can be called the **natural history method.** This longitudinal research strategy combines the rich detail of case studies with the generality of correlational investigations. Vaillant intensively studies a large number of individuals over a significant proportion of their lives, in some cases five decades or more. Particular attention is paid to the twists and turns of a person's life path. Because a number of individuals are studied in the same way, strong statements can be made about the natural course of people's lives.

As you can imagine, this method is highly appropriate for the investigation of developmental theories—like psychoanalysis. Just as natural historians chronicle the lives of wild animals and birds, the personality researcher can record the lives of people. This method makes available basic facts about personality and its development that elude other research strategies, while improving on Freud's case studies in that troubled individuals are not its exclusive focus. Generality is thereby served.

Vaillant's natural history method has mostly involved two samples of individuals. The first sample is 268 men chosen as college sophomores for their physical and psychological superiority: the most outstanding members of the 1938 through 1944 classes at a prestigious university. The average subject is now about 70 years old. The second sample is 456 men chosen as teenagers from inner-city Boston as a control group for a study of delinquency. These subjects originally joined the sample between 1940 and 1944, which means the average subject is now in his 60s.

Vaillant himself originated neither study. Instead, these samples have been handed down from the original investigators to other researchers and eventually to Vaillant. Each custodian of the samples has kept the available information in order and added to it. Most importantly, the custodians have kept the dropout rate to essentially zero.

What sorts of information are available? The overall focus of the original researchers was "health" broadly considered: physical, psychological, and social. Interdisciplinary investigation has been the rule, with anthropologists, social workers, psychologists, psychiatrists, and physicians making observations about each subject. These observations have been carefully recorded, and each subject's material fills several file folders to overflowing.

To investigate a particular question, the researcher reads the relevant files. Sometimes the data of concern are immediately present, such as a subject's higher level of education. In other cases, the data must be abstracted from the files. Vaillant (1983, p. 323) did this when he assigned each subject a score reflecting the degree to which they had achieved Erik Erikson's fourth developmental stage, industry versus inferiority. In other words, had the subjects shown in their behavior that they had begun to explore their skills and abilities? Vaillant looked for evidence in each of their records for such behaviors as summer jobs held between the ages of 11 and 16. Several judges rated the records independently, so agreement could be checked. Further, they were blind to adult outcome, so ratings were not biased by knowledge of what happened to the subjects once they became men.

How is the natural history method different than that of the typical case study? First, it is *prospective* instead of *retrospective*. Where Freud studied individuals after they had developed a problem, trying to understand which early events led up to it, Vaillant starts with the early events and sees where they lead. Second, the natural history method employs public evidence. Reliability can be checked by other individuals. Third, the method is not just intensive but also extensive. The simultaneous study of hundreds of individuals provides generalizations impossible to make from conventional case studies.

Why don't I regard the natural history method as simply a correlational research strategy employing longitudinal data? I might, since hypotheses are tested with correlation coefficients, and the generic precautions for such an approach (confounding by third variables, ambiguity of causality, and so on) should be honored. However, what makes the natural history method more of a case-study approach is that the original material consists of clinical details, not numerical responses to questionnaires.

Material is quantified after the fact. So, the natural history approach is both rich and—eventually—precise. Further, the approach allows longitudinal investigations of ideas not entertained by the original researchers. Vaillant coded Erikson's stage four from information obtained *before* Erikson described the psychosocial stage theory. This possibility allows efficient longitudinal research, because the original material already exists. Imagine how hard it has been to keep track of 600-plus individuals for 50-plus years. Many of us lose track of good friends just by moving to the other end of town. How convenient for future researchers that Vaillant and his predecessors have already done the hard work.

The natural history method is not foolproof. First, the subjects were not randomly selected. Women and minorities were excluded from the two samples I've described. This of course reflects the choice of the original researchers, and in retrospect, we see it as an unfortunate restriction.

Second, a subject's lengthy participation may have affected the very course of his life. The college sample has been interviewed on about 25 different occasions, with future interviews planned. Such scrutiny can create self-consciousness to an unusual degree.

Third, information of contemporary concern may be missing from the records, simply because the earlier researchers did not include it. Conversely, some information originally of interest may become irrelevant as theories and issues pass out of fashion. This material clogs the files and impedes their study.

Fourth, individual interviewers obtained much of the evidence, introducing unknown bias. Like Freud's original case studies, investigations using the natural history approach are only as valuable as the accuracy of their original evidence. Although attempts were made to standardize interviews and record information accurately, the practical considerations involved put a limit on the effectiveness of these attempts.

Nevertheless, this approach to personality research is exciting, yielding conclusions of enormous practical and theoretical significance, making it possible to investigate claims of psychoanalysis as well as other theories of personality development. For instance, Vaillant (1977) investigated the long-term consequences of using immature mechanisms like projection versus mature mechanisms like sublimation.

Vaillant ascertained an individual's habitual defense mechanisms by extracting from his records descriptions of how the person acted in times of crisis or conflict. Judges blind to other information about the individual categorized these extractions in terms of the defense mechanisms shown. Agreement among judges was good. Defense mechanisms were assigned scores reflecting their relative immaturity versus maturity, and each individual was then given an overall maturity score by combining the ratings of the defense mechanisms habitually employed.

When these overall scores were correlated with long-term outcomes, the results were striking. These scores predict adult social adjustment, economic achievement, and mental health. The more mature one's defense mechanisms, the better one adapts to life. Even more strikingly, the use of mature defense mechanisms throughout one's early life predicts one's health and longevity. These results underscore the importance ego psychologists place on the way people cope with difficulties.

Another important study by Vaillant (1983) that made use of the natural history method is his longitudinal investigation of alcoholism. As you well know, alcohol abuse is a serious problem in our society. Numerous investigations have attempted to understand what causes it, but most of the studies are seriously flawed. They start with a sample of individuals who abuse alcohol and then try to reconstruct their past. This is difficult under the best of circumstances, but what compounds the problem here is that alcohol abuse often entails problems with memory.

A better way to study the causes of alcoholism is by starting with a group of individuals early in their lives, before any have become problem drinkers, and then follow them to the point where they start to abuse alcohol. This is an expensive strategy, of course, which is why studies almost always work backwards. However, Vaillant's two samples of men allowed him to conduct a prospective investigation of alcoholism, which he has reported in a controversial book titled *The Natural History of Alcoholism*.

Many of his findings challenge our conventional beliefs about alcoholism. For example, we tend to think of "alcoholic" as a type of person, but Vaillant found no evidence that severe abusers form a discrete class of people. In other words, no clear distinction occurs between those who use alcohol and those who abuse it. Throughout life, people may oscillate from one extreme to another. Further, we tend to believe that personal problems lead people to abuse alcohol. Vaillant discovered just the opposite; problems follow in the wake of severe alcohol abuse more frequently than they precede it. Finally, he reported that conventional treatments for alcoholism—psychiatric or psychological—are not particularly effective. Whether or not men continue to abuse alcohol throughout their lives is unrelated to participation or not in a treatment program. However, if they join Alcoholics Anonymous, then they are less likely to continue abusing alcohol.

Vaillant's study of alcoholism is virtually unique because of its prospective nature. His conclusions have not gone unchallenged (e.g., Zucker & Gomberg, 1986). Nonetheless, they illustrate the power of his natural history method.

CORRELATIONAL AND EXPERIMENTAL RESEARCH STRATEGIES

Although case studies and their contemporary refinements are probably the best way to investigate psychodynamic theory, they are painstaking and inefficient, particularly if embedded in therapy. Other research strategies have thus been used to address the clinical predictions of psychodynamic theory. Though lacking the richness of case studies, these other strategies compensate for the shortcomings of that particular approach.

Psychodynamic researchers employ correlational studies to investigate differences among people: in character type, in defense mechanisms, in birth order, in psychological health and illness. A number of these investigations address developmental questions. What early childhood experiences give rise to particular character types? What are the long-term consequences of certain defense mechanisms? Is it really Mom's fault that we turned out soft-boiled? Other researchers use experiments to study the claims of psychodynamic theory about people's general characteristics: drives, unconscious motivation, the roles of humor, dreams, and fantasy. Because this approach is complex, most of these experiments use elaborate operationalizations and complicated designs.

In the rest of this chapter, I will describe investigations of psychodynamic theory that use correlational and experimental research strategies. In choosing studies, I have relied on the thorough surveys by Kline (1972, 1984), Fisher and Greenberg (1977), and Westen (1990, 1991), as well as others (for example, Eysenck & Wilson, 1973; Farrell, 1981; Sears, 1943). These various authors differ markedly in their enthusiasm for this kind of research, but they agree on which investigations are the most theoretically pertinent.

PARTICULAR LINES OF RESEARCH

Instincts and Drives

The most basic premise of psychodynamic theory is that people are energy systems. The life and death instincts provide this energy and are regarded as innate characteristics of all human beings. However, contemporary opinion within the social sciences does not accept human instincts. What brought about this skepticism?

Instinct: An innate pattern of behavior.

An **instinct** is defined as an innate pattern of behavior, arising from biological inheritance, not learning, and characterizing a species as a whole. A good example of an instinct is the song of the cowbird. All cowbirds sing the same song as adults, whether or not they heard it when they were young.

Studies with animals make use of isolation experiments to investigate instincts. Quite literally, the animal is isolated from environmental events that might confound the interpretation of some behavior as instinctive. Such experiments are impossible to conduct with people, so we cannot use these tests to say with certainty that humans have instincts. Further, anthropological observations challenge the idea that universal behaviors exist, whereas experimental investigations demonstrate the responsivity of people to the world.

The contemporary psychologist therefore dismisses the possibility of human instincts. The closest most researchers get to instincts is to speak of *biological drives.* Like an instinct, a biological drive is innate and universal; it motivates behavior. Unlike an instinct, a drive is expressed in a variety of ways sensitive to the environment. All people have a hunger drive, for instance, but it gives rise to all sorts of different activities to satisfy it. Some folks drive to

"And now, Randy, by use of song, the male sparrow will stake out his territory...an instinct common in the lower animals."

SOURCE: "The Far Side" cartoon by Gary Larson is reproduced by permission of Chronicle Features, San Francisco.

Wendy's; others raid the refrigerator; still others shake their neighbor's mango tree.

In all fairness to psychodynamic theory, then, Freud's life and death instincts should better be regarded as (potential) drives. And what is the evidence that these drives exist and work in the ways implied by Freud? Let us start by considering Eros: the twin urge for self-preservation and sexual satisfaction. We can regard the drive for self-preservation as obvious, and all of the mechanisms for seeking pleasure and avoiding pain serve this drive.

The evidence for the other half of Eros is less obvious. As adolescents and adults, we have a sex drive. We are motivated to satisfy this drive in one or more of the ways catalogued by Kinsey and his colleagues (Kinsey, Pomeroy, & Martin, 1948; Kinsey, Pomeroy, Martin, & Gebhard, 1953). However, psychodynamic theory additionally concerns itself with infant and childhood sexuality. Here considerable disagreement arises over what to make of the available evidence.

Although Freud theorizes extensively about childhood sexuality, research tends not to support the details of his hypothesizing.

Following Freud's original hypotheses, a number of researchers tested claims about infant sexuality through observations and interviews. They talked to parents and teachers about the practices of children. They sat in the corners of nurseries and playgrounds making notes. They interviewed adults about what they remembered from childhood. Sears (1943) provides an overview of this early research, which is unaltered by more recent findings (see, for example, Farrell, 1981; Fisher & Greenberg, 1977; Kline, 1972).

First, we know the genitals of infants are susceptible to stimulation. Newborn baby boys have erections, sometimes as many as 40 per day (e.g., Conn & Kanner, 1940). And vaginal lubrication has been observed in newborn baby girls. Both infant boys and girls manipulate their own genitals, and they may smile and coo while doing so.

Second, when slightly older, children show oral, anal, and phallic concerns. However, these do not fall into the simple progression hypothesized by Freud: oral to anal to genital.

Third, children evidence curiosity about sexual matters. As Freud proposed, children are quite interested in the origin of babies. They are also interested in sex differences, but there are few signs that children are confused about the difference between male and female genitals.

Fourth, at least in our society, children come to regard their sexual curiosity with shame. They hide their interest and any related activities from adults. And contrary to Freud's ideas of repression, the majority of adults recall such childhood secrets, even though they were associated with guilt.

If continuity between infant and child and adult sexuality is to be demonstrated, then one must show that pleasure is obtained through "sexual" activities across the lifespan. However, we don't know if infants and young children engage in certain behaviors because they are pleasurable or for some other reason (Farrell, 1981). For instance, erections among infant boys often occur at times of distress. This argues against the idea that infant erections are mainly sexual (that is, pleasure-driven) in origin and function. What looks like sexuality in the young child may not be sexuality in Freud's sense.

Let us turn our attention to Thanatos. Again, strict interpretation of Thanatos as an instinct is unreasonable. Even the most loyal of Freud's followers kept politely silent about the death instinct. How could it have evolved? If it did evolve, what prevents children from killing themselves? Suicide among the very young has been reported, but it is extremely rare when compared to suicide rates among adolescents and adults (Rosenthal & Rosenthal, 1984).

Freud pointed to the fact of self-defeating behavior as evidence of an inherent drive toward destruction. Contemporary opinion takes issue with this interpretation. Certainly, self-destructive actions take place all too frequently. However, in virtually all cases, people's failures and foibles can be explained without invoking a primary drive. People instead create problems for themselves because they favor short-term benefits over those in the long run, because depression or anxiety clouds their judgment, and/or because they unknowingly embark on nonproductive strategies (Baumeister & Scher, 1988; Curtis, 1989).

Most researchers have therefore interpreted Thanatos as a drive for aggression, usually directed against others. Konrad Lorenz (1966) and Robert Ardrey (1966), for instance, use animal evidence to argue that human aggression is innate—inherited from an animal past. Sociobiologists make the same point. Such arguments proceed first by showing that aggression in animals has a biological basis, then by invoking the similarity of human beings and animals, and finally by concluding that human aggression is the result of a biological drive (Mazur & Robertson, 1972).

In contrast, other psychologists have mustered a great deal of support for the notion that human aggression is a learned behavior. Bandura (1986) has shown, for example, that when children observe someone else act aggressively, then they are apt to do so themselves. And Berkowitz (1974) has demonstrated that someone's readiness to act aggressively can be influenced by the mere presence of stimuli that have in the past been associated with violence. We will return to these findings in more detail later when we discuss the cognitive-behavioral approach to personality. In the present context, the important point to remember is that studies like these argue against the notion that human aggression is a drive. Aggression seems too responsive to be the result of an innate impulse.

Berkowitz investigated another aspect of human aggression pertinent to Freudian theory: Are violent acts cathartic? If aggression is a drive, then it can be satisfied like hunger, thirst, or sex. And after satisfaction, the individual should be less likely to act in an aggressive way (Mook, 1987).

Examine your own beliefs about this possibility. Everyday language is filled with expressions that assume one's appetite for violence can be sated:

"Go ahead, get it out of your system."
"I got it off my chest."
"Make my day."

I think you can imagine how this notion can be tested. Researchers would assign their subjects to one of two experimental conditions: one where violence was perpetrated or observed, the other with no violence. All subjects would then be given the opportunity to act violently. In repeated experiments by Berkowitz and others, subjects exposed to violence acted *more* violently. Turning the other cheek is not only moral but also practical. And Freud is wrong that aggression is a drive.

So, the research argues against Eros and Thanatos. Does this mean that the essence of psychodynamic theory must be discarded? Not necessarily. For instance, we can draw the same conclusion as the neoFreudians in light of similar research evidence. A strictly biological interpretation of libido is untenable. However, people can still be described in energy terms. People have a variety of motives, chief among them those described by Freud and other psychodynamic theorists. But it is unreasonable to elevate any of these to the status of primary motives for all people, and it is even more unreasonable to argue that any are innate.

Unconscious Motivation

Contemporary psychologists have no trouble acknowledging the notion of unconscious mental processes (Kihlstrom, 1990). For example, when we speak, we necessarily "use" the rules of grammar to create sentences other people can understand. However, we are not aware of doing so; words simply appear on our tongue. When we drive a car, tie our shoes, or open a door, we similarly are not aware of what gives rise to our actions, yet necessarily some process must be going on within our minds that allows us to carry out these complex sequences of behavior.

An intriguing example of a nonconscious mental process is provided by the **mere exposure phenomenon.** In a series of studies, psychologist Robert Zajonc (1980, 1984; Kunst-Wilson & Zajonc, 1980) flashed pictures of various stimuli on a screen for extremely brief periods of time. His research subjects were unable to recognize any of the pictures. However, when later asked to rate stimuli according to how much they liked them, subjects showed a consistent preference for stimuli to which they had previously been exposed. Even though they had not consciously seen them, some aspect of their mind had been influenced, which led to increased liking.

The psychodynamic "unconscious" entails more than just a lack of awareness of mental processes; it is conceived as *motivated.* According to Freud and other theorists within the psychodynamic tradition, people are unaware of

Mere exposure phenomenon: The preference for stimuli one has been frequently exposed to, whether or not these have been consciously recognized.

certain thoughts and feelings because they are threatening. This conception of the unconscious has been more difficult to demonstrate. Conclusive evidence has been elusive, yet so many different lines of evidence point to the reality of the motivated unconscious that it seems a decent bet. Let me describe some of the relevant studies, and you can form your own opinion.

Perceptual Defense   Some of the earliest experimental investigations of the motivated unconscious were part of a psychology movement that argued that a person's literal perception of the world is influenced by needs and drives. An interstate highway traveler in dire need of stopping "sees" every miscellaneous road sign as an announcement of a rest area with comfort facilities. Further, the influence of needs and drives on perception can occur without an individual's awareness. This is most apt to occur when the stimuli are seen as threatening or upsetting.

Consider this experiment by McGinnies (1949). College students were shown words on a *tachistoscope,* a device that presents visual stimuli for extremely brief periods of time. As soon as they recognized the word, they were to push a button, and the time between initial presentation and recognition was recorded. During the experiment, their *galvanic skin response* (GSR), a measure of emotional arousal, was monitored.

Some words were innocuous, like *child, glass,* and *river,* whereas other words were somewhat "less than polite," like *whore, bitch,* and *Kotex.* Subjects took longer to recognize the risqué words than the innocuous words, and their GSR was higher while viewing them. These results are of course consistent with the notion of **perceptual defense,** and therefore with the notion of a motivated unconscious.

> **Perceptual defense: One's tendency not to readily recognize threatening stimuli.**

Or are they? If you think for a moment, you may have several objections (see, for example, Howes & Solomon, 1950). Perhaps the subjects recognized the taboo words as readily as the innocent words, but were too shy to call them out until they were sure. This would also account for the results.

Perhaps the subjects were less familiar with the taboo words than with the innocent words. Although subjects may indeed have taken longer to recognize them, the reason for the delay may well have been lack of familiarity, not perceptual defense. This objection has some trouble accommodating the GSR data, but perhaps the delay led to frustration and therefore to elevated GSR.

However, subsequent investigations vindicated the notion of perceptual defense against such charges (Maddi, 1980). Indeed, Matthew Erdelyi (1974, 1985) observes that current theorizing in cognitive psychology is quite amenable to phenomena like perceptual defense. Older theories tended to regard perception as unitary, an event that does or does not occur. At the present, perception is seen as a process characterized by selectivity at every stage. We are aware of only some of this selectivity.

I'll add one more idea here about perceptual defense. Although many experiments show that it exists, as psychodynamic theory predicts, most of these experiments also show an opposite effect for some subjects. These folks perceive threatening stimuli more readily than neutral stimuli. This is called **perceptual vigilance.**

> **Perceptual vigilance: One's tendency to readily recognize threatening stimuli.**

Does perceptual vigilance call into doubt psychodynamic theory? Yes and no. Freud described defense mechanisms that have the effect of attuning individuals to aversive occurrences—for example, *reaction formation* (Maddi, 1980). From this point of view, perceptual vigilance is another form of defense. Nevertheless, repression is thought to be the foundation of all defense mechanisms, even those defense mechanisms that attune the individual to threat. Reaction formation, for instance, obscures what is really threatening to the individual. From this point of view, perceptual vigilance is something other than just a defense, and it is thus difficult to accommodate with orthodox theory.

Repression and Memory Repression refers to keeping memories from our awareness because they are threatening. Several recent studies have investigated this process, thereby supporting the psychodynamic notion of a motivated unconscious. All used a similar procedure.

The tendency to repress upsetting memories had to be determined. This was done by having research subjects complete a questionnaire called the Marlowe-Crowne Social Desirability Scale (Crowne & Marlowe, 1964). This questionnaire ascertains the degree to which someone endorses statements that make a good social impression, despite being unlikely. So, "I never lose my temper" is one such statement. If subjects agree with a statement like this, we can conclude that they are placing themselves in the best possible light. Said another way, they are apt to be defensive.

Research subjects also complete a questionnaire asking about the extent to which they experience different symptoms of anxiety. Among nondefensive subjects—those scoring low on the Marlowe-Crowne Scale—we can take these reports of anxiety at face value. But among highly defensive subjects—those scoring high on the Marlowe-Crowne Scale—we suspect that when they report low anxiety, they may be repressing something.

Repression can therefore be defined in terms of the subject's pattern of responses to the Marlowe-Crowne Scale and a questionnaire asking about symptoms of anxiety. Support for this operational definition comes from studies showing that "repressors" so identified show the highest level of physiological arousal when threatened, despite maintaining that they feel no distress (e.g., Weinberger, Schwartz, & Davidson, 1979).

Studies have used this approach to investigate the sorts of memories repressors report (e.g., Davis, 1987; Davis & Schwartz, 1987; Hansen & Hansen, 1988). Consistent with psychodynamic theory, when the childhood memories of repressors were compared with those of nonrepressors, fewer negative memories are recalled. Also, the earliest negative memories of repressors do not date as far back as those of nonrepressors. These findings hold only when research subjects were recalling memories about themselves. Impersonal memories do not differ between repressors and nonrepressors.

Such findings suggest that repression entails limited access to memories that have negative associations. These studies are not as fine-grained as one would like, and alternative explanations are possible. For example, the psychodynamic interpretation proposes that negative memories are indeed present, yet the subject cannot recall them. But perhaps the repressors somehow ignored or overlooked negative events in the first place, which means they have no negative memories to recall.

Future investigations will no doubt test such alternative possibilities. For the time being, results appear highly consistent with the idea of a motivated unconscious. In general, the basic method holds great promise as a way to investigate what may lie beneath someone's surface thoughts.

Subliminal Stimulation   Psychologist Lloyd Silverman (1971, 1976; Silverman & Fishel, 1981) has conducted an extensive line of research investigating the motivated unconscious. Silverman is particularly concerned with the hypothesis that *psychopathology* expresses unconscious conflict. You have seen this idea in Freud's case studies. A patient's unconscious conflict showed itself in overt behavior.

Silverman's approach is experimental, making use of the tachistoscope. Stimuli thought to produce conflict, because they pertain to sexual or aggressive drives, are presented to subjects at *subliminal* levels, that is, for durations so brief that a person cannot consciously recognize the stimuli. Does this **subliminal stimulation** affect subsequent behavior? In particular, does it support the prediction that behavior will be disrupted by the activation of unconscious conflict?

Here is a representative experiment conducted by Silverman, Bronstein, and Mendelsohn (1976). Male college students participated in a competitive dart-throwing tournament. During a baseline period, they were exposed to one of three different subliminal messages: BEATING DAD IS WRONG, BEATING DAD IS OKAY, and PEOPLE ARE WALKING. The first message is thought to increase Oedipal guilt, the second to decrease it, and the third to be neutral. The dependent measure was the dart-throwing score obtained by the subjects after subliminal stimulation. Silverman and his colleagues predicted that guilt would impair dart-throwing. In keeping with this prediction, the subjects seeing the message BEATING DAD IS WRONG scored the lowest, whereas the subjects seeing BEATING DAD IS OKAY scored the highest. Subjects seeing the neutral message scored intermediately.

Silverman's research is extensive and intriguing. It is also controversial (see Balay & Shevrin, 1988; Weinberger, 1989). Critics point out that other research groups have failed to replicate it. Also, the studies are examples of what is known as *analogue research*. The "psychopathology" produced by Silverman's manipulations is only *analogous* to the psychopathology that brings people to the attention of mental health practitioners.

But the most fundamental criticism of the subliminal stimulation research, at least in the present context, questions the very notion of subliminal stimulation, a phenomenon with a controversial history (Bevan, 1964). How does Silverman ascertain that subjects are not aware of the stimuli presented by the tachistoscope? He chooses a tachistoscopic exposure level where "over 90% of the subjects cannot distinguish, at better than a chance level, one stimulus from another in a 'discrimination task' . . . even when they are offered a monetary incentive" (Silverman & Fishel, 1981, p. 63).

Subliminal stimulation: Stimuli below the threshold for awareness that nonetheless influence one's behavior.

You can see how this operationalization might be questioned. What about the other 10 percent? If they are perceptually vigilant, then they are *not* being stimulated subliminally. Might subjects who are aware of the stimuli respond to demand characteristics, giving Silverman the results his stimulus material seems to request? Counting against this latter possibility is the finding that none of the effects described is obtained when stimulus messages are presented at more lengthy intervals, when all subjects are conscious of their content.

Don't Think of a White Bear   As a youngster, author Leo Tolstoy was challenged by his older brother: "Stand in the corner until you are no longer thinking about a white bear." The point of this exercise is that thoughts can be difficult to suppress if that is one's explicit goal. We presume Tolstoy eventually left the corner. However, not all people have as much success in suppressing their thoughts. An intriguing research program by psychologist Daniel Wegner (1989) has investigated this phenomenon—thought suppression—and the results of his studies hold some important implications for the psychodynamic idea of a motivated unconscious.

Wegner's first experiment was inspired directly by the Tolstoy anecdote (Wegner, Schneider, Carter, & White, 1987). Research subjects sat alone in a room. They were given a microphone into which to speak. For five minutes they were to say anything that came to their minds. And they were to try not to think about a white bear. If this happened, they were to ring a bell. As might be expected, white bears made frequent appearances. On the average, they ambled into a subject's conscious mind a bit more frequently than once a minute.

The same subjects were next told to think of a white bear. Again, they were to ring a bell every time the bear showed up in their thoughts. Here's what is interesting: When compared to subjects who had not previously tried to suppress thoughts of a white bear, those subjects who had attempted to do so were *more likely* to think of a bear during this second phase of the experiment. In other words, prior attempts to suppress a particular thought led to a later preoccupation with that thought.

The relevance of these findings to clinical topics is obvious. Many of the problems people suffer from entail recurrent and intrusive thoughts—problems like depression, anxiety, schizophrenia, and most obviously, obsessive-compulsive disorders (Wegner, Shortt, Blake, & Page, 1990). Wegner's results suggest that individuals who try to put particular thoughts out of their minds thereby enter a vicious circle. The more they try *not* to think about a topic, the more readily it comes to mind.

Wegner also has found that given thoughts can most readily be suppressed by actively thinking of other topics, that is, by distracting oneself. In the typical case where one is trying to suppress a negative thought, positive distractions are obviously more effective than negative ones. However, those who habitually suffer from negative thoughts cannot readily come up with positive distractions (Wenzlaff, Wegner, & Roper, 1988).

Note that Wegner's research does not concern itself directly with the unconscious. In a way, its focus is the opposite, on consciousness run wild. But this technique has an important implication for how we think about the psychodynamic unconscious. Wegner argues that people who cannot suppress thoughts lack **mental control,** the ability to moderate thoughts and feelings. They are victims of whatever comes into their minds. They are not able to turn their minds to topics that would distract them.

So, the person who cannot suppress particular thoughts must at the same time be repressing other thoughts. The twist on this idea, from a psychodynamic perspective, is that the repressed thoughts are not necessarily threatening. They may be quite pleasant ones—and this is precisely why they are unavailable to the unhappy person's conscious mind.

Self-deception Ruben Gur and Harold Sackeim (1979) reported two studies pertinent to the motivated unconscious. Their concern was with **self-deception:** people lying to themselves. In everyday life, we presumably see frequent examples of self-deception by others: "My roommate actually thinks he'll get into medical school with a 2.33 grade-point average!" "Fred acts like his wife is going to return to him, but she left him 17 years ago and moved to Rio!"

Casual gossip is not the same thing as hard evidence. Are we really sure Fred expects his wife to return? Maybe he knows full well that she won't, and he's just putting up a front for any of a number of reasons. We can't tell. On the other hand, if Fred is lying to himself, then this act is an example of the motivated unconscious. One aspect of his mind (the unconscious) is deceiving another aspect (the conscious). Gur and Sackeim (1979, p. 149) took as their goal the creation of a laboratory phenomenon satisfying the definition of self-deception.

From the earlier discussion of perceptual defense, you know that the unambiguous demonstration of such behavior requires a complex method. Gur and Sackeim indeed employed a complicated procedure. Bear with me while I describe what they did and appreciate that their theoretical concerns demanded an intricate research strategy.

Research subjects listened to a series of different voices on audiotape. Some of these voices were their own and some of them were not. They were asked to identify their own voices. At the same time, their GSR was recorded. Previous studies have shown that a person's GSR is elevated when he hears his own voice on tape, even if he misidentifies it as someone else's voice.

So, in cases where someone misidentifies his own voice yet simultaneously shows an elevation in his GSR, it can be argued that he is holding contradictory beliefs. "That is not me," he says with his mouth; "That is me," he says with his physiology.

This operationalization is a subtle one. Gur and Sakeim do not equate an elevated GSR with a belief. Rather, they regard it as an indicator. At some level, the person must recognize the voice in order for his physiology to be influenced. However this recognition is mentally represented, it can be described as a belief.

What about the criterion of nonawareness? Again, Gur and Sackeim made use of information from previous research. When a research subject has identified a voice as his own, subsequent identification of a different voice as *not* his own is easier to make. This happens whether or not the initial identification

Mental control: The ability to moderate one's own thoughts and feelings.

Self-deception: Motivated lying to oneself.

is correct. Thus, by comparing the speed of identification following different types of responses, Gur and Sackeim could ascertain whether subjects were unaware that their own voices had been falsely identified. In other words, if someone falsely identifies a voice as his own and then shows rapid and correct identification of a different voice, it can be concluded that the person is unaware of the false identification. If he were aware he had made a mistake in identifying his own voice, then subsequent identification would not be facilitated.

Finally, how did the researchers show that self-deception is motivated? This was done in two different ways in two different experiments. In the first, subjects had earlier completed a measure of self-esteem. Subjects with poor self-esteem were assumed to have more of a motive to avoid self-confrontation than those with good self-esteem; accordingly, if self-deception is to be demonstrated, results should be more pronounced for subjects with poor self-esteem than for the others. In the second experiment, self-esteem was manipulated by the researchers just prior to the voice-identification task. Half of the subjects were given difficult verbal problems to solve, leading to failure and poor self-esteem, while the other subjects were given easy problems, leading to success and good self-esteem. Again, if self-deception exists, results should hold more strongly for subjects experiencing failure than for those experiencing success.

The results demonstrate the phenomenon of self-deception. GSR response to one's own voice was high, whether or not the voice was correctly identified. Following the incorrect identification of a stranger's voice as their own, subjects more quickly identified a different voice correctly. Finally, errors in identifying one's own voice were more likely for subjects with low self-esteem.

This research is important because it experimentally demonstrates the motivated unconscious. Is it definitive? No, because it is always possible to raise questions about research. But the demonstration is one of the best yet conducted, and it should give you a flavor of the challenge psychodynamic theory poses to the psychological researcher, and of the way sophisticated investigators have risen to the challenge. This research, in conjunction with the other studies mentioned in this section, convince me that a motivated unconscious exists.

Evaluation   I've described various experimental studies that have investigated the motivated unconscious. They converge in their support for this basic psychodynamic idea. Other investigations not surveyed here, like those of hypnosis (e.g., Stross & Shevrin, 1969) and others of defense mechanisms (e.g., Cramer, 1987; Cramer & Gaul, 1988), also suggest that the motivated unconscious exists. At the same time, the notion of perceptual vigilance arises from this research and it is difficult to accommodate within psychodynamic theory.

Case studies and experiments have different strengths and weaknesses. They are most sensibly employed for different purposes. The experimental studies described here, despite their circumscribed and qualified conclusions, accomplish what Freud's case studies cannot. They allow the researcher to get a handle on the motivated unconscious. Their demonstrations are repeatable, and the operative causes are identifiable.

Further, the experimental studies we have discussed give us a different way of thinking about the motivated unconscious, so they advance theory just as surely as did Freud's case studies. To use Kihlstrom's (1990, p. 460) phrase, experimental studies imply that the motivated unconscious is "kindler, gentler, and more rational" than the seething bundle of innate impulses depicted by Freud. Whether this characterization reflects the procedures and subjects employed by contemporary researchers or the fact that the motivated unconscious deserves to be called bland is unclear, but future studies should clarify the issue.

Oedipus Complex

According to Freud, the crucial determinants of adult personality reside in childhood. In particular, the way a child experiences the Oedipus complex is thought to determine the adult he or she becomes. What is the evidence the Oedipus complex exists and is played out according to Freud's scenario?

Fisher and Greenberg (1977) classify investigations of the Oedipus complex in terms of the specific question addressed. Does the newborn child show closeness to the mother? Do people show different attitudes toward the same-sex versus opposite-sex parent? Does the developing child come to identify with the same-sex parent? Is this identification brought about by anxiety? Do young boys experience castration anxiety? Do young girls experience penis envy? Does a person's moral sense develop from resolution of the Oedipal conflict?

Research provides affirmative answers to some of these questions, negative answers to others, and equivocal answers to the remaining. On the whole, support is lent to those early critics who questioned the Oedipus complex. But, like his assertions of infant sexuality, Freud's claims about Oedipal dynamics are not completely wrong. However, they are sufficiently off-center to warrant considerable doubt about this important aspect of psychodynamic theory.

Let me borrow from Fisher and Greenberg (1977) to explain where Freud's claims are supported by research and where they are not. On the positive side, young children of both sexes indeed show stronger attachment to their mother than their father. For instance, Schaffer and Emerson (1964) showed that infants reacted more negatively if separated from their mother than from their father. Of course, psychodynamic theory is not the only theory that predicts this finding.

Also on the positive side, developing children come to identify with the same-sex parent. In a variety of studies, children are first asked to describe themselves in response to a variety of questions about their beliefs, attitudes, and behaviors, and then to respond to the same questions from the perspective of their father and from the perspective of their mother. Usually, after age five or six, a child's responses resemble those of the same-sex parent more than the opposite-sex parent.

On the equivocal side, individuals often show attitudes that differ toward the same-sex versus opposite-sex parent. The differences themselves correspond to the Oedipal model: positive toward the opposite-sex parent, negative toward the same-sex parent. However, studies that have investigated the process by which these attitudes are formed yield results that do not exactly follow the Oedipal script.

Let me first describe two studies with adult subjects that support Oedipal predictions. Schill (1966) showed male and female college students a cartoon picture of a dog about to have its tail cut off by a knife. Research subjects were asked to speculate about which member of the dog's family was responsible for this impending doom (which you should recognize as symbolic castration). As Freud would expect, males saw the dog's father as the perpetrator of castration, whereas females saw the dog's mother as responsible.

Calvin Hall (1963) investigated Oedipal predictions through the content analysis of dreams. He operationalized hostility toward the father as the presence of a male stranger in one's dream. If this operationalization is plausible, then the validity of the Oedipal model would be supported if males dreamed more than females about male strangers. This is exactly what Hall finds.

Such adult studies do not, however, get at the process by which attitudes toward the mother and father are formed. A study is needed that looks at children across the age span when Oedipal feelings are presumably aroused and resolved. Friedman (1952) conducted one such study by asking children of different ages to tell stories in response to two different picture cues: one depicting a child with an adult male, the other depicting a child with an adult female. Boys told more stories containing conflict when the figure represented their father than when it represented their mother, whereas girls showed the opposite pattern. In these broad terms, then, the research once again confirms psychodynamic predictions. However, the details of Friedman's findings do not. Taking age into account fails to reveal the trends Freud proposed. Indeed, some of the age changes predicted by the Oedipal hypothesis occur exactly backward. From ages 5 to 16, girls showed conflict with their mother that increased, not decreased.

Along these same lines, Daly and Wilson (1990) examined the occurrence of murders within a family. Their findings do not support the Oedipal script, which predicts that murderous attacks should most frequently occur between fathers and sons and between mothers and daughters. Instead, males were the most frequent perpetrators of family murders, as well as the most frequent victims. Something other than Freud's hypothesized dynamics was going on in these families.

Also on the negative side, some research strongly disagrees with Freud's assertion that later identification with the same-sex parent is brought about by anxiety. Several studies show that little boys are most likely to adopt a masculine role if their father is warm, affectionate, and nurturant (e.g., Sears, 1953). More generally, Albert Bandura's investigations of modeling suggest that adult models will be followed to the degree that they are friendly instead of threatening. So,

The Cleaver family is a more accurate depiction of family dynamics than is the myth of Oedipus.

in personality development, as in other spheres of life, one gets further with honey than vinegar.

Finally, research somewhat disagrees with the idea of castration anxiety and altogether disagrees with the idea of penis envy. Studies show that males are more afraid of bodily damage than are females, but they have not shown that this fear particularly centers around loss of the genitals. Further, as Eysenck and Wilson (1973) have observed, the typical investigation of castration anxiety compares responses of males and females, and this is silly. Of course, boys are more likely to fear the loss of a penis than are girls: "If you ain't got nothing, you got nothing to lose!" Such investigations presuppose the Oedipal model they are trying to test.

How about the prediction that a person's moral sense develops from the resolution of the Oedipal conflict? By Freud's reasoning, father's strictness accelerates identification and superego formation. "Conscience" among boys should correlate positively with strictness of father. Many of you are no doubt rolling your eyes over this prediction, because you're thinking of the local juvenile delinquent whose father raised him like a drill sergeant.

Your skepticism corresponds with findings of a number of studies. Punitive fathers raise sons with weak moral standards. The development of conscience seems to be facilitated by nurturance and friendliness, not by punishment (Hoffman, 1963, Kohlberg, 1963, 1966). In sum, Freud was correct that parent-child interaction unfolds in complex ways. However, the specifics of his formulation, as captured in his notion of the Oedipus complex, often fail to square with the facts. In contrast to the myth of Oedipus, "Leave It to Beaver" seems a better model of what actually happens in the course of personality development. Friendly and supportive parents who provide good examples of how to behave produce healthy children.

Moral Development: Gilligan and Kohlberg

A related line of research compares the moral standards of males and females. As you recall, Freud argues that girls do not resolve the Oedipal conflict as neatly as do boys. So, their moral standards should not be as strong as boys' are. Freud is supported by some studies that show males have a superior moral sense to females, but other studies show females are superior morally to males, and yet other studies show no difference. Probably critical in deciphering these contradictory results is the particular operationalization of morality the researcher chose (Sears, Rau, & Alpert, 1965). Is conscience regarded as harsh and aggressive? Is it regarded as timid and acquiescent?

Rather than describe a number of studies and end up concluding that matters are confusing, I will instead discuss in detail the arguments of Carol Gilligan, whose 1982 book *In a Different Voice* points the researcher in a new direction for understanding sex differences in morality. Gilligan does not join the debate over which sex shows higher moral sense. Instead, she suggests that in our society males and females tend to have *different* moral standards. In attempting to compare them, one overlooks what is most interesting and most important.

Gilligan suggests that women's morality centers on not hurting others. In contrast, men's morality emphasizes rights. She describes the responses of two 11-year-old children faced with moral dilemma: Should a man steal a drug he cannot afford to save his dying wife? Jake, a young boy, argues that the man should steal the drug:

> A human life is worth more than money. . . . the druggist can get a thousand dollars later from rich people with cancer, but Heinz can't get his wife again. (p. 26).

Amy, a young girl, says the man shouldn't steal the drug:

> I think there might be other ways besides stealing it, like if he could borrow the money. . . . if he stole the drug, he might save his wife then, but if he did, he might have to go to jail, and then his wife might get sicker. (p. 28)

The critical contrast here is not that they recommend different courses of action, but that they justify them in different ways. Indeed, they see different moral problems. As Gilligan observes, "Jake [sees] a conflict between life and property that can be resolved by logical deduction, Amy [sees] a fracture of human relationship that must be mended with its own thread" (p. 31).

For a more personal example, let me describe what happens when my friend Lisa and I watch a sports event together. I always want "my" team to win. In contrast, before the game, Lisa roots for whatever team is the underdog. In the course of the game, she roots for the team that is behind. In contrast to my masculine vision of a 98–0 shutout by my team, Lisa wants frequent lead changes ending in a 98–98 tie.

Gilligan's ideas take issue not only with those of Freud but also with those of developmental psychologist Lawrence Kohlberg (1981). Like Freud, Kohlberg describes development in terms of stages. Moral reasoning develops from an egocentric stage, where moral decisions are based on one's own self-interest, to a principled stage, where moral decisions are based on considerations of justice. Gilligan criticizes Kohlberg's scheme of development because it embodies a masculine bias; Kohlberg (1981) seems to regard concern with rules as a more advanced moral stance than concern with the well-being of others.

Kohlberg (1984) has responded to Gilligan's criticisms, acknowledging that morality involves not just abstract principles but also care and concern for other people. His approach in the past has perhaps placed too much emphasis on justice. So, he agrees with some of Gilligan's arguments.

But he does not agree with all of her points. Most basically, he disagrees with her dichotomy of justice on the one hand and social concern on the other. Someone with a highly developed moral sense will consider both. Further, Kohlberg disagrees that men and women differ in the moral reasoning they employ (see Pratt, Golding, Hunter, & Sampson, 1988). He faults researchers who seem to show a sex difference for not taking into account potential confounds like education, employment status, and so on (see Boldizar, Wilson, & Deemer, 1989).

Gilligan's work remains important for challenging the way theorists and researchers have conceived morality. Attempts to measure all superegos against the psychodynamic standard and its masculine bias obscure the whole of moral reasoning. Gilligan recommends that each type of morality be studied in its own right (cf. Gilligan, Ward, & Taylor, 1988). And Kohlberg in effect agrees with her in recommending that the two be studied in conjunction with each other. In the present context, I second these recommendations. The Oedipal hypothesis has put blinders on researchers investigating morality for far too long.

Attachment

I noted in my discussion of Freud's case studies that Freud himself did not study children, despite his extensive theorizing about the impact of early events on a person's later personality. Contemporary developmental psychologists, in contrast, go directly to the source. Their investigations of children allow psychodynamic hypotheses to be directly evaluated. One of the most important lines of research undertaken by developmental psychologists looks at the emotional attachment between infants and their mothers. Consistent with psychodynamic thinking, the nature of these attachments has a pervasive effect on subsequent ways of behaving.

At about six months, most children begin to show a marked attachment to a single individual, usually their mother. They seek contact with this person, crawling after her, crying out to her, and so on. Strangers, in contrast, elicit fear. This pattern persists for several years.

Strange Situation Test: A laboratory procedure where an infant is briefly separated from his or her mother, then reunited; used to study attachment.

The **Strange Situation Test** is a research strategy for investigating attachments by young children (Ainsworth & Wittig, 1969). A mother brings her child to a developmental psychologist's laboratory. A carefully scripted series of events take place, where the mother leaves the child alone for a period of time and then comes back. The researcher watches the reactions of the child to being separated from the mother and then reunited. Three patterns of attachment are distinguished:

- *secure attachment*   The child is distressed when the mother leaves and relieved on her return; this pattern is shown by about 70 percent of children.
- *avoidant attachment*   The child is not distressed when the mother leaves and ignores her on her return; this pattern is shown by about 20 percent of children.
- *ambivalent attachment*   The child is distressed when the mother leaves yet not comforted when she returns; about 10 percent of children show this pattern.

These patterns can be highly stable ones (Ainsworth, 1989). As you might imagine, children whose attachment is avoidant or ambivalent grow up to have more psychological problems than children with secure attachments.

Some recent research implies that adults form romantic relationships in accordance with their attachment style as infants. Note that someone can relate to a lover in secure, avoidant, or ambivalent ways. Hazan and Shaver (1987) surveyed adults and classified their relationship style in these terms, finding proportions approximately equal to those shown by the comparable classification of infants: i.e., 70 percent, 20 percent, and 10 percent, respectively. Further, when questioned about the way their parents had raised them, these adult subjects answered as one would expect. Secure individuals remembered their parents as warm and supportive; avoidant individuals remembered their parents as cold and rejecting; and ambivalent individuals remembered their parents as inconsistent.

These findings have been replicated by Feeney and Noller (1990), although we must take studies that rely on retrospective accounts of childhood with a grain of salt. More conclusive evidence for the continuity of attachment styles will come as the children studied in the laboratories with the Strange Situation Test are followed through their lives. For the time being, we can conclude that research into attachment is consistent with broad psychodynamic claims about the importance of early relationships. The tentative finding that adults approach their romances in the same way they reacted to their mothers is particularly intriguing.

Birth Order

Now let me turn to Alfred Adler's account of personality development, with its emphasis on birth order. As you recall, Adler thinks a child's ordinal position within the family creates different social realities to which the child reacts.

Researchers have been intrigued by these predictions and have conducted a variety of investigations testing them. Here are brief descriptions of some of these lines of research.

Achievement   One line of birth-order research has looked at achievement, expecting firstborns to be particularly eminent. In a number of studies this is the case. For example, among United States presidents, firstborn sons are overrepresented (Wagner & Schubert, 1977). George Washington, Harry Truman, and Gerald Ford are examples. Interestingly, a preponderance of firstborn sons does not appear among defeated candidates for the presidency.

Intelligence   A related line of research has investigated intellectual development, again with the expectation that firstborn children will distinguish themselves because they have had the opportunity to tutor others. In a massive investigation of some 400,000 males from the Netherlands, Belmont and Marolla (1973) found that birth order was positively correlated with performance on the Raven Progressive Matrices, a nonverbal test of intelligence. However, you may be skeptical that family dynamics are responsible for this intriguing relationship. Aren't there other variables that might explain it? How about family income during one's childhood? How about the mother's age? In a study of how American students performed on the National Merit Test, Breland (1974) ruled out these and other confounds, showing that the relationship between birth order and intelligence occurred even when these factors were controlled.

Psychologists Robert Zajonc and Gregory Markus (1975) took an even closer look at the relationship between birth order and intellectual attainment. They reanalyzed the data of Belmont and Marolla (1973) and found that in addition to birth order, the spacing of children in a family affected intelligence. The more closely in time brothers and sisters are born, the lower their intelligence. This effect is particularly pronounced among the youngest children in the family.

To account for these findings, Zajonc and Markus proposed what they call a **confluence model.** This model makes three reasonable assumptions. First, people attain a given level of intelligence according to the amount of intellectual stimulation they receive from their family. Second, the amount of stimulation is determined by the average intelligence of the family members. Third, older children are more intelligent than younger children because of birth order.

Do you see how these assumptions explain the patterns in the Belmont-Marolla data? The more young children present in a family, the less intellectual stimulation the family provides to each. Firstborn children escape this handicap for at least their early years, while latter-born children are born into this situation. Particularly at a disadvantage, according to the confluence model, should be twins and triplets. And this is exactly what the data show. (I'm a twin, so I probably don't understand the confluence model as well as if I were not, but the point seems to be that "spaced out" siblings are advantageous.)

The confluence model provides a possible explanation for why SAT scores declined through the sixties and seventies: High school students taking the SAT tended to come from increasingly large families. Zajonc and Bargh (1980) tested

Confluence model: A theory of how the mutual influence among family members can affect the intellectual development of each.

this explanation and concluded that birth order and family size indeed account for some of this decline, but by no means all of it. Still, they predicted that SAT scores would start to rise again in the eighties and nineties, as the family composition of high school students again changed. And their prediction appears to be correct (Zajonc, 1986).

Although the confluence model points to a process linking birth order to intellectual attainment that is somewhat different from what Adler proposes, it is still in the spirit of his theorizing. A child's place in the family determines her or his environment, which in turn determines the sort of adult the child will become.

Affiliation   A final line of work has looked at patterns of affiliation as a function of birth order. Psychologist Stanley Schachter (1959) reported several intriguing investigations that support Adler's conjecture that firstborns are marked for life by the birth of a younger sibling, displacing them from the center of attention. Firstborns should therefore be made more anxious by threat than latter-borns, and they should be more likely to reach out to others (as parental figures) when they experience anxiety.

Schachter recruited female subjects for an experiment and told them that it would involve painful electric shock. While the experimenter was supposedly preparing the equipment, he gave them the option of waiting alone or with other women. Consistent with Adler's ideas, firstborn women reported more anxiety than latter-born women and were also more likely to prefer to wait in the presence of others.

Other studies similarly show that firstborn children are unlikely to pursue solitary and dangerous professions like being a fighter pilot or a skydiver; at the same time, they are more likely to seek help from a psychotherapist when experiencing problems (Freedman, 1982, p. 493). When an earthquake struck Los Angeles in 1971, firstborns reported that they spoke to more people immediately following the quake than did latter-borns, implying again the link among birth order, anxiety, and affiliation (Hoyt & Raven, 1973).

Some years ago, I conducted an informal study and asked students how they procrastinated during final exams. I also asked them their birth position. Two findings were interesting. First, almost everyone procrastinated when it came time for finals. The entire campus seethed with procrastination. But second, as a function of their birth order, students did different things while procrastinating. Firstborns wasted time socially, by going out to drink with others or by writing letters. Latter-borns wasted time alone, by playing video games or by alphabetizing their record albums. Again, these results are consistent with Adler's ideas about birth order.

Evaluation   Not all studies of birth order yield positive results (Ernst & Angst, 1983; Jones, 1931; Schooler, 1972). I've selected some of the investigations consistent with Adler's position to show its merit. Keep in mind all of the possible influences on the behaviors of concern in these studies. The fact that birth order has any effect at all is impressive; that these effects are consistent with Adler's ideas argues that we should take into account the child's position within the family in order to understand adult personality (Falbo & Polit, 1986).

Character Types

I want to conclude this section by describing research that supports the psychodynamic character types. These concepts have the most obvious relationship to personality as we usually think of it. What does the evidence say about the types of people proposed by the psychodynamic theorists? Actually, two hypotheses are embedded here. The first is a descriptive one, asking whether the characteristics of people cohere in the ways suggested by theory. For instance, is a constellation of anal traits identifiable? Do the same people tend to be stingy, neat, and stubborn? The second hypothesis is a developmental one, asking whether a particular character type is brought about by unusual events during the corresponding stage of psychosexual development.

In light of the research already described regarding the theory of psychosexual development, you can probably guess that little support exists for the developmental hypothesis. On the other hand, the descriptive hypothesis has been mostly supported by research (Fisher & Greenberg, 1977; Kline, 1972). People's characteristics do indeed cohere in ways predicted by the character types.

Oral and Anal Character Types A great deal of research has looked at the character types supposedly resulting from fixation at the oral or anal stages of psychosexual development. The oral character is thought to show a variety of characteristics:

- preoccupation with issues of giving-taking
- concern about dependence-independence and passivity-activity
- special attitudes about closeness and distance to others—being alone versus attachment to the group
- extremes of optimism-pessimism
- unusual ambivalence
- openness to novel experience and ideas, which involves enhanced curiosity and interest in investigating nature
- a hasty, restless, impatient orientation—wanting to be "fed" with events and things
- continued unusual use of oral channels for gratification, or compensatory denial of oral needs; for example, overeating, not eating enough, smoking, excessive talking (Fisher & Greenberg, 1977, p. 88)

If the idea of an oral character is to make sense, these characteristics should be correlated.

Similarly, the anal character is also thought to show a constellation of characteristics: the traits of obstinacy, parsimony, and orderliness. Borrowing from Abraham (1927) and Jones (1923), Kline (1972, pp. 10–11) elaborated this set of anal characteristics to include:

- procrastination followed by intense concentration
- a belief that nobody can do anything as well as oneself

- minute attention to detail
- strong drive to clean things
- profound interest in handwriting
- opposition of any attempt to guide one's conduct
- dislike of time being used up against one's will
- pleasure spoiled by small things out of place
- love of self-control
- interest in the backs of things
- love of exactitude, delight in organizing
- reliability
- hatred of waste
- pleasure in possessing something rare or unusual
- pleasure in statistics or tables
- dislike of spending money on perishable things

Researchers have tested these claims in dozens of studies. Most frequently, research subjects answer questions about various oral and/or anal characteristics. Responses are correlated with each other, and oral characteristics go together more frequently than one would expect by mere chance, as do anal characteristics (Fisher & Greenberg, 1977; Kline, 1972).

Blacky Test: A series of cartoon pictures of a dog ("Blacky"), used to investigate character types.

Some of the most intriguing of these studies use the **Blacky Test** developed by psychologist Gerald Blum (1949, 1962; Blum & Hunt, 1952). This is a projective test specifically designed to investigate psychodynamic character types. The name of the test refers to a dog, Blacky, who figures with its family in 12 cartoons depicting situations of psychosexual relevance. So, in one picture, Blacky is nursing. In another, Blacky is defecating. Earlier in this chapter, I described the Blacky picture used in Schill's (1966) investigation of castration responsibility: Blacky watches its sibling Tippy, who has a knife poised over its tail.

Blacky's sex is identified to the research subject as that of the subject. The subject then tells a story about each picture. What's going on? How do the characters feel? Stories are scored for the presence or absence of oral concern, anal concern, and so on. In the present context, we are interested in the designation of research subjects as oral (or not) and as anal (or not). Once subjects are so designated, do they act in ways consistent with their putative character type?

Various studies show that they do. Although inconsistencies exist, researchers have shown that oral subjects, as identified by the Blacky Test, are prone to suggestion and influence (Tribich & Messer, 1974), ambivalence regarding autonomy (Blatt, 1964), obesity (Friedman, 1959), excessive cigarette smoking (Kimeldorf & Geiwitz, 1966), and overindulgence in ice cream (Blum & Hunt, 1952). Anal subjects, as identified by the Blacky Test, show good memory for details (Adelson & Redmond, 1958), concern with order (Blatt, 1964), resistance to influence and suggestion (Tribich & Messer, 1974), and obsessive symptoms (Kline, 1968).

Let's move from these studies, which show that oral and anal characteristics tend to cohere, to studies investigating the developmental hypothesis about character types. Does excessive frustration or indulgence at a particular stage of psychosexual development show up later as the respective character type? Researchers have correlated adult characteristics with methods of child-rearing, especially stringency or leniency in weaning and toilet training. If the developmental hypothesis is correct, the child who nursed for too short or too long a time will show oral traits as an adult. Likewise, the child who was potty-trained in an extreme fashion will show anal traits as an adult.

Several types of these studies exist. Retrospective studies assess child-rearing practices after the fact, from the reports of the individual or the parents. These assessments are correlated with oral or anal personality measures (e.g., Thurston & Mussen, 1951). But prospective studies are methodologically preferable, because they assess child-rearing practices at the time they are occurring (Halverson, 1988). The children are followed for a period of time, it is hoped to post-puberty, where fixations show up, and then their character traits are measured and correlated with the child-rearing variables (e.g., Heinstein, 1963). Yet another type of study characterizes the weaning or toilet training typical of an entire culture and attempts to draw connections between these practices and the model personality of adults in that culture (e.g., Whiting & Child, 1953).

Regardless of how the studies are conducted, scant support arises for the developmental hypothesis (Fisher & Greenberg, 1977; Kline, 1972). Although some investigations have found relationships between child-rearing and personality, the links are not those specifically proposed by Freud's psychoanalytic theory.

Phallic Character Type In contrast to the large research literature investigating Freud's oral and anal characters, few studies have looked at the phallic character, which is presumably produced by unusual events at the phallic stage of psychosexual development, showing itself in the form of exaggerated sexuality and preoccupation with the self. However, a study by psychologists Donald Mosher and Mark Sirkin (1984) is relevant. These researchers were concerned with what they call the **macho personality constellation,** defined as *hypermasculinity* and measured by a questionnaire that asks subjects to endorse one statement from each of a number of pairs of statements like

Macho personality constellation: Hypermasculinity.

1. I like wild, uninhibited parties.
2. I like quiet parties with good conversations.

1. I like fast cars and fast women.
2. I like dependable cars and faithful women.

1. So-called prick teasers should be forgiven.
2. Prick teasers should be raped.

1. I like to drive safely, avoiding all risks.
2. I like to drive fast, right on the edge of danger.

1. Lesbians have chosen a particular life-style and should be respected for it.
2. The only thing a lesbian needs is a good, stiff cock.

The phallic character shows in exaggerated sexuality and preoccupation with the self.

Although Mosher and Sirkin do not explicitly link their research to the phallic character type, considerable overlap occurs between this character type and the macho orientation as they have measured it. In a study of 135 male college students, Mosher and Sirkin found good evidence for the coherence of the macho personality constellation. Subjects who choose the macho (phallic) alternative in one pair of statements from the questionnaire tend to choose the macho alternative in other pairs. Further, those who score high on the macho scale are apt to use drugs and alcohol excessively, to have physical fights, to get in automobile accidents, and to be sexually promiscuous.

In a follow-up study, Mosher and Anderson (1986) administered the macho personality questionnaire to another group of male college students, along with other measures. Those individuals who scored high on the macho scale reported a history of sexual aggression, using force or exploitation in order to have intercourse with the women they dated. When asked to imagine a rape, young men who scored high on the macho scale were more interested and sexually aroused than their non-macho counterparts. At the same time, the macho young men were also more distressed, afraid, ashamed, and guilty when imagining a rape. Consistent with psychodynamic theorizing, those with a phallic character type showed great ambivalence surrounding sexuality.

Evaluation Other lines of research have investigated the character types proposed by Carl Jung (e.g., Myers, 1962) and Erich Fromm (e.g., Fromm & Maccoby, 1970). Again, results show that particular traits cohere into types as hypothesized but that they do not develop in the way psychodynamic theorists have proposed. A different way of thinking about the origin of such character types is obviously needed.

Psychologist Abigail Stewart (1982; Stewart & Healy, 1989) provides a promising reconceptualization of the character types. She suggests that these styles are not permanently fixed categories but are instead strategies for coping with particular life demands. Accordingly, one's "type" is not constant but is instead dependent on his or her circumstances.

What Freud identified as an oral type, Stewart describes as someone with a *receptive* strategy. Receptive individuals view authority figures as benevolent. They tend to be passive and inactive, waiting for others to fulfill their needs. The anal type is seen as someone who is *autonomous* of other people. Autonomous individuals view others as critical and punitive, and they tend to protect themselves from their intrusions. The phallic types have an *assertive* strategy, and they try to use other people to achieve their own aims. Finally, the person with an *integrated* approach uses all of these strategies and is therefore flexible and mature.

At a descriptive level, Stewart's types correspond to the traditional character types of psychodynamic theory. But because she sees these as strategies of coping with the environment, she argues that people cycle through them many times in the course of life. Evidence seems to support this idea (Stewart, Sokol, Healy, & Chester, 1986).

Stewart classifies research subjects by asking them to tell stories in response to the ambiguous pictures of the Thematic Apperception Test (TAT). Depending on the themes they emphasize, subjects are designated as receptive, autonomous, assertive, or integrated. Then subjects are followed over time as they confront a new challenge. Later, they again respond to the TAT and are reclassified. Consistent with Stewart's ideas, and in contrast to the traditional conception of character types as fixed, most subjects show a regular progression from receptive through autonomous and assertive to integrated. For example, when students first begin college, they tend to be receptive. Once familiar with school, they show more advanced strategies. Similar results have been found for individuals when they first marry.

CONCLUSIONS: PSYCHODYNAMIC THEORIES IN LIGHT OF THE RESEARCH

The research shows that Freud was right about many of the general factors influencing personality, whereas his highly specific predictions are usually at odds with the evidence. In particular, his emphasis on sexuality as the prime human motive is not supported by the facts. This latter conclusion has considerable irony, because Freud's name is inextricably linked to the role of sexuality in personality.

What do we do with psychodynamic theory if we remove its sexual core? Does anything of importance remain? I think so. When we use research to strip away incorrect hypotheses, appreciate what is left: unconscious motivation, transference, defense mechanisms, character types, and the importance of early experiences. Taken together, these comprise a coherent statement about personality.

Said another way, Freud's hypotheses about *processes* underlying personality are often correct, but his claims about sexual and aggressive *contents* are often wrong. Freud may have been overly influenced by Victorian Europe and its strict prohibitions against overt sexuality, elevating this striking aspect of his culture to the status of universal human nature. The patients in his case studies clearly experienced conflicts with sexuality. However, people in other times and places have been less uptight about sex. Nevertheless, Freud's observations about the way people deal with these particular prohibitions lead to considerably general conclusions.

How is the composite theory presented at the end of the last chapter altered by these conclusions? Most of the points of view are vindicated. Those emphasizing instinctive, biological processes are not.

This revised theory sounds a neoFreudian one. However, this research-informed revision does not agree with the theory of any particular neoFreudian. Research fails to support claims that people are driven by a single dominant motive, be it sex, superiority, affection, approval, identity, integration, or whatever. The human family does not march to a single drummer. Lots of beats fill the air, and most of us listen to several.

What should you take with you after reading this chapter? First, appreciate that the common assertion that psychodynamic theory is impossible to test is wrong. The theory can be tested, and it has been tested. Second, appreciate that Freud and the other theorists were correct about a number of matters concerning personality. Their influence is felt throughout the entire field of personality psychology. The evidence suggests that this influence is warranted. Third, appreciate that research shows that Freud's emphasis on sexuality was incorrect.

SUMMARY

In this chapter, I described psychodynamic research. I started by considering the criticism that psychodynamic theory is impossible to test because its concepts are ambiguous and its predictions are muddled. I disagreed. These concepts can be operationalized if the researcher is willing to gather enough information to make a good inference about their presence or absence. Clear predictions can be made if the researcher distinguishes between clinical predictions (aspects of theory amenable to test) and metapsychological assumptions (bedrock aspects of a paradigm that underlie testable predictions).

I described several of Freud's well-known case studies. Despite their importance in providing the raw material for psychodynamic theory, these studies are only borderline instances of satisfactory research. Three contemporary refinements of the case-study research strategy are much more rigorous: the symptom-context method, the core conflictual relationship theme method, and the natural history method. Research that uses these approaches supports psychoanalytic predictions regarding symptom formation, transference, and defense mechanisms.

Finally, I described a variety of correlational and experimental studies investigating specific topics pertinent to the psychodynamic account of personality: instincts and drives, unconscious motivation, the Oedipus complex, moral development, attachment, birth order, and character types. Research support for psychodynamic predictions is mixed. In general, research bears out the neoFreudian criticism of a sexual libido.

PSYCHODYNAMIC PARADIGM: APPLICATIONS

reud's ideas about human nature reverberate not just through personality psychology but throughout all of contemporary culture. His ideas and terminology have been thoroughly assimilated by the Western world, as have those of the other psychodynamic theorists. We sprinkle our conversations with mention of defense mechanisms ("Now don't be defensive—you know that you do that"), with reference to one sort of complex or another ("Short men act that way"), with speculation about archetypes ("You've always been attracted to the earth mother type"). And we blame mother and father for how we turned out, sometimes to the point of suing them for incompetence.

But the influence of psychodynamic thought on contemporary life has been even more profound. Psychodynamic ideas, by virtue of their general acceptance, have literally changed the world and thereby changed who we are. Like Adam and Eve, we have tasted the fruit of our knowledge, and we are not the same. Once we accept the possibilities that our motives are hidden from us, that our sexuality is paramount, that behavior is over-determined, then we think, feel, and act differently, even if these possibilities are not strictly true.

Dissemination of ideas in the social sciences may have opposing consequences. On the one hand, through self-fulfilling prophecies, a theory's popularity sometimes leads to the appearance of an even greater validity as people act in expected ways. For instance, some managerial theories regard workers as lazy and disinterested; workplaces that embody these theories produce the very slackers assumed in the first place.

On the other hand, a theory's popularity sometimes leads to its own invalidation. Kenneth Gergen (1973) calls this an *enlightenment effect*. People may use their knowledge of the theory to act in ways not quite consistent with it. Slowly, the theory becomes wrong as people find the psychological equivalent of income tax loopholes.

As an example, consider the *unresponsive bystander effect* documented by social psychologists John Darley and Bibb Latané (1968). The more people

Is the unresponsive bystander effect a thing of the past?

witnessing an accident, the less likely anyone is to help. This phenomenon is attributed in part to the *diffusion of responsibility* among the bystanders. Everyone assumes the other fellow will help.

Diffusion of responsibility is an intriguing theory that explains what is otherwise puzzling: bystander apathy in cases of dire emergency. It is so intriguing, in fact, that it is taught to tens of thousands of students each year in social psychology courses. And what is the result? At least some of these students may do what I do when I see a stranger in distress: look to see how many bystanders are present. The *more* people around, the more likely I am to help. Bye-bye bystander effect!

Let's return to psychodynamic ideas. How about hysteria? Cases are much more rare today than during Freud's time. This may be an enlightenment effect: the result of widespread knowledge of Freud's ideas. People know that sensory systems don't stop working all of a sudden. If sudden blindness or deafness does occur, people know this may be a cop-out, a response to stress. People know that they have conflicts that may be outside their awareness. Such insights may preclude the bizarre hysteria cases Freud and Breuer and others of their era treated.

How about sex? By all estimates, sexual frequency and variety are up, as it were, from the turn of the century. Of course numerous factors are responsible, not least of which is the improved technology of contraception. Psychodynamic theory is another factor responsible for the sexual revolution. Freud is the father of the sexual revolution because his ideas have changed the way sex is regarded. He may not have agreed with the way sexual activities have evolved, but he certainly started the ball rolling.

And not only are sexual activities more common, but also our attitude toward them is different. It's okay and healthy to have a sex drive. We expect young children to be interested in sex, and we expect the same of senior citizens. Masturbation is harmless. No clear line is visible between normal and abnormal sexual practices. Thanks Sigmund, we needed that. Or maybe we didn't. Regardless, the times have changed with regard to sex, and so have we.

Against the context of Freud's profound influence on our times are also discrete instances where psychodynamic ideas have been applied. I've selected several topics where people have taken these ideas and done something with them. Although I'll comment on the general success or failure of these applications, let me remind you that application is not the same thing as research. Theories are not explicitly tested by applications. Reasonableness of a theory is assumed—not evaluated.

So, it is interesting that many of the applications I'll be discussing are concerned with notions of sexuality. This is the precise area of psychodynamic theory that the research evidence finds most contradictory. But undaunted by these facts, practitioners have gone ahead with libido-based applications. These applications have sometimes proven satisfactory, so perhaps they are produced by self-fulfilling prophecies.

PSYCHOPATHOLOGY: PRODUCED BY UNCONSCIOUS CONFLICTS

Hardly surprising is the widespread application of psychodynamic ideas to help understand psychological abnormality. After all, the important psychodynamic theorists have mostly been psychotherapists. The raw material of psychoanalysis was clinical material: facts about distressed people. In this section of the chapter, I will sketch this general formula for conceiving abnormality and then illustrate it by a number of examples.

Conception of Abnormality

The psychodynamic theorist sees psychopathology as a developmental problem, as an inevitable hazard of passing through the psychosexual stages to reach a compromise between instinctive drives and societal prohibitions. Because personality development is seen as cumulative, early events can be particularly traumatic, and, if adult personality is built on a flawed foundation, psychopathology results.

Persons experiencing difficulties with thoughts, feelings, or actions are regarded as poorly handling needs and drives. They hold them too much in check or not enough. As we used to say on the psychiatric ward where I worked: Check the lid on the id. Too tight, too loose, or missing altogether? Problems result from childhood events, from constitutional weaknesses, or from an interplay between the two.

Regardless, the symptoms a person experiences are viewed by psychodynamic theorists in two ways. First, they represent a literal tying up of libidinal energy that would be better employed elsewhere. What is mental health if not the abilities to love with joy and to work with joy (Vaillant, 1977)? Both take energy. Second, symptoms symbolize the particular conflict that underlies them. The woman who is hysterically mute, for instance, is thought to have a problem with something she might say and wishes she won't say it.

Hysteria

**Conversion disorder:
Hysteria.**

Hysteria is called **conversion disorder** (American Psychiatric Association, 1987). *Conversion* refers to the notion that the particular symptom results from the transformation of psychic conflict into physical malfunction. Before Breuer and Freud implicated the role of conflict in hysterical symptoms, the disorder was thought to be purely physical in nature.

Through the use of hypnosis and, later, free association, Freud showed that hysteria was a psychological disorder involving sexual conflicts that the patient was unable to acknowledge or resolve. Paralysis represented a solution to a dilemma, albeit a poor one. The psychodynamic account of conversion disorders is still widely accepted (e.g., Sackeim, Nordlie, & Gur, 1979), but the precipitating conflict is no longer seen as only sexual. A variety of conflicts give rise to hysterical symptoms including interpersonal strife, worries about money, and so on. Further, contemporary views emphasize the role of reinforcement in maintaining hysterical symptoms once they appear (Nemiah, 1980c).

Conversion disorders are not nearly as common today as they once were. In my personal experience, I have encountered only two individuals with clear conversion symptoms. Both fit the psychodynamic formula. One was a young woman who was hysterically deaf. She had grown up in a highly critical family and eventually turned off the criticism—literally. The other was a middle-aged man who was hysterically blind. He was married to a woman who in recent years had become obese, and he dealt with his anger at her appearance by blinding himself to it—again, literally.

Phobia

Excessive and inappropriate fears have been described throughout history. Hippocrates described phobias like that of Nicanor, who was deathly afraid of the sound of flutes, and that of Damocles, who was afraid to walk near cliffs or over bridges. In *The Merchant of Venice,* Shakespeare mentioned "some, that are mad if they behold a cat." Among famous people suffering from phobias were Augustus Caesar, Blaise Pascal, King James I of England, Samuel Johnson, and Sigmund Freud himself. The fact that sportscaster John Madden is afraid of flying is part of contemporary lore.

Before Freud, phobias did not receive much theoretical attention in their own right. They were regarded as just another manifestation of neurological disorder. Freud proposed a theoretical account of phobias per se, which we've already seen in the case of Little Hans (Chapter 5). A phobia is thought to result from displaced anxiety. Unlike hysterics, who blot anxiety from awareness, phobics still experience it. However, they attach it to an object or event that is not the original source of conflict.

Phobic objects are not chosen capriciously. They symbolize the real source of anxiety. According to Freud, Little Hans feared horses because they represented his father, in all of his sexual prowess and wrath. Or consider this case history:

A young woman suffered from a fear of insects, particularly cockroaches. She was so frightened that she might encounter a roach that she avoided all places where one might cross her path: restaurants, stores, even the homes of friends and family members. She removed almost all the furniture from her own apartment, fearful that an insect might be hiding underneath them. Because roaches rarely venture forth in bright light, she equipped all of her lamps with high wattage bulbs that burned continually. In the course of therapy, it was discovered that the woman's symptoms had started during adolescence, when she had a brief sexual encounter with a neighborhood boy. Her experience left her confused and frightened. She was attracted to the boy, but believed her parents would be greatly disappointed in her because of her sexual feelings. Not long afterwards, her fear of insects appeared: a symbol of sexuality best kept out of sight.

This particular phobia conforms well to psychodynamic theory.

Today, the psychodynamic account of phobias is not as widely accepted as it once was. While most clinicians acknowledge that some phobias represent displaced anxiety, even contemporary psychoanalysts look beyond sexual conflicts in explaining phobias (Nemiah, 1980b). As with hysteria, practitioners increasingly look to the environment to explain how phobias originate. Traumatic experience with the phobic object is now a popular etiological account (Marks, 1969). You can see how such explanations—based on principles of classical conditioning—are diametrically opposed to the symbolic explanation of psychodynamic theory. That phobic individuals may avoid unpleasantries by their fears is also a popular contemporary explanation. In the case of the woman who was afraid of insects, one might imagine how this fear serves to extricate her from difficult situations, like other dates where her sexual ambivalence would again become an issue.

Obsession and Compulsion

As noted in the Rat Man case described in the last chapter, Freud regards obsessions and compulsions as symbolic struggles. Conflicts regarding sex or aggression presumably underlie these problems. What we nowadays refer to as an **obsessive-compulsive disorder** is interpreted by psychodynamic theorists as anxiety displaced from one psychic realm to another. Recurrent thoughts (obsessions) and impulses to act (compulsions) are due to a reaction formation in the course of this displacement. So, the individual is consciously repulsed by what is unconsciously desired. Freud proposed that this process is not arbitrary. The obsessive idea or the compulsive behavior symbolizes the real conflict.

Consistent with this interpretation, the content of obsessions and compulsions tends to be limited to several themes: worry about dirt or disease; violence or loss of control; and religious blasphemy. All of these make sense within psychodynamic theory (Nemiah, 1980a). Obsessions involving cleanliness versus contamination reflect concerns of the anal stage, as do those about violence or loss of control. Blasphemy symbolizes anger against Dad and Mom for all their offenses, real and imagined.

Obsessive-compulsive disorder: A psychological problem characterized by recurrent thoughts (obsessions) and impulses to act (compulsions).

Here is a case I once encountered:

> A 35-year-old woman with two young children was obsessed with the idea that she would take a large knife and plunge it first into the heart of one child and then into the heart of the other. The thought repulsed her, since she loved her children, and it also frightened her, since she experienced the impulse as a very real one. When she found herself repeatedly opening the kitchen drawer containing knives, she started to hide the knives in unlikely places around the house. Then she feared that the hiding places were not all that secure after all, so she started to check them to make sure the knives were still there. The more she checked, the more accessible the knives seemed, and the more obsessive she became.

I talked with this woman on several occasions, eventually learning that she greatly resented the responsibility of raising two children with minimal help from her husband, who traveled for his employer. And while still a child, the woman had been assigned primary responsibility for raising her younger brother. From the viewpoint of psychodynamic theory, all of the facts of this case fit together. The one thing the woman does not want is to be responsible for others: her children, her husband, her brother, her parents, even herself. Her obsessive-compulsive disorder expresses her unconscious belief that others have robbed her of her freedom, because she has never been able to follow her own heart.

The psychodynamic explanation of obsessive-compulsive disorders has been challenged on two fronts. Cognitive-behavioral theories emphasize the consequences of the repetitive thought or act (Rachman, 1978). Such preoccupations can be highly reinforcing because they distract the individual from other sources of her anxiety. Biological theories point to brain differences between those with obsessive-compulsive disorders and those without, as well as to a strong genetic component for these difficulties (Willerman & Cohen, 1990). Missing from cognitive-behavioral and biological theories is an explanation of the particular content of obsessions and compulsions, so perhaps we should view the rival hypotheses as complementary.

Depression

Freud grappled with the problem of depression in his 1917 paper, "Mourning and Melancholia." Sadness occurs in both grief (mourning) and depression (melancholia), but only in the latter is it accompanied by loss of self-esteem. Depressed individuals, unlike merely sad ones, revile themselves as worthless and incompetent, responsible for all sorts of bad events.

To Freud, depressed persons seemed angry, and so Freud hypothesized that they are: angry at themselves. How does this come about? Remember, personality develops when we incorporate the characteristics of significant others, usually our parents. If these significant others disappoint us in some way—if we lose their love—then the anger that wells up within us in response to this loss of love seeks a target. According to Freud, we turn our anger inward, punishing the part of us that is them.

Sandor Rado (1928) elaborated Freud's account to argue that depressed people are inordinately dependent on others. By virtue of being raised in an inconsistent fashion, they need constant attention and love. At the same time, they are never satisfied with what they receive, because they do not trust it. Rado likened the depressive to a drug addict, in desperate need of love (the drug) when it is absent, indifferent when it is present.

Ronnie Fiske and I investigated some of Rado's hypotheses by surveying young adults, depressed and nondepressed, about their romantic relationships (Fiske & Peterson, 1991). Sure enough, the depressed individuals described relationships that were intense and tumultuous. Compared to nondepressed individuals, they described themselves as more dependent, self-sacrificing, angry, and unrealistic in their approach to romance.

Psychodynamic theory thus explains why suicide often accompanies severe depression. Suicide is symbolic murder of the self. It also explains why losses are common in the childhood of some depressives (Wolpert, 1980). Consider this case:

> A 45-year-old man had been depressed ever since his early 20s. His history revealed an austere childhood in an extremely poor family. He grew up without new clothes, toys, or vacations. He had few friends during his school years, although as a young man he had both a best friend and a fiancée. But then he was drafted into the army, and after several months he received a terse letter from his fiancée stating that she planned to marry his best friend. The man eventually married someone else, but his wife refused to have children, much to his disappointment.

This man felt cheated by his parents, by his country, by his best friend, by his fiancée, and by his wife. A psychodynamic therapist would focus on his presumed anger at all these people, anger he never expressed but instead turned against himself.

Contemporary opinion holds that depression has numerous causes, including biological and sociological determinants (e.g., Akiskal & McKinney, 1975). Some accounts emphasize the role of conscious thoughts in bringing about depressive disorders (e.g., Beck, 1967; Peterson & Seligman, 1984). Nevertheless, the psychodynamic idea of unexpressed hostility is still widely accepted as one of the determining factors (Lewis, 1981).

Paranoia and Homosexuality

We encountered the psychodynamic equation of paranoia and latent homosexuality in the case of Schreber. This case study has given rise to a number of related proposals. First, paranoia is a defense against unconscious homosexual impulses. Second, overt homosexuality results from a poorly resolved Oedipal conflict. Third, male homosexuality is associated with excessive castration anxiety, whereas female homosexuality is associated with excessive penis envy.

The proposals pertaining to overt homosexuality have been tested, and results have been largely equivocal for males and decidedly negative for females

(Fisher & Greenberg, 1977). Homosexual orientation may indeed result from childhood experiences, but the Oedipal script does not tell the whole story (Green, 1987).

What about paranoia? By definition, this disorder involves an unshakeable delusion of persecution. According to the psychodynamic model, paranoia is a defense against homosexual impulses, the projection of one's own unacceptable wishes onto another. So, the theoretical prediction is that male paranoids fret about other males, and female paranoids worry about the advances of other women. Actually, the evidence shows that *both* male and female paranoids fear males—not an unreasonable belief granted the more violent nature of men in our society (Lewis, 1981).

The content of paranoid delusions may include hints of homosexuality. For instance, Lehmann (1980) describes a letter written to a doctor by a paranoid patient. The patient scolds the medical staff for invading his bodily orifices, particularly his anus. They use secret machines that interfere with all of his organs: "I am at a loss to understand why those who are responsible are permitted to indulge in this peculiar pastime" (p. 1169). Along these same lines, I once worked with a paranoid patient who would walk up to me several times a day on the hospital ward, fix me with a stare, and announce in a loud voice, "I am *not* a faggot," as if I had made this accusation, which of course I had not. But the content of persecutory delusions is not limited to homosexual wishes; it encompasses the entire gamut of difficult-to-acknowledge impulses.

The causal role of repressed homosexuality in paranoia is no longer widely believed. However, more general psychodynamic ideas are still invoked to explain paranoid disorders. In particular, contemporary theories stress childhood events that lead to the use of the defense mechanism of projection (Walker & Brodie, 1980).

Multiple Personality

Multiple personality disorder: A psychological problem characterized by the existence within the same individual of altogether different personalities.

One of the most exotic of the psychological problems is **multiple personality disorder:** the existence within the same individual of altogether different personalities. These different personalities take turns being dominant, and barriers of amnesia typically exist between or among them. One personality may quite literally be unaware of another.

At one time, this disorder was thought to be virtually extinct, but in recent years new cases have been described and old cases have been reexamined (Rosenzweig, 1988). We are still far from understanding the causes of multiple personality disorder, but some intriguing hints are available.

Eugene Bliss (1980) interviewed a number of individuals diagnosed with multiple personality disorder and found the following common factors in their early histories:

- skill at self-hypnosis
- the creation of an imaginary playmate when between the ages of four and six
- the use of the imaginary playmate to defend against stress

These characteristics may well be the raw ingredients for this unusual disorder. Consider someone who responds to stress by creating an imaginary other to bear his or her burden. If this process is repeated often enough and done in a self-induced hypnotic state, the imaginary other may eventually become a personality in his or her own right.

Recent research documents physical or sexual abuse during childhood for as many as 97 percent of the individuals with multiple personality disorder (e.g., Putnam, Guroff, Silberman, Barban, & Post, 1986). This figure should be emphasized. Virtually no other finding in psychology is this robust. In Chapter 4, we discussed Freud's early hypothesis that sexual abuse during childhood played a role in later neuroses. He abandoned this theory, but these findings imply that sexual abuse deserves serious mention in *any* theory of psychopathology (cf. Browne & Finkelhor, 1986).

Drug Use and Abuse

In *Civilization and Its Discontents,* Freud (1930) describes alcoholism and drug addiction as slow suicide: manifestations of the death instinct. At a descriptive level, Freud is right. The toll that drug abuse—particularly alcoholism—takes on physical health is almost incalculable (Vaillant, 1983). But as a statement about the primary cause of drug abuse, Freud's hypothesis is unreasonable. Individuals start to drink or use drugs as the result of social and cultural factors. They continue to use drugs because of the biological phenomenon of addiction. A death instinct is superfluous to all of this. The persons may end up dead whether they wish to return to nothingness or not.

Among the consequences of drug use is an alteration in consciousness that some find enjoyable, though most explanations of drug use overlook this fact (Becker, 1953). Psychodynamic theory explains why drug use is sometimes enjoyable. Drug use puts secondary process on hold, gives the superego the night off, and opens a door—if only briefly—into a world where experiences and wishes seem to meld together.

Two other psychodynamic ideas about drug abuse warrant mention. First, theory links the potential to abuse drugs to childhood events, in particular to disturbances in the oral stage of development. For instance, alcoholics turn to the bottle as a substitute for Mother's breast. In keeping with their oral character type, they are passive and dependent. But research support for these possibilities is mostly negative (Fisher & Greenberg, 1977; Kline, 1972, Vaillant, 1983). If anything, dependency and passivity follow alcohol abuse rather than precede it.

Second, theory interprets the choice of a particular drug to abuse in symbolic terms: a representation of the underlying conflict giving rise to the abuse (Kernberg, 1975). As already seen, psychodynamic theory says that alcohol users react to dependency needs. Similarly, heroin users attempt to control an otherwise overwhelming environment. But little support for this neat explanation arises, and it cannot explain why many drug users are quite ecumenical in their chosen substances (Clayton, 1986).

Does the psychodynamic interpretation of drug use contain anything useful? On a general level, it is reasonable, because one must consider the significance of a drug to the person who abuses it. But although the causes of drug abuse are not found solely in physiology (Vaillant, 1983), the particular meanings assigned by psychodynamic theory are not generally accepted.

Evaluation

The influence of psychodynamic thought on our understanding of abnormal behavior cannot be overestimated. Almost all mental-health professionals accept certain psychodynamic notions as truisms: the role of unconscious conflicts, the use of defense mechanisms, the importance of childhood events, the coherence of symptoms and life-style. With respect to given types of abnormality, specific interpretations may or may not be popular today.

"So, Mr. Fenton . . . Let's begin with your mother."

SOURCE: "The Far Side" cartoon by Gary Larson is reproduced by permission of Chronicle Features, San Francisco.

Let me raise a question about the way psychodynamic theory views psychopathology. You may have raised a similar one while reading this section. Granted that similar conflicts precede a variety of different problems, what determines the exact symptoms a person develops? In response to the Oedipus complex, why did Schreber become psychotic but Dora hysteric? Psychodynamic theorists answer this question partly by positing constitutional weaknesses that predispose particular symptoms. But this is post hoc and circular, since we can know the weakness only by seeing the symptoms.

Psychodynamic theorists also answer this question by linking personality makeup to psychopathology. People with certain personality characteristics are at risk for analogous psychopathologies. For instance, obsessive characters develop obsessive-compulsive disorders. This is a compelling hypothesis, but research support is decidedly negative (Rosenhan & Seligman, 1989). So the question of symptom-choice remains important yet unresolved.

PSYCHOTHERAPY: RESOLVING UNCONSCIOUS CONFLICTS

In recent years, psychoanalytic therapy has become the favorite whipping boy of just about everybody. Close examination of its effectiveness has not been able to show that it works in the sense, say, that penicillin works or that relaxation training works. This criticism is important, and I will return to it later. However, concern with the effectiveness of psychoanalysis obscures some important ideas about this approach to alleviating human suffering.

First, psychoanalysis was regarded by Freud as a research technique, a way to investigate the unconscious. Freud and his followers sometimes claimed that it cured neuroses, but the fact remains that *psychoanalysis did not originate as a way of doing psychotherapy.*

Second, Freud himself was pessimistic that psychopathology could be changed much, that people could be liberated from unhappy life-styles that originated in early childhood. Is it fair, then, to criticize psychoanalytic therapy for failing to do what it regards as all but impossible?

Third, regardless of these disclaimers, and regardless of the lack of evidence about its effectiveness, psychoanalytic therapy has shaped the format of almost all contemporary psychotherapies, including those of demonstrated success. Other systems of therapy borrow psychoanalytic techniques and concepts extensively. In particular, consideration of the relationship between client and therapist occurs in all types of therapy, even behavior modification, and ranks as the outstanding contribution of psychoanalysis to clinical practice.

Conception of Cure

My intention is not to evaluate psychoanalytic therapy so much as to document its impact on how contemporary mental-health practitioners go about their business. One such impact is on how *cure* is regarded. Psychoanalysts move beyond circular definitions of health and illness that point to the absence of one to define the other, and vice versa.

Instead, psychoanalysis regards cure as the freeing of psychic energy from symptoms for use in working and raising a family. It is obvious that this embodies a value judgment, but attempts at value-free conceptions of health have always failed (Vaillant, 1977). Psychoanalytic theory takes the stance that it is better to do some things than others, and abnormality results when one is unable to pursue those activities deemed worthy. To be cured is to be no longer impaired.

At the same time, psychoanalysis does not regard cure as simply the alleviation of symptoms or the creation of occupational and social success. A businesswoman may gain continual promotions and be loved by her husband, but this need not mean that her ego has struck a healthy balance between the demands of the id and the superego. If she works at her profession 24 hours a day, if she drives without mercy people under her, if she regards success as the only possible outcome, then she is not healthy.

Instead, individuals become healthy by solving their unconscious conflicts. Their symptoms are thereby relieved, and their problems in living dissipate. Attention to underlying conflicts is the hallmark of the psychoanalytic conception of cure and has become popular among therapists of almost all theoretical persuasions.

Psychoanalytic Techniques

In *Principles of Psychoanalytic Psychotherapy,* Lester Luborsky (1984) describes three active ingredients in psychoanalysis. The first is self-understanding: The patient reaches insight regarding unconscious conflicts and their nature. A variety of expressive techniques are used to bring about self-understanding: free association, dream interpretation, and analysis of transference, for example. These techniques provide insights into the patient's unconscious and thus require the psychoanalyst to be a skillful listener.

Resistance: The unwillingness of a client to comply with therapy.

Accompanying each step toward insight is **resistance** on the part of the patient. Regardless of the patient's sincere intentions to solve his problems, considerable inertia exists:

> The patient pauses abruptly, corrects himself, makes a slip of the tongue, stammers, remains silent, fidgets with some part of his clothing, asks irrelevant questions, intellectualizes, arrives late for appointments, finds excuses for not keeping them, offers critical evaluations of the rationale underlying the treatment method, simply cannot think of anything to say, or censors thoughts that do occur to him and decides that they are banal, uninteresting, or irrelevant and not worth mentioning. (Meissner, 1980, p. 722)

Helping alliance: A relationship between a therapist and his or her client where both work to solve the client's problems.

Patients do not relinquish their neuroses easily, and resistance is an excellent defense against health.

The second important factor in psychoanalysis is the creation of a **helping alliance:** the patient's experience of the therapist and the therapy as useful. Ego psychology has contributed this idea to psychoanalysis, a reminder that therapy is the collaboration between two real people with real personalities that go beyond projected and imagined characteristics (Meissner, 1980). The patient and the therapist rely on the therapeutic alliance to weather the difficulties encountered in the course of therapy.

A good therapeutic relationship is determined in part by the personality characteristics the patient and the therapist bring to therapy. Additionally, therapists can make use of various supportive techniques. They allow patients to set their own goals in therapy. They convey understanding and acceptance of their patients. They are realistically hopeful. And so on. Luborsky (1984) regards the helping alliance as the most critical component of psychoanalytic therapy, even though self-understanding has received more attention over the years.

The third curative factor in psychoanalysis is the incorporation of gains occurring in the course of therapy. Backsliding is common in all forms of therapy. "Revolving door psychiatry" expresses the typical difficulty in helping patients maintain improvements brought about in therapy. How do you keep them out of therapy once it has finished? Luborsky (1984) suggests that the patient and therapist explicitly address the meaning of therapy termination. Patients may be anxious at the prospect of severing the therapeutic alliance and may react with a resurgence of symptoms.

Again, specific psychoanalytic techniques are deployed to handle this problem. When therapy ends, therapists frame it in terms of their clients attaining their goals, not as rejection. This leads to discussion of how clients felt about previous separations in their lives. And therapists encourage follow-up appointments.

Luborsky's (1984) depiction of psychoanalytic therapy moves beyond the stereotypes held by most of us: A bearded therapist tossing out obscure interpretations that have miraculous effects on the patient is a caricature of psychoanalysis. If only cures were so easy! Psychotherapy is not a one-liner, and no practicing analyst ever claimed it was. Insight is only one ingredient, and it is established slowly. Without a therapeutic alliance to overcome resistance and incorporate gains, insight is useless.

The therapy techniques I've described have also been assimilated by other schools of clinical psychology. Even therapists who have no use for the larger picture of psychoanalytic theory speak of insight, transference, the helping alliance, resistance, and termination anxiety. To repeat, the impact of psychoanalysis on psychotherapy in general has indeed been profound.

Therapy Effectiveness

I've already mentioned the belief among many that psychoanalytic therapy is not effective. In 1952, Hans Eysenck leveled one of the most serious criticisms against psychoanalysis. He claimed that 70 percent of individuals suffering from the sorts of problems psychoanalysts treat get better without treatment. They show what is called **spontaneous remission,** like when your sore throat goes away without you doing anything about it. Eysenck further claimed that the effectiveness rate of psychoanalytic therapy was less than 70 percent.

Spontaneous remission: Cure or recovery without professional treatment.

According to Eysenck (1952a), we now know what is worse than nothing: psychoanalytic treatment. Needless to say, the psychoanalytic community protested (e.g., Rosenzweig, 1954). Eysenck's figures have been challenged, along with his operationalization of therapeutic cure. Apparently, he failed to use the same criteria in judging spontaneous remission versus psychoanalytic cure.

Nevertheless, the fact that Eysenck overstated his criticism does not mean psychoanalytic therapy is effective. In a review of the research literature, Kline (1984) reports that he was unable to find a single investigation of the effectiveness of psychoanalytic therapy that was methodologically sound. This is still the case. So we are left without a firm answer to the question about the effectiveness of psychoanalysis.

Recent Developments in Psychoanalytic Therapy

Some psychoanalysts prefer to practice therapy the way Freud did. (It is somewhat difficult to pin down exactly what Freud did; some reports reveal him as a highly unorthodox "psychoanalytic" therapist, at least as we have come to understand the term; Roazen, 1975). But other analysts have followed the spirit of Freud's example while changing psychoanalysis in response to the times.

Luborsky (1984) describes three contemporary variants of psychoanalytic therapy. The first sets a time limit on the duration of therapy. Traditional analysis is open-ended. It has no time limit, and it may go on for years. In contrast, *time-limited psychoanalysis* sets an upper limit, usually 25 sessions. As a result, it is more organized and focused than open-ended therapy.

A second variant is family or group therapy conducted from a psychodynamic perspective. Here the therapist has a great deal of information available about how patients deal with each other. The therapeutic alliance is established not just between the patient and the therapist, but also between the patient and the group.

Finally, some analysts use medication in conjunction with conventional therapy techniques. In recent years, breakthroughs have occurred in the pharmacological treatment of anxiety and depression. However, Luborsky (1984) cautions against the overreliance on medication, which may mask symptoms, work against insight, and substitute for the therapeutic alliance. If medication is used, the patient and therapist should discuss its meaning in the context of therapy. What does it do? What does it not do? Some evidence suggests that medication plus psychotherapy is more effective than either alone, so I suspect this variant will become even more popular in the future.

PSYCHOSOMATIC MEDICINE: ILLNESS AS CONFLICT

As already discussed, Freud turned from treatment of individuals with neurological disorders to treatment of hysterics early in his career. However, one of the important applications of psychoanalysis goes back to the domain of physical disease and illness. It has been recognized for centuries that the mind can affect the functioning of the body, but psychoanalysis provides a specific account of how this might take place.

A **psychosomatic disorder** is defined as an organic pathology (that is, a physical problem) preceded by meaningful environmental stimuli (that is, mental representation). **Psychosomatic medicine** is the field that explains and treats these disorders. Freud's insight that hysteria involves unconscious conflict marked the beginning of the modern era in psychosomatic medicine. Although his work led to the conclusion that the hysterical symptoms did not represent actual physical dysfunction, it legitimized the attempts of subsequent workers to examine the possible relationship between psychological factors and physical illness.

The most famous of the psychosomatic pioneers is Franz Alexander (1939, 1950), who used psychoanalytic terms to explain someone's susceptibility to illness. He distinguishes between somatoform disorders like hysteria and psychosomatic disorders like peptic ulcers. Although both are responses to psychological events, conversion disorders are the symbolic expression of an emotion, whereas psychosomatic disorders are the physiological response to an emotion. In and of themselves, they convey no meaning and serve no purpose. To say it another way, Alexander distinguished conversion disorders from psychosomatic disorders by proposing the role of the voluntary nervous system in the former versus that of the involuntary nervous system in the latter.

The involuntary nervous system is involved in turning on and off the flight-or-fight response we have to danger. Our body's resources mobilize in response to an emergency: Our skin turns pale; our heart beats faster; our breathing becomes more rapid; our digestive process slows. When danger passes, these changes are reversed. According to Alexander, some people show chronic excitation of the emergency response. They are at risk for such illnesses as hypertension. Other people show chronic inhibition of the emergency response, and they are at risk for disorders like peptic ulcer.

Psychological factors enter into this process by dictating a person's chronic emotional state. A person who is hostile and competitive is always expecting combat and may develop hypertension. A person who is passive and dependent is always ready to be fed and may develop an ulcer.

Alexander theorizes about a number of psychosomatic disorders. Two of these have just been mentioned: hypertension and peptic ulcer. The other illnesses he discusses are asthma (linked to fear of being separated from Mother), arthritis (attributed to inhibition of hostility), colitis (produced by the inability to fulfill obligations), acne (traced to guilt over exhibitionism), and hyperthyroidism (linked to psychic trauma, like the loss of a mother during childhood).

What is Alexander's evidence for linking these illnesses to the chronic experience of particular emotions and hence to particular personality types? Some case studies provide startling confirmation. For example, Alexander (1950) described a young woman who experienced diarrhea when confronted with a financial obligation. Before she had married, her husband had loaned her money, which she had yet to repay. Whenever he teased her about this, she immediately had an attack of diarrhea.

Until her therapist pointed it out to her, the woman was unaware of the connection between her symptoms and the conflict she experienced surrounding her financial debt to her husband. But psychodynamic theorists have long equated money and feces, proposing that the symbolism originates in events surrounding the anal stage of psychosexual development. One hoards money as one retains feces; one spends money as one expels feces. Presumably, the young woman "paid off" her husband with diarrhea because she did not have the cash available.

Alexander also made an interesting observation about the preponderance of high blood pressure among black Americans. He attributed this finding to the inferior position relegated to blacks in our society. Blacks consequently need to maintain extraordinary self-control in the face of the associated indignities. Self-control is not achieved without a cost, and hypertension may represent the debit.

Grace and Graham (1952) investigated a more modest version of Alexander's psychosomatic theory. Rather than look for predispositions to illness within general personality characteristics established early in life, they ascertained the specific attitudes held at the time a given symptom appeared. They interviewed patients about how they felt and what they wanted to do at the time they experienced a particular symptom. Interviews with 128 patients suffering from 12 different symptoms/illnesses revealed striking similarities within symptom classes.

Here is a summary of the attitudes Grace and Graham identified. I've paraphrased a typical statement for each symptom from among the several quoted by these researchers.

1. *Urticaria* Patients suffering from this allergic reaction of the skin felt mistreated yet did not retaliate. A typical statement was, "They walked all over me, and I took it."
2. *Eczema* In this case, patients felt that other people were interfering with their activities. They felt frustrated. "My mother will not let me lead my own life."
3. *Cold hands* Patients with cold hands did not have "warm hearts" so much as an attitude that they should undertake some course of action without knowing quite what it was. "Somebody really should have done something."
4. *Vasomotor rhinitis* Nasal irritation was suffered by patients who wished to throw off responsibility for what was occurring. A typical statement was "I wish they'd go away."
5. *Asthma* Grace and Graham reported that patients with asthma expressed the same attitude as those with rhinitis, presumably to a much greater degree. "I really wish they'd go away."
6. *Diarrhea* Patients with diarrhea wanted to be done with some situation, to get it over with. "I wish final exams would end."

7. *Constipation* This symptom was associated with an attitude of grim determination to carry on in the face of insurmountable odds. "I'll do it even though it won't work."
8. *Nausea and vomiting* These patients reported thinking of an event they regretted. "I wish that had never happened" was a typical statement.
9. *Duodenal ulcer* Attacks of pain occurred with thoughts of revenge. "I'm going to get even with that son of a bitch if it kills me!"
10. *Migraine headache* Migraines followed the cessation of intense effort, whether or not it resulted in a successful outcome. "I had to get it there overnight."
11. *Arterial hypertension* Patients with this symptom felt under pressure from all sides. "Everyone depends on me; this place would fall apart if I were to leave."
12. *Low back pain* Such backaches occurred when patients wanted to carry out some activity involving the entire body, like walking or running away. "I wanted to walk out of the office and never go back."

What are we to make of these findings? On the one hand, they support the psychosomatic premise that psychological states can lead to particular symptoms. On the other hand, they have the typical weaknesses of case studies. The role of interviewer bias is highly possible. Grace and Graham (1952) claimed that the correlations they obtained between symptoms and attitudes were perfect. This is so high it is suspicious.

Further, the direction of causality is unclear. Diarrhea might result in the desire to be done with something (the attack of diarrhea), constipation in the determination to continue with something (attempts to move one's bowels), nausea with regret (about the retching), and so on. A better demonstration of the point would have been to show that attitudes precede symptoms.

As for the details of Alexander's theories, research finds most of them lacking. His elegant formulas linking specific diseases to specific conflicts are no longer accepted by contemporary workers (Weiner, 1977). So, while Alexander is honored as the first to link conflict to disease, current thinking sees this association as nonspecific (Friedman & Booth-Kewley, 1987). Instead, general states of helplessness and hopelessness are emphasized as bringing about a variety of illnesses (Engel, 1971). Also, conflicts are no longer located solely within the person, but are seen as involving stressful events in the immediate environment (Holmes & Rahe, 1967).

Interestingly, though, some recent research does support one of the important implications of psychodynamic theorizing about illness. One year after the event, psychologist James Pennebaker and his colleagues interviewed the spouses of individuals who had died by suicide or accident. The more frequently the research subjects had discussed their spouse's death with others, the less they ruminated about it and the fewer health problems they themselves experienced (Pennebaker & O'Heeron, 1984). Said another way, unburdening oneself to another person—a key ingredient of the talking cure developed a century ago by Breuer and Anna O.—is physically healthy.

In a follow-up study, Pennebaker, Hughes, and O'Heeron (1987) found that confiding in other people had measurable physiological effects that may produce benefits. In this line of work, we have documentation of Alexander's hypothesized links between conflict and illness. Furthermore, we see that one possible strategy for promoting someone's health is by encouraging her or him to cultivate supportive relationships with others.

The question of which diseases develop in response to stress remains pertinent and explains the renewed interest in recent years to link specific diseases to specific personalities. The **Type A coronary-prone behavior pattern** is the best known of these contemporary formulations (Jenkins, Rosenman, & Zyzanski, 1974). The Type A individual is time-urgent (living from deadline to deadline), competitive, ambitious, aggressive, and hostile. The Type A individual is also at risk for heart disease (Matthews, 1982). Some research suggests that this personality style predicts recurrent heart disease better than cholesterol and cigarette smoking (e.g., Jenkins, Zyzanski, & Rosenman, 1976).

It appears as if the hostility of the Type A individual is the active ingredient vis-a-vis the onset of heart disease (Barefoot, Dahlstrom, & Williams, 1983). This gives psychologists a specific target for change, so we are seeing attempts to help the Type A person learn to meet challenges with relaxation rather than a no-holds-barred attack (Levenkron, Cohen, Mueller, & Fisher, 1983). The hope is that if such individuals change their ways, they will thereby reduce their risks for heart disease.

Let me sum up this section by pointing out that modern psychosomatic medicine has incorporated the general formula of theorists like Alexander, linking conflict to susceptibility to disease. However, specific psychodynamic hypotheses are no longer taken seriously. Health psychology and behavioral medicine thrive in contemporary psychology. Although psychologists often apply the theories of other paradigms, students should appreciate that their roots lie in the psychodynamic paradigm.

Type A coronary-prone behavior pattern: A behavioral style characterized by incessant striving, time urgency, and hostility, believed to put someone at risk for heart disease.

CHILD-REARING

Because of its emphasis on early childhood, psychodynamic theory has greatly influenced the way we treat children in our society. Once psychodynamic ideas became generally known, parents and teachers grew determined not to raise contemporary versions of Anna O., the Rat Man, or Schreber. Their intentions led to changes in both child-rearing and educational practices.

Paramount among these changes was the desire to avoid frustrating the child. No frustration—no conflict . . . no conflict—no pathology. This formula oversimplifies psychodynamic theory almost to the point of contradicting it. Remember that overindulgence is just as damaging to personality development as is harsh discipline, but this was overlooked by many individuals who thought they were applying "scientific" ideas to cultivate happy children.

In this section, I will describe the views of two individuals who explicitly applied psychodynamic ideas to child-rearing. Benjamin Spock packaged psychodynamic notions in his book, *Baby and Child Care,* and made it one of the best-selling books ever. And A. S. Neill used psychodynamic ideas to create Summerhill, the prototype of experimental education.

In Search of Dr. Spock

To appreciate the impact of the "baby doctor," you have to understand that methods of child-rearing have changed dramatically over the years. His message fell on ears accustomed to quite different advice about how to treat children. Let me describe some of the earlier approaches to raising kids.

For an extreme example, consider this excerpt from the 1839 *Book of Health* written by the father of Daniel Paul Schreber, whom we met in Chapter 4:

> Crying and whimpering without reason express nothing but a whim, a mood, and the first emergence of stubbornness; they must be dealt with positively, through quick distraction of attention, serious words . . . or if all this be to no avail, through the administration of comparatively mild, intermittently repeated, corporeal punishments. . . . From then on one glance, one word, one single menacing gesture are sufficient to rule the child.
>
> This is also the best time to train the child in the art of renouncing. The mode of training here recommended is simple and effective: While the child sits in the lap of its nurse or nanny, the latter eats and drinks whatever she desires: however intense the child's oral needs may become under such circumstances, they must never be gratified. Not a morsel of food must be given the child besides its regular three meals a day. (Niederland, 1959, pp. 387–388)

Can you apply the theory of psychosexual development to the child raised in this way? Do you see why personality fixation is apt to result?

In the United States during the early part of the twentieth century, discipline was stressed. Parents were advised not to handle their babies under the assumption that handling would deprive the babies of their strength! Toilet training was to be initiated by the third month or earlier. (If you're not a parent, realize that modern kids are toilet trained at 14 months or later.) Behaviorist John Watson echoed such advice in his influential books on child-rearing: children should not be coddled or cuddled by their parents.

Against this trend of advice, Freud's ideas were revolutionary indeed. Freud held that harshness, restriction, and coercion harmed the emotional growth of the child and would show up later in severe disturbances in personality. In *Baby and Child Care,* first published in 1946, Dr. Spock drew liberally on Freud's theories as well as those of the philosopher and educator John Dewey. Note his comments in an interview:

"Freud was much too smart to get involved with child-rearing himself," Spock laughed. "Freud's philosophy was embodied in the idea that too much repression of sex and hostility created neuroses later in life. It was important to be loved by parents, rather than taught to fear." (*Newsweek,* 1968, p. 71)

Spock preached a message of flexibility and relaxation. In his own words, he attempted to take the "Thou Shalt Nots" out of raising children. He reassured new parents that they knew more than they thought.

Did Spock advocate permissiveness? Yes and no. On the one hand, his advice was permissive in comparison to immediately preceding dictates on child-rearing. Kids need not be fed on a rigid schedule, but only when they are hungry. Toilet training should not start until the child is ready. Learning occurs through exploration—not punishment. Above all, parents must express their love for the child. On the other hand, some parents followed Spock's relaxed advice to an extreme, becoming submissive to their children's demands at every juncture.

In the 1960s and 1970s, during the era of campus revolts and radical activities among young adults, Dr. Spock and his advice were blamed for producing an entire generation with no respect for authority. This perception was aided by the fact that Spock was an outspoken opponent of the Vietnam War and an unsuccessful presidential candidate in 1972 on the ticket of the radical People's Party (Viorst, 1972).

By the logic of this chapter, the thread of responsibility might thus extend beyond Spock to the turn of the century and the psychoanalytic ideas of Sigmund Freud. Definitive support for such a link is of course impossible, and the idea of Zeitgeist cautions us not to overattribute responsibility for society-wide changes to the activities of particular individuals. Still, if psychodynamic ideas about child-rearing did not directly bring about these social changes, they certainly accompanied the factors that did.

Through the many editions of his book, Spock has followed social change as much as he may have created it (Kellogg, 1976). In recent versions of *Baby and Child Care,* he has banished sexist pronouns and advises that the father should share equally in the mundane tasks of raising kids. Pictures of black parents and children have been added. New chapters address working mothers, day-care, drug use, hyperactivity, natural childbirth, and other topics of contemporary concern. Spock belatedly acknowledged the collaboration of his wife in creating the original book during the 1940s.

But regardless of these changes, two themes remain constant in Spock's advice. Coercion and harsh discipline have no place in the raising of children. Love and support must be abundant. The environment can thwart or facilitate development, but the motivating force lies within the developing child.

In an article on education, Spock (1984) once again stressed these themes. Responding to the National Commission on Excellence in Education report calling for more homework, longer school days, and longer school years, he sarcastically labeled it "A Plea for More Coercion in the Schools." He went on to say that schools are ineffective to the degree that they already coerce students. More of the same will not bring about excellent education.

Here's what Spock said about grading. Please don't throw these ideas in your teacher's face! Spock refers to the entire system of grading, not simply personality psychology grades assigned at the end of this particular school term. However, it might be productive to discuss in class the underlying model of human nature assumed by different strategies of assigning grades.

> I believe that grading is an abomination, misdirecting student efforts into memorizing for recitations and tests, and misleading teachers into thinking that the grades they give represent something gained from the course. What grades do measure, I would say, is the ability to memorize, freedom from learning disabilities, and conformity in thinking, which is not a valuable trait, to my mind. (1984, p. 29)

You can see once more the assumption that students are inherently motivated to learn, that excessive discipline can thwart this tendency toward growth.

Spock recommended that schools cultivate such personality traits as creativity, originality, initiative, and responsibility. Several ingredients are needed for this to occur. First, children must identify with teachers worthy of love and respect. Second, children must make school lessons part of their everyday activities, through learning by doing and through encouragement by teachers. It is no coincidence that these ingredients are similar to those identified by Lester Luborsky as crucial for effective psychoanalytic therapy. Both education and therapy involve behavior change; the application of psychodynamic theory to both of them ties this behavior change to underlying feelings and emotions.

In Search of Freedom

Over the decades, psychodynamic ideas have made their way directly into education. One notable avenue has been through Summerhill, the radical school founded in 1921 in England by A. S. Neill. Students at Summerhill were allowed total freedom of choice—in work and in behavior. The school's approach was derived in large part from the explicit application of psychodynamic ideas about child-rearing.

The most important premise of Summerhill is that children can be thwarted and perverted by harsh discipline and coercion. If they are unhappy, then they will not develop in a healthy way. They will not be able to learn. As Neill (1960) explained:

> In psychology, no man knows very much. The inner forces of human life are still largely hidden from us.
>
> Since Freud's genius made it alive, psychology has gone far; but it is still a new science. . . . Years of intensive work in child training has convinced me that I know comparatively little of the forces that motivate life. I am convinced, however, that parents who have had to deal with only their own children know much less than I do.
>
> It is because I believe that a difficult child is nearly always made difficult by wrong treatment at home that I dare address parents. . . . The difficult child is the

child who is unhappy. He is at war with himself; and in consequence, he is at war with the world.

    The difficult adult is in the same boat. No happy man ever disturbed a meeting, or preached a war, or lynched a Negro. No happy woman ever nagged her husband or her children. No happy man ever committed a murder or a theft. No happy employer ever frightened his employees.

    All crimes, all hatreds, all wars can be reduced to unhappiness. . . . Summerhill [is a place] where children's unhappiness is cured and, more important, where children are reared in happiness. (pp. xxiii–xxiv)

Summerhill began by renouncing discipline, direction, suggestion, moral training, and religious instruction. What took their place was what the child brought to the school: a nature that would develop to its potential if left alone. Courses were offered, but children were not required to attend. Examinations were given, but only as fun. Rigid distinctions between teachers and students were never defined.

Neill was greatly influenced by Wilhelm Reich, a onetime Freudian who melded psychodynamic ideas with Marxist politics. Among Reich's most important contributions to psychodynamic thought is the concept of *character armor:* the manifestation of conflict in a person's posture. The person may wear his problems like armor. A rigid and inflexible character shows in rigid and inflexible movements.

Reich is also known for his radical ideas about sex. Years before William Masters and Virginia Johnson became famous, Wilhelm Reich conducted sex therapy, under the assumption that people's sexuality had become so repressed by society that they no longer knew how to have pleasure. So he taught them. He dubbed his version of libido *orgone,* the energy of the orgasm, and regarded it as a tangible reality. Reich built a device to retrieve orgone from the sky and was eventually imprisoned in Pennsylvania for claiming that his orgone accumulator could regulate weather and cure cancer. Despite the bizarre nature of Reich's later theories, he was a profound thinker. His notions about emotional expression and freedom directly foreshadowed the human potential movement and provided an impetus for the sexual revolution.

At any rate, Reich and Neill were friends and they frequently discussed Summerhill. Neill was so impressed with Reich's warnings of the dire consequences of sexual repression that he came to advocate total honesty in sexual matters.

> The Summerhill pupils . . . appeared to have none of the normal inhibitions; they shared the same bathrooms, they would occasionally bathe in the nude, they used sexual swear-words freely, there was no censorship of their reading. They would fall in love. . . . There was no supervision of the students to keep them out of each other's beds. (Hemmings, 1972, pp. 122–123)

At the same time, Neill did not go out of his way to facilitate sex among his students, despite Reich's urgings that he do so. Contraceptives were not made available to Summerhill students. Neill feared—no doubt correctly—that his school would be closed down if he took such steps. Interestingly, not a single pregnancy occurred among Summerhill students in the 30-some years the school existed (Hemmings, 1972).

Neill was aware that his school existed within a larger society that was at odds with its principles of freedom. Children who came to Summerhill were inevitably products of repressive child-rearing, and despite the freedom of Summerhill, their early experiences left a residue. At best, the child with such a beginning could become semi-free. In contrast, a child reared with freedom from the beginning could become truly free.

Neill and his wife raised their only child, Zoe, with this goal. The only restriction placed on her was that she wear clothes when it was bitterly cold. Otherwise, she made her own decisions. She ate when and what she wanted. She acquired sphincter and bladder control on her own (much later than "normal" children). By reports, Zoe was happy and healthy, intelligent and friendly.

Zoe may be a special case. We know that we cannot generalize too far from single instances, no matter how compelling. Did the approach of Summerhill work for other children? This of course is a loaded question, because the criterion of "working" varies with one's value system. Neill regarded Summerhill as a success because it allowed children to live their own lives. Did it prepare children for the best universities? Did they win admission to law or medical school? Did they make a lot of money? Neill dismissed these criteria as irrelevant if they aren't goals freely chosen by individuals:

> You cannot *make* children learn music or anything else without to some degree converting them . . . into accepters of the *status quo*—a good thing for a society that needs obedient sitters at dreary desks, standers in shops, mechanical catchers of the 8:30 suburban train—a society, in short, that is carried on the shabby shoulders of the scared little man—the scared-to-death conformist. (Neill, 1960, p. 12)

In the battle between the individual and society, Summerhill championed the individual.

Do you think this is all pretty farfetched? Maybe it is, in the sense that few of you attend a school as permissive as Summerhill. On the other hand, consider pass-fail courses, independent studies, self-designed majors, and field placements. These are now standard curriculum components at most schools. They reflect the Summerhill philosophy and stem from the application of psychodynamic theory to education. Maybe Neill's ideas are not so farfetched after all.

PSYCHOHISTORY: PSYCHOANALYZING HISTORICAL FIGURES

Psychohistory is sometimes defined as the application of psychodynamic ideas to the understanding of historical figures and events (Friedlander, 1978). Although contemporary psychohistorians partake of additional psychological

Psychohistory: The use of psychological theories, usually psychodynamic in nature, to understand historical figures and events.

perspectives, the psychodynamic roots of the field are unmistakable (Runyan, 1988). Psychodynamic theory is well-suited to the analysis of historical material, particularly the roles played by individuals.

Psychohistories have been written from a psychodynamic view about Napoleon, Abraham Lincoln, Houdini, Socrates, Margaret Fuller, Isaac Newton, Emily Dickinson, Beethoven, Leon Trotsky, Benjamin Franklin, Bertrand Russell, Anne Hutchinson, Henry Kissinger, and—of course—Sigmund Freud himself (Anderson, 1978; Crosby & Crosby, 1981; Runyan, 1982). As previously noted, Freud pioneered this application of psychodynamic theory in his examinations of Leonardo da Vinci, Moses, and Fyodor Dostoyevski. Erik Erikson contributed to the development of the field by his psychohistorical studies of such individuals as Martin Luther, Thomas Jefferson, and Mahatma Gandhi.

Psychohistory remains a controversial endeavor. Terry Anderson (1978) describes the three major reactions to psychohistories as praise, neglect, or disdain and concludes that until quite recently, the latter two reactions were by far the most common. When Erik Erikson (1958) first published *Young Man Luther,* it was not even reviewed in history journals. Still, psychohistory shows no sign of going away, and scholars in and out of the field are taking increased note of it.

Although no overall agreement regarding the worth of psychohistory has emerged, there is consensus about its strengths and weaknesses. Let me summarize these for you. What are the advantages of psychohistory? To begin with, all historical analysis makes use of psychological assumptions at least implicitly; psychohistory makes these assumptions clear. History is not simply a chronicle of facts. The historian attempts to tie these facts together into a coherent whole. Psychodynamic theory may help do so by suggesting the motives of historical figures and linking them to prior events.

Because historical material is analogous to clinical material, psychodynamic theory allows it to be sifted for significance. It helps historians choose exactly where to look for motives. They pay attention to childhood events and relationships with parents. They place great emphasis on Oedipal dynamics.

Further, psychodynamic theory is one of the few approaches to history that recognizes and explains the historian's emotional reaction to the historical figure about whom he or she writes. This reaction is akin to the response of a therapist to a patient. In historical analysis as well as psychotherapy, these reactions must be worked through for an unfettered interpretation.

Finally, from its beginning, psychodynamic theory has grappled with the analysis of the single case. What can be concluded from the investigation of one life? What are the limitations of this approach? The strengths and weaknesses of case studies are well recognized within the psychodynamic paradigm, and the psychohistorian brings this sensitivity to a historical study.

Despite these reasons for expecting psychohistory to be viable, problems arise with the approach. Some of these are inherent difficulties. Others involve the way psychohistories have sometimes been conducted. As with our examination of case studies, we must distinguish the in-principle flaws of psychohistory from those brought about by sloppy execution.

Adolf Hitler has been the subject of several psychohistorical studies, yet very little is known about his childhood.

What are the difficulties that go with the territory, regardless of the care taken by the psychohistorian? First, the available research material is usually not of great interest to psychodynamic theory. Access to dreams is usually lacking, and often little evidence about a historical figure's childhood exists. Who would know that Junior would grow up to be a mover and a shaker of world history? Three of the most important people in the twentieth century—Adolf Hitler, Richard Nixon, and Mao Zedong—led childhoods that we know almost nothing about (Crosby & Crosby, 1981). Relatedly, a psychohistorian hardly ever interviews a subject face-to-face. Usually these subjects are dead, or if living, they do not submit to such an examination.

Second, the psychohistorian often studies an individual from another time and place. If that individual's behaviors are pulled from their cultural context, unwitting misinterpretation occurs. I've read about a psychohistorical analysis of Gandhi that placed great emphasis on his supposedly feminine characteristics, in particular his weaving. This "fact" is not at all striking if Gandhi's life is placed in the culture of India, where it of course belongs. In that context, weaving is not feminine in the same sense that knitting might be in contemporary America. Psychohistory proceeds best when the psychohistorian has a full appreciation of the subject's social world. When Erik Erikson discussed Hitler in *Childhood and Society,* he drew on his own experiences growing up in Germany in the first third of this century (Loewenberg, 1983).

Third, because of psychohistory's focus on the individual historical figure, the typical psychohistorian is often accused of reductionism. Attention to the roles of particular people with particular motives precludes the examination of the social and economic causes of historical events. Remember the ideas of Zeitgeist and Ortgeist? They pertain to historical as well as scientific change. Indeed, social psychologists argue persuasively against what is known as the great man (or woman) theory of leadership, the notion that a leader's influence resides in particular personality characteristics. Social factors are emphasized instead, which have nothing to do with an individual personality.

By extrapolation, this argument cautions the psychohistorian against reducing the course of history to the personalities of its players. Psychohistorical examinations of Hitler often emphasize the fact that his beloved mother Klara died of breast cancer despite the efforts of the family doctor, Eduard Bloch—a Jew (Crosby & Crosby, 1981). Although this incident was no doubt important to the young Adolf, to regard it as a primary determinant of his later anti-Semitism is to overlook the centuries-old reality of German prejudice.

Fourth, in keeping with the basic premise of psychodynamic theory, psychohistorians emphasize unconscious determinants of behavior. However, as I've already described, this is exactly the area where the historian has the least information. Accordingly, explanations via unconscious motivation strike many people as forced. For example, the Third Reich's military defeats have been attributed by some to Hitler's unconscious desires for self-punishment, but this is to ignore a host of more observable factors, like the bitterly cold winters in Russia (Crosby & Crosby, 1981).

Fifth, psychohistory is only as plausible as its foundation. As you saw in Chapter 5, psychodynamic theory cannot be regarded as simply right or wrong. Parts of it are reasonable and other parts are not. Psychohistory applies all of psychodynamic theory—a risky approach. In particular, it is dubious to transpose the emphasis on repressed sexuality to other times and places.

So much for the inherent difficulties of psychohistory. They are serious problems, and they have been widely recognized by those who conduct psychohistories. However, what about the other difficulties, those resulting from sloppy scholarship? It seems the list of such problems is long as well, and they apparently have not been as widely recognized. The psychohistory reviews I have read are highly critical of most studies.

One difficulty is that psychohistorians sometimes fill in factual blanks with what psychodynamic theory expects to be there. Childhoods are reconstructed from the wispiest of facts, and not surprisingly, Oedipal conflicts result. Motives and feelings are attributed to historical figures because it seems plausible to posit their existence. For example, Richard Nixon's mother is said to show "repressed anger" in photographs (Abrahamsen, 1978), quite a conclusion granted the meaning of repression! Psychohistorians would be better off if they just admitted gaps in their knowledge.

Another difficulty in the way psychohistorical studies have been conducted is an illness bias. Psychohistorians frequently diagnose historical figures as suffering from one neurosis or another, relegating important events to mere symptoms. When diagnosis from afar is done with living individuals, psychohistory becomes not just unreasonable but insidious. Kissinger has been called depressive, Nixon obsessive-compulsive, and so on. When these labels are assigned by "scientific" psychohistorians, the general public will see them as formal diagnoses rather than value-laden adjectives. Contemporary psychodiagnosticians regard it as unethical to diagnose a living figure on the basis of his or her public actions.

This ethical attitude stems in part from a 1960s flap when a survey of the American Psychiatric Association's members found 1,846 psychiatrists (of 12,356 polled) willing to take a stand on Barry Goldwater's psychological fitness for the presidency. Many were further willing to give him such diagnoses as megalomaniac, paranoid, narcissistic, psychotic, anal-compulsive, and schizophrenic. Goodness! Most of us have to wait in line to have a doctor tell us what is wrong with us. Needless to say, this survey has been blasted from numerous quarters, and it is a good bet that mental health professionals will not participate in a similar poll in the near future.

A final difficulty in the way psychohistories are conducted is that the investigator may not be sophisticated at historical research. Crosby and Crosby (1981) describe numerous psychohistory examples that violate fundamental tenets of historical inquiry. Psychohistorians may rely on biased sources, consult too few sources, or select only facts that fit the argument they are mounting.

Although what I've said so far has been largely critical of psychohistory, I'll conclude this section in the same way as the discussion of case studies in Chapter 5. Collectively, psychohistorical studies can be neither dismissed nor embraced. Psychohistory has a role to play in the larger field of history if its avoidable difficulties can be handled and its unavoidable difficulties acknowledged. Psychohistorical explanation on a case-by-case basis can be evaluated as good or bad, using much the same criteria as for a case study (Runyan, 1982).

Is it logically sound? Is it comprehensible? Does it survive attempts to prove it wrong? Is it consistent with available evidence? Is it superior to alternative explanations?

In an intriguing article, William Runyan (1981) posed the question, "Why did Van Gogh cut off his ear?" This well-known historical event might seem inexplicable because it is singular and bizarre. Nevertheless, it has stimulated considerable speculation in the historical literature. Indeed, Runyan described 13 different explanations for why it happened. All embody a psychodynamic flavor. For instance, some psychohistorians have suggested that Van Gogh was frustrated because his brother Theo became engaged. Others have suggested that he was struggling with homosexual impulses toward the artist Paul Gauguin. Perhaps he was inspired by bullfights, because the matador gives the ear of a vanquished bull to his favorite lady. (Van Gogh gave his severed ear to a prostitute.) Perhaps he followed newspaper stories of the then-contemporary Jack the Ripper, who sometimes cut off the ears of his victims. And so on.

Runyan sifted through a number of explanations to brand some of them good and others bad. For instance, there is no evidence that Van Gogh knew anything about Jack the Ripper. The "fact" of Van Gogh reading newspaper stories about the Ripper is merely assumed by psychohistorians favoring this possibility. On the other hand, Van Gogh's self-punitive reaction to frustration

Why did Van Gogh cut off his ear?

is well-documented. Explanations that point to frustration are therefore reasonable.

Runyan gave us no single answer to his question, but that is the point he is trying to make. Sometimes the best psychohistory can do is to winnow numerous possibilities to a few and then acknowledge that further choices cannot be made. Psychohistory thus becomes more eclectic and more tentative (McAdams, 1988). Perhaps it is also less sensational, but that is the price to be paid.

ADVERTISING: UNCONSCIOUS MOTIVES FOR BUYING

Sex sells products, or so we must assume from the ads where an outlandishly gorgeous man or woman tells us to buy oil filters, drain cleaners, exercise machines, laundry detergent, beer, cigarettes, used cars, hemorrhoid cream, and all sorts of other things that aren't sexy at all. Of course, this blatant appeal to sex is not uniquely suggested by psychodynamic theory. Common sense, as well as other psychological theories, tells us that the more attractive a product, the more likely we are to want it (or nothing at all). One way to make a product attractive is to show that its users are attractive. I've yet to walk into a tavern and see a racially mixed group of good-looking men and women toasting the winners of their recently completed volleyball game, sharing a table with several laborers in designer jeans. But I'll keep trying. I see this scene frequently on TV. How wonderful it all seems.

Where psychodynamic theory has made its own mark is in advertising's subtle use of sex to sell products by appealing to unconscious processes. I'll describe some of the possible ways this is done. I draw here from examples presented by Vance Packard in *The Hidden Persuaders* (1957) and Wilson Key in *Subliminal Seduction* (1973) and *Media Sexploitation* (1976). All three books are highly critical of the advertising industry, which is accused of using psychodynamic ideas to manipulate the buying preferences of an unknowing public. Their case is probably overstated in a number of instances, but if it is at all plausible, we have an intriguing and frightening example of applied psychodynamic theory.

The basic premise comes directly from this theory: People's motives are often hidden to them, including motives for buying one product over another. Most of us no doubt believe we buy a product because of its inherent qualities, but research has repeatedly shown that consumers are unable to distinguish among different beers, different cigarettes, and different gasolines when clues about their identity are removed. Nevertheless, we would rather fight than switch from (or to) Michelob, Camels, or Shell.

What's going on? Our preference extends beyond the product itself and embraces the image used to advertise it. According to Packard and Key, the real attraction of this image is below the level of awareness. Subliminal messages and symbols arouse our sexual interest, promising pleasure if only we buy the product. We don't get up from the couch in front of the tube and walk like a hypnotized zombie to the nearest convenience store and buy Doritos. However, some of us some of the time are subtly persuaded to grab one brand of munchies instead of another when we are in a store. That's all it takes for advertising to be successful.

In the 1950s, advertising researchers determined that buying preferences were hardly rational. In fact, ad campaigns based on "logical" assumptions were highly unsuccessful. For instance, the Chrysler Corporation surveyed consumers in the early fifties and found that people voiced strong opinions about the need for sensible and simple cars. So that's what Chrysler made available, and it promptly saw its share of the auto market drop from 26 percent in 1952 to 13 percent in 1954. Chrysler rebounded by producing the most extravagant cars possible (Packard, 1957). And the rest is history.

In searching for a way to understand consumer irrationality, advertising executives discovered the psychology of motivation. Psychodynamic theory was recognized as a good source of ideas about people's motives to buy. Clinical interviews were conducted to ascertain unconscious needs and desires. Hypnosis, free association, and projective techniques were borrowed from psychodynamic practice to identify desires that could be met by particular products. Ads were geared to satisfy these desires.

It was determined, for instance, that young people smoke cigarettes to appear old, whereas old people smoke cigarettes to appear young. So, everyone

Ivory Soap inadvertently cast X-rated film star Marilyn Chambers in a soap ad. Were Oedipal dynamics at work?

who appears in a cigarette ad should be youthfully mature, or maturely youthful, as the case may be. The Marlboro Man with his craggy face and full head of hair is a marvelous creation, a human Rorschach onto which young and old alike can project their ideal self. How old is he? You can't really tell, and that is the point.

It was also determined that people buy soaps and detergents because of a host of subtle fears and worries surrounding filth and odor, that is, concerns that originated in the anal stage. What better way to soothe these anxieties than by associating a cleaning product with mother's approval? Ivory Soap has taken this approach to an extreme. Perhaps their inadvertent casting of X-rated film star Marilyn Chambers as the maternal symbol is not so far removed from the Oedipal premise on which Ivory tries to capitalize.

One of the most insidious uses of psychodynamic ideas in advertising is a subliminal stimulation technique where messages urging the viewer to buy a particular product are flashed on television or movie screens below the level of conscious awareness. In 1956, an experiment was reported where a movie theater briefly flashed such messages as EAT POPCORN and DRINK COCA-COLA on the screen. Although these messages could not be consciously perceived, in a six-week period, popcorn sales in the theater increased 58 percent and Coke sales 18 percent!

The actual details of this experiment are elusive, because it apparently was reported only in the popular press, attributed to sources who wished to remain anonymous (Key, 1973; Packard, 1957). We know from the research reviewed in Chapter 5 that subliminal suggestion might sell products, but we also know that its influence is probably small. Whether or not invisible commercials are common or effective is a matter of speculation.

Does advertising make use of psychodynamic ideas to sell products? The answer is clearly yes. Are such techniques successful? The answer is probably yes, but the technique per se is only one of many factors that determine product preference. Are such techniques as widespread and outlandish as some suspect? The answer is probably no . . . at least, I hope that's the answer. When one considers the amount of money spent each year on advertising, one comes to the conclusion that few stones have been left unturned.

So it seems that contemporary advertisers are well aware of the power conveyed by certain images. I suspect that if Carl Jung were alive today, he would not need to study the mythology of exotic cultures to find examples of archetypes. He merely could turn on his television and flick the channel selector, not avoiding commercials but seeking them out. Archetypes abound!

For example, consider the many commercials today that feature splashing water. Everything from soft drinks to beer to blue jeans to chewing gum to automobiles makes a splash. Images of water are psychologically potent, Jung would argue, because they "tap" feelings of birth, renewal, and forgiveness. According to commercials, most people become joyously whole when they frolic in the surf or the rain. I just get wet.

Or ponder the delight that children take in "disgusting" objects, a need met by manufacturers of such items as Spit-Wads and Barfo Candy (*Time,* 1990). Anyone familiar with Freud's theorizing about the anal stage of psychosexual development would not find the appeal of these products too difficult to explain.

PROPAGANDA

Our discussion of advertising spills over into a related topic: the use of subliminal stimulation and similar techniques to influence people's opinions and values. None of the research we discussed in Chapter 5 gives us any reason to believe that deeply held beliefs can be subtly swayed by subliminal messages, yet this is a fear in some quarters.

The suspicion is expressed by some individuals that rock-and-roll songs contain subliminal messages urging listeners to worship the devil. These messages are presumably revealed when a song is played backwards. This is farfetched, to say the least, and implies a lot more about what credulous listeners expect to hear than what is actually contained in records.

Nonetheless, these possibilities were taken seriously enough to result in a 1990 lawsuit against the heavy-metal rock band Judas Priest (Henry, 1990). The members of the band and CBS records were sued—unsuccessfully, as it turned out—by the families of two young men who had shot and killed themselves after listening to Judas Priest songs. The case hinged on the presence in the record of subliminal messages saying "Do it!" This was apparently a reference to suicide. As you would guess, the musicians and their record company denied the existence of any such message.

I think it extremely unlikely that such messages are placed on records. There are certainly easier ways to damage individuals; I suggest poverty, prejudice, and war as tried and true approaches. But even if such messages do exist, their potential influence on someone's behavior pales in comparison to other factors. In the unfortunate case of the two individuals who shot themselves after listening to Judas Priest, shouldn't we take into account that they were drunk and stoned at the time? Shouldn't we take into account that they had histories of violence?

Let's turn from rock-and-roll to the use of images in political propaganda. Here the intent is to create or solidify negative attitudes against an enemy. Obviously, this can be done by depicting the enemy in ways calculated to be disgusting. Psychodynamic ideas are useful in explaining why certain images are more disgusting than others (cf. Rozin & Fallon, 1987).

In his book *Faces of the Enemy,* Sam Keen (1986) tells the reader how to create an enemy: "Dip into the unconscious well of your own disowned darkness . . . and . . . trace onto the face of the enemy the greed, hatred, carelessness you dare not claim as your own (p. 9)." Keen then proceeds to show striking similarities among propaganda posters from various times and places. In all cases, the "enemy" is shown as violent, dirty, blasphemous, greedy, and sexually perverted (see Figure 6–1).

Note that these are precisely the impulses that Freud hypothesized were lurking within each of us. In the course of socialization, we come to repress

FIGURE 6–1
The Enemy as
Disgusting

them. When we attribute such characteristics to others, we are engaging in the defense mechanism of projection. According to psychodynamic thought, we are also rationalizing our hatred of others and reducing them to something other than human—at least in our conscious minds.

Within the United States, we have seen in recent years an incredible increase in "negative" political campaigning. Candidates emphasize not simply their own credentials but additionally the weaknesses of their opponents. The content of many of these attacks conforms well to Keen's characterization of propaganda.

Remember how presidential candidate Michael Dukakis was criticized in 1988 for being "soft" on crime, particularly murder and rape? Remember how he was held responsible for polluting Boston Harbor? Remember how he was accused of being a spendthrift? The point here is that Dukakis—or any candidate, for that matter—could have been attacked on grounds of his platform, which would seem the most legitimate thing to do. However, it was the politically irrelevant, yet psychologically potent, attacks that were most compelling to the electorate.

CREATIVITY

Creativity has intrigued psychodynamic theorists since Freud (1900) analyzed plays by Sophocles and Shakespeare for Oedipal themes in *The Interpretation of Dreams*. Because of its emphasis on symbols and its assumption of over-determined behavior, psychodynamic theory is unique among psychological approaches in its ability to speak to the complexity of art and literature. Accordingly, psychodynamic pronouncements on these subjects have been widely noted.

Psychodynamic theory provides a cluster of related hypotheses about creative works, the act that gives rise to them, the personality of creative individuals, and the reaction of their audience. One important application is by critics who use it as a vantage point to aid our understanding of art and literature. Another important application is by artists and writers who use it intentionally as a source of techniques. You can see how this second application confounds the first, because the psychodynamic criticism of a work produced in explicit accordance with psychodynamic ideas is hopelessly complex. This epitomizes both the self-fulfilling prophecies *and* the enlightenment effects discussed at the beginning of the chapter. What does it mean when an artist consciously uses the language of the unconscious?

At any rate, Freud's (1908b) essay "Creative Writers and Day-Dreaming" proposes that some literary works are strictly analogous to dreams, little more than the disguised fulfillment of unsatisfied wishes. He argued that this is particularly the case for popular literature, what we call romances or pulps. Nevertheless, the basic psychodynamic formula for all art and literature is introduced here. Creative products satisfy unconscious wishes. These wishes are usually unacceptable, so they must be disguised. Artistic and literary techniques are deployed for this purpose.

In *Leonardo da Vinci and a Memory of His Childhood,* Freud (1910) elaborated on these ideas. He proposed that the famous artist and scientist suffered from an extreme inhibition of his sexual drive brought about by castration anxiety. His libidinal energy was then channeled into the well-known works of art and scientific discoveries. The *Mona Lisa*'s mysterious smile is no mystery to Freud. It is the smile of Leonardo's mother, rediscovered on the model and committed to canvas.

Freud's interpretation of Leonardo has been challenged on factual grounds (e.g., Schapiro, 1956), but the general equation of creativity and Oedipal conflict has transcended this debate. It often translates itself into an examination of what creativity and madness have in common. The person in the street often believes that genius and insanity are separated by the finest of lines, an opinion bolstered by statements of artists themselves. Salvador Dali is reputed to have said, "The only difference between myself and a mad man is that I am not mad" (Ades, 1978). Certainly, creative individuals may strike the rest of us as strange.

However, research does not support the hypothesis that the creative artist or writer is neurotic. If anything, creative individuals are particularly stable (Trilling, 1977). They may seem different because they tolerate ambiguity, show independent judgment, and are frequently curious (Singer, 1984). But these are strengths, not weaknesses.

According to Freud, the creation of art and literature and their appreciation reflect the same underlying process. What distinguishes the creative individual from others is an ability to represent fantasy in such a way that others can partake of it. Ernest Kris (1952) extends this idea and assigns the ego a more important role in the creative act than does Freud. In a process called **regression in the service of the ego,** the creative individual retreats into primary-process thinking for artistic insights and discoveries (Suler, 1980). Once the artist reaches an insight, he or she employs secondary-process thinking to turn the inspiration into a socially valued product. Creative individuals are skilled at this process; they are active masters of their unconscious rather than passive recipients of its impulses.

When LSD first became popular as a recreational drug, advocates touted it as an aid to creativity. No one makes this claim anymore, and the notion of regression in the service of the ego explains why. LSD facilitates primary-process thinking, providing all sorts of sparks and tickles, but it does not give an individual the technical skills to turn insight into creative products. That takes training, practice, and hard work . . . the result of mental control.

> **Regression in the service of the ego:** The ability of creative individuals to gain access to primary-process thinking for insights and inspirations.

Literary Criticism

Literary critics have made extensive use of psychodynamic theory to understand particular works and particular writers (Mollinger, 1981). Shortcomings of this approach parallel those already detailed for psychohistory. The psychoanalytic critic may focus too narrowly on the psychodynamic formula, sometimes losing the work itself in the process. And when this theory is applied to literary characters themselves, credibility is stretched. So, in his interpretation of Shakespeare's Hamlet, Jones (1910) speculates about Hamlet's childhood experiences.

Psychodynamic criticism is more reasonable when integrated with standard approaches to literary criticism. As C. S. Lewis (1941, p. 7) noted, the purpose of criticism is to answer the question, "Why, and how, should we read this?" Overly zealous critics brush aside this question in favor of a different one: "Why did he write it?" What results is no longer literary criticism.

In recent years, literary critics have turned from Freud's version of psychodynamic theory to that of Jung. This is not surprising. To Freud, symbols were ultimately personal. To Jung, symbols transcended the individual. Universal meanings could be sought. And, since literature often seeks to cross the boundary between the personal and the universal, Jungian theory is a more popular source of interpretations for symbols.

Marcel Duchamp, **Bicycle Wheel,** *1951 (third version, after lost original of 1913)*

Rene Magritte, L'Acte de Foie

Dadaism and Surrealism

One of the intriguing chapters in the intellectual history of the twentieth century is the relationship between psychoanalysis and the movements of dadaism and surrealism. The links are complex. Most agree, however, that the important dadaists and surrealists were influenced by Freud. A number of these artists and writers explicitly acknowledged psychodynamic theory as the source of techniques and themes.

What is dadaism? It was a creative movement within Europe toward the end of World War I. Painters and poets profoundly disenchanted with a world that produced the horrors of the first "modern" war criticized society on numerous grounds. Their criticism included art itself, which they saw as the product and prop of a decadent society (Ades, 1978). Mere convention dictated who was considered creative and who was not, and convention was a habit shaped by the bourgeois world (e.g., Becker, 1982).

But the dadaists were still artists and writers produced by the world that had deserted them. Their paradoxical position sometimes resulted in anger and frustration and sometimes in whimsical works that were deliberately made difficult to regard as art. In 1913, Marcel Duchamp pioneered the use of *ready-mades,* everyday objects exhibited as if they were classic paintings or sculptures. This is now a standard artistic technique, but at the time it attempted

Salvador Dali,
**Illumined
Pleasures,** *1929*

to show that art is produced merely by men and women, not by "artists" of special status.

If artistic conventions are distrusted and dismissed, what is left? In the early 1920s, André Breton seized on psychodynamic ideas to answer this question. In particular, Freud's notion of the unconscious provided a means to rail against coercive logic and rationality. Unfettered creativity was to be found only in the unconscious. So surrealism was born from the attempt of artists and writers to reach that place. Breton proclaimed the First Manifesto of Surrealism in 1924, defining the movement as

> SURREALISM, noun. Pure psychic automatism by which it is intended to express . . . the true function of thought. Thought dictated in the absence of all control exerted by reason, and outside all aesthetic and moral preoccupations. (Ades, 1978, p. 33)

Surrealist writers and artists developed a variety of techniques for tapping the unconscious: dream analysis, automatic writing and drawing, and hypnosis. They

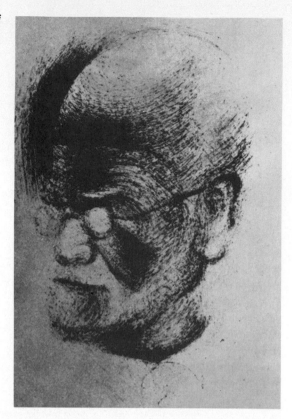

threw paint onto canvas and words onto paper at random. They imitated primitive art. They substituted rags for brushes. They dictated their poems and refused to edit them.

Two of the best known surrealists are painters René Magritte and Salvador Dali. Magritte painted memories of his dreams, and he is famous for the distortion of perspective in his works. Dali used Freudian symbols to depict explicit sexual themes: guilt, sex, incest, and masturbation.

Dali and Freud met in London shortly before Freud's death. They enjoyed their brief interaction and were impressed with each other. Dali sketched Freud, but it is much more difficult for psychodynamic theorists to capture what Dali and the other surrealists were about. Do their works validate the psychodynamic account of creativity or not? The entire movement defies such a question.

SUMMARY

By far the most generally influential approach to personality psychology is the psychodynamic paradigm. In this chapter, I described the application of psychoanalytic ideas within the fields of psychopathology, psychotherapy, psychosomatic medicine, child-rearing and education, psychohistory, advertising, propaganda, and creativity. What do these applications have in common? Most basically, the workers within these fields are attracted to psychodynamic theory because it is a theory that does justice to complex phenomena. The motivated unconscious is particularly attractive. Each application takes its particular formula more or less directly from Freud and uses it to predict, control, and/or understand a domain of human activity.

At the same time, the psychodynamic applications described here are controversial. Within each field are advocates and critics of equal fervor. Their debate is usually not over the pertinence of psychodynamic theory but instead is over the exclusive reliance on this perspective. Is this the best way to look at psychopathology, at history, at advertising, at literature? The answer is not found in any particular application. It resides in the judgment of the individual practitioner, shaped by the paradigm he or she accepts.

HUMANISTIC PARADIGM

The humanistic tradition is a long-standing one, dating at least to the fifth century B.C. philosopher Protagoras and his assertion that "Man is the measure of all things." This tradition has waxed and waned over the years. Often its ideological opponent has been the doctrine of **materialism,** which holds that all entities—including human beings—can be fully explained in terms of physics and chemistry. Humanists profoundly distrust what they see as the narrow view of science. They prefer instead to approach human beings as human beings, celebrating such irreducible human activities as art, music, and drama. Said another way, humanists believe that the needs and values of people must always take precedence over material things.

Materialism: The doctrine that all entities, including human beings, can be fully explained in terms of physics and chemistry.

Although we will discuss the humanistic paradigm as a whole in this chapter, some disclaimers are in order. This approach is probably less homogeneous than the other paradigms of personality. It spans intellectual traditions defined as much by their critical stance with regard to "scientific" psychology as by substantive features they share in common. Some humanistic theories present an upbeat and romanticized view of the human condition, whereas others stress what is dark and somber (see May, Rogers, & Maslow, 1986).

Also complicating any characterization of this paradigm is that it is sometimes entwined with the other paradigms of personality. Many of the important humanistic theorists were originally trained within the psychoanalytic tradition (McCall, 1983). When striking off on their own, they often brought psychodynamic ideas with them. And many of those who currently work within the cognitive-behavioral paradigm have borrowed traditional humanistic concerns like the self, goals, and consciousness. Be that as it may, the humanistic approach is sometimes called the **Third Force** to distinguish it from psychodynamic approaches on the one hand and cognitive-behavioral ones on the other. Appreciate, however, that some overlap exists.

Third Force: The humanistic approach to psychology.

Within personality psychology, the best-known proponents of the humanistic approach are Carl Rogers and Abraham Maslow. Both emphasize people's good and noble aspects and their inherent drive toward self-actualization. In this chapter, we will discuss their contributions, along with those of Rollo May—an influential existential theorist, and Ronald Laing—an important phenomenological theorist. We will also touch on representative research and applications.

THEORIES

Before we venture into specific theories, let me try to draw out some of their typical emphases (Urban, 1983). Not all humanistic theories share these features, but many do tend to cut across them. Taken together, these emphases provide a framework for understanding the humanistic view of personality.

The Family Resemblance of Humanistic Theories

First, *human beings and their behavior are distinctive.* They need to be thought about in a different way than other entities in nature. Here we see why humanistic theories stand in sharp contrast to other personality approaches, which model themselves quite intentionally on the natural sciences. Psychodynamic, trait, and cognitive-behavioral theorists are united in their search for the causes of what people do. They tend to be materialists. They tend to be reductionists. They tend to emphasize commonalities between people and animals, and even between living things and nonliving things.

Humanistic psychologists, in contrast, find these simplifying tendencies simply wrong. Any attempt to understand people must be at the level of what is unique about people—hence the humanistic interest in experience, existence, choice, and striving toward goals.

Second, *each and every individual is significant.* To the humanistic theorist, people are "significant" in two ways. Individuals are more important than anything else in the world, including social institutions. Humanistic psychologists lean to the left in their politics, if not further. In their theories, we find an impatience with the status quo, which is often held responsible for people's difficulties. R. D. Laing (1967), for example, who wrote extensively on schizophrenia, argued provocatively that madness is a sane response to an insane world. In the applications of humanistic theories, the world is changed to be compatible with people, never vice versa. The individual remains paramount.

Also, individuals are the only legitimate subject matter for psychologists to study. Other researchers may lump together groups of people and regard any variations among them as a methodological nuisance. In contrast, humanists regard such differences as the very essence of what it means to be a person. Remember the notion of idiographic goals introduced in Chapter 3, that the conclusions of personality psychology should pertain to individual people? Idiographic goals are readily embraced by most humanistic psychologists. Individuals are *always* regarded as unique.

Every individual reacts uniquely to a diagnosis of AIDS.

For example, Mullin (1990) recently investigated the reactions of individuals diagnosed with AIDS, with the goal of capturing what was unique about each person's response. Although many of those she studied managed to find something positive about this obviously devastating experience, regarding it as an opportunity, the particular door the diagnosis of AIDS opened differed greatly from person to person. Her different research subjects variously saw AIDS as an opportunity

- to be famous
- to be taken care of
- to be considered special
- to catalyze self-growth
- to be politically active

Merely concluding that people may find the diagnosis of AIDS to be an opportunity fails to capture the uniqueness of each individual's reaction.

To humanists, "generic" human nature is a fiction, so they hesitate to offer sweeping generalizations about people. Case studies are often used in research to show what is possible rather than typical. Abraham Maslow (1970), for example, wrote about self-actualization in terms of particular people he knew who had achieved it. Other researchers may relax this position, acknowledging that people share some characteristics in common with their fellows while having others that are unique. They may conduct familiar correlational investigations and experiments, yet they remain quite clear that these capture but part of what we mean by personality.

Third, *individuals are complexly organized.* Each and every person is seen as extremely complicated; at the same time, he or she is readily grasped as a coherent whole. Different theorists posit different principles that underlie this organization, and these are frequently phrased in terms of someone's goals and choices. The idea of self-actualization, which has such great importance to humanistic theories, proposes that people's activities cohere around their continued growth.

Let me pause and provide some background concerning self-actualization—a critical concept within this paradigm. The term was first introduced to psychology by Kurt Goldstein (1939), who studied brain-damaged soldiers following World War I. Goldstein was struck that these individuals—despite an injured nervous system—still had an integrity and wholeness about their personalities. He proposed that a person crystallizes personality in a meaningful way, even when injuries cause profound problems with memory, perception, and orientation. He termed this tendency self-actualization, and subsequent theorists who wished to emphasize the unity of the human spirit have found it a powerful notion indeed.

Fourth, *individuals are inherently active,* changing from day to day and even from minute to minute. When we think of personality, part of its very meaning is stability (Chapter 1). Yet many characteristics of people are in flux (Larsen & Diener, 1987), and to the humanistic psychologist these are among their most important. People are seen as flexible and changeable, as well as stable and invariant.

Several important ideas have been introduced by humanistic theorists to help explain these aspects of people. Let's start with the distinction between essence and existence. **Essence** refers to someone's fixed characteristics. Personality psychologists from other walks are often concerned with essence, that is, instincts, traits, habits, and cognitive styles. But humanistic theorists are more interested in **existence,** which refers to the continuing process of being alive as a human.

A further distinction is made between **being,** on the one hand—what already exists, and **becoming,** on the other hand—what does not exist at the moment but has the potential to do so. Once again, we can use the idea of self-actualization to illustrate these ideas. We may not be actualized at the moment, but we have the potential for it. Indeed, we are constantly striving to bring it about. *Becoming* refers not simply to a hypothetical future ("someday the Chicago Cubs will win the World Series") but to something more personal and plausible ("someday I will know myself").

Albert Bandura (1982) wrote an intriguing article where he pointed out that as we move through life, unpredictable events occur that can affect us profoundly. He used an example from his own life, when he was in graduate school. He found one of his assignments to be boring, and he and a friend went

Essence: A person's fixed characteristics.

Existence: The continuing process of being alive as a human.

Being: What already exists.

Becoming: What has the potential to exist.

off on the spur of the moment to play a round of golf. They found themselves playing behind two young women they did not know. The four of them struck up a conversation and finished the round of golf together. Eventually, Bandura married one of the women, and obviously things were quite different for the both of them. Suppose Bandura's assignment had been more interesting? Suppose his friend had wanted to play pinball rather than golf? Suppose one pair of golfers had not found the other pair congenial?

People differ in the degree to which they can be influenced by such chance encounters, and this is what is meant by the idea of becoming. We are predisposed to actualize certain possibilities but not others. And the predispositions themselves vary. We may be more "open" to new experiences at some times but not others. I always tease my graduating students that they will fall in love with someone the week before they leave campus forever. I'm often right, because transitions attune us to the possibilities we may be leaving behind. Part of the humanistic vision of mental health is a constant openness to chance encounters and the opportunities they present.

The idea that people are constantly in flux, always "becoming" as it were, means that we are inherently unpredictable. Humanistic psychologists do not hesitate to introduce notions such as choice and will, because these ideas explain why some people actualize their potential, whereas others do not. Other psychologists avoid these concepts like the plague, because the concepts are at odds with the common assumption that everything we do has causes. "Becoming" has no cause.

Fifth, *conscious experience is among a person's most important characteristics.* What sets a human being apart from other entities? Humanistic theorists grapple deeply with this question, and they indeed suggest different answers. But more often than not, an important part of each answer entails our conscious experience.

Conscious experience is difficult to define. Most definitions say that **consciousness** entails awareness of one's environment, one's psychological state, and finally one's very awareness. But awareness is usually defined as consciousness, so what we are left with is a circular definition. Difficult though it may be to define, consciousness is obviously important.

Consciousness: Awareness of one's environment, one's psychological state, and one's very awareness.

We saw in Chapter 2 that psychology began with Wilhelm Wundt's attempt to study consciousness. When the methods Wundt pioneered fell short, they were abandoned, along with the definition of psychology as the study of consciousness. Behaviorists argued that psychology should be concerned only with what could be seen and objectively measured. Although psychodynamic and cognitive-behavioral theorists freely allude to mental processes, they either distrust them or retreat into operational definitions.

Humanistic psychologists do not sidestep consciousness, despite its problems. Carl Rogers makes consciousness the keystone of his theory of personality. People literally are the way they experience themselves. Existential theorists similarly stress the importance of awareness.

Consciousness always has an object; in other words, we are always aware of something. Sometimes we are aware of being aware, which leads theorists to introduce the notion of the self as the entity responsible for this higher-order awareness. We discussed the self in Chapter 1, commenting that in most accounts of personality it proved both theoretically critical and elusive. Its link with consciousness explains both these characterizations.

Humanistic theorists acknowledge that consciousness may be flawed and our sense of self perhaps fragmented. Indeed, the typical criterion they suggest for wholeness is that the incongruities in our awareness be resolved, along with the discrepancies among our different senses of self. A key notion in many humanistic approaches is **alienation**— estrangement from one's own inner nature. Alienation makes no sense without awareness. Animals are not alienated. They may be unhappy or even in agony, but they are never alienated, because they lack the capacity to articulate a discrepancy between what is and what should be. Many humanistic theorists are therapists, and they see their task as one of facilitating awareness among their clients and thereby reducing discrepancies.

Alienation: Estrangement from one's own inner nature.

Sixth and finally, *people are self-regulating,* instigating transactions with the environment for particular purposes. Other approaches to personality see people as reactive, responding to their instincts or to environmental pushes and pulls. In contrast, the humanistic paradigm sees people as proactive; their behavior is spontaneous, emanating from within. Why are you reading this book? The humanistic theorist would stress your goals: to learn something about personality, to pass the course in order to earn your degree, to prepare yourself for a career, to tutor your friend who is failing the course.

These sorts of explanations are not encountered in the other approaches to personality. They are *future-oriented,* whereas psychological explanations phrased in terms of causes are necessarily concerned with the past, because that's how causes work, from events in the past to effects in the present. Humanistic explanations are *purposive.* We undertake what we do because we have goals to achieve. And they are *intentional.* We do what we do with awareness of the consequences we hope to produce.

Many humanists prefer the term "action" to describe what people do, rather than the term "behavior" used by other psychologists. The connotations of action are precisely those just described: future-oriented, purposive, and intentional. Behavior in contrast is a neutral term, stripped of anything human. Animals behave; automobiles behave; rainstorms behave; even our hair behaves (or not) when we try to style it. But only people engage in action.

In existential thought, the notion of self-regulation receives particularly close examination. As phrased by Jean-Paul Sartre (1956), life is absurd, which means that human existence has no ultimate meaning or purpose. We are abandoned into the world at birth, and we find ourselves simply being. In acting purposively, as we necessarily do, we not only initiate actions, we also create the very meanings with which we imbue what we do. Each and every individual must supply a meaning to life and then strive to fulfill it.

Existentialists greatly emphasize our choices, because in establishing a meaning for life, we necessarily choose the direction we want to follow. That we are conscious makes us free. We can entertain possibilities, and we can choose one route rather than another. We determine our goals, arrange our priorities, and embark on our travels. Again, both existential and humanistic theorists often introduce the notion of the self at this juncture as the entity that chooses a path and then moves along it.

With this overview of humanistic theories in mind, let us turn our attention to the particular ideas of several well-known theorists. As earlier noted, these theorists are not in perfect agreement with one another. Pay as much attention to their differences as to their similarities. We begin with the theory of Carl Rogers.

Carl Rogers: Self-Theory

Psychologist Carl Rogers (1902–1987) stressed the way people view themselves. He regarded self-perception as the critical characteristic of personality. His theory is therefore called **self-theory.** According to Rogers, people strive to make the most of their potential, to have a self-concept that is positive and consistent with their experience. As such, his perspective is both upbeat and hopeful; many have been drawn to the theory and the theorist himself.

Self-theory: Carl Rogers's theory of personality, which stresses self-perception.

Rogers's Life Rogers was born in Oak Park, Illinois. He attended seminary to become a minister, but when his interests changed, he transferred to Teachers College of Columbia, where he completed his clinical psychology degree in 1931. For the next 10 years, Rogers worked as a clinician in Rochester, New York, at a predominantly psychoanalytic clinic.

He at first tried to work within the Freudian system of psychotherapy but became disenchanted with the results. Rogers felt that when a clinician imposed "insight" on the client, it rarely led to a miraculous cure. He began to rely more and more on the client's own definition of his problem and on the client's own view of how best to solve it.

In 1940, Rogers took an academic position at Ohio State University, and he began a prolific career as a theorist. In 1942, he published *Counseling and Psychotherapy: Newer Concepts in Practice,* which criticized psychoanalytic theory and practice. In 1945, he went to the University of Chicago, where six years later he published his most famous book: *Client-Centered Therapy.* In this book, he described an alternative approach to psychotherapy based on a different vision of personality.

In subsequent years, Rogers elaborated his ideas and applied them broadly. The titles of some of his books give a flavor of the breadth of his concerns: *On Becoming a Person* (1961), *Freedom to Learn* (1969a), *On Encounter Groups* (1970), *Becoming Partners* (1972), *Carl Rogers on Personal Power* (1977), and *A Way of Being* (1980). He was always willing to present and argue for his view of human nature. His point-counterpoint with B. F. Skinner is well-known and makes for intriguing reading (see Rogers & Skinner, 1956). He also made a number of films where he demonstrated his therapy and discussed his ideas. Perhaps your instructor can show one of these films to your class.

Rogers's Theory Central to Rogers's theory is the motive toward self-actualization. People have an inherent need to survive, grow, and enhance themselves, always pushing toward increased complexity, independence, and social responsibility. People phrase these goals for themselves, and they are thus best understood from the individual's own point of view, what Rogers called **phenomenological reality.**

Phenomenological reality: Reality as defined from the individual's own point of view.

Organismic valuing process: According to Rogers, the inherent process within people that tells them what is good or bad for them.

Experience: According to Rogers, everything that is happening to a person at a given moment.

Awareness: According to Rogers, the part of experience that is symbolized, usually in words.

People interpret their ongoing experiences in terms of their actualizing tendency. Is self-actualization hindered or fostered by a particular experience? The answer depends on whether a person regards the experience as positive or negative. Rogers believed that an **organismic valuing process** is inherent within each person. According to this controversial notion, we do not have to learn what is good or bad for ourselves. We simply know it.

He illustrated this process with a study of infants given the opportunity to choose their own diet. By and large, their choices were nutritious, and the infants remained healthy (Davis, 1928). It should be noted, however, that foods containing refined sugar were *not* among the options available to the infants in this study. We know from our experience with Halloween and other holidays where candy is plentiful that children (and adults) may often indulge in sweets to the point of becoming ill. Obviously, particular environments can undercut the organismic valuing process.

Rogers distinguished between experience and awareness. **Experience** includes everything that is happening to a person at a given moment. In contrast, **awareness** is that part of experience we symbolize, usually in words. This distinction is important because we sometimes make mistakes when translating our experience into awareness. In other words, what we think is going on is at odds with what is really happening, and our mistaken awareness will interfere

According to Rogers, children simply know what is good for them, even what food is nutritious. Particular circumstances— such as Halloween—can undercut this process.

with the valuing process. This is unfortunate because we stop doing what is good for us because we quite literally no longer know what is good.

One example of this discrepancy occurs when our symbolic view of our own characteristics and their worth is at odds with our view of what is good and desirable. Crucial here is the concept of the **self,** which Rogers defines as one's view of and evaluation of one's own characteristics and one's perception of how one relates to others. The **ideal self** is what a person wishes to be. The valuing process should lead people to a congruence between self and ideal self, but as noted, this does not always occur. What goes wrong? To Rogers, the culprits are other people who convey negative opinions and evaluations about the person.

To understand personality development, we must look at how someone is treated by others. Warm and supportive parents tend to raise happy and adjusted children. Children who value themselves succeed in a variety of domains (Coopersmith, 1967, 1968). From the viewpoint of self-theory, these findings are to be expected. When parents make their child feel worthy, he has no major discrepancy between experience and awareness, between his self and his ideal self. His valuing process is not subverted. He *trusts* himself. He knows what is good for himself, he pursues it, and he benefits.

Self: According to Rogers, one's view of and evaluation of one's own characteristics, and one's perception of how one relates to others.

Ideal self: According to Rogers, what a person wishes to be.

To understand personality development, we must look at how someone is treated by others.

Carl Rogers developed client-centered therapy as a means of healing the damage done by conditional regard.

Conditional regard: Love and esteem that are contingent on what a person does.

In contrast, consider the child raised in a negative atmosphere. The critical views of her parents are assimilated and become a part of her awareness. Particularly damaging is when the parents provide **conditional regard:** "We love and value you to the extent that you conform to our wishes; if you fail to do so, you are no longer welcome in this house." Because the most important part of the child's experience is how her parents treat her, conditional regard exacts a severe toll. Because she relies on someone else's rules for self-definition rather than her own valuing process, self-actualization is thwarted. She becomes psychologically crippled.

As an academic adviser, I sometimes talk with students who are pursuing a particular course of studies because their family expects them to. Any attempt on their part to change their major is met with a great hue and cry from home. This is conditional regard, and you can see why these students are miserable. They cannot win. If they seek their own goals, their parents disown them. If they seek the goals of their parents, they disown themselves.

Client-centered therapy: The approach to therapy created by Carl Rogers, which attempts to undo the damage done by conditional regard.

Rogers's **client-centered therapy** consists of techniques to heal the damage done by conditional regard. Three factors are believed to be necessary for beneficial change in therapy (Prochaska, 1984). First, therapists must be *genuine* in their interactions with clients. People who have developed problems because of the way others have treated them are sensitive to phoniness or manipulativeness on the part of a therapist. Second, therapists must have an *empathic understanding* of clients, seeing the world from their vantage. Third, therapists must provide clients with *unconditional positive regard,* communicating that they are worthy people.

The intent in client-centered therapy is to create for clients conditions opposite those that generated their problem in the first place. The therapist accepts the statements made by clients, not interpreting them but rather trying to understand them as the clients do. Explicit directions and exhortations, common in other forms of therapy, are avoided because they send the message that the clients are deficient for not already doing these things. Instead, the therapist frequently reflects back to a client the client's thoughts and feelings:

> Client: I feel discouraged about the future. I'll never get a good job.
> Therapist: You seem to feel hopeless about things. Does that include your present job?

As the person talks about his thoughts and feelings, perhaps for the first time to a person who isn't harsh or critical, he begins to judge them more accurately against the evidence of the world.

The goal of client-centered therapy is to bring a client's experience and awareness back into congruence. Once this occurs, the client can correctly symbolize his experience. The valuing process is back on center stage. Self-actualization is again his central motive.

As noted earlier, humanistic psychologists are not always strong advocates of research, but Rogers was different. He was always interested in the empirical investigation of his personality theory and approach to therapy (e.g., Rogers & Dymond, 1954; Rogers, Gendlin, Kiesler, & Truax, 1967). One strategy he employed to measure a person's self-concept was the **Q-sort procedure** (Stephenson, 1953). In this research strategy, people are given a set of cards, each of which has the name of a particular trait printed on it. They are asked to sort these cards into piles, ranging from most characteristic of them to least characteristic. This is typically done two times, once with respect to the current self and once with respect to the ideal self.

> **Q-sort procedure: A card-sorting procedure for measuring one's self-concept.**

The similarity or dissimilarity of the two sorts is then ascertained by seeing where individual cards end up. To what degree do they fall in the same position with respect to the self and the ideal self? Consistent with Rogers's ideas, psychological distress is marked by low or negative correlations between one's self and ideal self. Psychological health is associated with a high correlation between the two (cf. Higgins, 1987).

Rogers has also taken a close look at the psychotherapy process. His basic premises seem to be supported (e.g., Gurman, 1977). Successful psychotherapy is conducted by therapists who are warm, sincere, and accepting. In the course of successful therapy, a client's self and ideal self converge, as Rogers predicted.

Evaluation   What should we make of Carl Rogers and his self-theory? Like Freud, his popularity transcends the realm of personality psychology and psychotherapy. His humanistic perspective serves as a correction to other views of human nature that downplay our positive aspects. So his ideas are widely applied: to education, politics, administration, race relations, and so on (Levant & Schlien, 1984). Toward the end of his life, Rogers was increasingly drawn to social and societal applications. This trend makes sense granted the importance he accorded to other people in our personality development and functioning. Said another way, each of us must bear some responsibility for the psychological well-being of those in our vicinity.

Indeed, all of us are "other people" to those whom we know, just as they are "other people" to us. The processes Rogers described occur within social systems. Happy people end up clustered together, because they mutually bolster each other's sense of worth. And unhappy people also feed into each other (cf. Locke & Horowitz, 1990). This is an apt example of how people seek equilibrium, not just within themselves but also between themselves and others.

In a fascinating essay, Carl Rogers and David Ryback (1984) extrapolated self-theory to a global level, using it to explain how international conflict might be avoided. For example, Rogers conducted an encounter group with Catholics and Protestants in Belfast, Northern Ireland. These individuals, whose bloody feuds are so well-known, were removed from their respective constituencies and met in an isolated retreat.

In just 16 hours of meetings, they began to express themselves openly, and the participants drastically modified their prejudices. Consider this exchange between Becky, a Catholic, and Dennis, a Protestant:

> Becky: Words couldn't describe what I feel towards Dennis from the discussion we had at dinner time. We spoke quietly for about 10 minutes and I felt that here I have got a friend and that was it.
> Dennis: We sat here at dinner time and had a wee bit of a yarn quietly when you were all away for your dinner—
> Becky: I think he fully understands me as a person.
> Dennis: I do, there is no question about that—
> Becky: And for that reason I am very grateful and I think I have found a friend. (p. 406)

What's going on? Presumably, when people are open with each other, they come to value themselves. And when they value themselves, no room exists for hatred and prejudice.

Rogers and Ryback (1984) recommended that wide-scale encounter groups might go a long way toward easing world tensions. They admitted that it sounds simplistic and utopian, but they noted that the individuals just described continued to meet after the encounter group was over. Might the billions of dollars spent on weapons and armies be more profitably spent on facilitating communication? These psychologists say yes.

At the same time, one can easily be critical of self-theory. It rests on some assumptions that are overly simple—if not downright incorrect. The valuing process is plausible to explain certain biological tendencies, but I'm not convinced that we have an internal barometer that helps us navigate the complex social world of values, morals, and politics. Answers to questions about what is good and bad for ourselves must be partly social conventions, because different societies value different practices.

In some cases, therapy works because it is nondirective. But in other cases, advice and recommendations are critical. For example, therapy for sexual difficulties often involves giving information (Masters & Johnson, 1970). Some matters individuals simply cannot figure out for themselves, regardless of an accepting context.

Finally, a world of unconditional positive regard might be a confusing place, a caricature of the "have a nice day" cliché so frequently hurled at us. Some people invariably impinge on others, and these people should be called to task for their actions. Still, if Rogers's notion is revised to mean regard for people per se and appropriate reactions to what they do, then he was probably right about the conditions that help us to be all that we can be (e.g., Harrington, Block, & Block, 1987).

Abraham Maslow: Hierarchy of Motives

Another important figure in the humanistic paradigm is Abraham Maslow (1908–1970). Maslow was born in Brooklyn, New York, the son of Russian immigrants. He first attended City College and Cornell University, and then the University of Wisconsin, where he was trained as an animal learning psychologist.

Maslow's first allegiance within psychology was to John Watson's behaviorism, but he turned away from this vision of human nature in response to several important life events. The birth of his first child and the outbreak of World War II were impossible for him to accommodate within behavioristic psychology (Hall, 1968). Further, he felt that the other dominant approach within psychology at that time—psychodynamic theory—also fell short of explaining them. Approaches to psychology based on animals or neurotics had little to say about the wonder of human development or the possibility of ending hatred and warfare.

To Maslow, behaviorism and psychoanalysis were psychologies of deficiency. People were viewed as victims of their environments or their drives. These approaches were pessimistic because they made no mention of the good and noble things people can accomplish.

So, Maslow (1970) self-consciously proposed "a positive theory of motivation" to encompass both "the highest capacities of the healthy and strong . . . as well as . . . the defensive maneuvers of crippled spirits" (pp. 35–36). He acknowledged the influences of William James, John Dewey, Max Wertheimer, Kurt Goldstein, and Alfred Adler. He elaborated on their suggestions that people strive toward goals higher than the satisfaction of physical drives. He stressed that people are inherently good and always moving toward health and wholeness.

Central to Maslow's humanistic approach is the notion that people have a variety of needs arranged in a hierarchy. This **hierarchy of motives** ranges from basic or *deficiency needs* that provide something lacking within the person, like food or air, to higher or growth needs that reflect uniquely human values, like truth and beauty (see Figure 7–1). People must satisfy lower needs before

Hierarchy of motives: Abraham Maslow's theory that one's needs can be arranged in a hierarchy according to the order in which they must be satisfied.

FIGURE 7–1
**Maslow's Hierarchy
of Motives**

Self-actualization

Esteem

Love

Safety

Physiological

SOURCE: Maslow, 1970.

they can satisfy higher needs. However, it is only in satisfying the higher needs that people can become truly fulfilled.

Maslow's hierarchy is an intriguing idea, capturing something important about the interrelation of human motives. When basic needs are salient, many higher needs are irrelevant. Who hasn't felt selfish desires crowd out other considerations? And what about the truism among revolutionaries that radical ideology is well-received when it is accompanied by food and safety?

My parents were teenagers during the depression, so their attitude toward employment is quite different than mine. This has made for a genuine gap in understanding over the years. I have sometimes complained to my parents that my job isn't as fulfilling as I would like it to be. They always ask, "But aren't you getting paid?" For them, growing up in a time of massive unemployment, jobs are regarded as vehicles only for basic needs. For me, growing up in a time of opportunity and affluence, jobs are the means to satisfy higher needs as well. But perhaps things are changing yet again as the job domain becomes increasingly uncertain. Maybe my children won't understand me either, but they'll see eye-to-eye with their grandparents about employment.

Here are postulates that present Maslow's (1970, pp. 98–100) ideas more formally:

1. Higher needs appear later in evolutionary development.
2. Higher needs appear later in personality development.

3. The higher the need, the less necessary it is for survival, the longer its gratification can be postponed, and the easier it is for the need to disappear.
4. Those who live at the level of higher needs show greater biological efficiency: better health, longer life, improved sleep and digestion, and so on.
5. Higher needs are less urgent.
6. The satisfaction of higher needs results in greater happiness and serenity.
7. As one pursues higher needs, one in general becomes more healthy.
8. Lower needs must be satisfied before higher needs, which means that higher needs have more preconditions.
9. Higher needs require suitable environmental conditions before they can be satisfied, more so than lower needs.
10. People who have gratified both higher and lower needs place greater value on the higher needs.
11. The higher the need level, the more widely and deeply one loves other people.
12. Those who pursue higher needs show social and civil concern.
13. Self-actualization is approached as one satisfies higher needs.
14. The pursuit and gratification of higher needs results in increased individualism.
15. Psychotherapy can better help those at higher need levels.
16. Lower needs are more localized, tangible, and limited than higher needs.

The problem with psychoanalysis and behaviorism is not in what they study, but in what they neglect. These approaches have limited their view of human nature by exclusively focusing on basic needs. In obvious contrast, Maslow inquired about higher matters.

Chief among these higher matters is self-actualization, which Maslow (1970, p. 150) defined as "the full use and exploitation of talents, capacities, potentialities, etc." He explored self-actualization by studying such individuals as Thomas Jefferson, Abraham Lincoln, Eleanor Roosevelt, Albert Schweitzer, and Jane Addams. He felt that these people were all self-actualized, possessing such characteristics as acceptance of self and others, spontaneity, autonomy, an interest in solving external problems, a need for privacy, creativity, and a philosophical sense of humor.

Maslow acknowledged that his studies of self-actualization were preliminary and impressionistic, based on his study of the biographies of people he admired. However, his ideas inspired the development of a questionnaire that attempts to measure one's degree of self-actualization (Shostrom, 1964). The **Personal Orientation Inventory,** as this measure is called, presents research subjects with pairs of statements. One statement reflects an aspect of Maslow's hypothesized characterization of self-actualization, whereas the other statement does not. Subjects choose the one statement in each pair that better describes

Personal Orientation Inventory: A questionnaire that attempts to measure one's degree of self-actualization.

themselves, and they are given a score based on how many of the self-actualization items they endorse.

The Personal Orientation Inventory has been widely used in research, yet its validity is in question. The measure may well be confounded by people's desire to present themselves in the best possible light. This would explain why substance abusers reportedly score higher on the Personal Orientation Inventory than do people in the general population (Weiss, 1987). Obviously, the Personal Orientation is not an ideal operationalization of Maslow's concept.

Peak experience: Feelings of intense enjoyment where the sense of self is lost.

Maslow further proposed that self-actualized individuals are likely to have **peak experiences,** feelings of intense enjoyment to the point where they lose their sense of self. Other writers have called this the mystical experience:

> Feelings of limitless horizons opening up to the vision, the feeling of being simultaneously more powerful and also more helpless than one ever was before, the feeling of great ecstasy and wonder and awe, the loss of placing in time and space with, finally, the conviction that something extremely important and valuable has happened, so that the subject is to some extent transformed and strengthened even in his daily life by such experiences. (Maslow, 1970, p. 164)

But where other writers interpret this experience in religious terms and regard it in all-or-nothing fashion, Maslow described it as a psychological phenomenon that exists in varying degrees and intensity in all people.

The frequency with which someone has peak experiences and the overall degree of self-actualization are critical dimensions of personality as Maslow saw it. More generally, his hierarchy of motives suggests that each of us can be characterized by the level of needs that are currently salient (Williams & Page, 1989). Although self-actualization and peak experiences are inborn potentials for all of us, most people most of the time are not at this level.

Why? Like Carl Rogers, Maslow pointed to the environment as the culprit that thwarts our natural development. Conflict, frustration, and threat make it difficult to satisfy our basic needs. In the absence of such satisfaction, the individual never proceeds to higher needs. Much of Maslow's writings are recommendations to society about how to encourage self-actualization among its members.

Maslow's ideas have greatly influenced psychology by focusing on the positive aspects of the human enterprise. Also, his attempt to specify relationships among needs is compelling. Nevertheless, problems arise with his approach. Once he left the animal learning laboratory, he did not conduct conventional research. Indeed, he conveys more than a hint of distaste for science in his books (e.g., Maslow, 1966).

Counterexamples exist with respect to his hierarchy. A mother may run into a burning building—ignoring safety needs—to save her children. A hungry man may give his money to another man who is starving. A highly religious woman may forego the satisfaction of basic needs because they conflict with her principles of faith. These instances all capture something worthy about people and are therefore consistent with Maslow's overall vision. But they also contradict the details of his theory. The hierarchy of motives is a good approximation of the order in which some people attend to needs, but it fails to describe matters for all of us (cf. Miner, 1984).

It is unclear to me just where Maslow obtained some of his notions. For example, in a discussion of sexuality among self-actualized people, he stated that orgasms were less important to these individuals yet at the same time more intense and satisfying (Maslow, 1970, pp. 186–192). This assertion sounds pleasing to listeners, at least to those poised at the verge of self-actualization and/or orgasm, but let's be skeptical for a moment. How could he know this to be true? He did not undertake any systematic study of sexuality. Even if he had attempted to do so, the comparison of the subjective aspects of orgasm across different people seems fraught with difficulty.

The conduct of science can never be fully separate from the values of scientists, but Maslow's approach to personality can be criticized for overly mingling his personal views with his pronouncements about human nature. The people he viewed as self-actualized were those whom he happened to admire. Surely the possibility of bias is here. Indeed, his particular characterization of a self-actualized individual (pp. 239–240) sounds curiously like a successful college professor. Some of my best friends are college professors, but I for one would not want to point to them as the epitome of human possibilities.

Rollo May: Existential Psychology

Existentialism cohered in Europe during the nineteenth and twentieth centuries. Danish philosopher Soren Kierkegaard (1813–1855) and German philosophers Friedrich Nietzsche (1844–1900), Edmund Husserl (1859–1938), and Martin Heidegger (1889–1976) set the stage for existential thought, which was popularized further by Albert Camus (1913–1960) and Jean-Paul Sartre (1905–1980). These ideas were first introduced to psychology by disaffected psychoanalytic therapists.

In the United States, the best-known proponent of existentialism as applied to psychology has been Rollo May (b. 1909). May completed his doctoral studies in clinical psychology at Columbia University (Reeves, 1977). He studied psychoanalysis with Alfred Adler and Erich Fromm. He was also influenced by Kurt Goldstein, who first suggested the notion of self-actualization.

In the 1940s, May contracted tuberculosis. The favored treatment in those days was rest in a sanatorium, so May spent more than a year in bed. He used this time to work on his book *The Meaning of Anxiety* (1950). In preparation for his writing, he read two previous accounts of anxiety, one by Freud and the other by the existential philosopher Kierkegaard.

He found the contrast between the two books striking:

> I valued Freud's formulations—his first theory, that anxiety is the reemergence of repressed libido, and his second, that anxiety is the ego's reaction to the threat of the loss of the loved object. Kierkegaard, on the other hand, described anxiety as the struggle of the living being against nonbeing—which I was immediately experiencing in my struggle with death. . . . What struck me powerfully was that Kierkegaard was writing about *exactly what my fellow patients and I were going*

through. Freud was not; he was writing on a different level, giving formulations of the psychic mechanisms by which anxiety comes about. . . . Freud was writing *about* anxiety. Kierkegaard . . . *knew* anxiety. (May, 1969, pp. 2–3)

May did not dismiss what Freud had to say, but he concluded that it was incomplete because it paid insufficient attention to one's experience of anxiety. Indeed, psychology as a whole paid scant attention to the sorts of concerns that most interested existentialists.

Dasein: Being-in-the-world.

Let's take a look at some of these concerns. Perhaps the central concept in existential psychology is **Dasein,** a German word that translates to being-in-the-world. The hyphens are deliberate, to convey the idea that people do not have any existence apart from the world. To exist is to be in the world. Existentialists object to a dichotomy between people and their environments, and the notion of Dasein removes this distinction. The goal of the existential psychologist is to describe someone's experience as accurately as possible. Usually included in a description of someone's Dasein is mention of one's psychological and physical self (termed the *Eigenwelt*), one's physical surroundings (the *Umwelt*), and one's interpersonal relations (the *Mitwelt*).

Modes: Different ways of being-in-the-world.

People differ in the way they express their being-in-the-world. Existentialists refer to these differences as **modes,** and various modes have been identified (Binswanger, 1963):

- singular mode: isolating oneself from others
- dual mode: merging oneself with another
- plural mode: living in a world of formal relations with others

World-design: The overall pattern of a person's different modes.

These different modes do not constitute a personality typology. A given person has many modes of being-in-the-world. Further, these cohere into an overall pattern, which is termed his or her **world-design.**

This discussion so far seems quite abstract, so appreciate that the goal of existential psychology is exactly the opposite, to give a concrete description of the experiences of a particular person. Remember May's distinction between theorizing about anxiety (as Freud did) and describing its experience (as Kierkegaard did). Typical psychology theorizes almost to the exclusion of description.

Existential psychology has a different way of proceeding, attempting to describe people in terms meaningful to them. For example, May (1983) presented the case of a Mrs. Hutchens, a client in therapy with him. She was a woman in her middle 30s, who sought out help because of a perpetual hoarseness thought to be hysterical, that is, without a physical basis. May's tentative explanation for her symptom was that her mother raised her in a harsh fashion. She was afraid to express what she really felt because she would be rejected if she did. This inhibition translated itself, as psychodynamic theorists would suggest, into the physical symptom of hoarseness.

With this all said, May (1983, p. 25) pointed out, "But if . . . I am chiefly thinking of these how's and why's concerning the way the problem came about, I will grasp everything except the most important thing of all . . . this person now existing, becoming, emerging—this experiencing human being immediately in the room with me." May went on to describe what was most central about Mrs. Hutchens, about her experience. Most basically, and like all individuals, she was preoccupied with herself. She took this to an extreme and made it her dominant mode of being-in-the-world. She experienced herself as constricted.

A previous therapist had casually told Mrs. Hutchens that she was too proper, and she promptly broke off therapy. Why? According to May, the therapist had failed to appreciate that being in control was of central importance to his client. It was the way she preserved her sense of safety.

At the same time, Mrs. Hutchens needed to interact with others. May described her hoarseness as a mingling of fear and hope, a tentative reaching out to him. This was not easy for her because it entailed risk. She was constantly vigilant. In the course of therapy, she often described incidents where her attempts to express herself to others were accompanied by intense anxiety. According to May, anxiety is what people experience when their very being is threatened. Like Kierkegaard, he depicted anxiety as indicative of a struggle, a primal one between life and death.

Existentialists believe that people choose their mode of being-in-the-world. They are ultimately responsible for their experience. This of course raises a question: If people exercise choice, then why do we have individuals who suffer so greatly, like Mrs. Hutchens? Did she choose to suffer? If so, why?

An existential psychologist would respond that people sometimes do not choose wisely. Suffering may not be their goal, but what they have chosen nonetheless brings them suffering. One reason for poor choices is our unawareness of possibilities in life. No one has infinite options available; we must be frank with ourselves about what is realistic. Otherwise, we are said to be inauthentic; **inauthenticity** leads to poor choices and eventually to unhappiness.

Another reason why people choose poorly is **existential guilt,** feelings that result from failing to achieve certain potentials. Some degree of existential guilt is inevitable, according to May, because no matter what we choose to do, we necessarily fail to do other things. We have only one route through life, and at some level we all feel guilty about the paths we have not taken.

In contemporary United States, we can find widespread attempts to deny this existential premise. College students speak glibly of "keeping their options open" until the time in their lives when they can "have it all." I am dubious that these strategies are viable. Existential psychologists would go further and brand them inauthentic, certain to result in unhappiness. Indeed, the current generation of young adults is reportedly up to 10 times more at risk for depression than their parents or grandparents (Seligman, 1988).

Another consideration that can thwart an individual is the **dread of nothingness.** This involves the fear of death, but more precisely it refers to the fear that death will bring a cessation of experience. One's being-in-the-world will be no more. Needless to say, we will all die, and we all know this, so the dread of nothingness constantly clouds our existence.

Inauthenticity: One's dishonesty with oneself concerning what is possible.

Existential guilt: The feeling of guilt that results from failing to achieve one's potential.

Dread of nothingness: The fear of the cessation of experience.

In some cases, we deny the dread of nothingness (Yalom, 1980). So, we may fail to acknowledge the possibility of death, acting as if the laws of nature apply to everyone but ourselves. Talk to a person who engages in unhealthy practices—smoking, drinking, or using drugs. Many people somehow believe that they are exempt from the consequences of their acts. The notion of being immune to the laws of nature may be at the basis of a number of common problems. A workaholic, for instance, may harbor the delusion that he or she is indispensable and therefore immortal.

Fusion: A strategy for denying death by losing one's self through identification with others.

Another strategy for denying death is **fusion,** where individuals cast their lot with other people to such an extent that their sense of self is lost. Fusion denies the special status of the individual as the one who has experiences and may happen when people become lost in their identification with a job ("company men"), a sports team (Bleacher Bums), or a rock-and-roll band (Dead Heads). Their mode of being-in-the-world denies the self and, with it, the possibility of the cessation of self. Don't misunderstand the point of fusion. Part of existence is becoming involved with other people; fusion goes beyond involvement to loss of personal identity. It is not an authentic way of being-in-the-world.

In fusion, people over-identify with others so much that their sense of self is lost.

One cannot read what Rollo May and other existential psychologists have to say without feeling that they are conveying something important about being human. The criticisms of existential psychology that most readily come to mind pertain to what this approach neglects. Because it deals with "serious" matters, it conveys a weighty picture of human existence. One searches in vain for commentary on the mundane. And with its insistence on individual choice and

responsibility, existential psychology seems to ignore the fact that people's lives are often shaped in large part by factors outside their control.

Ronald D. Laing: The Divided Self

Ronald D. Laing (1927–1989) was a Scottish psychiatrist best known for his phenomenological analyses of schizophrenia. In *The Divided Self,* Laing (1959) argued that schizophrenia could only be understood by grasping the experience of the patient. We have seen this suggestion throughout the chapter, but Laing is noteworthy for his clarity and vividness in describing the experiences of others.

He proposed that schizophrenia entails **ontological insecurity,** that is, profound doubts about one's own existence. One's self is thereby divided, and everything else about schizophrenia—the bizarre symptoms that capture the interest of most psychologists and psychiatrists—makes sense only in this context. Traditionally, these symptoms are described with colorful metaphors, terms like *word salad, loose associations,* and *poverty of speech,* which make schizophrenic individuals seem like broken machines. Laing counsels us instead to listen to what "abnormal" people tell us, because their experience, even when at odds with our own, is still their defining characteristic, just as our own experience defines us.

Laing recounted the case of Peter, a young man diagnosed as schizophrenic. Among Peter's symptoms was smelling something rotten that no one else could detect. One could simply call this an olfactory hallucination and be done with it, but Laing delved into Peter's experience. He discovered that Peter had been raised in a family where he was profoundly ignored. His parents fed and clothed him but otherwise paid him absolutely no heed. They went about their business in their small apartment as if Peter did not exist.

What resulted, according to Laing's analysis, was that Peter arrived at a highly idiosyncratic way of experiencing the world. He never developed a sense of *intersubjective reality:* the convention that certain experiences are public because other people treat them as real, whereas other experiences are private because other people do not acknowledge them. He never carved up his experiences this way, simply because his parents never validated or invalidated any of them. So what if someone else didn't smell what Peter smelled? No one had ever commented on anything that had seemed real to him.

At this point in his career, Laing (1959) did not claim that the way Peter's parents treated him caused his schizophrenia. That was not the point of Laing's phenomenological analysis. Rather, the way Peter was raised led him to experience the world in a certain way, and *we* cannot make sense of him until we understand his experiences. According to Laing, a diagnosis of schizophrenia is inadequate if our goal is to comprehend and eventually help another human being. Any theory of schizophrenia is uninformed until it takes into account the phenomenology of the schizophrenic individual. By implication, any theory of personality is uninformed until it takes into account the phenomenology of the individual.

Ontological insecurity: Doubts about one's own existence.

According to Laing, we can only understand schizophrenia from the inside.

Family systems: An approach to clinical psychology that regards individual problems as manifestations of dynamics within the family.

Laing was soon led from his phenomenological descriptions to consider why some people experienced themselves this way. He became convinced that the family was usually to blame for conveying to the young child impossible demands (Laing & Esterson, 1964). Here Laing converged with the **family systems** approach to therapy, which regards individual problems as manifestations of dynamics within the family.

Laing (1967) then took this criticism one step further and held the entire society responsible for making impossible demands on people. Those sensitive enough to the contradictions of the world became schizophrenic. Laing seemed to be saying that schizophrenia was a "higher" form of experience. So, his conception of schizophrenia evolved from viewing it as an unfortunate—although understandable—problem to viewing it as a state we should revere. At this point, most of those in the mental-health professions disagreed strongly with Laing's thinking. They admired his descriptions of schizophrenia and his obvious sympathy and understanding, but they would not take the next step and romanticize the problem.

The next phase in his career was the operation of a clinic in London called Kingsley Hall where "patients" were allowed to work through their schizophrenia, which Laing was now regarding as an experiential journey (Sedgwick, 1971). Travelers were not to be interrupted in this journey, because they would presumably emerge from it better off than they had been in the first place. Psychiatric intervention, such as drugs, constituted an interruption of a natural process and so should be avoided.

As you might imagine, Kingsley Hall—no longer in operation—was controversial. To the outsider it seemed chaotic. In the words of a resident:

> No one who lives at Kingsley Hall sees those who perform work upon the external material world as 'staff,' and those who do not as 'patients.' No caste system forbids people to move freely from one group to another, as it does in mental hospitals. No locus of institutional power subordinates everyone. . . . Each person at Kingsley Hall may choose to assume the obligations of a reciprocal bond with another person. . . .
>
> Some visitors are curious to know which of the residents had been labelled 'schizophrenic' by hospital psychiatrists before they came to live at Kingsley Hall, and which of the residents had previously worked as 'staff' at mental hospitals. . . . Their wrong guesses can be amusing. Guests, in staff positions at mental hospitals, sometimes suppose that those who had previously been labelled 'schizophrenic' are really doctors and nurses, and vice versa. (Schatzman, 1971, p. 267)

Mental breakdowns—that is, acute psychotic episodes—were not seen as cause for alarm. Residents were allowed, even encouraged, to smear feces on the walls, to refuse solid food, and to go for weeks without speaking to others.

Later in his life, Laing backed off from his strong stance and said that he never intended to glorify schizophrenia (McQuiston, 1989). His legacy is his initial work, the phenomenological description of schizophrenia. This is of great importance to personality psychologists as an example of how anyone's experience can be grasped, and of the benefits in understanding that ensue from this description.

RESEARCH

As repeatedly emphasized, many of the humanists have a distaste for conventional research. Accordingly, it is somewhat difficult to decide what should be discussed in this section. Some humanistic psychologists would argue that methods of phenomenology constitute the only legitimate approach to research (e.g., Keen, 1975), and thus our descriptions of experience comprise the only relevant data. If so, then we have already discussed research, every time we have paused for illustrative examples.

Other humanistic psychologists would say that theoretical concepts can be translated into terms amenable to conventional research via correlational investigations or experiments. This is a minority opinion, to be sure, but among those who expressed it was a prominent humanist: Carl Rogers (1969b). He called on researchers to operationally define such admittedly imprecise terms as *existence, becoming,* and *experience,* and then to study them. As you have seen, Rogers attempted to do this with respect to the important ideas in his own self-theory.

Yet another view on research within this paradigm starts with the distinction between metapsychological propositions and clinical propositions, which we discussed earlier with regard to psychodynamic theory and research. Some aspects of a theoretical approach—the metapsychological propositions—are bedrock assumptions that cannot be verified in particular studies. Rather, they serve as a foundation for other theoretical aspects that can be tested by research—the clinical propositions.

So, concepts such as *becoming, choice,* and *dread of nothingness* cannot be confirmed or disconfirmed in a study. Suppose we did a survey and asked people if these notions really existed. What would it mean if they said yes, or for that matter if they said no? Probably very little to the theorist who was already convinced about their status, one way or another. In contrast, imagine we just assumed the utility of these concepts, and then saw if other matters ensued as theory predicts. In this section, I'll follow this latter approach and discuss several lines of work that investigate clinical propositions derived from humanistic theories. Said another way, these investigations were inspired by the key ideas of the humanistic paradigm.

Private Experience

Many contemporary psychologists have heeded the humanistic demand that we should understand people from the inside out. In a recent commentary on personality psychology, Singer and Kolligian (1987, p. 536) noted "an increased emphasis on private experience," *the* central concern of humanistic psychologists.

Part of this emphasis entails a rediscovery of what William James (1890) had to say about conscious experience. James likened consciousness to a stream, stressing its continual movement. It always has a particular topic on focus; it is selective, personal, and pragmatic. James wrote outside of the phenomenological tradition, but his depiction fits well with the view of experience endorsed by contemporary humanistic psychologists (May, 1969).

After profound disinterest in consciousness throughout most of the twentieth century, psychologists in the final few decades have returned to its study with renewed enthusiasm (e.g., Ornstein, 1973, 1977). Consciousness has long been recognized as existing in qualitatively different states. Psychologists today study both the characteristics of these states and their consequences. The effects of meditation and psychoactive drugs on consciousness have been thriving areas of research. Religious experience has also become a legitimate topic for investigation (Wulff, 1990). And researchers study self-consciousness, self-awareness, and a host of related psychological states and processes (e.g., Baumeister, 1987; Linville, 1987; Markus & Nurius, 1986; Markus & Wurf, 1987; Ogilvie, 1987).

Daydreaming   As one example of this new interest in consciousness and experience, let's consider Jerome Singer's (1966, 1975, 1984) investigations of daydreaming. For years, the only interest psychologists ever showed in daydreaming was Freud's (1908b) pronouncement that only unhappy people engaged in it. No one checked out this assertion until Singer began his studies. What he found was at odds with Freud's conclusion.

According to Singer, daydreaming is close to a universal phenomenon, engaged in at one time or another by almost everyone. However, people report great variation in the time they spend daydreaming, from a few minutes per day to many hours. This appears to be a consistent individual difference.

In daydreams, a few themes are extremely common. Invariably, daydreamers assign themselves the central role in their fantasies, which take one of these typical forms:

- *self-recrimination*   People think back over actual events and wish they had said or done something differently.
- *thoughtful planning*   People plan future events and rehearse what they will do.
- *autistic*   People experience bizarre, dreamlike images.
- *self-conscious*   People imagine great adventures and triumphs.

To use my own daydreaming as an example, I fantasize about great athletic exploits on my part, in whatever sport is currently featured on television. My basketball, football, and baseball triumphs occur in regular succession throughout the year. Bo knows how lucky he is that my daydreams aren't really happening.

Singer suggests that daydreaming serves several functions. Daydreams provide escape from our everyday stress or boredom. They alter our mood and feelings. Quite obviously, daydreaming can enhance our sexual arousal. And finally, daydreams can be quite practical. When we rehearse what we might say during a conversation, the way we will drive across the country on a vacation, or how we might arrange the furniture in our living room, we may well come up with an optimal way to do things that is a lot simpler than relying on trial and error. In contrast to Freud's (1908b) conclusion that daydreaming is only for unhappy people, Singer's research suggests that it serves many adaptive purposes. In the language of humanistic psychology, daydreaming is a dress rehearsal for the process of becoming, a way to explore—and to realize—plans and possibilities.

Experience Sampling   Contemporary studies of private experience often make use of a new research method that is thoroughly high-tech. Called **experience sampling,** this approach "samples" a research subject's ongoing thoughts, feelings, and actions at many times throughout the day, while they are actually occurring (Hormuth, 1986). Typically in other approaches, when psychologists study individuals, they observe them at one point in time and then generalize to other points in time. They might ask subjects to perform a task in a laboratory or to complete a questionnaire, hoping that what is revealed is typical of the rest of the time. The problem with these procedures is that they are necessarily a step or two removed from the actual experiences in which the researcher is interested.

In experience sampling, people are provided with a beeper linked to a radio transmitter. The investigator programs the transmitter to sound the beeper at various intervals throughout a day. When the research subjects hear the beep,

Experience sampling: A research approach that ascertains one's ongoing thoughts, feelings, and actions while they are actually occurring.

they stop what they are doing and record their immediate thoughts and activities.

The most extensive use of experience sampling has been by psychologist Michael Csikszentmihalyi and his colleagues (1975, 1990; Csikszentmihalyi & Csikszentmihalyi, 1988; Csikszentmihalyi & Larson, 1984). For example, in one study, they gave beepers to a number of adolescents and beeped them over a period of several weeks. They were able to give in fine-grained detail the interrelations among these young people's thoughts, feelings, and activities.

For example, one of the important findings from experience-sampling studies is that our personalities are indeed in flux, as humanistic psychologists have asserted. Summary measures—such as questionnaires—necessarily ask subjects to generalize about how they usually feel or act. Experience sampling gets at the actual instances of experience, allowing variation to surface. Sometimes this variation proves substantial. Of particular interest to researchers has been the range of a person's mood, now recognized as an individual difference in its own right.

People with the eating disorder of bulimia, for example, report more extreme moods over time than do nonbulimic individuals (Johnson & Larson, 1982). They engage in bingeing and purging particularly when they feel lonely and depressed. Perhaps this is a clue about the causes of bulimia: People prone to this problem may be seeking a way to regulate their extremely fluctuating mood. Food makes someone feel better, and so a binge provides a temporary respite from unhappiness. But then the person feels guilty and ashamed and decides to purge.

Flow: The subjective feelings that accompany highly engaging activities.

Flow   Csikszentmihalyi (1990) has used experience sampling to study the experience of **flow:** subjective feelings that accompany highly engaging activities. It is similar to what Maslow referred to as a peak experience, and Csikszentmihalyi has been able to study these experiences as they happen. He does not have to rely on retrospective accounts that necessarily lose something in the retelling. Flow has been investigated in artists, athletes, and motorcyclists; it usually occurs during activities people most enjoy doing.

Flow takes place when a person focuses attention on the task at hand. The task must present an above-average challenge, and the skills brought to bear must be deployed with an above-average expertise. Critically, the challenges and skills must also be in appropriate balance. Without this balance, the person will not experience flow. Instead, what results is either worry (when challenges outweigh skills) or boredom (when skills outweigh challenges).

Flow experiences are reported by most people. Interestingly, flow occurs at work just as readily as it does at play, suggesting that too rigid a distinction between work and play—at least phenomenologically—is a mistake. As we might expect, flow occurs at work for people who are pleased with what they are doing, who work more at their job as opposed to less. So, again to use humanistic language, flow happens when people are authentic.

Let's examine the finding that challenges and skills must be above what the person usually experiences to result in flow. What this means is that a person must continue to change and grow; otherwise, flow will stop. Csikszentmihalyi

These runners are probably experiencing flow.

(1990) regards flow as the manifestation of a drive within us to develop psychologically (not physically). In sum, it is the feeling that accompanies the drive toward actualization long spoken about by humanistic theorists.

The Effects of Choice

We can offer the generic prediction from humanistic theories that choice is desirable. Indeed, choice should have all manner of beneficial consequences, because in choosing, people are acting in accordance with their nature. They are becoming. Experimental research nicely bears out this prediction (see Perlmuter & Monty, 1979).

In a typical study, research subjects are put in one of two situations: Either they are given a choice or they are given none. Following this intervention, some outcome of interest is studied. So, for example, individuals who *choose* to expose themselves to a painful stimulus are better able to tolerate the pain than individuals simply put into such a situation (Averill, 1973; Miller, 1979; Thompson, 1981). Individuals who *choose* to perform some task end up enjoying it more than individuals assigned to do the same task; they may do better at the task as well (Monty & Perlmuter, 1975).

One of the most dramatic experiments in the whole of psychology investigated the effects of giving choices to residents in a nursing home. Ellen Langer and Judith Rodin (1976) assigned half of the elderly residents to an experimental group where ample choices were provided. These residents were told by the staff that they themselves were responsible for their lives and their routines. They could choose how to arrange their room, when to schedule activities, and so on. The other half of the nursing home residents were assigned to a comparison group without these options. They were told by the staff that their needs would be taken care of and that they should be happy.

In point of fact, both groups were well-treated. Staff members were attentive and helpful. Material comforts were abundant. Medical care was readily available. The only difference between the two groups was the exercise of choices by the experimental subjects.

Several weeks after the experiment began, individuals in the two groups were compared with respect to happiness, activity, alertness, and health. On all these measures, subjects who had experienced enhanced choice scored higher, even though no differences between the groups existed before the intervention. Certainly, no humanistic theorist would have been surprised by these results, but they are obviously important, with practical and theoretical significance.

Eighteen months later, Rodin and Langer (1977) found an even more startling difference between the two groups. Thirty percent of the nursing home residents in the comparison condition had died, which was *twice as many* as those in the enhanced choice condition. So choice manifests itself not just in activity and alertness but also in longevity.

Hardiness

Another line of investigation that takes off from humanistic thought is Suzanne Kobasa's (1979, 1982) investigations of an individual difference she calls **hardiness.** She explicitly acknowledges the origin of this idea in existential theories (Kobasa, Maddi, & Courington, 1981). Briefly, she assumes that people differ in the degree to which they are actively engaged in meeting the challenges of life. Some people are passive and fatalistic, merely going through the motions. Other people, in contrast, approach the world with curiosity. They find meaning and interest at every turn. Stressful events are readily accommodated by these individuals, who recast them as challenges. These people are living an authentic life. As Kobasa puts it, they are hardy individuals.

Kobasa measures hardiness with a questionnaire that presents respondents with various questions tapping its components. To the degree that they agree with them, they are considered hardy. Studies show that hardiness measured this way predicts which people are less likely to fall ill when they experience stress. So, one study compared 100 working adults with numerous complaints of illness with 100 other working adults who had few complaints (Kobasa, 1979). Although each group had experienced the same number of stressful events, the second group proved to be hardier than the first.

One objection to this study is that it leaves unclear the direction of effects. Kobasa wishes to argue that hardiness produces resilience in the face of illness, but it might be that people who are resilient, for whatever reason, end up endorsing a "hardy" outlook. The counter to this objection is provided by a longitudinal study conducted by Kobasa, Maddi, and Kahn (1982), where the hardiness of individuals was measured at one point in time, and then intervening stressful events and health status were measured at a later point in time. In this study, hardiness predicted a person's immunity to illness in the face of stress.

Kobasa's research has been criticized (Funk & Houston, 1987). For example, critics observe that it can be difficult to identify the active psychological factors from among the many included in her questionnaire, which simply lumps all of them together (Carver, 1989; Hull, Van Treuren, & Virnelli, 1987). But regardless, hardiness is an example of an individual difference derived from humanistic thought with correlates and consequences consistent with theoretical prediction (see also Allred & Smith, 1989; Rhodewalt & Zone, 1989; Roth, Wiebe, Fillingim, & Shay, 1989).

Supportive Environments

We saw in our earlier discussion of humanistic theories that the environment is often assigned a negative role. People would be perfectly fine, developing and unfolding their inherent nature, if they were simply left in a benign setting. This claim as a whole is a metapsychological proposition, because it is impossible to verify the notion of an inherent human nature in an optimal environment. However, we can test the prediction that some environments better facilitate health and happiness than do others.

That extreme and brutal physical trauma take a toll on one's well-being is obvious and requires little documentation (but see Browne & Finkelhor, 1986). There exist more subtle ways to test this notion about inherent nature that yield some surprising results. We can talk not about physical trauma but instead about supportive contacts with other human beings.

Psychologists have extensively investigated the effects of such contacts under the rubric of **social support,** which refers to the various ways people can help one another (Cohen & Syme, 1985). Social support can range from the provision of tangible resources, like money and food, to practical advice about how to surmount a challenge, to affirmation, to purely emotional support—just being there with someone in distress.

Social support: The various ways people can help one another.

It is easy to summarize the vast research literature on social support; Support is almost always beneficial, by any and all criteria one might choose (Friedman & DiMatteo, 1989). People with rich and supportive friendships are happier and healthier than their socially estranged counterparts. They have more robust immune systems. They even live longer.

Social support is not simply a matter of receiving benefits from other people. It is necessarily a two-way street. And indeed, those who give to others are just as likely to benefit as those who receive. An intriguing study by House, Robbins, and Metzner (1982) illustrates this point. People who engage in volunteer work are healthier than those who do not, even when likely third variables such as initial health status, age, and social class are taken into account. Something is inherently beneficial about being engaged with another person, participating with them in the business of life.

Let's return to the notion of brutal, physical trauma and its obvious bad effects on people. Granted that the relationship between trauma and harm is so clear and common, we should be particularly interested in those few people who are traumatized yet do *not* suffer as much as we would expect. Researchers have looked at this possibility, and the findings are consistent with humanistic premises.

Invulnerable children: Children who thrive despite growing up with an abusive and/or extremely disturbed parent.

One line of work has looked at so-called **invulnerable children:** youngsters who grow up with an abusive and/or extremely disturbed parent. We would expect this experience to take a profound toll on the child, and indeed this often happens. But in some cases, the child in dire circumstance displays great skills and accomplishments:

> Mary was . . . the seventh of nine children, prematurely born with a congenital dislocation of the hip that was so inadequately treated at the city hospital that she developed a permanent limp. . . . Between two and five years of age, she was placed in a foster home with three of her siblings because the family living quarters had been condemned as overcrowded and unsanitary. The health visitor reported that the children were constantly exposed to the crude sexual behavior of the parents, especially when the father was drunk, which was fairly frequent. . . . He was brought before the court several times for physically abusing the children, particularly Mary, whom he called "the cripple." . . .
>
> When Mary was referred as a child at risk, I was struck by her immediate friendliness. The warm, comfortable, and trustful reaction took me completely by surprise, since I was expecting just the opposite. . . .
>
> I wondered how she spent her spare time. Her eyes lit up as she said enthusiastically, "I am collecting money for the poor children in India." (Anthony, 1987, pp. 38–39)

What makes such children possible? The research suggests that they share in common a solid relationship with some other human being, perhaps a brother or sister, a teacher, or a neighbor (Anthony & Cohler, 1987). For these children, this relationship helps them weather and even transcend their intolerable home life.

Another line of work studies post-traumatic stress disorders, which we discussed briefly in Chapter 4 as an example of Freud's notion of the compulsion to repeat. People with these disorders have experienced a severe trauma—assault, war, natural disaster, torture, internment in a prisoner-of-war camp—and later experience a host of debilitating symptoms of anxiety: trouble sleeping, difficulty concentrating, rumination, and social estrangement.

Like children exposed to abuse during their tender years, we would expect most people who have experienced severe trauma to show at least some psychological damage. Accordingly, those few individuals who display little effects of trauma become a particularly intriguing group to understand. One opinion among those who have studied survivors of trauma who are faring better than we might expect is that they have derived some sense of meaning or significance from the otherwise terrible event (e.g., Silver & Wortman, 1980).

Those who survived the horror of the Nazi death camps commonly reported that they wished to survive in order to bear witness to the Holocaust, to tell others about it so it would never happen again. This helped them deal with the trauma itself and its aftermath. As the existentialists suggest, people who

When trauma occurs, the person who is able to tie the experience to some purpose is better able to cope than the person who is not.

can place meaning on their life, no matter how absurd its events, fare better than those who do not (Frankl, 1963).

Do not misunderstand the point of these examples. Abuse and trauma are not simply in one's head; these are terrible things to be avoided and condemned. The point I am trying to make is that *if* these things happen, the person who is supported and is able to tie the experience to some purpose is better able to cope than the person who is not.

What you should appreciate about these investigations of private experience, choice, hardiness, and supportive environments is that psychology today is a different field than the one to which Rogers, Maslow, and other humanists originally objected. The most mainstream psychologist nowadays speaks of consciousness and experience. The humanists indeed have had an effect.

APPLICATIONS

If research stemming directly from within the humanistic paradigm is a bit difficult to find, the opposite is the case for the applications of this perspective on personality. Many walks of life have been touched by humanistic and existential ideas: therapy, health, business, and education. In this section, we will discuss several intriguing examples of these applications. Keep in mind the point I made about applications of psychodynamic ideas; they do not test theories so much as use them.

The Human Potential Movement

During the 1960s, Michael Murphy and Richard Price founded the Esalen Institute in Big Sur, California (Tomkins, 1976). This center for learning soon became well-known. It epitomized the 1960s counterculture, mixing together Eastern religions, radical politics, and the expansion of consciousness.

The Esalen Institute sprawls over several hundred acres where natural mineral springs flow. Murphy and Price envisioned Esalen as a health spa, a place where people could visit, take seminars, bathe in the springs, recuperate, and grow. Quite congenial, therefore, to those at Esalen were the ideas of humanistic psychologists writing at this time. In particular they found the writings of Abraham Maslow, with their emphasis on growth needs and self-actualization, to be inspirational.

One foggy night in 1962, Maslow and his wife just happened to be driving down the California coast, looking for a place to stay. They saw the lights at Esalen, pulled into its parking lot, and asked if they could have a room. Needless to say, the couple was enthusiastically received, and Maslow returned many times to lead seminars. This was the beginning of what came to be known as the **human potential movement,** the use of therapeutic techniques to enhance the functioning of already healthy individuals.

Maslow provided the rationale for this approach, and such therapists as Carl Rogers provided the actual techniques. Particularly popular were role-playing techniques whose roots were to be found in **psychodrama,** a strategy pioneered years earlier by the Romanian psychiatrist Jacob Moreno (1946). These techniques were used in group settings, in so-called encounter groups. People were encouraged—indeed, urged—to confront themselves and others. In the course of these intense encounters, their repressed feelings and thoughts would come to the surface, often resulting in emotional relief. Here we see a version of catharsis as encouraged by psychodynamic therapists, but in this case the people were not neurotics but normal. They experienced the release not as the removal of a burden but as a joyous fulfillment.

At the same time, other therapies stressing body awareness became popular at Esalen (e.g., Brooks, 1974). Their intent was to boost people's sensitivity to their own sensations, perceptions, and emotions. Meditation and yoga were employed for just this purpose. Ida Rolf came to the Esalen Institute, bringing a technique of deep massage that now bears her name: Rolfing.

The individual who came to symbolize the Esalen Institute, and indeed the entire human potential movement, was the controversial and charismatic Frederick (Fritz) Perls (1909–1971). Perls created **gestalt therapy,** which uses techniques of psychodrama and body awareness to force encounters among people. Gestalt therapy, by the way, has little to do with gestalt psychology as described in Chapter 2. Perls argued that people seek balance within themselves, in particular between their thoughts and feelings. In this sense we can speak of his approach as being concerned with meaningful patterns—wholes or gestalts. But little else in his approach can be traced to gestalt psychology (see Wertheimer, 1978).

Human potential movement: The use of therapeutic techniques to enhance the functioning of already healthy individuals.

Psychodrama: A therapeutic strategy employing role-playing techniques.

Gestalt therapy: The approach to therapy created by Fritz Perls that encourages people to achieve a balance between their thoughts and feelings.

Fritz Perls was an impatient therapist.

Instead, the roots of gestalt therapy are found elsewhere. Perls was originally trained as a psychoanalyst. His own analysts included Wilhelm Reich and Karen Horney (Clarkson, 1989). One can see their influence on gestalt therapy. From Reich came an emphasis on the body and the notion that neurotic people show their problem in their posture. If they can be encouraged to get "in touch" with their bodies, then they will benefit. From Horney came an emphasis on the role of other people in creating problems and fostering well-being. In Perls's encounter groups, people were encouraged to act out their conflicts with others: snarling and screaming at them, even wrestling and fighting with them if that was how they felt.

Perls was an impatient therapist. He felt that dramatic changes could be brought about in an extremely brief period of time. And so his gestalt treatment was an impatient therapy, cajoling people to bring their true natures to the surface, to get in touch with how they *really* felt, and to cut through the intellectualizations that hindered their growth.

He was bombastic and profane, yet people flocked to his encounter groups. One of his techniques was called the **hot seat,** which sounds perfectly dreadful to me, although people vied to be placed in it. In front of a group, the designated person would relate a recent dream. To Perls, each aspect of the dream—even its inanimate content—was symbolic. The person had to act out the dream in its entirety in front of the group. Someone who dreamed about a

Hot seat: A gestalt therapy technique where one person acts out a dream in front of a group.

chest of drawers had to "become" that chest of drawers and show what it meant to him or her. In the process, Perls and the other group members would notice something the person was avoiding or repressing and zero in on it. The individual would be forced to an emotional impasse, presumably followed by the recognition of its source and catharsis.

These kinds of encounters aroused strong opinions, both pro and con. Some saw them as the way to create a new species of human beings. In one project undertaken at Esalen, people were recruited to participate in an encounter group that lasted nine months, with the expectation that they would be permanently transformed by the experience. On the downside, others saw encounter groups as potentially damaging. Indeed, casualties of the encounters did occur: emotional breakdowns precipitated by the intense experiences. The human potential movement was billed as a program for healthy people, but certainly among those who were interested were some folks who were less than fully functioning. Confrontation and emotional tumult were not good for them.

Although the Esalen Institute became synonymous with encounter groups, they were only part of its agenda. Perls wanted to turn Esalen into a gestalt institute, but Murphy and Price resisted. He left in 1969 to form his own therapy center, but he died shortly thereafter.

Looking back on the height of the human potential movement, we can offer an evenhanded evaluation. The movement is no longer so popular, although Esalen remains alive and well. Our society has been forever changed by its existence. We all speak casually of self-fulfillment, finding our space, and doing our own thing. We use imagery to improve our golf swing or to survive a stressful job interview. We meditate on our coffee break. Even the current physical fitness boom can be traced to body awareness as promoted at the Esalen Institute.

At the same time, encounters are not the whole of existence. It is selfish to pursue them in a single-minded fashion. The human potential movement deserves some blame for fostering the "me" generation. The gestalt prayer popularized by Perls (1969, p. 4) now sounds terribly wrong:

> I do my thing and you do your thing.
> I am not in this world to live up to your expectations
> —And you are not in this world to live up to mine.
> You are you and I am I.
> If by chance we find each other, it's beautiful.
> If not, it can't be helped.

Also, the power of encounter groups to facilitate change was greatly exaggerated, by advocates and by critics. We now know that these experiences can prove tremendously exhilarating, while still leaving the person wherever he or she started.

The Will to Live

Contemporary America is remarkably health-conscious, and in the last decade we have seen an explosion of interest in the factors that influence our physical well-being. Chief among these are psychological states and processes, many of central concern to personality psychologists. At times, this interest in the psychological influences on health and illness becomes phrased in unambiguously humanistic language, as when we talk about a person's will to live. In this section, let's take a close look at some of these notions.

One of the best-known examples of this approach to physical well-being is recounted in the book *Anatomy of an Illness* (1981b) by writer Norman Cousins. He described how he fell ill in 1964 with a collagen disease: a problem with the connective tissue in his body. Cousins was able to move only with great difficulty. Nodules appeared under his skin. One specialist gave him but one chance in 500 of recovering.

Cousins decided that the one person out of 500 must do more than wait passively to see what would happen. He decided to take control of his illness. His reading convinced him that he had fallen ill in part because his adrenal glands were exhausted from too much stress.

How do you recharge your adrenal glands? Cousins chose a two-pronged approach. First, he stopped taking the aspirin prescribed for his pain, under the assumption that aspirin further taxed his adrenals. He substituted instead massive amounts of vitamin C, under the assumption that ascorbic acid combats collagen breakdown. Second, he mobilized his positive emotions—love, hope, faith, confidence, and laughter. Research has shown that negative emotions have harmful effects on the body's biochemistry. Does it follow that positive emotions have beneficial effects?

Cousins explored this possibility. Because he found his hospital room a depressing place, he left the hospital altogether and checked into a hotel. He

Norman Cousins combated a serious illness by mustering his positive emotions.

read humor books. From his friend Allen Funt, he obtained classic "Candid Camera" television episodes and watched them for hours at a time.

He recovered from this illness and then went on to write extensively about physical health and how it can be influenced by positive emotions and one's will to survive (e.g., Cousins, 1981a, 1983, 1989):

> I have learned never to underestimate the capacity of the human mind and body to regenerate—even when the prospects seem most wretched. The life-force may be the least understood force on earth. William James said that human beings tend to live too far within self-imposed limits. It is possible that these limits will recede when we respect more fully the natural drive of the human mind and body toward perfectibility and regeneration. Protecting and cherishing that natural drive may well represent the finest exercise of human freedom. (Cousins, 1977, p. 51)

One can easily imagine Rogers, Maslow, and other humanistic psychologists nodding in agreement.

Another contributor to this genre is Bernie Siegel, a physician whose best-selling books *Love, Medicine, and Miracles* (1986) and *Peace, Love, and Healing* (1989) brim with heartwarming anecdotes about how people's will to live helped them surmount serious disease. Siegel also makes a strong case that physicians have abdicated their traditional bedside manner and no longer know how to encourage health in their patients. Nowadays, they are more interested in equipment, tests, drugs, and money. They have lost track of the person who falls ill and struggles to regain his or her health. In other words, they have neglected to establish a "healthy" relationship with their patients.

Here again we see a statement highly compatible with the humanistic approach. Human beings are distinctive; they cannot be reduced to biology and chemistry. The physician who views a patient merely as the battleground between drugs and germs is missing the point about healing.

One more example of how ideas from the humanistic paradigm show up in thinking about health and illness is the work of Carl and Stephanine Simonton (1975; Simonton, Matthews-Simonton, & Creighton, 1978), who concern themselves with cancer. They regard this disease as a psychological phenomenon, brought about by a pessimistic way of viewing the world:

> Malignancy is . . . despair that has been experienced biologically, despair at the level of the cell. In this sense, suggest the Simontons, none of us *gets* cancer; we reach a point at which our deepest need and wish is to withdraw from life, and we therefore "choose" to develop cancer. . . . In the Simontons' view, the illness is a defective coping strategy used by someone who was not able to meet an adaptive demand. (Scarf, 1980, pp. 37–39)

The existential notion of choice is thus extended from how one lives to how one dies.

The Simontons believe that cancer can be combatted by encouraging a person to approach matters in a different way. An important part of their strategy is to instruct people in how to use mental imagery to envision a struggle between the body's defenses and the cancer cells that threaten life (see Figure 7–2).

Carl Simonton first hit upon this method of mental imagery while treating a 61-year-old man with advanced throat cancer. Simonton is a radiologist by training, and he was giving his patient daily radiation treatments. He asked the man to imagine how the radiation was affecting his cancer:

> The radiation therapy was to be visualized as a stream of tiny bullets of energy that struck all body cells, normal and abnormal, but destroyed only the weaker, aberrant, "confused" cells—the cancer cells. The patient was instructed to imagine his body's white blood cells coming in, swarming over the dead and dying cancer cells, and flushing them off (via the liver and kidneys) as one might remove the dead and dying enemy from the field of lost battle. Each imaging session was to close with the patient's visualizing his tumor as decreasing in size and his health as returning to normal. (Scarf, 1980, p. 37)

This particular patient recovered fully, and from there the Simonton method took form. The cancer patient fights his disease in his mind, willing himself to health by using thoughts and images (see Figure 7–2). A video game—"Killer T Cell"—has even been developed to help patients envision the process of zapping cancer cells.

Research support for these messages about health and illness is not nearly as abundant as we would like. The most compelling evidence comes from striking case studies, but these are often ambiguous. Who is to know what would have happened to Norman Cousins had he stayed in the hospital? Maybe his positive emotions had nothing to do with his recovery; maybe it was the vitamin C. Or maybe he was misdiagnosed in the first place, suffering only an acute episode of illness that would have resolved itself regardless of what he did.

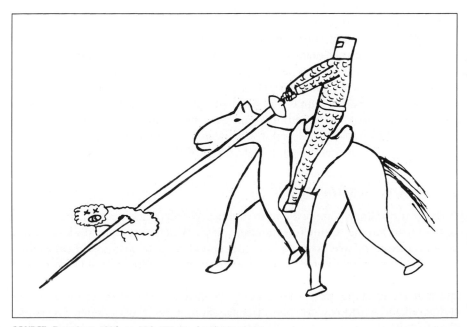

**FIGURE 7–2
Example of Cancer Imagery**

A patient has drawn a knight (a white blood cell) stabbing an armadillo (a cancer cell).

SOURCE: From Jaret, 1986, pp. 704–705. Used with permission.

Neither Cousins, nor Siegel, nor the Simontons recommend that people forego traditional medical care. Their humanistic message calls on people to supplement pills and surgery with hope, will, and supportive relationships. But some take their ideas one step further and place physical health solely in the lap of the individual: People can be healthy if they simply want to be. This is naive and perhaps destructive, as critics have pointed out (e.g., Angell, 1985; Peterson & Bossio, 1991; Kolata, 1980; Sontag, 1979).

Humanistic theorists argue that people cannot be fully understood in terms of cause-effect relationships, but this is not to say that people can suspend or transcend physical reality on demand. The causes of illness are many and complex, including genetic, biological, and environmental factors. It is absurd to ignore these in speaking about health and illness.

When psychological and social factors exert an influence on well-being, they probably operate through mundane channels. So, those with a negative outlook on life are indeed more apt to be ill than those without, but at least part of the reason for this is that many of these people don't take care of themselves. They smoke and drink and fail to watch their diet (Peterson, 1988). This is not an inevitable process toward illness, of course, because people can act differently. But neither is it the failure of a mysterious will to live (Lin & Peterson, 1990).

People who fall ill have enough to worry about without blaming themselves for being ill in the first place. However, the growing popularity of the "will to live" idea shows itself in people being apologetic for being sick. Cancer is seen as a personal failure. So is heart disease, which may have a substantial genetic basis.

In sum, the positive side of the humanistic approach to health and illness is that people can struggle back against what happens to them. They can take steps to combat illness or to prevent it from occurring. To the degree that they are happy and hopeful, loved and loving, they will increase not just the quality of their lives but also its quantity. The negative side of this approach is that it may be taken to an extreme, and people might start to think of their physical health as simply a matter of choice. Wouldn't it be nice if things were this simple? But bad things sometimes happen to good people (Kushner, 1981). And health-promoting practices carry with them no guarantees (Kaplan & Peterson, 1990). The most reasonable way to approach health and illness from a humanistic perspective is to say that people can choose how they cope with their lot in life.

Theory X versus Theory Y

Perhaps surprisingly, one of the most enthusiastic receptions of humanistic ideas has been within the business community. In particular, Abraham Maslow's ideas about motivation have been used to conceptualize how business organizations might be constituted in order to enhance motivation on the part of workers, and hence to increase their productivity. It is important to understand just where one's workers stand with respect to the hierarchy of needs. In most of the industrialized world, few workers operate solely at the level of deficiency needs. Organizations that try to enhance motivation in these terms only—using

Where does a worker stand with respect to Maslow's hierarchy of needs?

carrot-and-stick approaches—are bound to be ineffective, because they fail to reach workers at the level of needs most salient for them.

A well-known business application of Maslow's theories is found in Douglas McGregor's (1960) book, *The Human Side of Enterprise*. McGregor starkly contrasted two different approaches to management, which he termed Theory X and Theory Y. These approaches may not be explicit in the minds of particular managers, but they are implied by the way someone goes about his or her managerial tasks.

Theory X is the set of assumptions that guide traditional management: Workers are intrinsically lazy and so must be coerced into doing their job. Indeed, Theory X assumes that people prefer to be told what to do, that they wish to avoid responsibility, that they have no ambition, and that they seek security above all other concerns.

Theory Y embodies a humanistic view, assuming that workers are intrinsically motivated to expend physical and mental effort in their work. People prefer to exercise choice and control, rather than have these imposed on them. They seek out responsibility. Under the appropriate circumstances, workers can be counted on to be creative and innovative. They work not simply for a paycheck but also to fulfill less tangible needs, not least of which is the need to actualize their own potential, as workers and as people.

Theory X: The assumption that workers are intrinsically lazy and so must be coerced into doing their job.

Theory Y: The assumption that workers are intrinsically motivated to expend physical and mental effort in work.

Can you think of employers you have had who exemplify these approaches? If your employer constantly checked up on you, monitored your coming and going, and gave you a long list of "thou shalt nots," then you probably had a Theory X boss. If your employer instead assumed you would do your work and let you do it, asked your opinion about how to carry out various tasks, and praised your innovations, then you probably had a Theory Y boss.

Odds are that more of you have had personal experience with a Theory X boss than with one who endorsed Theory Y. McGregor harshly criticized typical managerial practices, which he argued "could only have been derived from assumptions such as those of Theory X" (p. 35). In general, work is set up as if it were a form of punishment to pay for satisfactions that can only be enjoyed away from the job. Consider the "incentives" provided by work organizations for their employees: salaries, bonuses, vacations, health and medical benefits, and pensions. None of these can be enjoyed at work; none of these has anything to do with work per se. If anything, they interfere with how people perform their jobs by creating arbitrary status differentials. According to McGregor, employees would see these distinctions as trivial if more effort were put into making work itself satisfying. But the Theory X boss assumes this to be impossible, so he never makes the attempt.

If Theory X is not as viable as Theory Y, then why has it been so popular, even to this day? McGregor provided two answers. The first is historical. Not all that long ago, workers indeed functioned at a deficiency level. The nature of their work—as slaves or indentured servants, in mines or sweatshops—guaranteed this. Indeed, such practices are still business-as-usual in some parts of the world. Management practices originally developed to deal with workers who literally were in physical danger. Of necessity, managers used carrots and sticks to coerce and bribe their employees. Theory X therefore made a lot of sense. Old managerial habits have been slow to change, especially because these include the notion that one need never talk to workers about what they might prefer.

A second explanation for the persistence of Theory X is that it can be a self-fulfilling prophecy. Despite lacking inherent validity, Theory X can become true if one acts as if it were (Argyris, 1975). The inner potential that Theory Y assumes people to possess can be destroyed by managerial practices stemming from Theory X. If a worker is mistrusted and threatened, then he or she will eventually act as if this treatment were justified. Remember the point made by Rogers, Laing, and other humanistic theorists that individuals live up (or down) to other people's views of them. That a song titled "Take This Job and Shove It" sold millions of copies some years ago sums it up well.

Along these lines is a series of intriguing studies of intrinsic motivation and how it can be undermined (Deci & Ryan, 1980). **Intrinsic motivation** refers to our pursuit of activities without an external reward for doing so. Instead, we do things because we derive pleasure from them. Consider someone who collects stamps as a hobby. Then suppose we give her a tangible reward for what she has been doing all along: 10 cents for every stamp she puts in an album. Then after a while, suppose we withdraw the reward. According to studies, our stamp collector is then less likely to engage in the activity she previously needed no

Intrinsic motivation: The pursuit of activities when without an external reward for doing so.

extrinsic reward for pursuing. Her motivation has been changed. Of course, people must be rewarded for their work. But if the *only* rewards are extrinsic, then their desire to do well comes too thoroughly under the sway of the rewards.

McGregor made the intriguing point that Theory Y sees no incompatability between the needs of the individual and those of the organization. Theory X, of course, sees workers and management locked in a struggle where the gain of one is the inevitable loss of the other. Consider the disputes in recent years that have torn apart professional baseball and football. To the onlooker, the athletes and the owners should be each other's best friends. Both are honored and adored beyond anyone's wildest dreams. Both have more money than they could possibly spend. But they butt heads periodically and refuse to compromise on trivial matters, probably because they think of labor-management relations in Theory X terms. The players go on strike, the owners lock them out, and both sides lose.

Another interesting point McGregor made is that typical ways of "rewarding" good performance can easily backfire by undercutting someone's drive for self-actualization. An organization may give employees raises that vary according to the quality of their work. Three problems exist with this common approach. First, in most cases, quality of work is exceedingly difficult to judge. Bias readily creeps into the process of judging it. Second, even if the quality of work could be gauged in a foolproof fashion, the difference in actual raises—say, 3 percent versus 5 percent—are usually so inconsequential that they are not worth the damage to morale they create. Third, there is no good reason to think "merit raises" really lead to better productivity. The United States, for example, has one of the biggest gaps between the highest and lowest salaries of workers, whereas Japan has one of the lowest gaps. None would argue that productivity is superior in U.S. companies.

Management today is well aware of these ideas and has great interest in learning how best to tap the potential of workers. We see innovations such as employees owning the company for which they work, signing the goods they produce, and being consulted regularly by management for advice. We see books like *In Search of Excellence* by Thomas Peters and Robert Waterman (1982) on the top of best-seller lists.

This book described a study of the most productive companies in the United States. It concluded that eight factors characterize most excellent corporations:

1. *A bias for action:* doing things and solving problems rather than simply talking about them.
2. *Closeness to customers:* learning from customers they serve about what works and what does not.
3. *Autonomy:* encouraging people in all parts of the company to be innovators.
4. *An emphasis on workers as people:* treating employees as sources of ideas and not just pairs of hands.

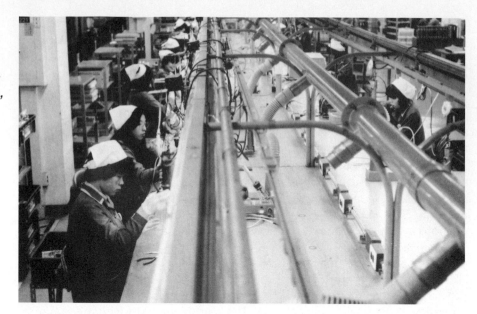

Japan has one of the world's smallest gaps between the highest and lowest salaries of workers, yet obviously Japanese productivity has not suffered.

5. *Focus on values:* making clear the basic philosophy of an organization and treating it as more than just a slogan.

6. *Sticking to what they know best:* never acquiring a business that no one knows how to run.

7. *A simple organization and a lean staff:* having the least cumbersome structure possible, so workers don't tumble over one another and trip on red tape.

8. *A fanatical emphasis on a few core values and great flexibility with regard to everything else:* being simultaneously "tight" with respect to what really matters and elsewhere "loose."

These features elaborate on Theory Y to embrace the humanistic vision of the individual as conscious, purposive, and significant, always in the process of becoming. Excellent corporations allow this nature to surface and serve company goals, rather than coercing or bribing workers into "behaving" according to a theory of organizational behavior that neglects their humanity.

Peters and Waterman (1982) pointed out that these characteristics of excellent companies are hardly surprising. They referred to them as "motherhoods," meaning they are so obviously "good" that none would argue against them. However, their list must be more than just common sense; otherwise, we wouldn't see so few companies putting them into practice.

What is the enemy keeping workplaces from excellence? Part of the problem, according to Peters and Waterman, must be laid at the feet of theorists and academics who espouse managerial ideas that have nothing to do with human beings. This echoes the humanistic criticism of traditional science, which misses what is obvious about human beings in its focus on causes and effects, numbers, and abstractions.

In Search of Freedom (Revisited)

One of the most influential applications of the humanistic paradigm is Carl Rogers's critique of education. In his 1969 book, *Freedom to Learn,* Rogers analyzed traditional educational practices and found them wanting. His self-theory suggests that the typical goals and strategies of education can only destroy a student's natural curiosity and deplete his or her self-regard. Rogers instead believed we should take a different approach to education.

He believed that traditional education is objectionable for two reasons. First, it is teacher-centered. The teacher sets the agenda and makes sure it is followed, deciding when the class will start and when it will end, what will be read and what will be skipped, which assignments will be completed and which will be scrapped.

Second, traditional education is evaluative. In fact, evaluation may be the most salient part of education for many students. Consider grade point averages, class ranks, and honors. These are all explicit evaluations of a person's worth. It's good to have high grades, an elite class rank, and all sorts of honors. It's bad to have low grades, a poor class rank, and no honors.

Rogers suggested that eduation be patterned on client-centered therapy, taking the focus off the teacher and letting the student make decisions.

Teachers, parents, and *Time* magazine may decry students' excessive concern with grades, but "grade-grubbers" are more in touch with the real world than their critics. Education is evaluative, and rewards and punishments are handed out according to these evaluations. The tragedy is that only a handful of students can win the race. One student gets good grades only because other students do not. One student can feel good about himself or herself only because other students feel crummy.

Rogers therefore believed that traditional education does psychological damage. Most students think poorly of themselves as a result of attending school. What should be the most exciting and important aspect of a young person's life becomes, all in all, a terrible experience.

He proposed a radical solution. Education should pattern itself after client-centered therapy. Take the teacher off focus, and let the student make decisions about what is to be learned and how best to go about this. The teacher switches his or her role from a drill sergeant to a resource, there to advise but not to direct. Students do not follow a syllabus handed to them the first day of class; rather, they design their own course of studies and make a contract with the teacher to follow it.

Just as importantly, grades are eliminated, because they are the academic equivalent of conditional love. And once you eliminate grades, tests become superfluous. Think about it. What is the purpose of the typical test? Only to help the teacher assign you a place in the Great Chain of Being. Rogers calls for open seating in a theater-in-the-round.

Let me put *Freedom to Learn* in context. I have used innovative techniques in my teaching. My favorite is to break the class into study groups and assign grades to a particular student that reflect only how his or her fellow students do. Competition becomes downright hazardous. And I've taught at a college without grades. The problem with Rogers's proposal is that education can't achieve it all at once. Small steps in the direction of student-centered learning have trouble surviving in a larger world diametrically opposed to the idea.

Many of my classroom innovations have fallen flat because my students blew off the course I was teaching in order to study for tests in their traditional courses. My unconditional regard, so to speak, was met with conditional regard on their part. And I cannot blame them. If they have a finite amount of time to do two assignments, and they will be punished severely for the lateness of one but not for the other, which one will they work on? Most anyone would make the same choice.

The college without grades where I taught went bankrupt. Among the school's problems was an insufficient number of students. Everybody agreed that we were doing something good, but our graduates needed grades to get admitted to law school or to obtain a job. The larger society wasn't ready for college students without a class rank. Would-be applicants figured this out before we did, and the school's demise was inevitable.

Rogers's vision of education therefore strikes me as utopian. It would be wonderful to work in a place where students felt free to learn, but I cannot find it in Barron's *Profiles of American Colleges*. Until I do, I'll remember what I said earlier in the chapter about self-theory: An important distinction occurs between people and what they do. This is certainly the case when we are talking about students on the one hand and their papers and tests on the other.

SUMMARY

The humanistic paradigm encompasses a variety of approaches defined as much by their critical stance with regard to conventional psychology as by substantive features they share in common. However, it is possible to describe a family resemblance for this approach to personality. Emphasized are the distinctiveness and significance of human beings, along with the importance of recognizing their complexity, activity, conscious experience, and self-regulation.

Several theorists have been particularly influential advocates of the humanistic approach. Carl Rogers proposed his self-theory, which stresses how people perceive their own selves. He felt that people have an inherent drive toward self-actualization. He is also well-known for devising client-centered therapy, an approach to treatment based on self-theory.

Abraham Maslow similarly argued that people are motivated to actualize their inner potential. He further proposed that people's motives exist in a hierarchy; lower-level motives must be satisfied before higher-level motives, such as self-actualization, become salient.

Existential psychologist Rollo May drew psychology's attention to people's experience. Existentialism provides a host of concepts for describing how people go about establishing their way of existing in the world. This approach assumes people choose their style of existence, sometimes wisely and sometimes not.

Ronald D. Laing was a Scottish psychiatrist best known for his phenomenological analyses of schizophrenia. He argued that schizophrenic individuals could only be understood as human beings whose experience is their defining characteristic, just as it is for all people.

Many humanistic psychologists are uninterested in conventional research. Nonetheless, humanistic ideas have had a great impact on the types of research now considered legitimate by personality psychologists. Among the contemporary lines of investigation inspired by humanistic concepts are studies of private experience, of the effects of choice, of hardiness in the face of stress, and of supportive environments.

A number of practical applications stem from the humanistic paradigm. Few walks of life have been left untouched by these ideas. I discussed examples from therapy, health, business, and education.

TRAIT PARADIGM: THEORY

The trait paradigm provides a commonsense approach to describing and explaining personality. Its key assumption is that people fall into categories or along dimensions defined by stable and pervasive characteristics, often of a biological nature. Researchers use various procedures to describe individuals with respect to these characteristics, but most frequently they gather information through questionnaires. This paradigm originated in the tradition of psychological testing, so its role model—for better or for worse—has been the IQ test. More generally, this approach to personality reflects Darwinian thought.

The importance of Darwin's (1859) theory of evolution to psychology in general and to the trait paradigm in particular cannot be overestimated. First, it focuses attention on biological characteristics, explicitly stating that they vary across individuals. Although genes as the mechanism of evolution were not recognized at the time of Darwin, subsequent elaborations of evolutionary theory were phrased in genetic terms. A topic of great interest to the trait paradigm is whether personality characteristics are inherited.

Second, the theory of evolution explains by pointing to the consequences of something, for example, an opposable thumb, an upright posture, or a large brain. These are known as *functional explanations*. Trait theories of personality have been functional as well, inspired by the success of evolutionary theory. But how are traits related to a person's adaptation to the world?

Literally hundreds of personality characteristics have attracted the attention of psychologists working within the trait paradigm. In each instance, a specific theory is proposed to explain the particular characteristic. I won't catalogue these circumscribed theories, but rather I'll talk about general trait theories because they address traits as a whole.

Some of the common questions posed by these theories include

1. What are the fundamental ways people differ? What is the best way to ascertain these differences?

2. How do individual differences determine adaptive or maladaptive behavior?
3. What is the origin of a particular individual difference? Can the relative contributions of nature versus nurture be determined?

Perhaps the most important question is how trait theorists discover individual differences. They use no single way. Sometimes a theorist takes a simple observation and turns it into a full-blown trait theory. Cesare Lombroso did this in the 1800s when he noticed (incorrectly) that criminals seemed to bear a physical resemblance to apes (Gould, 1981). So, criminals were thought to be evolutionary throwbacks, which in turn inspired an entire theory of moral behavior.

Sometimes a theorist deduces pertinent individual differences from an already-existing account of personality. Psychodynamic theorists have identified numerous traits in this manner. Donn Byrne (1961), for instance, started with the Freudian notion of repression and regarded it as a characteristic that people possess to varying degrees. At one extreme is repression, while at the other is *sensitization* (akin to perceptual vigilance).

And sometimes a theorist takes a striking behavior and turns it into a personality trait by finding out if people differ in terms of how frequently they show it. Christie and Geis (1970) fashioned the personality characteristic of *Machiavellianism* in this manner. Machiavelli was the fifteenth-century figure known for his advice to rulers that the end always justifies the means. Machiavellianism as a trait is the degree to which a person acts on this advice.

Regardless of the source of each personality characteristic, each is assimilated to the trait paradigm by the same process. Developing a way to measure individual differences in the characteristics is critical. This measure usually is a questionnaire completed by the person. Once a questionnaire is devised, and reliability and validity are ascertained, researchers investigate the relationship of the trait to function and dysfunction. Further, they explore the origins of the trait, looking for places where biology and environment contribute.

Against this common background are several different approaches to the trait paradigm. I'll describe these in this chapter. The first approach concerns itself with the very notion of a personality trait. The giant figure here is Gordon Allport, noteworthy because he set the agenda for the trait paradigm. He phrased the key issues that still define this approach to personality.

One of Allport's contemporaries was Henry Murray, who also made important contributions to the field of personality. Today he is best remembered for his approach to human motives. His theoretical and methodological innovations still influence the way we conceive and investigate motives, so we will discuss his approach as well.

Next, we'll look at two different approaches to understanding the interrelations among various traits. *Circumplex models,* as originally proposed by Timothy Leary and more recently by Jerry Wiggins, arrange traits in a circle according to their similarity or dissimilarity and then look for their basic structure. And *factor analytic models,* as popularized by Hans Eysenck and Raymond Cattell, use sophisticated statistical techniques to discover the central dimensions of personality.

Finally, we'll discuss several related approaches that address the biological basis of personality. The attempt to relate personality to biology dates back thousands of years. In the relatively recent past, theorists Ernst Kretschmer and William Sheldon attempted to explain individual differences in personality characteristics in terms of variations in people's physiques. More recently, personality psychologists have become interested in temperament— inborn styles of behaving—and the possible influence of one's genetic inheritance on these styles. And the most current biological approaches use notions from behavior genetics and sociobiology to clarify traditional personality concerns.

GORDON ALLPORT: SETTING THE AGENDA

What Sigmund Freud is to the psychodynamic paradigm, Gordon Allport is to the trait paradigm. Whether or not they agree with Allport, all subsequent trait theorists use his terminology and take positions on his issues. Let me therefore tell you about Allport the man before I describe Allport the theorist.

Allport's Life

Allport was born in 1897 in Montezuma, Indiana. His father was a country doctor and his mother taught school. In Allport's (1968b) own words, his "home life was marked by plain Protestant piety and hard work" (p. 379). Allport was a dutiful but uninspired student until he followed his older brother Floyd to college at Harvard University. There his eyes were opened to intellectual matters.

He studied psychology and social ethics, and he spent his time helping his brother with psychological research and doing social service: running a boys' club, working as a probation officer, helping foreign students, registering homes for war workers, and so on. Allport's later career can be seen as a sustained attempt to bridge science and social service. His concern with personality arose from this goal, since he felt that service programs must be grounded in an adequate conception of personality to be truly useful.

Before going to graduate school at Harvard, Allport lived abroad for a year, where he taught English and sociology in Constantinople. It was at this time that an intriguing event occurred: Allport met Freud for the first and only time. The meeting achieves significance in light of Allport's later theorizing, which starkly contrasts with the psychodynamic approach to personality.

As a twenty-two-year-old, he impetuously wrote to Freud, saying that he was in Vienna and would like to meet with him. Freud replied and invited him to his office. When Allport arrived, Freud received him but said nothing. He waited for him to state his mission. Allport became flustered and began to tell Freud of an incident that he had just witnessed on the train:

> A small boy about four years of age had displayed a conspicuous dirt phobia. He kept saying to his mother, "I don't want to sit there . . . don't let that dirty man sit beside me." (Allport, 1968b, pp. 383–384)

Allport intended to show his understanding of psychodynamic principles, because the boy's mother seemed overly prim and proper, just the sort to raise a child afraid of dirt. But when Allport finished his story, Freud asked him, "And was that little boy you?"

The question flabbergasted Allport, because he felt Freud had overlooked his obvious motive in order to seek something far below the surface. The incident convinced him that a personality theory based on neurotics was not very useful in making sense of most people's mundane behavior. Manifest motives should be fully explored before unconscious ones are sought.

This embarrassing incident at least allows a useful perspective on Allport's approach to personality. In a number of important ways, it breaks with the psychodynamic approach. While acknowledging the usefulness of psychoanalysis for understanding neurotics, Allport regards his theory as one for normal individuals. He emphasizes consciousness and rationality. It is a teleological theory with little to say about the influence of early traumatic events.

Once in graduate school, Allport suffered some misgivings. American psychology in the 1920s was a laboratory science of experiments concerned with molecular phenomena: sensation, perception, and learning. Comparing himself to his fellow students, Allport found he was without "giftedness in natural science, mathematics, mechanics (laboratory manipulations), nor in biological or medical specialties" (1968b, p. 384). Allport wanted to study such topics as social values and personality, but he had no role models.

So, with encouragement to pursue his own interests, he began to create what we now can see as personality psychology. His dissertation was the first investigation in the United States of the components of personality. In 1921 he published a paper (with brother Floyd) on the classification and measurement of personality traits, and in 1924 he taught the first personality course ever offered in the United States.

Except for four years at Dartmouth College, Allport spent his entire professional career at Harvard, where he made important contributions to the development of psychology. Among his academic pursuits, he investigated such social psychological topics as rumors, prejudice, and attitudes. And of course, Allport continued his investigation of personality. In 1937 he published *Personality: A Psychological Interpretation,* detailing his perspective on personality. In 1961 he revised this influential book under the title *Pattern and Growth in Personality.*

Unlike the other major personality theorists, Allport never developed a school of followers. This is mainly because his theoretical stance was eclectic and open-ended. He gave would-be disciples little dogma to embrace. Nevertheless, his particular ideas have been widely influential. Against the dominant trends of psychoanalysis and behaviorism, he forced attention on consciousness and intentionality. Allport was one of the few theorists conversant with all of the disparate strands of personality psychology, arguing persuasively that the field must pertain to the specific individual. "His work stands as a monument to a wise and sensitive scholar who was committed to the positive aspects of human behavior in terms that respected the uniqueness of every living organism" (Hall & Lindzey, 1978, p. 295). Humanistic psychologists found him to be a kindred spirit. Gordon Allport died in 1967.

Allport's Ideas

Here is Allport's (1937) definition of personality:

> Personality is the dynamic organization within the person of those psychophysical systems that determine his unique adjustments to his environment. (p. 48)

Let's focus on this definition, because Allport carefully chose each word.

Personality is *dynamic*—always changing. Personality is an *organization;* its components are coherently related to each other. Personality is *psychophysical,* neither just mind nor just body. To Allport, a person's mind and body work in concert. Personality is made up of *systems,* which means that its building blocks can be identified. The most important of these are an individual's traits. Personality *determines* behavior. It lies behind what a person does and has causal status. Finally, personality results in one's *unique adjustment* to the world. Each person is unlike all others in how he or she lives. According to Allport, personality psychology must recognize and explain this uniqueness or be doomed to misleading generalizations.

People's unique personalities can be captured by specifying their particular personality traits. Of the various terms available to describe personality, Allport opts for traits, defining a **trait** as a

> neuropsychic structure having the capacity to render many stimuli functionally equivalent, and to initiate and guide equivalent (meaningfully consistent) forms of adaptive and expressive behavior. (1961, p. 347)

Trait: According to Allport, a neuropsychic structure that initiates and guides behavior.

Again, Allport explicitly states that traits are real, that they underlie a variety of thoughts, feelings, and actions, and that they determine how we adapt to the world.

More specifically, traits filter the way we experience the world, and then they channel the way we respond to our experience. We all know people who treat every chance comment as a challenge, turning polite conversation into an argument. "Nice day." "What's right with it?" Other people—with different traits—bring calm to themselves and others.

Where do traits come from? According to Allport, we have no personality at birth. Through learning, maturation, and socialization, traits emerge. However, Allport did not dwell on an individual's history. He felt that behavior occurs because of contemporary factors—not past ones. He introduced the

According to Allport's functional autonomy of motives *concept, someone may originally undertake an activity for extrinsic reasons, yet continue it for intrinsic reasons.*

Functional autonomy of motives: The idea that behaviors originally undertaken to satisfy some extrinsic goal may become intrinsically satisfying.

concept of **functional autonomy of motives** to make his point explicit. According to this idea, behaviors originally undertaken to satisfy some extrinsic goal may become self-sufficient, continued because they are now intrinsically satisfying. A child may begin piano lessons under parental threat, but as an adult, she continues to play the piano because she loves it. The adult motive is autonomous. Unlike psychodynamic theorists, Allport liberated personality from its past.

Allport also anticipated the *consistency controversy*. To him, consistency does not mean that someone does the exact same thing in different situations. Someone who is chronically bored, for instance, may fall asleep during a movie, doodle during a lecture, and read the newspaper during a poker game. If we look only at the surface of what this person does, we see little consistency. On the other hand, if we take a look at the meaning of his activities, we see considerable consistency. In each setting, he is underwhelmed by the ongoing activity and does something else. His behavior is meaningfully consistent, if not literally so.

Why are people consistent? Like humanistic theorists, Allport felt the need to explain the coherence of our identity and continuity in our pursuit of future goals. However, he was reluctant to introduce the notion of the "self" because it seems like an actual entity, somehow calling the shots behind the scenes. To Allport, such an idea just made the explanation of consistency more complicated. Instead, he coined the term **proprium** to refer explicitly to the set of *processes* that define our personality. The proprium is not responsible for the consistency of our personality; rather, it is our personality.

It encompasses all the ways people project themselves into the future. According to Allport, we must understand an individual's hopes and fears, wishes and dreads. To understand personality, we must look to the individual's future intentions, and the person is usually aware of these intentions. Again, note the contrast with psychodynamic theorizing about personality.

Let's now examine in particular what Allport had to say about traits. He distinguished two types: **common traits** and **personal traits.** A common trait is used to characterize a group of individuals. Everyone is described with respect to the characteristic. So far in this book, I have described only common traits. Consider the strength of oral needs, as measured by the Blacky Test. We can array all people along this dimension, from not at all oral through somewhat oral to absolutely oral.

A personal trait is sometimes called an *individual disposition* and it is specific to the individual. It need not apply to anyone else. So, I know someone who loves small animals. This characteristic organizes her entire personality. She is the best friend that a dog or cat ever had. She won't eat veal marsala. Pictures of wide-eyed lion cubs hang inside her house, and bird-feeders hang outside. She is a volunteer guide at the Children's Zoo. Any description of her personality has to start with this trait of loving small animals.

Proprium: Allport's term for the set of processes that define personality.

Common trait: A trait that can be used to describe all individuals.

Personal trait: A trait that can be used to describe only a particular individual.

SOURCE: © 1971 S. Gross.

Can we place all people along a continuum called "loving small animals"? Not if we expect them to stay where we put them. Some people are as consistently hateful toward small critters as other people are loving, but most of us show no particular consistency one way or another. We love some small animals some of the time in some situations, while we hate other small animals at other times in other situations. No general trait organizes the way most of us behave here. The degree to which we love small animals does not characterize our personality. Thus, "loving small animals" is a personal disposition.

Allport further distinguishes among three types of personal traits according to their centrality to one's personality. Individuals who are stamped with a single personal trait have a **cardinal disposition.** It determines *everything* they do. Famous historical and literary individuals are remembered for the personality characteristics they so perfectly exemplify: Don Juan, Pollyanna, Don Quixote, Uncle Tom, Mata Hari, Puck, and so on.

Most of us do not have a cardinal disposition. Instead, we are characterized by 5 to 10 **central dispositions:** highly characteristic and frequently evidenced traits. Stop and think about the 5 to 10 traits you would use to describe your own personality. These are your central dispositions.

The third type of personal trait is a **secondary disposition,** which is more circumscribed than central dispositions. It does not appear in a variety of situations or give rise to a variety of behaviors. For example, I occasionally sing in the shower and whistle when I drive on I-94, but that's the extent of me and music.

Allport also discussed at some length how researchers should go about investigating personality. He distinguished between **nomothetic research,** which is concerned with establishing generalizations about all people, and **idiographic research,** which is concerned with the particular individual. Common traits fall within nomothetic research, whereas personal traits are the subject of idiographic investigation. Unlike other psychologists, who justifiably conduct nomothetic studies, the personality psychologist must do idiographic research.

The distinction between common traits and personal traits is therefore more profound than it first seems. All theorists within the trait paradigm accept common traits. Individual differences among these traits are investigated by using personality tests to place all people along the same basic continuums. But to accept personal traits is to step out of this research tradition. Personal traits are applied only to specific individuals, so they are antithetical to the typical use of personality tests. The relative placement of the individual with respect to others is at best irrelevant and at worst misleading.

Consider the danger of regarding the individual disposition of loving small animals as a common trait. How do we interpret people placed at the midpoint of the continuum ranging from extreme love at one end to extreme hate at the other? A person with "some" of this trait may indeed be consistent, showing moderately positive feelings toward small animals. But another person designated as having "some" of this trait may have extreme feelings from situation to situation. Or a person with "some" of the trait of loving small animals may live in a fancy apartment that has eradicated rats, roaches, and poodles; he has never

Cardinal disposition: A personal trait that determines everything a person does.

Central disposition: A highly characterized and frequently evidenced personal trait.

Secondary disposition: A circumscribed personal trait.

Nomothetic research: Research concerned with establishing generalizations about people.

Idiographic research: Research concerned with a particular individual.

had any personal contact with small animals but in the abstract thinks they are cute. You can see from examples like these why Allport argues for the necessity of personal traits to describe personality.

Although Allport's points are sensible, researchers have tended not to follow his suggestions about idiographic research. Case studies that focus on individuals remain much more popular among psychodynamic and humanistic psychologists than among trait psychologists. Indeed, much of Allport's own research was nomothetic, concerned with common traits.

For example, two of his well-known projects are the Allport-Vernon-Lindzey Study of Values (1960) and the Allport-Vernon study of Expressive Movement (1933). Both are instances of nomothetic research. In his study of values, Allport scores subjects from their endorsement of items reflecting one of six different values: theoretical, economic, aesthetic, social, political, and religious. Counseling psychologists widely use these scales to help people choose among different vocations. The study of expressive movement looks at the style in which people do what they do. In a series of studies, Allport and Vernon asked research subjects to do a variety of things: tap their finger, draw a circle, count, shake hands, and so on. Results showed that across diverse acts, people have a consistent style of expression (cf. Riggio, Lippa, & Salinas, 1990). Can you see that these investigations treat people's characteristics as common traits, not as individual dispositions?

The closest Allport (1965) got to idiographic research was his analysis of 301 letters written by a woman over a number of years. These *Letters from Jenny,* as they have come to be known, provide what Allport regards as the acid test for the personality psychologist. Can the researcher explain an individual life? By reading the letters, Allport identified eight personal traits: quarrelsome-suspicious, self-centered, independent-autonomous, dramatic-intense, aesthetic-artistic, aggressive, cynical-morbid, and sentimental.

From the perspective of the trait paradigm, the explanation of Jenny is complete, because she has been categorized (as quarrelsome, self-centered, and so on). But is this really idiographic research? Those reading Jenny's letters can only arrive at their conclusions by comparing Jenny to other individuals, as relatively aggressive, as relatively sentimental, and so forth. If pushed to the extreme, idiographic research implies that each individual merits unique theoretical language. And that is impossible.

Another problem with this kind of research is that different investigators might disagree about the central traits they identify. One way around this problem is to make the method of identifying traits explicitly quantitative. So, a researcher could literally keep track of all the personality terms a person uses as he or she speaks or writes. The most frequently used terms are arguably central to the individual. Additionally, the co-occurrence of different terms can be ascertained, revealing how the individual makes sense of people.

Swede and Tetlock (1986) took this approach in an investigation of how Henry Kissinger perceived world leaders as well as how he perceived himself. They read his book *White House Years* and wrote down all the traits he attributed to different world leaders. They found thousands of different descriptions. However, some clear patterns arose. Kissinger saw most leaders as falling into

Accoring to research by Swede and Tetlock (1986), Henry Kissinger saw most world leaders as falling into a small number of types. He did not see himself as fitting into any of these categories.

a small number of types: revolutionaries, patriots, personal friends, professional friends, able adversaries, and professional competitors. Interestingly and perhaps not surprisingly, Kissinger attributed traits to himself in a unique combination; in other words, he did not see himself as fitting into any of the categories into which other world leaders fell. This study therefore tells us how Kissinger saw the personalities of others as well as his own.

Perhaps the best way to regard idiographic versus nomothetic research is in terms of relative emphasis. Does the researcher make conclusions about people in general or one person in particular? A given investigation may emphasize one goal more than the other. The thing to remember here is Allport's important statement that personality psychologists should attempt to understand individual people.

Evaluation

Allport's contribution to the trait paradigm is that he set the agenda. He distinguished the trait approach from the psychodynamic approach. He made an articulate plea that personality psychology should study what is unique about individuals. He introduced concepts still employed today: functional autonomy of motives, proprium, common trait, personal trait, and idiographic versus nomothetic research.

On the negative side, Allport's theory failed to stimulate research, in part because particular techniques for achieving idiographic goals are problematic and in part because it makes few predictions. His theory is difficult to prove wrong, because uniqueness and functional autonomy serve as convenient escape clauses. Nevertheless, subsequent researchers have kept what is valuable about Allport's approach and discarded what is unwieldy to make the trait paradigm viable within personality psychology.

The topics we discuss in the remainder of this chapter can be viewed as elaborations of a particular aspect of Allport's vision of personality psychology. Where Allport failed to make clear just how traits were causes of behavior, Henry Murray did precisely this in his thorough examination of individual differences in motives. Where Allport took only preliminary steps toward identifying the range of traits, circumplex and factor analytic theorists attempt to specify the primary dimensions along which people differ. And where Allport sketchily discussed the biological basis of traits, subsequent theorists have taken a close look at how personality is grounded in biology and ultimately in evolution.

HENRY MURRAY: PERSONOLOGY

Henry Murray (1893–1988) was not a psychologist by original training. Born in New York City, he was a physician, biologist, and chemist who turned to psychology at about the age of 30. He changed his interests on reading Carl Jung's (1924) *Psychological Types.* Intrigued by the book, he used the opportunity of a visit to Zurich in 1925 to meet with the author. The two talked for hours, and Murray came away from the meeting dazzled by Jung's intelligence and by the notion of the unconscious. He was subsequently trained in psychoanalysis by Franz Alexander, the founder of modern psychosomatic medicine (see Chapter 6), and was influenced by psychodynamic theory throughout his career. Although some classify Murray with the Freudians and neoFreudians, I've placed him within the trait paradigm because he is best known for his catalogue of individual differences in needs and for his methods of assessing them.

On Murray's return to the United States in 1928 he was appointed director of the newly created Harvard Psychological Clinic. It was there that he developed his own theory of personality and broadly addressed the purpose and procedure of the field as a whole. He coined the term **personology** to stress that personality psychology should concentrate on the individual case: the person. He advocated the intensive study of a small number of individuals, rather than the cursory examination of large numbers, as is often the case within the trait paradigm.

To fashion his theories, he drew on biology, cultural anthropology, psychoanalysis, literature, and mythology. His fellow workers at the Harvard Psychological Clinic came from a variety of backgrounds, so his approach was interdisciplinary long before this was fashionable. Of the many men and women who worked with Murray, I cite Erik Homburger Erikson, because you have encountered him in Chapter 4. Murray importantly influenced the then-young

Personology: Murray's term for personality psychology, emphasizing that the field should concern itself with the person.

Erikson, and Erikson's psychosocial theory can be seen as an instance of Murray's personology.

Nowhere was the eclectic and interdisciplinary character of Murray's approach better represented than in his assessment strategy. He developed the *diagnostic council* to best describe the individual's thoughts, feelings, and actions. Different researchers from different backgrounds observe the same subject in a variety of settings. Each researcher employs the specialized techniques at his or her disposal to make these observations. For example, *Explorations in Personality* (Murray, 1938), a study of several dozen young men, employed questionnaires, interviews, projective tests, experiments, and so on, each administered by an expert. Then all of the experts bring their findings to a conference where the information is synthesized to characterize the personality of the individual.

Murray's aim was to observe the individual as a whole, in his or her natural setting. To this end, he developed a number of assessment techniques that allowed people to be themselves, providing rich information about their personalities. The best-known of these techniques is the **Thematic Apperception Test (TAT),** a projective test developed with Christiana Morgan. Subjects are shown an ambiguous picture and then asked to tell a story about what they see. The subject's responses are not constrained, so the ensuing story reveals the personality of the storyteller. In particular, the TAT is thought to reveal the needs of the person, because they are projected onto the characters in the picture (Morgan & Murray, 1935).

What is a **need?** In general terms, Murray called it "a push from the rear . . . an impulse which does not as a rule completely subside until a situation of a certain kind has been arrived at" (1938, p. 68). Needs arise from internal or external stimuli and directly catalyze action to appease or satisfy them. Each need is accompanied by a particular emotion.

We can identify a need in operation by observing how a person behaves. Several criteria are relevant in deciding that a particular person has a given need:

- Attention to certain aspects of the environment and not others
- Reports of particular feelings
- Repeated patterns of behavior
- Typical consequences of these behaviors
- Satisfaction with attainment of these consequences (and dissatisfaction with failure to achieve)

As an example, let's consider how one of the needs Murray described—the need to make an impression—might be identified. Some people have a higher need to be seen and heard than do others. They know of social opportunities, settings where they can be conspicuous (selective attention). They are vain and self-confident (particular feelings). They attempt to entertain others and to monopolize conversations (characteristic behaviors). They feel exuberant when they are noticed (typical consequences). And people with a high need to make an impression on others are pleased when their interactions go as planned and frustrated when lost in the shuffle (satisfaction versus dissatisfaction).

Thematic Apperception Test (TAT): Projective test used to measure the strength of people's needs.

Need: According to Murray, an impulse that motivates behavior aimed at achieving some specific form of satisfaction.

But you may or may not have a need to make an impression on others. Murray (1938) recognized that different people possess different needs. He identified approximately 20 needs (see Table 8–1 for brief definitions). Some of these have attracted more research attention than others, notably the need for achievement. We'll consider some of the research findings in the next chapter.

Murray's catalogue of needs is important not so much for the specific motives he included as for their range. At the time he wrote, most theorists recognized a handful of clearly biological motives; other needs were presumably derived from these via processes of conditioning. The prevailing opinion was that all needs, directly or indirectly, served to reduce biological drives. Murray's catalogue was a forceful reminder that human motivation could not possibly be so simple. It legitimized a richer view of human motivation and indeed of personality as a whole (Hilgard, 1987).

His view of needs encompasses a variety of distinctions: between more versus less biological involvement, between direct versus indirect expression, between more versus less reliance on particular environmental circumstances, and so on. The strength of people's needs differ, and personality is characterized by the particular mix of these needs.

Two other concepts of Murray's are important. First is that of the **press.** Unlike many personality theorists, Murray explicitly recognized the environ-

Press: According to Murray, an environmental property that determines whether or not a person reaches a given goal.

TABLE 8–1
Murray's Needs

Need	Characterization
Abasement	Need to submit to external forces
Achievement	Need to accomplish
Affiliation	Need to form and maintain friendships
Aggression	Need to overcome opposition
Autonomy	Need to be free of restraint
Counteraction	Need to make up for failure
Defendance	Need to defend self against criticism
Deference	Need to admire a superior
Dominance	Need to control one's environment
Exhibition	Need to make an impression
Harmavoidance	Need to avoid physical harm
Infavoidance	Need to avoid humiliation
Nurturance	Need to assist the helpless
Order	Need to put things in order
Play	Need to have fun
Rejection	Need to snub
Senitence	Need to enjoy sensuous feelings
Sex	Need to have sexual intercourse
Succorance	Need to have one's need gratified by another
Understanding	Need to ask and answer questions

SOURCE: Murray, 1938.

ment's role in facilitating or thwarting behavior. A press is an environmental property that determines whether or not a person reaches a given goal. What a person does is not simply a function of his or her needs but also of the existing environmental press. An important distinction here is between the individual's perception of the environment *(beta press)* and the reality of the environment *(alpha press)*. Murray suggests that behavior occurs in response to the beta press. The local tavern is just a shabby building (alpha press), but it may also be the only place where someone feels accepted (beta press). The latter is more important in understanding the person's behavior at the tavern than the former.

Thema: According to Murray, the combination of an operative need and a prevailing press.

The second concept is Murray's notion of the **thema,** which is the fundamental unit of behavior and the building block of personality. Quite simply, a thema is the combination of an operative need and a prevailing press. Themas range from a single episode (you feel hungry in the presence of a bag of M & M's) to a series of episodes (you bring a high need for understanding to a challenging university) to an overarching style of life (you have a high need for nurturance and thus you become a veterinarian). The full description of personality places the person in context—physical, social, and cultural.

Murray's personology is important because it argues that a variety of motives are crucial, while at the same time suggesting procedures for identifying and measuring these motives (Hall & Lindzey, 1978). Murray influenced an entire generation of personality psychologists by directing their attention to the whole person, to the importance of the environment, and to the need for sophisticated assessment. His influence may have waned through the 1960s and 1970s, but at present a renewed interest in his approach to personality is occurring (e.g., McClelland, 1989).

CIRCUMPLEX APPROACHES

Let us now turn to attempts to understand the interrelations among various traits, starting with *circumplex* approaches. These find their theoretical rationale in the writings of Harry Stack Sullivan (1892–1949). Sullivan received his medical degree in 1917, and then undertook psychoanalytic training in the 1930s. The Chicago School of Sociology, which embraced the perspective known as **symbolic interactionism,** strongly influenced Sullivan. In this view, people are defined by their relationships with others and how they symbolize these relationships to themselves.

Symbolic interactionism: The view that people are defined by their relationships with others and how they symbolize these relationships to themselves.

According to Sullivan (1947, 1953), personality is the pattern of a person's relationships with others. This takes the neoFreudian position to an extreme (Chapter 4); personality is not only influenced by other people—it literally is how one relates to others. Sullivan proposed that people attempt to achieve satisfaction on the one hand and security on the other. Satisfaction entails biological drives like those emphasized by Freud. By security, he meant social needs like those that concerned Karen Horney.

Sullivan was particularly interested in the motive for security. Development, for him, is the process by which a person achieves security. Because interpersonal disruptions threaten our security by producing anxiety, our development is directed toward achieving harmonious relationships with others. Different strategies exist for achieving security. What are they? In attempting to answer this question, subsequent theorists ended up with a general statement about the whole of personality.

Circumplex models represent one possible way to depict the range of interpersonal events and therefore traits; these models depict possible transactions in a circle reflecting their similarity versus dissimilarity. If two interpersonal events are highly similar, they are close to one another. If they are dissimilar, then they are far apart.

Circumplex model: A depiction of traits in a circle reflecting their similarity versus dissimilarity.

Timothy Leary

One early attempt to describe interpersonal behavior in a circumplex was presented by Timothy Leary (1957) in his book *Interpersonal Diagnosis of Personality*. Yes, this is the same Timothy Leary who later became well-known for his experiments with LSD at Harvard, and for his slogan "turn on, tune in, drop out." Prior to being a psychedelic guru, Leary was a personality psychologist strongly inspired by Sullivan's ideas. He made contributions to the trait paradigm that are still influential today (Andrews, 1989).

Leary believed that Sullivan presented a powerful conceptual approach to understanding personality but that he had provided no method for putting it into practice. So Leary thought he himself could provide an appropriate method via a circumplex approach. Figure 8–1 shows the circumplex model Leary (1957) proposed for classifying interpersonal behavior.

Before achieving fame as a psychodelic guru, Timothy Leary made important contributions to personality psychology.

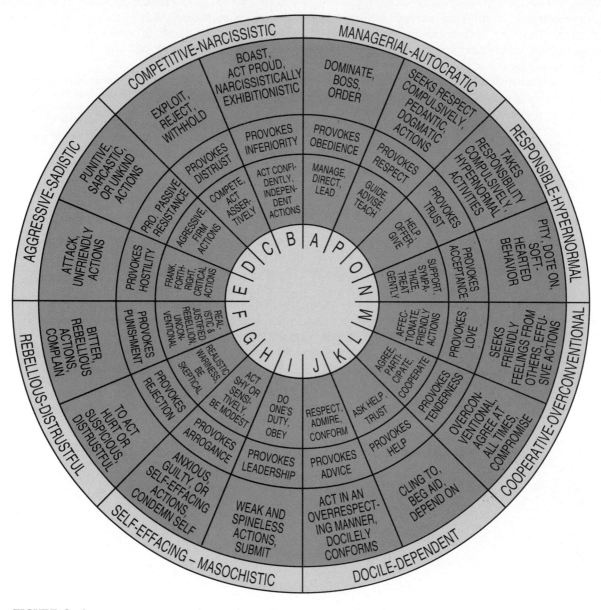

FIGURE 8–1
Leary's (1957)
Circumplex Model

The innermost circle has arbitrary letter abbreviations—*A, B, C,* and so on—that Leary introduced as a shorthand way of describing the categories. In the next circle are illustrative behaviors; note that all are ways of acting vis-a-vis another person. In the next circle are the behaviors these actions typically provoke in others, which makes explicit the social nature of personality. In the next circle are labels for what Leary terms reflexes, the behaviors in question carried out habitually and rigidly. Finally, the outer ring of the circle suggests labels for these behaviors as they are displayed at different intensities. So, "aggressive" is forthrightness to a moderate degree; "sadistic" is forthrightness

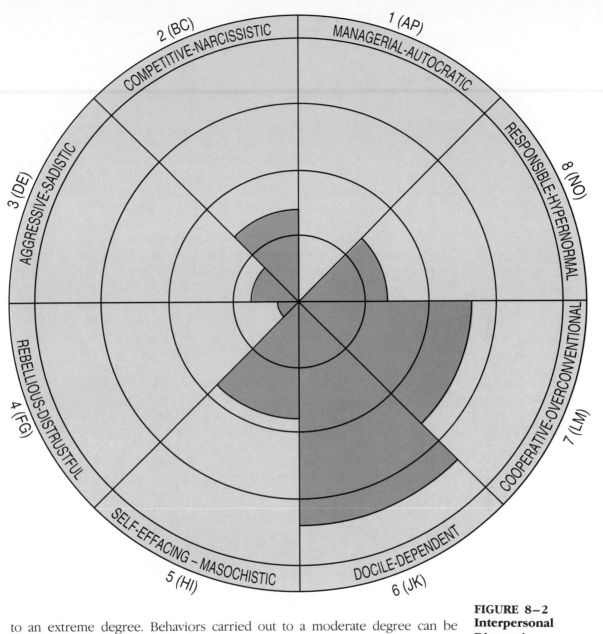

FIGURE 8-2
Interpersonal
Diagnosis

*The extent of the
shading represents
the frequency this
individual behaved
in particular ways
during
psychotherapy
(Leary, 1957).*

to an extreme degree. Behaviors carried out to a moderate degree can be adaptive, as Sullivan proposed. But when taken to the extreme, they become pathological.

What are the uses of such a circumplex? Although Figure 8-1 is complicated, appreciate how much information it efficiently conveys. This figure is not only a catalogue of personality traits, but also a theory of social psychology, as well as a statement concerning abnormality. Leary used his circumplex to "diagnose" (describe and explain) an individual's personality. So, information about someone's behavior was obtained and classified by expert judges using the different categories of the circumplex. Then the results were graphed onto it.

For example, Leary studied how a patient in therapy interacted with his therapist over the first 20 hours of therapy. Several thousand "interaction units" were identified, classified, and graphed. As can be seen in Figure 8–2, this particular individual was frequently docile and dependent toward the therapist, avoiding hostility and competitiveness. We can ascertain changes in the course of therapy by comparing the patient's graphs from different points in time.

Circumplex models have several virtues. First, we can ascertain the completeness of a theoretical view by seeing if gaps exist anywhere around the circle (Stern, 1970). Second, a circumplex can be specified with varying degrees of detail, while always maintaining its completeness. For example, a very simple circumplex might have only four categories. This would arguably be complete, because all four quadrants are defined. However, the quadrants could be further subdivided, as we saw in Leary's circumplex. Third, because the circumplex is a structural depiction of traits, we can take a step back from it and theorize about the nature of its organization. What dimensions define the overall scheme?

Here we begin to see the importance of circumplex models of personality. They help the theorist understand the basic ways that people differ. Remember from Chapter 1 how Allport and Odbert (1936) identified more than 18,000 trait terms in the English language. How might these be simplified and explicated? One answer is to arrange them in a circumplex, then look for the dimensions that define the arrangement.

Leary hypothesized that two dimensions underlie his particular model: hate versus love and weakness versus strength (again see Figure 8–1). Each of his categories represents a particular combination of these two dimensions. For example, "docile-dependent" blends love and weakness.

No inherent need requires a circumplex model to be limited to two dimensions. A three-dimensional model is possible, with traits arranged in a sphere and defined by three underlying dimensions. Four- and five-dimensional models are mathematically possible as well, although they can no longer be visualized. Most theorists prefer two-dimensional representations (Benjamin, 1974).

Jerry Wiggins

Jerry S. Wiggins (1979, 1980, 1985) is a psychologist at the University of British Columbia who devised what today is the most widely accepted circumplex model. He used more rigorous statistical procedures than did Leary in order to decide just how to arrange traits in a circle (e.g., Wiggins, Steiger, & Gaelick, 1981). In numerous samples, Wiggins asked research subjects to rate themselves as possessing (or not) various traits. He then calculated correlations between all possible pairs of traits. That is, he determined the degree to which subjects attributed the same traits to themselves. If two traits correlated positively with one another, they were placed close together on the circle. If the correlation was zero, then the traits were placed at right angles. If negative, then they were placed on opposite sides of the circumplex.

Wiggins' research led to the particular model shown in Figure 8–3. The two dimensions that seem to underlie his model are much the same as those that

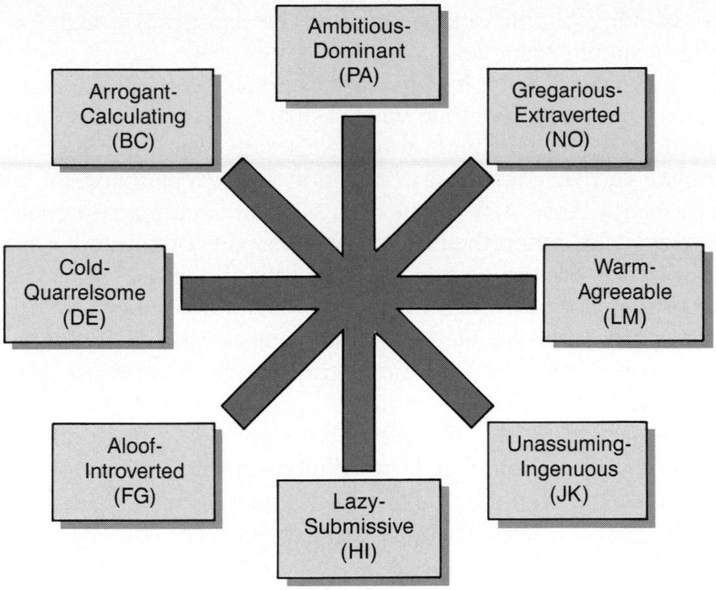

FIGURE 8-3
Wiggins' (1980)
Circumplex Model

Ambitious-
Dominant
(PA)

Arrogant-
Calculating
(BC)

Gregarious-
Extraverted
(NO)

Cold-
Quarrelsome
(DE)

Warm-
Agreeable
(LM)

Aloof-
Introverted
(FG)

Unassuming-
Ingenuous
(JK)

Lazy-
Submissive
(HI)

define Leary's circumplex—that is, hate versus love and weakness versus strength—although the particular categories differ. Wiggins' "opposites" are more clearly opposed than those Leary suggested, both conceptually and empirically (Paddock & Nowicki, 1986).

Many psychologists who work within the trait paradigm concern themselves in particular with one given trait, to the exclusion of all the other traits that might be studied. Circumplex models provide an extremely useful framework for making sense of the disparate activities of trait researchers (Carson, 1969). A glance at a circumplex can tell an investigator what other traits might be related to the one in which she or he is interested. This is an important step beyond the original view of traits proposed by Allport.

The major drawback to circumplex models, at least as so far devised, is that they tell us more about the *linguistic* relationships among traits than they do about people's actual behaviors. Although language provides a good starting place, these models must eventually be validated against what people actually do. Researchers are now beginning such investigations, relating Wiggins' circumplex model to people's moods (Wiggins, Phillips, & Trapnell, 1989), social behaviors (Gifford & O'Connor, 1987), and adaptation (Romney & Bynner, 1989).

FACTOR ANALYTIC APPROACHES

Another strategy for understanding the interrelations among various traits is the statistical technique of **factor analysis** (Child, 1970; Gorsuch, 1974). This is a procedure for analyzing a complex set of correlations among various measures to form what one hopes is a simpler pattern. The actual mathematics involved in

Factor analysis: A statistical procedure for analyzing a complex set of correlations among various measures to form a simpler pattern.

factor analysis are daunting, but the rationale behind the statistics is straightforward. Let's consider a simple example.

Suppose research subjects complete dozens of personality questionnaires, each measuring a somewhat different trait. What results is an exceedingly large amount of information. Is there a simple way to describe what's going on in these data? We might start by computing correlation coefficients between all possible pairs of measures. As we saw in our discussion of circumplex models, these correlation coefficients reflect the degree to which pairs of traits co-occur (or not). We might notice, for the sake of our example, that scores from the odd-numbered questionnaires correlate positively with one another and are independent of the scores from the even-numbered questionnaires. We might further notice that scores from the even-numbered questionnaires are also positively correlated with one another.

One way to describe our data, therefore, is to say that despite all the different measures our subjects completed, two dimensions underlie our data. The first dimension is reflected by the odd-numbered questionnaires. Suppose these questionnaires measure such traits as thrift, reverence, courtesy, and bravery; we feel justified in calling this first dimension the "Boy Scout" dimension. The second dimension is reflected by the even-numbered questionnaires, and it is similarly interpreted by abstracting the gist of the meanings of the relevant traits.

Real data are rarely so simple that their organization can be discerned by simply looking at a set of correlation coefficients. Here is where the statistical procedure of factor analysis enters into the picture—to reveal underlying dimensions that would otherwise be hidden. The identified dimensions are usually called **factors,** and they provide a way to describe one's data in simple terms.

Factors: Presumably basic dimensions identified through factor analysis.

Many researchers are not content to use factor analysis just as a tool to simplify their data. Instead, they go further and interpret factors as composing the basic structure of personality itself. However, the distinction between the description of factors and their interpretation is an important one. Interpretation is nowhere as easy as our earlier example implied. Applied to data, factor analysis will always identify underlying factors. Whether these factors have substantive meaning is another matter. Stephen Gould (1981) described the biggest pitfall in the interpretation of factors:

> Factorists have often fallen prey to a temptation for *reification*—for awarding *physical meaning* to all strong [factors]. . . . Sometimes this is justified . . . but such a claim can never arise from the mathematics alone, only from additional knowledge . . . of the measures themselves. (p. 250)

Factors cannot reflect reality unless the component scores themselves do. And even then, interpretation may run afoul. Here is Gould again:

> Nonsensical systems of correlation have [factors] . . . as well. . . . A factor analysis for a five-by-five correlation matrix of my age, the population of Mexico, the price of Swiss cheese, my pet turtle's weight, and the average distance between galaxies

during the past 10 years will yield a strong [factor] . . . since all the correlations are so strongly positive. . . . It will also have no enlightening physical meaning whatever. (p. 250)

In other words, the analysis revealed the passage of time as the confound of all the correlations here, and the single latent "factor" revealed by factor analysis reflects merely this confound. My point is to suggest that this statistical tool cannot be used blindly. It does not create theory out of data by an automatic process.

Personality psychologists are understandably reluctant to use factor analysis only as a descriptive tool. After all, they are not really interested in the questionnaire scores of particular people at a particular time under a particular circumstance. They want to go beyond these particular data. They especially want to assume that questionnaire scores reflect personality traits and that factors reflect the underlying structure of personality. So they interpret the factors they discover by assigning substantive meaning to the questionnaire scores and then looking for common meanings reflected in a given factor.

In the hands of skillful theorists, factor analysis can be an extremely useful way to process an overwhelming amount of information about people. The two most famous theorists are Raymond Cattell and Hans Eysenck, and it is to their research programs and resulting theories that we now turn.

Raymond Cattell

Raymond Cattell was born in England in 1905, the son of middle-class parents. He attended the University of London as a chemistry major but then changed his mind. Here is how Cattell describes his switch into psychology:

> On a cold and foggy London morning in 1924 I turned my back on the shining flasks and tubes of my well-equipped chemistry bench and walked over to Charles Spearman's laboratory to explore the promise of psychology. . . . This seemingly quixotic act . . . sprang from my broader reading having led me to see that psychology was the really new, challenging frontier of science, and the source of rational hopes for human progress. (1984, p. 121)

(By the way, Spearman was an early investigator of intelligence and one of those who helped invent factor analysis in the beginning of the twentieth century.)

After receiving his doctorate in psychology, Cattell worked for five years as a clinician. He came away unimpressed with the merits of psychotherapy, concluding that psychology's biggest need was for basic research on learning and personality. In 1937 he was able to follow through on his belief when E. L. Thorndike of Columbia University invited him to come to the United States and be his research assistant. Cattell said yes and has stayed there ever since. He has held appointments at several universities, most notably at Harvard and at the University of Illinois (where he stayed for almost three decades: 1946–1973).

Cattell's basic scientific premise is that the scientist's topics should dictate the methods used to investigate them. Personality demands a method that can simultaneously take into account its numerous facets. Experimentation has little value. Instead, multivariate statistics in general and factor analysis in particular are the preferred methods for personality psychology:

> Whereas the physicist or the bivariate brass instrument experimenter [that is, experimental psychologist] can hope to reach a law with a few bits of wire and glass and a couple of checking experiments the [personality] psychologist in his multidetermined uncontrollable world needs say 200 subjects, 30 variables in five hours of measurement, and some repetitions of it all. This prospect turns off the less dedicated Ph.D. and many others toward easier—if more trivial problems. (Cattell, 1984, p. 172)

Throughout his long career, Cattell has used factor analysis to identify the underlying structure of the various aspects of personality.

What are these aspects? Among the more important are traits, attitudes, sentiments, drives, moods, roles, and environments. Personality is the combination of all these into what Cattell calls a *specification equation,* the goal of which is to predict exactly what a person will do in a given situation. So, Cattell regards personality as an equation that predicts behavior.

Cattell has investigated traits most thoroughly, defining them as relatively permanent and pervasive tendencies to respond. An important distinction arises between surface traits and source traits. **Surface traits** are the innumerable differences we see among people. Language gives us the total domain of surface traits. Remember the list of trait names compiled by Allport and Odbert (1936)? Cattell began his personality research with the same list. He eliminated synonyms and obscure traits, leaving 171 surface traits, such individual differences as flexibility, conscientiousness, and eccentricity. He then asked observers to rate people they knew with respect to these traits. Factor analysis revealed the underlying structure of these surface traits, what Cattell calls **source traits.**

The **Sixteen Personality Factor Test (16PF)** is a questionnaire that measures the most important source traits. Table 8–2 gives brief descriptions of

Surface traits: According to Cattell, the innumerable differences that can be observed among people.

Source traits: According to Cattell, the dimensions that underlie surface traits, identifiable through factor analysis.

Sixteen Personality Factor Test (16PF): A questionnaire that measures the 16 source traits identified by Cattell.

TABLE 8–2
Source Traits (As Measured by Cattel's 16PF)

Casual versus Controlled	Placid versus Apprehensive
Conservative versus Experimenting	Practical versus Imaginative
Emotional versus Stable	Relaxed versus Tense
Expedient versus Conscientious	Reserved versus Outgoing
Forthright versus Shrewd	Shy versus Venturesome
Group-Tied versus Self-Sufficient	Sober versus Happy-Go-Lucky
Humble versus Assertive	Tough- versus Tender-Minded
Less- versus More-Intelligent	Trusting versus Suspicious

SOURCE: From Cattell, 1984.

these traits in terms of their endpoints. Appreciate that each of these traits represents a dimension along which people vary. In Allport's terms, they are common traits.

Cattell has no place for personal dispositions, but his 16 source traits allow a dazzling variety among people. Suppose each trait has just three levels: high, medium, and low. How many unique combinations are there? Three to the 16th power, which is in excess of 43 million "types" of people!

Although many personality psychologists assess traits only with a questionnaire, like the 16PF, Cattell recognized that one should not rely on a single source of data. So he gathered and analyzed not only responses to questionnaires, which he called **Q-data,** but also information from the individual's life **(L-data),** such as whether or not someone is married, and information from objective observations **(T-data)** as well, such as how a person behaves during a driving test.

Cattell looks for convergence among the source traits found in the three types of data. So far, these efforts have not been entirely successful. Some traits "appear" only in one or two types of data. Thus, the exact number of source traits deemed critical by Cattell is uncertain. Usually, Q-data and L-data are in better agreement with one another than either is with T-data, perhaps because "objective" performance is determined more by situational demands than by personality traits.

The factors themselves also have been subjected to factor analysis. Let's stop for a minute and look at what this procedure provides: a simpler (and even more abstract) structure of underlying personality. Two of these *second-order factors* are noteworthy. The first is identified as *introversion-extraversion* (after Jung's dimension) and the second as *anxiety* (Maddi, 1980). Taken together, these suggest four basic types of people: introverted-anxious, introverted-nonanxious, extraverted-anxious, and extraverted-nonanxious.

More of Cattell's work deserves mention. Influenced by his English mentors, Cattell has investigated the heritability of personality characteristics (Cattell et al., 1955, 1957). He developed a statistical technique for this purpose—*multiple abstract variance analysis (MAVA)*—that estimates not only the presence or absence of genetic influence, but also the degree to which a trait has a genetic basis. Results from the MAVA technique suggest that traits such as intelligence and assertiveness have a relatively strong genetic underpinning, whereas traits like conscientiousness and control do not (Loehlin, 1984).

Cattell also has been interested in psychopathology. He's investigated the structure of the "abnormal" personality (Cattell & Scheier, 1961). Additional factors are used to explain emotional disorders, and Cattell draws on psychodynamic notions to interpret them. People with problems tend to be highly anxious, and the source of this anxiety is twofold: a genetic predisposition to be sensitive to threats and a family environment where conflict and inconsistency dominate.

A final interest of Cattell's is sketched in his 1972 book *A New Morality from Science: Beyondism.* This book is a bold attempt to use the techniques of science—that is, multivariate statistics—to decide which system of morality is the best! Cattell proposes that societies throughout the world be characterized

Q-data: Question-naire responses.

L-data: Information concerning people's lives.

T-data: Objective observations.

first by their differing religions, social systems, and political organizations and then by the degree to which they achieve "the greatest good for the greatest number" of their citizens. It is then a simple matter to see which morality is most highly correlated with this measure. Needless to say, this is controversial and unlikely to be taken seriously by world leaders. This may be just as well, but Cattell's *Beyondism* epitomizes the only person who rivals and perhaps surpasses Freud as a personality theorist of scope and audacity.

Hans Eysenck

The other major figure in factor analytic studies of personality is Hans Eysenck (b. 1916). Comparisons between Cattell and Eysenck are inevitable and intriguing. Here is what they have in common. Both are immigrants: Cattell from England to the United States, Eysenck from Germany to England. Both studied at the University of London where they were influenced by psychologists and statisticians who can trace their intellectual ancestry to scientist Francis Galton. Both believe measurement is fundamental to personality psychology. Both employ factor analysis to identify the underlying structure of personality. Both believe that important aspects of personality are inherited. And both have been extremely prolific throughout their careers.

At the same time, important differences remain between them. Cattell is influenced by psychodynamic ideas and speaks approvingly of Freud's intuitive insights into personality, while Eysenck is vehemently opposed to psychoanalysis. Also unlike Cattell, Eysenck has always been interested in therapy and has been a proponent of behavior modification. Finally, through their respective versions of factor analysis, Cattell and Eysenck arrive at different underlying structures of personality. Where Cattell points to at least 16 factors of personality, Eysenck believes no more than three are necessary.

Eysenck is a controversial figure within psychology. Part of this controversy is inevitable, since he advocates the politically unpopular idea that personality and intelligence are inherited. But part of the controversy is also due to Eysenck's style of writing and speaking (Gibson, 1981). He is critical of other psychologists to the point of sarcasm. He has written a number of books calling things as he sees them. To give you a flavor of this, the titles of two of Eysenck's better-known books are *Sense and Nonsense in Psychology* (1953) and *The Inequality of Man* (1973).

Eysenck has used a variety of procedures for gathering data about research subjects: questionnaires, ratings by others, assessments of physique and physiology, objective psychological tests, and biographical information. These data are factor analyzed to find the basic structure that underlies personality. In his early research, Eysenck found two factors: **introversion-extraversion** and **neuroticism.**

> Extraversion is defined in behavioural terms by the various traits that are correlated together to define this factor, traits such as sociability, impulsiveness, activity, carelessness, liveliness, jocularity, and so forth. (Eysenck, 1976, p. 11)

Introversion-extraversion: According to Eysenck, one of the basic dimensions of personality, reflecting one's shyness versus sociability, caution versus impulsiveness, and so on.

Neuroticism: According to Eysenck, one of the basic dimensions of personality, reflecting one's emotionality.

Neuroticism is conceived of as strong, labile emotionality, predisposing a person to develop neurotic symptoms in case of excessive stress. Traits correlating to define this 'type' are moodiness, sleeplessness, nervousness, inferiority feelings, irritability. (pp. 15–16)

Note that Eysenck's two factors are essentially the same as the two second-order factors Cattell identifies, implying that they are approaching the structure of personality at different levels of abstraction (cf. Mershon & Gorsuch, 1988).

More recently, Eysenck has found a third factor: **psychoticism.** He is still describing this dimension but provides a sketch of the individual high in psychoticism

Psychoticism: According to Eysenck, one of the basic dimensions of personality, reflecting one's insensitivity, oddness, and detachment from others.

as being solitary, not caring for people . . . often troublesome, not fitting in anywhere. He may be cruel and inhumane, lacking in feeling and empathy, and altogether insensitive. He is hostile to others, even his own kith and kin, and aggressive, even to loved ones. He has a liking for odd and unusual things, and a disregard for danger. (Eysenck, 1976, p. 19)

Psychoticism can characterize the extremely disturbed individual, but Eysenck conceives it as a personality dimension along which all people can be arrayed.

An intriguing aspect of Eysenck's approach to personality is his attempt to specify a physiological basis for each of his personality dimensions. Introversion-extraversion is linked to chronic levels of excitation in the cortex. Introverts are overaroused and hence easy to stimulate; for this reason, they avoid situations apt to overwhelm them. In contrast, extraverts are underaroused and thus difficult to stimulate; accordingly, they seek out exciting situations. Neuroticism is thought to reflect the degree to which the autonomic nervous system reacts to stimuli. The more reactive a person, the more neurotic he or she is. Finally, Eysenck tentatively links psychoticism to one's level of male sex hormone. (It's bad enough that excess testosterone makes us bald; does it have to make us peculiar as well?)

A theory of psychopathology emerges from this physiological interpretation of the dimensions of personality. The person who is high on neuroticism and introversion is at risk for anxiety disorders: fears, phobias, obsessions, and compulsions. The person who is high on neuroticism and extraversion is a candidate for psychopathy (antisocial personality).

In this theory, disorders do not occur automatically. They befall a person with the appropriate predisposition and environmental circumstances. People *learn* their problems. Because of one's particular personality, one tends to learn some things more easily than others, so different personalities are associated with different problems (Patterson, Kosson, & Newman, 1987). For example, the introverted neurotic will easily associate fear with objects in the environment. A phobia may result.

Traits and therapy are usually strange bedfellows. A trait is a fixed characteristic of an individual, and if one believes traits to be the basic units of personality, then one usually believes personality to be fixed as well—resistant to change, including therapy. But Eysenck's interest in behavior modification follows naturally from his theory of emotional disorders. What has been learned can be unlearned. The physiological account of traits explains how therapy can work. Traits represent *predispositions to learn.* As people learn and unlearn particular behaviors, their traits do not change, although their behavior does. To Eysenck, a trait is thus a vehicle for change.

Similarly, Eysenck's physiological theory allows him to combine interests in heredity and learning—the traditionally opposite nature versus nurture. What is inherited is the biological apparatus that makes learning possible. So, the physiological underpinnings of personality make Eysenck's approach to personality extremely powerful. At present, though, not enough research supports his hypothesized processes of the brain and nervous system.

Conclusion: Factor Analysis and Personality

Factor analytic approaches to personality have probably not received the attention and acclaim they deserve. The theories of Cattell and Eysenck are complex enough to capture the richness of personality, and at the same time they are grounded in empirical research of a type acceptable to most psychologists. More than any other approach described in this chapter, these theories bring Allport's original vision of personality psychology into reality.

What's the problem then? I think the technique of factor analysis is largely to blame. The statistics involved are difficult to understand, since they require mathematical sophistication that many personality psychologists do not want to acquire. Further, because of this, the pitfalls of factor analysis are easier to understand than its potential contributions. Cattell and Eysenck have painstakingly tried to show that their factors are more than just statistical abstractions. In large part they have succeeded, but this success has gone unnoticed (Cattell, 1990).

The theorists themselves often fail to make their techniques more comprehensible to a larger audience. Both Cattell and Eysenck fill their articles with technical quibbles about the theoretical and procedural shortcomings of the other theorist. I suspect that readers are turned off by what appears as massive disagreement between the major proponents of factor analysis. If Cattell and Eysenck are so critical of one another, why should the rest of us take them seriously? When factor analysts emphasize what is common to the different approaches, this strategy will be more accepted (Zuckerman, Kuhlman, & Camac, 1988).

BIOLOGICAL APPROACHES

Typology: A set of categories describing discrete personality types.

Theorizing about personality is probably as old as humanity itself (Martindale & Martindale, 1988). The early personality theories were **typologies:** mutually exclusive and exhaustive categories of types of people (Jastrow, 1915). Some of the pigeonholes of the early categories were based on a moral or religious view of the world. Types were characterized by a predominant virtue or vice, which catalyzed everything a person thought, felt, or did. Taken together, these virtues made up an all-encompassing perspective on the universe and people's place within it.

Other early typologies were based on differences in biology. Unlike moral typologies, variants of these are still very much a part of contemporary personality psychology. Biological approaches assume people differ in personality because they differ physically. These physical differences are usually regarded as fixed and pervasive characteristics inherited from one's ancestors. Taken together, biologically based personality theories comprise an important line of theorizing within the trait paradigm.

Over the years, many psychologists in the United States have been reluctant to believe that differences among people have a biological basis, preferring instead the notion that learning is responsible for all individual differences. The problem with this reasoning is that it approaches the nature-nurture controversy in too stark a fashion. A more evenhanded view starts by acknowledging the importance of both nature and nurture, and then proceeds to understand how they interact to determine our behavior (Crawford & Anderson, 1989).

Important Evolutionary Ideas

A variety of biological approaches to personality exist. What unites them is the theory of evolution, which provides the dominant perspective on the whole of biology. In this section, we'll briefly discuss some important evolutionary ideas, focusing on those most relevant to the understanding of personality.

Natural Selection In discussing evolution, we must first distinguish between the *fact* of evolution and the *explanation* of this fact. That species change over time is well established, supported by the fossil record, the success of animal and plant breeders, and the recurrence across different species of basic anatomical structures.

Granted that species change, how can we explain these changes? The English naturalist Charles Darwin (1809–1882) provided a persuasive explanation of evolution in his 1859 book *The Origin of Species*. His theory was inspired at least in part by the way pigeon breeders artificially produce a new breed. To create a pigeon with brightly colored feathers, let us say, pigeon fanciers would choose the most colorful birds and breed them together. Among the offspring would be some number of even more colorful birds. These birds would in turn have offspring. As this process is repeated across many generations of birds, what results, for the sake of our example, is an extremely garish pigeon.

Darwin proposed that this process of selection also occurs in nature. His theory of evolution therefore emphasizes the role of **natural selection** in producing change. Nature plays the role of the breeder, although of course it has no final goal like Day-Glo feathers. Feathers become more colorful only if changes in this direction aid survival every step of the way.

Natural selection: Charles Darwin's theory of evolution, which proposes that species evolve in the direction of characteristics that lead to successful reproduction.

Here are the main postulates of Darwin's theory of natural selection:

- The members of particular species have characteristics that vary.
- These variable characteristics can be passed on from parents to offspring.
- Some of these characteristics aid survival.
- Species produce more offspring than survive to be adults.

Across time, as one generation begets another generation, characteristics that aid survival become more prevalent. Those that hamper it become less prevalent. Wholly new species can develop.

According to Darwin's theory, any two species existing today at some point had a common ancestor. In some cases, one need not look back too far to find the common ancestor; in other cases, the common ancestor is lost in the dawn of time. When one speaks of human beings as related to the great apes (chimps, gorillas, and orangutangs), one means that these species share a common ancestor about 15 million years ago. One most definitely does not mean that people descended from the great apes. Evolutionary theory proposes that contemporary species are the *cousins* of human beings, not our ancestors.

Genes   Darwin proposed his theory of natural selection without knowing how parents passed on characteristics to their offspring. This piece of the puzzle fell into place with the publication of studies conducted by Austrian monk Gregor Mendel (1822–1884). Mendel investigated the inheritance of characteristics among pea plants. His work eventually led to modern genetics.

Theorists of today regard the **gene** as the mechanism of inheritance. Genes are tiny structures found within each cell of the body, composed of DNA (deoxyribonucleic acid) molecules. Genes are blueprints for biological development, determining whether we become human beings, chimpanzees, or petunias. They determine whether we are males or females, tall or short, dark-haired or fair. They may also influence our personality.

Human beings may have as many as 100,000 different genes, arranged along chromosomes. Chromosomes are inherited from our parents. An individual's complete set of genes—from both parents—is called his or her **genotype.** Along with environmental events, the genotype determines the characteristics that the individual actually shows, which are called his or her **phenotype.** A phenotype does not perfectly reflect a genotype, because events occurring during development affect just how the plan contained in the genes is actually executed.

Genes exist in pairs. In the simplest case, one member of the pair is dominant, determining the phenotype. To use a well-known example, brown-eyed genes dominate blue-eyed genes; hence, the gene for brown eyes is considered dominant. Much more common is **polygenic inheritance,** which refers to the determination of particular characteristics by more than one gene at a time.

Gene: The mechanism of inheritance, composed of DNA molecules and passed from parents to offspring.

Genotype: An individual's genetic inheritance; the blueprint for development provided by the genes.

Phenotype: An individual's actual characteristics, produced by one's genotype in combination with the environment.

Polygenic inheritance: The determination of characteristics by several genes working in combination.

Behavior Genetics   The field of **behavior genetics** studies how genetic differences within a species are related to behavior differences (Hirsch, 1967; Wimer & Wimer, 1985). Behavior geneticists do not study instinctive behaviors, which are behaviors all members of a species show and are minimally influenced by environmental input. Instead, behavior geneticists study behavioral differences among people brought about by the complex interaction of genetic and environmental influences. So the relevance of behavior genetics to personality psychology is obvious.

The key concept in the field of behavior genetics is **heritability,** which refers to the proportion of a trait's variation due to genetic factors. The more a trait's variation in a group of individuals is due to genetic factors, the greater its heritability. A number of personality traits show a fair degree of heritability, meaning that differences among people in these traits reflect at least in part differences in their genes.

Heritability should not be equated with any simple notion of inheritance. I am *not* saying that personality traits are inherited, passed directly from parents to children. Heritability is a more abstract concept. It refers to a group of people and not to an individual. It refers to the variation in traits across these people, not to their traits per se. To repeat: Behavior geneticists attempt to link *variation* in traits or behaviors on the one hand to *variation* in genes on the other.

Fitness and Inclusive Fitness   The slogan "survival of the fittest" is frequently used to summarize Darwin's theory of evolution. However, it deserves some scrutiny. **Fitness** refers simply to successful reproduction, not strength or longevity. An organism is fit if it successfully passes its genes into the next generation. "Survival" thus refers to the continuation of genes, *not* individuals. Fitness therefore transcends an individual to encompass all those sharing genes in common.

Under certain circumstances, laying down one's life for the sake of another can be evolutionarily advantageous—so long as the two share genes in common. If the "sacrifice" of one's life enhances the reproductive success of a close relative, then this act ends up enhancing the survival of one's own genes. **Inclusive fitness** is defined as the fitness of an individual plus the influence of the individual on the fitness of his or her relatives (Hamilton, 1964).

Sociobiology   The notion of inclusive fitness extends the traditional interpretation of fitness, allowing evolutionary theory to be applied to topics that previously seemed outside its limits. The field of **sociobiology** rests on this idea. Sociobiology is the application of modern evolutionary theory to social behavior (E. O. Wilson, 1975, 1978). Complex social interaction invariably proved a stumbling block to previous evolutionary theorists, because any society requires cooperation, compromise, and occasional sacrifice by its members. How could natural selection have led to selflessness?

Sociobiology answers this question via inclusive fitness, which allows "altruism" to be explained in biological terms by referring to genes that two individuals share in common. Sociobiologists can use inclusive fitness to

Behavior genetics: The field that studies how genetic differences within a species are related to behavior differences.

Heritability: The proportion of variation in some characteristic due to genetic variation.

Fitness: The ability to reproduce successfully.

Inclusive fitness: The fitness of an individual plus the influence of the individual on the fitness of relatives sharing genes in common.

Sociobiology: The application of modern evolutionary ideas—particularly the notion of inclusive fitness—to social behavior.

interpret social behavior just as they interpret individual characteristics: as adaptive. People behave as they do because certain social conventions helped our ancestors pass their genes on to subsequent generations.

With this introduction to important evolutionary ideas in mind, let us turn to some of the ways psychologists have applied these notions to personality. At present, interest in these approaches is great. They speak to a number of issues of long-standing concern within the trait paradigm (Buss, 1990).

Physique and Personality

Asthenic: Kretschmer's term describing a thin body build.

Athletic: Kretschmer's term describing a muscular body build.

Pyknic: Kretschmer's term describing a fat body build.

Dysplastic: Kretschmer's term describing a "rare and ugly" body build.

Endomorphy: The degree to which one's physique is round.

Mesomorphy: The degree to which one's physique is muscular.

Ectomorphy: The degree to which one's physique is slender and angular.

Somatotype: The description of one's physique along the dimensions of endomorphy, mesomorphy, and ectomorphy.

One of the most enduring beliefs is that personality differences reside in the physique. Hence, as mentioned before, typologies based on body build have been proposed since the time of the early Greeks. Most have suggested that three basic body types exist: round, muscular, and thin (Eysenck, 1967).

The modern era in theorizing about physique and personality began in 1921, when German psychiatrist Ernst Kretschmer proposed a theory that linked physique to mental illness. He observed that individuals suffering from the two dominant forms of psychosis—schizophrenia and manic-depression—tended to have different body builds. Schizophrenics were thin and frail, while manic-depressives were plump and round.

To test this informal observation, Kretschmer studied the differences in people's bodies. Consistent with previous theorists, he identified three major types of body build. The linear physique he called **asthenic,** the muscular he called **athletic,** and the roly-poly he called **pyknic.** (A fourth type, the **dysplastic,** was comprised of those rare individuals with inconsistent body builds that struck the observer as "ugly.")

Kretschmer then found support for his speculations. He classified psychiatric patients by their body build and by their diagnosis and found that schizophrenics were apt to be asthenic, while manic-depressives tended to be pyknic. However, he didn't control for the age of his patients. With age, we all tend toward a pyknic physique, as well as toward an increased risk for bipolar depression (Hall & Lindzey, 1978).

Kretschmer believed that his theory could be extended to normal individuals as well, although he presented no evidence to support this. It remained for the American William Sheldon (1940, 1942) to build on the earlier ideas of Kretschmer and extend them to the normal individual.

Sheldon was a psychologist and physician who worked mainly at Harvard and Columbia Universities. In the course of his career, he published a number of books on the human physique, on human temperament, and on the relationship between the two. His major contributions to biological theories of personality are twofold. First, he suggested that physique be described along continuous dimensions, not in terms of discrete types. Second, he described in great detail how one should characterize physique.

So, Sheldon proposed that each physique held three components: **endomorphy** (round), **mesomorphy** (muscular), and **ectomorphy** (linear). Bodies are rated on 7-point scales in accordance with each of these components. These ratings yield a person's **somatotype:** his or her profile of the three components of physique. Manute Bol, for instance, might be rated 117, since he is low on endomorphy and mesomorphy (11) but high on ectomorphy (7). Bo Jackson would probably be rated 171. You and I, on the average, are 444.

According to Sheldon, each component of physique is associated with a particular personality style. Endomorphic individuals are "calm, easygoing, affable, sympathetic, affectionate . . . amiable, jovial" (Metzner, 1979, p. 23). Mesomorphy is associated with the action-oriented. These people are "the actors, the athletes, the executives, the achievers, the fighters" (p. 25). Finally, ectomorphic individuals are overly sensitive, erratic, and inhibited: "critical, superior, judgmental, and suspicious . . . guarded and cautious" (p. 28).

What is the evidence that people of different physiques indeed have different personality characteristics? Some exists, although Sheldon has been criticized for overestimating the strength of the correlation. Still, it does seem that mesomorphic individuals tend toward active and outgoing behaviors like pursuing sports or members of the opposite sex (e.g., Hendry & Gillies, 1978). The consistency of such behaviors exceeds what one would expect by chance.

But such correlations between physique and personality do not address a fundamental premise of this approach, that physique directly brings about characteristic thoughts, actions, and feelings. Notice that the personality traits thought to be associated with endomorphy, mesomorphy, and ectomorphy correspond well to society's stereotypes about fat people, muscular people, and thin people. Perhaps young people with a given body build incorporate the "appropriate" stereotype and act it out. Or a muscular youth might find success

Professional athlete Bo Jackson would probably score 171 in Sheldon's game.

at sports comes easily and thereby develops competitiveness. These would produce correlations between physique and personality, although not because physique has a simple causal role.

This is an important caution about biological theorizing in general. A demonstrated correlation between a biological characteristic and a personality characteristic need not imply that biology has directly influenced personality. Something else might be going on, and until an actual mechanism linking biology and personality has been found, we are left with an inherently ambiguous association.

Regardless of the causal links, it would be a mistake to dismiss physique from our explanation of personality. As Brian Wells (1983) observes, "the physical self is always an important element in our previous history, present self-perception, and future expectations" (p. vii). But the effects of physique on personality are likely to be subtle and complex and in many cases mediated by our own beliefs as well as those of others.

Temperament

Temperament: A biologically based style of behaving.

Another approach to the biological basis of personality is concerned with **temperament,** usually defined as a biological predisposition that encourages a person to respond to events in some ways but not others. Temperament refers to a person's way of interacting with the world, particularly by his or her emotional style. (By the way, the word "temper" is derived from temperament.) Many theorists distinguish between temperament and personality, viewing the former as one of the raw ingredients of the latter. This may be too fine a distinction, but it underscores the notion that temperament is a biologically based style of behaving and not the whole of personality.

Temperament theories have been proposed throughout the century (e.g., Diamond, 1957; Eysenck, 1947; Thomas, Chess, Birch, Hertzig, & Korn, 1963) and are currently enjoying new popularity in research programs that use techniques of behavior genetics to investigate how personality styles are inherited (Collins & Gunnar, 1990).

The young of many species show wide variation in behavior almost from birth, suggesting a biological basis (Scott & Fuller, 1965; Yerkes, 1943). Perhaps the most striking variation is that observed among human infants. Thomas and Chess (1977) describe the original impetus for their study of temperament:

> Like innumerable other parents, we were struck by the clearly evident individual differences in our children, even in the first few weeks of life. There were differences in the regularity of biological functions such as sleep and hunger, in levels of motor activity, in the intensity of laughter or crying, in the initial reactions to new stimuli, in the ease with which the baby's reactions could be modified. . . . In many, though not all . . . children, there appeared to be a remarkable persistence of at least some of these characteristics of individuality as they grew older. (pp. 3–4)

Of course, this example does not prove a strictly genetic basis for individual differences.

Prenatal occurrences and birth itself affect subsequent behavior. Dangers of maternal malnutrition, drug use, and illness during pregnancy are well-known examples. In some cities, signs are posted in bars warning pregnant women not to drink. (Maybe the nonpregnant should be warned about drinking as well.) Compared to infants of nondrinking women, those born to drinking women show not only physical differences but also behavioral differences. These newborns are likely to be tremulous and irregular in their sleep. They tend to cry in a way that is aversive to listeners and to dramatically swing from drowsiness to excitation and vice versa. These ways of behaving—although present at birth—are not genetic.

Similarly, the way parents react to children affects the way their kids behave. This process occurs very early in life. Again, we are tempted to identify those differences as genetic, but they may really be the result of the environment. How many differences between little boys and girls are due more to the way their parents react to them than to the difference between an X and a Y chromosome? Or remember Alfred Adler's ideas about birth order. Infants may behave quite differently because they are born into different social environments.

It is a mistake to try and classify complex behaviors into two neat piles of those determined by nature and those determined by nurture. Temperament theorists agree and try to show that *aspects* of behavior—not behaviors as a whole—are influenced by hereditary factors. This is why they call temperament a style, a way of engaging in activities that themselves have numerous determinants.

As noted earlier, biological explanation within personality psychology has always been controversial. Much of this controversy stems from the political and social implications of the argument that racial differences in intelligence are genetically based. Hitler's pronouncements about pure and impure human races did nothing to win acceptance of the notion that aspects of personality are inherited. Finally, American ideology about all men (and women) being created equal is often at odds with the intent of temperament theorists.

Nevertheless, we have equal reason to distrust an extreme environmentalism that dismisses biology and particularly genetics as irrelevant in understanding what people are about. Thomas and Chess discuss one of the dangers of this position:

> As mental health professionals we became increasingly concerned at the dominant professional ideology . . . in which the causation of all child psychopathology, from simple behavior problems to juvenile delinquency to schizophrenia itself, was laid at the doorstep of the mother. . . . The guilt and anxiety created in mothers whose children had even minor behavioral deviations were enormous. (1977, p. 5)

Thomas and Chess dub this ideology the *Mal de Mere* syndrome, literally the "sickness of the mother," arguing that excessive guilt on the part of the mother could indeed screw up her kids, completing a self-fulfilling prophecy.

What are the basic temperaments? Early attempts to catalogue temperaments were hampered by the aforementioned difficulties in determining

Twin method: A method for disentangling the effects of nature and nurture by comparing the resemblance in characteristics of identical versus fraternal twins.

whether or not a genetic influence was present. Recent attempts have been more successful because they use Sir Francis Galton's **twin method** for disentangling nature and nurture (see Chapter 2). The behavior of identical and fraternal twins is ascertained and then compared. Do identical twins resemble each other more than fraternal twins? If so, a case is made for a genetic influence on the behavior being studied. Notice that this is not foolproof. As a correlational research strategy, the twin method is subject to various confounds, and one can draw the wrong conclusion. Stop and think of reasons other than heredity why identical twins might behave more similarly than fraternal twins.

Did you think of the possibility that identical twins are treated more similarly than are fraternal twins? They are often dressed alike, given similar names, confused by friends and family members, and treated as a pair rather than two individuals. Here we have a likely confound in the twin method, but surprisingly, it does not seem to be relevant. Researchers have classified twins based on the degree to which their environments are the same, finding that this classification is essentially unrelated to how similar the twins are with respect to their personality characteristics (Loehlin & Nichols, 1976; Plomin & Daniels, 1987; but see Baker & Daniels, 1990).

This finding—if it holds up—is extremely important, and not just because of what it says about the heritability of traits. It implies that the family environment children *share* is not a particularly important influence on the personalities they develop. Most psychologists accept as a truism the importance of one's family on development, but this finding suggests that family influence varies from child to child within the same family.

In some domains of investigation, the twin method is refined to include comparisons not only of identical and fraternal twins, but also of twins raised together and twins raised apart. The assumption here is that twins in the same family are exposed to the same environmental determinants, while twins in different families are not. With this approach, the effects of similar versus dissimilar "nature" and similar versus dissimilar "nurture" can be examined simultaneously.

Family study: A method for disentangling the effects of nature and nurture by comparing the resemblance in characteristics of family members having varying degrees of biological relatedness.

Researchers have supplemented the twin method with other research strategies (Plomin, DeFries, & McClearn, 1980). One intriguing method is to compare the similarity of identical twins with respect to some characteristic to the similarity of fraternal twins mistakenly regarded by their families as identical (Scarr, 1968). (Researchers ascertain whether twins are identical or not by comparing blood proteins, while parents do so just by looking at their children.) This method presumably holds "nurture" much more constant than in typical twin studies. Researchers also employ **family studies**—comparing the similarity of family members according to the distance of their relatedness (the more distant a relative, the less genetic similarity), and **adoption studies**— comparing the resemblance of children to their biological versus adoptive parents.

Adoption study: A method for disentangling the effects of nature and nurture by comparing the resemblance in characteristics of parents and adopted versus biological offspring.

Arnold Buss and Robert Plomin (1975, 1984) have identified three temperaments that have good evidence for a genetic basis: emotionality, activity, and sociability. As styles of behavior, each temperament is inferred from actual behavior by quantifying responses in terms of frequency (how many responses per unit of time), duration (how long each response lasts), and amplitude (how intense each response is).

So, *emotionality* is reflected in the frequency with which one cries, pouts, or throws tantrums; in the duration of these outbursts; and in their intensity. *Activity* is shown by the rate one walks or talks, by the persistence at high-energy activities, and by the tendency to be in constant motion: bouncing or pacing. *Sociability* is estimated by the number of social contacts one initiates, by the amount of time spent with others, and by the degree to which one is socially responsive.

Note that these measures can be adapted for infants, children, and adults. Individuals are arrayed along each of these quantitative dimensions according to "how much" (frequency, duration, and amplitude) of the temperament they show in their behavior. It's easy to find the extreme of each temperament: Haven't you noticed that emotional, active, and sociable people usually sit in front of you at the movies?

Research converges to support Buss and Plomin's contention that these three styles of behaving are heritable. With respect to these temperaments, identical twins resemble each other much more than do fraternal twins. In fact, the tendency is for fraternal twins to show a slightly negative correlation. So, if Twin A is high on emotionality, Twin B is likely to be somewhat low. Buss and Plomin term this a *contrast effect* and suggest that it's due to labeling on the part of the parents:

> Parents might contrast their fraternal twins, labeling one as active and the other as inactive. The twins might contrast themselves and become more differentiated behaviorally. One twin partner, who might be slightly more active than the other, converts this slight edge into a consistent advantage in initiating activities, and the other twin relinquishes the initiative to his partner. (1984, p. 119)

This might not happen with identical twins because parents are more likely to stress their similarities. At any rate, remember my earlier point that temperament studies do not necessarily ignore the role of the environment in determining personality. The contrast effect, although emerging from heredity investigations, leads to an insight about the special social environment of twins.

Granted a particular set of behavioral styles, how does a person's temperament interact with the other determinants of personality to bring about a behavior? Temperament theorists stress that the answer is a complex one. Thomas and Chess (1977) cite the example of a child who is highly active. In an urban environment, she "is more apt to get burned and bruised, to break things, to dart out into the street in front of an oncoming car and to interfere unintentionally with the activities and comforts of others than is the child with a moderate or low activity level" (p. 73). She will bring down on herself a whole host of prohibitions and punishments, which will have profound effects on her entire personality.

But suppose this same child was in a rural environment. Her high activity style would not put her at risk for so many dangers and would not bring about parental restriction. Being in a different environment, she would grow into quite a different person than her urban counterpart. We can think of many other environmental factors that would interact with particular temperaments to influence the course of personality development (Kagan, 1989).

An interesting extension of the research on temperament is examining how heritability changes with age (Plomin & Nesselrode, 1990). As we grow older, does the influence of genetics decrease, stay the same, or increase? One's intuitive answer would be that genetic influences decrease with age as the importance of socialization necessarily increases. However, the available evidence implies just the opposite. Heritability increases with age, which means that variation in temperament is more closely linked to genetic variation among adults than infants. The best way to interpret this trend is not yet clear. It may reflect biological processes, environmental ones, or interactions between the two. If nothing else, these findings underscore the point that genetic influences on temperament can be highly complex.

The Heritability of Traits

Several recent studies have used methods of behavior genetics to investigate the heritability of personality traits. Note that this line of investigation is somewhat different from studies of temperament, which we took pains to define as our *style* of behaving. Studies of traits, in contrast, get at the actual *content* of our behavior. Research shows that a number of traits are heritable. Before I describe these studies, let us remember one more time that heritable does not mean that traits are inherited as a whole. Rather, it means that the variation in a trait has a basis in genetic variation.

I'm dwelling on this distinction because it is easily misunderstood. The popular press has reported these new studies in sensationalistic fashion. "Major Personality Study Finds that Traits are Mostly Inherited," proclaimed a *New York Times* headline (Goleman, 1986), when this was not at all what the study found. Further, a moral danger arises in confusing heritable with inherited. If our personalities are seen as inherited, we might overlook the role played by the immediate environment in shaping our behavior. Social reforms might be dismissed as futile. But if our personalities are seen as heritable, the importance of the environment remains undiminished.

Over the years, personality researchers periodically administered questionnaires to sets of twins. The typical finding was greater similarity in traits between identical twins than between fraternal twins (e.g., Newman, Freeman, & Holzinger, 1937). Other researchers conducted family studies, comparing the similarity in traits across individuals of differing biological relatedness. Again, they typically discovered greater similarity between close relatives than between distant relatives (Crook, 1937).

Several problems plagued these early studies, so they were met with limited acceptance. First, the sample sizes were extremely small, which made the resulting differences look like flukes. Second, many of these studies used questionnaires of unknown reliability and validity, again making the results suspect (Eysenck, 1990). Third, statistics for quantifying the extent of genetic influence—that is, for estimating the degree of heritability—did not exist, and

thus comparisons across studies were hampered. Fourth, twin studies and family studies represent less-than-foolproof research designs. Any given investigation could be criticized by someone skeptical of genetic influences on personality. Such skeptics existed in abundance.

Conditions have since changed, as more acceptable studies have been conducted. Researchers have used larger sample sizes, better questionnaire measures of traits, and newly developed statistics that allow comparisons across different investigations (e.g., Rose, Koskenvuo, Kaprio, Sarna, & Langinvainio, 1988). Finally, several recent studies have employed the most sophisticated version of the twin method, comparing twins raised together and raised separately (e.g., Pedersen, Plomin, McClearn, & Friberg, 1988; Tellegen et al., 1988).

The conclusions from these studies echo those from earlier studies: Many personality traits show a moderate degree of heritability. Indeed, because these newer studies have been conducted in a variety of countries—the United States, England, Finland, Sweden, and Australia—they possess generality seldom encountered in psychological research.

Just which personality traits are heritable? The answer is essentially every trait researchers have examined. Eysenck's personality dimensions of introversion-extraversion and neuroticism have been the most frequently investigated; studies consistently find these to be heritable (Plomin, Chipuer, & Loehlin, 1990). In other investigations, personality inventories such as the MMPI and the 16PF have been used, and once again, the majority of scales prove heritable (Loehlin, Willerman, & Horn, 1987; Rose, 1988). The importance of these latter studies is that personality inventories attempt to encompass the entire range of individual differences.

Granted a genetic basis to variation in traits, what is the extent of this heritability? Exact estimates vary from study to study, but they seem to converge at about 40 percent (Plomin, 1986). In other words, about 40 percent of the variation in personality traits across people is due to underlying genetic variation. By way of comparison, estimates of the heritability of intelligence range from 50 percent to 70 percent (Snyderman & Rothman, 1987). So, the heritability of personality traits is less than that of intelligence, yet still of the same order of magnitude.

Let us put these findings in context. First, we must not overinterpret the importance of genetic factors on personality. Most of the variation in traits is due to nongenetic sources. Second, a consistent discrepancy occurs in the heritability estimates of twin studies versus adoption studies (Plomin, Chipuer, & Loehlin, 1990). Twin studies yield higher estimates of heritability than adoption studies, when of course they should agree. The reason for the discrepancy is not clear, but it is possible that the assumptions used to derive heritability estimates are too simple and require modification. Third, almost all studies to date have measured personality traits with questionnaires. As we will discuss at length in the next chapter, such operationalizations are not ideal. Fourth, the entire approach of behavior genetics leaves unanswered basic questions about how genes influence personality.

Linkage study: A method for investigating genetic inheritance by determining the link between particular characteristics and others known to be determined by single genes, such as color blindness.

The research just described gives no clue about which genes influence personality. We can strongly suspect that polygenic inheritance is at work. If single genes were responsible, these would probably have been identified already through **linkage studies.** In these studies, the link is investigated between personality traits and physical characteristics known to be determined by single genes, such as color blindness. Such links seem not to exist (McKusick, 1986).

Relatedly, research to date provides few answers concerning the biological pathway leading from genes to behavior. Investigations along these lines are now under way, comparing the physiology of those who differ with respect to particular traits. If researchers find differences, then it might be possible to infer how these are genetically programmed.

But the most basic question that can be asked about the heritability of traits is why it exists in the first place (Buss, 1990). For the most part, evolution has worked to minimize the variation of our physical characteristics. Virtually all people have the same number of fingers and toes. So why should they differ with respect to their personality?

This question has not gone unexamined. Tooby and Cosmides (1990) sketched several different answers, although they acknowledged that we currently have no basis for choosing among them. One possibility is that the survival of the species as a whole is served by having variation across individuals with respect to personality traits. This guarantees maximum flexibility in adapting to different environments. Another possibility is that personality traits, at least within normal ranges, are irrelevant for survival and so have never been selected against. And a third possibility is that this variation is a coincidental byproduct of other characteristics of people, such as the structure or function of the nervous system, which do vary for evolutionary reasons.

Has the survival of our species as a whole been served by having great variation across individuals?

Biology and Human Nature

So far, in our discussion of biological approaches to personality, we have focused on individual differences. Another way biological considerations shed light on personality is by helping us understand what different people share in common. In other words, biological approaches suggest their own model of human nature, one phrased in evolutionary terms. This model assumes that people have evolved with characteristic ways of surviving and reproducing; these quite literally comprise our nature.

Evolutionary-minded psychologists attempt to discern these aspects of human nature in several sources of information. First, they study the behavior of our close cousins the primates as they live in their natural environments (e.g., Smuts, 1985). Second, they study certain human cultures such as the !Kung of the Kalahari, the Aborigines of Australia, and the BaMbuti of the Congo; these people still exist in much the same way as their ancestors did tens of thousands of years ago (e.g., Shostak, 1981; Turnbull, 1962). And third, they study archaeological evidence in order to re-create the lives and personalities of people long ago (e.g., Festinger, 1983). The premise of all of these approaches is that we can learn about human nature by understanding how people evolved.

The picture that emerges from these studies is consistent, although we would want to know much more. Our species came into existence about 200,000 years ago. The very first people lived in small groups. They were nomads, constantly on the move. Males in these groups hunted large animals, while females gathered plants. The degree of social cohesion within these groups was notably great, and sociobiology explains why. All the members of these small tribes were closely related, so in helping any individual, someone was increasing his or her own fitness.

This view of human nature, stressing cooperation and interaction among people, differs markedly from earlier biological metaphors for human nature that were uninformed by modern evolutionary ideas. Consider the Freudian view of people as inherently selfish; it is at odds with what is now believed about our ancestors (see Parisi, 1987). Nonetheless, in emphasizing sexual and aggressive aspects of people, Freud was at least looking at the sorts of activities that make a difference in evolution.

Mate selection: The process men and women use to choose their reproductive partners.

David Buss (1984, 1990, 1991) has called on personality psychologists to take greater account of evolutionary considerations in proposing theories and designing studies. In particular, he believes the topic of **mate selection**—how men and women go about choosing their partners—can be enlightened by an appreciation of evolution. Buss argues that men and women have different needs in their respective partners, and that these should be reflected in differences in preferred characteristics. So, men should prefer younger and good-looking women, because these characteristics foreshadow the ability to bear children successfully. Females should prefer older and industrious men, because these characteristics signify the ability to provide resources for a family.

Buss (1989) investigated these hypotheses in a questionnaire study carried out in 37 different cultures around the world, and they were for the most part supported. He argued that findings that occur across different cultures have a biological basis, but this line of reasoning has been disputed (cf. Howard, Blumstein, & Schwartz, 1987). These results may simply imply that people in different cultures face the same situational demands and pressures.

Regardless, evolutionary ideas in general and those of sociobiology in particular have become popular, yet at the same time controversial. The controversy has two sources. First, sociobiologists propose that many of our species-typical activities are the product of evolution and somehow adaptive. Eyebrows are raised when this line of reasoning is applied to rape, infanticide, and war. Let me stress that many sociobiologists would disagree with these particular applications, but the ensuing arguments color the entire endeavor (Archer, 1988).

Second, sociobiology is sometimes used to explain differences between human groups as biologically based. This may then lead to the implication that some groups are superior and others inferior. To propose that men and women are fundamentally different because of evolutionary reasons is to undercut, perhaps, social and political movements for equality between the sexes. To propose that ethnic groups are fundamentally different because of evolutionary reasons again implies that attempts to change an inequitable status quo are pointless, perhaps even wrong.

Despite questionable extrapolations by some theorists, biological approaches to personality have become an important addition to the trait paradigm. They flesh out the details of Allport's original vision of traits as psychological *and* biological. If theorists can avoid the temptation to explain every aspect of personality in biological terms, these approaches should have substantial "fitness" in the years to come.

SUMMARY

This chapter described the major theories of those who work within the trait paradigm. All share the assumption that personality is best described in terms of how people differ from one another. These differences—called traits—are regarded as stable and pervasive characteristics, often with a biological basis. They are usually measured with questionnaires.

Gordon Allport is the father of modern trait theory, and I described his approach to personality in some detail. He set the agenda for later trait theorists, introducing terminology and phrasing issues still of concern today.

Henry Murray was a contemporary of Allport who was particularly interested in individual differences in needs that motivate our behavior. He proposed an influential catalogue of human needs and devised methods for measuring them.

What traits exist, and how are they related to one another? One approach to this issue is through a circumplex model: the arrangement of traits in a circle according to their similarity or dissimilarity. Timothy Leary and Jerry Wiggins proposed particularly well-known circumplex models. Another approach is through the statistical procedure of factor analysis, which attempts to identify the basic dimensions of personality. Raymond Cattell and Hans Eysenck have been the most influential personality psychologists to use these techniques.

An issue of long-standing concern within the trait paradigm is the relationship of biology to personality. Studies of physique and temperament have been conducted, and personality has been examined from the perspectives of behavior genetics and sociobiology.

TRAIT PARADIGM: RESEARCH

Because the trait paradigm is concerned with the classification of personality, its research goals are straightforward. As you saw in Chapter 8, theories are phrased in terms of individual differences, and investigations test predictions by calculating correlation coefficients between measures of these variables. Which individual differences correlate with each other? Are correlations more likely under certain circumstances than others? Can confounds be ruled out?

In principle, individual differences can be measured in many ways (Craik, 1986). Trait psychologists could observe people as they go about their lives. They could interview them. They could talk to their friends or relatives They could analyze their autobiographies. But by far the most widespread method of assessing individual differences is with questionnaires. Why is the use of questionnaires so popular within the trait paradigm?

The most compelling rationale for questionnaires is their efficiency. All personality researchers use questionnaires, but the trait paradigm in particular leads to their use. Besides underlying a variety of thoughts, feelings, and actions, a trait should also underlie responses to personality questionnaires. To the degree one is anxious, for instance, one will answer questions in an anxious fashion. To the degree one has a high need for achievement, one will show it in response to questions. Why bother to study the particulars of a person's life if responses to a questionnaire can provide the same information, saving lots of time and energy?

Unfortunately, responses to personality questionnaires do not always provide the same information. Some critics go so far as to claim that questionnaires give no useful information whatsoever. Others are more lenient. However, all agree that questionnaires should be used with caution.

Unlike intelligence tests, which usually present research subjects with actual problems to be solved and thus sample some aspect of "intelligent" behavior, personality questionnaires simply ask subjects to report on behaviors that reflect different traits. For instance, here are some questions about introverted or extraverted behaviors:

1. Do you wish for excitement?
2. Do you consider the alternatives carefully before you act?
3. Would you rather go to a party or to a library?
4. Do you move quickly?
5. Would you be unhappy if you constantly had to interact with other people?

On the face of it, responses to these questions indicate how introverted or extraverted a person is. However, one must assume that the responses accurately describe what the person actually does.

What should the cautious researcher consider when evaluating the adequacy of a personality questionnaire? Here are some common pitfalls. First, people may not answer questions truthfully if the accurate answer puts them in an undesirable light. Psychologist Donald Fiske (1971) studied the way research subjects regard personality questionnaires. (By the way, he interviewed and observed people; he did *not* ask them to fill out questionnaires about filling out questionnaires.) He concluded:

> To test a person is to try him, and a person on trial is threatened by the possibility of being found wanting. When we give a subject a test, we must recognize that he perceives the possibility of the test's indicating that he is inadequate in some way, that he does not meet the standards set by himself and others. (pp. 205–206)

Because personality traits often relate to adaptation, they have "good" and "bad" endpoints. None of us wants to function at the level of deficiency needs, and high levels of neuroticism or psychoticism are clearly not attractive. So, if personality questionnaires let subjects present a desirable view, then they will do it. This problem is referred to as contamination by **social desirability** (Edwards, 1957). The opposite confound may also occur if some payoff exists—like access to psychotherapy, educational programs, or disability pensions—for being scored as sick, helpless, or feeble.

Social desirability: The tendency to answer a questionnaire in order to put oneself in the best possible light.

Several popular strategies minimize the role of social desirability. Some questionnaires are rewritten so different responses to the same question are equally desirable. And researchers can use a questionnaire specifically designed to measure the degree that someone gives self-enhancing responses. Scores of these questionnaires are then compared to scores of other questionnaires to see how strongly they correspond. If the correlations are high, then social desirability is probably playing a role. Also, theorists reinterpret certain personality traits to incorporate their social value. By this view, traits are interpersonal strategies, and social desirability stops being a confound and becomes an important component of what is being measured. Coyne (1976) reinterprets depression in this way by looking at depressive symptoms as a way of relating (poorly) to others and not as a property of the person per se.

A second common pitfall occurs when people do not answer questions accurately because they simply don't know the answers! A person cannot convey every matter relevant to personality. Remember the psychodynamic concepts that pertain to the unconscious? Asking people about their unconscious makes absolutely no sense because responses will be inaccurate (see e.g., Nisbett & Wilson, 1977). Researchers can avoid this problem if they have a good handle on the meaning of the trait they're measuring. Theory dictates method, and sometimes questionnaires are precluded.

A third pitfall is that people might answer questions according to idiosyncratic styles that have nothing to do with the content of the questions. These styles are called **response sets** (Cronbach, 1946). They can be identified by correlations between tests with similar formats (like 7-point rating scales or yes-no answers) that appear too high granted the meanings of the traits being measured. Fiske catalogued some of the styles identified in this way:

Response sets: Styles of answering questionnaires that have nothing to do with the content of questions.

Acquiescence: agreeing with . . . statement; marking the "yes" alternatives;

Extremity: marking the more extreme alternatives on a graded list, as in a multistep rating scale;

Evasiveness or cautiousness: unwillingness to commit oneself; marking the "?" or "can't say" alternatives;

Carelessness: making inconsistent judgments;

Deviance: marking many unusual responses;

Position set: tendency to mark an item, especially on a multistep rating scale, in the same general position as the mark for the preceding item. (1971, p. 214)

Response sets are a particular problem when subjects complete a number of questionnaires with common formats. Suppose positive correlations are found. Do these reflect associations among traits—a finding with consequences for trait theory? Or do these merely reflect one or more response sets—a finding with no consequences for trait theory?

One can minimize response sets by varying the format of questions used within a particular test or across tests. To control for acquiescence, for instance, the researcher makes sure that "yes" answers do not always count toward the presence of a trait and that "no" answers do not always count toward its absence.

It is not my intention to build a case against using questionnaires to assess traits. In some cases, questionnaires pose questions about behavior that people can and do answer accurately. In other cases, questionnaires are calibrated against what people actually do, just as IQ scores are calibrated against actual academic performance. Questionnaires may even sample the behaviors being studied. Any personality questionnaire demands scrutiny. The reliability and validity of scientific procedures are constantly threatened, and personality questionnaires are hardly exempt. Instances arise when a researcher decides a particular trait should *not* be measured with a questionnaire.

Some critics have added to this list of problems by suggesting that there are no such things as traits (e.g., Fiske, 1973; Mischel, 1968; Peterson, 1968; Vernon, 1964). If there is nothing general and stable about personality, then a questionnaire can hardly measure it. This criticism is more profound than the other problems I've sketched because it doubts the basis of the entire trait paradigm.

In Chapter 1, the consistency controversy was mentioned as an important debate that has recently raged throughout personality psychology. At the end of this chapter, we will discuss this controversy in detail and how it has been resolved. First, though, let us get a flavor of the sort of research conducted within the trait paradigm.

INVESTIGATIONS OF PARTICULAR TRAITS

Most of the research within the trait paradigm is concerned with particular dimensions of personality. Literally hundreds of traits have been proposed and studied, but I'll focus only on eight of the most important ones.

Achievement Motivation

Achievement motivation: The drive to accomplish something difficult in situations characterized by a standard of excellence.

For two reasons, research in **achievement motivation** is traced to Henry Murray (1938). First, he included the need for achievement among his list of human motives, defining it as the drive

> to accomplish something difficult. To master, manipulate, or organize physical objects, human beings, or ideas. To do this as rapidly and independently as possible. To overcome obstacles and attain a high standard. (p. 164)

Second, using Murray's TAT, one could measure the need to achieve. Researchers prefer the TAT over standard questionnaires as a measure of the need for achievement because motives seem more likely to "appear" in people's fantasies than in questionnaire responses (McClelland, 1980). So, our needs influence the themes of stories we create in response to the TAT's ambiguous pictures.

Psychologist David McClelland (1961) provides these two stories told about a picture of a boy sitting at a desk with a book in front of him:

> A boy in a classroom who is daydreaming about something. He is recalling a previously experienced incident that struck his mind to be more appealing than being in the classroom. He is thinking about the experience and is now imagining himself in the situation. He hopes to be there. He will probably get called on by the instructor to recite and will be embarrassed. . . .

> The boy is taking an hour written. He and others are high-school students. The test is about two-thirds over and he is doing his best to think it through. He was supposed to study for the test and did so. But because it is factual, there were items he saw but did not learn. He knows he has studied the answers he can't remember and is trying to summon up the images and related ideas to remind him of them. (p. 41)

The second story clearly reflects a high need to achieve, while the first one does not. McClelland scores the TAT by counting the number of achievement-related ideas per story. The higher the count, the higher the motive to achieve.

The high-need-to-achieve trait predicts good performance in situations where a standard of excellence is present (McClelland, Atkinson, Clark, & Lowell, 1953). For instance, students high in need for achievement get better grades than other students, if the grades are in courses relevant to their long-term goals (Raynor, 1970). Otherwise, achievement motivation is unrelated to performance.

How does achievement motivation originate? Some researchers trace it back to our early socialization, perhaps to when our parents encouraged us to be independent and to succeed (Weiner, 1978). No one argues whether achievement motivation has a genetic basis. Instead, McClelland and others emphasize that achievement motivation can be changed by life experiences, whenever they may occur.

One of the most intriguing lines of research in achievement motivation (as well as in personality psychology in general) is McClelland's study of the economic development of nations and how it might be fostered. His research program has been in two stages. First, in *The Achieving Society,* McClelland (1961) argues that societies with large proportions of people who have a strong need for achievement show impressive economic development. One finding that supports this argument is the positive correlation between the number of achievement-related ideas in a particular country's grade-school textbooks in

Lee Iacocca has come to represent achievement motivation.

1925 and the economic growth of that country in 1950! Second, in *Motivating Economic Achievement,* McClelland and Winter (1969) describe training programs for businesspersons in different countries that foster their need for achievement by stressing the importance of self-responsibility. These programs appear to be effective.

More recent investigations of the achievement motivation trait continue to show that it is an important determinant of actual achievement (Jenkins, 1987). However, its effect on someone's performance can be complex. For example, Biernat (1989) showed that achievement motivation leads to actual achievement only when someone values achievement. In her research, achievement motivation as ascertained by the TAT and achievement value as measured by a questionnaire were independent of one another. Here we have a reminder that questionnaires may not tell us everything we want to know about a trait (McClelland, Koestner, & Weinberger, 1989).

Androgyny

In the 1960s, we questioned everything basic in our society: politics, religion, and morality. Sex and gender were scrutinized as well, leaving us with a richer vocabulary to describe what it means to be a man or woman. Where previous generations used terms like masculine and feminine interchangeably with biological maleness and femaleness, we now use masculinity and femininity to describe dimensions of personality that may apply to both biological males and females.

Psychologist Sandra Bem (1974) extended this trend by suggesting that some males and females can be described as both masculine and feminine: as psychologically androgynous. **Androgyny** reflects the degree to which an individual shows both traditionally "masculine" and traditionally "feminine" traits. Bem used 7-point rating scales to measure androgyny by asking subjects to indicate how well different personality characteristics describe themselves. Some of these traits are considered masculine: aggressive, ambitious, and independent. Others are defined as feminine: affectionate, gentle, and yielding.

Ratings are used to classify subjects as masculine (high on masculine traits, low on feminine traits), feminine (high on feminine traits, low on masculine traits), androgynous (high on both), or undifferentiated (low on both). Bem's (1974) approach to combining masculine and feminine ratings has been criticized (e.g., Pedhazur & Tetenbaum, 1979), and alternative scoring rules have been suggested (e.g., Bobko & Schwartz, 1984; Hall & Taylor, 1985). Still, all preserve Bem's idea that the androgynous individual shows characteristics traditionally regarded as masculine and feminine.

Androgyny is thought to be most likely fostered among children whose parents are warm and encouraging (Kelly & Worrell, 1976), but androgyny is still a recently described trait, so no prospective studies have yet been conducted. Common sense suggests that parents' gender stereotypes are an important factor in producing androgynous children or not, and retrospective studies seem to agree (see Costos, 1986; Jackson, Ialongo, & Stollak, 1986; Sedney, 1987). I have

Androgyny: The degree to which an individual shows both traditionally masculine and traditionally feminine traits.

The androgynous individual blends stereotypical masculine and feminine characteristics.

friends who intentionally dress their little boys in pink and little girls in blue and other friends who just as intentionally do the opposite.

Bem (1975) proposed that androgyny has advantages in a society like our own that puts complex demands on its members. The individual who is tough and tender, logical and emotional, aggressive and tactful—as the situation requires—has an advantage over the individual who isn't so flexible. In two experiments, Bem found that "androgynous subjects of both sexes display 'masculine' independence under pressure to conform, and 'feminine' playfulness when given the opportunity to interact with a tiny kitten. In contrast, all of the nonandrogynous subjects were found to display behavioral deficits of one sort or another" (1975, p. 634). Several studies have found androgyny to be correlated with happiness and psychological well-being, further supporting Bem's research (e.g., Flaherty & Dusek, 1980; Shaw, 1982).

On the other hand, the relation of androgyny to individual adjustment has important qualifications (Taylor & Hall, 1982). First, the correlation is stronger for women than for men. Alan Alda and Phil Donahue notwithstanding, society accepts the androgynous female more than the androgynous male. Second, the reason "androgynous" women fare better in the world may be due to their masculine traits—not the blend of these characteristics with feminine traits. Perhaps research on androgyny is simply rediscovering the societal truism that men and the things of men, including their traits, are more valued (Broverman, Vogel, Broverman, Clarkson, & Rosenkrantz, 1972).

Several recent studies support this interpretation. For example, Dimitrovsky, Singer, and Yinon (1989) administered Bem's measure of androgyny to several hundred men and women recruits prior to basic training in the Israeli army. The type of job for which the recruits were then trained—traditionally masculine or traditionally feminine—was determined. Finally, at the completion of training, success ratings by the recruits as well as by their peers and their commanding officers were obtained. The most highly rated in all cases were men and women who scored high on masculinity. Androgyny proved beneficial only insofar as it reflected masculine traits (see also Signorella & Jamison, 1986).

Definitive answers about androgyny and its relationship to individual adjustment are not yet fully known. Like other personality psychologists working within the trait paradigm, Bem is criticized for neglecting the situation where a particular behavior occurs. In some settings, androgyny is advantageous, whereas in others, it creates profound difficulties (Porter, Geis, Cooper, & Newman, 1985). So, imagine androgynous behavior in San Francisco, California, and Smalltown, U.S.A. Society is still undergoing change with regard to sex roles and how they are received, with some areas of the country changing more rapidly than others. What is true of androgyny in the 1990s may not be true in the decades to come (see Mednick, 1989).

Anxiety

A key concept in personality psychology is anxiety. Freud and other clinically oriented theorists treat anxiety as an emotional state that defines psychopathology. Other theorists, like Cattell and Eysenck, expand its conception to include a personality dimension along which all individuals can be placed. Charles Spielberger (1966) terms this **trait anxiety** and has developed a questionnaire that measures the degree to which a person responds to situations with apprehension and uneasiness. Here are the sorts of questions that reflect trait anxiety:

Trait anxiety: The degree to which a person habitually responds to situations with apprehension and uneasiness.

> Read each statement and indicate which is the most appropriate description of how you *usually* feel with respect to it: never, sometimes, often, always.
>
> 1. I am not confident in my abilities.
> 2. I ruminate about my failures.
> 3. I have "butterflies" in my stomach.
> 4. I perspire a great deal.
> 5. I experience trouble falling asleep.

Measures using questions like these usually correlate well with other measures of anxiety, including the questionnaires devised by Cattell and Eysenck (Lamb, 1978).

Where does trait anxiety come from? Remember from the last chapter that Eysenck (1967) argues that anxiety has a genetic basis. Twin studies and family studies support this contention (e.g., Roubertoux, 1985). At the same time, early socialization and later life experiences are also critical in determining trait anxiety (Phillips, Martin, & Meyers, 1972). If children experience frequent bad events—like failure in school or parental disapproval, they will grow up anxious. Studies with animals also show that unpredictable and uncontrollable situations produce chronic fear and anxiety (Mineka & Kihlstrom, 1978).

At its extreme, trait anxiety is dysfunctional. Excessive apprehension accompanies neuroses like phobias, panic attacks, and obsessions, as well as disorders like depression, schizophrenia, anorexia, and bulimia. Does this mean trait anxiety is always maladaptive? Not exactly, because research shows that moderate levels of anxiety may facilitate both classical and instrumental conditioning (e.g., Spence, 1960; Spielberger, 1966). Moderate anxiety may thus facilitate learning and performance and bring about positive adjustment to the world.

Before you work yourself into a tizzy over your next class exam, consider these further qualifications of the relationship between anxiety and performance:

1. On a simple task, subjects high in anxiety perform better than subjects low in anxiety. . . .
2. On more difficult or complex tasks, subjects high in anxiety perform more poorly than subjects low in anxiety—particularly in the early stages of the task.

Research suggests that anxiety is dysfunctional in the extreme, yet beneficial in moderate amounts.

As learning proceeds, the performance of . . . anxious subjects will improve and often surpass that of subjects low in anxiety. (Phares, 1984, p. 463)

A good illustration of this complexity is found in studies of test anxiety (Sarason, 1980). As most of you well know, if you have mastered the material for a course, some arousal (anxiety) helps you to zip through a test and do well. But if you are not on top of the course material, your arousal during the test works against you.

Field Dependence

Field dependence/ independence: The degree to which people function autonomously of the world around them (field independence) or not (field dependence).

The personality dimension of **field dependence/independence** is "the degree to which people function autonomously of the world around them" (Goodenough, 1978, p. 165). At one end of the dimension is the field independent person, who uses internal frames of reference to interpret incoming information. At the other end is the field dependent person, who uses external frames of reference to interpret the world.

Field dependence and independence are conceived in extremely broad terms and are thought to affect not only perception, but also intellectual, social, and cultural matters. This dimension does not, however, lend itself easily to a "bad versus good" interpretation; depending on the situation, both field dependence and field independence have assets and drawbacks.

Interest in field dependence arose from studies by Herman Witkin (1949) of how people use cues to perceive what is upright in space. He investigated situations where different types of cues conflicted. Usually, we rely on some combination of visual cues (horizontal or vertical lines) and bodily cues (the pull of gravity) to tell us which way is up, and it doesn't matter which cues we use since they agree. But what happens when they disagree, when what we see doesn't jibe with what we feel?

Researchers use an apparatus that may be familiar to you if you have taken a course in the experimental psychology of perception. The Tilting-Room/ Tilting-Chair Test is a device well-explained by its name. A subject sits in a chair

Field dependence/independence can be measured with the Tilting-Room/ Tilting-Chair Test.

that tilts from a horizontal position; the chair is in a room that also tilts from a horizontal position. The subject is asked to move the chair so that it is upright. Does he or she use an external frame of reference (position of the room) or an internal frame of reference (bodily sensations)?

Witkin and his colleagues (1954) discovered that subjects differed with respect to the cues they habitually employed. The individual difference of field dependence/independence was thus defined, and simpler ways of measuring the trait were developed. Today one of the simplest is the Embedded Figures Test, a puzzle where "hidden" designs must be located (see Figure 9–1). The quicker and more accurately individuals can find the designs, the more field independent they are.

Studies find that field dependence/independence relates to social interaction. The field dependent person, for instance, is more likely to rely on others for guidance in ambiguous situations (Culver, Cohen, Silverman, & Shmavonian, 1964), to base judgments on the opinions of others (Oltman, Goodenough, Witkin, Freedman, & Friedman, 1975), to attend to social stimuli (Nevill, 1974), to disclose personal information (Berry & Annis, 1974), and to be popular (Oltman et al., 1975).

Goodenough points to child-rearing practices for the origins of this trait:

> The evidence supports the common sense hypothesis that when socialization practices encourage separation from parental control, then development proceeds toward great field independence. However, when the course of development is either governed by a tightly organized, strictly enforced set of rules and prescriptions for behavior, or when parental nurturing and protective functions inhibit separation, then greater field dependence ensues. (1978, p. 195)

His comments are consistent with the finding that men in our society tend to be more field independent than women, perhaps because boys are more frequently encouraged to separate from their families than are girls. Field dependence/independence may also be heritable (Vandenberg, 1982), but this has not been well documented.

Researchers have also compared the field dependence/independence of people in different cultures (Goodenough, 1978). Societies like the Eskimo of

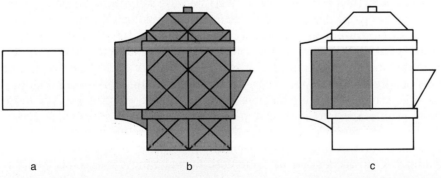

a b c

FIGURE 9–1 Embedded Figures Test

An Embedded Square. Find the square (a) that is camouflaged in the coffeepot (b). The solution is shaded in (c).

SOURCE: P. 175 in D. R. Goodenough. Field dependence. In H. London and J. E. Exner, Eds., *Dimensions of personality*. Copyright © 1978. Reprinted by permission of John Wiley & Sons, Inc., New York.

Baffin Island tend to have members who are field independent, while those like the Temne of Sierra Leone tend to have members who are field dependent (Berry, 1966). This difference maps neatly into the characters of the two societies. The Eskimo are migratory, with little social organization or political authority, and the Temne are sedentary, with intricate social and political stratification. Clearly, field dependence and field independence are useful traits for members of these respective cultures.

Introversion-Extraversion

This personality dimension also plays a role in many formulations. The *introvert* is quiet, retiring, and reflective, whereas the *extravert* is sociable, outgoing, and impulsive. **Introversion-extraversion** is usually measured with questions like those described earlier in this chapter, although G. D. Wilson (1978) reports an alternative measure of dropping lemon juice on a subject's tongue and measuring how much saliva is produced. Saliva increase is substantially correlated with introversion as measured by questionnaire ($r = .70$), a finding that supports Eysenck's physiological interpretation of introverts as overaroused and easily stimulated.

Introversion-extraversion: A personality dimension reflecting whether one is quiet and retiring (introversion) or sociable and outgoing (extraversion).

Because introversion-extraversion reflects general levels of arousal, this trait pertains to adaptation in a number of ways. For instance, introverts have a lower pain threshold than extraverts (Eysenck, 1971), which means that aversive stimuli have a greater impact on them. Imagine the innumerable situations that people will seek out (or avoid) granted a particular pain threshold (Geen, 1984). If people can match their chronic arousal to the demands of a particular setting, they'll adapt quite well. Otherwise, they'll be in trouble. Following this line of reasoning, researchers find that extraverts outperform introverts as salespersons and personnel directors, whereas introverts outperform extraverts in more solitary professions. Furthermore, extraverts are more likely to wind up in prison, to get venereal disease, and to change jobs frequently (G. D. Wilson, 1978).

As noted in the last chapter, the evidence strongly supports the heritability of introversion-extraversion (Plomin, Chipuer, & Loehlin, 1990). Indeed, this trait may explain the heritability of such temperaments as excitability, activity, and sociability (Buss & Plomin, 1975, 1984), because it arguably subsumes them. What remains to be determined in detail is the physiological underpinning of introversion-extraversion. In a recent review, Stelmack (1990) noted numerous physiological differences between introverts and extraverts. However, he concluded that their overall pattern is at odds with Eysenck's hypothesis that levels of cortical arousal are the foundation for the trait. Work here continues.

Interestingly, there is a hint that identical twins raised apart are even *more* similar with respect to introversion-extraversion than those raised together (Shields, 1976). Stop for a minute and think about this. It implies both genetic influence (to account for the overall similarity between twins) and environmental influence (to account for the difference between those raised together and those raised apart).

Power Motivation

Another motive originally described by Murray (1938) is **power motivation:** the need to have an impact on others, to be in charge of people and situations. The strength of this motive is usually measured with the TAT by counting the number of times a subject mentions social impact in stories.

Power motivation: The drive to have an influence on other people.

David Winter (1973, 1988) has investigated the relationship between power motivation and leadership. If ever there were people who would score high on this motive, we would expect them to be leaders. This proves to be the case for both men and women. Power motivation is correlated with holding elective office. It also predicts who will pursue careers in fields like teaching, psychotherapy, journalism, and management. In all these professions, one exerts an influence over others.

According to Winter, among men—but not women—power motivation is associated with impulsive behaviors like aggression and sexual exploitation. Again, these activities all have something to do with exerting influence over others. Finally, power motivation is correlated with the number of credit cards one possesses. Commercials for VISA and Mastercard would have us believe that power follows from these cards, but perhaps a better interpretation is that the *need* for power leads to their acquisition in the first place.

In an intriguing study, Winter (1987) scored power motivation for political leaders by treating their speeches as if they were TAT stories. In other words, he counted the frequency in the speeches of themes of social impact. Although political leaders on the average score high on power motivation, it also varies from leader to leader. For example, among United States presidents during the twentieth century, Theodore Roosevelt, Franklin Roosevelt, Woodrow Wilson, John Kennedy, and Lyndon Johnson scored particularly high. Scoring much lower were William Taft, Herbert Hoover, and Dwight Eisenhower. Small numbers should make us cautious about generalizations, but note that Democratic presidents seem higher on power motivation than Republican presidents. Note also that those presidents who were in office when the United States entered a war were high in power motivation.

David McClelland (1975, 1989) has looked at the relationship between power motivation and physical well-being. Specifically, he finds that people with a high motive for power who chronically hold this motive in check (a tendency operationalized by counting the number of times "not" appears in their TAT stories), are at increased risk for a variety of physical ills. They show elevated blood pressure, respiratory disease, and immunological dysfunction (Jemmott & Locke, 1984).

Just how one's motives translate themselves into poor health is not presently known, although McClelland (1982) hypothesized that people who experience conflict between power motivation and its restraint put a strain on their sympathetic nervous systems. This in turn may produce physical vulnerability. The line of reasoning here is reminiscent of Franz Alexander's (1950) theorizing about psychosomatic illness, as discussed in Chapter 6. Because many of Alexander's formulations did not stand the test of time, we should probably be careful about accepting McClelland's conclusions until we have further confirmation at hand.

What are the origins of power motivation? Among its raw ingredients may be one's temperament, in the form of predispositions to be active, impulsive, and sociable. However, it is clear that socialization plays a major role in determining the particular ways power motivation is satisfied (Winter & Stewart, 1978). Let's return to the finding mentioned earlier that men high in power motivation may act in socially responsible ways, such as becoming teachers, or, unlike women, in socially irresponsible ways, such as being aggressive and exploitative. Winter (1988) made sense of this behavior pattern by taking into account whether or not the men in question had children or younger siblings. If so, they had the opportunity to learn to be responsible to others, and their power motivation was channeled in a constructive direction. If not, then their power motivation became manifest in harmful ways.

Self-Esteem

Self-esteem: The degree to which individuals have high regard for themselves.

Another personality dimension that has attracted a great deal of attention is **self-esteem:** the degree to which individuals have high regard for themselves. Self-esteem is associated with a host of desirable outcomes. It is measured with questionnaires like the Coopersmith (1967) Self-Esteem Inventory. Such questionnaires ask research subjects to indicate whether they see themselves as popular, easygoing, and fun to be around. In brief, self-esteem reflects the extent to which people like themselves.

Here is how Singer (1984) summarizes the results of research with elementary school children:

> Children characterized as high in self-esteem are more active, more expressive, and more confident than children scoring at either low or moderate levels. They are better at assessing their own or others' abilities, more successful in schoolwork, social, and athletic activities; more creative and less willing to be influenced in their judgments by pressure from authorities. They also show more curiosity and exploratory behavior. By contrast, children who score low on a measure of self-esteem are more socially isolated, physically weaker and incapable of defending themselves, more fearful in interpersonal encounters and more preoccupied with "inner" problems. (pp. 266–267)

No wonder books urging you to be your own best friend are best-sellers. A person benefits from high self-regard. These benefits then heighten self-esteem even further. On the dark side, low self-esteem can also become a self-fulfilling prophecy. Individuals with poor opinions of themselves eventually get others to agree with them (e.g., Coates & Wortman, 1980). Most theorists believe that self-esteem results from our actual successes and failures, as well as from the way friends and family treat us (Sears, 1970). Being a member of a group, particularly one that is well-regarded, also enhances self-esteem (Brown & Lohr, 1987). And finally, a person's accomplishments relative to his or her peers are also important (Marsh & Parker, 1984).

Sensation Seeking

This personality dimension grew out of research looking at the effects of *sensory deprivation* (Zuckerman, 1974, 1978, 1985). What happens when people are placed for some period of time in situations with minimal stimulation? This question has practical implications (for example, anticipating the consequences of prolonged spaceflight) as well as theoretical importance. Psychoanalysis and certain versions of learning theory propose that people seek out quiescence; however, results from sensory deprivation experiments show that "quiescence" can be extremely disconcerting. It produces anxiety, hallucinations, and delusions.

Theorists have therefore suggested that people have optimal levels of arousal and stimulation. Sensory deprivation is unpleasant because it brings people below these optimal levels. Marvin Zuckerman (1969a, 1969b) further suggests that these levels are stable and general individual differences. Because some people have higher optimal levels than others, they are more likely to seek out extra stimulation from the environment. These people are high on the trait that Zuckerman (1978) calls **sensation seeking,** measured with questions that ask research participants whether or not they prefer experiences that strongly stimulate the senses, like roller coasters, airplane flights, walks in the rain, and so on. In each case, it is obvious which response alternative counts toward a high sensation-seeking score.

Considerable evidence has been gathered in support of Zuckerman's original notion that sensation seeking is a general trait. Here are some of the

Sensation seeking: The tendency to seek out stimulation from the environment.

behaviors correlated to sensation-seeking scores: quantity and variety of sexual activity; drug use; cigarette smoking; preference for spicy, sour, and crunchy foods; gambling; skydiving; volunteering for unusual psychology experiments (like studies of hypnosis); preference for complex designs; and tolerance for primary process thinking (Zuckerman, 1978).

How does sensation seeking relate to adjustment? Again, the particular setting must be taken into account. People low in sensation seeking are fearful in novel or dangerous settings (Mellstrom, Cicala, & Zuckerman, 1976), while those high in sensation seeking are bored and restless in bland or confining situations (Zuckerman, 1974). At either extreme, sensation seeking is associated with psychopathology. Some evidence shows that psychopaths are particularly high sensation seekers, whereas schizophrenics are particularly low (Montag & Birenbaum, 1986; Zuckerman, 1978).

Zuckerman has extensively explored the biological bases of sensation seeking. It is clear that this individual difference is heritable (e.g., Fulker, Eysenck, & Zuckerman, 1980). Sensation seeking among people has counterparts in other species, from lizards to rats, implying that it serves some adaptive purpose (Zuckerman, 1990). Indeed, it is easy to explain why the survival of our species has been well-served by the existence of some people who are predisposed to boldly explore the environment and others who are predisposed to be more cautious.

Individuals high in sensation seeking may go to great lengths for new experiences.

Zuckerman (1985, 1988, 1990) has also investigated psychophysiological correlates of this trait to discover just how the genetic basis of sensation seeking is translated into behavior. Although the evidence here is still incomplete (Eysenck, 1990), researchers have some reason to suspect the involvement of the neural enzyme monoamine oxidase (MAO). Sensation seeking is negatively correlated with MAO levels (Schooler, Zahn, Murphy, & Buchsbaum, 1978). What does this mean? MAO apparently functions to reduce the level of neurotransmitters such as norepinephrine and serotonin. Low levels of these neurotransmitters are linked to reduced activity and in the extreme to depression (Baldessarini, 1975). So, persons high in sensation seeking have low levels of MAO and therefore high levels of neurotransmitters; they end up biologically predisposed toward activity.

Evaluation

I've reviewed research approaches and findings for eight personality traits. I might have considered additional dimensions of personality, but these are among the most interesting and best investigated. And conclusions and criticisms concerning these traits apply to research for other traits as well.

On the positive side, research findings leave me convinced that individual differences in personality can be defined and measured. Many of these differences are associated with positive and negative adjustment to the world. We know something about their origins. In general terms, then, at least part of the vision of Gordon Allport has been achieved.

Also on the positive side, most trait psychologists have recently arrived at a consensus concerning the basic individual differences (Digman, 1990; John, 1990). In a variety of studies, the same five dimensions show up time and again. First described by Warren Norman (1963), these dimensions are now known as the **Big Five** to signify their presumedly basic status as traits:

- neuroticism (i.e., worried, nervous, emotional)
- extraversion (i.e., sociable, fun-loving, active)
- openness (i.e., imaginative, creative, artistic)
- agreeableness (i.e., good-natured, soft-hearted, sympathetic)
- conscientiousness (i.e., reliable, hardworking, neat, punctual)

Big Five: The presumably basic dimensions of personality— neuroticism, extraversion, openness, agreeableness, and conscientiousness.

These dimensions are independent of each other, which means that someone who falls on the extreme end of one of these may be high, middling, or low with respect to any of the others.

Research support for the Big Five comes from factor analytic studies. Even the questionnaires devised by Cattell and Eysenck yield these 5 dimensions, rather than the 16 claimed by Cattell or the 3 by Eysenck (Noller, Law, & Comrey, 1987). In passing, we should again note that the technical details of factor analysis can be quite complex. So, minor variations in how these analyses are carried out can identify different numbers of factors. In view of this fact, the agreement concerning the existence of the Big Five is all the more impressive.

The Big Five shows up when research subjects rate themselves, acquaintances, strangers, and even hypothetical people (McCrae & Costa, 1987; Peabody

& Goldberg, 1989; Watson, 1989). It shows up when concrete behaviors are studied (Botwin & Buss, 1989). And it is apparent in studies conducted in different countries (e.g., Church & Katigbak, 1989; John, Goldberg, & Angleitner, 1984).

The five dimensions of personality captured by the Big Five are necessarily broad individual differences, and the implication is not that researchers should stop investigating the more specific traits that often interest them. Rather, the point is that the Big Five provides a potentially useful road map for understanding trait theory and research. In a series of studies, psychologists Robert McCrae and Paul Costa have shown that the Big Five is sensibly related to other attempts to organize individual differences, such as Murray's catalogue of needs and the circumplex model proposed by Wiggins (e.g., Costa & McCrae, 1988a; McCrae & Costa, 1989a, 1989b). These investigators have also devised a questionnaire measure—the **NEO PI,** an acronym for Neuroticism, Extraversion, and Openness Personality Inventory—that explicitly operationalizes the Big Five (Costa & McCrae, 1985). This inventory promises to become widely used as a measure of broad individual differences.

But there is also a negative side to research within the trait paradigm. A number of important questions remain unanswered. First, although the Big Five gives a general picture of the range of traits, the fact remains that most researchers understandably study more specific individual differences. How are these related to each other? No doubt some overlap exists. What is the significance of correlations between, let us say, achievement motivation and extraversion? Is one characteristic derived from the other? Do both reflect a more basic trait? Research doesn't tell us, because most investigations that correlate one trait measure with another do so to establish *discriminant* validity. The focus has been on what is different rather than on what is the same.

Second, in their concern with function and dysfunction, have trait researchers neglected neutral traits in favor of those with value-laden end points? Further, is it any coincidence that the "desirable" ends of these personality dimensions describe the personalities of upper-middle-class university professors? Subtle bias is introduced when characteristics are termed field independence, androgyny, introversion, and self-esteem rather than autism, sex-role inconsistency, social withdrawal, and conceit (respectively).

Third, what is the exact process by which a given individual difference originates and develops? It is important to know that a personality trait does or does not show a genetic influence, and that certain family practices are more apt to produce certain characteristics than others, but research has been rough-grained. Can it really be that high androgyny, low anxiety, and high self-esteem are all produced by the "Leave It to Beaver" Cleaver family? Prospective studies are needed to see exactly what occurs within families to produce individual differences. We also need more thinking along the lines of Eysenck to specify the physiological mechanisms responsible for the heritability of personality characteristics.

Fourth, in assuming that traits are biologically based, have researchers looked past the contribution of cultural factors? Personality psychologists do not analyze individual differences as a function of group membership other than gender. But surely our social class, occupation, ethnic group, and religious

NEO PI: Neuroticism, Extraversion, and Openness Personality Inventory; a measure of the Big Five dimensions of personality.

affiliation have some effect on who we are. These classifications do not map into biological factors, and they have therefore been neglected. A mature trait theory would ground individual differences in a particular culture and historical period. If nothing else, this would allow a better perspective on the adaptive value of particular traits. More profoundly, it might allow the discovery that some individual differences are universal (field dependence/independence, for example) and others culturally bound (androgyny, for example).

Fifth, are traits the best way to conceive individual differences? Most of the research I've described focuses on the individual to the exclusion of the setting. Perhaps individual differences reflect consistencies in a person's environment more than the manifestation of inherent personality traits. This of course is the essence of Mischel's (1968) criticism of the trait paradigm and his reconceptualization of personality. The next section considers his arguments in detail.

MISCHEL'S CRITIQUE: BEHAVIOR IS NOT CONSISTENT

So far I've discussed typical trait research, and the results certainly support the utility of this approach to understanding personality. But as I have emphasized, questions can still be raised. In recent years, the most basic question asked by critics concerns the very existence of traits. This sort of question is not asked within the trait paradigm itself, because the existence of traits is a bedrock assumption—a metapsychological proposition, as it were—on which the paradigm itself rests.

From outside the trait paradigm, psychologist Walter Mischel (1968) raised this question in his book *Personality and Assessment,* proposing that if traits exist, then the thoughts, feelings, and actions that reflect a given trait should be highly correlated across different situations. This issue is not exactly the one of concern to researchers whose studies I described in the previous section. These investigators looked at the antecedents and consequences of a particular trait, or—more exactly—of a measure of a particular trait (usually a self-report questionnaire). They were interested in whether or not relationships exist. Mischel instead asked about the size of these relationships.

This debate entails how best to interpret the absolute magnitude of correlation coefficients. Remember that a correlation coefficient, which is usually abbreviated as *r,* ranges from -1.00 through zero to 1.00 (Chapter 1). The farther away *r* is from zero, the more it reflects a substantial association between two variables, positive or negative as the case may be. If *r* hovers near zero, then the two variables are not associated. Needless to say, if behaviors reflecting a particular trait are correlated near zero, then the entire trait paradigm is called into question.

Although trait consistency per se had not been a major focus of trait research, over the years a number of studies investigated the topic, and Mischel surveyed these studies in his book. Let's consider the investigation by Hartshorne and May (1928) of cross-situational consistency in children's moral conduct. In different situations where one could lie, cheat, or steal, is there evidence of a general trait of honesty versus dishonesty? Would one group of kids transgress at every opportunity and another group hold themselves in check? Or would the conduct of children in one situation be unrelated to their conduct in another?

Using common sense as well as prominent personality theories (like Freud's or Maslow's or Cattell's), we would expect substantial consistency: evidence for the presumed trait of honesty. However, this is not what Hartshorne and May found. They observed thousands of kids when at home, the classroom, parties, sports events, and so on. Moral conduct was not highly consistent. What children did in one situation correlated no higher than $r = .30$ with what they did in another situation. These correlations exceed what would be expected by chance, but Mischel claimed that they are surprisingly small granted the pronouncements of common sense and personality theory.

Further, as situations became more dissimilar, correlations decreased. For instance, measures of deceit within the classroom correlated on the average $r = .26$ with each other, but only $r = .17$ with measures of deceit outside the classroom. Mischel used these findings to argue that the situation is of paramount importance in explaining moral conduct. The "trait" of honesty is superfluous to the explanation of actual behavior.

What other "traits" did Mischel include in his indictment? According to the investigations he reviewed, any trait that pertains to attitudes toward others, sexual identification, dependency, aggression, rigidity, avoidance, and conditionability is suspect because there is little evidence that behaviors reflecting these individual differences are consistent. Appreciate that this list is not an arbitrary set of human characteristics; it includes notions that reside at the core of the major psychodynamic and trait theories.

Mischel noted some exceptions. Behaviors reflecting "intelligence" are relatively general across situations and stable across time, achievement strivings show consistency as well, and diverse behaviors reflecting field dependence/independence correlate as highly as $r = .50$. But remember that Mischel considered these exceptions rather than the rule. Further, unlike other individual differences, these traits are explicitly defined with respect to the setting. Their consistency therefore results from the similarity of these situations.

If one is to question the utility of traits to personality psychology, one must answer two important counterarguments. First, if traits are useless concepts, then what is it that trait research has been looking at for the last 70 years? Second, if traits have no basis in people's behavior, then why do so many personality psychologists and ordinary people believe they exist?

In the remainder of *Personality and Assessment,* Mischel (1968) attempted to answer these questions. To explain what trait research has actually investigated over the years, he made the valid point that much of this research employs self-report questionnaires. This procedure is open to confounds (see, e.g., Nicholls, Licht, & Pearl, 1982). Mischel argued that many of these confounds have not been ruled out and that "trait" research may be questionnaire research in the most trivial sense:

> Typical of the fate of . . . personality measures is the fact that . . . [they are] most strongly correlated with other paper-and-pencil measures, but much less system-

atically associated with nonquestionnaire measures. . . . Indeed, the phrase "personality coefficient" might be coined to describe the correlation between .20 and .30 which is found persistently when virtually any personality dimension inferred from a questionnaire is related to almost any conceivable external criterion involving responses sampled in a *different* medium—that is, not by another questionnaire. (1968, p. 77)

So, Mischel stated that typical trait research is based on a flimsy foundation of response sets, low correlations, and confounds.

Turning to why so many mistakenly believe traits exist, Mischel argued that "consistency" exists largely in the eye of the beholder. In other words, our preconception that people have traits encourages us to see their behavior as more consistent than it really is. We may bring to bear on our observations all sorts of biases that lead to the "construction" of consistency and the mistaken conclusion that people have traits.

A study by Chapman and Chapman (1969) is illustrative. These researchers showed subjects a series of responses to different Rorschach cards supposedly made by psychiatric patients. The subjects also saw the diagnosis of each patient. The responses and diagnoses were arranged so they showed no relationship to each other: they were *uncorrelated.* However, when subjects were asked to report on relationships present in the series of cards, most affirmed that they saw strong correlations. For example, a diagnosis of homosexuality was seen as associated with Rorschach responses mentioning rear ends. What's going on here? Chapman and Chapman (1969) term the phenomenon of "seeing" nonexistent relationships consistent with stereotypes **illusory correlation.** Mischel argues that illusory correlation and similar biases are responsible for the widespread belief in traits.

Illusory correlation: The perception of a correlation between variables when none actually exists.

If you believe your best friend is competitive, you *interpret* many of her behaviors to reflect this trait, even though another person assigns quite different meanings to what she does. You *notice* her competitive acts more than her cooperative ones: "There she goes again." You *remember* instances of her competitiveness better than her other behaviors.

Mischel closed *Personality and Assessment* with a call for personality psychology to throw out the outmoded approach of the trait paradigm: "This conceptualization of man, besides being philosophically unappetizing, is contradicted by massive experimental data" (p. 301). In its place, he called for a psychology of personality based on learning theory, one that reflects the sensitivity of behavior to the situation.

Mischel's arguments stimulated so many reactions within the trait paradigm that he is today regarded as responsible for a renaissance in personality research (West, 1983). Before I describe these research reactions, let me make some general points that blunt Mischel's criticisms.

First, in his 1968 book, he was careful to say that some traits—like field dependence/independence—are supported by the evidence. Many who read Mischel heard stronger claims than he actually made.

A second point I wish to make about Mischel's argument is that it is unclear which trait theory or theories Mischel attacks in his book (see, e.g., Eysenck,

1982; Hogan, deSoto, & Solano, 1977; Pervin, 1985). None of the trait theories reviewed in Chapter 8 make the bold claim that people will act the same regardless of the situation. Yet this is the hypothesis Mischel evaluates in *Personality and Assessment.*

Third, Mischel by and large ignores research bearing on the biological and genetic bases of personality, important aspects of the trait paradigm. It is difficult to dismiss the results of twin studies as due to response sets or illusory correlations. Interestingly, Hartshorne and May (1928) report that measures of dishonesty correlate between siblings, even if they are orphans. From the same data used by Mischel to argue against traits, Hartshorne and May concluded that a hereditary factor was present.

Finally, Mischel did not deny that behavior is consistent across situations, or that personality questionnaires predict what people do. In both cases, correlations of $r = .30$ are found, and these exceed what we would expect by chance. So, Burton (1963) did a factor analysis of Hartshorne and May's (1928) original data and found evidence for one general factor: honesty versus dishonesty.

Mischel's argument is that the typical correlations are too small to be of any practical value. However, far smaller correlations are taken seriously in medical research, meteorology, economic planning, election forecasting, genetic counseling, parole decisions, and so on. The absolute magnitude of a correlation coefficient is tricky to evaluate in cases where it is not .00 or 1.00. Mischel dismisses the $r = .30$ typical of trait research much too glibly.

The issue of "how big" a correlation coefficient must be before one takes it seriously has been addressed by several researchers. Robert Rosenthal and Donald Rubin (1982) observe that correlation coefficients are difficult to interpret because their values are not intuitive. What does a correlation coefficient of $r = .30$ mean in everyday life? Here's an interesting answer that Rosenthal and Rubin provide. Suppose you are seriously ill and have a 65 percent chance of dying. A medical treatment is available that will reduce your chance of dying to 35 percent. Would you be interested in receiving the treatment? Of course you would, so appreciate that if the relationship here between treatment (or no treatment) and your chances of living (or dying) were expressed as a correlation coefficient instead of percentages, the absolute magnitude would be exactly $r = .30$. Is this too small to take seriously?

Rosenthal (1990) gave another example showing how tricky it is to make sense of the size of correlation coefficients. You may remember the recently completed medical study showing that a single aspirin per day resulted in a decreased likelihood of a heart attack. This study received a great deal of publicity in the popular media, and it has affected medical practice. However, when the relationship between taking an aspirin and reducing the risk of a heart attack is expressed as a correlation coefficient, the figure looks miniscule: $r = .03$.

Another perspective on interpreting the absolute magnitude of correlation coefficients is provided by David Funder and Daniel Ozer (1983). They start with Mischel's assertion that situations have a greater impact on behavior than do personality traits. What is the evidence for this claim? Usually it is not specifically tested. Instead, a researcher shows that a trait measure correlates .30 with some behavior, then observes that this doesn't seem like a strong relationship, and finally concludes that situations are overwhelmingly important. On the face of it, this seems like okay logic, because what is not due to traits must be due to situations.

Right? Wrong—random variation also occurs, in behavior associated with neither traits nor situations. Maybe the research subjects have the flu. Maybe the measures are unreliable. Regardless, if one wishes to say situations are more important than traits, one must explicitly look at how strongly each is related to behavior.

We already know that the typical correlation between traits and behaviors is $r = .30$. How strongly are situations correlated with behaviors? This statistic is usually not calculated by experimental psychologists, the researchers who study the impact of situations on behaviors.

It is an easy matter, though, to express the strength of situational effects in terms of correlation coefficients. This is exactly what Funder and Ozer (1983) did, computing the correlations between situational factors and behaviors for such well-known experiments as the investigation of destructive obedience by Milgram (see Chapter 1) and the study of bystander apathy by Darley and Latané (see Chapter 6). Guess what? These barely exceed .30, essentially the same as the typical correlation between traits and behaviors.

Yet another way to think about the magnitude of correlation coefficients comes from a mathematical analysis by Ahadi and Diener (1989). If traits do determine behaviors, it is unlikely a one-to-one relationship occurs between given traits and given behaviors. Instead, particular behaviors probably reflect the simultaneous influence of several traits. What happens if these traits are independent of one another, as are the Big Five dimensions? An upper limit is thereby set on the magnitude of correlations between any two behaviors.

Consider the case of two behaviors, each influenced by three traits (see Figure 9–2). If only one trait affects both behaviors, then the highest correlation that can be obtained between these two behaviors is the familiar $r = .30$. You should see a theme running through this discussion, namely that correlations in

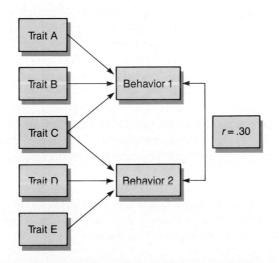

FIGURE 9–2
The Influence of Traits on Behaviors

If two behaviors are each influenced by three independent traits, only one of which is the same for both, then the upper limit to the correlation between these two behaviors is $r = .30$.

the vicinity of .30 are not grounds for dismissing traits. If anything, just the opposite conclusion follows, once the meaning of correlation coefficients is grasped.

REACTIONS TO MISCHEL'S CRITIQUE

Despite these qualifications over Mischel's conclusions, his criticisms had great impact. Personality psychologists at first ignored *Personality and Assessment,* but other psychologists read the book and took seriously its criticisms of the trait paradigm. In response to the growing belief (among these other psychologists) that personality as a whole was a dying field, trait researchers undertook various lines of research designed to show that personality concepts were indeed sensible.

Trait Stability

One of the first reactions to the charges against traits was the mustering of evidence showing that measures of traits are highly stable over time. Personality characteristics we show when young are those we show when old. Consider this well-known description of personality stability from a lecture by William James (1890):

> Already at the age of twenty-five you see the professional mannerism settling down on the young commercial traveller, on the young doctor, or the young minister, on the young counsellor-at-law. You see the little lines of cleavage running through the character, the tricks of thought, the prejudices, the ways of the "shop" . . . from which the man can by-and-by no more escape than his coat-sleeve can suddenly fall into a new set of folds. On the whole, it is best that he should not escape. It is well for the world that in most of us, by the age of thirty, the character has set like plaster, and will never soften again. (p. 121)

Research reviewed by Hogan et al. (1977), Conley (1984a), Pervin (1985), Stein, Newcomb, and Bentler (1986), Costa and McCrae (1988b), and others show that a variety of individual differences stay much the same over decades: temperament, vocational interests, achievement, neuroticism, psychopathology, antisocial behavior, sex-role adherence, expressiveness, moral conduct, introversion-extraversion, aggression, altruism, and so on.

One of the most impressive demonstrations of personality consistency across the life span is by Jack Block (1971). In his research, Block surmounted a procedural problem that plagues longitudinal research: Personality measures valid for one age group are inappropriate for another age group. There are aggressive children and aggressive adults, for instance, but the behaviors reflecting aggressiveness differ. If this is the case, how can we ascertain correlations over time? Giving subjects the identical tests or questionnaires is silly. Small correlations will perhaps reflect lack of trait consistency, but they could also result from noncomparable measures.

Block's solution is ingenious. Approximately 170 individuals were studied as early adolescents, late adolescents, and adults—a period spanning almost 30 years. At each stage in life, extensive information about each subject was gathered from interviews, objective tests, reports of others, school and work records, and so on. (Note the similarity between this procedure and George Vaillant's natural-history approach described in Chapter 4). Clinical psychologists then read through each subject's material at each stage in life. They judged the relative importance or unimportance to the subject's personality of a standard set of trait descriptions—for example, is a talkative individual; tends to be self-defensive; is calm, relaxed in manner. The raw data available at different points in life differed, but they were used to make ratings with respect to the same personality characteristics.

This procedure is called a *Q-Sort,* which Carl Rogers used to investigate self-concepts. As Block employs this procedure, it is a compromise between nomothetic and idiographic personality assessment. The same set of traits is used for all subjects (nomothetic procedure), but the salience of traits for a given subject is ascertained by comparing it to his or her other traits (idiographic procedure). In Block's research, different judges rated a subject's personality at different points in time, thus precluding illusory correlation.

Personality consistency is ascertained by seeing if traits salient (or nonsalient) for an individual at Time One remain salient (or nonsalient) at Time Two. Although his findings are complex, Block reports that a number of traits are stable over years:

> The unity or consistency of personality is compellingly apparent in these data and is manifest in so many and diverse ways as perhaps to establish the unity principle once and for all. Personality coherency has always been assumed by personologists because it *must* be assumed. But the empirical support for this proposition has appeared to be weak or contrary . . . vigorous arguments against the very *idea* of personality consistency have been mounted.
>
> I view the sets of empirical relationships . . . as sufficient proof for the principle of personality consistency. (1971, p. 268)

For instance, among the traits studied by Block are **ego-control** and **ego-resiliency.** The former trait is the degree to which people can control their impulses. Someone high in this trait can eat just one potato chip. The latter trait is the degree to which people are flexible in response to environmental demands. Someone high in this trait can eat one million potato chips if no other food is available, while refraining altogether under other circumstances. These traits show impressive stability throughout childhood and into adult life (see, e.g., Funder, Block, & Block, 1983). They relate to a variety of behaviors and characteristics, like delay of gratification, irritability, attentiveness, and aggression.

Do you see how Mischel could answer these findings? He did not deny the reality of individual differences—he took issue with their interpretation in terms of traits. According to Mischel, people are consistent to the degree that the situations where they find themselves are consistent. I bet that the subjects

Ego-control: The degree to which one can control his or her impulses.

Ego-resiliency: The degree to which one is flexible in response to environmental demands.

studied by Block and other longitudinal researchers stayed within characteristic settings across the life span (see Caspi & Herbener, 1990). The stability of their "personality" may reflect the stability of the context in which their behavior occurred. Angry young individuals become angry old ones not because they have a trait of anger but because they are found in places, such as corporations, that elicit and reward expressions of anger.

The Act-Frequency Approach

One of the problems with the studies reviewed in *Personality and Assessment* is that many arrived in an unsystematic fashion at the specific behaviors assumed to reflect particular traits. It simply seemed to the researcher that these sorts of behaviors reflect this sort of trait. But says who? A less arbitrary way of deciding which behaviors reflect which traits should be possible. Psychologists David Buss and Kenneth Craik (1984) give us such a procedure in their **act-frequency approach.**

Act-frequency approach: A procedure for determining which behaviors (acts) reflect which traits.

Buss and Craik start by assuming that personality dispositions summarize the general thrust of a person's thoughts, feelings, and actions. For example, Stanley is bold to the degree that he thinks bold thoughts, experiences bold feelings, and performs bold deeds. Although Stanley occasionally acts like a wimp, bold is a reasonable summary of his behavior. Dispositions are ascertained by counting the number of pertinent acts occurring within a certain time limit.

The first task of the personality psychologist is therefore to ascertain which acts map into which dispositions. Following this, several other questions can be answered. Among the most important is which acts are central to a trait and which are more peripheral? Asked another way, which acts are good examples of a trait and which are poor examples?

Here is an example of how Buss and Craik proceed in characterizing a disposition. They solicit nominations of acts that exemplify a particular trait by asking a large number of individuals to

> think of the three most extraverted males (or females) you know. With these individuals in mind, write down five acts or behaviors they have performed that reflect or exemplify their extraversion.

Nominated acts are combined until they have a list of approximately one hundred acts for the disposition of extraversion. Other individuals judge each of these acts in terms of how good or poor an example it is of the trait in question. Table 9–1 presents some examples of acts.

A particular person is assigned an extraversion score according to how many of the extraverted acts he or she performs in a given time period—two weeks, four weeks, and so on. Ideally, scoring constantly monitors what a person does, but Buss and Craik have so far been unable to surmount the technical difficulties involved. Instead, research subjects are asked to rate the frequency of their acts retrospectively. These ratings are then checked against comparable ratings by friends and relatives, and agreement has been substantial.

TABLE 9–1
Extraverted Acts

I told several jokes in a row.
I got people together to play a sport.
I addressed a group of people.
I went to a bar to socialize.
I threw a big party.
I sang loudly in the street.
I organized a group gathering.

SOURCE: From Buss & Craik, 1984.

Buss and Craik have investigated such dispositions as extraversion, introversion, dominance, submission, quarrelsomeness, agreeableness, gregariousness, and aloofness. They have established that these dispositions are composed differently. Some dispositions (like agreeableness) have highly prototypical acts, whereas others (like aloofness) do not.

What is the relevance of this approach to Mischel's critique of personality traits? Buss and Craik (1984) found that prototypic acts (with respect to a particular trait) are more consistent than other acts. Further, prototypic acts correlate more highly with personality questionnaires. In these cases, the $r = .30$ "limit" is exceeded. Perhaps the studies reviewed by Mischel (1968) were unfair tests of personality consistency because they only assessed peripheral acts, those reflecting the influence of several traits.

Of course, the act-frequency approach is not foolproof (see Block, 1989). The frequency of acts exemplifying dispositions is not the only parameter. Indeed, frequency of acts may be irrelevant in attributing certain dispositions. How many people must someone kill to be considered murderous? Is Charley Manson eight times as murderous as Sirhan Sirhan?

Also, some dispositions are defined by things a person does not do. Buss and Craik acknowledge that their approach is biased towards acts of commission rather than omission. Judges had difficulty nominating representative acts for aloofness, because an aloof person is mostly refraining from acts a non-aloof person performs. The act-frequency approach seems incapable of studying many of the dispositions of concern to psychodynamic theory, an account of personality based in large part on what people do not do.

Finally, practical problems arise with the act-frequency approach. It is only as useful as the assessment of act frequency. Retrospective measurement is subject to bias and distortion (see Borkenau & Ostendorf, 1987). And a given act reflects more than one disposition. Suppose you punch out your boss and walk off your job. How are these acts to be apportioned among the various personality traits they reflect?

Buss and Craik are aware of the difficulties in implementing the act-frequency approach to personality dispositions, and, for the moment at least, we should regard their strategy as preliminary but promising. The approach offers a sophisticated way to think about traits and their relationship to behavior, improving on previous approaches because it tells the researcher which behaviors reflect which traits. Such information is obviously an important prerequisite for investigation of trait consistency.

The Modified Idiographic Approach

Gordon Allport anticipated the possibility that individuals don't act consistently across situations. It was for this reason that he did not regard common traits as the main units of personality. In contrast, the research reviewed by Walter Mischel (1968) was exclusively concerned with common traits—personality dimensions along which all subjects can be placed. Allport would not be surprised at the results of Mischel's review; in fact, some of the studies that figured prominently in Mischel's negative view were cited by Allport (1937, 1961) in his own books.

But as you recall, Allport did not discard traits in light of these studies. Instead, he proposed that different traits apply to different people: People are consistent across situations only with respect to their personal dispositions, which are different from those of someone else. But Allport's call for an idiographic approach to personality went unanswered because research procedures for idiographic assessment were not readily available.

In 1974, Daryl Bem and Andrea Allen resurrected Allport's ideas to champion the commonsense belief in behavior consistency. Bem and Allen suggested that for any given trait, some people are more consistent with respect to it than other people. In other words, the degree a trait is relevant to behavior is an individual difference. They argued that "one simply cannot, in principle, ever do any better than predicting some of the people some of the time" (p. 512). But this ain't bad relative to Mischel's view of the matter.

How do you identify people who are consistent or inconsistent with respect to a given trait? Here is what Bem and Allen did: they asked their research subjects how consistent versus inconsistent they were. This approach seems simple, but it is an important approximation to Allport's goal of idiographic assessment, a step taken some four decades after Allport's (1937) call for the study of personal traits.

Bem and Allen described the hypotheses of their research in the following way:

> Individuals who identify themselves as consistent on a particular trait dimension will in fact be more consistent cross-situationally than those who identify themselves as highly variable. . . . The cross-situational correlation coefficient of the self-identified low-variability group should be significantly higher than the coefficients of the high-variability group. . . . We tested this hypothesis twice on the same population of subjects, using two orthogonal personality traits, friendliness and conscientiousness. (1974, p. 512)

The same 64 college students were asked to rate "How much do you vary from one situation to another in how friendly and outgoing you are?" The same rating was made with respect to conscientiousness.

Friendly (or unfriendly) behavior was assessed in six different ways, including reports by self and others and by observations. Conscientious (or nonconscientious) behavior was assessed in seven different ways. To test their predictions, Bem and Allen divided their sample in two at the midpoint of self-rated consistency with respect to friendliness and then calculated correlations between measures of friendly behavior for the two groups. In the consistent group, correlations averaged $r = .57$, while in the inconsistent group, they averaged $r = .27$. So, Mischel's .30 personality coefficient can be exceeded if the researcher limits attention to subjects for whom the trait in question is more of a personal disposition, rather than a common trait.

The results for conscientiousness were not so straightforward, but they are informative. When subjects were divided into two groups on the basis of self-rated consistency or inconsistency, and intercorrelations computed among measures of conscientiousness within these two groups, the findings for friendliness were *not* replicated. However, further information available to Bem and Allen revealed that the subjects did not agree with them regarding the behaviors reflecting conscientiousness. For instance, Bem and Allen used neatness and cleanliness of one's hair as an index of conscientiousness, an interpretation at odds with the subjects. Failure to replicate the friendliness findings is not so surprising. More generally, personality researchers need to check *their* assumptions that behaviors reflecting particular traits have the same meaning for their research subjects.

Kenrick and Stringfield (1980) used the approach of Bem and Allen to investigate consistency of Cattell's 16 source traits. Research subjects used 7-point scales to describe themselves with respect to each of these traits. For each of the subjects, one of their parents and one of their friends used the same scales to describe the subject. Subjects also rated how consistent or inconsistent they were with respect to each trait and were asked to nominate their single most consistent trait. Finally, Kenrick and Stringfield further refined Bem and Allen's approach by asking subjects to rate the degree that their behavior with respect to each trait was publicly observable. The thinking here is that some people might be consistently anxious, for instance, but hold this in check, preventing the observer from seeing the "true" consistency.

Results strongly confirmed the findings of Bem and Allen. When self, parent, and peer ratings were intercorrelated, they averaged only $r = .25$. (There's that limit again.) But when analyses were limited to the most consistent trait, average intercorrelations increased to $r = .61$. And when analyses were further limited to the most consistent traits that were also high in observability, correlations entered the $r = .7$ to .9 range.

This *modified idiographic approach* pioneered by Bem and Allen (1974) is noteworthy (Tellegen, 1988). However, criticism is not lacking (see, e.g., Chaplin & Goldberg, 1984). Mischel and Peake (1982), for instance, repeated the original study with another group of subjects, assessing conscientiousness in the same way as Bem and Allen. They also extended the original study by including additional measures of conscientiousness. Results were confusing. If you recall, a number of Bem and Allen's measures were based on observer ratings. When Mischel and Peake looked at agreement among raters for consistently conscientious versus inconsistently conscientious subjects, correlations with the self-identifications were much higher for consistent subjects than for inconsistent subjects. But when they looked at consistency among behaviors, correlations were uniformly low regardless of the subject's consistency or inconsistency.

Mischel and Peake (1982) explained these results by suggesting that global ratings are distorted. Suppose Joey regards himself as consistently belligerent. His friends and family are aware of this self-definition and come to accept it. So, all parties involved agree when asked to rate how belligerent Joey is. But this is not the same thing as showing that Joey actually behaves in a belligerent fashion. Mischel and Peake argue that he probably does not. Bem and Allen's (1974) research is thus dismissed.

Or is it? Bem (1983) rebutted the Mischel and Peake (1982) article (see also Conley, 1984b; Epstein, 1983b; Funder, 1983; Jackson & Paunonen, 1985; Moskowitz, 1988). Perhaps Mischel and Peake chose inappropriate behaviors. Remember that Bem and Allen (1974) also ran into trouble when they studied conscientiousness. Subjects' beliefs about what constitutes conscientious behavior differs not just from those of the experimenter but also from each other. Perhaps conscientiousness fails to be a personal disposition for anyone.

A study by Amabile and Kabat (1982) bears directly on the argument by Mischel and Peake that global ratings are distorted by self-definition, and it suggests that their argument is wrong. In this experiment, subjects saw a videotape of another person. Manipulated in the videotape were both self-definition (as an introvert or extravert) and actual behaviors (reflecting introversion or extraversion). Although both self-definition and behavior influenced the subjects' global ratings, when these conflicted, subjects paid more attention to the behaviors. In other words, "actions speak louder than words" because global ratings reflect actual behavior more than self-definition.

Psychologist David Funder has extensively investigated the ability of observers to judge accurately the traits of other people (see Kenrick & Funder, 1988). This research program shows that people are generally good at such judgments, so long as they know each other well (e.g., Funder & Colvin, 1988). Another factor that affects the accuracy of trait judgments is whether the traits are visible (e.g., Funder & Dobroth, 1987). For example, people's introversion or extraversion is obviously manifest in social interaction and thus can be accurately judged by other people. In contrast, their neuroticism may show itself in more private ways and therefore is less easy to judge.

Funder's work is important for two reasons. First, it shows that personality consistency is *not* just in the eye of the beholder. Illusory correlations are most apt to bias perceptions in genuinely ambiguous situations. One's visible traits are usually clear enough to observers that the traits themselves determine judgments. And second, the studies by Funder imply that trait researchers might profitably make greater use of the judgments of observers in order to ascertain individual differences.

The Aggregation Approach

Seymour Epstein (1979) also took issue with Mischel, proposing that we can predict "most of the people much of the time" if we take the simple but painstaking step of improving the reliability of the way we measure behaviors reflecting traits. Epstein observed that many studies assess single behaviors in several settings and then look at their correlation. The correlation will often be low.

What would happen if a researcher asked students in a math class to work one long-division problem, and then followed them into an English class and asked them to conjugate one verb. If students were scored as right versus wrong at each of these tasks, would these scores correlate highly? Would they correlate highly with an intelligence test?

Of course not, because any given behavior—even if it reflects the individual difference studied, be it intelligence, conscientiousness, or friendliness—has innumerable determinants. It is only when we look across a variety of behaviors that we see convergence. Level of mathematical ability becomes evident when students work many long-division problems over many days in many courses. Verbal competence similarly shows its characteristic level only in repeated instances. Summary measures of the two correlate appreciably, and both in turn correlate with intelligence tests.

Can the personality researcher apply the same mentality to the issue of personality consistency? They do so routinely when they create questionnaires; all have multiple items. They do not do so when they study actual behavior. In his research program, Epstein demonstrates the benefits of multiple assessment of behavior. He calls his strategy one of **aggregation.** Epstein obtains repeated measures of behavior across different days. Scores on any 2 days may not be appreciably correlated, but scores over 7 days, 14 days, or longer cohere. Averages computed across the days correlate highly with questionnaire measures of the traits these behaviors presumably reflect (Epstein, 1979). The $r = .30$ limit is often exceeded.

> **Aggregation: A measurement strategy that combines multiple assessments.**

For instance, Epstein (1979) asked subjects to make daily ratings of their spontaneity, outgoing feelings, and number of social contacts they initiated. Averages across 14 days respectively correlated $r = .45$, $r = .47$, and $r = .52$ with Eysenck's questionnaire measure of extraversion. Because one expects an extravert to be spontaneous, outgoing, and social, these findings make a strong case for the utility of trait concepts.

Can we criticize anything about Epstein's aggregation approach? In his original demonstrations, two considerations got in the way of the strongest possible answer to Mischel. First, as the last example illustrated, Epstein relied a great deal on ratings by subjects; these ratings may not be the same thing as the behaviors they attempt to summarize. Second, Epstein used data regarding stability over time to make conclusions about generality across situations (Mischel & Peake, 1982).

However, Epstein's (1984) more recent studies corrected these flaws. Objectively measured behavior shows substantial coherence if aggregated over a sufficient number of instances and situations. And psychologists are increasingly aware that aggregation improves their ability to predict behavior (Rushton, Brainerd, & Pressley, 1983). Aggregation is now a standard tool of the personality researcher (see, e.g., Woodruffe, 1984). However, as Epstein (1984) notes, all of this attention is welcome but somewhat ironic because the approach really began with Henry Murray's (1938) *Explorations in Personality*. What was the diagnostic council if not a procedure for aggregating vast amounts of information about people's behavior?

The Interactionist Approach

A final reaction to Mischel's criticism of traits is one that integrates both trait approaches and situation approaches to personality. This position proposes that both the person and the situation are critical in determining behavior. One popular version of this position holds that it is the **interaction** between individuals and their environment that is important to understanding what they do.

Interaction: The joint influence of traits and the environment on behavior.

Interaction here is used in a particular sense. Suppose we have two people: a prototypic extravert and a prototypic introvert. Suppose we have two situations: a crowded party and a quiet library. And suppose we are interested in studying happiness. Can we say who is happier: the extravert or the introvert? Not unless we know the setting they are in. Can we say which setting is more likely to lead to happiness? Not unless we know which person is in the particular setting. This is what is meant by an interaction between person and situation. The effect of an individual difference depends on the setting; the effect of the setting depends on the individual difference (see Figure 9–3).

The call for personality psychologists to study interactions of this type was raised by several people, following the appearance of Mischel's *Personality and Assessment,* most notably by Kenneth Bowers (1973), Bo Ekehammar (1974), and Norman Endler and David Magnusson (1976a, 1976b). Suggesting that person-

**FIGURE 9–3
Person-Situation
Interaction**

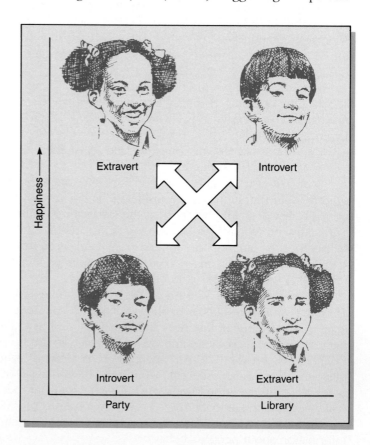

ality psychology should study the person in the situation is nothing new. In the 1930s, Kurt Lewin stressed that the field can go awry in two ways: by making statements about types of people without reference to settings and by making statements about types of settings without reference to people. Allport, Murray, Maslow, Cattell, and others had similar views, despite their interest in individual differences. All said that the relevance of any particular personality characteristic depends on the situation.

But like many theoretical insights, the importance of interactions was not translated into actual research until years later (Magnusson & Endler, 1977). Then an explosion of studies appeared demonstrating that such interactions were indeed important. Most had a similar research design. Subjects were recruited and given a personality test. On the basis of their test scores, they were divided into two groups: high and low with respect to some trait (achievement motivation, androgyny, anxiety, and so on). They were then randomly assigned to one of two experimental treatments that were chosen because the researcher believed the factor distinguishing the two treatments would interact with the personality trait under study. An appropriate behavior was assessed for all subjects.

Bowers (1973) summarized a number of such studies, the consistent finding being that interactions were important in explaining the observed behavior. Consideration of just the personality trait or just the experimental manipulation didn't account for behavior, since the results of these studies took the form depicted in Figure 9–3.

What can we conclude? According to the interactionist approach, people are consistent, although consistency isn't in their literal behavior. Rather, it resides in the process of how they respond to situations. Traits are important inasmuch as they determine this process. But they are not useful for predicting behavior in the absence of information about situations.

When the modern interactionist approach took shape in the 1970s, the tendency was to regard the person-situation interaction in monolithic terms: All interactions were regarded as equally important and powerful in determining behavior. But recent extensions regard interactions with increasing sophistication (A. H. Buss, 1989). So, one line of research finds that some settings are more apt to interact with personality dimensions than are others. A highly constrained environment, one with strong pressures to behave in certain ways, does not allow a trait to manifest itself (see, e.g., Monson, Hesley, & Chernick, 1982; Price & Bouffard, 1974; Schutte, Kenrick, & Sadalla, 1985). One of the things funerals and final examinations have in common is highly uniform behavior on the part of the people present. The trait researchers would have little to study at such events. However, other settings allow more variability in behavior, and consistent individual differences are evident.

For instance, Epstein (1983a) studies the relationship between personality traits and the behavior of people in a threatening situation: their first parachute jump. Correlation coefficients go sky-high, so to speak. But when the analogous study is conducted in a laboratory, using a different and less threatening circumstance (an anticipated electric shock), the link between traits and behaviors is not nearly so robust.

Sid has less need than most to know exactly
where he's going.

SOURCE: "The Neighborhood" cartoon by Jerry Van Amerongen is reproduced with special permission of
King Features Syndicate, Inc.

Another line of research finds that some types of people are more apt to be influenced by situations than are others. Whether or not someone is well-described by simple trait notions, by simple situationalist notions, or by interactions may itself be an individual difference. Mark Snyder (1983), for example, studies a personality characteristic called **self-monitoring.** High self-monitors guide their behavior by attending to situational feedback about how appropriate that behavior is and then modifying how they act. Low self-monitors guide their behavior by attending to inner states and feelings. I suspect Miss Manners and Roseanne Barr live at opposite ends of this dimension. At any rate, Snyder finds that high self-monitors do not act consistently across situations (because they are responsive to particular demands within each), while low self-monitors act consistently (since they are oblivious to situational demands).

Self-monitoring: The degree to which one guides his or her behavior by attending to situational feedback.

Yet another spin-off of the interactionist perspective is that of Daryl Bem and David Funder (1978), who chided researchers for neglecting the "personality" of situations. *What?* A given setting can be described in terms of the characteristic behaviors shown by people within it. If these characteristic behaviors are phrased in trait language, then it is possible to assess the fit between actual people and actual situations. When the fit is good (that is, when the personality of the person is similar to the personality of the situation), then the person behaves in typical fashion there—consistently with her traits. When the fit is poor, she will act inconsistently with her traits. However, this does not mean that traits do not exist, only that the setting in question is a poor one in which to look for trait-relevant behavior of that person. A favorite theme in books and movies places a "down home boy" in the company of stuffed shirts amid grand surroundings. In the story, the protagonist triumphs by remaining himself. In real life, he probably does not behave in such a situation like he used to down on the farm.

Bem and Funder (1978) demonstrate these arguments in several studies using Q-sort procedures to describe both people and situations in the same trait terms. Prediction of behavior was greatly enhanced when people were matched to situations instead of mismatched.

A corollary of this matching notion is that behavior will be consistent across two situations to the degree that the situations are perceived to be similar. Lord (1982) demonstrates this for behaviors reflecting the trait of conscientiousness. The more similar a person regarded two situations (via a Q-sort), the more likely he or she was to behave consistently in them.

Finally, one more version of the interactionist approach is the discussion by David Buss (1987) of the ways people end up with a given environment as opposed to another. In *selection,* people choose to enter or avoid existing settings, a point Gordon Allport made years ago (Wachtel, 1973). Once in these settings, the patterns of rewards and punishments determine what they do there. And their experiences influence their future selections.

In *evocation,* people unintentionally elicit certain reactions from other people. For example, depressed people may act in ways so others reject them (Coyne, 1976). Twins may each evoke similar treatment simply by virtue of being twins (Neale & Stevenson, 1989). And introverts have very different social interactions than do extraverts (Thorne, 1987). The point of such examples is again that one's traits influence one's environment, which in turn may influence these traits (Feather & Volkmer, 1988).

In *manipulation,* people intentionally deploy tactics to alter the world in which they live. The tactics chosen are influenced by a person's traits, but to continue the refrain, the consequences of the tactics end up influencing the person. Buss, Gomes, Higgins, and Lauterbach (1987) asked couples how they attempted to get what they wanted from their partners. Six strategies were reported most frequently:

- being charming
- giving the "silent treatment"
- threatening or yelling
- reasoning
- acting childishly
- grovelling

Certainly, all of these are familiar to us, on both the giving and receiving ends. However, people differ in terms of the manipulative tactics they prefer, in accordance with their traits. For example, neurotic individuals tend either to stop speaking to their partner or to act childishly—sulking and pouting. The responses they elicit may end up making them more neurotic.

So, is behavior better described in terms of traits or situations? Both person-oriented and situation-oriented approaches to personality are relevant, depending on the aspect of the trait under scrutiny. In fact, Walter Mischel's (1973, 1977, 1979, 1984, 1986, 1990) more recent statements about personality endorse the bidirectional influence of person and situation. The interactionist approach strikes many as a compelling perspective.

CONCLUSIONS:
TRAIT THEORIES IN LIGHT OF THE RESEARCH

As the Grateful Dead sing, "What a long, strange trip it's been"—from the theories covered in Chapter 8 through the research described here in Chapter 9. Sophisticated accounts of personality stressing individual differences gave rise to simplistic research that gave rise to criticisms that gave rise to conclusions that we need sophisticated accounts of personality stressing individual differences. Maddi (1984) noted the wry fact that "despite Allport's (1937, 1961) outspoken criticism of common trait theorizing . . . in many textbooks . . . [he is] ironically criticized with his own criticisms" (p. 12). With any luck you won't leave this chapter with this mistaken view of Allport and the other theorists who work within the trait paradigm.

Allport stressed the importance of the situation by defining personal dispositions in terms of their ability to render different settings the same. (Doesn't this sound like Bem and Funder's matching approach?) Murray and Maslow approached personality in terms of needs, so of course the situation is important to behavior. The situation determines whether a given need is satisfied or not. Hungry people eventually stop eating. High-achievers eventually take a break from the rat race.

Mischel's (1968) critique applied to typical trait research, not typical trait theory. Even staunch defenders of the trait paradigm admit that much research is "mindless" (Hogan, deSoto, & Solano, 1977). The culprit is the ubiquitous questionnaire, which lets the researcher study "personality" and "behavior" without seeing research subjects do anything more than fill out computer-scored answer sheets.

Here are some of my conclusions about trait theories in light of the research—both good and bad. First, results underscore the importance of individual differences. These differences are often stable, often consistent, and often related to adaptation. Second, results also underscore the importance of the setting where behavior occurs. In particular, the consistency (or inconsistency) of individual differences cannot be understood unless situational factors are simultaneously on focus. Current researchers have developed a variety of procedures for accomplishing this. Third, the general thrust of trait theories is supported by research (although no particular theory is supported over any other). Still, I suspect the most important research within the trait paradigm has yet to be conducted.

Here are my ideas about a future research agenda for the trait paradigm. Researchers should move beyond the questionnaires typically used to measure "traits" of personality. They should go out into the world and observe what people do and the circumstances in which they do them. Additionally, researchers can ask friends and family members to report what people are all about. Following Cattell and Eysenck's earlier example, these researchers should then look for the range and structure of individual differences in behavior (as well as in questionnaire responses). Using some variant of the act-frequency approach, they should map traits and behaviors into each other. (The exact equation will probably vary with the setting.)

Then, trait research should begin in earnest. Issues of stability, change, consistency, and person-environment fit can be studied definitively with respect to behavior. Contributions of biology and socialization can be specified more exactly (Rowe, 1987). Understanding of adaptation can be advanced more certainly.

Actually, researchers already know how to do all this. The best research within the trait paradigm (that on achievement motivation, androgyny, anxiety, and so on) has always supplemented questionnaires with other assessment procedures, has always studied behavior in settings where the relevant individual difference is highly pertinent, and has always acknowledged the complexity of the subject matter. When mindless research is eradicated, the trait paradigm will remain, more viable than ever.

SUMMARY

I described trait research in this chapter, beginning with a discussion of the rationale behind the use of questionnaires to study individual differences and the problems inherent in this strategy. I then described research concerning eight individual differences: achievement motivation, androgyny, anxiety, field dependence/independence, introversion-extraversion, power motivation, self-esteem, and sensation seeking. In each case I asked how is the trait measured, how is it related to adaptation, and how does it originate.

The next section shifted gears, looking in detail at Walter Mischel's 1968 book *Personality and Assessment* and at his conclusion that trait conceptions of personality are of little use because people do not behave consistently across situations. This criticism stimulated studies of trait stability over time as well as a great deal of research into issues of behavioral consistency: studies such as the act-frequency approach, the modified idiographic approach, the aggregation approach, and the interactionist approach. I concluded that consistency indeed exists, but it is complicated and affected by a variety of factors, the most important of which is the nature of the situations where behaviors occur.

This conclusion is ironic, because it was the starting point of Gordon Allport and other early theorists within the trait paradigm. Trait research has gone the long way around the barn, but perhaps this was necessary. Research sophistication now matches theory sophistication, and, I predict, the most intriguing trait research still lies ahead.

TRAIT PARADIGM: APPLICATIONS

o you have a number-two pencil?

We all know what follows this question: more questions, to be answered by filling in little circles on a computer-scored answer sheet. Right now, you run across such tests mainly in the classroom, but you won't leave them behind when you finish school. You'll be asked about that number-two pencil for the rest of your life.

Many of the questionnaires you'll complete will be measures of individual differences: abilities, opinions, interests, values, needs, and so on. These individual differences are examples of personality as viewed from the trait paradigm. Not surprisingly, then, the purpose of questionnaire measures is to decide about your fitness relative to that of others.

We can recognize applications within the trait paradigm by their concern with individual differences, with assessment, and with function or dysfunction. Many such applications exist within our contemporary world, and I'll survey some of the more intriguing ones in this chapter. First, though, let me make some general comments.

In Chapter 6, I described applications within the psychodynamic paradigm, pointing out that many focused on the sexual aspect of psychodynamic theory and were thus out of touch with research findings. Applications within the trait paradigm are different. In one important way, these applications converge with contemporary research results: They usually recognize that behavior is not highly consistent across situations. If a measure of an individual difference is to be useful in predicting success or failure, then the measure needs to be specific. To the degree an application stays within a specific domain of behavior, it is likely to be sensible: predicting typing performance from a typing test, for example. To the degree it generalizes wildly across situations, it is likely to be silly: predicting managerial skill from a golf score. (Don't think this isn't done by some people with the utmost of sincerity!)

Here's another general point. As you are well aware, the ethics of psychological tests are often questioned. Because important decisions are based

on test results, it is not uncommon to scrutinize the whole endeavor. Tests and the use of tests are obviously unethical when the measures are invalid. But the deeper issue involves measures that are only somewhat valid.

Validity is not an all-or-none thing, because it is usually judged by patterns of correlation coefficients, which are difficult to interpret. After reading Chapter 9, you can imagine that most applied measures of individual differences "work" after a fashion. Mischel's (1968) personality coefficient of $r = .30$ shows up in applied domains as well.

What can we make of this? Well, these measures are valid for nomothetic purposes: for making generalizations about people. But they are not as valid for idiographic purposes: for making specific statements about Peter, Paul, or Mary. Because no test correlates 1.00 with what it is predicting, mistakes are inevitable. While society as a whole may be satisfied that medical school admissions tests see to it that doctors tend to be pretty smart, you or I would not be satisfied if the test results said no to the application of a good friend, whom we *know* to be more intelligent than many doctors.

Another problem is that tests can become self-fulfilling prophecies by perpetuating the status quo. Suppose we want to use a personality test to determine if someone should be allowed to drive an automobile. The ideal way to do this would be to gather hundreds of 16-year-olds who don't know how to drive a car and administer all sorts of questionnaires to them. Then we would give them cars and let them drive for a few years. At the end of this period, if they (and we) are still alive, we would see who had good or bad driving records. Then we would look at the questionnaires and see if any of their answers discriminate the good from the bad drivers. If so, we have a valid test.

But this isn't how it's done. Society can't allow all potential drivers behind the wheel in order to develop a procedure that determines who should not be allowed there in the first place. And the same holds for would-be doctors, lawyers, police officers, and soldiers. What happens in actuality is that psychologists work backwards: How do people who are already driving, doctoring, or lawyering respond to questionnaires? Their answers are used to choose future drivers, doctors, and lawyers.

This strategy differs from the first. It perpetuates the status quo. It has to, since the past determines the future. The potential harm is that the measures may not have as much to do with their stated purpose as they should.

Consequently, a refinement of this strategy is often followed. First, see what responses determine great drivers from good drivers, great doctors from good doctors, and so on. Then compare these responses with those of people to be screened. This strategy has its merits, but it is based on the fine distinction between what it means to be *great* versus what it means to be *good*. The finer the distinction, the more difficult it is for a test to be reliable and valid in making it.

Think about cooking. Good cooks are different from bad cooks because they know how to follow a recipe. But a great cook departs from a recipe. If we studied just good cooks and great cooks, we would see if a potential cook departs from a recipe. Then we would hire a lot of cooks who do not follow recipes to work in our restaurant chain. And we would go broke.

The trait paradigm encourages us to think in terms of single dimensions. We rank everything and believe our rank reflects a pervasive and eternal dimension. No wonder we are so perplexed when rankings fall apart. Why can't a sports team win year after year? Why isn't this beautiful person a brilliant worker?

Some critics argue that psychological tests should be abandoned. Tests work for individuals and the society only by perpetuating the status quo. But we are not likely to see an end to testing. People will, however, be more cautious in using them. In some professional schools, tests are *not* required anymore, and "truth in testing" laws have been passed requiring to be made public the details of tests used to screen individuals for work and school (Bersoff, 1981).

Within psychology, principles for the ethical use of tests are widely available (London & Bray, 1980). Here, for example, is Principle 8 of the American Psychological Association's (1981) "Ethical Principles of Psychologists":

Assessment Techniques. In the development, publication, and utilization of psychological assessment techniques, psychologists make every effort to promote the welfare and best interests of the client. They guard against the misuse of assessment results. They respect the client's right to know the results, the interpretations made, and the bases for their conclusions and recommendations.

Principle 8 goes on to say that psychologists must provide to their clients a full explanation of the nature and purpose of any psychological test they are administered, in language the clients can understand. Further, in reporting the results of tests, psychologists must explicitly qualify their conclusions in light of what is known about the reliability and validity of the tests in question. Finally, they must recognize that tests can become obsolete, and that it is unethical to use a test if they know it to be outdated. These principles reflect the opinion that tests themselves are neither fair nor unfair. It is how people use them that makes them reasonable or unreasonable.

Another point is that employers, teachers, and others charged with making decisions about people do indeed make judgments about personality. The issue is not whether they will do this, but rather how. Should they rely on their intuitions or on psychological tests? I think you can see that the alternative to psychological testing has its own problems.

In the following sections, keep these ethical issues in mind. How many applications within the trait paradigm adhere to Principle 8? Also keep in mind the relationship of application to theory and research. Applications are based on acceptance of a paradigm; they do not question its key assumptions. As a result, applications may not be scrutinized the way Principle 8 mandates.

PSYCHODIAGNOSIS: IDENTIFYING PEOPLE'S PROBLEMS

Intelligence testing is the most popular application of the individual differences approach. I've scattered enough ideas about intelligence testing throughout the book that I won't give it a separate section here. Rather, I'll describe the second most popular application within the trait paradigm: the use of psychological tests to diagnose abnormality.

The first clinical psychologists did not do psychotherapy. Instead, they gathered information to help psychiatrists identify a patient's particular problem and plan the best way to treat it. They observed, interviewed, and gave psychological tests. In fact, one of the first questionnaires ever developed—the Personal Data Sheet of Woodworth (1919)—was devised to screen neurotic men from military service during World War I. Although the role of the modern clinical psychologist is much more varied, **psychodiagnosis** in general and psychological testing in particular remain central activities.

Psychodiagnosis: The identification and description of a person's psychological problems.

Personological assessment: An approach to psychodiagnosis using rich information about particular individuals.

Psychometric assessment: An approach to psychodiagnosis using carefully developed quantitative measures.

Korchin and Schuldberg (1981) distinguish two general approaches to psychodiagnosis. The first they call **personological assessment;** its "primary purpose is to describe the particular individual in as full, multifaceted, and multilevel a way as possible" (p. 1147). The second approach is **psychometric assessment,** which emphasizes carefully developed measures that place people along a well-defined continuum. "Objectivity is sought both in the acts required of the client and the examiner; judgment and inference are minimized. . . . Test reliability and validity . . . are of central importance" (p. 1148).

As examples of these respective approaches, consider the Rorschach and the MMPI. Some clinical psychologists prefer the Rorschach because it reveals rich information about the person responding to it. I once administered the 10 inkblots of this test to a young man who carefully looked at not just the front of each card, where the inkblot is printed, but also at the back of the card (blank except for a copyright in the corner). He also inspected the edges! I trust you'll agree that my characterization of him as suspicious seems reasonable.

At the same time, the Rorschach is easy to criticize on the grounds of poor reliability and validity (Anastasi, 1982). Different psychologists arrive at highly discrepant diagnoses of the same individual. And the diagnoses suggested by the Rorschach don't always relate to other information about the individual. Remember the "illusory correlation" study described in the last chapter? Chapman and Chapman (1969) did not arbitrarily choose the Rorschach for this research. They wanted to make a point about the invalidity of this projective test.

Other clinical psychologists prefer the MMPI because of its objectivity. The MMPI was developed through a procedure of criterion validation. It includes only questions that have in the past distinguished groups of individuals with a given psychiatric diagnosis (for example, depression, schizophrenia, hysteria) from "normal" individuals not under a doctor's care. Depending on the way the MMPI is scored, about a dozen different scales are possible (Butcher & Keller, 1984). A person who responds to the MMPI receives a profile of scores along these scales.

The MMPI has been administered to hundreds of thousands of individuals, in more than 90 foreign-language translations, and information about the range of scores and the behaviors that correlate with them is extensive. It has recently been revised and updated (Butcher et al., 1989). The MMPI is frequently scored in a mechanical fashion, using what is known as a *cookbook approach*. If a person has a certain profile (scores above cutoffs on particular scales and below cutoffs on other scales), then a given diagnosis and treatment recommendation can be found in a book. (And because we live in the 1990s, we can now read them directly off a computer printout; Matarazzo, 1986.)

Critics of the MMPI acknowledge its objectivity and usefulness in making broad generalizations about people, but they point to its inability to speak to the concrete individual. After all, the patient involved is a single person. Thus, an idiographic approach is needed.

The personological and psychometric traditions came into sharp conflict when psychologist Paul Meehl (1954) produced strong evidence that clinical intuition was less accurate in predicting individual behavior than cookbook formulas. Granted certain information about a patient, how best to combine it in order to predict future behavior? If we have Rorschach responses and/or MMPI profiles, what is the best way to use this information to predict that patient Jones will profit from group therapy, will have a fistfight with an orderly, or will pay bills on time?

Meehl argues that the clinician who mulls over the available information and makes the best prediction will consistently do worse than someone who mechanically predicts that patient Jones will act the same as other people with similar Rorschach responses or MMPI profiles have acted in the past. Knowing this patient as a "person" is not as helpful as knowing about patients in general.

Needless to say, Meehl's argument in favor of statistical prediction raised controversy (see, e.g., Holt, 1970). Was he saying clinical psychologists were useless? Not exactly, because clinicians have to decide what information to gather in the first place (Meehl, 1957). But he was saying that the personological approach to psychodiagnosis failed by its own test: making predictions about the individual.

I wonder if idiographic approaches to psychodiagnosis would be resurrected if Bem and Allen's (1974) strategy of dividing subjects into consistent versus inconsistent groups was extended to clinical assessment. By this logic, we would make predictions based on information only about consistent individual differences. While we might still use a cookbook in making treatment recommendations, different patients would warrant different recipes.

Finally, let's look at two future trends in psychodiagnosis. First, clinical psychologists are turning from personality-like tests to actual observations of behavior (Korchin & Schuldberg, 1981). **Behavioral assessment,** as this strategy is known, is a reaction to the same misgivings with trait conceptions of personality that Walter Mischel (1968) expressed.

Behavioral assessment: An approach to psychodiagnosis using actual observations of behavior.

In behavioral assessment, the clinician describes what a person actually does and the circumstances where he or she behaves in that particular way (Goldfried & Kent, 1972). Treatment recommendations are presumably based less on inference than with traditional assessment. So, one strength of behavioral assessment is its recognition of the situation in which behavior occurs.

A second trend in psychodiagnosis was set into operation by the American Psychiatric Association's (1980) third revision of their diagnostic manual: DSM-III. If you have taken a course in abnormal psychology, you know that previous versions of this widely used catalogue of disorders embody psychodynamic notions of abnormality and describe problems in terms of underlying mental processes and states. These processes and states were inferred from what the patient did. A reasonable way to accomplish this goal of determining behavior was with psychological tests.

However, DSM-III and its revision, DSM-III-R, are not strongly committed to Freudian dynamics. Problems are more often defined in behavioral terms. A depressed person is not someone who has turned anger inward, but rather someone who shows sadness, appetite disturbance, and low self-esteem. Diagnosis using DSM-III and DSM-III-R categories requires less inference and more observation. This means that the traditional tests of clinical psychologists are less relevant to the contemporary needs of the mental health profession.

THE HERITABILITY OF PSYCHOPATHOLOGY

As we discussed in Chapter 9, genetic influences on personality traits have recently been demonstrated in studies showing certain traits to be heritable. Such demonstrations have their counterpart within psychiatry, where we see great interest in the possibility that particular forms of psychopathology also show a genetic influence. As a branch of medicine (Chapter 2), psychiatry has long interpreted psychopathology in biological terms. Disorders have been conceived as bodily illness, injury, or defect, and as such they have been treated with physical interventions such as drugs, shocks, and surgery (Bromberg, 1959). Granted this perspective on abnormality, a reasonable next step is asking if disorders are heritable.

That many forms of psychopathology run through families is well-established (Kessler, Price, & Wortman, 1985), but this fact alone sheds no light on the origin of these disorders. They could be due to shared biological factors, but just as plausibly they could result from similar environments. What we need are more sophisticated research designs, such as twin studies, that allow us to estimate heritability. Such studies are now being conducted, and various disorders do appear to be heritable (Willerman & Cohen, 1990), including

- alcoholism
- autism
- bipolar depression
- obsessive-compulsive disorder
- panic disorder
- schizophrenia
- unipolar depression

However, some qualifications need to be made concerning these demonstrations, which parallel our discussion of the apparent heritability of particular personality traits.

First, these studies do not show that psychopathology is inherited as a whole. They show instead that variation in some disorders is associated with variation in genes. Each of the disorders just listed has environmental risk factors, so we should not conclude that genetic influence precludes situational causes.

Second, we do not have a good idea of the particular genes that predispose psychopathology. Several linkage studies have apparently found particular genes associated with bipolar depression (Egeland et al., 1987) and with schizophrenia (Bassett et al., 1988). However, these studies have been difficult to replicate. It may well be that no simple pattern of genetic influence will ever be discerned. After all, psychological disorders are complex clusters of thoughts, feelings, and actions. The route that lies between one's genetic code and one's behavior is necessarily complex and indirect.

Third, and relatedly, we do not have a handle on the physiological underpinnings of disorders. To the degree that disorders show a genetic influence, this can only take place through the intermediary of physiology. Theories galore have been proposed concerning the biological basis of psychopathology (Andreasen, 1980), but it is fair to say that no great consensus has emerged. Indeed, theorists are not even sure where to look in the body for these supposed mechanisms. And they are not even sure at what level to look: in terms of biochemistry, or anatomy, or whatever.

For example, consider the finding that alcoholism is heritable. This is intriguing, to be sure, but what does it mean? Certainly no neural or hormonal structure impels someone to enter a bar and order a double martini. The mechanism must be more subtle, perhaps influencing one's affective response to intoxication, but it is as yet unidentified. Numerous studies have compared the physiology of alcoholics and nonalcoholics, but definitive conclusions are hampered by the fact chronic alcohol abuse takes a toll on the body. In other words, numerous differences exist between alcoholics and nonalcoholics, but it is difficult to decide if they are causes or effects.

Fourth, we do not understand the evolutionary significance of psychopathology. Granted that some disorders are heritable, it is plausible to ask if in some way they are adaptive. This is a different way to look at abnormality, which almost by definition is considered maladaptive. But perhaps the types of behavior we deem abnormal today were more functional during the past evolution of our species (cf. Glantz & Pearce, 1989). Depression, for example, might once have been a useful response to frustrating circumstances. Or perhaps some disorders entail exaggerated versions of behaviors that prove useful when less extreme (cf. MacDonald, 1988). Then again, perhaps psychopathology is without evolutionary significance.

Let me close this discussion on the heritability of psychopathology by drawing out one possible implication. Suppose research continues to show that genetics have something to do with psychological abnormality. Suppose it becomes possible someday to identify people who—by virtue of their genes—are at increased risk for problems such as alcoholism or depression. Then what happens?

On the one hand, we might attempt genetic replacement or repair, removing someone's vulnerability to genetically influenced problems by literally changing his or her genes (Weatherall, 1985). Along these same lines, we might see interventions somewhere in the process by which genetic blueprints are carried out. So, to take a hypothetical example, if schizophrenia proves to be predisposed by the failure of the body to synthesize a given enzyme, then that enzyme can be provided from without, thereby preventing schizophrenia.

On the other hand, we might see the removal of undesirable genes from the gene pool (Gardner & Sutherland, 1989). In other words, those carrying genes that put them at risk for one or another psychological disorder might be told not to have children. Or pregnant women might be advised to undergo **amniocentesis:** tests of the fetus before birth. A decision whether or not to have an abortion would then be made in view of the test results.

Amniocentesis: Tests of the fetus before birth.

Difficult ethical questions are raised by these possibilities, which make eugenics (Chapter 2) much more than an abstraction (Nash, 1990). Genetic counselors have already been confronting these issues with respect to physical illnesses that are genetically influenced, such as Huntington's chorea, Tay-Sachs disease, cystic fibrosis, and certain forms of cancer (Kessler, 1979). Knowing what to do will become no easier if and when these matters are extended to psychological disorders.

Some fear that abuse will follow the development of sophisticated techniques for genetic screening (Nelkin & Tancredi, 1989). We already hear reports of genetic discrimination: people being turned down for insurance coverage or employment because their family histories put them at risk for genetically influenced diseases (e.g., *Consumer Reports,* 1990). Should this be allowed? Ponder the implications of a whole class of people shunned for genetic reasons.

PERSONALITY DISORDERS

Nowadays typologies reside mainly in casual gossip or in the history of personality psychology. But typologies are also alive and well in the psychiatric notion of a personality disorder. **Personality disorders** seem to be based on these assumptions:

Personality disorder: A pervasive style of behaving that is inherently dysfunctional.

1. Types of people exist.
2. Some types are inherently dysfunctional. That is, these individuals experience chronic distress and consistently show impairment in their work and relations with others.
3. Each type predisposes a more severe psychopathology; under stress, a person with a personality disorder breaks in a particular way.
4. These types of people are set in their ways early in life through some interplay of biological and environmental factors. However, the biological factors are emphasized.
5. Mental health professionals regard these people as poor clients, because they resist change.

You can see how personality disorders are particularly good examples of the trait paradigm.

Personality disorders also exemplify what is wrong with the trait paradigm. Not all mental health professionals recognize the existence of personality disorders, pointing to problems with the concept. First, the entire notion ignores the social and cultural context in which people live. Second, psychiatry rarely agrees about the basic types of people. Throughout the years, drastic revisions in the catalogue of personality disorders have been the rule, not the exception. Third, the evidence that personality disorders lead to particular psychopathologies is mostly negative. Fourth, the belief that someone with a personality disorder resists therapeutic change may be a self-fulfilling prophecy. (The label may reflect the therapist's frustration and inadvertently be used to rationalize half-hearted attempts at future therapy).

DSM-III-R describes 11 personality disorders (American Psychiatric Association, 1987). Where did the ideas for these particular disorders originate? Their sources are varied, echoing the diversity of the origins of personality traits themselves. One source of particular personality disorders is—quite bluntly—confusion. The *borderline personality disorder* arose from the observation that some patients appeared psychotic (out of touch with reality) part of the time and neurotic (too much in touch with reality) at other times (Gunderson & Singer, 1975). How do you classify people who fall at the metaphorical border between psychosis and neurosis? Call them borderline personality disorders.

A second inspiration for particular personality disorders has been clinical experience. If therapists stumble across certain types of people frequently enough, they assume something basic is going on. The notion of *antisocial personality disorder* originated this way. Some people are just no damn good. (As you will see, the antisocial personality disorder is the best-supported "type" among all those described by DSM-III-R.)

A third suggestion for disorders, and the most popular, is from some theory used to deduce basic types of deficient personalities. Psychodynamic theories have been particularly popular sources of ideas. Some personality disorders—like the dependent personality disorder—have been defined in terms of the stage of psychosexual development where a person is thought to be fixated. Others—like the paranoid personality disorder—are defined by a person's predominant use of a given defense mechanism. With such a variety of sources of personality disorders, no wonder the endeavor is chaotic.

Psychologist Theodore Millon (1981) brings some order to the personality disorders described in DSM-III-R by classifying them into three clusters. Cluster One is made up of people who are dramatic, emotional, and erratic: soap opera characters.

The *histrionic personality disorder* applies to a person who is melodramatic and intense. "You won't believe what just happened to me!" These people incessantly draw attention to themselves, crave excitement, overreact to minor events, and throw tantrums.

The *narcissistic personality disorder* takes its name from the mythological character who fell in love with his own reflection. "I've talked enough about myself. Why don't you talk about me now?" A person with this disorder has an overblown sense of self-worth.

The *antisocial personality disorder* describes people who can't get along with others. In adolescence, it shows itself as truancy, delinquency, persistent lying, vandalism, promiscuity, and fighting—"Smoking in the boys room," plus a whole lot more. As adults, these people fail to meet obligations as workers, spouses, parents, or citizens. They get themselves (and others) into trouble.

The final personality disorder in the soap opera cluster is the *borderline personality disorder,* which has already been mentioned. Borderline individuals are unpredictable, unstable, and intense. They act in self-damaging ways—overdoing sex, gambling, and shopping. They cannot tolerate being alone, but their relationships with others are volatile and ambivalent. Once I was the therapist of a man who fit this characterization. In our first few meetings, he praised me to my face and behind my back (so I heard). Then one day I told him about a clinic procedure that he didn't like; all of a sudden I was the world's worst therapist.

Millon (1981) identifies Cluster Two of personality disorders as comprising people who are chronically anxious and fearful: cartoon characters, shy woodland creatures who lurk in the corners hoping no one will notice them.

People with an *avoidant personality disorder* are so sensitive to rejection that they beat others to the punch. They refuse to enter relationships without guarantees. Before a first date, they want to know about a second date; they may even want to choose names for the children. Avoidant personalities want acceptance but tend not to find it. As you might imagine, their self-esteem is low.

A *dependent personality disorder* refers to people who let others run their lives for them. Other people make their decisions. They subordinate their own needs: "No that's okay. I don't mind going to a restaurant that specializes in prime rib. Sure, I'm a vegetarian, but I can eat the crackers."

Obsessive-compulsive personality disorders are perfectionists who insist that others submit to them. I work with some people like this. I let them do everything from the start, since they always end up doing everything anyway. According to DSM-III-R, to warrant this label, a person must additionally show an inability to express feelings and have an excessive devotion to work. "Oh you know Mabel, she's married to the job."

The final personality disorder in this cluster is the *passive-aggressive* individual who resists the social and occupational demands in a variety of indirect ways. He procrastinates, dawdles, and forgets. He is intentionally inefficient. "But you told me to call you if the hot water line broke. This is the *cold* water line! I just did what you told me to do." Hostility is at the root of this person's ineffective passivity.

Cluster Three describes personality disorders characterized by oddness and eccentricity. These people are weird, and others feel uncomfortable around them.

Someone with a *paranoid personality disorder* lives a life of suspicion and mistrust. He is always looking for trickery on the part of others, and he continually questions the loyalty of friends and family members. He is secretive, overly jealous, and quick to take offense.

The *schizoid personality disorder* describes someone who is cold and aloof. She is indifferent to praise, criticism, or the feelings of others. This type of person has only one or two friends, at the most.

Finally, the *schizotypal personality disorder* is a person who combines undue social anxiety with peculiar ideas and habits. This person has problems with reference: reporters on the evening news, bumper stickers, and subway advertisements are directed specifically at him. He says things that don't fit into the ongoing conversation. "Speaking of the price of tea in China, have you noticed how Mrs. Green has painted her shutters chartreuse? I wonder who will be elected president in the year 2000?" The schizotypal individual establishes poor rapport with others (are you surprised?) and tends to live an isolated life.

I've described the 11 personality disorders currently recognized by the American Psychiatric Association (1980). On the face of it, this typology has a ring of truth, since we can easily recognize one or two people in our immediate vicinity who fit nicely into each of the categories. But this is a superficial test of the typology's validity—or the validity of our "diagnoses."

Let's return to the original assumptions about personality disorder. Many of them are not supported by available evidence. Although some individuals are more dramatic, more timid, or more bizarre than others, they don't exist in discrete clumps like four-leaf clovers or condominiums. These "types" are much more ill-defined than DSM-III-R assumes. So, the reliability with which mental health professionals can diagnose personality disorders is notoriously low (Mellsop et al., 1982).

The assumption that personality disorders have a biological basis has also not been sustained by research, with one striking exception. The antisocial personality disorder has a physiological underpinning. People who lack a conscience also lack the ability to learn to avoid punishment, perhaps because they experience little anticipatory fear (Lykken, 1957). Most of us lead reasonably ordered lives because we learn early on that certain transgressions lead to punishment. If we suddenly want to take a walk on the wild side, the anticipation of punishment makes us fearful, so we stay on the boring side. But suppose we did not experience a welling up of fear? Suppose our nervous system was such that this fear simply did not occur? Then we would be predisposed to a reckless existence. This may be the case for people with an antisocial personality disorder (Hare, 1970). Notice that this argument does not point to biology as a necessary and sufficient cause of antisocial behavior—it is a predisposition that interacts with other characteristics of the person and the environment to eventually lead to this dysfunctional style.

Yet another reason to be skeptical of these personality disorders is that they don't predispose severe problems. As you read my descriptions of these disorders, I'm sure you saw the seeds of later psychopathology within each. The histrionic personality disorder encourages hysteria. The avoidant personality disorder makes fears and phobias more likely. The obsessive-compulsive personality disorder is the training school for obsessions and compulsions. And the schizotypal individual is a schizophrenic waiting in the wings. So goes the logic, but none of this works too well in actuality (Rosenhan & Seligman, 1989). People diagnosed with a given personality disorder are not particularly likely to develop the corresponding psychopathology.

This topic seems a mess. Is there any way to bring order to it? Well, it's reasonable to say that some people have trouble making it in the world. We just have to read the newspaper or walk down the sidewalk to know this is true. Where the assumption goes astray is in attempting to separate "them" from "us" with a typology grounded in biology. Function and dysfunction must refer to particular environments, and for people this means the social and cultural context of their behavior. As noted earlier, personality disorders are described without reference to this context.

If we acknowledge that disordered personalities exist in particular settings, we have a more sophisticated perspective on dysfunction, one compatible with recent research in the trait paradigm (Chapter 9). The basic types of dysfunction do not transcend time and place. Instead, the social nature of dysfunction is explicit: difficulties with friends, family, and work are not consequences of a personality disorder—they *are* the disorder. Personality disorders are exaggerations of roles a particular society provides.

A great hue and cry has been made about sex differences in the prevalence of personality disorders (e.g. Kaplan, 1983). Some disorders apply mainly to women and others mainly to men. Does this represent a bias in DSM-III-R or not? Not from my view. Of course women are more apt to be dependent, and of course men are more apt to be antisocial. Traditional sex roles pushed to their respective extremes and acted out in an inordinately rigid way bring about such personality disorders.

"New" personality disorders will therefore always appear. What happens when an androgynous individual raises his or her androgynous role to the nth power? I don't know, but I bet a disorder will result, just as the exaggeration of any social role leads to difficulties.

CRIMINALITY: A BIOLOGICAL PREDISPOSITION?

In Chapter 8, I mentioned the work of Cesare Lombroso. This nineteenth-century criminologist proposed that some criminals were evolutionary throwbacks, marked by their ape-like characteristics. Research did not support his speculations, and Lombroso's theory faded away. As criminology became part of the larger discipline of sociology, explanation of crime in terms of personality characteristics also faded away.

But recent years have seen a resurgence of interest in possible personality predispositions to crime. This is an aspect of the Zeitgeist: Concern with law and order accompanies the belief that crime originates within the individual and not with social conditions. At any rate, in *Crime and Human Nature,* James Q. Wilson and Richard J. Herrnstein (1985) argue that individual differences determine criminality. The factors they identify are mainstay constructs of the trait paradigm, in particular those personality characteristics with a genetic basis.

Wilson and Herrnstein's book is controversial, because in some ways it is a modern version of Lombroso's thesis (Leo, 1985). However, their thesis is more sophisticated; they argue that individual differences interact with environmental conditions to produce criminals. No gene produces crime; rather, genes determine individual differences that make crime more or less likely granted certain situations.

Who do Wilson and Herrnstein identify as the potential criminal? Here is their description:

> People who break the law are often psychologically atypical. . . . Offenders are, for example, disproportionately young, male, mesomorphic . . . and from the low normal or borderline region of the distribution of intelligence test scores. (p. 173)

> [They are] emotionally unstable, impulsive, suspicious, hostile . . . ego-centric . . . unhappy, worried, and dissatisfied. (p. 179)

Note that these are individual differences in physique, intelligence, and constitution—characteristics that are genetically influenced.

Wilson and Herrnstein describe studies showing that chronic violation of the law runs in families, even when criminal parents give up their children for adoption to noncriminal parents. For instance, Mednick, Gabrielli, and Hutchings (1984) investigated almost 15,000 adoptions in Denmark between 1924 and 1947. Adoptive parents and the child's corresponding biological parents were

According to Wilscn and Herrnstein, criminals tend to be young, male, and mesomorphic.

classified as "criminal" if either parent of a pair had an on-record conviction. Children were similarly classified. (Too few daughters were ever convicted of a crime to include in the analyses, so results are limited to the sons.) Table 10–1 summarizes the findings of this study. As you can see, the criminality of biological parents affects the criminality of their sons more than the criminality of the corresponding adoptive parents does.

Additional findings from this study also point to the role of heredity in predisposing crime. Across the decades covered by the study, the results were unchanged by such social upheavals as a major depression, a world war, and occupation by a foreign power. The age at which children were adopted did not affect the results, and neither did the timing of crimes by the biological parents—before or after adoption. Finally, the results held even when the

TABLE 10–1
Proportion of Sons Convicted of Crime

Biological Parents Convicted	
Adoptive Parents Convicted	24.5%
Adoptive Parents Not Convicted	20.0%
Biological Parents Not Convicted	
Adoptive Parents Convicted	14.7%
Adoptive Parents Not Convicted	13.5%

SOURCE: Mednick, et al., 1984.

criminal records of the biological parents were unknown to the adoptive families.

Further evidence that criminality can be attributed to personality traits comes from studies showing that the predispositions Wilson and Herrnstein identify are consistent across situations and stable across time. Consider *impulsiveness,* which is plausibly linked to criminality in several ways—for instance, by making immediate rewards (of crime) seem attractive and distant punishments unlikely. Impulsiveness is measured with a simple paper-and-pencil task: the Porteus Maze Tests, where subjects trace their way without lifting their pencils through different mazes. Impulsiveness is shown by lifting one's pencil, cutting corners, straying from the path, and so on, and these behaviors are found to distinguish criminals from noncriminals (Riddle & Roberts, 1977).

Similarly, *misconduct* is highly stable across time. In a longitudinal study started in the 1930s, Glueck and Glueck (1950, 1968) followed 500 delinquent boys and 500 nondelinquent boys into adulthood. (By the way, the nondelinquent sample is the one also studied by George Vaillant, 1983, as described in Chapter 5.) Of the delinquents, originally chosen at 14 years of age, 354 were arrested between the ages of 17 and 25, and 263 were arrested between 25 and 31. In contrast, only 62 of the nondelinquents were arrested before the age of 31. So, breaking the law (or not) is a stable individual difference.

Where does this leave us, as individuals and as a society? Let's first consider some criticisms of the approach of these authors. The studies they review are correlational and therefore subject to various confounds. As Wilson and Herrnstein point out, not all available data lead to the same conclusion about the causes of crime. For instance, national differences in crime point to explanations transcending personality characteristics. Here are some intriguing facts pulled from *Crime and Human Nature*. In Japan, total crime fell 20 percent between 1962 and 1972, while it almost tripled in New York City. In 1976, the risk of being robbed in Japan was about 1/200th of the risk of being robbed in the United States!

Clearly, culture has something to do with criminality. Wilson and Herrnstein counter this by saying that whatever this something might be, it doesn't explain differences within a culture. Yes and no. Cultural factors that distinguish Japan and the United States with respect to crime rates may not vary appreciably within a particular culture, but then again they may. We simply don't know. Perhaps Japanese are more law-abiding than Americans because they wish not to bring shame to their families. But perhaps some Americans are more law-abiding than other Americans for the exact same reason: They want to protect their families from what the neighbors would think.

One of the bothersome things about the research reviewed in *Crime and Human Nature* is that most studies operationalized criminality in terms of conviction by the authorities. This is far from a perfect measure of criminality. Is it implausible to argue that young, unintelligent males with mesomorphic builds and an inability to take the future into account are more likely to be accused and convicted of crimes than other types of people, even if these other types do the same sorts of criminal things?

Studies using self-report of criminal activity give the same results as those using conviction to operationalize criminality, but this need not mean that the two measures are valid. I wouldn't admit on a questionnaire that I'd broken the law. Maybe the person who would admit this is the same sort of person who would admit it to casual acquaintances, some of whom tip off the police.

Still, I'm not fully convinced by my own arguments that Wilson and Herrnstein are wrong. At the same time, I'm not fully convinced they are right. Regardless, in the years to come, the application of trait ideas to criminality will become more popular, so let's consider what this means.

Suppose society accepts the argument that criminality can be explained by individual differences in personality, and that personality can be explained by genetic predispositions. Personal responsibility is the cornerstone of the legal system. Does this argument excuse criminals from responsibility for their misdeeds? "Hey, it's the fault of my ancestors. I just live with it."

Wilson and Herrnstein address this idea, noting that "if society should not punish acts that science has shown to have been caused by antecedent conditions, then every advance in knowledge about why people behave as they do may shrink the scope of criminal law" (1985, p. 504). This is true whether crime is explained in terms of social conditions or in terms of personality traits. However, Wilson and Herrnstein further argue that punishment would still be necessary. Indeed, they believe that individual differences affect the likelihood of crime in large part because of the way they lead people to choose courses of action with different payoffs. To the degree a given crime is punished swiftly and surely, all people—regardless of their personality—will be less likely to choose it.

I have another point of view. The debate between the personal responsibility of the criminal versus the scientific explanation of his crime is an echo of the idiographic-nomothetic debate within personality psychology. The legal system takes an idiographic approach to the criminal, who is after all an individual. This approach assumes free will (that is, personal responsibility) unless it has a good reason not to assume it. This is the way society attempts to understand the individual.

The scientific research of Wilson and Herrnstein (1985) and other criminologists takes a nomothetic approach to crime, generalizing across individual criminals and the circumstances of their behavior. This approach cannot accommodate free will. This is the way psychology attempts to understand people.

As you know from Chapters 8 and 9, the idiographic and nomothetic approaches are never fully compatible. They are appropriate for different purposes. The idiographic approach may not be appropriate for the purpose of science, except as an ideal goal for personality psychologists, yet it is indispensable for a legal system like our own that recognizes individual rights. To throw personal responsibility out of the courts is to invite the use of Meehl's cookbook—not to make predictions but to make justice. It won't work.

Let me raise one more point about applying the trait paradigm to criminality. Is it ethical to conduct and report research of the kind surveyed by Wilson and Herrnstein? These authors do their best to call the data as they see them. They try to be cautious and fair. But what will the public do with this book? Will the qualifications be overlooked, but the juicier "facts" remembered?

I became aware of *Crime and Human Nature* through a *Time* magazine review under the title "Are Criminals Born, Not Made?" (Leo, 1985). This question is *not* the thesis of Wilson and Herrnstein. They believe criminals are made—with physique, intelligence, gender, and constitution being among the ingredients. A great deal of their book is devoted to examining how these individual differences interact with particular situations to produce criminality (or lack of criminality). So, they are in keeping with contemporary interactionists. I doubt John and Jane Public will be as sophisticated in their consumption of the book, as shown by the title of the *Time* review. I doubt all of our nation's lawmakers and judges will consider the possible distinction between idiographic and nomothetic understanding.

Should we fault Wilson and Herrnstein for publishing a book that may be used in a bad way, like similar books on race differences in intelligence have been used? Should we fault physicists and engineers for providing the ideas used to build nuclear arsenals? What do you think?

RACIAL DIFFERENCES IN PERSONALITY?

If you think Wilson and Herrnstein's (1985) ideas about criminality have disturbing implications, then you will be even more disconcerted over some recent theorizing by psychologist J. Philippe Rushton (1985, 1988, 1989; Rushton & Bogaert, 1987) about racial differences in personality. You may remember that in Chapter 9 I suggested trait researchers should locate personality within its cultural context. Accordingly, the investigation of how ethnic groups differ with respect to given traits might provide interesting and important information about the cultural influences on personality.

Rushton starts with differences between ethnic groups, but then uses them to offer conclusions about biological influences. In so doing, he resurrects racial stereotypes that should have been put to rest a long time ago. I deliberated over whether to dignify Rushton's ideas by covering them in this book. I decided to discuss them in a critical fashion, with the hope they will be refuted rather than further publicized.

At any rate, what does Rushton have to say about racial differences in personality? He wanted to know how people of African, Asian, and European descent differ from one another. He focused on a number of behaviors reflecting sexuality, and in particular on a variable he termed **sexual restraint:** the degree to which a person approaches sexuality in a reticent and controlled fashion. Those high on sexual restraint have a low sex drive, infrequently engage in intercourse, avoid promiscuity, experience guilt surrounding sex, and so on; those low on sexual restraint approach sex with great enthusiasm and few inhibitions.

Rushton reviewed previous studies conducted over the years to conclude that those of Asian ancestry are more sexually restrained than those of European

Sexual restraint: The degree to which a person approaches sexuality in a reticent and controlled fashion.

ancestry, who in turn are more restrained than those of African ancestry. He further concluded that these differences have their basis in biology, an argument he made by pointing to physical differences among these groups, such as genital size, frequency of ovulation, length of gestation, and the like.

Rushton's final argument is that these differences reflect evolutionary considerations. From population biology, he borrowed the notion that species differ with respect to their reproductive strategies. At one extreme is **r strategy,** which describes species such as oysters that produce an incredible number of offspring but provide no parental care. At the other extreme is **K strategy,** which describes species such as elephants that produce a small number of offspring for which they provide extended care. On the whole, human beings exemplify the K strategy, but Rushton proposed that within our species, we can make distinctions along the r versus K dimension. So, according to him, the degree of sexual restraint that characterizes a group reflects its reproductive strategy. More restrained individuals are following the K strategy, and less restrained individuals, the r strategy.

Putting all of these arguments together, Rushton ended up concluding—bluntly—that Asians are prim, proper, and devoted to their children, whereas blacks are promiscuous, uninhibited, and indifferent to their children. Whites are intermediate. He attempted to support these arguments further by quoting statistics on divorce, illegitimacy, infant mortality, and so on.

What we have here is a pretty clear statement that blacks are a morally inferior group who are closer to animals than are other human groups. I need not belabor the sorts of purposes to which these "scientific" conclusions might be put. The world already has enough prejudice without sketching future directions it might take.

Needless to say, Rushton's arguments can be rebutted (Lynn, 1989; Zuckerman & Brody, 1988). Perhaps the first place to start is with the notion that three groups of human beings—the so-called races—exist that are biologically distinct. The line of reasoning here is suspect. In biology, *race* is a term that refers to geographically separate groups that do not interbreed. These criteria are *not* satisfied by the so-called human races, which are better regarded as culturally defined groups. The physical differences to which we may attach significance—skin color, hair texture, and the like—are distributed continuously across the human species. Biologically speaking, only one group of human beings exists, although individuals of course vary greatly.

Is it justified to make a distinction *within* a single species using concepts originally devised to make distinctions *between* species? Only if one could show that the components of r versus K strategy were heritable, and no evidence shows this is the case. Indeed, Rushton presented no heritability estimates in support of his arguments. As we saw in Chapter 9, these estimates are needed to argue that a characteristic is influenced by genetics.

Another point to make about his argument is that the particular studies he cited as showing differences among groups vary greatly in their methodological rigor. Few studies employed anything approaching random sampling, which of course is of prime importance if one wishes to offer conclusions that apply to literally billions of people.

r-strategy: A species-wide reproductive strategy where many offspring are produced and given no parental care.

K strategy: A species-wide reproductive strategy where few offspring are produced and given extended parental care.

He ignored differences *within* groups, lumping together Koreans, Eskimo, and Chinese-Americans; Swedes, Italians, and Portuguese; and Nigerians, Haitians, and African-Americans. When he reported differences among "racial" groups, he rarely provided information about the range of scores within them. We can suspect that in many cases greater differences occurred within groups than between them.

Also, Rushton ignored the role of culture and socioeconomic status in determining the characteristics he studied (but see Rushton & Bogaert, 1988). The investigations he cited were conducted for the most part in the Western world, where it is simply a fact that people of African ancestry are most likely to be poor and subject to discrimination. Might not these facts have something to do with the relatively high rates of infant mortality found in this group?

I confess to being confused as to why anyone would devote such energy to "proving" biologically based racial differences, particularly in the face of the evidence and common sense. What is the implication of this kind of work? Is an inequitable status quo excused or even legitimized? Are unstated personal issues afoot (cf. Wicklund & Braun, 1987)? As you could tell from Chapter 9, I find biological theorizing to be an exciting aspect of the trait paradigm. It would be a shame if the entire endeavor were tarnished by wild extrapolations such as those just described. I trust common sense will prevail.

CAREER COUNSELING: MATCHING PEOPLE TO CAREERS

Sorry, Charlie, but you're just not cut out for a career in crime. But the trait paradigm can still help you choose another career. One of the more popular applications of this approach to personality is the use of **interest inventories** by vocational counselors. As Zytowski (1973) describes these questionnaires, they fit round pegs into round holes by matching a person's interests with those apt to be satisfied by a particular profession.

Interest inventory: A questionnaire for assessing vocational interests.

The **Strong Vocational Interest Blank** (SVIB) is the best-known of these interest inventories. You may have completed this questionnaire at some point in your life—it's been around since 1927. (Because David Campbell has taken over the SVIB since its creator Edward Strong's death in 1963, it is often called the Strong-Campbell Inventory.) The format and underlying logic of the SVIB are simple. From a list of hundreds of activities, individuals indicate their reactions to each as "like," "indifferent," or "dislike." Here are some sample items (Campbell, 1971):

Strong Vocational Interest Blank (SVIB): The most widely used interest inventory, developed by Edward Strong and David Campbell.

1. Actor
2. Advertising Man
3. Architect
4. Military Officer
5. Artist
6. Astronomer
7. Athletic Director
8. Auctioneer
9. Author of novel
10. Author of technical book
11 Auto Salesman
12. Auto Racer

13. Auto Mechanic	17. Building Contractor
14. Auto Pilot	18. Buyer of Merchandise
15. Bank Teller	19. Carpenter
16. Designer, Electronic Equipment	20. Cartoonist

The person's profile of responses is then compared to the average responses of individuals working successfully in different occupations. The greater the match, the more seriously someone should consider choosing that occupation.

This is a cookbook procedure. Administration, scoring, and interpretation of the SVIB are now fully automated via a computer program. Results of the SVIB are useful in matching people to occupations they are interested in and in steering them away from others. If one is interested in a profession, one is more likely to stay with it and do well (Reeves & Booth, 1979). But the SVIB does *not* measure ability. If I'm interested in being an auctioneer, but I stutter, I'd be better off not pursuing this career.

As a self-report measure of individual differences regarding interests, the SVIB fares well. Scores are highly stable over time (Johansson & Campbell, 1971) and predict which professions people actually enter (Hansen, 1984). Further, the interest profiles associated with different professions have stayed the same over the decades. Despite incredible social changes during the past 50 years, chemists in the 1980s express the same likes and dislikes as did chemists in the 1930s. The same is true for workers in other occupations (Hansen, 1984).

The biggest problem with the SVIB and related interest inventories is that they use already-existing groups to provide the bottom line. So they are tied to the status quo. Still, those who use interest inventories are sensitive to the

Interest inventories are of little use in counseling a woman who is considering a career typically reserved for men.

possibility of bias on the basis of race or gender. If most chemists are white males, is it reasonable to use the SVIB procedure to counsel a black female if she is considering chemistry as a career? Traditionally, separate questionnaires for men and women respondents have been used to solve this problem, but this falls short if an insufficient number of women (or men) work at a particular profession.

At one time, the SVIB was printed on blue paper for men and pink paper for women! David Campbell has himself labeled this a blunder, and I mention it to show how insidious bias can be. But the problem lies not in the tests themselves. Our society encourages men and women to consider different vocations, and the majority follow this advice. The SVIB is not to be faulted for reflecting this social reality.

The more general shortcoming of interest inventories is that jobs themselves change. In particular, someone taking the SVIB today may be ideally suited for an occupation that does not yet exist. If the interests associated with future jobs overlap with those of past jobs, then interest inventories will help steer people toward them. But if future jobs combine interests in novel ways, then these questionnaires will not help respondents choose them.

Interest inventories have also been criticized because they lack a theoretical basis. To some degree, this is untrue, because they apply the basic tenets of the trait paradigm (if not the particulars of a given theory). Regardless, a notable exception to this criticism is John Holland's (1966, 1985) theory of vocational personalities.

Holland assumes that "the choice of a vocation is an expression of personality" (1985, p. 7). This is fully compatible with the perspective on personality I presented to you in Chapter 1. And Holland corrected a serious shortcoming of many personality theories: They ignore what most people do 40 hours a week, 50 weeks a year, from age 18 to age 70.

From Holland's assumption, we can conclude that interest inventories are personality inventories. Factor analysis of interest inventories reveals six clusters of interests, and therefore six basic types of people:

■ Realistic types: People who prefer the manipulation of objects, tools, machines, and animals.
■ Investigative types: People who prefer to observe and investigate physical, biological, and cultural phenomena.
■ Artistic types: People who prefer to create art forms or products.
■ Social types: People who prefer to work with other people, informing, training, developing, curing, or otherwise "enlightening" them.
■ Enterprising types: People who prefer to work toward organizational goals or economic gains.
■ Conventional types: People who prefer the systematic manipulation of data and the keeping of records.

Holland believes these types are culture specific. So, in Tolkien's Middle Earth, we would expect the typology of hobbits, ents, goblins, and trolls each to involve different interests.

Holland further proposes that environments can be classified. Because the most important aspect of the environment is other people, this classification mirrors that of his personality types. Accordingly, he names six environments: the realistic, the investigative, the artistic, the social, the enterprising, and the conventional. The "press" (see Murray, 1938) or "personality" (see Bem & Funder, 1978) of each environment is derived from the character of the people who congregate in it, and it demands certain behaviors from the individual.

In a study of college instructors, John Smart (1982) found support for these ideas. He classified academic disciplines as realistic, investigative, artistic, social, enterprising, or conventional (see Table 10–2) after instructors completed a questionnaire that assessed their teaching goals. The teachers in a particular discipline agreed among themselves about the importance of certain goals, and these goals in each case reflected their particular discipline. Instructors in realistic fields felt education should prepare students for careers. Instructors in social fields believed character development of students was important. And so on.

Holland's theory goes far beyond the modest intent of the SVIB and related questionnaires. His is a sophisticated vision of personality in keeping with the interactionist approach. A key postulate is that a match between the person and the setting is beneficial: The individual is satisfied and productive and has an

TABLE 10–2
Typology of Academic Disciplines

Academic Environment	Representative Disciplines
Realistic	Agricultural Education Civil Engineering Forestry
Investigative	Economics Geology Mathematics
Artistic	Art English Music
Social	History Political Science Sociology
Enterprising	Law Marketing Personnel Management
Conventional	Accounting Business Education Finance

SOURCE: From Smart, 1982.

identity and a circle of friends. The organization that serves as the setting is pleasant, stable, and successful.

And a mismatch is not beneficial. Have any of you transferred from another college because it just wasn't you? Were you the only student there who listened to classical music—or the only one who didn't? Holland's approach to person-environment fit explains your discomfort. If you feel like a square peg right now, find comfort in the possibility that there is a place for you elsewhere.

PERSONNEL SELECTION: CHOOSING PEOPLE FOR CAREERS

As you have just read, one application of the trait paradigm assists people in choosing occupations. Another application is involved with the other side of this process: helping business and industry choose employees. **Personnel selection** is concerned with individual differences leading to good and bad job performance. Accordingly, personnel psychologists often embrace the orientation of the trait paradigm.

Personnel tests are nothing new. Thousands of years ago, tests were used in Greece and China to select workers for particular jobs (Dunnette & Borman, 1979). The modern impetus for these tests began with World War I, when almost two million men were screened using group-administered intelligence tests. Similarly, Woodworth (1919) developed a test for identifying psychiatric disturbance among soldiers. His inventory was adapted for civilians and used by employers during the economically troubled 1930s to select "stable" and "cooperative" workers (Hogan, Carpenter, Briggs, & Hansson, 1984).

A second impetus came with World War II. Henry Murray went to work for the Office of Strategic Services (OSS), where he was charged with "judging the suitability of each candidate for a proposed assignment overseas" (Murray & MacKinnon, 1946, p. 76). Murray brought to bear his considerable assessment skills. The OSS wanted a simple "in" or "out" judgment to be made, but this was not the only decision required. Granted that a recruit was not grossly unfit, just how effective was he or she likely to be? Murray and MacKinnon fretted that "screening devices . . . efficient in distinguishing people . . . incapable of functioning effectively are not so successful in discriminating degrees of effectiveness among those whose test scores fall above the usual level of acceptability" (1946, p. 76).

Realize that the OSS was the forerunner of the CIA and that Murray was responsible for recommending people for particularly dangerous assignments, like being a spy or a resistance leader. He couldn't just rely on the SVIB to pick men and women for these missions impossible. Instead, he developed a series of tests that mimicked situations likely to be confronted in the field. He inferred how a person would act in actual situations from how that person performed in mock situations. So, several decades prior to Mischel's (1968) critique of the trait paradigm, Murray devised two of the later considered "contemporary" reactions

Personnel selection: The process of choosing particular workers for particular jobs.

to this critique: looking at actual behavior rather than questionnaire responses and taking the situation into account.

Here are two of the many tasks Murray and his fellow psychologists developed. Imagine the situations these tasks try to mimic:

> *Construction Test.* The candidate was shown a glorified tinker-toy with which he was instructed to build a 5-foot cube with 7-foot diagonals in ten minutes with the aid of 2 helpers whom he was to direct. The "helpers" were members of the junior staff who soon turned the situation into a test of the candidate's frustration-tolerance by becoming increasingly lazy, recalcitrant, and insulting. No candidate ever finished the task, and there were those who became either markedly upset or enraged by the humiliations they suffered.

> *Stress Interview.* The candidate was told to assume that he had just been caught going through a secret file in a government building in Washington, and, after ten minutes in which to think up an innocent and plausible explanation for his presence there, he reported to a basement room where, under the glare of a spotlight, he was given a grilling cross-examination on the details of his story in an attempt to confuse and disquiet him as much as possible. (Murray & MacKinnon, 1946, p. 78)

In yet another test, candidates were invited to a party and encouraged to get drunk: "The party which lasted usually long past midnight often revealed aspects of the candidates' personalities not seen in soberer states" (p. 79). *In vino veritas.*

Information from all these tests was collated by a diagnostic council, which characterized a candidate's traits and recommended assignments accordingly. We therefore see Murray's approach to assessment: a variety of tests and observations carried out by a variety of experts to describe the whole person. The specifics of Murray's recommendations are shrouded in military secrecy, but his program succeeded at a general level. Of the hundreds of men and women who were assessed by the diagnostic council, only a handful proved unsatisfactory in the eyes of their superiors or colleagues. When it was possible to calculate them, correlations between initial assessment and subsequent performance were positive, although modest (Office of Strategic Services, 1948).

After World War II, personnel selection exploded. Trait psychologists turned away from the situational tests favored by Murray and used the more efficient personality inventories being developed (like the MMPI and the 16PF) to predict subsequent job performance. Paralleling the history of trait research, enthusiasm for personality assessment in selection waned in the 1960s. The .30 "limit" was encountered in personnel selection, and some called for personnel psychologists to discard personality assessment (e.g., Ghiselli, 1973; Guion & Gottier, 1965).

Hogan et al. (1984) suggested that several factors led to decreased enthusiasm. First, some of the popular personality inventories—like the MMPI—were best suited for predicting psychopathology. Scores were largely unrelated to job performance. Second, many personality scales were used to

"Well, Mr. Cody, according to our questionnaire, you would probably excel in sales, advertising, slaughtering a few thousand buffalo, or market research."

SOURCE: "The Far Side" cartoon by Gary Larson is reproduced by permission of Chronicle Features, San Francisco.

predict performance at jobs that had nothing to do with the traits being measured When the individual difference is pertinent to the job, successful prediction is possible. For instance, introversion-extraversion relates to the ability to work well in quiet or noisy settings (Hockey, 1972). Once again, the "problem" with personality questionnaires resides not in the measures themselves but in the purpose to which they are put.

Recent developments within personnel selection handle individual differences and their assessment with more sophistication (Guion & Gibson, 1988). We see the realization that individual differences are better assessed by observing what people actually do as opposed to what they say they do. Simulations like those developed by Murray are popular once again, and aggregation is used to bolster the reliability of assessment. Personnel psychologists now define the specific requirements of jobs in behavioral terms, fitting people to these settings.

One of the notable success stories of personnel selection has been chronicled on the sports pages (Deutsch, 1990). In conducting its annual draft of college athletes, the National Football League straightforwardly applies the trait paradigm. Which individual differences lead to good or poor adaptation (that is, victories or losses)? How can these individual differences best be measured?

Once upon a time, the Dallas Cowboys were the acknowledged innovators here (Furlong, 1971; Maule, 1968). In the early 1960s, Tex Schramm approached IBM about the possibility of using computers to assist in scouting the hundreds of college players he might use on his football team. IBM assigned Salam Qureishi (from Aligarh, India) to work with Schramm, and what ensued was a profitable collaboration between a Cowboy who knew nothing about computers and an Indian who knew nothing about football.

What are the qualities that make for a good football player? Qureishi talked to numerous coaches and distilled their answers down to eight individual differences: character, quickness and body control, competitiveness, mental alertness, strength and explosiveness, weight, height, and speed. Scouts rated prospects on 9-point scales corresponding to these categories. Recognizing potential problems in subjective ratings, the Cowboys developed objective measures of these qualities. This is where the now-familiar statistics on the 40-yard dash and the bench press came from. Believe it or not, even IQ is figured into the formula. "Character" is harder to quantify, of course, but the Cowboys inferred it from lack of drug use (a prophetic operationalization, granted subsequent scandals in sports).

A player's scores on the different scales are summed, and those with higher scores are drafted sooner. Does the system work? In 1964, the procedure produced this order of players: (1) Joe Namath, (2) Dick Butkus, (3) Gale Sayers, and (4) Fred Biletnikoff. Although none of these players played for the Dallas Cowboys, they all had successful careers in professional football, eventually reaching the Hall of Fame. And the Cowboys traditionally identified future stars overlooked by other football teams, like Calvin Hill.

Over the years, other football teams have caught up with Dallas in personnel selection (and victories). The newest horizon is the use of similar quantifying techniques to select adaptive versus maladaptive plays. The San Francisco 49ers, for instance, have given computers to their assistant coaches (Compton, 1984). The success or failure of particular plays in particular circumstances is constantly monitored, and the head coach uses this information throughout the game. In my reading, I haven't encountered the exact correlation coefficients involved, but I bet they exceed the .30 limit because they are based on aggregated information obtained from actual situations. The only thing missing to maximize the predictability of outcomes is the Bem and Allen procedure of distinguishing consistency versus inconsistency. But maybe the 49ers achieve consistency by virtue of their superior personnel.

PREDICTING PREFERENCES

What do Coca-Cola, George Bush, "M*A*S*H," and people accused of crimes ranging from murder to conspiracy share in common? All of them have benefited from an application of the trait paradigm. Just as NFL teams predict the success of football players from individual differences, people involved with these four examples predict their own success (that is, popularity) from individual differences. The techniques of opinion polling have become highly refined and are used in marketing products, charting political careers, selecting television shows, and even choosing sympathetic jurors. But at the bottom, they all embrace a similar logic stemming from the trait approach to personality.

It is assumed that people's likes and dislikes are both stable and general individual differences. Much of society rises and falls according to preferences of the citizens, so information about predisposing individual differences is powerful indeed. In this section, I'll describe some representative investigations of public preference.

Political Polls

Polling is a way to gauge public opinion. The best-known polls predict the outcomes of elections for public office. As early as 1824, newspapers tried to forecast the presidential election by surveying a sample of voters (Gallup, 1972). And in 1883, the *Boston Globe* sent reporters into specially selected precincts the night of an election. This system is still used to project final returns. ("With 2 percent of the precincts reporting, we give New Jersey to Smith.")

With a few famous exceptions (like the Dewey-Truman presidential race in 1948), modern political polling has been highly accurate in its forecasts. Accuracy results from randomly selecting respondents. Early polls were based on *convenience samples:* people on the street corner, people who mail back a postcard, people who answer the telephone. But since the 1930s, it has become clear that such samples are confounded because political leanings tend to correlate with socioeconomic class. Any convenience sample that disproportionately samples rich people or poor people introduces a political bias. And most convenience samples do precisely this.

Modern polling began with George Gallup's random samples in the 1930s. Imagine a list of all 325 million people in the United States. If you want to know what presidential candidate is favored by these millions of people, you can get a highly accurate estimate by interviewing *no more* than 1,500 of them—so long as they were chosen at random, which means that every one of the 325 million has an equal chance of being included in the sample.

How does this work? It may not be intuitive, but the random sample guarantees accuracy. Gallup (1972) compares the process to a cook making soup. He wants to know how it tastes, so he stirs it a bit and sips a small spoonful. The spoonful tastes fine, so he assumes the whole kettle of soup does. He does not worry that he has sampled only a small fraction of the soup, since his stirring "randomized" the potential spoonfuls. Had he not stirred the soup, his spoonful would have been a convenience sample, perhaps unrepresentative of the soup as a whole.

Would *more than* 1,500 people in a random sample of the United States population improve accuracy? Of course, but not enough to warrant the increase in time and energy. Gallup (1972) reports that such a sample yields estimates that are accurate within 3 percent. (Most of us would be thrilled if our checkbook balance were that close to reality.)

National polls do not start with a list of millions of names and then randomly choose 1,500. That would be too unwieldy. Instead, they use a simpler procedure that yields essentially the same representative group of respondents. One variant starts by selecting at random a small number of precincts within the country. Then residences within these precincts are selected at random. And finally people within these are selected at random.

So far, I've described polls that ignore individual differences among respondents, since presidential election polls are only interested in overall national opinion. But many polls subdivide their sample by individual differences and make separate projections within groups defined by age, sex, race, religion, amount of education, type of employment, and place of residence.

Information about preferences due to individual differences allows political candidates to chart their campaigns, and here polling changes from a means of estimating opinion to a strategy of capitalizing on opinion or even creating it. Suppose a candidate for governor of your state finds that she is extremely popular with affluent college graduates and extremely unpopular with poor people of limited education. She might decide to direct her time, energy, and money toward swaying the opinions of the people in-between. No need to visit the fancy suburbs or the inner cities, since those people have already made up their minds.

Suppose the candidate finds out from polls that uncommitted voters are particularly concerned with law and order, or with possible threats to the nuclear family, or with economic issues. She can tailor her campaign speeches accordingly, just as a psychotherapist tailors treatment to a patient's illness. It's the exact same strategy, one that has been so refined in the United States that no serious candidates are without polling experts on their campaign staffs.

Consumer Behavior

Cynics have noted that candidates for political office are products to be sold to the public. Once upon a time, this was not as insulting as it is today, since marketing was product-oriented. Advertisements stressed the qualities of a particular product, and it was assumed that good products sold better than poor products.

But, by the 1950s, marketing had become consumer-oriented. So many products were available, and they were so similar, that advertisements began to stress the qualities of the *consumer*. It was assumed people bought products for reasons other than the nature of the product itself. To the degree a product touched on these reasons, it would sell.

The trait paradigm provided a number of ideas here, and the psychology of consumer behavior is thus an application of this paradigm (Cohen & Chakravarti, 1990). Trait theories, particularly those stressing needs, are used to predict, understand, and manipulate the buying of products. When you go to the 7-Eleven to get a six-pack of beer, you may regard this as a simple act to prepare for watching TV that evening. But Big Business, from the viewpoint of the trait paradigm, sees you as satisfying a number of needs, none of which has anything to do with beer or television.

Let's consider Murray's theory. Remember how it catalogues needs people have to varying degrees? Some people have a high need for play, while other people have a high need for achievement. Think about beer commercials. They can be classified as appeals to play versus appeals to achievement. "Play" beers are used to have a good time—Miller Lite, for example, while "achievement" beers are used to reward yourself for meritorious actions—Löwenbräu, for example. These types of beer are marketed to appeal to different groups of people, in accordance with their dominant needs.

Sometimes beers change their image (though not their taste) to capture a larger market. Are you old enough to remember that Miller used to be the "champagne of bottled beer" and Michelob reserved "for special occasions"? These former achievement beers have become play beers. Indeed, with Michelob, you can have it all, which makes it a self-actualization beer.

Why settle for champagne?

These are not silly examples. I've taken them all from a standard textbook of *Consumer Behavior* by James McNeal (1982). Any of you who take courses in marketing know the great extent this field is influenced by the trait paradigm. The need profiles of different markets are carefully ascertained by businesspersons, and products are advertised to appeal to prevailing needs. This is called *segmentation of the market*.

Although a person's needs are assumed to be stable and general, they can also wax and wane. So, advertising tries to arouse needs. You saw examples in Chapter 6 of how products may be linked to sexual needs. Sex sells, but so does play, achievement, power, affiliation, nurturance, and so on. Different advertisements try to tickle these different needs. And, although we are not always fully aware of the process, sometimes we are. A while ago, I bought new Michelin tires for my car in direct response to television commercials showing an infant crawling through tires while her mother and father talked off-camera about the merits of cheap versus expensive tires. Whoever designed that commercial is a genius.

Television Polls

TV shows are a different sort of product, but network executives are similarly interested in the results of polls. Two specific matters concern them. First, which shows should make it onto television in the first place? Second, of those shows that do premier, which should be kept and which scrapped? To answer these questions and related ones (like the particular time slot when a show will be most successful), preference polls are taken.

The three major networks use slightly different procedures to choose among pilot programs (Gitlin, 1983). CBS passes out free tickets to tourists in Los Angeles and New York. The ticket entitles the holder to view pilot shows in special studios equipped with chairs having two buttons: If you like what you see, you press the green button; if you don't like what you see, you press the red button. After a show is seen, viewers complete questionnaires asking for more specific reactions to the show. ABC has its pilots screened through Preview House, an independent firm specializing in market research. Preview House contacts potential viewers by phone and invites them to come in and rate shows. NBC uses yet another procedure. It shows pilots on cable television in certain areas, and then phones viewers to ask their opinion.

None of these samples is chosen randomly, so the networks try to achieve representativeness by weighting responses according to sex, race, and age. Problems nevertheless remain. It is frequently charged that racial minorities do not appreciably enter into this process. Bias may also be introduced by response sets and considerations of social desirability. For instance, respondents said that they would be interested in a miniseries based on the life of Martin Luther King (because this seems like the appropriate thing to say), but the series itself was unsuccessful (Gitlin, 1983).

Still, the system is reasonably accurate in predicting which shows will be popular or unpopular once they make it on the air. Testing figures from CBS for the years 1957 through 1980 show that whether or not a show ends up in the top half of all shows can be predicted from initial piloting over 80 percent of the time (Gitlin, 1983). However, spectacular exceptions are well-known. "All in the Family" screened to below-average ratings, but "clinical intuition" prevailed, and the show became a great success. Still, screening is successful enough that almost all shows that wind up on television have to survive the process.

Sometimes screening is used to fine-tune a show. The name "Dynasty" was chosen over the initially favored "Oil" by using a phone survey. Testing showed that American audiences preferred "M*A*S*H" with a superimposed laugh track, whereas British audiences preferred it without. (That gives rise to some interesting conclusions about national differences.) Preview House tried out new Angels for Charlie and found a replacement for Suzanne Somers when "Three's Company" shrank to two.

Preference polls are refined to take into account individual differences among viewers. Different sorts of people watch television at different times and on different days, and networks try to tailor their shows to the available market. So, according to Gitlin (1983), comedy shows are planned for 8 P.M. slots, and dramatic shows for 10 P.M. slots. Advertisers are particularly interested in audience composition, because—as we have seen—different products are packaged to appeal to different groups of people.

Once shows are on the air, the Nielsen Company informs us about which shows are most watched. Recording devices are attached to television sets in several thousand homes across the country. They keep track of whether the set is on or off, and if on, what channel is being watched. This information is collated every two weeks to give network television a report card based on the absolute and relative popularity of different shows.

Like the use of screening polls, the Nielsen ratings are criticized for nonrepresentative samples and for possible distortion. But when checked by other procedures, like telephone questionnaires or viewer diaries, ranking of shows is essentially the same (Gitlin, 1983). So, we may conclude that the Nielsen Company will continue to be an important part of television for the forseeable future.

Jury Selection

By now you are familiar with the way applications of the trait paradigm are carried out. If preferences of a group of people can be ascertained and related to individual differences, then one can predict future preferences from information about these individual differences. One of the most controversial forms of this application is the choosing of jury members.

Juries are usually chosen by a procedure known as *voir dire*. Prosecution and defense lawyers interview prospective jurors, and each is allowed to dismiss a certain number on suspicion of bias. In practice, of course, the lawyers not only dismiss jurors who are biased against them but also select those who are biased in favor.

The lawyer cannot simply ask a potential juror if he is favorably biased. Justice is supposed to be blind, but this is a naive assumption. Because of individual differences brought into the courtroom, jurors differ markedly in the degree to which they are predisposed to reach a given verdict. If one has a handle on these predispositions, then one can "stack" the jury.

Knowing this, some lawyers have enlisted the help of psychologists to conduct the *voir dire*. Since jurors for any given trial are drawn from a specific place, the psychologist may interview a random sample of individuals living there. Following the procedure of the political pollsters, the interviewer asks their opinion of the pending court case and asks a number of other questions, often about demographic and socioeconomic matters. The psychologist then determines which of these answers to these latter questions predict predisposition to convict or acquit.

During the examination of prospective jurors, a lawyer informed by these patterns of correlations asks these same "other questions," not because answers to them are interesting in their own right, but because they predict strict or lenient predisposition (bias). Jurors are dismissed or accepted accordingly. This procedure may sound a bit like science fiction, but it has been used with success in a number of cases (Brigham & Wrightsman, 1982).

Is this ethical? So far, jury surveys have been conducted only by defense lawyers, and some therefore argue that they serve to protect the accused's presumption of innocence. This argument would evaporate if prosecutors made use of the strategy. Others argue that lawyers have always attempted to stack the jury; surveys just help them do it a little better. I'm not impressed with any of these arguments, but the procedure of *voir dire* leads almost inevitably to jury surveys. For a number of reasons—and jury selection is but one—our justice system deserves scrutiny and change.

SHORT-CIRCUITING THE SYSTEM: CAN YOU BEAT THE SCHOLASTIC APTITUDE TEST?

Because important decisions are based on the results of psychological tests, the question arises whether people can short-circuit the process. Granted that a high score on a test can lead to fame and fortune, can someone achieve these scores without possessing the attributes the test tries to assess? The answer is obviously yes, although how takes many forms—from downright cheating (stealing the answer key to a personnel selection test) to practicing (working sample items from the law boards), from being coached (taking a course in preparation for a test) to beating the system (figuring out the rationale of a test's right or wrong answers).

Disagreement exists concerning the ethics of these various strategies for scoring well on a test. It is predictable that the powers-that-be who create, administer, and use tests for important decisions wish that people would just take them and receive scores reflecting their "true" aptitude or interest. It is also predictable that the people whose lives hang on the results of tests do not always comply with this wish. They seek every advantage.

Claims and counterclaims about "getting a leg up on" the trait paradigm are most numerous with respect to tests of academic ability, in particular the

Scholastic Aptitude Test (SAT), used by many colleges and universities to make admission decisions. So I'll focus on the SAT.

Most of you probably took the SAT, and you may remember that the test booklet advised you not to do so repeatedly, because scores are highly stable. Although the test booklet did not elaborate, do you see how this advice follows directly from a bedrock assumption of the trait paradigm? Individual differences are regarded as fixed characteristics, like eye color or height, since they have a genetic underpinning.

By this logic, repeatedly taking the SAT results in essentially the same scores, within the limits of reliability. Also by this logic, a student cannot prepare for the SAT, since scores cannot be shoved around at the last minute. And in particular by this logic, a student cannot be coached to do well on the SAT anymore than someone can be coached to have blue eyes or a tall stature.

So why is the SAT coaching business a thriving endeavor? Try this answer on: because coaching improves scores! If you are from a small town, or if your family lacks the money to tune you up for the SAT, then you don't have the same opportunity to improve your SAT scores that someone from an affluent or urban environment has. And you may not get into a highly selective university.

Am I being cynical here? Perhaps. SAT scores do matter, but SAT scores are not quite as fixed as higher education would like to believe. Although estimates vary about the degree to which coaching can improve scores, reviews of studies assessing the effects of testing agree that scores do improve following coaching (e.g., Kulik, Bangert-Drowns, & Kulik, 1984; Messick & Jungeblut, 1981). And some methods of coaching are more effective than others. As a rule, the more contact time between the test-taker and the coach, the greater the improvement.

Some argue that the SAT remains a valid way of assessing academic aptitude, because extensive coaching in effect changes the exact quality (intelligence) the test purports to measure. This may be, but the argument is at odds with the typical interpretation of intelligence as a relatively fixed individual difference. It is also at odds with the procedures used in coaching, like memorizing lists of vocabulary words. That ain't intelligence.

Probably the most controversial attempt to coach SAT scores is reported by David Owen (1985) in his book *None of the Above,* in which he describes a plan for beating the system altogether, a way to get high scores while knowing nothing except how the SAT is put together.

Most of us know that if we eliminate a few answers on the SAT as obviously wrong, it is to our advantage to choose randomly among those that remain. Odds are that we'll get some of these right. The SAT instruction booklet gives this same advice.

Owen goes one step further by explaining how to guess among answers. Although his strategy has not been proven effective, it is based on sound reasoning. Questions on the SAT are there because they discriminate between respondents. Questions that are so easy that everyone gets them right do not exist, nor do questions that are so hard that everyone gets them wrong. So, the SAT-taker is faced with the task of guessing answers correctly that other people guess incorrectly.

He or she can be taught to recognize so-called distractor answers—those that seem plausible to Joe or Josephine Ordinary, but not to Brad or Buffy Elite. Owen catalogues a number of recognition strategies. One is to eliminate "obvious" answers. Here's an example:

> A literary agency's editors read 4 out of every 20 scripts submitted. What is the ratio of unread to read scripts?

The answer here is 4 to 1, because there are 16 unread scripts to every 4 that are read. But one of the alternatives is 5 to 1, which snares some respondents because it is an obvious (although wrong) answer: 20 divided by 4 equals 5. The general strategy here is to add, subtract, divide, and multiply the numbers contained in a problem, and then *eliminate* the answers to these permutations. Look elsewhere for the answer.

Another strategy recommended in *None of the Above* is to know the location of sections within the SAT that are experimental and thus unscored. The Educational Testing Services includes these sections for the purpose of developing new items for subsequent tests. If experimental items correlate well with other items on the SAT, they are kept for future versions of the test. But Owen tells test-takers to skip these experimental items and spend their time on the parts of the test that count for them. (By the way, the experimental section can be recognized because its items are particularly ambiguous and difficult.)

Owen claims that such strategies can improve SAT scores by several hundred points. This claim is disputed by spokespersons of the Educational Testing Service (Bowen, 1985), and I have no way of knowing who is right. However, I do know that Owen's logic is sound. All tests and measures have confounds—factors that produce high (or low) scores that have nothing to do with the quality ostensibly being measured. To the degree these confounds can be imparted to a test-taker, the system can be beat.

This is simply one more example of an enlightenment effect. Knowledge of the trait paradigm can be used to defeat the purpose of its applications. Realize that the dynamic I've just described plays itself out as well in other domains where the trait paradigm is applied. Consider disability pensions based on psychiatric illness. Individuals who manifest the "right" set of symptoms can retire from the work force and receive a monthly stipend. While many disability decisions reflect the facts of the matter, it's not bizarre to suggest that at least some decisions reflect instead a strategic presentation of symptoms. When working as a clinician, I always got a kick out of the handful of patients who answered the question "How are you feeling?" with a list of symptoms *in the exact order* listed in DSM-III-R. These patients were invariably looking for some redress from the system, and they knew the rules well.

Similarly, producers of television shows sometimes try to take advantage of the way pilots are evaluated (Gitlin, 1983). It is believed, for instance, that comedies preview particularly well, since laughter in a large audience is contagious. A pilot show contains more jokes than the actual series that comes from it, because a humorous pilot should test high.

Students often complete teacher evaluation forms at the end of a course. On the face of it, these forms measure teaching ability, and school administrations use them to make personnel decisions. Teachers keep the importance of evaluation forms in mind, passing them out under circumstances that create high instead of low ratings by students. Distribute them the day you cancel the final examination, or the day you finally deliver a good lecture, or the day your young children and aging parents visit the class and sit in front of the room. Beat the system.

AN ALTERNATIVE ROLE MODEL: MULTIPLE INTELLIGENCES

To conclude, I would like to consider a topic that points toward a more upbeat future for applications within the trait paradigm. Remember that I keep saying that this paradigm shows the influence of the intelligence testing tradition. It reflects the assumption that intelligence is fixed, unitary, and measurable with a test.

But what would the trait paradigm be like if influenced by a different conception of intelligence? A book by psychologist Howard Gardner (1983) describes a different way to think about intelligence. The subtitle of the book is *The Theory of Multiple Intelligences*. Gardner criticizes the assumption that intelligence is a single entity captured by a single score on an IQ test.

Instead, Gardner proposes that we have several intelligences, largely independent of each other. Intelligence measured by an IQ test is but one of these. An individual may be endowed with more versus less of each of the intelligences discussed by Gardner, so each person must be described with a *profile*.

Let me give you some background. Alfred Binet originally devised intelligence tests to distinguish retarded children from those who did poorly at school for other reasons. Nothing inherent in Binet's tests would suggest that they can make subtle distinctions along a continuum. And nothing inherent in the tests would suggest that the continuum they define captures the whole of what we ordinarily mean by intelligence.

These extrapolations of Binet's tests were brought about by the social and intellectual context in which they first appeared. Intelligence tests were rapidly assimilated to the newly provided viewpoint of Darwin. The theory of evolution might seem to imply that all species can be arranged in order from most primitive to most advanced and that all individuals within a species can be similarly arrayed. But this is *not* what the theory of evolution says. All species currently existing are as advanced (or as primitive) as any others. People are *not* more advanced than gorillas, or chimpanzees, or kangaroo rats, or cockroaches, or creeping bent grass—merely different. As stressed in Chapter 8, these are our cousins, not our ancestors.

Further, fitness as used by evolutionary theorists is *not* an across-the-board characteristic some people possess more of than others. Fitness must be specified with respect to a particular environmental niche. Some characteristics render an individual fit in one setting but not in another. And fitness means the capacity to reproduce. Oversimplified versions of the theory of evolution overlook these distinctions.

These are not difficult ideas, but psychologists concerned with intelligence have often misinterpreted them. "Intelligence" has been used as a synonym for fitness, although its criterion has been success in school and not reproductive capacity. (That's a topic for discussion: What do school success and procreation have in common?) Intelligence tests have been used to arrange people in rank order according to their presumed fitness.

Steven Gould (1981) observes that people are tempted to create over and over again what is called *The Great Chain of Being:* the ultimate rank order. We see this in the handicapping of tennis players, in record countdowns on Top 40 radio stations, in class ranks. Darwin's theory was made palatable, perhaps, by using it to create yet another chain, one with people at the top end (and with Englishmen as the epitome of the epitome). And intelligence tests fit nicely into this distortion of Darwinian thought, because they confirmed the assumptions by English and American psychologists about the relative standing of different ethnic groups. Intelligence was seen as unitary, because only one line in which to stand existed, and intelligence was biologically based, because—after all—fitness and worth run in families (and races).

Intelligence tests were used to screen immigrants at Ellis Island.

Howard Gardner disagrees with almost all of these ideas about intelligence. In particular, he criticizes the assumption that intelligence is unitary. Other critics have also suggested that humans have several independent capacities, but their efforts have foundered because they relied on a single line of evidence to identify what these might be. In contrast, Gardner looks for convergence among several sources of evidence:

> Studies of prodigies, gifted individuals, brain-damaged individuals, *idiot savants,* normal children, normal adults, experts in different lines of work, and individuals from different cultures. (1983, p. 9)

What does Gardner look for to identify an intelligence, which he regards as a relatively autonomous human competence? He looks for its isolation in special populations (like individuals with brain damage). He looks for its development in specific individuals (like prodigies) or cultures. And he looks for agreement among experts about the core abilities involved in a particular skill.

Gardner takes a good scientific tack, looking for evidence from sources that have proven difficult for previous theories. No better example of such a troublesome source from the perspective of typical views of intelligence exists than that of **savants:** individuals who possess an extraordinary ability that stands out against mediocrity or even deficiency in all other areas (Treffert, 1989). That a person who is "retarded" by the measure of a typical intelligence test is capable of creating a beautiful sculpture, or of playing flawless music, or of performing lightning-fast calculations is impossible to explain if intelligence is regarded as unitary. But if independent intelligences exist, such striking individuals are no longer anomalous.

Similarly, Gardner looks for evidence of precocious accomplishment. Thanks to *Amadeus,* we are all familiar with Mozart's musical feats at an early age. Gardner cites other examples from different domains. Jean-Paul Sartre was a thoroughly fluent speaker and writer by age five. Saul Kripke worked through algebra on his own by the time he was in fourth grade. Other than their singular skills, each of these prodigies was otherwise a child, and this is precisely Gardner's point when he argues that people have multiple intelligences. One intelligence may far outstrip all others.

He requires that an ability be plausibly linked to the evolutionary history of our species. Can a case be made that a particular competence has been adaptive, granted what we know about the niche of our ancestors? Does linguistic skill, for instance, confer an advantage on a population of early hominids? Notice that Gardner does *not* use circular reasoning to argue that intelligence has an inherited basis.

From the convergence of the various lines of evidence, Gardner identifies these intelligences:

- Linguistic
- Musical
- Logical-Mathematical

Savants: Individuals who possess an extraordinary skill while displaying mediocrity or even deficiency in all other areas.

- Spatial
- Bodily-Kinesthetic
- Personal

All of these are self-explanatory except the last intelligence, by which Gardner means the ability to have access to one's own feelings and the ability to make distinctions among others.

Gardner admits that his particular scheme of multiple intelligence is tentative. The evidence he cites was not gathered for the purpose of testing his theory, and, to date, no full-blown investigation of the theory has occurred. Measures for all the intelligences do not yet exist.

Still, I think Gardner's theory is important enough to be included here. It is important because it is a sophisticated application of the theory of evolution to individual differences. It shows that a biologically based scheme of human capacities need not be simplistic. It need not assume The Great Chain of Being. It need not be circular, since it starts with each capacity, not an ambiguous measure.

Suppose trait theorists had followed this example rather than the one they did? Gardner begins with the capacities he wants to explain. He proceeds by taking into account findings from biology, neurology, anthropology, and so on. In short, he is concerned with behavior. Contrast this with personality psychologists who start with a trait and then search for the behaviors to which it might apply. Gardner gives examples of how people differ in terms of a particular intelligence: what they concretely do or do not do that shows a given level of intelligence. He shows how intelligences determine adaptation, not just for contemporary people, but for our ancestors.

Gardner's approach contrasts with typical theories of intelligence because it is hopeful. It does not reduce all ability to a single number; instead, it allows for variety in the way people combine their different intelligences. Consider government leaders. They can do their jobs well in any of a number of ways: with linguistic intelligence (making speeches), with mathematical intelligence (planning budgets), with personal intelligence (telling citizens what they need to hear). Imagine the numerous ways these skills can be meshed.

Gardner takes great pains to explain that these intelligences are not immutable. In fact, his ultimate goal for the theory of multiple intelligences is to speak to educators about the ways these different abilities can be cultivated. In particular, he hopes his theory will bring about an end to the Western tendency to devalue all intelligences except the logical-mathematical.

Imagine the trait paradigm had it been modeled on the theory of multiple intelligences. First, trait theorists would start with specific behaviors in particular settings, rather than with broad traits. Second, attention to a single dimension of personality would be secondary to consideration of profiles of traits. Third, applications would cultivate traits instead of merely measure them. As you saw in Chapter 9, contemporary trait psychologists are now doing such things, but it took decades of "false starts."

Applications within the trait paradigm are numerous and controversial. Individual differences are assessed in a variety of domains and used to predict people's successes and failures. In this chapter, I described several such applications of the trait paradigm: psychodiagnosis, the heritability of psychopathology, personality disorders, criminality, racial differences in personality, career counseling, personnel selection, political polls, consumer behavior, television polls, and jury selection. These applications are controversial because they may not accomplish their stated purpose. In some cases, assessment procedures give the wrong answer. I described how individuals may deliberately confound applications of the trait paradigm, creating for themselves high scores on tests and measures used to make important decisions.

I concluded the chapter by considering how these applications would differ if the trait paradigm had once upon a time been influenced by a different conception of intelligence. To this end, I described Howard Gardner's theory of multiple intelligences, which proposes that "intelligence" is not a single entity.

COGNITIVE-BEHAVIORAL PARADIGM: THEORY

he last of the personality paradigms I want to consider is the most recent to take form. The cognitive-behavioral paradigm combines earlier cognitive theories with learning theories to result in a view of the person as engaged in a constant give-and-take with the world. Importantly, the "world" is defined in terms of how individuals see it, so their thoughts and beliefs are accorded central importance. Also importantly, the "person" is seen as highly responsive to the demands of the world, so personalities are expected to be very much in flux, across both time and situation.

After discussing common theoretical emphases, I will describe the origins of the cognitive-behavioral paradigm. It stems from the work of gestalt psychologists on the one hand and behaviorists on the other. Then I'll consider George Kelly's personal construct theory, an account of personality based on an elaboration of the person-as-scientist metaphor, discussed earlier in the book (Chapter 1). If you are looking for a giant figure in this chapter—a counterpart to Freud, Maslow, Rogers, and Allport—then Kelly certainly fits the bill. Next I'll consider different versions of social learning theory, which uses principles of learning to explain complex social behavior. Over the years, as social learning theory has been revised and updated, it has come to epitomize the cognitive-behavioral approach.

THE FAMILY RESEMBLANCE OF
COGNITIVE-BEHAVIORAL THEORIES

The basic premise of the cognitive-behavioral paradigm is that people are best understood in terms of their interdependence with the world. The two determine each other. Indeed, in the typical cognitive-behavioral theory, it is impossible to separate the person from the world. Kurt Lewin (1951), for example, made the apparently simple statement that

$$B = f(P,E)$$

Behavior (B) is a function (f) of the person (P) and the environment (E). This becomes a more sophisticated proposal when we realize that Lewin defined the environment as a perceived reality that can only be understood from the viewpoint of the individual. And individuals in turn are defined by their perceptions of the relationship between themselves and the world. In other words, they can only be understood by taking into account their settings. And here we enter a hall of mirrors. The world reflects the person, the person reflects the world, and so on and so forth.

The distinction between physical reality and perceived reality is critical to this paradigm. For example, environmental psychologists speak of *density* on the one hand (how many people are packed into a particular space) and *crowding* on the other (the psychological experience of density). Sharing the backseat of a subcompact is usually an unpleasant experience, unless the person shoved up against you is your sweetheart. Then you feel warm all over. How you interpret the situation dictates your reactions to it. And your reactions in turn determine your future interpretations. Suppose you find that you don't like sharing a backseat with someone? You will probably not fantasize about spending the rest of your life with that person.

So, once reality is conceived in terms of a person's perceptions, then what and how he or she thinks become important. All cognitive-behavioral theories regard cognition as critical. Other theories so far described are also cognitive in that they recognize the importance of a person's mental life. Psychoanalysis can be conceived as a cognitive theory (Erdelyi, 1985), as can Allport's approach. What sets cognitive-behavioral theories apart from these other theories is their assumption that individuals' thoughts are primary characteristics of their personalities.

The distinction between cognitive-behavioral theories and humanistic theories is more subtle. In both, an emphasis is placed on conscious thoughts. Those who work within the cognitive-behavioral paradigm are highly sympathetic to the goal of phenomenology; they assume people can convey much of what is pertinent about their thoughts and beliefs through introspection and self-report. However, in contrast to the humanistic approach, cognitive-behavioral theories are unabashedly deterministic. One's thoughts reflect not choice and will but rather processes of learning (Bandura, 1989). Granted that individuals have learned a given way of seeing the world, they behave accordingly. They cannot help but do so.

At the same time, cognitive-behavioral theorists assume that a person's personality can and does change quite readily in response to a particular situation. Here is where processes of learning become so important to this approach. As people interact with the world, they come to discern its texture, not least of which is the pattern of rewards and punishments. Most of these theorists assume people are **hedonists** who try to maximize pleasure and minimize pain. This hedonistic tendency drives the learning process.

Hedonist: One who seeks to maximize pleasure and minimize pain.

Indeed, most cognitive-behavioral theories see people as active agents who do more than simply react to stimuli. They additionally try to understand their world to make it an easier place in which to live. Theories typically assume that people try to make their understanding more accurate, more precise, and more consistent. On the whole, these tendencies should lead them to greater happiness.

Despite everyone's supposed goal of happiness, not all achieve it. Hedonism is thwarted for several reasons. People may find themselves in a setting that does not provide plentiful rewards. They may lack the skills to attain these rewards. Or they may be operating under assumptions that prove unproductive. For example, people's attempts to be consistent in their thinking can backfire if they are thereby led to overlook alternatives.

The good news here is that change is possible, in either the world, the person, or both. Many cognitive-behavioral theorists are therapists, and they have devised a variety of strategies that facilitate change. As you might imagine, their techniques stress the interplay between the person and the world. We saw in Chapter 6 that the success of psychoanalytic therapy has long been doubted. Cognitive-behavioral therapies, in contrast, are seen as unambiguously successful, so much so that these approaches dominate contemporary clinical psychology.

Is there a downside to cognitive-behavioral theorizing? Although it sounds reasonable to propose that "people and their worlds constantly influence each other," this statement leads easily to the assertion that "everything is related to everything." This only invites muddling. Not knowing where to start, theorists and researchers can only throw up their hands in the face of what seems like overwhelming complexity.

It is true that the cognitive-behavioral paradigm gets muddled at times. Problems can be avoided, however, by keeping the focus concrete. Let me explain. Cognitive theories pay attention to a person's thoughts and beliefs about the world—not a general world but the specific one in which he or she lives. Any given transaction between the person and the world therefore has a particular causal structure (Bandura, 1986). In the abstract, everything is potentially related to everything else, but in the concrete, relations are often much more simple, because causes work over time (Kihlstrom & Harackiewicz, 1990).

Despite similarities, the various cognitive-behavioral theories differ. Some emphasize cognition more than behavior, or vice versa. Each theory favors particular cognitive constructs, which means that the cognitive-behavioral paradigm ignites the same debate that occurs within the trait paradigm over the theoretical terms most suitable for describing personality. Perhaps the biggest point of contention is the degree to which cognitive terms are general versus circumscribed. Some theorists propose broad styles of thinking deployed across all situations. Other theorists regard cognitive variables as closely tied to particular situations and hence not at all general.

Cognitive content: Particular thoughts and beliefs.

Here is a rough classification of terms used by cognitive theorists. **Cognitive content** refers to a person's particular items of knowledge, beliefs, attitudes, and values: "Space is the final frontier." "My telephone number is 476-0013." "I detest cabbage and all things made with cabbage." "The grade I will get in this course has nothing to do with how hard I work." "The most important goal for humanity is the continuation of humanity." Note that each statement contains a specific item of information.

Cognitive style (structure): Inter-relations among thoughts and beliefs.

Cognitive style (or **structure**) describes the interrelations among a person's beliefs. So, in thinking about political events, you might have a simple view of matters: "My political party is composed of good people who favor good policies, while other political parties are composed of individuals who are simply trying to get rich." Or you might have a complex view of yourself: "I'm not a good student, but I'm an excellent athlete; as a friend, I'm getting more and more conscientious, but I'm not where I want to be yet." Note how specific items of information are related to each other—redundantly in the first case, independently in the second.

Cognitive process: Ways thoughts and beliefs originate or change.

Cognitive process refers to the ways a person arrives at beliefs or changes them. Many theorists suggest that our beliefs are characterized by harmony or balance. We therefore admit new information readily if it confirms already-held beliefs. In contrast, we resist new information to the degree it contradicts what we already think. By this view, first impressions can be highly influential, because they provide the framework for understanding second impressions. I remember a "Peanuts" cartoon where Linus explained that he only shined the front halves of his shoes, because it didn't matter what people thought of him when he left the room.

More exactly, perhaps, people interpret future experience in light of past experience. Beliefs have inertia, and theories of change must acknowledge this aspect of the process.

The distinctions among content, style, and process are not always easy to draw, so you should regard these categories as rough. They help me decide what about cognition I can ascertain by simply asking someone questions, and what about cognition I should assess in other ways. Content—but not process—is usually available to a person's awareness.

ANTECEDENTS OF COGNITIVE-BEHAVIORAL THEORIES

As mentioned several times, the cognitive-behavioral paradigm results from the relatively recent combination of two earlier lines of theorizing, one stemming from gestalt psychology and the other from behaviorism. Before we talk about particular cognitive-behavioral approaches, let us discuss these ancestors, starting with gestalt psychology.

Gestalt Psychology and Personality

In Chapter 2, I sketched several key assumptions of gestalt psychology. First, the basic substance of psychology is not elements but relationships. Indeed, the word *gestalt* means whole, pattern, or configuration. Second, some relationships are more psychologically basic than others, so we have an automatic tendency to move toward these so-called good gestalts. Third, people are self-regulating systems, tending toward balance and harmony.

Although the original gestalt psychologists were concerned with molecular activities like perception and learning, other theorists applied these basic assumptions to complex behavior, including what we mean by *personality*. Particularly notable here is Kurt Lewin (1890–1947). Lewin immigrated to the United States from Germany prior to World War II. His subsequent influence on personality psychology was immense.

Lewin (1935) called the psychological field where behavior occurs the **life space,** which he defined as the sum of all forces acting on a person at a particular time. By *forces* he means both internal and external factors, everything from biological needs to environmental stimuli, that can potentially influence behavior. Note the use of the qualifier "potentially"; whether a particular factor indeed affects what someone does depends on the other forces present and their particular mesh. Lewin included only contemporary forces, not influences from the past or the future. This emphasis on the here-and-now was an important aspect of his approach to personality, one that still characterizes many cognitive-behavioral theories in general. The past and the future affect behavior only to the degree that representations of them appear in the present life space.

The life space is divided into regions or sections. Lewin stressed that people are not perfectly unified; to varying degrees, personality is segmented. Each region has a particular *valence;* that is, it may be positive or negative for the individual, depending on whatever needs are operating at that particular moment. If you are hungry, then a bag of Fritos probably has a positive valence for you. If you are feeling discouraged, then a difficult school assignment probably has a negative valence.

Lewin revealed his gestalt background by his interest in *states of equilibrium:* conditions where forces are perfectly balanced. What happens when disequilibrium prevails? The pattern of needs and valences present at a given moment sets into motion activities aimed at reducing the tension an individual is experiencing. This process restores equilibrium to the life space and allows the individual to attain a good gestalt.

Equilibrium can be restored in any of a number of ways. The hungry person can eat the Fritos, for instance, and thereby reduce his hunger. Or he can count the money in his pocket and realize that he doesn't have enough to buy Fritos and must buy a candy bar instead. Or he can think of the inches around his waist that he wants to lose and see the Fritos as threatening his goal, thereby changing their valence from positive to negative.

Lewin described various properties of the life space, one important characteristic being the number of regions present at a given time. A life space with numerous regions has more **differentiation,** so we can expect behavior

Life space: According to Lewin, all the forces acting on a person at a particular time; also, a person's mental representation of the relationship between the self and the world.

Differentiation: According to Lewin, the degree to which one's life space is divided into numerous regions at a given time.

within it to be more complex in the sense that it is influenced by more forces. In contrast, a life space with few regions is undifferentiated. Consider the example of terror (Hall & Lindzey, 1978). You hear a bump in the night while walking down a dark street, and you are overcome with fright. At that moment, the noise is the only "fact" in your psychological reality, and you respond to it (and nothing else). You freak out! As time passes, we hope your life space becomes more differentiated. You perceive a safe area under a street light. Now your life space has two "facts," and you act accordingly: You flee danger and seek safety. You may, however, dart across the street and into the path of a passing car, which has a tangible existence in physical reality but not in your psychological reality.

One of Lewin's most famous experiments demonstrated that 4-year-old children when frustrated behave like 2-year-old children (Barker, Dembo, & Lewin, 1941). This experimental study of *regression* shows that frustration can simplify an individual's life space. Behavior becomes more primitive because the life space has fewer regions.

More generally, Lewin conceived personality development in terms of differentiation of the life space. Although regression may occur, as just described, people on the whole develop an increasing number of regions (Hall & Lindzey, 1978). So, consider how distinctions along the dimension of time (past, present, and future) allow people to view themselves and the world differently: "That was yesterday!" Similarly, distinctions along the dimension of reality lead to a more differentiated life space: "You're dreaming!"

Organization is another key concept for understanding development in Lewin's terms. Not only do the regions of a life space become more numerous over the life span, they also become more interdependent, coordinated, and integrated—adults are more able than children to combine separate activities into a whole. What makes this possible is an organization of life space regions into a hierarchy. Children's regions exist at the same level; influence among them is a simple give-and-take. Adults' regions exist at different levels; influence is thus more complex. A 5-year-old girl fingerpaints because she loves it; her 30-year-old father paints the outside of their house *in order to* improve its appearance, *in order to* increase its value, *in order to* sell it at a profit, *in order to* move to a neighborhood with better schools, *in order to* educate the little girl as well as possible because he loves her and her fingerpainting.

Another important characteristic of the life space describes the nature of the connections among its regions. According to Lewin, regions have varying degrees of influence on each other. He called this influence **accessibility** and proposed that the more accessible two regions were, the more they could mutually influence each other. Accessibility is a direct function of the number of barriers between two regions. Suppose you still have a hankering for Fritos, and they are on sale at the local convenience store. But suppose further that you have no money on hand, that the only place to cash a check is on the other side of town, that your car has a flat tire, that it is freezing cold outside, and that you don't have a heavy coat. You can surmount all of these problems, I would think, but the number of intermediate steps between you and the Fritos makes it unlikely the steps will influence you to get them.

Organization: According to Lewin, the interdependence, coordination, and integration of one's life space.

Accessibility: According to Lewin, the degree to which two cognitive regions influence one another.

Yet another characteristic of the life space is the rigidity versus fluidity of boundaries between regions. In some life spaces, regions respond slowly and inflexibly to the influence of other regions. These are *rigid* boundaries and may be illustrated by an individual whose political beliefs (in Region A) are unswayed by available information to the contrary (in Region B). In contrast, other regions have *fluid* boundaries. Influence occurs across them suddenly.

In presenting his ideas, Lewin took a mathematical approach, phrasing his concepts with formal equations borrowed from physics. These mathematical representations proved overly metaphorical and were never much accepted by other psychologists (e.g., Cantril, 1935; London, 1944). Nevertheless, Lewin's general approach to personality remains influential. His view of human nature still characterizes the cognitive-behavioral paradigm. People are conceived as complex systems acting in accordance with their view of things and seeking equilibrium within themselves and the world. Each individual's life space is different, thereby defining his or her unique personality. Terms used by later theorists have their counterparts among concepts first introduced by Lewin. None of these constructs should be confused with traits, because each is expected to change across time and situation.

Behaviorism and Personality

As noted briefly in Chapter 2, behaviorism began with John Watson's (1913) manifesto calling for psychology to concern itself with the overt actions of people and animals instead of unobservable mental events. From this beginning, the term **behaviorism** has evolved to include a broad set of emphases:

Behaviorism: The approach to psychology that concerns itself with the overt actions of people and animals.

1. The explanation of observable behavior is the most important goal for psychology.
2. Behavior can be explained from the bottom up, by emphasizing what animals and people have in common.
3. The most basic explanations are those phrased in terms of the environment.
4. Learning is the most important psychological process.
5. The method of choice for psychology is laboratory experimentation, using animals as well as people for research subjects.

Not all behaviorists endorse all of these emphases. Indeed, no single behaviorist camp exists.

Radical behaviorists are those who completely disavow all reference to unobservables. The mind and the characteristics we ascribe to it are regarded as fictions that impede the progress of psychology. Radical behaviorists are no doubt horrified by the emergence of the cognitive-behavioral approach, because they see this as a contradiction of terms (cf. Ledwidge, 1978).

Other behaviorists are willing to use mentalistic notions in their theories. These psychologists maintain the behaviorist goal of explaining overt behavior, but they believe explanation is best served by using some constructs that must be inferred rather than directly observed. It is these individuals who have contributed most directly to the cognitive-behavioral paradigm.

Learning: A change in behavior due to interaction with the environment.

From its beginning, behaviorism has concerned itself with how we interact with the environment and how our behavior changes as a result of that interaction. These changes are called **learning.** As a sophomore in college, I took Psychology 248—Learning, and I expected the course to be devoted to what I did in the library Sunday through Thursday evenings: studying lecture notes, outlining book chapters, working problems, and so on. Instead, the course was devoted to how dogs came to salivate in the presence of Russian scientists, to how cats learned to escape from boxes where they had been imprisoned by Ivy League professors, and to how lists of nonsense words like GLP, BZT, and XRM were memorized by German philosophers. This information was interesting enough, and I "learned" it pretty well. But I had trouble understanding why psychologists regarded these activities as instances of learning. I now understand. Maybe I can save you similar confusion.

Psychologists interested in learning take a broad view of their subject matter. They start by considering all possible changes in behavior, some of which can be attributed to biological processes like maturation or fatigue. The rest can only be due to one's interaction with the environment. From a broad view, these latter changes share more in common with each other than not. All are considered learning. (To reserve "learning" for changes in behavior resulting from higher education is overly restrictive and ultimately arbitrary.)

Behaviorists are interested in simple examples of learning precisely because of their simplicity. If one assumes that all forms of learning share a common essence, then why not study forms that are easy to study? With hindsight, we can criticize this assumption made by the early learning psychologists (see, e.g., Gardner, 1985). At the same time, we can see it as a reasonable strategy on their part. If physics and chemistry have profited greatly by studying pared down versions of their subject matter in the laboratory, then why not psychology?

Among learning theorists, considerable debate has occurred about the best way to depict learning. Do different types of learning exist, or is one type primary? If one form of learning is primary, which one is it? Instead of giving you an overview of this debate, I will describe the major types of learning stressed by different behavioral theories. In each case, I'll try to sketch the role this type of learning plays in human behavior. Keep in mind that at least some behaviorists regard each type as a general explanation of behavior and behavioral change.

Classical Conditioning **Classical conditioning** is the form of learning first described by the Russian physiologist Ivan Pavlov at the turn of the century. You should be familiar with classical conditioning and its terminology from your introductory psychology course. An **unconditioned stimulus** that elicits some **unconditioned response** is repeatedly paired with some environmental event, like a sound. This event eventually becomes a **conditioned stimulus** and comes to elicit a version of the original behavior, now termed a **conditioned response.**

Classical conditioning: A form of learning where an originally neutral stimulus, when paired with another stimulus capable of eliciting a reflexive response, comes to elicit that response itself; also called Pavlovian conditioning.

Unconditioned stimulus: In classical conditioning, the stimulus that can elicit a particular behavior as a reflex, without learning.

Unconditioned response: In classical conditioning, the behavior elicited by the unconditioned stimulus.

Conditioned stimulus: In classical conditioning, the originally neutral stimulus paired with the unconditioned stimulus.

Conditioned response: In classical conditioning, the behavior elicited by the conditioned stimulus.

Russian psychologist Ivan Pavlov described classical conditioning at the turn of the century.

A familiar instance of classical conditioning is the phenomenon of taste aversion (Logue, 1979). Have you ever drunk too much alcohol and become horribly ill? Suppose this happened, and the culprit was tequila. The alcohol in this liquor is the unconditioned stimulus, and your vomiting is the unconditioned response. The former led to the latter not through learning but through a biological reflex that protects you from poisoning yourself.

When you later smell tequila and feel queasy as a result, the smell is the conditioned stimulus and your queasiness is the conditioned response. Note that alcohol was what made you sick, not the smell or taste of tequila per se. But because of classical conditioning, you have learned to respond this way to tequila.

Classical conditioning was enthusiastically endorsed by John Watson as the key to understanding all of human learning. But a more circumscribed view is now in favor: Classical conditioning is implicated mostly in our learning of emotional reactions (Schwartz, 1984). This is still an important aspect of the human condition.

Extinction: In classical conditioning, the cessation of pairing of the unconditioned stimulus and the conditioned stimulus.

Fears and phobias may arise through classical conditioning. I was once mugged on a dark street by a group of young men. For years afterward, my heart beat faster when I walked along a street at night and had to pass an alley. If I saw a group of fellows on the street, I came close to panicking. But, over the years, my fear has gradually undergone **extinction,** because dark streets and young men were never again paired with trauma. In other words, the conditioned stimulus (dark street) no longer occurred with the unconditioned stimulus (mugging), so the conditioned response (fear) went away.

Good emotions can also be interpreted in terms of classical conditioning. A television commercial for a perfume captures this well. A young woman sees her lover on the other side of a crowded restaurant. She sprays her perfume on a piece of paper, and the waiter delivers the scent. The young man breathes deeply from the paper, becomes sexually aroused, and makes a pass at the waiter. (Well, not exactly, but you get the point.)

Some psychologists question whether these kinds of examples really reflect the operation of an automatic process of conditioning (Schwartz, 1984). Cognitive theorists, for instance, argue that emotional reactions cannot be imprinted on us without accompanying mental activity. My being fearful on dark streets after I was mugged might have been due to an expectation of danger rather than to a pairing of a stimulus with a response. If I'd been mugged in broad daylight, I'd probably still be wary on dark streets, even more so than on well-lit streets.

Instrumental Conditioning   Shortly after Pavlov described classical conditioning, the American psychologist Edward Thorndike (1911) began to study how cats learned responses that allowed them to escape from boxes. Through trial-and-error, his animal subjects learned that some responses had desirable effects (allowing them to escape), while other responses did not. The cats repeated the former responses but not the latter. Thorndike summarized this type of learning with the **Law of Effect,** so termed because animals (and people) learn behaviors according to their effects on the environment.

Law of Effect: Thorndike's proposal that reward strengthens behavior, whereas punishment weakens it.

This type of learning is called **instrumental conditioning** to stress the pragmatic (instrumental) nature of behavior. Animals and people do things that work—actions that lead to good things and avoid bad things. Another name for this is **operant conditioning,** which implies a similar point—that learning involves operations (movements) on the part of an animal or a person, followed by some consequence that determines whether or not the organism will repeat the operations in the future. In classical conditioning, environmental stimuli elicit particular responses from people or animals. In operant conditioning, the organism does something first, and then environmental stimuli follow.

This type of learning casts *hedonism* in psychological terms. Pleasure becomes positive reinforcement, whereas pain becomes punishment. Current learning psychologists use the terms reinforcement and punishment in a particular fashion, though, that cuts them loose from the mentalistic connotations of pleasure and pain. So, **positive reinforcement** is any stimulus that increases the frequency of a behavior it follows. And **punishment** is any stimulus that decreases the frequency of a behavior it follows. Note that one must see the behavioral consequences of a stimulus before one decides it is reinforcement, punishment, or neither.

By the way, a frequently misused term is **negative reinforcement,** so be careful in reading this paragraph. Negative reinforcement is not the same as

Instrumental conditioning provides a technology for training animals—and people.

Instrumental conditioning: A form of learning where a response is associated with its consequences, becoming more likely if followed by reinforcement and less likely if followed by punishment; also called operant conditioning.

Operant conditioning: See *Instrumental conditioning*.

Positive reinforcement: A stimulus that increases the frequency of a behavior it follows.

Punishment: A stimulus that decreases the frequency of a behavior it follows.

Negative reinforcement: A stimulus whose removal strengthens the frequency of a behavior it follows.

punishment. It is reinforcement because a person or animal—by definition—increases the frequency of the behavior it follows. What they achieve, though, is relief from some stimulus. For example, a negative reinforcer is the threat of a poor credit rating that someone can avoid by paying a bill before it is due.

In and of itself, the Law of Effect is somewhat limited in terms of what it can explain. However, as elaborated over the years by different theorists, most notably B. F. Skinner (1938), instrumental conditioning has become an extremely powerful explanation of human behavior. In fact, additional concepts have been introduced precisely to bolster the Law of Effect in the face of questions about its breadth.

For instance, if behaviors must be emitted before they can be reinforced, how can we learn to do things we've never done before? The idea of **shaping** answers this question. We learn new behaviors by having our past behaviors gradually shaped into them through reinforcement and punishment. A common example is teaching your dog to roll over. You don't sit around holding some treat in your hand waiting for Fido to flip. The treat will spoil before the dog performs the behavior you want to reward him for. Instead, you start by rewarding Fido first for holding still on command. When he starts to do that pretty well, you reward him for his occasional listing to one side. Eventually he'll fall on the ground. (Maybe because he's weighted down from the 10,000 treats you've given him.) You keep reinforcing him for *successive approximations* to the desired behavior. If the two of you are patient enough, he will learn to roll over. According to learning theorists, all complex behavior is learned in this way.

Relatedly, what accounts for the novelty of behavior? We don't always do things in exactly the same way or in exactly the same situation. Students don't have to be shaped from scratch each time they take a class. They know to raise their hands to be called on, to bring pencils and notebooks to class, to go to the bookstore for texts, and so on. What they are doing is termed **generalization** of past learning to new circumstances.

And if generalization of instrumental conditioning occurs, why is it not rampant? Students learn to raise their hand to be called on in class; however, they usually do not do so on a date or on the job. Generalization of learning is curbed by **discrimination.** What we learn is taken to new situations, but hardly to all of them. The more dissimilar two situations, the more likely we are to discriminate between them.

Why does behavior occur in the absence of obvious reinforcement? This is the biggest problem in using instrumental conditioning to explain the bulk of human behavior. Mundane reality presents us with neither pleasure nor pain; to encounter either one, we usually have to wait for Friday afternoon and Monday morning (respectively). But we keep on behaving at other times.

Here are several concepts that explain why we behave in the absence of obvious reinforcement. The first is **chaining.** Suppose we learn some response that leads to a reward. No problem. Well, we will also learn a second response that gives us the opportunity to perform the first response (that leads to the reward). And we will learn a third response that leads to the second that leads

Shaping: A process by which complex behaviors can be gradually learned; successive forms of the desired behavior are reinforced as they come to resemble the target behavior.

Generalization: The performance of behavior in situations where it was not originally learned.

Discrimination: The nonperformance of behavior in situations where it was not originally learned.

Chaining: A process by which a sequence of behaviors can be learned, only the last of which is rewarded; first the last behavior is learned, then the next to last, and so on.

to the first that leads to the reward. In other words, we chain responses together. Responses at the beginning of the chain occur without obvious reward, but they ultimately lead to it. Consider grocery shopping. Early in our lives we learned that if we stood in front of the candy bars in aisle seven and pointed, someone would buy one for us. As we grew older, though, we learned a more complicated sequence of events: making a grocery list, clipping coupons, driving to the grocery store, and ending up in aisle seven once again.

A second concept is that of **secondary reinforcement.** Some stimuli are reinforcing because of their biological character: food, water, safety, and so on. Other stimuli become reinforcing through association with these primary reinforcers. Social approval, for instance, is a secondary reinforcer for most of us, because we learned as infants that approval from our parents went hand-in-hand with attention to our basic biological needs.

A final way to explain behavior in the absence of obvious reinforcement is with the notion of **schedules of reinforcement** (Ferster & Skinner, 1957). People (and animals) need not be reinforced after every particular response in order to learn that response. Instead, reinforcement can be delivered on a variety of schedules: after every third response, after four minutes have elapsed, on alternate Fridays, and so on. These different patterns of reinforcement all maintain behavior. In fact, under some circumstances, highly intermittent reinforcement can lead to a frenzy of responding. Some learning theorists cite gambling as an example of behavior reinforced by the most infrequent of rewards.

Secondary reinforcement: An originally neutral stimulus that becomes reinforcing because it has been paired with reinforcers.

Schedules of reinforcement: Patterns by which reinforcement occurs—after every behavior, after every 10th behavior, and so on.

Intermittent reinforcement can lead to highly persistent responding.

With concepts like shaping, generalization, discrimination, chaining, secondary reinforcement, and so on, instrumental conditioning has wide applicability. I sometimes ask my students to think of an example of some behavior or response that appears *not* to be the product of operant conditioning. They have a lot of trouble doing this.

Prepared Learning   Some things are easier to learn than other things. Everybody knows this, but appreciate that this truism is not included in traditional accounts of classical and instrumental conditioning. Instead, learning theorists have assumed that all learning occurs in the same fashion. In light of this assumption, any differences in learning are dismissed as unimportant. However, this simplifying assumption has been successfully challenged in recent years. Some theorists argue that learning can be difficult or easy according to an organism's biological predispositions (e.g., Revusky & Garcia, 1970; Rozin & Kalat, 1971).

Think back to my example of taste aversion. This phenomenon is so common that we overlook one of its striking characteristics. When we drink too much tequila and get sick, what is it that later makes us nauseous? Classical conditioning predicts that we should be conditioned to all stimuli associated with the experience. But this doesn't happen. We are nauseated by the smell and taste of the liquor—not by bottles or glasses, or salt, lemons, or bars. Taste aversion is highly specific. We associate illness with tastes and smells, not with other stimuli.

This observation has been confirmed in studies with rats (e.g., Garcia & Koelling, 1966). The association between illnesses and tastes is easy for rats to learn. But even when sights or sounds are repeatedly paired with illness, no conditioning occurs. Martin Seligman (1970) suggests that the ease versus difficulty of learning such associations can be explained by considering the evolutionary significance of the learning.

An animal that readily associates particular tastes or smells with gastric disturbance has a survival advantage over other animals, because it will therefore learn to avoid foods that will make it sick. Over the eons, animals that learn this link quickly will survive and pass on their predisposition. Seligman calls such predisposition **prepared learning.**

In contrast, an animal that readily associates sights or sounds with gastric disturbance is a confused creature, since that's not the way its body works. Again, through evolution, this tendency has therefore been selected against. What results, in Seligman's terminology, is **contraprepared learning.**

Placing learning in an evolutionary context goes against typical behaviorism and its emphasis on the particular environment in the here and now. And while the full implications of prepared learning are still being explored, some agree that human phobias can be explained in these terms (e.g., Ohman, Fredrickson, Hugdahl, & Rimmo, 1976; Seligman, 1971). What is striking about phobias is how narrow they are. People develop phobias to spiders and snakes, not to electric outlets and guns. Are these arbitrary facts, or do they reveal something about the evolution of our species?

Prepared learning: According to Seligman, learning that occurs quite readily because of natural selection.

Contraprepared learning: According to Seligman, learning that occurs with great difficulty because of natural selection.

Insight Learning   Classical and instrumental conditioning share the assumption that learning is a gradual process, built up by repeated pairings of stimuli and responses. Prepared learning suggests that this process can be speeded up if it involves a biologically predisposed link, but it still emphasizes that learning results from an accumulation of associations.

Some psychologists disagree that learning is a gradual process. They argue that learning can occur in leaps and bounds, that people have "Aha" experiences. As you might imagine, these psychologists invoke cognitive language to explain learning. We don't learn associations between stimuli and responses through some automatic process; instead, we learn relationships, solutions, plans, and schemes through an active process of problem solving and hypothesis testing. Learning occurs when we see the answer.

There is a drastic difference between learning achieved through associations and learning achieved through insights. Both interpretations of learning attribute changes in our behavior to our interactions with the environment. But where conditioning stresses learned responses, **insight learning** stresses cognitions. What happens when a rat learns to run through a maze in order to get some food? A conditioning explanation would say he has learned to run 20 paces forward, turn left, run 10 more paces, and turn right. A cognitive explanation would say he has learned a map of the maze.

Insight learning: A form of learning characterized by the sudden grasping of relationships, solutions, or plans.

In support of cognitive learning, psychologist Edward Tolman (1948) has argued that rats (and people) learn by forming mental representations. In his experiments, he tested his explanation against the alternative notion that learning involves only responses. Take, for example, the rat who learned to run the maze. Suppose we flood the maze, so the rat must swim through it to get the food, soggy though it may be. If all the rat had learned to do was chain together different responses, then he should not be able to find the treat. These responses are irrelevant in a flooded maze. But if he has a cognitive map, he can successfully traverse the maze, even though the required responses are now entirely different. And when Tolman tested this, the rat was actually able to swim the maze, illustrating his argument.

Another example of insight learning comes from the research of Wolfgang Kohler (1924), whom I mentioned in Chapter 2. Kohler was one of the founders of gestalt psychology, so he was interested in relations. According to Kohler, learning consisted of seeing how one's means could lead to one's ends. He studied problem solving among chimpanzees, placing them in situations where trial-and-error learning was not possible. If a banana is hanging from the ceiling beyond one's reach, and if a stick is in the room, then "insight" leads to the use of the stick to reach the banana. Learning occurs all at once.

Who is right—those who emphasize conditioning or those who emphasize insight? In my view, both emphases are warranted, depending on the particular behavior learned. As I mentioned earlier, learning theorists have argued long and hard about which type of learning is primary. A more profitable strategy might instead be to ask which type of learning is implicated in which type of behavior.

SOURCE: "The Far Side" cartoon by Gary Larson is reproduced by permission of Chronicle Features, San Francisco.

Insight learning is clearly an important component of so-called intelligent behavior. If I've locked the keys inside my car, I don't start emitting behaviors at random. Instead, I study the situation and consider various ways to gain entry. Are any windows open? Have I left spare keys anyplace? Can I force the door? Where can I get a coat hanger? Do I have the money for a locksmith?

Trial-and-error learning also has its place. If I've found a coat hanger to open the door, I have to fish around with it before I master the process. I have to experiment with bending little hooks at its end. And if I do open the door this way, it wasn't because I achieved insight into the way to manipulate the coat hanger. I was lucky, and the next time I lock my keys in the car, I'll again have to go through a number of failed responses before one works.

Conclusions   On the face of it, the different types of learning vary greatly in their complexity. Classical and instrumental conditioning seem by far the most simple, ostensibly automatic processes by which associations are formed through repetition. Insight learning seems much more complex because it relies on active thinking.

However, the opinion among some learning theorists today is that all types of learning, including conditioning, involve cognitive processes. These theorists stress the fact that conditioning occurs most readily to informative stimuli (e.g., Kamin, 1969). In other words, animals and people only learn associations that tell them something new about the world. Once this perspective on learning is taken, we begin to see all types of learning as adding to one's knowledge. What is learned must therefore have a mental representation.

The important point is that such a view of learning is highly compatible with theories like Lewin's. Both end up stressing thoughts and how they are influenced by what goes on in the world. Both end up agreeing that personality is defined by how one acquires, represents, and utilizes knowledge. In sum, what we have is the beginning of the cognitive-behavioral paradigm. Subsequent theorists have fleshed out the details of this view, and it is to their contributions we will shortly turn.

In passing, let me note that not all behaviorists have joined forces with cognitive theorists. The well-known psychologist B. F. Skinner (1904–1990) never departed from his stance as a radical behaviorist, always regarding cognitive approaches as obstacles to psychology as a science (e.g., Skinner, 1987). His view of human nature has no room for thoughts and beliefs. Indeed, it has no room for what we typically mean by personality.

Remember from Chapter 1 that *personality* refers to characteristics that are general, characteristic, enduring, integrated, and functional. Behaviorists like Skinner tend to believe that these aspects of people do not exist. Rather, people and their behavior are shaped entirely by the pattern of rewards and punishments that prevails in a particular environment. As the environment changes, so, too, does behavior, and we are thus left with nothing general, characteristic, enduring, or integrated for personality psychologists to explain.

The only place where radical behaviorism makes contact with the typical goals of personality psychology is in a shared concern with human function and dysfunction. Here, radical behaviorists provide persuasive explanations of how and why people's behavior may go awry. And their techniques of behavior modification often help to alleviate such problems. We will return to the radical behaviorists in Chapter 13, where our focus will be on applications within the cognitive-behavioral paradigm.

GEORGE KELLY: PERSONAL CONSTRUCT THEORY

The intellectual history of George Kelly is difficult to uncover. Who and what influenced his personal construct theory? Unlike other major personality theorists, who can be readily placed in historical and cultural contexts that explain why their theories took the form they did, Kelly seems to be a natural. He did not grow up in a cosmopolitan city like Vienna. He did not attend a notable school like Harvard University or the University of London. He did not have a famous mentor like Galton, Freud, or Jung. Instead, he worked largely on his own, publishing his personality theory in two volumes in 1955, to the literal astonishment of the academic community. In a review of the work, Jerome Bruner (1956) termed it "a genuine new departure and spirited contribution to the psychology of personality" (p. 356). George Kelly, in a very real sense, is the Rocky Balboa of personality psychology.

Kelly's Life

The details of Kelly's life are certainly no mystery, and they do shed some light on the origins of his personal construct theory. And many who review these facts locate Kelly's theory in his life experiences—not in his formal education.

Kelly lived from 1905 to 1967. Among other activities, like studying physics and mathematics, Kelly was a self-taught clinician. He worked in Kansas during the Great Depression, trying out a variety of approaches, keeping those that worked and discarding those that did not. There he began to develop a system of therapy that focused on a client's interpretation of events. He saw that a variety of interpretations were always possible and that some were more functional than others. The seeds of his personal construct theory were planted by these insights. Indeed, in the preface to his 1955 books, Kelly describes how the theory originated in a handbook of clinical procedures.

After World War II, Kelly was appointed the director of the clinical psychology program at Ohio State University. It was here that he formally developed his theory, attracting students who have since done much to make his personal construct theory popular. One of his students was Walter Mischel, and you will see later in this chapter how Mischel's cognitive person variables bear a strong resemblance to Kelly's personal constructs.

I have asserted that cognitive theories have been influenced by gestalt psychology. Is this true of personal construct theory? Sort of, but it's hard to tell because Kelly was not one to reference the work of other psychologists (Neimeyer, 1985). He was clearly familiar with gestalt psychology; one of his earliest publications (1933) was concerned with the relationship between brain structure and perception. And in his 1955 books, Kelly says his theory is concerned with what Lewin calls the life space (p. 279).

But most people believe Kelly arrived at his cognitive theory largely through his clinical experiences on the plains of Kansas. So, although personal construct theory is consistent with many of the tenets of other cognitive approaches to personality psychology, it is not derived from them in any direct fashion.

Kelly's Theory

Constructive alternativism: Kelly's assumption that all interpretations of the universe are subject to revision or replacement.

Personal construct theory is based on a single philosophical assumption, a position Kelly terms **constructive alternativism.** According to this bedrock notion, all present interpretations of the world are subject to revision or replacement: People can always change their minds. And because they can change how they think, they can change who they are. Is this a radical idea? In the abstract, most of us would agree that one can look at events in different ways.

But in the concrete, most of us have trouble doing so. We assume our views of the world reflect the way the world really is. Views other than our own are confused, wrong, or even bad (Berger & Luckmann, 1966).

I remember vividly the first time I visited San Francisco. A friend somewhat familiar with the city gave me a tour in his car, and he kept getting lost. Twice we took a wrong turn and went over the Golden Gate Bridge. I became increasingly upset as I envisioned running out of gas, falling through the bridge, having the bridge collapse, straying into a dangerous neighborhood, and worst of all, not finding a place to go to the bathroom. The second time across the bridge, my friend turned to me and said, "Isn't this fun? I love driving across the Golden Gate Bridge."

I looked at him like he was crazy, but then I realized it was possible to view our excursion as fun. We weren't trying to go anyplace—we were just cruising San Francisco. And the bridge is one of the highlights of the city. By this time, I knew as much about the Golden Gate Bridge as did many San Francisco natives.

This is what Kelly means by constructive alternativism. I changed my interpretation of the car trip from disaster to delight, and these different interpretations had profoundly different emotional consequences (although I still had to go to the bathroom).

Lodge owner Harold Shuffle saw only the negative side of things.

SOURCE: "The Neighborhood" cartoon by Jerry Amerongen is reproduced with special permission of King Features Syndicate, Inc.

Embedded here is a statement about human nature and its relationship to the world. People do not simply respond to an objective environment. Rather, they creatively represent the environment and then respond to their representations. If you see the world as an adventure, then you embark on life with vigor and excitement. If you see the world as an obstacle course, then you run through it with fear. In other words, Kelly echoes Lewin's earlier emphasis on perceived reality. He captures it in what he calls the *fundamental postulate* of personal construct theory: "A person's processes are psychologically channelized by the ways in which he anticipates events" (Kelly, 1955, p. 46). Kelly elaborates this postulate with a number of corollaries. Together, these proposals constitute personal construct theory.

Unlike Lewin, Kelly is not interested in motives and needs. In Kelly's view of things, people seek to predict and control the world, which is not necessarily the same thing as achieving equilibrium with it. So, in Kelly's theory we find an explicit statement of the person-as-scientist metaphor. Just as scientific theories are regarded as tentative, so, too, are the "theories" of everyday people. They hold onto their views of the world as scientists do—because these views are useful in predicting and controlling events.

Sometimes people's theories get them into trouble, but they still don't discard them. For instance, consider how many problems result from our implicit assumption that others are mind readers. We may eventually discover that they were not so good at telepathy as we had assumed for so long: "Didn't you know I hated that restaurant?" "How could you forget our anniversary?" "Wasn't it obvious I didn't like that purple and orange dress?" "You surely know I hate burned toast and raw eggs more than anything in the world!"

Do examples like these invalidate the person-as-scientist metaphor? Not at all, because scientists can be as wrongheaded as everyday people. You can conduct an experiment that cannot possibly prove a particular theory wrong. We've seen this as a charge against psychodynamic research, for instance, when all possible evidence is consistent with "theoretical" prediction. When everyday people metaphorically conduct such nonfalsifiable experiments with the world, we say they are setting into operation *self-fulfilling prophecies,* acting in such a way that their beliefs cannot be proven wrong.

Imagine someone who thinks he is a social loser. Because of this belief, he doesn't speak to others, doesn't go to parties, doesn't pursue friendships. And as a result, all the evidence he confronts about himself points to the conclusion that he is indeed a loser. But this is not an objective and unchanging fact. It is the product of a particular interpretation of the world. Kelly's techniques of psychotherapy, which we will consider in Chapter 13, aim at breaking a person out of these circular interpretations.

So far I've been referring to a person's interpretations of the world in general terms. Let's get more specific. Just how do individuals frame their understanding of things? According to Kelly, the basic unit of a person's cognitive activity is the **personal construct.** In terming it *personal,* he stresses that cognitive activity belongs to a particular person. No interpretations arise without people, and all people have their own interpretations. In terming it a

Personal construct:
A category of experience.

construct, he emphasizes that the individual actively builds (constructs) his or her view of the world. Personal constructs are not imposed on a person; they are chosen.

Personal constructs are how people categorize their experiences, sorting ongoing life into bundles. Think of constructs as the pigeonholes we use as we categorize. Embedded in the idea of personal constructs is a statement about human nature: People are inherent classifiers.

Kelly proposed that personal constructs are bipolar. In other words, they have meaning only when a person classifies some experiences as *similar* and others as *dissimilar.* Consider this simple example: "I live with three other people. Two of them are college students, and the other one dropped out last year." The construct—being in college—makes sense only when there are those who fit into it and those who do not.

Individuals make sense of their experiences by assigning recurrent events to different categories. To the degree this process helps them predict and control future events, the current system of categories is kept. To the degree errors occur, their personal constructs are revised. Back in the 1960s, when I was in college, a female friend of mine always had crushes on men with long hair and beards. She explained to me that her brother had long hair and a beard, and he was a wonderful person, so she assumed other men with these characteristics would also be wonderful. She eventually discarded this assumption, because it brought her more heartbreak than not. Would-be boyfriends were no longer categorized in terms of whether or not they were hairy.

People have many constructs, and it is the total of these, what Kelly calls one's **construct system,** that defines one's personality. Perhaps you are now shaking your head and thinking that personal construct theory is hopelessly complex. Don't people have an infinite number of constructs? After all, more than 18,000 words can be used to describe personality traits (Chapter 1), and what happens when distinctions are made using "kind of . . . ," "sort of . . . ," "extremely . . . ," and "never on Sunday"?

Matters are not as complicated as you might think. People do not have an infinite number of personal constructs, because their constructs are not equivalent to their vocabulary. Consider someone who thinks all his friends are thrifty, reverent, courteous, and brave; he regards his enemies as wasteful, blasphemous, rude, and cowardly. How many personal constructs does he have? Only one, because he categorizes people—friends and enemies—redundantly with respect to thrift, reverence, courtesy, and courage. He can have an extremely rich vocabulary but a highly simple construct system. Even though he sorts his experiences into only a few categories, he uses several labels to describe these categories.

Kelly developed a procedure for measuring personal constructs, the **Role Constructs Repertory Test,** usually referred to as the **REP Test.** In one of its typical forms, the REP Test gives people the names of 20 social roles: mother, father, brother, sister, employer, friend, acquaintance, and so on. For each role, the respondent is asked to think of someone who fills it in his or her life. Then the person is asked to consider a particular triad of these people: for instance,

Construct system: A person's entire set of personal constructs.

REP Test (Role Construct Repertory Test): A procedure for assessing an individual's personal constructs; he or she is presented with triads of objects and asked to specify how two of them are alike and different from the third.

brother, employer, friend. The subject then writes down how two of these people are alike yet different from the third. Then the respondent is given another particular triad, and the procedure is repeated 15, 20, even 30 times.

Kelly assumes the REP Test gives an insight into the constructs a person uses in thinking about other people. However, the adequacy of the REP Test is hotly debated. Let me just note one obvious shortcoming of the typical form of this test: It relies on a respondent's verbalization. As I've already pointed out, personal constructs are not the same thing as words. In many cases, of course, we use verbal labels to tag our personal constructs. But we can imagine "categories" of experience that are nonverbal, that channel our behavior yet elude our labels. Clinical psychologists are usually interested in precisely these kinds of constructs.

For instance, suppose a husband is extremely resistant when his wife asks for help with the chores and errands. He suddenly remembers he has to do work at the office, call a friend on the phone, or write a letter to his brother. He never gets around to helping his wife. To the outside observer (and to his wife), it is obvious this man has a personal construct making "requests from wife" equal to "imposition → ignore." But he is unable to verbalize this category. Indeed, he may even call himself a conscientious spouse.

Assuming the comparisons and contrasts elicited by the REP Test bear a resemblance to someone's personal constructs, how is the test scored? Unlike the questionnaires described in Chapter 9 (measures of anxiety, extraversion, and the like), the REP Test does not yield a single score. Instead, a subject's responses can be used to assess a variety of cognitive characteristics.

The simplest thing you can do is to look at the substance (or meaning) of the constructs a person uses. Do any particular constructs show up repeatedly? A person might categorize others mainly by their gender, or age, or friendliness. A frequently used construct is similar to a favorite shirt or pair of shoes. You bring it into many situations, and it is an important aspect of your personality.

You may also examine more abstract properties of the constructs. Kelly proposes that a construct's **range of convenience** is the set of events it can be applied to. Not all of our constructs are used to make sense of all the experiences we have. We may think of our family members in terms of their generosity (or not), but never use this category when thinking about people outside our family.

A construct's **focus of convenience** is the set of events where it does its best job, allowing the person to make highly accurate predictions about the world. Consider someone who spends many hours every day working in a restaurant. She has a number of personal constructs that help her understand customers and fellow employees. What happens when these constructs are applied outside that circle? They probably don't "work" as well, because she is attempting to understand events that fall outside the focus of convenience of her constructs. A fish out of water tries to swim, but it doesn't do too well. Similarly, a person who is using the wrong set of cognitive categories to understand events does a lot of gasping and flopping about.

Another important property of a personal construct is its **permeability**: the degree to which it can be applied to new events. A person with a permeable

Range of convenience: The topics to which a personal construct applies.

Focus of convenience: The topics to which a personal construct best applies.

Permeability: The degree to which a personal construct can be applied to new events.

construct readily interprets new experiences with it. In contrast, an impermeable construct is of no use to someone who encounters different events. So, a person who likes to travel to new places and eat in strange restaurants no doubt has permeable constructs. In contrast, someone else who shows little tolerance for the unusual or the irregular has impermeable constructs. This person has trouble switching from an automatic transmission to a manual, from a microwave oven to a campfire, or from a day job to a night job.

You can also score the REP Test for the entire construct system it reveals. How is one's construct system structured and organized? One important property is the *differentiation* of the construct system, which is called **cognitive complexity** (Bieri, 1955). Remember the earlier example about the man who regards his friends as good people and his enemies as bad people? Contrast him with a woman who believes some of her friends are bad people, whereas some of her enemies are good people. She uses the constructs of friend-enemy and good-bad independently, and thus her construct system is more differentiated than that of the man, who uses the constructs redundantly.

Cognitive complexity: The degree to which one uses personal constructs independently of one another.

Kelly argues that a construct system is organized in a *hierarchical* fashion, because some constructs are more important than others. This way individuals are able to choose among constructs when they lead to contradictory predictions. When in conflict, they use **superordinate construct** to anticipate events. Think of the superordinate constructs your different friends use. For one friend, it is religion. For another, it is family.

Superordinate construct: A personal construct that subsumes others.

Kelly views personality development simply as the elaboration of personal constructs. A person tries out different worldviews, keeping those that help anticipate events and discarding those that do not. On the whole, he or she comes to possess an increasingly complex and accurate set of constructs. However, development may go awry. Particular constructs may be impermeable, or they may be nonverbal, which can preclude attempts to examine and change them.

Evaluation

Since his death in 1967, Kelly has become increasingly popular. Psychology in general and personality psychology in particular have become more cognitive in orientation, and Kelly's use of the person-as-scientist metaphor is now seen as ahead of its time. The theorists I discuss in the remainder of this chapter all acknowledge Kelly's influence on their own cognitive views of personality (Jankowicz, 1987).

Nevertheless, personal construct theory has some problems. I have already mentioned the first one: Personal construct properties are difficult to assess. Despite obvious questions about the REP Test's validity, researchers tend to rely almost exclusively on it, which means that support of Kelly's theory is not as solid as one would expect, given the popularity of the approach.

A second problem with personal construct theory involves Kelly's rather glib dismissal of motivation. Kelly argues that a psychological theory requires motivational constructs—needs, drives, instincts, and so on—only if you assume that the natural state of a person is at rest. Then you have to explain activity. In contrast, if you assume a person is inherently active, then motivation is superfluous. Well, yes and no. Much of what Kelly says about motivation is reasonable, particularly when psychodynamic theory shows us that excessive concern with drives can produce an unwieldy account of personality. At the same time, though, some notion of motivation is necessary. Not all people are active all of the time. What about depression, apathy, and procrastination, occasional friends to us all?

Here's another difficulty: Do all people attempt to predict and control the events in the world? Again, we know of instances where people do not. Remember Erich Fromm's argument that people sometimes "escape from freedom" by aligning themselves with totalitarian political groups? Remember Marvin Zuckerman's trait of sensation seeking, which impels people to jump out of airplanes or ski recklessly—activities marked by lack of predictability and elusiveness of control? Personal construct theory is silent on such topics.

And another problem common to most cognitive theories is that passion and emotion are given "intellectual" interpretations, which means that their essence is overlooked. In his overview of cognitive approaches, Gardner (1985) described the *computational paradox:* The more scientists attempt to describe the mind by stressing reason and rationality, the more clear it becomes that people do not work this way. As these terms are used, emotions and cognitions are different, and cognitive theories like Kelly's subsume the former under the latter. Debate about the wisdom of reducing emotions to cognitions is considerable.

A final problem with personal construct theory takes issue with the scientist metaphor. This has an important limitation which may have occurred to you as you read about Kelly's ideas. Science is basically an *interpersonal* endeavor, but Kelly and other cognitive theorists usually apply it *intrapersonally.* What does this mean? Scientists typically work by proposing theories and conducting research to support their predictions. Other scientists attack these theories and try to falsify them. The generation and modification of scientific theories is a social process.

In contrast, personal construct theory argues that this process also occurs within each person. People change their minds about things, and they benefit by doing so. But is the process of change within an individual strictly analogous to the process of change within a science? When change occurs, is it for the same reasons? Personal construct theory does not explore such questions.

These problems with personal construct theory are not fatal flaws. The theory is quite flexible, and there is no reason why it can't be modified to more satisfactorily address motivation, emotion, and belief change.

SOCIAL LEARNING THEORY

The term **social learning theory** has been used by several generations of theorists to describe an approach to personality stressing the social context in which learning occurs. The organization in this section will be chronological, covering in the order they appeared several important versions of the social learning approach. We will start with the very first social learning theory, presented by John Dollard and Neal Miller in their 1950 book *Personality and Psychotherapy*. In this book they attempted to explain complex aspects of personality in the simple terms of stimulus and response.

Social learning theory: An approach to personality that stresses the social context in which learning occurs.

Background: Clark Hull's Behaviorism

To explain Dollard and Miller's work, I must first give you some background on their Yale University colleague, Clark Hull, because Hull's version of behaviorism provided them with their basic learning concepts. At one time, it was one of the most influential of the behavioral theories. Skinner's version of behaviorism may be better known today, but Hull's (1943) system has influenced personality psychology to a much greater degree.

This is true for several reasons. First, while Skinner (1950) downplayed theory in favor of documenting empirical relationships among stimuli and responses, Hull's theory is phrased as a formal theoretical model, replete with postulates, equations, and the like. As you have seen throughout this book, one of the common threads in personality psychology is theory. Hull's approach to psychology, however divergent its details, represents a strategy of science that personality psychologists understand.

Second, Hull's behaviorism does not disavow unobservables. Indeed, one of his central theoretical notions is the **drive**, defined as any stimulus that impels action. A drive originates in the environment (as when we step on the hot sand at the beach and are motivated to dash furiously into the water), or it originates inside the person (as when we get the munchies and are motivated to dash to the refreshment stand at the end of the beach). Behaviors are reinforced to the degree that drives are reduced.

Drive: According to Hull, any stimulus that impels behavior.

Third, Hull had an important impact on personality psychology because he worked with an interdisciplinary group at Yale University, a group whose interests extended to the sorts of topics that concern personality psychologists. Hull's behaviorism was one of the guiding frameworks for his colleagues, who included sociologist John Dollard and psychologist Neal Miller. Let us now turn to their work.

John Dollard and Neal Miller

After accepting positions at Yale's Institute of Social Relations, Dollard and Miller collaborated on several important books. One of these projects proposed the well-known **frustration-aggression hypothesis** (Dollard, Doob, Miller, Mowrer, & Sears, 1939), stating that frustration is a necessary and sufficient condition for aggression. Frustration is viewed in broad terms as the interruption of any goal-directed activity. Almost everyone knows not to pet a dog while it is eating—even Lassie might bite you if you get between her and her Purina. And almost everyone knows not to change the television channel when someone is watching his favorite show—even a good ol' friend might bite you if you get between him and "The Simpsons."

Frustration-aggression hypothesis: The theory that frustration is a necessary and sufficient condition for aggression.

The strong statement that the frustration-aggression hypothesis makes is no longer accepted today, but it has survived in a weaker form (Baron & Byrne, 1984). Frustration that is intense or arbitrarily imposed indeed leads to aggression. Your friend might not bite you if you just flipped the channel during the commercials, or if a hurricane were threatening and you switched to the 24-hour weather channel. At any rate, the frustration-aggression hypothesis exemplifies well the Hullian approach to psychology. It is phrased in strong theoretical language, it lends itself to empirical test, and it stresses drives (that is, frustration) as causes of behaviors (that is, aggression).

Similar emphases are evident in Dollard and Miller's (1950) treatment of personality and psychotherapy. Someone's "personality" is viewed in terms of specific **habits:** links between stimuli and responses established by learning. They believe all behavior—normal and abnormal—is established in the same way by the same process of drive reduction. Habits may produce anxiety and misery, but they are nonetheless learned.

Habit: A stimulus-response link established by learning.

So, you may learn to fear cats because you were scratched by one as an infant. Your fear response is established by classical conditioning. This fear then functions as a drive itself. Whenever you see a cat, you experience fear, and you leave the situation. Your fear is therefore reduced, and you continue to leave situations where you encounter cats. What may seem a puzzling phobia to someone who only sees the measures you take to avoid cats is easily understood by someone else who knows your learning history.

By this view, psychotherapy involves learning new habits to replace old habits. Your fear of cats can be overcome if you lock yourself in a room where several kittens are frolicking about. You will be overwhelmed with fear and will try to escape, probably to the great amusement of the kittens, who will (we hope) start to lick your quivering fingers and purr into your pounding ears. After some time, your fear will extinguish itself, because you are finally in a situation where you will confront the fact cats will not harm you.

Dollard and Miller similarly interpreted a variety of clinical phenomena. Consider repression, which plays a key role in psychodynamic formulations of abnormality (Chapter 4). These theorists explain repression in an elegant fashion, defining it as *not* thinking, and then arguing that a person is reinforced for not thinking about a topic because anxiety is thereby reduced. Do you remember what you said at that disastrous job interview last week? Not exactly, because every time you thought back over what ensued, you became anxious. And every time you stopped thinking, the anxiety went away. Voila: repression.

Contrast this with Freud's view of repression. In both cases, repression is viewed as a motivated activity. But while Freud regarded repression as the person banishing a particular cognitive content to a place called the unconscious, Dollard and Miller saw it simply in terms of the person not thinking about those contents. The unconscious is not a place but a deficit.

Another example of their theorizing is regression, also an important Freudian concept (Chapter 4). As you remember, regression is when a person faced with stress retreats to an earlier mode of behaving. Examples include pouting, sucking your thumb, or sticking out your tongue when you feel at a loss. Freud interpreted regression as a defense mechanism, as a return to a more primitive way of acting in response to an overwhelming situation. In contrast, Dollard and Miller explained it more simply by citing animal research demonstrating that conditions of high drive disrupt poorly learned responses while facilitating well-learned ones. This phenomenon is familiar to any of you who have sung, danced, or acted in front of an audience. The audience arouses you. If you have practiced your performance, you do well with the audience; if you have not practiced, you bomb out (Zajonc, 1965).

Habits acquired early in life are apt to be much better learned than those acquired later in life. So, anxiety has the dual effect of disrupting new habits and rekindling old habits. According to Dollard and Miller, this is exactly what happens in regression.

Also like Freud, Dollard and Miller sketched development in terms of an interplay between one's biological drives and one's social setting. Parents can produce conflicts in their children in the domains of hunger, elimination, sexuality, or aggression by punishing attempts to reduce drives. If the child learns to deal with anxiety through repression, the pattern is set for neurotic behavior later in life.

Suppose parents punish their young child severely for touching his genitals while at the local McDonald's. (That would make an interesting theme for a commercial: Mc-no-no.) The parents' intention may be simply to curtail masturbation in public. However, the child may generalize the punishment to include all behaviors associated with pleasure and his body. As an adolescent and adult, he experiences severe anxiety in sexual situations. Notice how Dollard and Miller ended up with the same predictions as Freud by taking a behavioral route.

These theorists were greatly interested in how individuals resolve conflicts. Their paradigm case is the **approach-avoidance conflict,** now a part of everyday language. You want to eat a Twinkie because you are hungry, but the snack will make you fat. What do you do? The conflict is resolved by the relative strengths of your drive to approach it versus your drive to avoid it, by how close or far you find yourself from the Twinkie, and so on. Neurotic individuals experience particular difficulty resolving their approach-avoidance conflicts, hovering in the vicinity of whatever plays the part of a Twinkie in their life, neither eating it nor leaving it.

Approach-avoidance conflict: A situation that possesses both desirable and undesirable aspects, which simultaneously draws and repels the individual.

Like all behaviorists trying to explain "personality" topics, Dollard and Miller sometimes ran into trouble. Habits are too small to account for the generality attributed to personality and too fragile to account for its stability. The two theorists were aware of these problems and attempted to deal with them.

So, they accorded great importance to language, an unusual emphasis among behaviorists. To them, words arouse drives, playing the role of sticks and stones. Words also reduce drives, smoothing ruffled feathers. Language is also critical in determining the generalization and discrimination of our learning. By introducing language into their learning theory, Dollard and Miller made their approach more applicable to personality.

Dollard and Miller also proposed that potential responses exist in a hierarchy. For a particular person, some responses are consistently more likely than other responses. Again, this notion helps them explain the consistent and stable aspects of human behavior, since it explains why a particular behavior is chosen over others time and again.

How well did Dollard and Miller succeed in explaining personality and psychotherapy? Their effort was heroic, and many of their particular interpretations are ingenious; however, the bulk of the research supporting their claims about personality is indirect. They derive their ideas from carefully conducted experiments with animal subjects and extrapolate them to people, sometimes without further testing (Hall & Lindzey, 1957).

In my view, Dollard and Miller's biggest shortcoming is that their use of learning theory sometimes is metaphorical. Although thoughts and beliefs can be spoken of as "covert" stimuli and responses, this stretches what these latter terms actually mean. Perhaps the behaviorists would have been better off using cognitive terms in the first place, rather than appropriating notions from animal learning experiments and forcing them inside the head.

Julian Rotter

Clark Hull also influenced a second generation of behavioral theorists interested in clinical topics. Among these, Julian Rotter deserves special mention. In contrast to Dollard and Miller, Rotter (1954, 1966, 1975, 1990) freely used cognitive terms in his version of social learning theory. Where Dollard and Miller treated stimuli as properties of the objective world, Rotter regarded them in terms of people's perceptions and interpretations. This makes Rotter's social learning theory very much an example of the contemporary cognitive-behavioral approach.

Reinforcement plays an important role in Rotter's view of learning. All things being equal, people are more likely to act in ways that have been rewarded than punished. However, reinforcement by itself does not allow accurate predictions of what someone will do in a complex situation. The choices faced by a person are obviously more numerous than those faced by a rat or pigeon in an experimental laboratory. The hungry animal can either push a lever for food or starve to death. That's pretty stark. The hungry person can invite himself next door for dinner, or heat up leftovers, or order a pizza to be delivered, or walk to a restaurant, or drive to a grocery store, or feed spare change into a vending machine. Those are a lot of choices, all of which have rewarding consequences. Which one is the hungry person apt to do?

To answer questions like this, Rotter (1954) introduced additional concepts. People can respond in a variety of ways to a particular situation. This is the idea of *behavior potential:* each behavior has a certain likelihood of occurrence (or potential) in a certain situation. The greater the likelihood, the more apt the person is to perform that behavior rather than another. Behavior potential in turn is determined by the person's **expectancy** that the behavior

Expectancy: One's belief that a behavior will lead to a particular outcome.

will lead to a given goal and by the **reinforcement value** of that goal (its valence). All of these must be specified with respect to a particular *psychological situation,* because Rotter recognized the importance of the setting in determining someone's particular expectancies and reinforcement values.

Back to the hungry fellow in the above example. How he chooses to respond to his growling stomach can be predicted if we know what he believes about the alternatives available to him. Suppose he has a low expectation that some of the ways to get fed will succeed. The vending machine he has in mind tends to keep his money. The pizza place may not deliver after midnight, and it's already 11:55 P.M. His neighbor may be out of town. At the same time, suppose he also has a poor opinion of the cooks at the local restaurants; they're almost as inept as he is! The grocery stores are all closed. So, all things considered, he has only one choice with both high expectancy and high reward value: heat up the leftovers.

Like Dollard and Miller, Rotter needed to explain the stability and consistency of human behavior. Part of the burden for explaining why people act in a similar fashion can be placed on the environment; people act the same to the degree they find themselves in the same psychological situation. How many times has our friend raided the refrigerator for leftovers? More than once, we can be sure.

But stability and consistency are also explained by Rotter in terms of **generalized expectancies,** beliefs of the person that transcend particular settings. One generalized expectancy is **locus of control,** which is an individual difference that ranges from *internal* orientation on the one hand (when the person believes rewards are brought about by his or her own actions) to an *external* orientation on the other (when the individual believes rewards are due to chance factors, fate, or powerful others). Locus of control is measured by a questionnaire Rotter (1966) devised. This questionnaire shows respondents pairs of sentences, one reflecting internality and the other externality. The subject chooses the sentence from each pair with which she or he most agrees:

Generalized expectancy: According to Rotter, expectations that apply across situations.

Locus of control: The generalized expectancy that rewards are brought about by one's own actions (internal orientation) or are due to chance, fate, or other people (external orientation).

    a. Regardless of what you do, some people will never appreciate it.
    b. If you try hard enough, everyone will like and respect you.

    a. The grades I get in classes are completely under my control.
    b. My particular grades are mainly due to my teachers.

One's locus of control is determined by calculating the number of internal versus external statements endorsed.

Literally thousands of investigations have examined locus of control. Phares (1984) summarized the thrust of these studies by noting that

> our survey . . . has revealed the typical internal [individual] to be one who actively comes to grips with the world. Compared to the external [individual], the [person who is] internal is resistant to social pressure and dedicated to the pursuit of excellence. (p. 295)

In a responsive environment—and this qualification is critical—individuals with an internal locus of control receive all sorts of benefits that elude those with an external locus of control.

Internality sounds like it is always desirable, so let me underscore the point that it is beneficial only in situations where one's efforts do pay dividends. In situations that elude control, people are better off resigning themselves to this fact, rather than beating their heads into an unyielding wall (Janoff-Bulman & Brickman, 1980). Along these lines, a study of college students found those with an internal locus of control to be more satisfied with unstructured instruction, whereas those with an external locus of control were more satisfied with a structured approach (Forward, Wells, Canter, & Waggoner, 1975). Similarly, the finding that ethnic minorities, women, students, prisoners, paraplegics and other groups with restricted access to the goodies in the world usually score in the external direction of Rotter's (1966) scale seems to reflect an accurate view of current affairs. The fit between the person and the world is indeed critical.

Interpersonal trust: The generalized expectancy that the word of others can be trusted or not.

Another generalized expectancy identified by Rotter (1967, 1971) is **interpersonal trust,** defined as the extent someone relies on the word of others. Trust is also measured by a questionnaire, one that asks people to endorse trustful versus distrustful statements—for example, "Elected officials usually keep their promises" versus "Take the advice of others with a grain of salt." Research shows that people high in trust act as we would expect (Phares, 1984). They are less likely to lie, they respect the rights of others, and they give people a second chance.

What does interpersonal trust have to do with learning? You might take my word that it does, but let me explain anyway. Like all social learning theorists, Rotter believed learning occurs in a social context. People high in trust rely on what other people say about the world. They allow others to shape their expectancies ("You'll never finish that assignment in an hour") and to define their reinforcement values ("That's a great movie"). People low in trust are more suspicious of others and as a result may go about their learning in a less direct fashion.

For example, a graduate student I know frequently asks me for advice: where to find a particular reference, how to write a computer program, what career possibilities to consider, and so on. Over the past year, it has become clear to me she does not trust what I tell her. She ends up asking the same questions of literally dozens of other people. I do not find this flattering, because I think I give good advice. So, I have begun to be increasingly abrupt with her. And now she indeed has little reason to trust what I say. This dynamic illustrates the give-and-take between the person and the world stressed in the cognitive-behavioral approach. She and I are each part of the world of the other, and we have mutually influenced each other and thereby ourselves.

Rotter had more to say about the consequences of one's expectations than about their origins. So, "learning" is not the focus of his social learning theory, which of course is a bit ironic. The importance of his approach is that he emphasized the individual's thoughts and beliefs as the critical determinants of behavior. It remained for subsequent social learning theorists to take a close look at how these thoughts and beliefs develop.

Walter Mischel

Walter Mischel was a student of George Kelly's at Ohio State University and was originally trained as a clinical psychologist. You know him so far in this book as the critic of trait psychology whose 1968 book *Personality and Assessment* argued against the notion that people behave consistently across different situations. Mischel is also an important social learning theorist, so in the present context, let's rephrase his thesis in a different way: People are highly sensitive to the particular settings in which they find themselves.

Remember also that Mischel argued in his 1968 book that people go beyond the information given to "see" personality consistency that may not be there. Again, in this context, let's say this differently: People have theories about themselves and the world that affect how they interact with the world.

Taken together, these two restatements reveal Mischel as a cognitive-behavioral theorist. Indeed, most of his writing since *Personality and Assessment* has elaborated his version of social learning theory (e.g., Mischel, 1973, 1979, 1984, 1986, 1990). He proposes that the appropriate units of personality are cognitive **person variables,** so termed to distinguish them from traits. To Mischel, a person variable is an individual difference produced by someone's interaction with past environments that in turn influences interaction with future environments. Person variables thus span both the person and his or her world. They are circumscribed because they are tied to given settings (Wright & Mischel, 1987, 1988). And they are in constant flux.

Person variable: Mischel's term for cognitive individual differences closely tied to particular settings.

Mischel regards a number of person variables as important. *Competencies,* for example, refer to people's abilities to use information to accomplish their goals. Goals range from immediate—like how to flag down a taxi during a rainstorm, to distant—like how to have a satisfying career or marriage. Regardless, people can only do what they know how to do (Cantor & Kihlstrom, 1987). Because they differ greatly in terms of what they know, their behaviors show a corresponding diversity.

Encoding strategies are the ways the individual categorizes experiences. These in effect are personal constructs. Different people make sense of the same environmental event in widely different ways. And once they interpret an event in a particular way, then their "theory" affects the way they behave. Imagine you work unsuccessfully at some task. You might conclude that your failure reflects on your own lack of ability, and you become despondent. But someone else in the same situation might conclude that her failure reflects the inherent difficulty of the task, and she feels challenged, ready to try again. A contemporary concern within the cognitive-behavioral paradigm is to describe in detail people's encoding strategies and to document their influence on subsequent behavior. I'll describe some of this research in the next chapter.

People's *expectancies* are their beliefs about the likely consequences of their actions, and Mischel proposes that people act in accordance with these beliefs. If my pocket calculator does not work, I give it a slam, because I expect this will jar it into action. If my personal computer does not work, I do not smash it, because I expect this will make matters worse. We have already discussed expectancies in terms of Rotter's notions of locus of control and interpersonal trust. However, Mischel is skeptical that one's expectancies are really this general (cf. Mischel, Zeiss, & Zeiss, 1973). He conceives of them as highly specific, linked to given outcomes in given settings.

People differ as well in terms of the *subjective values* they place on different outcomes. Mischel proposes that all people are purposive, intent on pursuing goals. Their pursuits differ because their goals differ. In emphasizing subjective values—preferences, as it were—Mischel brings feelings and emotions into his theory. In discussing Kelly earlier, I noted that emotions may be shoved aside when cognitions are on center stage. Here is Mischel's attempt to accord emotions the importance in personality they certainly deserve, by suggesting that they shape the goals toward which people strive.

Finally, included among the important person variables are the ways people control their own behavior. In Mischel's terms, people are *self-regulatory systems*. They intentionally change their environment in order to make some of their own behaviors more likely than others. For example, if I want to remember to take a stack of books to the library, I will place them at my front door, so I cannot help but encounter them on my way out. This is an extremely simple example. In more complex cases, people impose goals and standards on themselves, and they monitor their performance in view of them. They may reward or punish themselves accordingly. People differ greatly in how they go about self-regulation, and again Mischel's version of social learning theory makes sense of the great diversity seen among people.

Delay of gratification: The self-imposed postponement of rewards.

Let me illustrate some of these ideas by discussing Mischel's long-standing research program investigating how people tolerate **delay of gratification:** the self-imposed postponement of rewards (e.g., Mischel, Shoda, & Peake, 1988; Rodriguez, Mischel, & Shoda, 1989). The ability to delay immediate gratification makes possible a host of important human activities: higher education, arts and crafts, healthy living, marital fidelity, obeying laws against theft and assault—in short, any activity that extends over time, where long-term benefits outweigh short-term benefits, if one can resist the quick fix. Temptation is not always easy to ignore; we all know why grocery stores display candy bars, cigarettes, and sleazy tabloids next to the checkout line.

Everyday people explain delay of gratification in terms of willpower, whereas psychodynamic theorists talk about ego strength (cf. Funder & Block, 1989). Mischel takes a closer look at the topic, investigating what people actually do in the course of resisting temptation. He studies preschool children who are shown objects, like toys or snacks, one being more desirable than the other. If a child can sit alone in a room until the experimenter returns, he gets the more desirable object. If a child is unable to sit and wait, and instead calls for the experimenter to return, he gets the less desirable object. Mischel is interested in what makes waiting more versus less likely.

One of the most effective strategies used by the children who successfully delay gratification is to distract themselves from the objects. They sing or talk out loud, inspect their feet, or even cover their eyes with their hands. In short, they think about things other than the reward that awaits them.

Another strategy that works well is to think about the reward in ways that make it less tasty and tantalizing. It is easier to delay your lunging at

Delay of gratification makes important achievements possible.

marshmallows if you cognitively transform them into clouds or cotton balls or worse. Thinking about them as mouth-watering delicacies doesn't help you resist them.

This is a good example of the interplay between the person and environment that the cognitive-behavioral paradigm assumes is so critical to understanding personality. Here it takes place via cognitive person variables. Appreciate that the child who effectively delays her gratification changes the world in which she lives. Because of her particular competencies, she eventually experiences greater rewards and opportunities. These in turn affect her ability to further master the world.

In sum, Mischel's list of person variables is an important catalogue of cognitive factors that deserve the attention of theorists and researchers in the cognitive-behavioral tradition. This list can also be criticized for being just that, a list. The difficult business of actually combining the person variables into an overall theory of personality is just now getting underway.

The most ambitious example to date is Cantor and Kihlstrom's (1987) discussion of **social intelligence,** which they define as the ability to meet the mundane demands of everyday life. According to Cantor and Kihlstrom, people differ markedly in their social expertise and how they deploy it. Underlying these individual differences are the person variables Mischel has identified:

Social intelligence: The ability to meet the mundane demands of everyday life.

competencies, encoding strategies, expectancies, and the like. I will discuss their research program in the next chapter.

Albert Bandura

The last social learning theorist I will examine is Stanford University psychologist Albert Bandura. Bandura was a student of Kenneth Spence at the University of Iowa in the 1950s, and Spence earlier was a student of the behaviorist Clark Hull at Yale. So, in contrast to Mischel, Bandura has intellectual roots clearly and deeply embedded in the learning theory tradition.

However, as Bandura's thinking evolved, he introduced a number of ideas that took him ever further from traditional learning theory and closer to cognitive theory. Here are some of the most important of his concepts.

Observational learning (modeling): A form of learning where someone watches what other people do and how they are reinforced or punished.

First, Bandura places great emphasis on **observational learning,** which refers to changes in a person's behavior as a result of watching what other people do and how they are reinforced or punished. Observational learning is often called **modeling.** Unlike the other forms of learning discussed earlier in this chapter, observational learning does not require the learner to do anything overt. Rather, to use Bandura's (1977b) phrase, learning occurs vicariously.

Observational learning explains why complex and novel behavior often appears out of the blue, when it is implausible that shaping played any role at all. We learn where to mail letters, how to order meals at a restaurant, how to dissect a frog, when to say "please" and "thank you," and all sorts of behaviors by watching others perform them. These people are our **models,** and we pay attention to the consequences of their actions. If they are rewarded for doing something, then we are apt to do the same. If they are punished, then we are apt to restrain ourselves.

Model: In observational learning, the person who is observed.

Bandura (1974) feels that classical and instrumental conditioning exist, but he further believes that these types of learning don't have nearly the applicability to complex human behavior that observational learning has. Observational learning is responsible not just for isolated behaviors, but also for complex actions like creativity and sex roles (Bandura, 1986). Indeed, our very "personality" can be viewed as a product of social learning (Bandura & Walters, 1963).

Bandura's interest in observational learning developed through his studies of aggression. In a series of studies, Bandura (1973) investigated whether a child exposed to a violent model would later act violently. His results are consistent with the perspective sketched here. If the model is rewarded, the child is likely to act in an aggressive way. If the model is eventually punished, the child is less likely to be aggressive. Further qualifications exist as well. For instance, the status of the model and the relationship of the model to the child influence the course of observational learning (Bandura, 1986).

Such research is behind the attempts to limit violence in the movies and on television, or at least to ensure that violence is ultimately punished. Arnold Schwarzenegger's character in *The Terminator* wreaks havoc on the world but is eventually dispatched. This may satisfy the letter of Bandura's theory, but

Much of what we learn comes from observing others.

hardly its spirit; regardless, censors to date seem satisfied to see that villains eventually fail.

Second, Bandura interprets learning and performance in cognitive terms, emphasizing a person's expectancies as critical. He makes a distinction between two types of expectations (Bandura, 1977a). One is **outcome expectation:** the belief that a given behavior produces a given outcome. The other is **efficacy expectation:** the belief that one can perform a particular behavior. So, a basketball player is certain that her team can win the championship game if it can score 100 points (outcome expectation); however, she is extremely doubtful her team can do this (efficacy expectation).

Much of Bandura's (1986) recent research has looked at people who differ with respect to their **self-efficacy** vis-a-vis some behavior: their relative confidence they can perform it. Studies show that an individual's self-efficacy for a given response ("I am certain I can give this speech") is a better predictor of performance than past success or failure in performing it. One of psychology's few truisms is that past behavior predicts future behavior. Bandura has shown that attention to self-efficacy improves on this truism, strongly underscoring the importance of cognition.

Outcome expectation: One's belief that a given behavior produces a given outcome.

Efficacy expectation: One's belief that a particular behavior can be performed.

Self-efficacy: One's confidence that a particular behavior can be performed.

Third, Bandura introduces the notion of **reciprocal determinism** to explain the mutual influence among cognition, behavior, and the environment. Early in this chapter, I mentioned Lewin's notion that behavior is a function of the person and environment. Reciprocal determinism is an even more sweeping statement, because it proposes that each term in Lewin's equation is a function of the other two.

Fourth, in both his theory and his research, Bandura endorses what he calls a **microanalytic strategy.** He limits his analyses to particular behaviors by particular people in particular settings. Granted the assumption of reciprocal determinism, this strategy simplifies what otherwise would be a daunting task. But Bandura's real reason for following his microanalytic strategy is his belief that cognition and behavior indeed are closely tied to particular settings. All expectancies are necessarily specific ones.

His version of social learning theory looms as the next grand theory of personality. Because Bandura's theory is still being developed, it may be unfair to criticize it just yet. Still, several pitfalls seem possible. The first is a danger in pushing the microanalytic strategy too far. As we have stressed, *personality* includes aspects of behavior that are general, enduring, and integrated. Too narrow a focus precludes understanding the whole of what we mean by *personality*.

The second danger is that much of Bandura's theory, when stripped of its jargon, seems terribly commonsensical and necessarily true (Smedslund, 1978). That a theory is reasonable is hardly a strike against it, but some critics charge that his social learning theory tells us nothing we didn't already know. Bandura (1990) disagrees strenuously with this criticism, as you might imagine, pointing to the success of therapeutic strategies derived from his view of personality, particularly the idea of modeling. If his theories are so obvious, why did it take so long for someone to develop behavior modification based on the notion of observational learning?

SUMMARY

The cognitive-behavioral paradigm of personality considers the interplay between individuals and their world as the essence of personality. Thoughts and beliefs are accorded great importance, along with processes of learning. Cognitive-behavioral theories emphasize the content of a person's thoughts, their organization or structure, and the process by which they change.

This approach to personality has its roots in two different psychological traditions. From gestalt psychology, and in particular the ideas of Kurt Lewin, comes its concern with reality as perceived by the individual. From behaviorism comes its concern with learning, including, in particular, processes of classical and instrumental conditioning.

Perhaps the most important figure in the cognitive-behavioral tradition is George Kelly, whose personal construct theory is an extended elaboration of the person-as-scientist metaphor. According to Kelly, people seek to predict and control events in the world by using categories—personal constructs—to interpret them.

Social learning theory includes several approaches to personality that stress the social context in which learning occurs. The first social learning theory was proposed by John Dollard and Neal Miller, who used Clark Hull's version of behaviorism to explain topics of traditional concern to personality psychologists. The next social learning theory to emerge was that of Julian Rotter, who argued that learning can only be understood in terms of someone's expectations. Contemporary social learning theories have been proposed by Walter Mischel on the one hand and Albert Bandura on the other. Both rely greatly on cognitive notions to explain people's behavior.

COGNITIVE-
BEHAVIORAL
PARADIGM:
RESEARCH

The psychodynamic paradigm is dominated by the case history approach. The trait paradigm frequently uses questionnaires. What is the favorite research technique of the cognitive-behavioral paradigm? The answer is not simple. Various strategies for "getting inside the head" have been employed, with no single procedure being the overwhelming favorite of cognitive-behavioral researchers (Taylor & Fiske, 1982).

Thoughts and beliefs—the subject matter of the cognitive-behavioral paradigm—create the problem. Cognition is not observable in the same sense that we can see smiles or frowns. Instead, a person's thoughts and thought processes must be inferred from what he or she does. So far, this is no different than the psychodynamic paradigm, in which the researcher makes inferences from what can be observed to what cannot be observed. But the cognitive-behavioral paradigm is more complicated because of its assumption that people are conscious, active, and rational agents. These assumptions assign great importance to self-report in assessing an individual's cognitions.

But as I've said before, self-report about cognitive matters may be suspect, regardless of how conscious, active, or rational someone might be. We have seen that cognitions are not the same thing as vocabulary. Stated another way, cognitions are not the same thing as reports on cognitions. Although most researchers subscribe to this truism, it's not clear what one should do with it.

Let's distinguish two general approaches. The first asks for a person's self-report on beliefs, attitudes, and the like. This approach shares much in common with questionnaire approaches in the trait paradigm, except that the person reports thoughts instead of behaviors. To the degree that these thoughts are available to awareness and not distorted by confounds like social desirability, then self-report is a valid strategy. So, investigators concerned with self-efficacy typically ask subjects about their beliefs: "How confident are you that you can let the spider crawl up your arm?"

The other popular strategy in studying cognition borrows from experimental psychology. For instance, subjects may be given reaction-time tasks or memory tasks. At first glance these procedures seem identical to those used for 100 years by experimental psychologists interested in molecular processes. But when personality psychologists use these procedures, it is not to study recall or reaction time per se but to make inferences about the underlying structures and processes that characterize personality. So researchers interested in depression look at how well depressed individuals recall their good versus bad experiences. Someone who is depressed is apt to remember bad events more accurately than good events; someone who is not depressed exhibits the opposite pattern of recall (Blaney, 1986).

Like self-report measures of cognition, these experimental probes are problematic. It is time-consuming to use these procedures. Subjects must be studied one at a time, sometimes for several hours, and even with such an extensive period of study, only a handful of cognitive domains can be investigated. While this is in keeping with the cognitive-behavioral paradigm's distrust of broad dispositions and concern with specific cognitions, it interferes with a goal of all personality psychologists—to study what is *general* about an individual's behavior.

To help me decide which general approach (questionnaires or experimental tasks) is better for studying cognition, I distinguish between cognitive content and cognitive process. My rule of thumb is that cognitive content is studied through self-report, while cognitive process is studied with the complicated laboratory procedures pioneered by experimental psychologists. (Cognitive style can be studied with either approach.)

Nevertheless, here are some qualifications. As I mentioned in Chapter 11, it is not always clear where content ends and structure and process begin. Those cognitions in awareness are not always easy to identify. More basically, cognitions are not necessarily "real." They do not refer to entities that literally exist in a person's mind. When I've talked about cognition so far, I've used a casual way of speaking, one that treats cognitive contents, structures, and processes as if they pertain to real things.

Category mistake: A metaphor taken literally.

But when the subject is examined carefully, such usage is impossible to justify. English philosopher Gilbert Ryle (1949), in his book *The Concept of Mind,* reminds us that "things" of the mind are not identical to "things" of the physical world. Ryle coins the term **category mistake** to explain the dangers of metaphorical speaking that does not recognize the metaphor. So, both everyday people and cognitive theorists speak of the mind in metaphorical terms, using expressions from the physical world. Consider these examples:

> I see what you mean.
> My thoughts are jumbled.
> I crammed for the examination.
> That information is at my fingertips.
> Then again, perhaps it's not so clear.

I lost my way.

Let's go over that again.

It is a category mistake to forget that these expressions, though applied to cognition, are really taken from physical objects. Indeed, the basic distinctions I make among cognitive content, structure, and dynamics should sound familiar to those who have studied physics. Over the years, cognitive theorists have explicitly borrowed these terms.

Are cognitions real? The answer is no, at least in the way we speak about them. Cognitive terms are best regarded as **intervening variables,** as notions that the theorist devises to account for observations (MacCorquodale & Meehl, 1948). However, the researcher should not go one step further and regard these terms as referring to something tangible.

This is not to say researchers should give up looking for something tangible that corresponds to thoughts and beliefs. The search for the physiological basis of cognition is a thriving endeavor (e.g., Allport, 1986), and rightfully so. Instead, my point is that it will be extremely unlikely that future researchers will discover a one-to-one relationship between theoretical terms in contemporary cognitive-behavioral theories on the one hand and structures and functions of the brain on the other.

Essentially *all* cognitive constructs—at least at this time—are best thought of as intervening variables. And intervening variables should be measured with more than one operation. As hypothetical entities in a conceptual domain, their meaning can only be captured with a host of measures that presumably triangulate and converge. Unfortunately, this is not frequently done.

When cognitive-behavioral researchers stay with one procedure, it can be frustrating to those of us who study their work. Cognitive-behavioral theories have considerable overlap and are readily translatable from one to another. For example, Kelly's personal construct theory can be used to give an account of Rotter's social learning theory, or vice versa. But this is never done. We are left with researchers interested in personal construct theory who use the REP Test exclusively, researchers interested in generalized expectancies who use Rotter's scales exclusively, and so on. The relationships among measures associated with different theoretical traditions are simply not known.

Is there hope? Yes, because the situation is really brighter than it seems. Within each line of work are solid and interesting empirical findings. What is missing to date is an overall picture of research within the cognitive-behavioral paradigm, where links between different theories have been forged by relevant studies. But as I have emphasized, this paradigm is the most recent approach to personality to take form. We should be patient. At present, it is a hotly researched area, and the big picture is in the making.

We will start by discussing the two major research approaches to assessing cognition: questionnaires and process analysis. Then we will look at several lines of research that demonstrate the central importance of cognition. We will conclude by examining some of the important theoretical issues within the cognitive-behavioral paradigm in view of what research to date has revealed.

Intervening variable: A theoretical term, with no necessary counterpart in reality, introduced to explain what can be observed.

ASSESSING COGNITION WITH QUESTIONNAIRES

As you've seen, many of the important cognitive theorists favor a particular questionnaire to assess an individual's cognition. Within each line of research, these questionnaires have been elevated to a rather sacred status, hampering methodological refinement. In this section, I'll describe a notable exception to this trend: the efforts of psychologist William A. Scott (1969, 1974). First at the University of Colorado (where he was my professor) and then at Australian National University, Scott developed a number of questionnaires for measuring individual differences in cognition. He has investigated important issues within the cognitive-behavioral paradigm that other approaches to the paradigm—with their undue reliance on single procedures—have not been able to address.

Object: According to Scott, the things about which we think.

Attribute: According to Scott, the ways we group or distinguish objects.

Cognitive domain: According to Scott, a group of objects to which the same set of attributes can be meaningfully applied.

Scott views cognition as how someone describes objects in terms of particular characteristics he calls attributes (Scott, Osgood, & Peterson, 1979). **Objects** can be living or nonliving things, abstract or concrete; objects are nouns. **Attributes** refer to any of the ways we might group or distinguish objects; attributes are adjectives. For example, my class roll contains a list of my students (objects), followed by their class level and major field of study (attributes). You think about your friends (objects) in terms of their endearing features (attributes).

Scott also introduces the notion of a **cognitive domain,** defined as a group of objects to which the same set of attributes can be meaningfully applied. So, the various roles you play in life probably comprise a sensible cognitive domain, because you appraise them in the same terms. And in contrast, perhaps you think of your friends in a completely different way than you think about your family members; if so, these are distinct cognitive domains for you. In limiting his attention to particular cognitive domains, Scott avoids making the assumption that people have highly consistent ways of thinking about disparate topics. This may prove true, and we can investigate this possibility directly by comparing the ways people think about different domains.

The value of Scott's approach to cognition is that it is compatible with each of the more formal theories discussed in the previous chapter. Although the theories use their own language to describe people's thoughts and beliefs, they each have counterparts to objects, attributes, and domains. Indeed, in every case, the equivalents of these are extremely important notions. Consider, for example, the person variables Mischel (1990) enumerates. These can be described in object-attribute terms, presumably in highly circumscribed domains. Or take Rotter's (1966, 1971) generalized expectancies; again, these can be recast in terms of the characteristics (e.g., trustworthiness) attributed to objects (e.g., other people).

The object-attribute approach becomes awkward when we use it to describe certain aspects of cognition, such as one's knowledge of the rules of chess. But Scott argues that his view of cognition nonetheless applies in a straightforward way to many topics of concern within the cognitive paradigm. Further, and here is why we are focusing on these ideas in the present context, Scott has developed an array of questionnaires for assessing the ways people assign attributes to objects. These measures show how certain aspects of cognition can be ascertained with questionnaires.

Here are descriptions of some of these questionnaires. Each asks respondents to describe objects with attributes:

> *Listing and Comparing Objects.* The respondent generates 20 objects in a particular domain, such as friends. He identifies the degree to which he likes each object. Then he groups objects together that are similar in an important way. He identifies the way they are similar. Finally, he groups those objects together that are different in this respect.
>
> *Free Description of Objects.* The respondent is provided with 20 objects in a particular domain, such as nations of the world. Then she describes each in her own words in terms of its important characteristics. Finally, she rates how pleasant or unpleasant each characteristic is.
>
> *Checklist Description of Objects.* Respondents indicate whether each of 72 adjectives (representing 36 synonyms, half evaluative and half neutral) applies to 20 objects in a particular domain, such as family activities. They also indicate the degree to which they like or dislike each object.
>
> *Rating of Objects.* The respondent uses 10 bipolar rating scales, including both evaluative and nonevaluative dimensions, to describe each of 10 objects in a particular domain, such as self-roles.

Scott has also devised additional questionnaires with other formats. In all cases, though, research subjects describe objects in terms of attributes, and a given questionnaire is specific to a single cognitive domain.

These questionnaires can each be scored in a variety of ways to yield scores of individual differences in cognitive content and cognitive style. Let's first consider cognitive content. Among the important attributes a person can ascribe to objects is an evaluation: good, bad, ugly, or indifferent. So we can ask about the degree to which objects in someone's cognitive domains are generally liked or disliked. We can also ask about the degree to which someone shows **ambivalence:** attributing both good and bad characteristics to the same object.

Do you see how overall liking versus disliking can be scored from the questionnaires described earlier? From the *Free Description of Objects* measure, for example, we can calculate the average "pleasantness" of characteristics attributed to objects. And from the *Checklist Description of Objects* measure, we can ascertain the degree to which someone describes objects with positive rather than negative or neutral adjectives.

These measures can be analogously scored for other aspects of cognitive content. People differ in terms of the **complexity** with which they view objects, using many versus few attributes to describe them. Someone who has expertise in a given domain, for example, sees objects there in complex terms. The richness of their thoughts allows them to select from alternatives unthinkable to others.

Think about the domain of things to do on a vacation. Now think specifically about camping. With what complexity do you view this activity? Regardless of where you find yourself on the complexity spectrum, appreciate

Ambivalence: The attribution of good and bad characteristics to the same object.

Complexity: According to Scott, the degree to which an object is described with many attributes.

the extensive range of possible positions, and each translates into a characteristic way of camping on one's vacation.

Another characteristic of cognitive content that can be scored from Scott's questionnaires is the **centrality** of particular attributes. In other words, how frequently is a given attribute used to describe objects? Often-used attributes have a wide range of convenience, to use George Kelly's phrase. We can literally glimpse at how someone else sees the world by determining their most central attributes. Contrast people for whom "good-looking" is a highly central attribute in the cognitive domain of friends and acquaintances with those who think of others in terms of how "interesting" they are.

One more characteristic of cognitive content that can be scored from Scott's questionnaires is the **precision** of an attribute: the number of distinctions it allows a person to make. A highly precise attribute is comprised of many categories. Perhaps you have had the same experience that I have in the presence of a wine connoisseur: absolutely no idea what she is talking about when she appraises a particular bottle with terms like woody, dry, subtle, or delightful. Though esoteric (to me), her attributes are precise. In contrast, mine are much less so: red versus white, cork versus no cork, and cheap versus forget it.

Let's next take a look at characteristics of cognitive style: the interrelations among a person's thoughts and beliefs. All cognitive-behavioral theories assume that someone's cognition has an organization to it. Theories differ in terms of the exact basis of this organization: whether it reflects consistency, complexity, accuracy, or whatever. Scott's measures allow these different hypotheses to be tested. Can we say that one mode of cognitive style is more dominant than others?

Because Scott construes various cognitive styles as individual differences in their own right, we can also ask more subtle questions. For example, do different topics tend to be thought about with different styles? How general are cognitive styles?

Here are some of the cognitive styles Scott identifies. **Evaluative centrality** is the degree to which evaluative attributes are more central than nonevaluative attributes. Do you see how this can be scored from his various questionnaires?

Consider the prototypic gossip: Nothing passes his lips that is not an evaluation. Contrast what you hear from him with error messages in a typical computer program, which patiently tells you that ERROR 237 was made 453 TIMES. No evaluation is given here, just a description.

Another cognitive style is **image comparability:** the degree to which all objects in a cognitive domain are described with the same attributes. Said another way, image comparability is an index of the coherence of a cognitive domain. For an example of a domain with a high degree of image comparability, consider how physicists view the world. They describe the entire physical universe in a single scheme of the same basic properties: mass, space, and time. For an example of a domain with a low degree of image comparability, consider Gordon Allport's vision of personality psychology as idiographic, describing

Centrality: According to Scott, the frequency with which an attribute is used to describe objects.

Precision: According to Scott, the number of distinctions one can make with a particular attribute.

Evaluative centrality: According to Scott, the degree to which evaluative attributes are more central than nonevaluative attributes in a cognitive domain.

Image comparability: According to Scott, the degree to which all objects in a cognitive domain are described with the same attributes.

each person with a unique set of traits. Because many consider high image comparability a prerequisite for science, or at the very least an incredible help, you can see why Allport's approach has not been widely accepted.

Another property of cognitive style is **affective-evaluative consistency:** the degree to which someone assigns favorable characteristics to liked objects and unfavorable characteristics to disliked objects. Consider Festinger's (1957) cognitive dissonance theory, which proposes that any form of inconsistency (such as in the attributes one ascribes to the same object) is aversive to individuals and motivates them to change evaluations. In contrast, Scott suggests that this "universal" tendency toward consistency might be an individual difference. Some people only have friends who are saints and enemies who are dirtbags, but other people have friends with drawbacks and enemies with virtues. The former individuals are high on affective-evaluative consistency, while the latter individuals are low on this property of cognitive style.

Finally, a cognitive domain has a characteristic level of **dimensionality,** what other cognitive theorists refer to as cognitive complexity (e.g., Bieri, 1955). Does a person bring a variety of perspectives to bear on a particular topic? Does she have numerous personal constructs? When ascribing attributes to objects, does she use them independently or redundantly? A person with high dimensionality makes numerous distinctions among objects. Imagine Julia Child talking to you about food. A person with low dimensionality makes few taste distinctions. (Pass the ketchup, please.)

Let's take stock. Scott provides a variety of questionnaires that assess individual differences in cognitive content and style. The benefit of his approach, with its reliance on multiple measures, is best appreciated by contrasting it to other questionnaire approaches within the cognitive-behavioral paradigm. As noted earlier, many of the paradigm's dominant theories tend to rely on a single questionnaire measure.

You already know that relying on a single questionnaire has considerable risk. A confound may distort a respondent's answers, but in the absence of a converging measure against which to validate the questionnaire, the confound remains undetected. Consider the REP Test as described in the last chapter. Research shows that cognitive complexity is sometimes correlated with general intelligence (e.g., Vannoy, 1965) and with social desirability (Goldstein & Blackman, 1976). Do high cognitive-complexity scores reflect the independent use of constructs, as personal construct theorists intend? Or do they instead reflect intelligence and/or acquiescence to social conventions? If the latter is at all true, interpretation of findings involving the REP Test must be drastically revised.

The REP Test is often administered to individuals with profound problems like depression or schizophrenia. Their responses invariably differ from those of people without such difficulties. Do these differences reside in the use of constructs per se (which are accurately reflected in REP Test responses), or do they reflect more general states like confusion, apathy, or suspicion? To repeat the point: Sole reliance on one operationalization precludes the disentangling of such possibilities.

My purpose here is not to pick on the REP Test. Let me qualify my criticisms. First, I'm suggesting skepticism about questionnaire measures of cognition, not dismissal of the approach altogether. Second, I'm using the REP Test as a representative example. In a general review of questionnaire assessment of cognitive variables, Goldstein and Blackman (1978) criticize virtually all these tests. Third, researchers are well aware of the questions I raise, and they are trying to develop alternative questionnaire measures. Indeed, personal construct researchers are in the forefront of this attempt to broaden assessment.

I have discussed William Scott's work in this section because he has long recognized the difficulty of using questionnaires in cognitive-behavioral research. His approach has not yet infiltrated the whole of the paradigm, but it represents a notable improvement over other questionnaire strategies. One reason why many researchers have yet to discover his questionnaires is ironic: his methodological focus. Scott has devoted much of his research program to developing his measures—to such an extent that theory has taken a back seat. Researchers in the cognitive-behavioral paradigm are attracted to innovative ideas and findings, not to innovative procedures per se.

Scott has used his multimethod strategy to investigate certain questions about the role of cognition in personality. Let me describe some of his findings. Keep in mind how these bear on the theories described in Chapter 11.

Do Different Measures of the Same Characteristics Agree?   Appreciate that this is an extremely important question for personality psychologists interested in cognition. Yes, measures correlate, but the magnitude of these correlations is often close to the familiar .30 limit (Scott, Osgood, & Peterson, 1979). This means that even with respect to our thoughts about the same topic, we are far from showing perfect consistency. As Epstein recommends for measures of overt behavior, these results imply that cognitive researchers should aggregate as many measures of individual differences as possible.

Are Cognitive Properties General Across Domains or Topic Specific?   Again, appreciate that this is important to know. Theorists like Rotter (1966) hypothesize generalized expectancies, whereas Mischel (1990) and Bandura (1986) prefer a much more circumscribed view. The answer is complex: evidence exists for consistency across different domains, but evidence also exists for topic specificity (Peterson & Scott, 1975). Depending on the purpose, the researcher can speak about cognition in general or with respect to a particular topic.

What Is the Effect of Increased Experience and Information on Cognitive Structure?
A variety of studies indicate that the more familiar you are with a cognitive domain, the greater your dimensionality with respect to it (Scott, Osgood, & Peterson, 1979). These findings support the general assumption by cognitive theorists that our thoughts and beliefs move toward increased sophistication and accuracy (at least if we assume that the world itself is a complicated state of affairs best understood in complicated terms).

What Is the Principle That Describes Cognitive Organization? The cognitive theories described in Chapter 11 propose that in the course of development, cognitions become more complex and at the same time more interconnected. The different theories hypothesize that various principles dictate this latter process. For instance, Kelly suggests that constructs become arranged in a hierarchy. Note that several of Scott's variables describe modes of integration among cognitions: evaluative centrality, image comparability, and affective-evaluative consistency. Are any of these predominant? The answer is no (Scott, 1974). Different people show different types of integration, and the type favored by the same individual may well vary across cognitive domains. This should give pause to theorists seeking a single tendency guiding cognitive development.

How Does Cognitive Style Pertain to Psychological Well-Being? Scott and Peterson (1975) found that well-adjusted college students (as judged by themselves and their friends) think about self and others as positive, unambivalent, and high in affective-evaluative consistency. These results are consistent with a humanistic view of mental health, as well as with that of the neoFreudians who link personal adjustment with harmonious social relations.

Let us conclude by noting that several drawbacks to Scott's approach are evident. First, research subjects must expend an inordinate amount of time and effort to complete the measures. Not all potential subjects have the inclination or ability to answer questionnaires for 8 to 10 hours. Second, Scott's lack of a strong theoretical stance cuts both ways. While it frees him from certain assumptions that may prove limiting, it also cuts the methods adrift. Third, Scott has tended not to investigate how overt behaviors relate to his properties of cognitive style.

ASSESSING COGNITION WITH PROCESS ANALYSIS

In contrasting measures of cognitive content with measures of cognitive process, Susan Fiske and Shelley Taylor (1984) asked their readers to compare a snapshot to a movie. What information does each convey? More important, what information does each fail to convey?

Like a photograph, questionnaires can freeze cognition for a moment and give a detailed look at content. William Scott's questionnaires represent the state of the art in capturing content. But whether a questionnaire resembles a Nikon or an Instamatic, it cannot capture cognition in use. How does cognitive style develop? How does it shape behavior? How does it change in response to the world? These are questions about our thought processes, and they require assessment procedures sensitive to time.

Like a movie, such procedures follow the action over a period and depict the sequence of cognitive events. What complicates matters for cognitive psychologists is that cognitive events can never be literally glimpsed. Their presence or absence can only be inferred from observable actions of research subjects. How many words are remembered? In what order are items recalled? How quickly is a decision made?

Answers to these questions can give insights into cognitive processes when coupled with a theoretical statement about how we make sense of the world (Fiske & Taylor, 1984, 1991). However, in the absence of hypotheses, data about recall and reaction time are just numbers of no interest whatsoever to the personality psychologist. Contrast this with the approach of William Scott, where descriptions can be important in their own right.

Perhaps you are wondering why researchers don't use questionnaires to measure process, because they could give researchers considerable latitude. Remember my familiar warning: Cognitive processes are not typically available to someone's awareness. Go back and read the preceding sentence carefully. It does *not* say people are unaware of what they are thinking. It merely says people cannot report on how they arrived at their thoughts, on why their beliefs change, or on what determines their beliefs.

I've mentioned several times Richard Nisbett and Timothy Wilson's (1977) argument that respondents to a questionnaire will "tell more than they can know" if posed questions about cognitive processes. If asked what factors influenced their preference among a series of consumer goods placed on a table, subjects will give an elaborate account of how they arrived at their decision. No one mentions the possibility that they were influenced by the location of the goods on the table, although subjects clearly prefer whatever item is on the far right.

The Nisbett and Wilson (1977) argument is an important caution to cognitive researchers: Don't confuse one's reports on a cognitive process with the process itself. But some hear their argument as saying more than it really does, as arguing against self-report altogether in studying cognition, since people don't know what they're talking about. This is an unwarranted generalization.

First, such an extreme version of Nisbett and Wilson's conclusion ignores the useful distinction between content and process. The experiments reported by Nisbett and Wilson ask a person to give his preference, for instance, with no second-guessing of the validity of *this* self-report. Second, even if a person is wrong about what determines her thoughts and beliefs, a psychologist trying to understand her personality is interested in this information. The central tenet of the cognitive-behavioral paradigm is that one's thoughts and beliefs lie at the center of feelings and actions. This is true whether one's thoughts are reasonable or unreasonable.

But if researchers wish to understand cognitive process, then they must go beyond self-report questionnaires and study cognition across time. Fiske and Taylor (1984) provided a useful catalogue of techniques to do this. All start with a hypothesis about the presumed process, and then gather information to decide if the hypothesis is plausible or implausible.

Schema: A cognitive structure that represents one's general knowledge about a given concept or concept domain.

Central to most of these efforts is an interest in what a person knows and how this knowledge is represented. Theorists often refer to this aspect of cognition as a **schema:** "a cognitive structure that represents one's general knowledge about a given concept or concept domain" (Fiske & Taylor, 1984, p. 13). Someone uses a schema to make sense of the world, to go beyond immediate information to make inferences.

Suppose you have a schema about sororities and their members. One of your classmates wears a sweatshirt emblazoned with Greek letters, so you assume she is a member of a sorority. She mentions she will be busy the next weekend, so you assume she is involved in the whirl of parties planned for the school's homecoming. In class the next Monday she looks tired, and her eyes are red, so you assume she stayed up late drinking too much.

Your assumptions may be correct, but notice that you did not directly observe any of the events and behaviors that seem plausible to you. Your schema gives rise to your assumptions, and in this example, you can see some of the beliefs that make it up:

- Young women who wear sweatshirts with Greek letters on them are sorority members.
- Sorority members go to parties on homecoming weekend.
- At parties, sorority members drink too much.

Notice that these beliefs are associated with each other. One leads to another. Given certain information, certain beliefs are entertained; given those beliefs, other beliefs are entertained, and so on.

But suppose your classmate is an exchange student from Athens. Suppose her family visited her in the United States for the first time in several years. Early Monday morning she bid them a tearful farewell at the airport. Your sorority schema, although sometimes quite useful in making sense of the world, has steered you wrong.

Measures of Attention

Many cognitive theories of personality liken schemas to filters. They determine what we pay attention to in the world and what we ignore. Following this logic, the researcher can work backwards from information about someone's attention (or inattention) to make conclusions about the person's cognition. Various strategies for assessing attention have thus been developed, ranging from technologically sophisticated videotapes of eye movements (where one's eyeballs are directed, and for how long) to primitive measures of how long someone stares at different items on a bulletin board.

For instance, Mischel, Ebbesen, and Zeiss (1973) had college students take a battery of personality tests. Then they prepared two notebooks for each student, one containing information about the supposed positive aspects of his or her personality and the other containing information about the supposed negative aspects. Next, each subject took a bogus intelligence test. The researchers told half of the subjects that they had scored particularly well and the other half that they had scored particularly poorly. (Whether a given subject "succeeded" or "failed" was determined randomly.) After hearing about their intelligence test performance, the subjects were left alone with their "personality profile" notebooks for 10 minutes.

The experimenters were curious about the amount of time subjects spent looking at positive information about themselves versus the amount of time spent looking at negative information. Success on the intelligence test led to greater attention to one's assets, whereas failure led to greater attention to one's liabilities, supporting the idea that people's thoughts and experiences seek congruence.

Measures of Memory

One way to map out a schema is by studying an individual's memory, seeing how and what a person remembers about a particular experience under the researcher's control (Sherman, Judd, & Park, 1989). Because the researcher knows what the facts actually are, any departures evident in a subject's recall or recognition suggest a schema is operating. Suppose a subject is given a list of words that describe personality traits, some positive (for example, bright-eyed and bushy-tailed) and some negative (for example, dazed and confused). Ten minutes later he is asked to recall as many of these words as possible. What does it mean if he comes up with most of the negative traits and none of the positive ones? Some conclude that he has a "depressive" schema organized around negative views of himself and the world (e.g., Derry & Kuiper, 1981). Most people remember more of the positive traits.

Do you see the interplay between the person and the world, and how the schema is the locus for this transaction? If the depressed person is attuned to bad things by virtue of his depressive schema, he will become more and more depressed as he thinks about his life, since he remembers what is bad. And if the nondepressed person is attuned to good things, she will be robust in the face of disappointments, since she remembers what is good about her life.

What a person does or does not remember is important to personality psychology, not just because the content of memory is an intriguing individual difference (which it is), but because it channels the way we interact with the world. One of my male colleagues used to remember the names of all the female students in his undergraduate classes but not the names of the male students—not even one. You don't need to be a psychologist to see what this reveals about the workings of his mind, but appreciate that this mental bias also affected his behavior and in turn the world in which he lived.

How do *you* react to a teacher who knows your name versus one who does not? Odds are that you are friendlier in the former case, you are more likely to attend class and sit in the front row, and you may even try harder to do well in the course. It is not surprising that my colleague believed that female undergraduates were excellent students but that male undergraduates were not. So, memory pertains to more than isolated facts about the world; it is an important meeting ground between the person and the environment.

Measures of Decision Making

Reaction time: The speed with which someone responds to a stimulus.

A final set of measures used by cognitive-behavioral researchers to understand underlying processes looks at the ways people make decisions based on the information they receive. A favorite parameter here is the speed with which someone makes a decision: in other words, his or her **reaction time.**

Suppose your roommate badly cuts his finger. Through the window you see a car with lights on the roof. You run out and flag it down. The policewoman behind the wheel administers emergency first aid and then takes your roommate to the hospital. When you later visit the hospital, you remark to your roommate how lucky he was that a police car was passing by. You might also thank the schema that helped you decide—quickly and accurately—that a car with lights on the roof was a police car.

This is the logic behind using reaction-time measures to assess cognition: Someone who has a particular schema recognizes and uses information relevant to it in an efficient (and usually rapid) manner. Hence, rapid reaction times for decisions or judgments about a given topic suggest that a schema is present.

Psychologist Hazel Markus (1977, 1980) has used reaction-time measures to study schemas concerning the self. In one experiment, she had female subjects respond to several questionnaires measuring whether they were independent or dependent. She assumed that subjects who scored in an extreme direction (independent or dependent) had a self-schema incorporating this personality characteristic. Subjects scoring in the middle of these scales were termed *aschematic,* the assumption being that their self-schema did not include the dimension of independence or dependence.

Markus then asked the subjects to perform a variety of tasks. One involved presenting subjects a list of personality trait terms, one at a time with a slide projector, and asking them to push a button in each case indicating whether it was "like me" or "unlike me." The terms included synonyms of "independent" (such as individualistic, outspoken, and assertive), synonyms of "dependent" (such as conforming, submissive, and timid), and neutral words. She measured the speed with which subjects made the "like me" or "unlike me" decision for each type of word.

Granted the meaning of self-schemata, what results do you expect? Markus found that independent subjects more rapidly judged whether independent traits characterized them than did dependent subjects or aschematic subjects. She also found that dependent subjects more rapidly judged whether dependent traits characterized them. These results nicely support the existence of self-schemas, because they demonstrate that people differ in the efficiency with which they process certain classes of information.

Evaluation

Measures of attention, memory, and decision-making have recently been adopted by cognitive-behavioral personality researchers, and results to date are promising. However, not everyone familiar with these approaches is convinced they are the techniques of the future, and several criticisms have been raised.

First, the schema concept used to make sense of many of these experimental approaches strikes some as ambiguous. Perhaps schemas are overly complicated ways of explaining research findings. For instance, need we invoke a depressive schema to explain why depressed people say negative things about themselves (Segal, 1988)? After all, this is what depression means, and it may have a biological basis. What does a hypothesized cognitive style add to our understanding of depression?

Further research is needed, and I suspect that the schema concept will be vindicated. Markus, Smith, and Moreland (1985), for instance, have demonstrated that all sorts of experimental measures converge with each other. In a particular cognitive domain, people recognize, organize, remember, and employ information in characteristic ways. Schemas cease being unclear and start being parsimonious when they help the theorist make sense of disparate findings.

Second, researchers fond of these experimental techniques have failed to explore exactly how individual differences in memory and reaction time relate to other aspects of people's behavior (Markus & Zajonc, 1985). So, research that shows how particular schemas influence the processing of relevant information would be more impressive if it further demonstrated that information processing in turn influenced how people acted outside of the laboratory.

Third, you may have noticed that these techniques rely excessively on words. Although our understanding of the world is often phrased verbally, cognition, as noted, is not the same thing as vocabulary. One of the most serious criticisms raised against the research techniques borrowed from experimental psychology is that they still are used to study how words are recognized and recalled. Subjects are now shown words like "ambitious" or "introverted" instead of words like "horse" or "dog." But is this enough of a change to say that researchers are studying the whole of personality? I think not.

It is ironic that cognitive schemas and the use of experimental probes to assess them received a big boost from Mischel's (1968) criticism of trait research as making infrequent contact with "real" behavior. Experimental techniques were an alternative to mindless investigations correlating one questionnaire with another. Yet schema research is subject to much the same criticism as past trait research. It's removed from "real" behavior.

In light of my criticisms, I have some suggestions for cognitive-behavioral researchers. I advise them not to forget the hard-won realizations of the trait researchers. Studies of how people respond to abstract stimuli (be they questions on a questionnaire or trait words flashed on a screen) cannot substitute for studies of how people respond to the real world.

I recommend that researchers study attention by watching people as they mingle at a cocktail party or shop in a mall, for instance. Who and what is noticed? Maybe researchers could study memory by assessing what people remember and forget in the course of their everyday life. Why do some people remember to buy postage stamps but not diapers? Why do other people know what's on television but not in the newspaper? Finally, I suggest that researchers study decision making by interviewing parole officers, abortion counselors, or car salespersons.

Actually, psychology researchers study behavior in all of these settings, which is why I chose them as examples. What has yet to be done is for personality researchers interested in the schema approach to venture into these arenas. For the time being, researchers using experimental techniques to study personality are staying close to their laboratories. While they gain control and reliability in their research, they sacrifice generality and validity.

THE IMPORTANCE OF COGNITION

Research within the cognitive-behavioral paradigm is booming, so I cannot possibly discuss every line of inquiry currently being pursued. What I can do is examine the central claim of this approach to personality, namely that thoughts and beliefs are the essence of a person. They affect, in a crucial way, everything else about the person. Perhaps this strikes you as extremely plausible; as philosopher René Descartes argued, "I think, therefore I am." But not all individuals who address the matter agree about the primacy of cognition.

As we have discussed, behaviorism was ushered into psychology by John Watson's (1913) dismissal of mental life as not an appropriate or important topic for psychology. Ever since, radical behaviorists like B. F. Skinner (1971) have echoed this assertion. Cognition, if not a downright myth, is no more than an **epiphenomenon,** an irrelevant derivation of the real essence of a person. Some behaviorists may acknowledge the existence of cognition, then disavow its importance by likening thoughts to exhaust fumes coming from a car's tailpipe. They accompany the movement of the car but do not make the car run.

The best way for cognitive psychologists to answer these criticisms is with research demonstrating that thoughts and beliefs do indeed lie at the center of human activity. How can they show that people's thoughts determine what they do? At first this question seems to have an obvious answer. You simply assess thoughts and actions, and show a substantial link between the two. But a closer examination reveals that this procedure is not foolproof, because it relies on a

Epiphenomenon: A secondary phenomenon accompanying and caused by some primary phenomenon.

Radical behaviorist B. F. Skinner dismissed cognition as an appropriate or important topic for psychology.

correlation between thought and deed. Correlations do not always reflect a direct causal sequence. Perhaps the behavior in question led to the particular thought. Perhaps both the thought and behavior reflect some third variable.

For instance, consider a study that asks whether students who believe a particular instructor is an effective teacher do well in this instructor's class. This hypothesis is consistent with the central claim of the cognitive-behavioral paradigm that thoughts (beliefs about an instructor) determine actions (class performance). But it is also consistent with other possibilities. Maybe students decide after they've received grades whether a teacher did a good job or not: "That creep—look at how he marked me down!" Or maybe the students' beliefs and performance result from something the teacher does, like grading leniently or harshly. Beliefs and performance end up being correlated with each other—but not because a direct link exists between them.

These pitfalls are generic problems for researchers within the cognitive-behavioral paradigm. They must be surmounted if one is to argue that thoughts and beliefs are primary characteristics of personality. Researchers buttress their cognitive arguments in various ways.

One obvious strategy is to assess cognition *prior* to assessing behavior. Causes don't work backwards in time. If you still find a link between thoughts and actions, then you've eliminated the argument that cognition is the effect rather than the cause. Consider the earlier example. If students give their opinions about their teacher's effectiveness before they write any papers or take any exams, and a correlation exists between their beliefs and their eventual achievement, one cannot argue that their performance led to their belief.

Eliminating third-variable arguments is not as easy. Researchers usually get rid of such confounds by conducting experiments holding extraneous factors constant while manipulating the potential "cause" and measuring the conse-quence of this manipulation on the "effect" being studied. Cognitive researchers attempt to do this by trying to manipulate cognitions and assessing behaviors. So, we might tell students in one class that their teacher is effective and students in a second class just the opposite. What is the effect on student performance?

Unfortunately, researchers cannot directly manipulate cognitions. Remem-ber that thoughts are not literal "things" with a tangible existence. They can only be shoved around metaphorically, and our shoves will inevitably affect other aspects of a person. Any experimental study of cognition has only the guise of an experiment. In actuality, all such studies yield correlational data, and we must be continually alert for third variables.

Because experimentation doesn't automatically relieve cognitive research-ers from the threat of third variables, what are they to do? They employ two further strategies, usually in conjunction. The first involves so-called *manipula-tion checks:* measures of the hypothesized cognition and attempts to demon-strate that the manipulations correlate with these measures and that these measures in turn correlate with the effects being studied. If cognition is indeed involved, then both these correlations will be significant, and manipulations will not correlate with effects except insofar as the cognitive measures mediate this link. The logic here is diagrammed in Figure 12-1. (This strategy is brought to a high degree of mathematical sophistication in the statistical technique of *path*

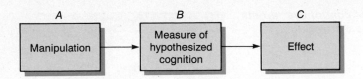

analysis, which uses patterns of correlation coefficients to trace the path of causal influence among variables; Kenny, 1979.)

In our classroom example, we'd want to measure afterward whether the students thought the teacher effective or ineffective. Is there an overall difference between the two classes? If so, we conclude that the instruction manipulation "took." Did the students who believe the teacher was effective do better than those who believe he was ineffective? If so, we conclude that beliefs mediate the link between the instruction and the performance.

The second strategy involves formulating likely third variables and then eliminating them by explicit test. To the degree that we test for plausible confounds and find them unlikely, we conclude that our original hypothesis is correct.

Let's return once more to the classroom example. We unobtrusively observe the students in the two classes and count the number of smiling versus frowning faces we see at any point in time. Maybe we calculate attendance. Or suppose we count how many students in the two classes are listening to music on their headphones. If none of these measures bears any relationship to the manipulated cause or the measured effect, then we can be confident that thoughts indeed affect behavior.

So much for the commonsense notion, "I think, therefore I am." To this maxim, we have to add temporal considerations, experimental manipulations, internal checks, and scrutiny of third variables. Descartes had an easier time than the researcher working within the cognitive-behavioral paradigm.

Conclusions from cognitive research rest ultimately on a plausibility judgment. Someone can always think of a possible third variable, of a way to argue that thoughts and beliefs do not play an important role in personality. The bottom line is slippery: Does the third variable strike one as more or less plausible than an appeal to cognition? At present, most personality psychologists agree that the case for the importance of cognition has been persuasively made. Let's discuss some of the lines of research that have convinced them.

Personal Control

A host of theories within psychology talk about an individual's sense of **personal control:** beliefs about how well he or she can bring about good events and avoid bad events. These theories stress that such beliefs do more than reflect one's past competence in controlling events; they also determine a person's future actions with respect to events. A heightened sense of personal control is associated with emotional, behavioral, and even physiological vigor in the face of challenge. A diminished sense of control accompanies helplessness, apathy, and illness.

Personal control: One's belief about how well he or she can bring about good events and avoid bad events.

Lack of control over events may be distressing.

For instance, if you are well-prepared and confident about a test you are to take, you will approach the exam in a forthright fashion. You'll arrive on time and your pencils will be sharp. If your exam is missing a page, you'll notice it immediately and tell the proctor. You are in charge.

But if you are poorly prepared for a test, you will take the exam as a wimp would. You'll arrive late, and you'll bring a pencil when you need a pen—or vice versa. And it's only as you hand in the exam that you realize it was missing an entire page. Oh no! You are not in charge: The exam is.

These extremes capture the endpoints of personal control. Although a person's sense of control is shaped by the facts of the matter, it is not identical to them. So, confident students high on personal control may be overestimating their mastery of the material, while unconfident students low on personal control may be underestimating their knowledge. What is intriguing and important about personal control is that these beliefs have effects on subsequent coping beyond the facts. All things being equal, the individual with a sense of control outperforms the individual without a sense of control. This happens even when all things are not equal.

The roots of contemporary theories of personal control go back to Alfred Adler and the neoFreudians, who proposed that people are driven to interact effectively with their environment. And, as you recall, Henry Murray introduced the achievement motive. In an important paper, Robert White (1959) drew these early ideas together and labeled the motivation to be competent **effectance motivation.** He called the experience of effective interaction with the environment a feeling of *efficacy.* Remember learning to catch a baseball, thread a needle, or choose a course schedule that let you sleep until noon? The exhilaration you felt as you mastered these activities is what White means by efficacy. Even today, you are impelled to do these things well, for no other reason than the pleasure that comes from doing something in a competent way.

Effectance motivation: One's drive to interact with the environment in a competent fashion.

The work of Adler, Murray, and White does not fall directly within the cognitive-behavioral paradigm, because their constructs stressed the motivational aspects of a person's sense of control. But the cognitive revolution of the 1960s transformed these motivational theories by rephrasing them in the new language of information processing. Effectance changed from a motive, with biological connotations, to an idea (belief, expectation, attribution, or perception). Where the early theorists emphasized one's drive to master the environment, the new generation of theorists spoke instead of one's beliefs about whether or not this could be done.

Recasting effectance motivation as beliefs has two important implications. First, the attention of researchers is directed toward specific aspects of the person, because beliefs are always about something. Motivation can be general, but beliefs are always specific. The specificity of beliefs about personal control distinguishes them from traits and improves our ability to predict future behavior from them. Second, the cognitive transformation of personal control encourages researchers to look to the environment and the way a person interacts with it. Where motives reside within a person, beliefs refer to both the person and his or her world. Again, because beliefs in personal control span the person, the environment, and their interaction, one's ability to predict future behavior is enhanced.

The consequences of people's beliefs about control were examined in a variety of studies beginning in the 1960s. "Control" was operationalized in different ways: as ability to choose, as ability to predict, and so on. Regardless, research results converged to show that control is usually beneficial (Janis, 1983). Further, people do not need to exercise control in order to benefit from it (Averill, 1973; Miller, 1979; Thompson, 1981). The mere perception of control is sufficient to reduce stress, increase motivation, and encourage performance.

For instance, Glass and Singer (1972) exposed research subjects to bursts of an unpleasant noise. Half the subjects were told they could shut off the noise by pushing a button; the other subjects were not given the option. All were then given a proofreading task. The subjects who believed they had control over the original noise (even though they never pushed the button) made fewer proofreading errors than the other subjects. This is a striking illustration of the notion that behavior occurs in a psychological environment sometimes at odds with the physical world.

As noted, numerous theories of personal control compete in the professional literature (Peterson & Stunkard, 1989). In Chapter 11, we mentioned two of these: Rotter's locus-of-control concept and Bandura's notion of self-efficacy. Another well-known account of personal control is **learned**

Learned helplessness: Inappropriate passivity resulting from a belief in helplessness learned from experience with uncontrollable events.

helplessness, a theory of why people (and animals) act in an inappropriately passive way and fail to cope with demands fully within their competence.

Psychologists Steve Maier and Martin Seligman (1976) suggest that individuals act helplessly because they have learned to be helpless. The critical determinant of such helplessness is experience with uncontrollable events. What happens when individuals repeatedly encounter bad outcomes, regardless of what they do or don't do?

According to Maier and Seligman, they learn that bad outcomes are indeed uncontrollable. This learning leads to a general expectation that future outcomes will be uncontrollable. The diminished sense of personal control thereby produces ineffective behavior.

Learned helplessness was first investigated in dogs and rats. Maier and Seligman exposed animals to a series of uncontrollable shocks. Twenty-four hours later, the animals were tested in a shuttlebox. In a shuttlebox an animal receives a shock it can turn off by moving from one end of the box to the other (that is, by shuttling). Most animals learn to shuttle with no difficulty.

In striking contrast, though, the animal previously exposed to uncontrollable shocks fails to learn how to escape. It sits there and passively absorbs the shocks. In a word, the animal is *helpless*. You might be thinking that the helpless animal was traumatized by the shocks the day before, but this is not the case. Dogs or rats exposed to physically identical shocks that they can control have no trouble learning to escape in the shuttlebox.

Seligman (1975) argues that learned helplessness occurs among people as well as animals. Research shows that a host of psychological and physical difficulties follow bad life events outside a person's control—like unemployment, death of a spouse, or victimization. The generalization of helplessness theory from animals to people is far from perfect, though, because research also shows that people exhibit a variety of responses to the same life events.

What determines people's helplessness versus vigor in the face of uncontrollability? In a refinement of helplessness theory, Lyn Abramson, Martin Seligman, and John Teasdale (1978) argued that one important influence on reactions to uncontrollability is a person's causal interpretation of the original bad events.

When people encounter an uncontrollable event, they ask why it happened. Their answer channels their particular response to the event. Three aspects of causal explanation are important. An *internal* explanation ("It's me") makes self-esteem loss more likely than an *external* explanation ("It's the economy"). A *stable* explanation ("It's going to last forever") leads to more prolonged helplessness than an *unstable* explanation ("It's just one of those days"). A *global* explanation ("It's going to screw up everything I do") produces more pervasive deficits than a *specific* explanation ("It's the heat in that place").

Explanatory style: One's habitual way of explaining bad events involving the self.

Individuals show a characteristic style of offering causal explanations for bad events, habitually favoring certain explanations instead of others. **Explanatory style** is therefore an individual difference, ranging from pessimistic (when uncontrollable bad events are explained with internal, stable, and global causes) to optimistic (when the opposite explanations are invoked). People with

TABLE 12–1
Example of a Questionnaire Item Measuring Explanatory Style

Please try to imagine yourself in the situation that follows. If such a situation happened to you, what do you feel would have caused it? While events may have many causes, we want you to pick only one—the major cause if this event happened to you.

Please write the cause in the blank provided after each event. Next we want you to answer three questions about the cause you provided.

Event: You have a serious fight with your best friend.

A. Write down the one major cause: _____

B. Is the cause of this something about you or something about other people or circumstances? (circle one number)

totally due to others	1	2	3	4	5	6	7	totally due to me

C. In the future, will this cause again be present? (circle one number)

never present	1	2	3	4	5	6	7	always present

D. Is this cause something that affects just this type of situation, or does it also influence other areas of your life? (circle one number)

just this situation	1	2	3	4	5	6	7	all situations

a pessimistic explanatory style are presumably at greater risk for helplessness in the wake of actual bad events than are their optimistic counterparts (Peterson & Seligman, 1984).

Explanatory style is measured in one of two ways I helped to develop. The first way is with a questionnaire that presents research subjects with hypothetical bad events for them to explain (Peterson et al., 1982; Peterson & Villanova, 1988). They imagine each event happening to themselves and then write down its "one major cause," which they rate according to its internality, stability, and globality (see Table 12-1). These ratings are combined to yield an overall explanatory-style score for each subject.

The second way of measuring explanatory style is with content analysis. When people write or speak about events involving themselves, they frequently include explanations for why these events happened. A researcher can locate these explanations in letters, diaries, interviews, speeches, and the like, and rate them for their internality, stability, and globality (Peterson, Schulman, Castellon, & Seligman, 1991). Again, ratings are combined into an overall explanatory-style score for each subject.

Learned helplessness theory and particularly the notion of explanatory style have been widely applied to human ills. For example, studies have shown that those with a pessimistic explanatory style, when compared to those who are optimistic, are more likely to be

- depressed (Sweeney, Anderson, & Bailey, 1986)
- getting bad grades in school (Peterson & Barrett, 1987)
- performing poorly at work (Seligman & Schulman, 1986)
- lonely (Anderson, Horowitz, & French, 1983)
- in poor health (Peterson, Seligman & Vaillant, 1988)

We will discuss some of these applications in detail in the next chapter. In the present context, their significance lies in showing the importance of cognition.

Learned-helplessness researchers have long tried to show that cognitions are responsible for the phenomena to which their theory has been applied. When Steve Maier and Martin Seligman first described their helpless dogs, other researchers proposed explanations unrelated to cognition. Some argued that the animals were physiologically traumatized by their exposure to uncontrollable shock. Others argued that the animals had learned to hold still during the initial shocks, thereby decreasing the intensity. And still others suggested (tongue in cheek, I hope) that Maier and Seligman were using dead animals in their studies. Physiological trauma, holding still, and death do not involve beliefs in response-outcome independence or expectations of uncontrollability.

Maier and Seligman (1976) conducted a series of studies to rule out these alternative explanations and support their cognitive hypothesis. Central to these studies was the *triadic design,* a procedure using three different groups of animals. Animals in Group One are exposed to shocks that can be terminated by some response, like pushing a lever. Animals in Group Two are *yoked* to those in Group One, which means they are given the exact same shocks with the critical difference that no control over their offset is allowed. Animals in Group Three receive no shock whatsoever, controllable or uncontrollable.

All three groups are then tested at the same task. What does it mean when animals in Group Two act passively in comparison to those in Groups One and Three? Obviously, they are helpless. More interesting, though, is that one cannot plausibly attribute their passivity to trauma, because Group One animals experienced the same physical events.

What about the argument that "helpless" animals have learned to hold still, and that their inactivity produces helplessness in the later situation? In an ingenious experiment, Maier (1970) ruled out this possibility by arranging matters so that animals in Group One could control shock *by doing nothing.* If they made a movement, shock would continue. If they held still, shock would cease. If the argument that learned helplessness involves learning to hold still is a good one, then Group One animals should be impaired at the test task. This was not the case, so Maier concluded that helplessness was mediated by a belief in uncontrollability.

When learned helplessness was first studied in people, researchers borrowed the triadic design to support the inference that cognitive factors are involved. Consistent with the animal studies, human studies found that people exposed to uncontrollable bad events—usually problems that could not be solved—behaved differently than those exposed to controllable bad events (or to no events at all). Perseverance, problem solving, aggression, and sense of humor are just some of the activities affected by uncontrollable bad events (Seligman, 1975).

These studies suggest that cognitions are responsible for the observed behaviors. This conclusion is further supported when manipulation checks (questions about perceived control) distinguish among groups in the triadic design and map into the particular deficits that comprise learned helplessness. Interestingly, manipulation checks don't always work out (Tennen, 1982). Whether subjects report they have control or not may have little to do with whether they act helpless. This may mean that subjects cannot report with validity on their "control."

Although it seems clear that learned-helplessness effects are produced by cognitions, debate is spirited concerning the exact nature of the thoughts that intervene between uncontrollable bad events and listless behavior. According to helplessness theory, the critical belief concerns personal control. But some theorists have suggested that helpless individuals are ruminating about their past experiences (Kuhl, 1981); they do poorly at subsequent tasks because they are distracted. And still other theorists have proposed that helplessness is produced by someone giving up in order to save face (Frankel & Snyder, 1978). In other words, following an initial failure, one may stop trying in order to protect one's self-esteem; presumably one feels less shame in failing when one does not try again than in failing when one does (cf. Berglas & Jones, 1978).

Let's turn to studies of explanatory style and how researchers have attempted to demonstrate that cognitions indeed are the critical factor. As I have already discussed, a correlation between two variables at the same point in time is inherently ambiguous with regard to causality. Many studies of explanatory style can be criticized because they take this approach, simultaneously measuring explanatory style and some supposed consequence, such as depression or poor performance. Correlations between explanatory style and this other characteristic may mean that explanatory style is the cause, but they may just as plausibly mean something else (Peterson & Seligman, 1984).

Longitudinal studies where explanatory style is ascertained at one point in time and its supposed consequence at a later point are more persuasive. This research design rules out the possibility that the explanatory style is in actuality determined by its hypothesized consequence. Seligman and Schulman (1986) measured the explanatory style of insurance agents as they began their careers, then followed them for a year. The pessimists were more likely to quit than the optimists, and among those who stayed on the job, the pessimists failed to sell as many policies as the optimists.

And more persuasive still are longitudinal studies that explicitly investigate the role of possible confounds. If cognitions in the form of explanatory style are important, a link between explanatory style and a supposed consequence should be demonstrable even when third variables are held constant. Peterson and Barrett (1987), for example, showed that a pessimistic explanatory style among college freshmen predicted a low grade point average at the end of their first year, even when their Scholastic Aptitude Test scores were taken into account.

This shows that the third variable of "ability" does not account for the correlation between explanatory style and grades.

When explanatory style is used to predict subsequent difficulties, one of the most likely third variables is the initial degree of problems an individual experiences. Pessimistic explanatory style has been linked to poor health in longitudinal studies, for example, but it might well be that sickly individuals are pessimistic *and* stay in poor health. This would still result in a correlation between explanatory style at Time One and poor health at Time Two, but without cognition being important.

The way around this confound is to additionally measure someone's health status at Time One and show that the relationship between his or her initial explanatory style and subsequent poor health still holds when the initial health status is taken into account. Peterson, Seligman, and Vaillant (1988) did exactly this in showing that a pessimistic explanatory style among young men predicted poor health 35 years later, regardless of their initial health status.

Not all psychologists are convinced that explanatory style is as pervasive in its effects as I have been implying. The way it is measured has been criticized (e.g., Carver, 1989), as has its conception as a stable and pervasive individual difference (e.g., Cutrona, Russell, & Jones, 1985). Some studies have found that people's optimism or pessimism rises and falls with their level of depression, implying that explanatory style may not always cause depression (Hamilton & Abramson, 1983). It is reasonable to conclude, therefore, that research into explanatory style is unfinished business (Peterson, 1991). Regardless, the points raised in this discussion about how to show that cognition is important remain valid ones. Any and all cognitive notions introduced by cognitive-behavioral theorists need to be scrutinized in the ways I have discussed.

Let me close this section by speaking in general about the psychology of personal control. I have written a paper with psychiatrist Albert Stunkard arguing that the various theories of personal control are more alike than different (Peterson & Stunkard, 1989). We combined locus of control, learned helplessness, self-efficacy, and another dozen or so similar theories. Here is the composite we created:

1. Personal control is one of the important ways people differ from each other.
2. Personal control resides in the transaction between the person and the world; it is neither just a disposition nor just a characteristic of the environment.
3. Personal control may take the form of believing that one can effect actual outcomes, choose among them, cope with their consequences, and/or understand them.
4. In a responsive environment, personal control is desirable; it encourages emotional, behavioral, and physiological vigor in the face of challenge.
5. Personal control may be thwarted by failure and encouraged by success, although it does not bear a one-to-one relationship to past patterns of success and failure.

So, personal control is both a cause and a consequence of the way people respond to their environment.

Stunkard and I believe that theories of personal control are popular today because personal control is a salient matter in the world. Perhaps it is *the* salient issue of the times, in a way it has never been before. Several historical factors combine to make the 1990s the age of personal control.

First is the unlimited number of choices we face among material goods: What kind of car? What color refrigerator? What brand of running shoes? What kind of personal computer? These choices may sometimes overwhelm us, but they underscore the control we have over the trappings of the material world.

Second is the series of assassinations of charismatic American leaders: John F. Kennedy, Martin Luther King, and Robert Kennedy, along with the rash of terrorism and highjacking. The fact a lone gunman can bring about profound changes in the course of world events is an unparalleled realization. Assassins and terrorists have control, and in the face of their deeds, everyday people have no control.

Third is the Vietnam War and the generation that protested against it. Raised in accordance with Dr. Spock, who counseled parents to follow their children's lead in choosing when and where to eat, sleep, and be toilet trained, the young people of the 1960s exercised the personal control encouraged within them. However murky the Vietnam era may be, it is clear that millions of individuals decided against all precedent *not* to participate in a war. And they didn't. Personal control became the badge of this generation, some of whom are now leading figures in the social sciences.

Fourth, and perhaps most important, since Hiroshima, we have been faced with the possibility that a single individual can end life for all of us simply by pushing a button, regardless of anything the rest of us might do. Again: Personal

Senseless bad events, like the murder of John Lennon, may threaten the personal control of all people in our society.

control ranging from total to nil is illustrated in a way never so clear to previous generations. Is it surprising that psychologists within the cognitive-behavioral paradigm accord such importance to one's belief in personal control?

In pursuing the topic of personal control, psychologists must be careful not to focus exclusively on the individual and thereby overlook the role of reality in shaping his or her beliefs. Personal control is a belief, and people do not have infinite choices over what they believe. They certainly should not be blamed if they happen to lack a sense of control, because their belief may well have a basis in the facts of the matter.

Schemas

Another line of work within the cognitive-behavioral paradigm that demonstrates the importance of cognition is investigating schemas. As I earlier discussed, a schema is a cognitive representation of what one knows. A person uses a schema to go beyond immediate information. The notion of a schema is similar to Lewin's life space, Kelly's construct system, and Scott's cognitive domain. The basic idea is that what we know is organized, and the details of the organization dictate our attention, recall, and use of information. In short, a schema channels our behavior and so helps to define our personality.

Schema notions have long been popular in experimental psychology's study of cognition, particularly among theorists who regard memory as an active process of interpretation (Bartlett, 1932). In other words, people use their schemas to construct memories as they need them. They provide the raw material for these constructions.

Contrast this with another view of memory that sees the process as essentially passive, as making a carbon copy of the sensations and perceptions we experience and retrieving the copy whenever we remember anything. This is a commonsense perspective, but experimental psychologists have proven it wrong (Neisser, 1967). Memory instead involves the interpretation of events through their assimilation to existing knowledge. The notion that memory is active has been shown in numerous experiments that find that people "remember" events that never occurred if these events are congruent with other beliefs and experiences. So, in the earlier example of the Greek student, you are positive that she told you she was in a sorority because all of your other ideas lead you to this (mistaken) memory.

On the other hand, experiments also have shown that people fail to remember events that actually did occur if these events are incongruent with their general knowledge. Again, the Greek student may have once mentioned that she was familiar with the Parthenon, but this fact did not stay with you, because it didn't jibe with your view of her.

More generally, people may not know that they go beyond the information available. Because one's inferences are often correct, the line is fuzzy between them and actual facts about the world. This is an example of the give-and-take between the person and the world that is critical to the cognitive-behavioral paradigm. One's schema is the meeting point between the two.

The original proponents of the schema concept were interested in molecular activities like learning and memory. Schema ideas began to be applied to personality when gestalt psychologists like Kurt Lewin transported gestalt ideas to complex behaviors. They argued that social behavior needs to be understood by attending to the individual's interpretations, and further that these interpretations have a particular structure or pattern—what is now called a schema.

An early application of the schema idea to personality was **implicit personality theory** (Schneider, 1973), another instance of the person-as-scientist metaphor. Most people have a "theory" about personality: about which traits go with each other. They use these theories to make sense of themselves and others. Like all cognitive strategies, sometimes these theories prove useful in predicting, understanding, and even controlling what happens. Other times, these theories get the person into trouble.

Implicit personality theory: Someone's beliefs about what traits tend to co-occur with one another.

Psychologist Daryl Bem gives us insight into the implicit personality theories of students who take one of his large classes and find him "open, personable, and friendly before a sea of 300 faces" (Bem & Allen, 1974, p. 509). Their "theory" about personality leads them to assume that Professor Bem will be even more outgoing when they visit him in his office. Instead, he is "rather formal" in this different setting, and they become confused. He appears "blatantly inconsistent" (p. 509). The careful way of describing his inconsistency is *not* to attribute it to the discrepancy between what he does in one setting versus another so much as to say inconsistency occurs between what he does and what his students believe he should do.

You saw in Chapter 9 how Walter Mischel (1968) used the idea of schemas to criticize trait theories of personality. According to Mischel, people "see" consistency that isn't really present because their schemas concerning personality traits includes the assumption of consistency. They fill in the blanks and make consistency out of nothing at all.

Nancy Cantor and Walter Mischel (1977, 1979) argued that the trait terms popular in personality psychology are really ideal categories (or *prototypes*) used by people to make sense of themselves and others. These categories reflect on the one hand actual characteristics of people and on the other hand implicit "theories" about people. In their research, Cantor and Mischel demonstrated how prototypes affect what we perceive and remember about a person. So, if we are told that someone we are to meet is an extravert, we tend to notice their outgoing behaviors and recall them later. By using such schemata to understand other people, we exaggerate the consistencies they show.

However, an interesting thing happened to this particular criticism of personality consistency: Theorists became interested in schemas as personality characteristics in their own right. After all, a schema well satisfies much of what we mean by personality, as discussed in Chapter 1. They are obviously psychological in nature; they have a degree of generality and stability; they differ from person to person; they are related to other characteristics of a person; and they influence adaptation.

At the same time, let me emphasize that a schema is not a trait. First, by definition, a schema is tied to a particular domain. It refers to a subset of the world. The situational specificity of a schema is part of its meaning. Our schema for sports cars, let us say, is irrelevant to the way we thinks about family members.

Second, a schema is not fixed. We use it to interpret events we encounter, but at the same time, a schema changes as we use it. Schemas have inertia; they do not always change rapidly in the face of contrary facts, and sometimes they do not change at all. But schemas do not blind us completely to information inconsistent with them (Higgins & Bargh, 1987). I've been known to misread the thermometer outside my window and leave my apartment without bringing a coat. Despite my belief that it is warm outside, my chattering teeth and blue fingers soon persuade me that I am wrong. The same happens with respect to any schema, although individual differences exist in the responsiveness of schemas to contrary information.

Self-schema: Organized beliefs about one's own self.

A full-blown theory of personality based on schemas has yet to be proposed. However, steps in this direction are currently being taken by researchers who conceptualize the self in schema terms. A **self-schema** can be defined as knowledge about one's own self. Markus and Wurf (1987, p. 300) elaborated this definition to propose that the self is "a dynamic interpretive structure that mediates most significant *intrapersonal* processes . . . and a wide variety of *interpersonal* processes." This view of the self in schema terms has several important implications.

For starters, the self is no longer conceived as monolithic. Because schemas by definition are tied to specific content areas, we should expect that one's self-schema is similarly multifaceted (Sande, Goethals, & Radloff, 1988). In other words, someone's sense of self is really a collection of different cognitive representations: my self as a friend, my self as a son or daughter, my self as a student, my self as an athlete, and so on. Great variation across different people exists in the content and structure of such self-representations.

The most obvious way self-representations differ is in terms of their content. Sandra Bem (1981, 1984), whose work on androgyny I discussed in Chapter 9, has more recently interpreted people's sex-role orientations in terms of the schemas people possess about the appropriate characteristics and behaviors of males and females. Many people in our society intermingle these **gender schemas** with their self-schemas, resulting in individuals for whom gender—their own and that of others—is front and center in all interactions (Frable, 1989).

Where does androgyny fit into this view? Bem has suggested that androgynous individuals do *not* view the world through the framework of a gender schema, which is to say they differ from "traditional" masculine and feminine individuals. Bem's particular view of androgyny has been challenged by other psychologists (e.g., Edwards & Spence, 1987; Forbach, Evans, & Bodine, 1986; Payne, Connor, & Colletti, 1987). The major point of contention is her hypothesis that androgynous individuals lack gender schemas. A different hypothesis is that androgynous individuals possess schemas that combine masculine and feminine characteristics and roles.

This argument is supported in a reaction-time experiment conducted by Markus, Crane, Bernstein, and Siladi (1982). Subjects completed Bem's questionnaire measure of sex-role orientation (Chapter 9) and were classified as masculine, feminine, or androgynous. They were then shown a list of trait words (one at a time) and asked to make a "like me" or "unlike me" decision in each case. Words were masculine, feminine, or neutral in connotation.

Masculine subjects made quicker decisions about masculine words than did feminine subjects. Feminine subjects in turn made quicker decisions about feminine words than did masculine subjects. What about androgynous subjects? Bem (1981) proposed that these individuals are aschematic with respect to gender and so would predict their reaction times to be slower than sex-typed subjects for both masculine and feminine words. But this was not the case. Instead, androgynous subjects reacted as quickly to masculine words as did masculine subjects and as quickly to feminine words as did feminine subjects. These findings imply that androgynous individuals are not blind to gender stereotypes. Rather, they think about themselves in terms that blend masculine and feminine characteristics. They interpret information to fit their multiple-gender self-schemas.

Beyond this debate, a schema interpretation of androgyny is more powerful than the previous conception of it as a trait. It spans the person and the world, and so explains where androgyny is adaptive and where it is not. It also implies how androgyny might originate and change. Perhaps most important, a gender schema has just as much to say about traditional individuals as it does about androgynous ones.

Self-representations also differ in terms of their importance to the individual. Self-conceptions that are central to an individual tend to be complex

Gender schema: Organized beliefs about the appropriate characteristics and behaviors of men and women.

and pervasive in their influence. For example, my sense of self as a teacher is central to me. It is a highly elaborate and detailed schema, composed of many different beliefs. It includes all the things I know how to do as a teacher, what Mischel calls competencies. I know how to prepare a syllabus, give a lecture, write an examination, grade a paper, and defuse classroom strife. I know the sorts of films to show in class. I know to check the calendar for religious holidays before scheduling midterms.

In contrast, my sense of self as a bicyclist, let us say, is not at all central. I recently bought a bicycle, and I am slowly beginning to use it, riding around my neighborhood on the weekends. I have not been on a bicycle in years, and I quite literally do not know what I am doing. Shifting gears, avoiding potholes, and choosing a route that doesn't go in a circle are very difficult. The point is that my schema for riding a bicycle is clearly a crude one, and it is reflected in my ineptness. I am not embarrassed about being a fool on my new bicycle, because this activity so far is peripheral to my thoughts about who I truly am. If I gave a lecture as poorly as I ride my bicycle, I would be highly distressed.

Yet another way self-representations differ is in terms of whether they have been achieved or not. I already am a teacher, for example, so this aspect of my self-schema refers to something that actually exists. But myself as a champion bicycle racer, to continue the contrast, is merely a possible self.

Markus and Nurius (1986) have discussed the importance of such possible selves. They may be desired or undesired, and in either case, the more strongly a person feels about a possible self, the more it influences present behavior. If you are in school preparing for a career, you may well possess a possible self that depicts you as a doctor, lawyer, or teacher. Your everyday activities are obviously channeled and influenced by the goal you have set for yourself (Van Hook & Higgins, 1988). Other possible selves are negative ones, and if these are the only ones people envision, they may be one step closer to achieving these as well (cf. Oyserman & Markus, 1990).

Along these lines, some researchers have been particularly interested in the self-representations of chronically depressed people. They suggest that depression is maintained at least in part by a **depressive schema:** a cognitive structure that tunes in negative information about the self while tuning out positive information (Bargh & Tota, 1988). One insidious way depressive schemas may exacerbate depression is by facilitating recall of negative memories (Blaney, 1986; Johnson & Magaro, 1987). Think about it. Depressed individuals more readily recall disappointments; these in turn make them even more depressed.

Another implication of viewing the self in terms of schemas is that the self is seen as dynamic, meaning that aspects of it are in constant flux, depending on situational demands. Theorists introduce the notion of the **working self-concept** to describe the aspect of the self salient at a particular moment. When I am riding my bicycle, my schema of self as a bicyclist—however primitive it may be—is nonetheless engaged. When I pursue other activities, this particular schema is no longer salient. Highly central aspects of the self remain chronically salient (Higgins, King, & Mavin, 1982), which means that one's self also possesses the continuity theorists wish to attribute to it.

Depressive schema: Organized beliefs that maintain depression by attuning the person to negative information about the self.

Working self-concept: The aspect of the self schema salient at a particular moment.

From the perspective of self-schemas, people are seen as controlling and directing their own actions, with the self as the center of this activity. Granted their particular self-schemas, they set certain goals for themselves, plan certain behaviors to achieve these goals, carry them out, monitor their progress, and evaluate their eventual success (Bandura, 1978). Individual differences exist at all stages in this process of self-regulation.

Psychologist Anthony Greenwald (1980) provided an interesting perspective on self-regulation, by comparing the self to a totalitarian state. In both cases, he argued, information is ruthlessly controlled and shamelessly altered to fit current needs. So, people constantly revise their personal history in light of current events (Ross, 1989). They highlight and aggrandize their own roles. They ignore inconsistencies (Swann, Pelham, & Krull, 1989). They shirk responsibility for failure while embracing success.

The totalitarian nature of our self-schemas is not necessarily bad. After reviewing the research literature on making excuses for oneself, Snyder and Higgins (1988) concluded that excuses are often beneficial, at least for the person who makes them. The typical excuse shifts blame for negative outcomes in such a way to allow a person to preserve self-esteem: "Yes, I know I didn't complete the work I promised, but I was taking care of a sick friend, and I knew you would understand." Excuses may also help people believe they have control over outcomes, even if they did not exercise it. In the example just given, the implication is clear that the excuse-maker believes she or he could have done the work. Failures ordinarily take a toll on personal control, but excuses allow you to have it both ways.

In a related line of research, Shelley Taylor (1989) has catalogued the **positive illusions** many people hold. Individuals typically think they are above average in looks, intelligence, sense of humor, and popularity. They typically think tomorrow will be better than today. They typically expect to be free of headache and hassle.

Positive illusion: The pervasive belief that one's lot in life is better than it actually is.

I once administered a questionnaire that asked, among many other questions, how long the respondent expected to live. I then devised a coding sheet where I planned to transfer the answers I obtained. I allocated two spaces on the coding sheet for the answer about expected age. However, I should have allocated three spaces, because the typical subject expected to live in excess of 100 years. Needless to say, virtually all of them will be wrong.

So, most people have a pervasive tendency to see their lot in life as better than it is. The punchline is that these people are happier and better adjusted as a result (Taylor & Brown, 1988). Among the handful of individuals who fail to embrace positive illusions, unhappiness, social isolation, and even poor health are common.

Psychodynamic theorists identify positive illusions as instances of denial and expect them to be associated with emotional difficulties. That just the opposite seems to be the case is striking and leads us to rethink what it means to be healthy and insightful. Indeed, some theorists have provocatively argued that depression results from seeing things as they really are (Alloy & Abramson, 1979).

Throughout the book, we have seen that many personality theorists have felt the need to propose that people have a self: an entity that somehow integrates diverse characteristics and results in behavioral continuity. Freud proposed the ego to fill the role, and Allport suggested the proprium. Cognitive-behavioral theorists have turned to schemas to make sense of the self (Schlenker, 1985; Suls & Greenwald, 1983). This endeavor has been productive to date, although several problems do seem to exist.

First, the schema notion strikes some as mushy (Fiske & Linville, 1980). Despite the methodological rigor of schema research, theorizing has not always kept pace, and the very meaning of a schema is debated. Second, schemas are seen as nothing new (Fiske & Linville, 1980). Is a schema different than a system of personal constructs? At a conceptual level, perhaps not. However, at a research level, they are quite different, because schema research reveals cognitive processes in a way personal construct research does not. Third, in common with other cognitive-behavioral perspectives on personality, the schema approach does a better job explaining "cold" activities like perception and memory than "hot" activities like motivation and emotion (Pittman & Heller, 1987).

Social Intelligence

The cognitive-behavioral approach to personality shifts our attention from what people have—such as traits—to what people do (Cantor, 1990). One obviously important thing people do is to think, and in our discussion of personal control and schemas, we saw how people's thinking has great consequences for everything else about them. Yet another line of research concerned with what people do is Cantor and Kihlstrom's (1987) work on social intelligence, which we briefly mentioned in Chapter 11 while discussing Mischel's version of social learning theory. Let's now take a closer look at social intelligence, because it is a good illustration of research within the cognitive-behavioral paradigm.

Social intelligence: The knowledge people bring to bear on the problems encountered in everyday life.

Cantor and Kihlstrom define **social intelligence** as the knowledge people bring to bear on the problems they encounter in everyday life. It is instructive to contrast social intelligence with the sort of intelligence psychologists over the years have tried to measure with IQ tests. "Intelligence" as operationally defined with an IQ score is presumably stable and general. Intelligence in this sense is thought to transcend the particular content of what someone knows and reflect his or her capacity for knowing.

Because social intelligence refers to expertise at particular tasks, it is necessarily tied closely to given domains. Here we see agreement with the view of intelligence championed by Howard Gardner (1983), as discussed in Chapter 10; many different ways to be intelligent exist, because many different settings in which to display one's expertise exist. Social intelligence is further regarded as highly malleable. When we learn to do something better, we necessarily become more intelligent.

Traditional approaches to intelligence are not particularly concerned with the psychological processes responsible for intelligent behavior (Sternberg, 1985). But Cantor and Kihlstrom are greatly concerned with how people acquire expertise and with how they then use it. Their approach is very much in keeping with the thrust of the cognitive-behavioral paradigm, because it focuses attention on how cognition mediates a person's learning and performance.

Cantor and Kihlstrom have borrowed heavily from experimental psychology's study of cognition. Experimental psychologists typically study such cognitive processes as memory, judgment, decision making, and concept formation by seeing how research subjects in laboratory experiments respond to tasks involving simple stimuli. Subjects may be asked to memorize lists of nonsense syllables, unscramble anagrams, or interpret brief stories. Such investigations have suggested various notions that Cantor and Kihlstrom believe can be used to understand how people think about the complex tasks of real life.

Not all agree with this assumption (Ostrom, 1984). The tasks of real life differ from laboratory studies because they usually involve thinking about other people. And people differ from simple stimuli in a number of obvious ways (Heider, 1944, 1958):

■ People intentionally influence the environment.
■ People think about us as we are thinking about them.
■ People may change under our scrutiny, and we may change under their scrutiny.
■ People's actions often demand explanation and justification.

Some argue, therefore, that theoretical concepts from experimental psychology's study of cognition must be generalized only with extreme caution (Fiske & Taylor, 1984). Indeed, many psychologists use the term **social cognition** to describe how people think about the social world, with the explicit intent of distinguishing social cognition from cognition per se.

Social cognition: Thoughts and beliefs about the social world.

Regardless, Cantor and Kihlstrom (1987) believe considerable continuity occurs across social and nonsocial domains in the ways our knowledge is structured. Of course the content of our knowledge differs, depending on whether we are thinking about how to do long-division on the one hand versus how to make friends on the other. But the manner in which our knowledge is acquired, organized, and used may be highly similar, regardless of the domain of thought. Perhaps the best way to resolve a debate of this nature is to test the assumption in actual research. If cognitive theories lead to new insights about personality, then we can be satisfied that their generalization is legitimate.

I have so far spoken glibly of the "problems" people encounter in their everyday lives. I am referring not just to broken zippers and bounced checks but to a whole array of things you may not ordinarily think of as problems. Psychologists who specialize in problems and their solutions give us a quite broad definition of a **problem:** any discrepancy between what we know and what we want to know. In many cases, this discrepancy is easily resolved because someone knows how to proceed. The solution is readily available, so the problem is solved. But it was still a problem, no matter how briefly it existed.

Problem: A discrepancy between what one knows and what one wants to know.

With this view of problems, you can see that much of everyday life consists of encountering problems and then trying to solve them. Among my typical activities every morning are waking up, making coffee, cooking breakfast, retrieving my mail, planning my classes, and so on. All these activities are problems in that I have to do something to achieve what I want. But none of them is problematic because in each case I have the necessary expertise.

Other activities of life are both problems and problematic. Here we lack the skills to reduce the discrepancy between what we know and what we want to know. Suppose you have a bad day, and you feel down on yourself. You'd love to have a boost. Some of you know how to achieve this goal, say by calling up a good friend on the phone, by watching a Grade B horror movie, or by going to bed early. But others of you quite literally do not know what to do in order to feel better. You may therefore do nothing, hoping your bad mood will go away by itself. Or more insidiously, you may do something that makes you feel even worse, like getting in touch with a former boyfriend or girlfriend who never fails to make you feel like a loser.

Problem space: A cognitive representation of a problem.

Critical in solving a problem is depicting it in a given way to yourself. Psychologists refer to the cognitive representation of a problem as a **problem space,** and it is comprised of your current state, your desired end state, and the permissible steps for getting yourself from the former to the latter. Expertise shows itself in the way people create a particular problem space and then in how they go about solving the problem.

Interestingly, an expert in a given domain may actually spend more time thinking about a problem—representing a problem space—than a novice does (Larkin, McDermott, Simon, & Simon, 1980). An expert has a greater repertoire of possible solutions, as well as the ability to recognize which strategy will work for which problem variations. An expert also knows when enough is enough and stops trying to solve a problem when doing so creates more drawbacks than benefits. Said another way, an expert in a particular domain is able to set priorities concerning which problems are worth solving well, poorly, or not at all.

Life task: A self-defined problem to which an individual devotes time and energy during a given period of life.

These ideas about solving problems are brought to bear by Cantor and Kihlstrom (1987) in studies of how people pursue various **life tasks:** self-defined problems to which individuals devote their time and energy during a given period of life. So, life tasks are important to an individual. If and when a life task is achieved, the person will be significantly different. Life tasks entail major goals, dreams, and hopes. We might describe them as a style of life someone is trying to achieve.

You have encountered similar ideas earlier in the book. Alfred Adler, for example, proposed that all people share the goal of striving for superiority (Chapter 4). This can be seen as a universal life task. Similarly, evolutionary theorists regard survival and reproduction as universal life tasks (Chapter 10). Cantor and Kihlstrom make no assumptions about the universality of given life tasks; they see different people pursuing different tasks, depending on the circumstances of their lives.

They do observe that people in similar circumstances tend to pursue similar goals, citing Erik Erikson's psychosocial stage theory of development as an important catalogue of the life tasks in which people may be engaged at different points in their lives (Chapter 4). But at the same time, Cantor and Kihlstrom see nothing inevitable about the sequencing of most life tasks. Unlike Erikson, these theorists propose great variation in the tasks that concern individuals and in when—if ever—they choose to pursue them.

Life tasks span both the demands of given situations and the desires of given people, and so resemble the thema notion introduced by Henry Murray to encompass environmental presses and dispositional needs (Chapter 8). People know what their life tasks are and they can give an account of the activities they pursue that are relevant to these tasks. At the same time, life tasks qualify as ill-defined problems, meaning that optimal solutions are not readily available to the individual. Indeed, optimal solutions may not even exist, so part of "solving" a life task entails deciding what qualifies as a solution.

I spend a great deal of time speaking to my students about what they wish to do with their lives following graduation. With those who have an occupational goal clearly in mind, we discuss the steps they might follow in achieving it. If they wish to go to graduate or professional school, for example, they must make sure that they sign up for the required tests, that they obtain and complete applications, that they ask teachers and supervisors to write letters of recommendation on their behalf, that they send transcripts, that they buy nice clothes for interviews, that they remove offensive messages from their telephone answering machines, and so on. With those students who are unclear about the occupation they wish to pursue, we talk about how they might solve this problem, and the steps obviously differ.

Even with the same life task, people show great variety in how they construe it and thus in how they pursue it. Here Cantor and Kihlstrom have been influenced by the personal construct theory of George Kelly, because different interpretations of a task result in different approaches to its solution. Let us consider the simple example of whether someone approaches a task with optimism or pessimism: expecting the best or the worst. The optimist shows greater flexibility in the solutions he or she attempts, as well as greater perseverance (Scheier, Weintraub, & Carver, 1986). Assuming that some sort of solution is possible, then the optimist is obviously more likely to hit on it than is the pessimist.

Earlier in this chapter, I discussed positive illusions. Research on optimism versus pessimism gives us another take on these. Optimism may start out as an illusion, but it often ends up helping the person achieve a goal by sustaining effort and morale. Is optimism that proves useful still an illusion? Perhaps not. Regardless, what we have is an excellent example of the give-and-take between the person and the world. One's expectations, for the better or for the worse, end up influencing the world in which one lives, which in turn shapes future expectations, again for the better or for the worse (Miller & Turnbull, 1986).

Psychologists use the term **script** to describe someone's beliefs about the sequence of behaviors to follow in a particular setting for a particular purpose (Schank & Abelson, 1977). For example, most of us have a restaurant script that we follow so we can be seated, order a meal, and pay the bill. Other scripts are more idiosyncratic in that different people proceed in altogether different ways to achieve the same goal. Social intelligence—or its lack—is very much evident in the scripts people follow in their pursuit of life tasks.

Script: One's beliefs about the sequence of behaviors to follow in a particular setting for a particular purpose.

Much of Cantor and Kihlstrom's research into life tasks has involved college students. Their studies show that most of the life tasks pursued by typical students fall into these general categories:

■ Making friends
■ Being on one's own

- Establishing an identity
- Getting good grades
- Establishing a future direction
- Managing one's time and getting organized

These should be familiar to you, not just because you are a college student, but also because these concerns have been extensively studied by other personality psychologists, who have identified them variously as intimacy, achievement, self-actualization, and the like.

Cantor and Kihlstrom's unique contribution lies in viewing these concerns as problems to be solved and then taking a close look at what people actually do in trying to solve them. What has ensued is a great appreciation of individual variation in the pursuit of life tasks. Further, the mutual interdependence of thinking and acting is clearly evident.

Consider the life task of making friends. Langston and Cantor (1989) asked first-year college students to rate the importance of this task to themselves as well as to describe in questionnaires and interviews various other ways they regarded it. Most subjects described making friends as an important goal, so it qualifies as a shared life task. But different subjects thought about this life task in different ways. While many viewed making friends as a rewarding and simple thing to do, a minority regarded this task as difficult and fraught with anxiety. Subjects were then followed through time to ascertain how they pursued friends and how satisfied they were with the results.

According to the basic premise of cognitive-behavioral approaches, different appraisals of the same life task should have far-ranging ramifications. This is exactly what happened. Langston and Cantor (1989) showed, for example, that the subjects who were anxious about making friends approached this task quite differently than those who felt confident. Anxious subjects tended to put themselves down and see others as more appealing. Not surprisingly, many of them took a passive approach to making friends, letting other people make decisions and judgments for them.

This particular script had some benefits for subjects. Granted that someone was anxious about making friends, taking a passive approach to the task resulted in greater satisfaction and less stress. Said another way, subjects who were anxious about making friends yet did *not* follow a passive and de-pendent script were most likely to be displeased with their performance in this domain. And this approach took its toll. Anxious individuals who "solved" the problem of how to make friends actively also were on average less satis-fied with the results than those who did otherwise. I wonder if part of the reason for this pattern of results is that anxious people who are less satisfied with their friendships tend to associate with those who are not themselves rewarding people.

Langston and Cantor's (1989) study also showed that one's approach to a given life task is highly specific to that task. In other words, they studied the ways their subjects approached other life tasks and found little generality. Subjects who were passive with respect to making friends were not necessarily this way with respect to their school work.

Let's consider another life task of concern to most college students: being on one's own. In the same sample of subjects just described, Zirkel and Cantor (1990) identified two groups who appraised this task in quite different ways. Both viewed being on one's own as an important goal, but in one group, subjects regarded the task as easy and enjoyable, whereas in the other group, it was seen as difficult, stressful, time-consuming, and challenging. Again, the researchers' concern was the degree to which these appraisals influenced how subjects pursued the life task in question.

Perhaps most interesting about this study are results involving how subjects described the specific activities they saw as contributing to the solution of the "problem" of being on one's own. Subjects who saw the task as difficult regarded a greater number of activities as relevant than those who saw the task as simple. Further, those who regarded the task as difficult described relevant activities in extremely broad terms, such as "not having Mom and Dad to turn to" and "not missing my high school friends." In contrast, the other subjects mentioned as relevant such mundane and circumscribed activities as "balancing my checkbook."

"Not missing my friends" is both more pervasive and more nebulous than "balancing my checkbook." Consequently, not missing one's friends is a lot more difficult to do. I'm not even sure how individuals would know they have successfully done this. In contrast, balancing one's checkbook is straightforward in that the steps for doing so are explicit, and one can judge success by looking at the bank statement. Is it surprising that subjects who pursued the life task of being on one's own in a vague fashion experienced more stress and less satisfaction than those who followed a more mundane script?

Don't misunderstand these results. They do not mean that subjects who regard the activities relevant to a given life task in circumscribed terms care less about the life task or are somehow less thoughtful about it. To the contrary, these individuals are arguably more thoughtful because the problem space they have created for themselves is more detailed.

All behavior is necessarily specific and concrete. Social intelligence entails seeing how given behaviors relate to broader goals (Carver & Scheier, 1981). The subjects Zirkel and Cantor (1990) studied who regarded the task of being on one's own exclusively in sweeping terms were therefore at a loss in knowing how to achieve their goals.

As one more example of social intelligence research, let us consider the task of getting good grades. Norem and Cantor (1986) studied college students who all had an excellent track record. Yet within this group, different strategies were used to achieve good grades. One group Norem and Cantor identified as optimists. They expected to do well on tests and papers, they pursued their school work with confidence and good cheer, and they indeed did well. Another group they identified were students who were pessimistic about the grades they would eventually receive yet who also did well.

Earlier we saw how positive expectations translate themselves into success and negative expectations into failure. Norem and Cantor's pessimistic subjects are an exception to this generalization. What was going on with them? These researchers discovered that this group of subjects, despite high ability and prior success, were extremely anxious about their school performance. They voiced negative expectations as a way of curbing their anxiety. By expecting the worst, they made school work less imposing. They were then able to do well. Norem and Cantor describe this phenomenon as **defensive pessimism** and conceptualize it as a strategy for achieving good grades.

Defensive pessimism: One's expectation of a negative outcome in order to curb anxiety concerning performance.

The two researchers brought defensive pessimists into a laboratory and gave them a task to perform. They provided some of the subjects with a pep talk prior to the task, telling them how well they were sure to do. When the performance of these subjects was compared to that of other defensive pessimists not given a pep talk, the former ended up doing worse. The pep talk had interfered with their strategic use of negative expectations. I hasten to add that negative expectations are usually damaging to an individual because they result in passivity (Seligman, 1975). The defensive pessimists Norem and Cantor studied are a special group because they have the ability to do well as long as they can calm themselves.

The social intelligence approach of Cantor and Kihlstrom is a promising line of research within the cognitive-behavioral paradigm. It uses ideas from experimental psychology's study of cognition to yield some genuinely new ways of regarding personality. Defensive pessimism is one example. From another perspective, we might view defensive pessimists as anxious or irrational and then move on. But from the social-intelligence perspective, their ostensibly "neurotic" behavior can be seen as functional, a good solution to a particular problem they happen to face.

The drawbacks of the social intelligence approach are those shared by the entire cognitive-behavioral paradigm. It may rest on too rational a view of people, without enough attention to their passionate and tumultuous aspects. Similarly, it may place too much emphasis on conscious thoughts and beliefs. We saw in Chapter 6 that there is good reason to believe that people's motives can be unconscious, and the social intelligence approach, at least as so far carried out, is silent on tasks that people cannot verbally report. Finally, Cantor and Kihlstrom's assumption of extreme domain specificity places them in the same bind as Bandura, studying topics removed from what is typically meant by personality. To be fair, however, it is precisely this different view of personality that makes the social intelligence approach notable (Cantor, 1990).

CONCLUSIONS: COGNITIVE-BEHAVIORAL THEORIES IN LIGHT OF THE RESEARCH

As mentioned before, of the four paradigms of personality psychology covered in this book, the cognitive-behavioral paradigm is the newest. Not surprisingly, then, research is at an uncertain stage. This helps to explain why the field has yet to agree on a particular research strategy. Both questionnaires and experimental probes are employed, but rarely by the same researcher or even within the same research tradition.

Perhaps because cognitive-behavioral research has so recently taken form, much of the relevant research can only be described as exploratory. Many investigators have labored mightily just to show the utility of looking at what and how a person thinks. These demonstrations were necessary, granted an intellectual climate in American psychology throughout much of the twentieth century that regarded *mind* as a semi-dirty word. The case for the importance of cognition has now been well made, but more specific questions are just starting to be investigated.

Let me nevertheless offer some tentative conclusions about cognitive-behavioral theories. Let's start with what this research tells us about personality. First, as illustrated by the studies reviewed in the previous section, cognition is clearly important. People's thoughts and beliefs affect their behavior, motivation, and mood. Even physical well-being is influenced by thinking. Second, the content and style of thought are in turn sensitive to the situations in which people find themselves. Thinking does not bear a one-to-one relationship to reality, but neither is it completely estranged from the way things actually are. Putting these two conclusions together, we find support for the central premise of the cognitive-behavioral model: People are engaged in a constant give-and-take with the world that is mediated by what and how they think.

"I paint what I see, child."

SOURCE: Copyright © 1971 by Gahan Wilson. Reprinted by permission of Simon & Schuster, Inc.

On the downside, this research has a great deal yet to tell us about personality. Cognitive-behavioral research supports the gist of all the theories within the paradigm without supporting any particular theory above any other. Maybe this is to be expected. Because the theories reviewed in Chapter 11 are so similar to each other, it may be impossible to distinguish among them empirically.

These theories do make differing claims about the principle that describes how cognitions are organized. Scott's research, as discussed earlier in the chapter, cautions us that no single organizational tendency is at work for all people. This insight has yet to be incorporated into the theories in question.

Another way the theories differ is on the generality versus specificity of cognitive characteristics. Rotter, for example, proposed that people entertain highly generalized expectancies. And in contrast, Bandura argued that cognitions are closely tied to particular situations. Research implies that these extreme positions are both wrong; an intermediate position that recognizes a degree of generality as well as a degree of situational specificity is more reasonable (see Peterson & Scott, 1975). Again, this conclusion has yet to be incorporated into the competing theories.

As mentioned several times, cognitive-behavioral researchers have tended to neglect "hot" cognition: the passionate aspects of thoughts. People are conceived as cool, calm, and collected processors of information—even when this information is noncool, noncalm, and noncollected. It is clear that cognitive processes are entwined with feelings, so this neglect needs to be corrected.

Relatedly, cognitive-behavioral theorists may need a better vocabulary for describing the whats and hows of the mind. Current terms force them to juxtapose thought and feeling and ask which causes which (Zajonc, 1980). Such contrasts may be strained, if not downright silly. Can cognition be better described so it does not lead us into such quandries?

We don't know enough about the origins of cognitive characteristics, which is ironic granted the importance accorded to learning by cognitive-behavioral psychologists. Research, however, tends to look more at the consequences of thought than its origins, so we have only a dim idea of why some cognitive styles develop rather than others.

Finally, most cognitive-behavioral psychologists have devoted little attention to the physiological bases of cognition and behavior. In other fields of psychology, a great deal has been learned about how the brain and nervous system work. Much of this knowledge should also be of interest to cognitive-behavioral theorists and researchers. Consider the differences in information processing believed to characterize the left versus right hemispheres of the brain (Springer & Deutsch, 1985). Consider the possibility that people differ in which hemisphere is dominant. Here is an intriguing individual difference just waiting for personality psychologists to scrutinize it (Singer, 1984). This work has yet to be assimilated into the cognitive-behavioral paradigm, where it would readily fit. The traditional opposition between mind and body may work against this assimilation. Perhaps it is time to banish this dualism and speak of people as integrated entities, not as cognitive ghosts residing in a physiological machine.

SUMMARY

The subject of this chapter was research conducted within the cognitive-behavioral paradigm. Critical in understanding the current state of research is knowing that no single procedure is universally accepted. Some researchers favor questionnaires for assessing cognition, whereas others prefer experimental techniques originally developed to study attention, memory, and decision making.

I described the questionnaire approach of William Scott, who has developed a variety of procedures for measuring individual differences in cognitive content and cognitive style. Then I described some of the techniques borrowed from experimental psychology and how they have been adapted by personality researchers.

Research converges to support the central premise of the cognitive-behavioral paradigm: People are engaged in a constant give-and-take with the world, mediated by their thoughts and beliefs. Several lines of research—on personal control, schemas, and social intelligence—were described to illustrate the type of studies conducted within the cognitive-behavioral paradigm.

Research supports the thrust of cognitive-behavioral theories in general but no single theory in particular, perhaps because these theories differ in so few ways. Future investigations within this paradigm should be concerned with the relationship between cognition and emotion, with the origins of cognitive characteristics, and with the biological basis of cognition and behavior.

COGNITIVE-
BEHAVIORAL
PARADIGM:
APPLICATIONS

"It's all in your mind."

"Take another look at it."

"Try to picture it this way."

"You don't see how to do it."

"It all depends on how you choose to see it."

"With an attitude like that, no wonder you're unhappy."

In everyday conversation, we endorse the main premise of the cognitive-behavioral paradigm: People are moved not simply by the events in the world but also by their views of those events. Accordingly, if thoughts and beliefs about these matters are changed, people and their worlds will also change.

Over the years, a number of applications of the cognitive-behavioral paradigm have developed. They share in common an attempt to explain matters by looking to a person's thoughts and beliefs, how they are acquired and how they are used. Just as for applications within the trait paradigm, individual differences are important. These are assessed by questionnaires and other procedures and are used to make decisions about people in the clinic, the classroom, or the workplace. And like applications within the psychodynamic paradigm, those within the cognitive-behavioral paradigm focus on change. Techniques for altering someone's thoughts and behaviors are used in various settings to help people adjust to difficulties there.

To date, cognitive-behavioral applications to clinical topics like psychopathology and psychotherapy have predominated, so I'll concentrate on them in this chapter. But first, I'll discuss the common pitfalls of such applications.

Two pitfalls are particularly hazardous. The first is inherent in the entire cognitive-behavioral paradigm: the short shrift of feelings and emotions. Some of the most intriguing work by cognitive-behavioral psychologists *derives* particular feelings from particular ways of thinking. But as we saw in Chapter 12, emotions also determine thoughts. Applications that ignore the possibility of a bidirectional influence often fail.

For instance, psychologists argue that conflict between people and groups may result from cognitive factors (e.g., Balke, Hammond, & Meyer, 1973). The two sides don't understand each other; they have mistaken beliefs; they don't appreciate that their opponents see things differently. Techniques for resolving conflict have made it possible for ideological opponents to walk a mile in each other's shoes, so to speak. And this is often highly successful, but at other times it simply doesn't work. Individuals and groups may hate each other for any of a number of reasons that have nothing to do with individual differences in cognition—historical events, religious doctrines, economic competition, and so on. Their hatred in turn leads to cognitive conflict, but resolving their differences in opinion doesn't change their hatred.

The second problem found in some applications is not an inherent one. Instead, it results from an oversimplification of the cognitive-behavioral approach to personality. Problems are viewed as located *solely* between someone's ears, and the possibility that the world also determines the nature of things is overlooked. Just because "it's all in your mind" is frequently said by everyday people as well as psychologists doesn't make it so.

This phrase additionally means that "it's also not in the real world." This implicit message removes the E from Lewin's equation that $B=f(P,E)$. Problems are reduced to hallucinations or projections, and they are attacked without reference to their context. This is a conservative view that may lead us to blame victims for whatever misfortune has befallen them. Indeed, a well-documented phenomenon in the social psychology literature shows that people assign responsibility even to those who suffer a clearly capricious bad event—like a rape, a car accident, or a serious injury.

Relatedly, psychologist Melvin Lerner (1971) argues that most of us need to believe in a *just world* where good and bad events are meted out according to our virtues or sins. Belief in a just world is a good gestalt since it allows us a harmonious perspective. But often the world isn't just. Innocent people suffer. And the good die young.

We tend to overlook the evidence otherwise to endorse the notion that the world is just and harmonious. We assume, for instance, that someone is on welfare because he is lazy, that someone was raped because she asked for it, that someone is ill because he doesn't take care of himself, that someone is unhappy because she is looking at things the wrong way. We ignore the possibility that the world has as much to do with these matters (including our thoughts and beliefs about it) as people themselves do.

So, in reading about applications within the cognitive-behavioral paradigm, be wary of these two shortcomings. Is the cognitive practitioner justified in looking mainly to thoughts and beliefs to explain behavior and to determine the best intervention? And in examining cognition, is the practitioner neglecting the fact the real world plays a role in shaping these cognitions?

PSYCHOPATHOLOGY AND PSYCHOTHERAPY

Synonyms for the problems suffered by people who seek out psychiatrists and clinical psychologists usually stress the physical or emotional aspects of their difficulties: mental illness, emotional disturbance, nervous breakdown, and so on. But in recent years, a new synonym has been introduced: **cognitive disorder.** This term implies that one's thoughts and beliefs lie at the center of one's problems in life. The growing popularity of this approach as applied to psychopathology can be traced directly to the growing popularity of the cognitive-behavioral perspective within personality psychology as a whole.

Contemporary psychologists are additionally excited about the cognitive-behavioral approach to psychopathology because it leads naturally to another application: psychotherapy techniques deployed against a client's harmful way of viewing matters. Granted that thoughts and beliefs lie at the center of one's problems, and granted that thoughts and beliefs are somewhat malleable, cognitions are a natural target for the therapist. To the degree that people are like computers, they can be reprogrammed. To the degree that people are like scientists, they can be given new theories.

For many years, psychotherapy meant psychoanalysis in one form or another. But with the recent popularity of the cognitive-behavioral paradigm, an alternative now exists. Techniques of **cognitive psychotherapy** provide clinical psychologists with different ways of going about their work. In this section, I'll describe some of the cognitive approaches to psychopathology and psychotherapy.

Cognitive disorder: A form of psychopathology caused and/or maintained chiefly by particular ways of thinking.

Cognitive psychotherapy: An approach to therapy that targets a client's thoughts for change.

George Kelly's Approach

George Kelly (1955) has made the most thorough attempt to explain psychopathology in cognitive terms. Using the language of personal constructs, he redefines the traditional emotional disorders. For instance, *anxiety* is defined as an individual's awareness that the events in his or her life are outside the range of convenience of available constructs. Consider our fear when driving along a remote stretch of a Nebraska interstate and seeing that the fuel gauge needle is quivering on empty. Something bad is happening, and we may not have the wherewithal to construe it. Do we have to stay stranded on the side of I-80 for the rest of our lives? If we know that the state police patrol the highway regularly, on the lookout for fools like us, then we have a construct to make sense of our experience. We'll be angry, or humiliated, or even amused. But we won't be anxious. Kelly believes anxiety results only when we are aware that our cognitive map doesn't correspond to the territory we are traversing.

A related emotion with a related cognitive interpretation is *threat,* which individuals experience when they realize their construct system is about to be shaken up. In other words, they are about to confront a massive invalidation of the way they view the world. Maybe the letter from the graduate school admissions committee has just been delivered. Is it a rejection? Her blind date is knocking on the front door. Is he a rejection? Her fiancé is late to the wedding.

Is she a rejection? In each case, assuming the possible event becomes a real one, she must change her constructs. The more central the construct involved, the more threatened she feels when it is attacked.

We do more than sit and quake in response to the world. Sometimes we do battle. So, Kelly interprets *hostility* as a person's effort to extort validation from the world for a prediction that has already been proven wrong. Some people are bullies not because they are inherently mean but because they have made incorrect predictions about the way things are. Rather than change their constructs, they try to change the world. Haven't we all been on one side or the other of unrequited love? At first, it is paradoxical that one human being will be hostile to another human being for the "offense" of not reciprocating a crush. But by Kelly's view, this hostility makes perfect sense. Love is never having to say you're wrong.

Depression is interpreted as a condition where constructs are constricted. Their range of convenience has shrunk to the point where they apply to almost nothing. The depressed person therefore experiences almost nothing. Symptoms that reflect constricted constructs predominate among the DSM-III-R diagnostic criteria for depression: loss of pleasure and interest in usual activities, decreased sex drive, decreased appetite for food, difficulty in concentrating, increased sleep. If you are depressed, you avoid everything. From the viewpoint of personal construct theory, you do so because your constructs are not sufficient for everyday life. Taking constricted constructs into the complex world is like taking a skateboard onto the Long Island Expressway.

The opposite of depression is *mania,* usually regarded as excessive and inappropriate elation. Kelly's cognitive rendering of mania points to dilated constructs, constructs stretched and expanded to the point that they fit everything. Manic individuals are grandiose and expansive. Nothing gets them down or counts against their plans. They undertake reckless activities in apparent disregard of their bad consequences. Why? Because their constructs have no room for disaster.

Neither the depressed person, with constricted constructs, nor the manic person, with dilated constructs, can ever be proven wrong. Remember the scientist metaphor? Imagine a scientist whose theories are so circumscribed that the right conditions for testing them can never be arranged. Imagine a scientist whose theories are so general they can encompass all possible evidence. These caricatures are the respective analogues of depression and mania.

Real science as well as real people must walk the line between the constriction and the dilation of theories. In order to refine our predictions about and our understanding of the world, we must dare to be wrong about things. By this view, both depression and mania reflect a lack of explanatory derring-do.

A final example of how psychopathology can be explained with personal constructs is Donald Bannister's (1963, 1965) interpretation of schizophrenia. Bannister administered REP Tests to schizophrenic patients to see how they used personal constructs. He found that these patients applied constructs to themselves and others in ways that were idiosyncratic and inconsistent. Bannister then asked what could give rise to this particular use of personal constructs.

The answer to this question is his *serial invalidation hypothesis,* which states that schizophrenics live in a world that continually invalidates their constructs. In other words, their experience contradicts their predictions. As a response to continual invalidation, schizophrenics metaphorically loosen their constructs. They apply them differently than other people (that is, idiosyncratically) and apply them differently from one moment to the next (that is, inconsistently). The result is twofold. The good news is that invalidation is avoided. The bad news is that this worldview literally makes no sense.

Bannister hypothesizes that schizophrenics randomly organize their personal construct system. Experience is therefore *kaleidoscopic* (Adams-Webber, 1979, p. 66). Imagine all AMTRAK passengers with different train schedules. Imagine that each schedule changes from minute to minute. (If you've ever ridden AMTRAK, this is easy to imagine.) Suppose your entire experience was this disordered. According to Bannister, this is the essence of schizophrenia.

In support of his theory of schizophrenic thought disorder, Bannister conducted laboratory experiments with normal individuals, asking them to make predictions about hypothetical people. Subjects were then told that their predictions were wrong. This process was repeated several times. In keeping with his prediction, Bannister found that serial invalidation does indeed lead subjects to make inconsistent predictions. Over time, subjects flip-flop between opposite poles of an invalidated construct, sometimes choosing one and sometimes another.

Bannister's serial invalidation hypothesis is similar to the explanation of schizophrenia proposed by R. D. Laing, which I discussed in Chapter 7. Remember that Laing attributed schizophrenia to profound inconsistency on the part of one's family members. Bannister elaborated on this notion by suggesting a cognitive mechanism that leads from the inconsistency to which one may be exposed to one's disordered experience.

You have seen how Kelly explains psychopathology. As you might therefore imagine, he tries to undo problems by targeting a client's personal constructs for change. **Fixed-role therapy** uses role-playing to alter someone's construct system. The client quite literally is given the script of someone with a different personality and is asked to play it. The therapist designs this script so the client will end up trying out new constructs while following it.

Fixed-role therapy: George Kelly's psychotherapeutic approach, where clients try out different roles and their associated personal constructs.

The ultimate goal of fixed-role therapy is for clients to see that their "personality" is just as much a fiction as that of the character each has played. The clients learn they are able to choose the terms of their personalities. *All* theories can be revised, even the near and dear belief that personality is fixed. Because we are what we think and we choose our categories of thought, then it follows that we can choose who we are.

Jack Adams-Webber (1981) provided a concrete description of fixed-role therapy. A client "Joan" is asked to write a character sketch of herself from the viewpoint of someone who knows her well. The purpose of the sketch is to provide the therapist with the constructs that Joan uses to understand herself. With this sketch as a reference, the therapist then writes another sketch of a different person, "Nancy." The second sketch emphasizes the constructs Nancy uses to predict and understand events in the world. These are quite different than Joan's favored constructs.

Joan (the client) is given the sketch of Nancy (the role) and asked to play it. She is instructed to interact with other people in such a way that they leave with an impression of Nancy—not Joan. So, although Joan sees herself as quiet, Nancy sees herself as talkative. In following the script, the client must use a different personal construct. As she labors to interact with the world in different terms, the new construct becomes part of her worldview. If it leads to more accurate appraisals, this is not lost on her.

The therapist and the client meet frequently to plan how she is to enact the role. The therapist takes on the role of director, treating the client as if she were "in character." If the client acts like Joan, the therapist acts surprised. (You may recognize this as one of the strategies of method acting, where performers immerse themselves in the roles they are playing, temporarily becoming the character.)

In fixed-role therapy, the therapist plays the parts of important people in the client's life, so she can practice her new role. They also change parts, which means the therapist becomes Nancy, while the client becomes Joan's father, mother, husband, or employer. Switching roles accomplishes yet another change in perspective: The client comes to see that other people construe her, as she construes them.

At the end of therapy, Joan returns, presumably enlightened by the experience of seeing the world through Nancy's eyes. The therapist suggests that Nancy go into retirement, no matter how exciting she may have been. The important point is not the particular role one plays, but that one can choose a role, revise it, and discard it, again and again. The client is left with the injunction to create a new Joan.

Role-playing is also used in other systems of psychotherapy to help people express their repressed emotions or perfect the skills with which they perform particular behaviors. These purposes are not the major concern of fixed-role therapy because Kelly's therapy tries to effect cognitive change. The skill with which the person plays a role is not crucial, and neither are the role's emotional aspects. Indeed, the client who feels awkward and uncomfortable with a particular role is apt to benefit most from the role-playing, because it provides a particularly different construct system.

Fixed-role therapy is not widely used (van Rillaer, 1970), perhaps because it requires a great deal of ingenuity on the part of the therapist as well as the client. Extensive studies of its effectiveness have not been conducted. However, my sense is that it would be most effective for individuals who are anxious as opposed to depressed, because they would have the energy to give it a try. Also, I suspect that a client has to be bright enough to engage in the "as if" thinking required to construct and carry out a new role.

Aaron Beck's Approach

Psychiatrist Aaron T. Beck presents another cognitive interpretation of psychopathology. Although he is best known for his theory of depression (Beck, 1967), he has also looked at how thoughts and beliefs produce anxiety (Beck & Emery,

1985). In contrast to the typical treatments of these psychopathologies, which regard them as emotional disorders, Beck believes that cognition is the primary characteristic and determinant of each.

Depression   Depressed people are characterized by both the content and the process of their thoughts. In contrast to the nondepressed, depressed persons have an excessively negative view of themselves, their world, and their experiences. (That doesn't leave much out, does it?) Further, they think about matters in such a way that their pessimism and hopelessness are perpetuated.

Consider this brief case history of a man whose wife has unexpectedly left him:

> The deserting wife has been the hub of shared experiences, fantasies, and expectations. The deserted husband . . . has built a network of positive ideas around his wife, such as "she is part of me"; "she is everything to me"; "I enjoy life because of her." . . . The more extreme and rigid these positive concepts, the greater the impact of the loss . . .
>
> If the damage . . . is great enough, it sets off a chain reaction. . . . The deserted husband draws extreme, negative conclusions that parallel the extreme positive associations to his wife. He interprets the consequences of the loss as "I am nothing without her"; "I can never be happy again"; "I can't go on without her." (Beck, 1976, pp. 109–111)

If not interrupted, these ways of thinking escalate. The man may generalize his negative view of himself as a spouse to other areas of his life. He may doubt his abilities at work and his competence as a friend. He may curtail his everyday activities and become withdrawn from the world and the satisfactions it offers. He then has even more cause for being depressed. His sleeping and eating might suffer as well, and the resulting physiological effects will only make him feel worse. Finally, suicide might seem like the only possible escape from a life that has become too painful.

This case nicely illustrates the basics of the cognitive-behavioral approach to personality. The deserted husband is depressed not simply because his wife left him but because of how he has interpreted the event. His interpretation sets into operation all sorts of processes that in turn feed back to his views of himself and the world.

Beck emphasizes that depression is *not* an inevitable consequence of a serious loss. Many men and women whose spouses leave them get on with their life in a satisfactory fashion. The difference between them and the depressed husband lies in how they look at their loss: as a lesson, as good riddance, as something outside of their control, and so on.

While most of us can place bad experiences within a cognitive context that minimizes their depressing consequences, the depressed individual employs **errors in logic** when thinking about these bad experiences. Their conclusions are always disastrous. Here are some of the errors Beck has identified.

Arbitrary inference is a conclusion drawn in the absence of any evidence to support it. Suppose you want to get to know someone better, so you suggest a cup of coffee and a dash of conversation. However, the person says, "No, thank

Errors in logic: According to Beck, the styles of thinking that cause and maintain depression.

you, not today." What do you make of all this? The reasonable answer is nothing, because it is an isolated incident involving someone you do not know. But the depression-prone individual doesn't just shrug his shoulders and put the incident out of his mind. He'll draw an inference from it: "She hates me because I'm a boring person. She doesn't like the way I look. I'll never find anyone who will want to grow old with me."

A related error is *selective abstraction,* taking a detail out of context and focusing on it rather than on more general aspects of an experience. One Monday morning, a friend of mine was horribly depressed. I asked her what had happened, and she told me that she'd gone to a party that weekend and spent some time with an attractive man. So? According to her, "I was at the party for five hours, and for three of those hours, he didn't say a word to me!" When I remarked that it sounded like he had talked to her for two hours, which seemed like a long time, she stared at me with a puzzled look on her face. "That never occurred to me," she finally said.

Depressed people often *magnify* the impact of bad experiences. I usually get worked up when I can't find a parking place on a crowded street. I automatically assume my failure foretells doom in all domains of my life. This is what Beck means by magnification. The other side of the coin is *minimization,* when we dismiss or trivialize good experiences. Modesty may be a virtue, but if taken to an extreme, it sets a person up for depression. "Oh, it's nothing. Anybody could have won the Olympic Gold Medal that day. The wind was blowing right."

Finally, *personalization* is another depressive error in logic: taking responsibility for bad events in the world that you are not connected with at all. Have you caught yourself apologizing to a friend whose car always breaks down, simply because your car always runs? You were probably personalizing matters.

Anxiety　　Let's turn from Beck's explanation of depression to his explanation of anxiety. He starts by underscoring the importance of the **emergency response** that all living beings, from paramecia to people, show in response to threat. We (and they) have guaranteed our survival because we can rapidly mobilize our body's resources for fight or flight.

In people the emergency reaction is directed by our thoughts. We recognize danger, we judge our ability to cope with it, and we decide among response alternatives. Are you amazed that we can merge onto high-speed expressways with only occasional accidents? We do this so well because we are mindful of the potential dangers.

Anxiety disorders (like panic attacks or phobias) occur when we treat nonemergency situations as if they were emergencies. A racing heart, rapid breathing, tremors, and flushed skin are "natural" responses to a giant truck or a saber-toothed tiger closing in on us. These become symptoms of anxiety in the absence of any objective threat, when our appraisal of a situation is at odds with the facts of the matter. We get in trouble when we confuse a classroom examination, a date, or a shopping mall with an 18-wheeler run amok.

What leads to misappraisal? Similar to his explanation of depression, Beck argues that cognitive biases lead individuals "logically" to anxiety. These

Emergency response: The body's response to threat, in which one is readied for fight or flight.

tendencies conspire to make them view themselves as exceedingly vulnerable. If you regard yourself as made of spun glass, then you're going to be a timid and fearful person. Vulnerability can also be produced by a perception of *skill deficits* ("I've never taken a course in public speaking"), by *self-doubt* ("I'll forget to bring my notes"), and by *catastophizing* ("They'll laugh at me and then walk out"). Needless to say, anxiety interferes with the performance of many activities, so the person's sense of vulnerability is vindicated. Like depressed people who create a depressing world for themselves, anxious people do their part in creating a world of threat and danger.

Cognitive Therapy   Beck developed his cognitive explanation of depression in conjunction with a treatment known as **cognitive therapy** (Beck, Rush, Shaw, & Emery, 1979). The therapist helps the depressed client identify the thoughts that produce depression, challenge them, and eventually replace them with a more productive view of matters. Beck calls his approach *collaborative empiricism,* because the therapist and the client work together to test the client's beliefs against the facts.

> **Cognitive therapy:** Beck's therapy for depression, based on the assumption that depression is caused by negative and illogical thinking.

The central tenet of cognitive therapy is that depression is the result of an unduly pessimistic view of the self and the world, maintained by slipshod thinking. The depressive is not motivated to be unhappy (as psychodynamic theories hold). Instead, he or she has a mistaken view. When such erroneous beliefs change, the depression goes away.

In the initial stages of cognitive therapy, clients learn the basics of Beck's theory of depression. The therapists emphasize the possibility that thoughts produce emotions, urging clients to examine their own emotions to see the particular thoughts that precede them. At first this is difficult for the client to do, since these thoughts may be highly routinized, a bad cognitive habit that occurs with little awareness.

These bad habits are called **automatic thoughts,** a running commentary on a person's experience that occurs so readily the person is not conscious of it. What is apparent, however, is the depression it produces. Imagine your worst enemy doing the play-by-play of your life. After years of hearing put-downs, you turn down the voice in your head. But the depressing effects remain. The cognitive therapist helps clients become aware of automatic thoughts. Once an automatic thought is out in the open and scrutinized as a hypothesis, it is often found to be lacking.

> **Automatic thoughts:** Unbidden and habitual thoughts, usually self-critical, that cause or maintain depression.

Suppose Steve gets depressed at work when given an assignment. The automatic thought that produces his depression may be, "I'll never finish things by the deadline, and my boss will think I'm incompetent." As long as this thought occurs automatically, it is naturally depressing. Once Steve identifies the thought, though, it can be evaluated in light of the steady raises and promotions he has received ever since he began working. It seems implausible that he is incompetent.

If any doubts linger, Steve might be encouraged to ask his boss about the significance of the deadline. Suppose his boss says, "Oh, that's just a guess on my part. You know the work better than I do, so I figure you'll tell me if my deadline is off-base." See how much anguish and misery could be avoided if we simply asked people what *they* think about things, rather than basing what *we* think on clairvoyance?

Through exercises like this, cognitive therapists help depressed clients use available evidence to draw better conclusions about their experiences. Most of these conclusions cast the clients in a better light, and their depression will lift. But perhaps in some cases the negative inference is justified. Maybe Steve's boss is indeed firm on deadlines and gets annoyed when employees take too long to finish assignments. If this is ascertained, Steve still need not conclude that he is incompetent. Rather, he could see that he needs to change things. He can learn to manage his time better, stand up to the boss when deadlines are unreasonable, or shrug off such fussing as a small price to pay for raises and promotions. The cognitive therapist is prepared to help the client do one or all of these things. Keep in mind that the important goal of cognitive therapy is to lead the depressed individual to a positive point of view.

Beck's cognitive therapy has become an incredibly popular treatment for depression, and well-controlled studies have shown it to be as effective as antidepressant medication without—obviously—the side effects (Hollon & Beck, 1986). The approach is currently being extended in many directions (Persons, 1989). It is used to help people who have trouble with eating disorders, sexual intimacy, schizophrenia, personality disorders, and physical complaints (e.g., Beck & Freeman, 1990; Perris, 1989). Versions of cognitive therapy programs have been devised for couples as well as for groups (e.g., Freeman, 1983).

Despite the deserved popularity of cognitive therapy, some loose ends exist in our understanding of how it works. Beck and other cognitive therapists make frequent use of the schema concept to explain the success of cognitive therapy. Presumably, what happens in therapy is that a depressed person's self-schema is attacked and changed. In fact, though, researchers have not taken such a fine-grained look at the cognitive changes that occur during cognitive therapy. Perhaps changes in self-schemas are responsible for changes in depression, but perhaps not (Segal, 1988).

Relatedly, we can argue with Beck's basic premise that depressed people are illogical. Remember our discussion of positive illusions? These are biased ways of thinking that nondepressed people bring their experiences that lead them to think matters are better than they really are. It may well be that nondepressed people are illogical. Some studies imply that depressives judge themselves more realistically, which is to say much more harshly, than nondepressives regard themselves (e.g., Lewinsohn, Mischel, Chaplin, & Barton, 1980). By this view, cognitive therapy for depression entails not the destruction of illogical self-schemas but rather their creation.

Learned Helplessness Approach

As discussed in Chapter 12, Martin Seligman (1974, 1975) has suggested that learned helplessness is a model of depression. What does this mean? Remember the general discussion of models in Chapter 2. A model is a metaphor for understanding some complex phenomenon. If learned helplessness is to be a

model for depression, then parallels should exist between the two at a number of points: causes, symptoms, cures, and so on. For almost two decades, Seligman and his colleagues have explored these parallels. The concept of explanatory style was added to the learned helplessness theory largely to strengthen the link between learned helplessness and depression (Abramson et al., 1978).

How does learned helplessness fare as a model of depression? I think it fares pretty well (Peterson & Seligman, 1985). Consider the parallels established between helplessness produced by uncontrollable events and naturally occurring depression:

- Symptoms: Passivity, negative cognitions, loss of self-esteem, sadness, hostility, anxiety, loss of appetite, reduced aggression, and neurotransmitter depletion.
- Causes: A belief that responding is futile because it is independent of important outcomes.
- Therapy: Changing beliefs in response futility, electroconvulsive therapy, antidepressant medications, sleep deprivation, and the passage of time.
- Predisposition: A pessimistic explanatory style.

Learned helplessness is not exactly the same thing as depression, but it seems to capture many of the essential features of this disorder.

Much of my own work as a researcher has been in collaboration with Seligman, testing the hypothesis that explanatory style is a risk factor for depression. On the basis of a number of studies, we conclude that people who typically offer internal, stable, and global explanations for bad events become depressed when such events occur (Peterson & Seligman, 1984). For instance, adult men entering a prison are apt to become depressed while serving their time if they have a "depressive" explanatory style. I've also found that elementary school children become depressed over a six-month period if they make internal, stable, and global explanations for bad events. The same appears true for college students.

The learned helplessness theory of depression suggests several therapeutic strategies (Abramson et al., 1978; Seligman, 1981). All attempt to prevent or undo the particular thoughts that produce and maintain helplessness. They should therefore be effective in treating depression once it exists, as well as in preventing it in the first place. So, depression can be combatted by the strategy of *environmental enrichment*. With desirable outcomes made more likely, and undesirable ones made less likely, the individual can avoid the circumstances that produce helplessness altogether.

If bad events cannot be eradicated, then the individual can undergo *personal control training* which changes expectations from uncontrollability to controllability. As with Beck's approach, the therapist must be aware of the facts of the matter. If a person indeed has the ability to control outcomes but believes otherwise, then personal control training challenges the erroneous expectation. But if the person indeed lacks the ability to bring about desired events, then the therapist must impart new skills.

Sometimes control remains elusive, and *resignation training* must be undertaken. In other words, such persons must reduce the attractiveness of nice things that remain beyond their grasp. ("Medical school has its drawbacks.") And they must similarly reduce the aversiveness of crummy things that are inevitable. ("God has a plan for everyone.")

Finally, explanatory style provides a convenient target for therapy. *Attribution retraining* attempts to change someone's explanations of failure from internal, stable, and global causes to external, unstable, and specific causes, and to do the opposite for explanations of success. What does this accomplish? Remember that helplessness theory assigns particular roles to each of these three dimensions of explanatory style. If success is explained internally and failure externally, then self-esteem is bolstered. If success is explained stably and globally and failure unstably and specifically, then triumphs are savored and setbacks are dismissed.

These therapeutic strategies have yet to be explicitly packaged and deployed against depression. Seligman (1981) argues that cognitive psychotherapies like those of Beck (already discussed) and Ellis (to be discussed) are in effect using these tactics already in their treatment of depression. He further states that psychotherapy of depression is effective to the degree it specifically changes the cognitions deemed important by helplessness theory.

In a recent study, Seligman and his colleagues (1988) studied 39 depressed patients undergoing therapy at the University of Pennsylvania Center for Cognitive Therapy, which is under the direction of Aaron Beck. The patients were followed over the course of their therapy. On the average, they were seen once a week over a six-month period, and then for one year afterwards. A comparison group of 10 "normal" (nonpatient) individuals were recruited through the media and matched to the patients in terms of sex, age, and education.

Explanatory style was measured by a questionnaire at three points in time: at the beginning of therapy, at the end of therapy (i.e., after six months of successful treatment), and then one year following termination. As we might expect, the patients started therapy with a more pessimistic explanatory style than the nonpatient comparison group. Further, the explanatory style of the patients improved from pessimistic to optimistic in the course of therapy. The more optimistic they became, the greater was the extent to which their depression lifted. The gains in optimism, on the whole, were maintained during the one year follow-up period. Some erosion—toward pessimism and depression—occurred among some patients one year after the end of therapy; these were individuals who were somewhat pessimistic at the time therapy ended.

The findings of this study are consistent with the learned helplessness approach, although we can still raise questions. An obvious chicken-and-egg problem arises here, because depression and explanatory style moved in lockstep during and after therapy. In a way, this is not surprising, granted the close link between the two. But consequently, we do not know the exact process by which cognitive therapy changes explanatory style. For instance, it may directly affect someone's beliefs. Or it may first improve a patient's mood, which in turn changes his or her beliefs.

The idea that helplessness is analogous to depression has been controversial and is far from generally accepted (see Arieti & Bemporad, 1978; Brewin, 1985; Coyne & Gotlib, 1983; Weiner, 1990). Many critics argue that depression involves more than passivity in the face of uncontrollability. If you recall what is meant by a model (Chapter 2), this is a somewhat misguided criticism. From the start, we should expect learned helplessness to fall short of capturing the whole of depression. Shortcomings are inherent in any model.

The parallels between learned helplessness and depression are generalizations: summaries of how most helpless people (or dogs or rats) and most depressed people behave. Not all instances of helplessness and of depression parallel one another. For example, thoughts of suicide accompany depression but not learned helplessness as produced in the laboratory. And although women are much more likely to be depressed than are men (Nolen-Hoeksema, 1990), no corresponding sex difference occurs in susceptibility to laboratory helplessness.

Nevertheless, in a number of cases, helpless individuals act depressed, and depressed individuals act helpless. Seligman (1978) has speculated that future diagnostic systems will include a category for *helplessness depression,* a disorder that helplessness theory describes particularly well (see also Abramson,

Metalsky, & Alloy, 1989). It would be defined as a depressive episode that follows in the wake of an uncontrollable event and is maintained by one's expectations of future uncontrollability.

Granted that at least some good examples of depression as learned helplessness exist, another matter must be addressed in judging whether or not the analogy is worthwhile. As a metaphor of human ills, learned helplessness is rich indeed. It can be applied to a wide variety of failures at adaptation, so long as they are marked by passivity and preceded by uncontrollable events (Peterson & Bossio, 1989). So, some theorists suggest that helplessness is involved not only in depression, but also in academic failure, child abuse, test anxiety, drug use, epilepsy, physical illness, loneliness, voodoo curse, and problems of the lower class. Learned helplessness has even been linked by some writers to the escalation of the Vietnam War, to the plight of hapless sports teams, to the crises of faith described by Paul in the New Testament, and to the woes of the Third World!

Does learned helplessness play a role in all of these problems? If so, then its specificity with respect to any one of them is nil. In particular, one is led to question whether it applies to depression. To establish specificity, researchers must do more than document analogies. In addition, they must demonstrate that these parallels do not hold true for other cases. The surface has only been scratched here.

Researchers have mainly looked at the distinction between depression and schizophrenia with respect to helplessness. It appears that helplessness better captures depression than it does schizophrenia. Bad events are more likely to precede depression than schizophrenia (Thoits, 1983), and depressed individuals are more likely to offer internal, stable, and global explanations for such events than schizophrenic individuals (Raps, Peterson, Reinhard, Abramson, & Seligman, 1982). But the issue of specificity to depression is still very much up in the air, because other studies have found that a pessimistic explanatory style is linked as closely to anxiety as it is to depression (e.g., Ganellen, 1988; Nezu, Nezu, & Nezu, 1986).

Rational-Emotive Therapy

One of the earliest cognitive approaches to therapy was introduced by Albert Ellis (1962, 1973). **Rational-emotive therapy** is as simple as *ABC* (Prochaska, 1984). According to Ellis, personality can be understood in terms of *Activating* events, *Beliefs* used to interpret these events, and emotional *Consequences* of these beliefs. This formula nicely summarizes the cognitive perspective, regarding beliefs as central in determining people's responses to the world.

Beliefs are rational or irrational. Rational beliefs produce pleasant or productive consequences for the person, whereas irrational beliefs lead to misery. Rational-emotive therapists assume their clients are troubled because they entertain irrational beliefs. Therapy thus tries to identify these beliefs and eradicate them.

Ellis identifies several irrational beliefs commonly held by members of our society. How many of these strike you as familiar? How many of these have produced anger, guilt, or frustration in you?

Rational-emotive therapy: The approach to therapy developed by Albert Ellis, based on the assumption that problems are caused by irrational thinking.

- The basic human desires are needs.
- Certain events, like standing in line or being rejected by a lover, are intolerable.
- Our worth as human beings is determined by our material success.
- The world should treat us fairly.
- I can't live without love.
- We cannot be happy unless people approve of everything we do.
- Things must turn out as we plan them.
- We can't go without cigarettes, or beer, or donuts.

Characteristic of irrational beliefs are their absolute nature and the fervor they inspire. In Kelly's terms, irrational beliefs are superordinate. Despite the difficulties they produce, we cling to them because it is inconceivable to us that we can (or may) let them go.

Ellis criticizes other forms of therapy that focus on the *A's* or *C's* of personality and ignore the *B's*. In particular, he lambasts psychoanalysis, arguing that insight into the past (the *A's*) and recognition of one's feelings (the *C's*) don't solve a client's problems. The client's crooked thinking (the *B's*) must be changed, and this is done by *D*isputing her or his beliefs. "Where is it written down that life is fair?" "Who says that you'll die if your marriage ends?" "What evidence do you have that being promoted will make you happy?"

Rational-emotive therapy has been compared to an educational process (Prochaska, 1984), an apt analogy since this form of therapy strives to change one's beliefs. To this end, clients are given homework assignments to test for themselves the consequences of their particular beliefs. Suppose a student believes she cannot speak up in class because she will be laughed at. The therapist may ask her to find out if this will really happen. So she speaks up in class. And no one laughs; they don't even wake up. Her irrational belief has been challenged.

Reattribution Therapy

Yet another cognitive approach to therapy takes off from one of the classic psychology experiments. You may have encountered in your introductory psychology course the study by Schachter and Singer (1962) where research subjects were injected with adrenaline (identified to them as a vitamin), creating heightened physiological arousal. Different subjects were then placed in different situations designed to produce varying interpretations of why they felt as they did. In one condition, subjects were left with someone who made jokes and in general acted silly. In another condition, subjects were insulted and treated rudely by another person. When asked to report the emotion they were experiencing, subjects reported feelings appropriate to the situation: happiness versus anger, respectively.

According to Schachter and Singer (1962), these research subjects used the information present in their particular social situation to make sense of their arousal. The cognitive label they placed on their bodily sensations defined the nature of the emotion they experienced. Schachter and Singer's study is an intriguing demonstration of the importance of cognition. People's emotions varied with how they thought, even when their physiology was explicitly controlled.

Once Schachter and Singer reported their results, clinical psychologists quickly seized on an intriguing implication of this research. A client's negative emotions, particularly fear and anxiety, could be changed into positive emotions if the client could be induced to reattribute their source. Several psychologists described techniques for doing this, and **reattribution therapy** was born (Harvey & Galvin, 1984).

Reattribution therapy: An approach to therapy in which people are encouraged to explain events or feelings in a way that minimizes their distress.

The general strategy of reattribution therapy requires the client to switch from internal attributions for negative emotions and behaviors to external attributions. (Note the similarity to Seligman's, 1981, proposed reattribution training.) An experiment by Michael Storms and Richard Nisbett (1970) illustrates the benefits of reattribution. Insomniacs were recruited and given a pill to take before they went to bed. Although the pill was a *placebo,* half the subjects were told it would increase their arousal, whereas the other half were told it would relax them. The results may surprise you. Insomniacs given the "arousing" pill reported that they fell asleep more quickly than usual, and insomniacs given the "relaxing" pill found it harder to fall asleep than ever.

These results are consistent with Schachter and Singer's theory. Think through the logic. Insomniacs have trouble sleeping because they are aroused, and they attribute this arousal to some defect in themselves: "Here I go again. I'll never be able to fall asleep." This self-attribution only increases their arousal. Suppose they have a plausible source for their arousal that has nothing to do with themselves? Then they can attribute their nervousness elsewhere and relax. The "arousing" pill provides precisely this external source of arousal. In contrast, the "relaxing" pill only compounds the worries of the insomniac. The pressure of having to relax only heightens arousal further: "My goodness. I've taken a tranquilizer, and I'm still not sleepy. This is going to be one of those nights."

Reattribution therapy has been used to treat problems such as fear of public speaking, shyness, and cigarette smoking (Harvey & Galvin, 1984). But it has not always worked, and the current opinion about reattribution therapy is that it must be integrated into a more complete strategy of psychotherapy.

Perhaps clinical psychologists were naive to think that a single instruction about the source of negative emotions could overturn long-standing cognitive and emotional habits, particularly when the instruction is at odds with the facts. So, insomniacs really do have trouble falling asleep, cigarette smokers really do experience cravings during withdrawal, and shy people really do feel nervous around others. The therapist who tells these people they are wrong about these matters risks his or her own credibility.

One area where I think the reattribution approach has considerable promise is in the treatment of sexual dysfunctions. Here, misinformation abounds. For all the importance of sex and sexuality, many people don't even know the basics about how their bodies work. For instance, occasional impotence is common among men and has little significance—unless someone draws a conclusion to the contrary. Such a conclusion may create anxiety, which leads to further sexual difficulty. Information about the frequency of impotence can head all this off at the pass.

In this case, reattribution doesn't try to change a plausible interpretation into an implausible one. Instead, it moves toward increasing plausibility. If a person finds that a new point of view leads not only to decreased anxiety, but also to more accurate predictions and successful control of events, then the person will seize on this perspective.

Here is an example from a case study I once read. A man sought out therapy because of recurring impotence. This sexual problem was leading to all sorts of other problems in his marriage. He viewed himself as less than a man. His wife viewed herself as less than a woman. Needless to say, these attributions did not create an atmosphere conducive to sexual arousal, trapping the couple in a vicious circle.

After talking to the man and achieving rapport, the therapist asked to see a picture of his wife. The client pulled a photo out of his wallet, and watched as the therapist studied it carefully. "What a beautiful woman!" the therapist finally said. "Any man would be spellbound in her presence."

And what a beautiful intervention by the therapist! Do you see how this new perspective liberates the client and his wife from their damaging self-attributions? "I'm anxious around my wife because she's so attractive." Fear turns into desire. His impotence is no more.

Another area where reattribution therapy has promise is academic counseling. Again, misinformation may lead students to self-damaging attributions. If these can be changed, then their morale and grade point average will rise. Wilson and Linville (1982, 1985), for instance, noted that college freshmen tend to get particularly low grades. Various factors are responsible for this, and many have nothing to do with a particular student's intellectual ability. Consider what freshmen confront as they start college: harsh grading curves in introductory courses, no curfew, noisy dormitories, no curfew, bizarre roommates, no curfew, mysterious study habits, no curfew, and so on. Yet freshmen with a report card full of C's and D's and F's may look past these plausible explanations for their poor performance and attribute it instead to deficient ability.

And then they give up. In subsequent years, their grades continue to be low, even though renewed effort would pay off. Suppose students were encouraged to attribute low grades during their first year to external and unstable factors. Wilson and Linville (1982, 1985) made precisely this intervention. Guess what? Grades indeed improved following a brief message like that in the preceding paragraph. Students who did not receive this message showed less improvement in their grades.

Cognitive-Behavioral Therapy

Rational-emotive therapy and reattribution techniques can be criticized for neglecting the real world. I'm troubled by some of the beliefs Ellis terms irrational, because these beliefs sometimes mirror the way things really work.

Consider the belief that the world treats good-looking, wealthy, and successful people better than it treats the rest of us. Is this an irrational belief? Ellis would say it is, but any social psychology textbook describes research proving that this is *exactly* the case. The fact that the world works this way is lamentable, but the person who recognizes it is hardly irrational.

As I mentioned in connection with reattribution therapy, cognitive interventions are apt to succeed to the degree they are consistent with the events the person is likely to experience. In some cases, as with the case of impotence just described, a new perspective doesn't get the person in trouble at all, and therapy can be "purely" cognitive. In many other cases, though, the person's thoughts—despite their association with misery—bear some resemblance to reality. Therapy must then address not only cognitions but also the world.

In recent years, cognitive psychotherapists have increasingly made behavior modification techniques part of their therapeutic repertoire, to such an extent that we can speak of **cognitive-behavioral therapy** as a coherent approach. Cognitive-behavioral therapists recognize the interdependence of the person and the world, and they stress the importance of both learning and cognition. Let's take a look first at traditional behavior modification. Then we'll discuss how traditional techniques have been incorporated into cognitive approaches to therapy.

Cognitive-behavioral therapy: Therapeutic approach that combines techniques of cognitive therapy and behavior modification.

Behavior modification: Therapeutic strategies derived from learning theory.

Traditional Behavior Modification

Behavior modification refers to therapeutic strategies derived from learning theory. Literally hundreds of behavior modification techniques exist, but all reflect the assumption that behaviors—normal or abnormal—are learned (Bellack & Hersen, 1985). Hence, they can be relearned or unlearned, as it were. As noted in Chapter 11, behaviorists from the very start have been optimistic about the ease with which behaviors can be changed through environmental manipulations.

Classical conditioning techniques attempt to change people's emotional reactions by pairing objects with stimuli that elicit different emotional reactions from their typical ones. After repeated pairings, the objects will eventually give rise to new emotions.

One of the best known of the classical conditioning techniques is **systematic desensitization,** originally developed by psychiatrist Joseph Wolpe (1958). Systematic desensitization is deployed against fears and phobias. The therapist first shows the client how to relax thoroughly, because relaxation is incompatible with anxiety. Then the therapist and the client devise a hierarchy of scenes and situations reflecting the client's particular fear. Suppose the person is scared to death of speaking in class. An item low in the hierarchy might involve the client nodding agreement to a professor's rhetorical question. An item intermediate in the hierarchy may have the client asking the teacher to repeat a definition. Finally, an item high in the hierarchy would be the client disputing the instructor's conclusion in front of classmates.

Systematic desensitization: A classical conditioning technique used to treat fears and phobias; the client relaxes while imagining feared objects.

Therapy proceeds by having the client relax and visualize the scene lowest in the hierarchy. As long as the imagery is tolerated without anxiety, the client holds on to it. If and when anxiety occurs, the client again relaxes until she or he can imagine the scene comfortably. Gradually, the client works up through

"Listen... You've got to relax... The more you think
about changing colors, the less chance you'll
succeed... Shall we try the green background again?"

SOURCE: "The Far Side" cartoon by Gary Larson is reproduced by permission of Chronicle Features, San Francisco.

the hierarchy, so the feared scenes are repeatedly paired with relaxation instead of anxiety. In this way, fears and phobias are vanquished. Success rates have been reported as high as 80 to 90 percent, and success is maintained years later (e.g., Paul, 1967).

Systematic desensitization has been deployed against an incredible variety of fears. Bernstein and Nietzel (1980) report that it has been used to treat "fear of balloons, wind, the year 1952, feathers, violins, dirty shirts, and short people" (p. 368).

Sex therapists William Masters and Virginia Johnson (1970) use an analogous procedure in their treatment of sexual dysfunctions occasioned by excessive anxiety (like impotence or inhibited orgasm). In **sensate focus,** couples kiss and caress with the goal of giving pleasure to their partner, not as a prerequisite for intercourse. Performance anxiety is reduced and relaxation is increased, with both emotional states becoming associated with caressing.

Sensate focus: A classical conditioning technique used to treat sexual dysfunction; clients kiss and caress in order to feel pleasure, not to prepare for intercourse.

This year's Irrational Fears Grand Champion worries, from her home in Madison, Wisconsin, about being caught up in a deadly lava flow.

SOURCE: "The Neighborhood" cartoon by Jerry Van Amerongen is reproduced with special permission of King Features Syndicate, Inc.

Flooding: A classical conditioning technique used to treat fears and phobias; the client is exposed to feared objects until the fear extinguishes.

Aversion therapy: A classical conditioning technique used to encourage avoidance; the client confronts the object or situation to be avoided while experiencing pain or nausea.

Eventually, their lovemaking progresses to intercourse and orgasm, but the path leads through classical conditioning.

Another technique of this type is **flooding** (Marshall, Gauthier, & Gordon, 1979). Here, the person is exposed to the object or situation feared and is not allowed to flee from it. (We assume the therapist has not miscalculated, that no objective danger exists in the confrontation.) The fear eventually extinguishes. Needless to say, flooding must be used with caution. If the person leaves the situation before fear is alleviated, we have good reason to think the fear will be exacerbated.

In **aversion therapy,** a therapist tries to induce a client's avoidance of some object by pairing that object with a negative experience. Alcoholics and drug users may be given a particular chemical that reacts violently with the abused substance, making them deathly ill. The hope is that some variant of taste aversion will be conditioned, and the clients will avoid alcohol or drugs. Similarly, child molesters may be shown pictures of children while they are given painful electric shocks. The hope again is that their initial positive response will be changed to a negative one through classical conditioning.

Aversion therapy seems to work in the short run, but determined individuals can undo the conditioning by playing "b-mod therapist" themselves (Bernstein & Nietzel, 1980). Someone determined to drink will go ahead and drink in the face of conditioned nausea. Eventually this learning will be extinguished, and the person can drink without feeling queasy. I believe the lesson here is the same one learned by practitioners of all forms of psychotherapy. No miracle treatments exist; success must involve hard work by the client. This includes the need for "booster" sessions with the behavior therapist, where the original learning is repeated.

Instrumental conditioning techniques try to increase the frequency of desired behaviors by **selective reward** and to decrease the frequency of undesired behaviors by **selective punishment.** The rationale behind these strategies is that once people are engaging in positive behaviors while refraining from negative ones, their natural environments will take over and maintain this style of behaving. Accordingly, the therapist who uses these techniques studies carefully the actual settings to which the person will take the new skills. If these settings are not conducive to the new skills, if the desired behaviors will not be rewarded in them, then the therapist must change the situation. No point in teaching people to say "please" and "thank you" if they live in a hostile and rude environment.

So, behavior modification sometimes need not involve the "client" at all. A therapist can deal with a child's noncompliance by instituting **parent training,** teaching parents to be behavior therapists for their child. Perhaps they have been unwittingly rewarding the child's outbursts while ignoring or even punishing occasional moments of calm. When parents start to pay more attention to how they respond to what their child does, his or her behavior changes for the better.

Sometimes people have problems in the world because they quite literally do not know how to win reward and avoid punishment. In this case, a therapist might undertake **social skills training,** teaching individuals specific ways of interacting positively with others. This is a popular approach to the treatment of depression, particularly when depressed individuals find little satisfaction in the world around them because they don't have the required skills to do so (Lewinsohn, 1974).

Behavior modification can also be carried out on a large scale (see Skinner, 1986). For example, a **token economy** implements instrumental conditioning on an entire psychiatric ward (Kazdin, 1977). Patients earn tokens for positive behaviors like staying awake, making eye contact, initiating conversations, keeping clean, and so on. They lose tokens for negative behaviors, like acting bizarre, picking fights, or shirking assigned duties. Tokens then can be used to "purchase" desired commodities—cigarettes, candy, weekend passes, movie tickets, whatever. Token economies represent the behaviorist view of the way the world really runs, except that the system of rewards and punishments in a token economy is explicit and coherent.

Another behavior modification technique based on instrumental conditioning is **biofeedback.** Most biofeedback applications stem from Neal Miller's (1969) suggestion that physiological responses like one's heart rate, glandular secretions, skin temperature, and brain waves can be altered through rewards and punishments, just like overt responses. People have difficulty identifying these responses because they are covert. Biofeedback solves this problem by monitoring bodily responses with an appropriate machine and providing the person with the pertinent information (or feedback). Then, individuals can

Selective reward: An instrumental conditioning technique for increasing the frequency of some behavior by rewarding it.

Selective punishment: An instrumental conditioning technique for decreasing the frequency of some behavior by punishing it.

Parent training: The instruction of parents in behavior modification techniques they will then use with their children.

Social skills training: A therapeutic strategy in which individuals are taught specific ways of interacting positively with others.

Token economy: Operant therapy carried out on a large scale; individuals earn tokens for positive behaviors and lose them for negative behaviors; tokens in turn are exchanged for desired commodities.

Biofeedback: An instrumental conditioning technique in which people learn to modify their bodily responses by attending to information monitored by a machine.

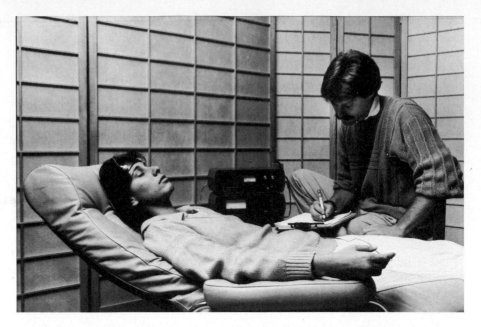

Biofeedback makes covert responses overt, in the hope that a person can learn to control them.

change their bodily responses. The basic premise of biofeedback has been questioned, because researchers have found it difficult to replicate Miller's original studies showing that responses of the autonomic nervous system could be conditioned. Nevertheless, biofeedback is a thriving enterprise, used to combat migraine headaches, insomnia, pain, and high blood pressure.

Behavior Modification Today   As I have discussed, radical behaviorists have no room, in their approach to psychology, for unobservable mental events. Many traditional behavior modification therapists regard themselves as radical behaviorists, but if you read the preceding section carefully, you perhaps saw some inconsistencies with this stance. For example, systematic desensitization—a supposedly behavioral technique—entails mental imagery. Biofeedback works insofar as a person "knows" which responses are being rewarded or punished. And virtually all the techniques discussed here are described to clients first so they can help carry them out. Something other than simple learning seems to be involved in behavior modification.

This realization was eventually reached by a number of influential behavior modifiers, who concluded that cognition played a central role in this form of therapy (Kendall & Hollon, 1979; Mahoney, 1974; Meichenbaum, 1977). Rather than pretending mental events are not important, behavior modifiers should explicitly include them as targets of therapeutic change.

Among the first psychologists to devise techniques exemplifying this "new" brand of behavior modification was Albert Bandura (1986). In a series of studies, he showed how fears could be banished through observational learning. Suppose Ann is afraid of cats. This fear creates serious problems, because she avoids places where she might come across a cat. She won't visit friends who have cats as pets. She won't go on walks because she might encounter a cat. Bandura attacks problems like this on two levels, cognitively *and* behaviorally.

Ann might be asked to watch another person hold a kitten, either in person or on a videotape. Then she is encouraged to hold a kitten herself. Through observational learning in the first case and enactive learning in the second, she develops a new ability: how to hold a cat without being scratched or bitten. Now she can visit her friends. Now she can take walks.

This therapy has done more than just change Ann's behavior. It has also changed the way she thinks about herself. Specifically, her self-efficacy with respect to cats has been altered. Ann now regards herself as master of the little beasts, and her sense of personal control further reduces her fears. She may even get a kitten of her own, because cats now remind her of her competence in confronting the world.

More generally, all of the traditional behavior modification techniques I have previously discussed can be enhanced by attending to the thoughts that accompany learning and performance. Indeed, Bandura (1977a) has argued that behavior change can *only* take place to the degree people's cognitions change. Psychologists who work within the cognitive-behavioral paradigm would certainly agree (Smith, 1989).

Behavior modification today entails changing both thoughts and behavior, under the assumption that changes in the one supports changes in the other. For an example, let's consider how cognitive-behavioral therapists help people cope with stressful events. They start with the premise that the stressfulness of a particular situation depends on how someone appraises the situation and his or her ability to meet the demands posed by it (Lazarus, 1966, 1982, 1990; Lazarus & Folkman, 1984).

Primary appraisal refers to the individual's interpretation of what is at stake in a given situation. Suppose you get a traffic ticket for failing to signal a turn. No one likes to get a ticket, but your emotional reaction will vary depending on whether you are required to go to court, how much you might be fined, whether your driving record is good or bad, and if your car insurance rates might be raised. What superficially is the same event—receiving a traffic ticket—takes on greatly different forms depending on how you appraise its consequences.

Secondary appraisal refers to the individual's assessment of the resources he or she has available to cope with a stressful event. Some stressful events are seen as easily resolved: by waiting them out, by talking to someone responsible, by regarding them as a good lesson. One's distress following such events is minimal. Other negative occurrences are regarded as not so easy to cope with, and considerable distress follows.

A general distinction is made between coping strategies that are problem-focused versus emotion-focused. In problem-focused coping, one tries to change the world to remove the source of stress. In emotion-focused coping, one tries to change how one is feeling about an event. No coping strategy is best for all circumstances, because the most effective coping depends on individuals and on the particular stressors they face.

From this perspective on stress, cognitive-behavioral therapists help people "manage" stress by instructing them in a variety of strategies that reduce the negative impact of aversive events. They may suggest that individuals

- relax in the face of stress by breathing deeply and regularly
- get in good physical condition
- think about things differently, remembering past triumphs
- give themselves pats on the back when they do well
- take breaks and vacations
- turn to other people for advice and support

None of these suggestions is meant to be profound advice, although it is remarkable how few people do these things on their own. Notice how these *stress management* techniques target both thoughts and behaviors for change.

We need not wait for stressors to occur in order to cope with them. Instead, we can anticipate stress and take preventive steps. Cognitive-behavioral psychologists have developed programs of *stress inoculation* that teach people skills and strategies for coping with stress before it occurs (Kendall & Turk, 1984). These programs usually entail three steps.

First, individuals are encouraged to become aware of the relationship between how they think about events and how they then react to them. Then they are instructed to try out different ways of thinking about potentially stressful events. Suppose someone is about to undergo surgery, and the goal of stress inoculation is to help him reduce his anxiety about the procedure. He is told to regard the surgery not as something that may end his life but instead as something that will soon allow him to do new things.

Second, people are given specific instructions in how to cope. It is pointless to tell them "just don't worry" if they do not know how to accomplish this. So, they are instructed in anxiety-reducing techniques like those I have been discussing.

Third, the clients practice their newly acquired skills. In the example of the man about to undergo surgery, he might visit the hospital and take a tour of the ward where he will stay as a patient. He will no doubt experience some anxiety, but he can combat it with the strategies he has learned. Stress inoculation programs like the one just described prove successful in helping people meet a variety of challenges (e.g., Kendall et al., 1979; Langer, Janis, & Wolfer, 1975).

Conclusions

Cognitive-behavioral therapy has become incredibly popular, in large part because it works (Hollon & Beck, 1986). What we do not yet know is exactly why this approach to therapy works as well as it does. Each version of cognitive-behavioral therapy nominates its own active ingredients—typically changes in particular contents and styles of thought—but research has yet to take a fine-grained look at the hypothesized process of improvement. Such studies are currently under way (e.g., Ozer & Bandura, 1990).

To close, let's compare cognitive-behavioral therapy with psychoanalytic therapy as described in Chapter 6. To the cognitive-behavioral therapist, the client is seen as in error, not in conflict. Therapy is conceived as education, not energy release. When progress is slow, this is due to inertia, not resistance. Perhaps most importantly, the cognitive-behavioral approach is much more optimistic about the prospects for improvement than is psychoanalysis. Eventual harmony is expected between the person and his or her world.

Cognitive-behavioral psychotherapy is not diametrically opposed to psychoanalytic therapy at all points (Meichenbaum, 1990). Remember, psychoanalysis provided the example for all other talking therapies. Before developing their own strategies, Kelly, Beck, and Ellis all conducted therapy from a psychoanalytic perspective. So a psychoanalytic flavor still remains. Cognitive-behavioral therapists accord great importance to the therapist-client relationship. Also, they sometimes blame the external world for the problems their clients face. Finally, they usually adopt a weak version of the unconscious. People's thoughts and beliefs may work below the level of their full awareness. However, these therapists do not join with Freudians in attributing this lack of awareness to motivation. Instead, they see it as a skill deficit, and therapy as the process of imparting not insight but expertise.

PERSONAL CONTROL AND HEALTH

A historical view of health care suggests three stages (Taylor, Denham, & Ureda, 1982). From the time of the earliest healers to the 1800s, the focus was on the *treatment* of disease. But Edward Jenner's discovery of vaccination in 1796 introduced the era of disease *prevention,* leading to a drastic reduction or eradication of such ills as smallpox, malaria, poliomyelitis, and diptheria. Today, we have entered a third stage in health care: the active *promotion* of healthy lifestyles. As we enter this third era, psychologists find they have a great deal to contribute.

The most basic difference between health promotion and disease treatment and prevention lies in what is required of those who will benefit from health-care strategies. Disease can be successfully treated if patients passively comply with physicians. Disease can be successfully prevented if citizens passively comply with public health officials. Health cannot be promoted, though, unless the individual actively participates in the effort.

Recent years have seen the formation of a new field: **health psychology** (Genest & Genest, 1987; Krantz, Grunberg, & Baum, 1985). Health psychologists are concerned with the psychological aspects of health and illness, and they attempt to answer two basic questions. First, what links behavior and illness? Second, what can be done to change these links?

Health psychology: The field of applied psychology concerned with the psychological aspects of health and illness.

Many health psychologists find personal control to be a highly useful concept (Rodin & Salovey, 1989; Taylor, 1990). Lack of personal control is associated with poor health. Remember the research mentioned in Chapter 12 that found a correlation between pessimistic explanatory style at one point in life and illness at a later point (Peterson, Seligman, & Vaillant, 1988)? This finding has been replicated in a variety of samples using such criteria for good versus bad health as the number of symptoms and their duration, physicians' diagnoses, immune responses, and total lifespans (Peterson & Bossio, 1991). Related lines of research have established similar correlations between other cognitive factors and health (e.g., Miller, Brody, & Summerton, 1988; Scheier & Carver, 1985).

Explaining the Association between Personal Control and Health

Granted the reality of these correlations, how can we explain them? We should start by assuming that the path between personal control on the one end and physical well-being on the other is highly complex. It is unlikely any single factor is solely responsible for the correlation between the two. Several possible mediators must simultaneously be considered.

Those with diminished personal control may have problems with their immune system and hence be unable to fight off disease. Some studies with animals suggest that uncontrollable aversive events lead to immune system suppression and increased vulnerability to illness (Maier, Laudenslager, & Ryan, 1985). Perhaps a similar process is triggered in people who perceive little control over the important events in their lives.

Those with diminished personal control may be unable to prevent or contain stressful events. As these accumulate, they exact a toll on health (Rabkin & Struening, 1976). In contrast, people high in personal control are better able to navigate life. They experience fewer disappointments and setbacks and therefore less stress.

Those with diminished personal control may be socially estranged. A well-established epidemiological finding is that individuals with a rich network of friends and family members are healthier and live longer than those who are isolated from others (House, Landis, & Umberson, 1988). Because those low in personal control tend to be lonely, they fail to reap the benefits of supportive contacts with others (Cobb, 1976).

They may also end up being less healthy simply because they have negative expectations. The positive belief that one's health is good and will continue to be good may actually translate itself into good health, even when "objective" health status is held constant (Kaplan & Camacho, 1983; Mossey & Shapiro, 1982). As discussed in Chapter 12, what starts out as an illusion may not end up as one, because it becomes a self-fulfilling prophecy.

Plus, those with diminished personal control behave in a helpless fashion, which means they may fail to take the necessary steps to promote health. Individuals with a pessimistic explanatory style, for example, do not watch their diet as carefully as do their more optimistic counterparts (Peterson, 1988). When they fall ill, pessimists do not take as many active steps as optimists in order to feel better (Lin & Peterson, 1990). In the short run, this passivity may not make much difference to one's health, but in the long run, it no doubt decreases both the quality and quantity of one's life (cf. Scheier et al., 1989).

Promoting Health

The concrete problem faced by health psychologists is how to induce someone to take the long view, to sacrifice immediate pleasures for the promise of the future. To date, this problem has not been fully solved. Health promotion programs are all somewhat successful, in reducing obesity, cigarette smoking, use of salt, and so on (Gebhardt & Crump, 1990). But none is completely successful. Programs to date have failed to reach substantial segments of the intended population. Notoriously unresponsive to health promotion programs are members of the lower socioeconomic class and minority groups.

Why aren't programs more successful than they have been? The glib answer is that they are bucking human nature. It's hard for people to change. My view is a bit more specific. I think today's health-promotion programs have not fully taken into account individual differences in personal control (Peterson & Stunkard, 1989). Surely it is no coincidence that the groups most unresponsive to health promotion are precisely the groups that rank lowest in the belief that they can bring about important events. Fatalism and pessimism do not psych someone up to go jogging or eat oat bran muffins.

Health promotion starts with epidemiological findings. What factors have researchers linked with subsequent illness? Here are some of the most common: poor nutrition, obesity, lack of exercise, immoderate use of alcohol, smoking, and stress (Taylor, Denham, & Ureda, 1982). Notice that every one of these risk factors involves behavior. Unlike earlier eras, where people were more likely to die from accidents and plagues that they had no control over, in our era, Americans are apt to die from their own bad habits.

Accordingly, health promoters are attempting to change these risk factors, which means psychologists are called on to help individuals and groups change their unhealthy habits into healthy ones. Psychologists have expertise in changing behavior, and health promotion is analogous to psychotherapy. In the one case, the goal of therapy is to alleviate misery, and in the other case, the goal is to promote health and longevity.

Health promotion programs are going on all around you. If you listen to the radio or watch television, you are constantly reminded that you should curtail drinking and driving, that only dopes use dope, that high blood pressure has no overt symptoms, that you should adopt a low-fat, low-cholesterol diet. The grocery store where I shop has a video monitor in the produce section that constantly runs brief clips on how to prepare vegetables without losing vitamins. If you live in Palo Alto (CA), Pawtucket (RI), Minneapolis (MN), Lycoming County (PA), or North Korelia (Finland), then you know that teams of health professionals have worked for years to help you reduce the risk of coronary disease. Pamphlets, public service announcements, phone calls, and volunteer groups have all been deployed toward this goal.

Psychotherapy and health promotion differ in one critical way. A neurotic life-style makes one unhappy: depressed, anxious, and unproductive. But an unhealthy lifestyle makes one happy (in the short run): fat, sassy, and complacent. Exercise hurts. Saying no to gooey deserts, aromatic cigars, and

exotic liqueurs is a drag. To the degree someone lives in the here and now, health promotion is impossible.

Health promotion programs must do more than provide information and moral exhortation. They must also change our beliefs about what we can or cannot do. Before embarking on a long trip, we have to believe that the directions we will follow are correct and that we are capable of following these directions. As discussed in Chapter 11, Bandura (1986) calls these beliefs *outcome expectations* and *efficacy expectations,* respectively. People must feel confident about both before they will change their behavior. So far, health promotion has emphasized the former (yes, good nutrition leads to longer life) but ignored the latter (and yes, you can do what is required to achieve good nutrition).

Preliminary evidence suggests that health promotion that targets personal control over specific behaviors can be highly successful. So, Condiotte and Lichtenstein (1981) demonstrated that self-efficacy with respect to not smoking predicted who would or would not relapse following a smoking cessation program. As you may know, it is easy to give up smoking. Mark Twain supposedly remarked that it was so easy he had done it dozens of times. The real trick is not to backslide. The same is true for losing weight, eating right, exercising, and so on. Good intentions carry a person through an initial flurry of beneficial activity, but they do not sustain permanent changes in behavior.

Perhaps those small numbers of people who successfully alter their unhealthy habits are those with an enhanced sense of personal control. In a review of research on risk-factor reduction, Anne O'Leary (1985) concluded that personal control is important:

> The evidence taken as a whole is consistent in showing that people's perceptions of their efficacy are related to different forms of health behavior. In the realm of

substance abuse, perceived self-regulatory efficacy is a reliable predictor of who will relapse and the circumstances of each person's first slip. Strong percepts of efficacy to manage pain increase pain tolerance. . . .[Personal control over] eating and weight predicts who will succeed in overcoming eating disorders. Recovery from the severe trauma of myocardial infarction is tremendously facilitated by the enhancement of the patients' and their spouses' judgments of their physical and cardiac capabilities. And self-efficacy to affect one's own health increases adherence to medical regimens. . . .

While specific strategies may differ for different domains, the general strategy of assessing and enhancing self-percepts of efficacy to affect health . . . has substantial general utility. (pp. 448–449)

In the future, health promotion programs need to assess the personal control of the targeted population. Different strategies would unfold depending on the level of control. Those with an efficacious orientation toward their health need little more than information about what's healthy and what's not. Those with a helpless orientation need their personal control bolstered before information per se will have any effect on their behavior. To this end, some of the techniques of cognitive psychotherapy may be useful.

ENVIRONMENTAL PSYCHOLOGY

Environmental psychology is concerned with how and why the physical environment influences people's behavior. Granted this definition, you might find it unusual that I've included environmental psychology in a chapter devoted to applications of the cognitive-behavioral paradigm. Cognitive-behavioral theories contend that behavior occurs in a psychological world, not a physical one. Meaningful reality consists of one's interpretation of events, not the events themselves.

> **Environmental psychology:** The field of applied psychology concerned with how and why the physical environment influences people's behavior.

Yes and no. As I've noted several times, personality psychologists concerned with people's thoughts and beliefs may retreat too far "into the head" and forget that cognitions pertain to the real world as well as to the person. But the physical environment should be of obvious concern to cognitive psychologists, because people think about the physical world.

Similarly, people's cognitions should be of obvious concern to environmental psychologists, because people apprehend the physical world in terms of thoughts and beliefs. Compare attending a standing-room-only concert to waiting in the back of a crowded elevator as it stops at each floor of a 21-story building. In each case, your toes are crushed, your nose is offended by other people's body odor, your clothes are rumpled, and you can't see or hear a thing. But you're having the time of your life at the concert, while you're feeling incredibly angry in the elevator. The physical stimulation in both cases is essentially the same, so we must look to your interpretations to understand your differing reactions.

Environmental psychologists agree that cognitions mediate people's responses to crowding, to aversive noise, and even to pollution. I'll describe some of this work in the present section. Then I'll conclude by considering an intriguing research area that applies Lewin's idea of the life space to the physical environment.

Crowding

Since the early 1960s, when fears of overpopulation became widespread, literally hundreds of researchers have looked at the psychological consequences of crowding. You may have heard about James Calhoun's (1962) experimental study of overcrowded rats. He confined rats to a room of fixed size, providing them with ample food and water. The rats reproduced freely, increasing the population size, and social pathology was the eventual result. As the rats became more densely packed in the room, they acted in negative ways. They fought with each other. They cannibalized their young. They became physically ill. They let their voter registrations lapse. They stopped supporting public television.

So, crowding can be harmful. Studies with human subjects support this conclusion (Baron & Byrne, 1984). As population density goes up in a town, so, too, does the crime rate. In a college dormitory, crowded conditions lead to interpersonal friction, low grades, and even illness.

But not all research concludes that crowded conditions are harmful. Perhaps this shouldn't surprise you. Many of our fellow citizens love to live in cities, and those of us who do not often visit shopping malls just to rub shoulders with the milling masses. What's going on here?

People appear less affected by overcrowded conditions than animals. People can mitigate the harmful effects of physical crowding with cognitive

People may cope with annoying stimuli by ignoring them.

Crowding is not always aversive—it depends on how the individual interprets the experience.

strategies. For instance, we can limit our attention to external stimuli. Occasional visitors to large cities are aghast when they see residents walk down a sidewalk oblivious to unconscious bodies. The morality of the passersby is often criticized: "New Yorkers don't care about people." This is probably unfair. Instead, city dwellers have learned to shut such unpleasant stimuli out of their awareness (Milgram, 1970). Calhoun's rats exhibited pathology in part because of physiological changes brought about by too much stimulation. City residents protect themselves against *stimulus overload* by walking fast, by looking the other way, and by avoiding eye contact. (They also avoid being shot.)

Relatedly, our perceived control over crowding determines its effect. Take my example about the difference between a rock concert and a slow elevator. In both cases, aversive stimuli are present. But the person at the concert chose to go and feels free to leave, while the person in the elevator is literally trapped. Indeed, in a study of elevator passengers, Rodin, Solomon, and Metcalf (1978) found that people standing near the control panel felt less crowded than those standing far away from it.

According to laboratory studies, control over crowding mitigates its negative consequences. For instance, Dru Sherrod (1974) crowded subjects into a laboratory room. Some subjects had access to a button they could push to summon Sherrod to remove them from the room. Although these subjects did not exercise this option, they were less distressed by the crowding than other subjects who didn't have access to an escape button.

These cognitive insights into the effects of crowding have been used by architects and urban planners to design environments so personal control is enhanced (and perceived crowding is decreased). One strategy is to arrange settings so interactions are more predictable. For instance, houses built on cul-de-sacs tend to keep strangers away. You are more apt to encounter people familiar to you, enhancing your control over ensuing events. Similarly, college dormitories arranged with rooms on short hallways or in suites minimize uncontrollable interactions; students in these dorms are happier and healthier than their counterparts in rooms on long hallways. If school administrators believed suite residents would make more money once they graduated (which they of course would donate to the school), you better believe dormitory renovations would ensue on every campus!

Sometimes settings are designed to be unpleasant so people won't feel comfortable and settle into them. Waiting rooms at bus and train stations are intentionally miserable, and the more modern they are, the more misery they cause. They offer no way to escape from the gaze of others, no place to put your feet up, and no way to control the events that occur. Do these designs keep out panhandlers and bums? Maybe so. On the other hand, they might add to the ranks of the undesirable. Craig Zimring (1981) describes reports that the Dallas-Fort Worth Airport, which is laid out in a vast circle, is so disorienting it sometimes precipitates psychiatric disturbances!

Noise and Pollution

The conclusions environmental psychologists make about crowding are the same they make about noise. In broad terms, noise has negative consequences. Unwanted noise can mask what we want to hear, it can lead to auditory damage, and it can make us irritable and inattentive (Cohen & Weinstein, 1981). But if we take a closer "look" at noise, we find that how people interpret it determines their psychological reactions.

Context is important in determining whether noise is unpleasant or not. Crashing surf on the beach at Malibu is exhilarating, while whispers in the back of Carnegie Hall are intolerable. Also, the control we perceive over noise is important. Consider a dormitory where everybody has to ask everybody else to turn down their stereo. No one finds their own tunes annoying. Personal control has something to do with this form of hypocrisy.

Psychologist Sheldon Cohen and his colleagues (1980) conducted an important study that found that children whose school was under the flight paths of an airport solved problems more poorly than other children who were not subject to uncontrollable noise. Further, Cohen and his fellow researchers (1981) later found that these effects could be reversed (though not totally) by reducing classroom noise (see also Bronzaft, 1981).

These studies are correlational. That is, it is not clear whether these harmful consequences were due to physical trauma, to uncontrollability, or to some unknown third variable. However, laboratory studies suggest uncontrollability is a possible mechanism.

David Glass and Jerome Singer (1972) ran a series of experiments exposing subjects to aversive noise. Half the subjects were led to believe they could terminate the noise if they wished. The other half were given no such instruction. Although subjects with control did not exercise it, they still outperformed the other subjects on problem-solving measures. Interestingly, performance differences were only evident after subjects were exposed to the noise, suggesting that the noise produced learned helplessness. (Notice the similarity to the studies done on the effects of crowding?)

In other words, people's interpretation of noise affects not only their immediate reactions but also their long-term reactions. Maybe this is why airplane pilots show no harmful effects from hearing jet engines, while the school children they fly their airplanes over fall victim. Indeed, some research even implies that people living close to airports are at increased risk for psychiatric illness (Cohen & Weinstein, 1981). Other studies challenge these findings, and I wonder if the debate could be resolved by comparing psychiatric admissions of those who lived in an area *before* an airport was built versus those who moved there *after* it was operating. If personal control is critical, I'd expect the former group to be more at risk than the latter group, who presumably chose to expose themselves to the noise.

Let me change the topic from noise to air pollution. Again, we have an example of the physical environment impinging on the individual. The effects of air pollution (by definition) are harmful: illness, death, irritability, aggression, lack of altruism, sleep disturbance, auto accidents, and so on. But beyond the physical consequences of air pollution, one's interpretation of it channels one's exact reaction. Once again, a person's perceived control is important. Evans and Jacobs (1981) describe research modeled on Glass and Singer's investigations of uncontrollable noise: Bad odors seen as uncontrollable disrupt performance to a greater degree than the same odors believed to be controllable.

In this context, realize that most Americans regard pollution as here to stay (e.g., Swan, 1972). Perhaps this fatalism will exacerbate the negative consequences of pollution. On the other hand, some researchers believe people can accommodate pollution, at least in a psychological sense. When new versus old residents of smog-ridden Los Angeles were compared, the long-term residents reported better health, less concern with smog, and decreased likelihood of curtailing activities in the face of pollution alerts (Evans & Jacobs, 1981). In other words, air pollution had ceased to be an important aspect of their life space. Whether this is foolish or brave is a matter for debate; it proves, however, that people will keep on keeping on in the face of physical reality, with particular ways of thinking making this possible.

Cognitive Maps

The life space depicts the person's view of his or her environment. For the most part, psychologists in the cognitive-behavioral tradition construe "environment" in the broadest sense, including other people, goals, plans, and fears. But some environmental psychologists look specifically at how people view the physical layout of their neighborhood, their town, or their nation. Striking individual differences in these **cognitive maps** have been discovered, and further research finds that these individual differences relate to other characteristics of people.

Cognitive map: A cognitive representation of a physical place.

I sometimes demonstrate cognitive maps with a classroom exercise. I ask my students to draw a map of the building where our class meets: "Put in as much detail as you can." The male students draw a building with several

FIGURE 13-1
Cognitive Maps of
Los Angeles

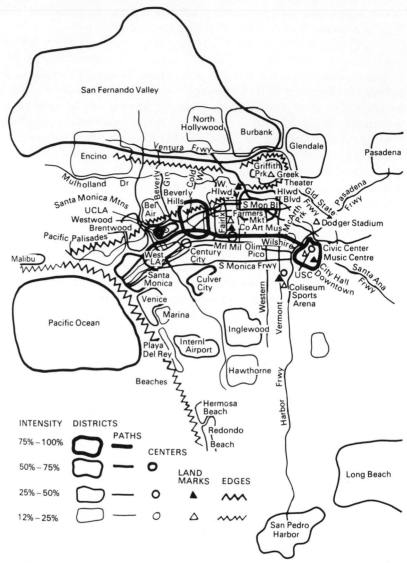

SOURCE: P. Gould & R. White (1974), *Mental Maps*. New York: Penguin, p. 36.

restrooms for men, but none for the women. And the female students draw a building with several women's restrooms, but none for the men.

What's my point? Our cognitive maps are practical creations. They contain features that are meaningful in our day-to-day transactions with the real world. They don't contain features that are personally irrelevant. The student in a wheelchair knows where all of the ramps and elevators are in a building, and students without the need to know this don't. Left-handed students know where "left-handed" desks are located in a classroom. The rest of us may not even know these desks exist.

In a similar exercise, I've asked my students to draw a map of our town. I can interpret the people by looking at their maps. I usually know who is of legal

Pasadena

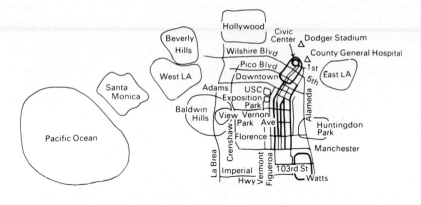

INTENSITY   PATHS   DISTRICTS   CENTERS   LANDMARKS   EDGES

25% – 50%

12% – 25%

City Hall △ Union Station
Little Tokyo
Downtown
Brooklyn Ave
1st st
6th st
Bus
Depot

INTENSITY   PATHS   DISTRICTS   CENTERS   LANDMARKS   EDGES

50% – 75%   △

25% – 50%

12% – 25%

drinking age, because they locate all 17 of the town's bars on their maps. I usually know who has children, because their maps contain the local hospital, the preschool, and the convenience stores that sell Pampers 24 hours a day. I usually know who drives a car, because parking lots and stoplights abound. And I usually know who is a pedestrian, because alleys and paths connect the different parts of the town, whereas streets hardly exist.

Geographers Peter Gould and Rodney White (1974) describe systematic investigations of people's cognitive maps that support these informal conclusions. Techniques exist for creating composite cognitive maps for a group of individuals. Look at the maps in Figure 13–1. All depict Los Angeles, but notice the vast contrast in detail as you move from the left map to the right maps. The left map shows the rich knowledge of the city possessed by upper-class, white residents of Westwood. The top right map shows the more restricted view of black residents in Avalon (near Watts). And the bottom right map shows the extremely circumscribed sense of Los Angeles possessed by Spanish-speaking residents in Boyle Heights. As Gould and White note, "Their collective map includes only the immediate area, the City Hall, and, pathetically, the bus depot—the major entrance and exit to their tiny urban world" (1974, p. 37).

Don't misinterpret what Gould and White mean by pathetic. They are commenting not on the cognitive maps of a particular urban group so much as on our stratified society. It's obvious to us all that people have different amounts of money, but it's cause for alarm when we see so graphically how money translates itself into access to the world. Access in turn leads to a rich and differentiated worldview, which can only make the world more accessible. And so it goes.

Gould and White also have asked Americans in different parts of the country about where they prefer to live and how much they know about different areas. Preference and knowledge go together and are inversely related to what is called the *confusion matrix:* the tendency to confuse adjacent states with each other. Most Americans show a regional bias, preferring their own state and knowing a great deal about it. If they don't live near the following sets of states, they tend to confuse Vermont with New Hampshire, Mississippi with Alabama, and Illinois with Indiana.

We don't need to be social scientists to see that ignorance is a potential breeding ground for all sorts of problems. No wonder Americans favor locating nuclear waste dumps someplace, as long as it is over there in Utah, or Iowa, or New Jersey, or wherever they don't know anything about. Regional prejudices make more sense once we see (literally) how people in one part of the country ignore the other parts.

However, cognitive maps need not be depressing. They provide information that can be used to change the physical environment so people can interact more forthrightly with it. Gould and White describe several lines of research that can lead to practical interventions. What do people view as the central landmarks of their city? Skyscrapers are not usually depicted as such, which makes sense when you think about it. People can't see skyscrapers. Instead, buildings and places at street level are much more frequently included in cognitive maps. To me, this means that city planners should worry less about how a city looks from a helicopter or airplane and more about how it looks from a car or on foot.

How do people draw neighborhood boundaries? Again, research results are at odds with "theories" of certain urban experts. Everyday people mark out their neighborhood area by its physical area, not on the density of its population. To me, this suggests a need for drastic revision in the way buildings, neighborhoods, and towns are designed.

Finally, where do people feel at danger? Research finds consensus among neighborhood residents about safe versus dangerous places. Maybe street lights and police patrols should be concentrated where cognitive maps indicate fear. And, on the other hand, research also suggests that people are sometimes completely oblivious to environmental hazards, even when explicitly asked to indicate them. Even after the well-publicized earthquake in the Bay Area in 1989, few people seem to represent in their cognitive maps the virtual guarantee of future quakes in this area. The West Coast is one of the few parts of the country that almost all Americans regard as highly desirable. To me, the West Coast would be even more desirable if concrete plans for coping with the aftermath of an earthquake were in place. This won't happen as long as the possibility of earthquakes is not represented in people's cognitive maps.

SUMMARY

The subject of this chapter was applications of the cognitive-behavioral approaches to personality. The most extensive of these have been to psychopathology and psychotherapy. Cognitive-behavioral interpretations of problems-in-living abound, as psychopathologists have identified characteristic contents and styles of thinking at the base of problems such as depression and anxiety.

Cognitive-behavioral therapies also abound, and all target maladaptive thoughts for change, under the assumption that a different perspective will alleviate suffering. Sometimes the best way to encourage a different perspective is by changing the world in which one lives. This can be done by teaching the person new skills so rewards become more readily available.

I also touched on two other areas where the cognitive-behavioral approach has been applied: health psychology and environmental psychology. In both cases, applied psychologists look at people's thoughts and beliefs and at how these mediate the interplay between people and the worlds in which they live. Specific cognitions may create problems; changing them may therefore provide solutions.

REFLECTIONS ON PERSONALITY PSYCHOLOGY

We've covered a great deal of material in this textbook, and we've still but introduced the study of personality. Even though our overview of the field has not been exhaustive, it at least has been representative. By now you should have a good sense of the sorts of theories, research, and applications that concern personality psychologists. The purpose of this brief concluding chapter is to reflect on the topics we have examined, discussing some questions our journey has raised.

IS THE PARADIGM NOTION USEFUL?

I have used the notion of a paradigm in order to organize the field. A paradigm of personality psychology is a coherent set of assumptions about how personality should be explained. It underlies theory, research, and application. Four paradigms were discussed: the psychodynamic paradigm (Chapters 4–6), the humanistic paradigm (Chapter 7), the trait paradigm (Chapters 8–10), and the cognitive-behavioral paradigm (Chapters 11–13). In each case, the theories, research, and applications within a paradigm hang together as a whole.

Is an organization in terms of paradigms really the most sensible way to bring order to the field of personality psychology (Emmons, 1989)? Other textbook authors have used a similar device, discussing personality topics under several large headings similar to the ones used here. However, their treatments differ somewhat from our book and from one another in terms of the particular paradigms they use.

Does this invalidate the idea of personality paradigms? I think not. Indeed, we expect some disagreement. As I noted in Chapter 3, the various approaches to personality psychology are *like* the scientific paradigms Kuhn (1970) discussed with respect to physical sciences, but not exactly so. Several exist at the same time, and they overlap to a degree. And over time, different paradigms have converged and even merged with one another—for example, cognitive and behavioral approaches.

An organization in terms of paradigms makes sense because the alternatives are not nearly as useful. One might discuss personality psychology in terms of a series of discrete topics—like sex roles, aggression, fantasy, and so on. One might discuss personality psychology in terms of research strategies—like questionnaires versus experiments. Or one might focus on different aspects of the person—like intrapersonal versus interpersonal dynamics. The trouble with such alternatives is that we have no guarantee any of their headings will have any sort of longevity.

Certainly the substantive topics of concern to personality psychologists have changed over the years. In the 1950s, for example, psychodynamic theorists were greatly interested in the effects of weaning and toilet training on adult personality. As we saw in Chapter 5, the yield of this work was meager, and now little concern arises over these particular topics. However, interest in the childhood determinants of adult personality still flourishes. And a psychodynamic perspective is still brought to bear on this topic. What survived was not the specific topic of toilet training but the more general psychodynamic perspective from which it was approached.

We are thus brought back to viewing personality psychology in terms of the paradigms. Indeed, psychologists within the field usually do *not* take an ecumenical approach to substantive topics (McAdams, 1990). They are informed by a larger perspective. The paradigm notion is obviously useful in understanding these larger perspectives.

WHERE ARE TODAY'S GRAND THEORISTS?

Throughout this textbook, I've put a great deal of emphasis on the contributions of particular theorists: Freud, Rogers, Maslow, Allport, Murray, and Kelly, among others. Some contemporary personality psychologists see no need for this continued homage to past theorists (Mendelsohn, 1983), likening it to a walk through a graveyard. By their view, personality psychology today no longer rests on the contributions of grand theorists. For that matter, neither does it depend on the contributions of modern theorists with the stature of Freud, Allport, or Kelly, because such people do not exist. The era of grand theorizing concerning personality is long gone (Sanford, 1976).

I disagree. The influences of Freud, Allport, and Kelly are still very much in evidence today. Contemporary personality psychologists still use the concepts these earlier theorists first introduced and still try to resolve the issues they first phrased. And this argues strongly for the continuity of personality psychology.

It further seems to me that grand personality theorists are alive and well today. Certainly, the object relations theorists qualify as both influential and contemporary. So, too, do the social learning theorists, especially Albert Bandura (1986), who has tirelessly extended his ideas in a number of directions. Other grand theorists may well emerge in the years to come from among the ranks of those who investigate such topics as evolution, the self, and social cognition. Perhaps those who lament the supposed dearth of grand theorists today are merely nostalgic for the good old days in personality psychology. But the future of this field seems even brighter than its past.

DOES RESEARCH INFLUENCE THEORY?

One can acknowledge the continued existence of grand personality theorists yet still be skeptical that theories of the scope they propose are able to be touched by empirical studies. By this view, personality psychologists really engage in two activities, theorizing and researching, and the two have little to do with one another (Lamiell, 1987). Again, I think this position misrepresents what is really going on.

No one investigates psychodynamic theory as a whole, to be sure, but no one has ever been able to do this. Aspects of a paradigm are always going to be nontestable—remember the notion of metapsychological propositions mentioned at several junctures. Other aspects—the clinical propositions—are testable, but any given study examines only one or two clinical propositions at a time. Gradually, the results of these individual studies feed back on the paradigm as a whole and influence it.

Some argue that psychology today has only **midrange theories** that concern themselves not with the whole of the human condition but just a small aspect of it. A midrange theory is a bit more general than a specific hypothesis, but it is much more circumscribed than Freud's psychoanalytic account of personality. Learned helplessness, for example, represents a midrange theory. It does not constitute an entire personality theory, and it does not attempt to do so.

However, we can unambiguously locate learned helplessness within the cognitive-behavioral paradigm, because it shares with the other theories located there a common view of theory, research, and application. The same is the case for most any midrange theory.

Research influences midrange theories—obviously—but in having this influence, it also feeds back, eventually, to change the paradigms where the midrange theories are embedded. Perhaps to those of us in the here and now, such changes are imperceptible, but in the future these influences may well seem like scientific revolutions (Kuhn, 1970).

Indeed, the personality paradigms have changed profoundly over the years. Within the psychodynamic paradigm, for example, we see much less emphasis nowadays on biological drives. And we see correspondingly more emphasis on social influences, ego functions, and mental representations of self and others.

Within the humanistic paradigm, we see ideas originally thought to be resistant to empirical investigation now studied in imaginative ways. More generally, we see the humanistic criticism of traditional psychological research influencing the way research is done in all paradigms.

Within the trait paradigm, we see how the consistency controversy sent shock waves throughout the entire approach, resulting in a more sophisticated view of traits. And we see an exciting era about to begin as the concepts and

Midrange theory: An explicitly circumscribed account of some aspect of a phenomenon.

methods of behavior genetics are used by personality psychologists interested in the evolutionary significance of traits.

The cognitive-behavioral paradigm literally took form in a recent years, as cognitive ideas and behavioral ideas were combined into a coherent statement about human nature. Within this paradigm, we see ideas from experimental psychology's study of cognition used to clarify concerns of long-standing interest to personality psychologists.

WHAT IS THE FUTURE OF PERSONALITY PSYCHOLOGY?

It is difficult to tell the future, but we can speculate about it by extrapolating current trends (Carson, 1989; Pervin, 1990). We can expect, perhaps, that personality psychology will become more specialized, that it will rely more on sophisticated methods and statistical analyses, and that it will evolve into less of an ivory-tower endeavor. Personality psychologists will no longer stay in their traditional haunts—the clinic and the university—but will move farther into industry, hospitals, schools, and campaign staffs of politicians. We may even see a psychologist well-versed in statistical inference appointed in some advisory role to the Supreme Court, because so many matters of justice and injustice rest nowadays on the ability to discern patterns among complex data.

Perhaps we will see an integrated perspective emerge in the field, one that borrows the most useful ideas from the current paradigms and combines them into a view of personality with which most can agree. This integrated perspective will then serve as a powerful springboard for future theory, research, and application. What might the contributions be from the existing paradigms?

From the psychodynamic paradigm, we would certainly want to take the notion of *overdetermined behavior:* the assumption that even the most trivial of actions has numerous determinants. We would want to borrow the notion of *unconscious motives:* Some of the chief determinants of what we do are hidden from our conscious awareness. We would also want to borrow the idea that *childhood events* can influence adult personality, if not in the exact way psychodynamic theorists propose, then at least in some way. More generally, we would want to borrow the idea that personality shows a sensible *development* over one's lifespan.

From the humanistic paradigm, we would probably start with its central tenet that people are not simply machines. An important aspect of what it means to be a person is *experience,* and unless we grasp this, we know little else about personality. We would also want to include some version of *self-actualization,* to capture that part of people always striving toward goals. Finally, we would want to take as our own the humanist's *skepticism concerning "scientific" methods.*

From the trait paradigm, we would borrow the notion of *individual differences,* recognizing that people differ in basic ways from one another, and that these characteristics can be highly stable and pervasive. At the same time, we would wish to qualify this view of broad individual differences with an appreciation of *interactionism,* the joint effect of traits and situations on what people actually do. Finally, we would want to take from the trait paradigm the possibility that aspects of personality are *heritable,* influenced by genetics although not inherited as a whole.

From the cognitive-behavioral paradigm, several ideas would be useful as well. *Learning* would be one essential ingredient for our integrated perspective. And we would want to include the idea of *cognition* mediating the give-and-take between the person and the world. Finally, we would want to take from this paradigm the notion of *situational specificity:* What we do can be highly sensitive to the particular setting in which we find ourselves.

These are undeniably useful ideas, but some seem to contradict others. I've suggested, for example, that an integrated view should incorporate the insights that personality reflects learning and genetics, that what we are all about is fixed as well as in flux, that conscious thoughts are important as well as unconscious motives.

These seeming contradictions should sound familiar to you, however, because they in effect restate the fundamental issues that have always concerned personality psychology. We discussed them in Chapter 3 (pp. 70–72), where they were identified as pushmi-pullyu issues. Each end of an issue needs the other end to be sensible.

My conclusion, therefore, is that these issues taken as a whole reveal something important not only about personality psychology but also about personality. People are incredibly diverse. We must recognize this diversity if personality psychology is to advance and grow. The only fundamental issue discussed in Chapter 3 that has been resolved is the one of simplicity versus complexity: A century of personality psychology leads us without hesitation to say that personality is complex. That both ends of the other issues can be reasonable is not contradictory once we take a view of people across situations and across time, with the expectation that sometimes one end of an issue will describe what is going on, and sometimes it will be the other.

This is hardly a new insight. The Bible tells us that "For everything there is a season" (Ecclesiastes 3: 1–5). If and when we can make sense of the circumstances in which each end of each fundamental issue applies, then we will have an integrative approach to personality.

SUMMARY AND FAREWELL

In this brief concluding chapter, I reflected on some of the issues raised by our coverage of personality psychology. Though not all personality psychologists would agree with me, I speculated that (a) paradigms are the most useful way of organizing the field; (b) theorists of great scope still exist, (c) research indeed influences theory and eventually even the paradigms of personality psychology; and (d) the future of personality psychology may well see an integrated perspective that combines ideas borrowed from the paradigms that exist today.

Thank you and good night.

REFERENCES

Abelson, R. P. (1963). Computer simulations of "hot" cognition. In S. S. Tomkins & S. Messick (Eds.), *Computer simulation of personality*. New York: Wiley.

Abraham, K. (1927). *Selected papers*. London: Hogarth.

Abrahamsen, D. (1978). *Nixon vs. Nixon: An emotional tragedy*. New York: New American Library.

Abramson, L. Y., Metalsky, G. I., & Alloy, L. B. (1989). Hopelessness depression: A theory-based subtype of depression. *Psychological Review, 96,* 358–372.

Abramson, L. Y., Seligman, M. E. P., & Teasdale, J. D. (1978). Learned helplessness in humans: Critique and reformulation. *Journal of Abnormal Psychology, 87,* 49–74.

Adams-Webber, J. R. (1979). *Personal construct theory: Concepts and applications*. Chichester, U. K.: Wiley.

Adams-Webber, J. R. (1981). Fixed role therapy. In R. J. Corsini (Ed.), *Handbook of innovative psychotherapies*. New York: Wiley.

Adelson, J., & Redmond, J. (1958). Personality differences in the capacity for verbal recall. *Journal of Abnormal and Social Psychology, 57,* 244–248.

Ades, D. (1978). *Dada and surrealism*. Woodbury, NY: Barron's.

Adler, A. (1907). Organic inferiority and its compensation. In H. L. Ansbacher & R. R. Ansbacher (Eds.), *The individual psychology of Alfred Adler*. New York: Harper, 1964.

Adler, A. (1910). Inferiority feeling and defiance and obedience. In H. L. Ansbacher & R. R. Ansbacher (Eds.), *The individual psychology of Alfred Adler*. New York: Harper, 1964.

Adler, A. (1927). *The theory and practice of individual psychology*. New York: Harcourt, Brace & World.

Adler, A. (1931). *What life should mean to you*. Boston: Little, Brown.

Adorno, T. W., Frenkel-Brunswik, E., Levinson, D., & Sanford, N. (1950). *The authoritarian personality*. New York: Harper.

Ahadi, S., & Diener, E. (1989). Multiple determinants and effect size. *Journal of Personality and Social Psychology, 56,* 398–406.

Ainsworth, M. D. S. (1989). Attachments beyond infancy. *American Psychologist, 44,* 709–716.

Ainsworth, M. D. S., & Wittig, B. A. (1969). Attachment and exploratory behavior of one-year-olds in a strange situation. In B. M. Foss (Ed.), *Determinants of infant behavior* (Vol. 4). London: Methuen.

Akiskal, H. S., & McKinney, W. T. (1975). Overview of recent research in depression. *Archives of General Psychiatry, 32,* 285–305.

Alexander, F. (1939). Emotional factors in essential hypertension. *Psychosomatic Medicine, 1,* 139–152.

Alexander, F. (1950). *Psychosomatic medicine: Its principles and applications.* New York: Norton.

Alloy, L. B., & Abramson, L. Y. (1979). Judgment of contingency in depressed and nondepressed college students: Sadder but wiser? *Journal of Experimental Psychology: General, 108,* 441–487.

Allport, G. W. (1937). *Personality: A psychological interpretation.* New York: Holt.

Allport, G. W. (1961). *Pattern and growth in personality.* New York: Holt, Rinehart & Winston.

Allport, G. W. (Ed.). (1965). *Letters from Jenny.* New York: Harcourt Brace Jovanovich.

Allport, G. W. (1968a). The historical background of modern social psychology. In G. Lindzey & E. Aronson (Eds.), *The handbook of social psychology* (2nd ed., Vol. 1). Reading, MA: Addison-Wesley.

Allport, G. W. (1968b). *The person in psychology: Selected essays.* Boston: Beacon.

Allport, G. W., & Allport, F. H. (1921). Personality traits: Their classification and measurement. *Journal of Abnormal and Social Psychology, 16,* 6–40.

Allport, G. W., & Odbert, H. S. (1936). Trait-names: A psycho-lexical study. *Psychological Monographs: General and Applied, 47* (1, Whole No. 211), 171–220.

Allport, G. W., & Vernon, P. E. (1931). *A study of values.* Boston: Houghton Mifflin.

Allport, G. W., & Vernon, P. E. (1933). *Studies in expressive movement.* New York: Macmillan.

Allport, G. W., & Vernon, P. E., & Lindzey, G. (1960). *A study of values* (Rev. ed.). Boston: Houghton Mifflin.

Allport, S. (1986). *Explorers of the black box: The search for the cellular basis of memory.* New York: Norton.

Allred, K. D., & Smith, T. W. (1989). The hardy personality: Cognitive and physiological responses to evaluative threat. *Journal of Personality and Social Psychology, 56,* 257–266.

Altman, I. (1975). *The environment and social behavior: Privacy, personal space, territory, and crowding.* Monterey, CA: Brooks/Cole.

Amabile, T. M., & Kabat, L. G. (1982). When self-descriptions contradict behavior: Actions do speak louder than words. *Social Cognition, 1,* 311–325.

American Psychiatric Association. (1980). *Diagnostic and statistical manual of mental disorders* (3rd ed.). Washington, DC: Author.

American Psychiatric Association. (1987). *Diagnostic and statistical manual of mental disorders* (3rd ed., rev.). Washington, DC: Author.

American Psychological Association. (1981). *Ethical principles of psychologists.* Washington, DC: Author.

Anastasi, A. (1979). *Fields of applied psychology* (2nd ed.). New York: McGraw-Hill.

Anastasi, A. (1982). *Psychological testing* (5th ed.). New York: Macmillan.

Anderson, C. A., Horowitz, L. M., & French, R. des. (1983). Attributional style of lonely and depressed people. *Journal of Personality and Social Psychology, 45,* 127–136.

Anderson, T. H. (1978). Becoming sane with psychohistory. *The Historian, 41,* 1–20.

Andreasen, N. C. (1980). *The broken brain: The biological revolution in psychiatry.* New York: Harper & Row.

Andrews, J. D. W. (1989). Integrating visions of reality: Interpersonal diagnosis and the existential vision. *American Psychologist, 44,* 803–817.

Angell, M. (1985). Disease as reflection of the psyche. *The New England Journal of Medicine, 312,* 1570–1572.

Ansbacher, H. L. (1980). Alfred Adler. In H. I. Kaplan, A. M. Freedman, & B. J. Sadock (Eds.), *Comprehensive textbook of psychiatry* (Vol. 1, 2nd ed.). Baltimore: Williams & Wilkins.

Anthony, E. J. (1987). Risk, vulnerability, and resilience: An overview. In E. J. Anthony & B. J. Cohler (Eds.), *The invulnerable child.* New York: Guilford.

Anthony, E. J., & Cohler, B. J. (Eds.). (1987). *The invulnerable child.* New York: Guilford.

Archer, J. (1988). The sociobiology of bereavement: A reply to Littlefield and Rushton. *Journal of Personality and Social Psychology, 55,* 272–278.

Ardrey, R. (1966). *The territorial imperative.* New York: Atheneum.

Argyris, C. (1969). Some unintended consequences of rigorous research. *Psychological Bulletin, 70,* 185–197.

Argyris, C. (1975). Dangers in applying results from experimental social psychology. *American Psychologist, 30,* 469–485.

Arieti, S., & Bemporad, J. (1978). *Severe and mild depression.* New York: Basic Books.

Averill, J. R. (1973). Personal control over aversive stimuli and its relationship to stress. *Psychological Bulletin, 80,* 286–303.

Baker, L. A., & Daniels, D. (1990). Nonshared environmental influences and personality differences in adult twins. *Journal of Personality and Social Psychology, 58,* 103–110.

Balay, J., & Shevrin, H. (1988). The subliminal psychodynamic activation method: A critical review. *American Psychologist, 43,* 161–174.

Baldessarini, R. J. (1975). The basis for amine hypotheses in affective disorders. *Archives of General Psychiatry, 32,* 1087–1093.

Balke, W. M., Hammond, K. R., & Meyer, G. D. (1973). An alternate approach to labor-management relations. *Administrative Science Quarterly, 18,* 311–327.

Bandura, A. (1973). *Aggression: A social learning analysis.* Englewood Cliffs, NJ: Prentice-Hall.

Bandura, A. (1974). Behavior theories and the models of man. *American Psychologist, 29,* 859–869.

Bandura, A. (1977a). Self-efficacy: Toward a unifying theory of behavioral change. *Psychological Review, 84,* 191–215.

Bandura, A. (1977b). *Social learning theory.* Englewood Cliffs, NJ: Prentice-Hall.

Bandura, A. (1978). The self system in reciprocal determinism. *American Psychologist, 33,* 344–358.

Bandura, A. (1982). The psychology of chance encounters and life paths. *American Psychologist, 37,* 747–755.

Bandura, A. (1986). *Social foundations of thought and action.* Englewood Cliffs, NJ: Prentice-Hall.

Bandura, A. (1989). Human agency in social cognitive theory. *American Psychologist, 44,* 1175–1184.

Bandura, A. (1990). Some reflections on reflections. *Psychological Inquiry, 1,* 101–105.

Bandura, A., Ross, D., & Ross, S. A. (1963). Imitation of film-mediated aggressive models. *Journal of Abnormal and Social Psychology, 66,* 3–11.

Bandura, A., & Walters, R. (1963). *Social learning and personality development.* New York: Holt, Rinehart & Winston.

Bannister, D. (1963). The genesis of schizophrenic thought disorder: A serial invalidation hypothesis. *British Journal of Psychiatry, 109,* 680–686.

Bannister, D. (1965). The genesis of schizophrenic thought disorder: Re-test of the serial invalidation hypothesis. *British Journal of Psychiatry, 111,* 377–382.

Barefoot, J. D., Dahlstrom, W. G., & Williams, R. B. (1983). Hostility, CHD incidence, and total mortality: A 25-year follow-up study of 255 physicians. *Psychosomatic Medicine, 45,* 559–570.

Bargh, J. A., & Tota, M. E. (1988). Context-dependent automatic processing in depression: Accessibility of negative constructs with regard to self but not others. *Journal of Personality and Social Psychology, 54,* 925–939.

Barker, R. G., Dembo, T., & Lewin, K. (1941). Frustration and regression: An experiment with young children. *University of Iowa Studies in Child Welfare, 18* (1). Described in C. S. Hall & G. Lindzey (1970). *Theories of personality* (2nd ed.). New York: Wiley.

Baron, R. A., & Byrne, D. (1984). *Social psychology: Understanding human interaction* (4th ed.). Boston: Allyn & Bacon.

Bartlett, F. (1932). *A study in experimental and social psychology.* New York: Cambridge University.

Bassett, A. S., McGillivray, B. C., Jones, B. D., & Pantzar, J. T. (1988). Partial trisomy chromosome 5 cosegregating with schizophrenia. *Lancet, 108,* 799–801.

Bateson, G., Jackson, D. D., Haley, J., & Weakland, J. (1956). Toward a theory of schizophrenia. *Behavioral Science, 1,* 251–264.

Baumeister, R. F. (1987). How the self became a problem: A psychological review of historical research. *Journal of Personality and Social Psychology, 52,* 163–176.

Baumeister, R. F., & Scher, S. J. (1988). Self-defeating behavior patterns among normal individuals: Review and analysis of common self-destructive tendencies. *Psychological Bulletin, 104,* 3–22.

Beck, A. T. (1967). *Depression: Clinical, experimental, and theoretical aspects.* New York: Hoeber.

Beck, A. T. (1976). *Cognitive therapy and the emotional disorders.* New York: International Universities Press.

Beck, A. T., & Emery, G. (1985). *Anxiety disorders and phobias: A cognitive perspective.* New York: Basic Books.

Beck, A. T., & Freeman, A. (1990). *Cognitive therapy of personality disorders.* New York: Guilford.

Beck, A. T., Rush, A. J., Shaw, B. F., & Emery, G. (1979). *Cognitive therapy of depression.* New York: Guilford.

Becker, H. (1953). Becoming a marijuana user. *American Journal of Sociology, 59,* 235–242.

Becker, H. (1982). *Art worlds.* Berkeley: University of California Press.

Bellack, A. S., & Hersen, M. (Eds.). (1985). *Dictionary of behavior therapy techniques.* New York: Pergamon.

Belmont, L., & Marolla, F. A. (1973). Birth order, family size, and intelligence. *Science, 182,* 1096–1101.

Bem, D. J. (1983). Further deja-vu in the search for cross-situational consistency: A response to Mischel and Peake. *Psychological Review, 90,* 390–393.

Bem, D. J., & Allen, A. (1974). On predicting some of the people some of the time: The search for cross-situational consistencies in behavior. *Psychological Review, 81,* 506–520.

Bem, D. J., & Funder, D. C. (1978). Predicting more of the people more of the time: Assessing the personality of situations. *Psychological Review, 85,* 485–501.

Bem, S. L. (1974). The measurement of psychological androgyny. *Journal of Consulting and Clinical Psychology, 42,* 155–162.

Bem, S. L. (1975). Sex role adaptability: One consequence of psychological androgyny. *Journal of Personality and Social Psychology, 31,* 634–643.

Bem, S. L. (1981). Gender schema theory: A cognitive account of sex-typing. *Psychological Review, 88,* 354–364.

Bem, S. L. (1984). Androgyny and gender schema theory. *Nebraska Symposium on Motivation, 32,* 179–226.

Benjamin, L. S. (1974). Structural analysis of social behavior. *Psychological Review, 81,* 392–425.

Berger, P. L., & Luckmann, T. (1966). *The social construction of reality.* New York: Doubleday.

Berglas, S., & Jones, E. E. (1978). Drug choice as a self-handicapping strategy in response to noncontingent success. *Journal of Personality and Social Psychology, 36,* 405–417.

Berkowitz, L. (1974). Some determinants of impulsive aggression: Role of mediated associations with reinforcements for aggression. *Psychological Review, 81,* 165–176.

Bernstein, D. A., & Nietzel, M. T. (1980). *Introduction to clinical psychology.* New York: McGraw-Hill.

Berry, J. W. (1966). Temne and Eskimo perceptual skills. *International Journal of Psychology, 1,* 207–229.

Berry, J. W., & Annis, R. C. (1974). Ecology, culture, and psychological differentiation. *International Journal of Psychology, 9,* 173–193.

Bersoff, D. N. (1981). Testing and the law. *American Psychologist, 36,* 1047–1056.

Bevan, W. (1964). Subliminal stimulation: A pervasive problem for psychology. *Psychological Bulletin, 61,* 81–99.

Bieri, J. (1955). Cognitive complexity-simplicity and predictive behavior. *Journal of Abnormal and Social Psychology, 51,* 263–268.

Biernat, M. (1989). Motives and values to achieve: Different constructs with different effects. *Journal of Personality, 57,* 69–95.

Binet, A., & Simon, T. (1913). *A method of measuring the development of the intelligence of young children* (3rd ed.). Chicago: Chicago Medical Books.

Binswanger, L. (1963). *Being-in-the-world: Selected papers of Ludwig Binswanger.* New York: Basic Books.

Blaney, P. H. (1986). Affect and memory: A review. *Psychological Bulletin, 99,* 229–246.

Blatt, S. J. (1964). An attempt to define mental health. *Journal of Consulting Psychology, 28,* 146–153.

Bliss, E. L. (1980). Multiple personalities: Report of fourteen cases with implications for schizophrenia and hysteria. *Archives of General Psychiatry, 37,* 1388–1397.

Block, J. (1971). *Lives through time.* Berkeley: Bancroft Books.

Block, J. (1989). Critique of the act frequency approach to personality. *Journal of Personality and Social Psychology, 56,* 234–245.

Blum, G. S. (1949). A study of the psychoanalytic theory of psychosexual development. *Genetic Psychology Monographs, 39,* 3–99.

Blum, G. S. (1962). A guide for the research use of the Blacky pictures. *Journal of Projective Techniques, 26,* 3–29.

Blum, G. S., & Hunt, H. F. (1952). The validity of the Blacky pictures. *Psychological Bulletin, 49,* 238–250.

Bobko, P., & Schwartz, J. P. (1984). A metric for combining theoretically related but statistically uncorrelated constructs. *Journal of Personality Assessment, 48,* 11–16.

Boldizar, J. P., Wilson, K. L., & Deemer, D. K. (1989). Gender, life experiences, and moral judgment development: A process-oriented approach. *Journal of Personality and Social Psychology, 57,* 229–238.

Boring, E. G. (1950). *A history of experimental psychology* (2nd ed.). New York: Appleton-Century-Crofts.

Borkenau, P., & Ostendorf, F. (1987). Retrospective estimates of act frequencies: How accurately do they reflect reality? *Journal of Personality and Social Psychology, 52,* 626–638.

Botwin, M. D., & Buss, D. M. (1989). Structure of act-report data: Is the five-factor model of personality recaptured? *Journal of Personality and Social Psychology, 56,* 988–1001.

Bowen, E. (1985, April 22). Cracking the SAT code. *Time,* p. 61.

Bower, G. H. (1981). Mood and memory. *American Psychologist, 36,* 129–148.

Bowers, K. S. (1973). Situationism in psychology: An analysis and critique. *Psychological Review, 80,* 307–336.

Bowlby, J. (1969). *Attachment and loss.* New York: Basic Books.

Breland, H. M. (1974). Birth order, family constellation, and verbal achievement. *Child Development, 45,* 1011–1019.

Breuer, J., & Freud, S. (1895). Studies on hysteria. *Collected works* (Vol. 2). London: Hogarth.

Brewin, C. R. (1985). Depression and causal attribution: What is their relation? *Psychological Bulletin, 98,* 297–309.

Brigham, J. C., & Wrightsman, L. S. (1982). *Contemporary issues in social psychology* (4th ed.). Monterey, CA: Brooks/Cole.

Brody, B. (1970). Freud's case load. *Psychotherapy: Theory, Research, and Practice, 7,* 8–12.

Bromberg, W. (1959). *The mind of man: A history of psychotherapy and psychoanalysis.* New York: Harper & Row.

Bronzaft, A. L. (1981). The effect of a noise abatement program on reading ability. *Journal of Environmental Psychology, 1,* 215–222.

Brooks, C. V. (1974). *Sensory awareness: The rediscovery of experiencing.* New York: Viking.

Broverman, I. K., Vogel, S. R., Broverman, D. M., Clarkson, F. E., & Rosenkrantz, P. S. (1972). Sex-role stereotypes: A current appraisal. *Journal of Social Issues, 28,* 59–78.

Brown, B. B., & Lohr, M. J. (1987). Peer-group affiliation and adolescent self-esteem: An integration of ego-identity and symbolic-interaction theories. *Journal of Personality and Social Psychology, 52,* 47–55.

Brown, J. A. C. (1964). *Freud and the post-Freudians.* New York: Penguin.

Brown, N. O. (1959). *Life against death.* Middletown, CT: Wesleyan University Press.

Browne, A., & Finkelhor, D. (1986). Impact of child sexual abuse: A review of the research. *Psychological Bulletin, 99,* 66–77.

Bruner, J. S. (1956). You are your constructs. *Contemporary Psychology, 1,* 355–357.

Bursten, B. (1979). Psychiatry and the rhetoric of models. *American Journal of Psychiatry, 136,* 661–666.

Burton, R. V. (1963). Generality of honesty reconsidered. *Psychological Review, 70,* 481–499.

Buss, A. H. (1989). Personality as traits. *American Psychologist, 44,* 1378–1388.

Buss, A. H., & Plomin, R. (1975). *A temperament theory of personality.* New York: Wiley.

Buss, A. H., & Plomin, R. (1984). *Temperament: Early developing personality traits.* Hillsdale, NJ: Erlbaum.

Buss, D. M. (1984). Evolutionary biology and personality psychology: Toward a conception of human nature and individual differences. *American Psychologist, 39,* 1135–1147.

Buss, D. M. (1987). Selection, evocation, and manipulation. *Journal of Personality and Social Psychology, 53,* 1214–1221.

Buss, D. M. (1989). Sex differences in human mate preferences: Evolutionary hypotheses tested in 37 cultures. *Behavioral and Brain Sciences, 12,* 1–49.

Buss, D. M. (Ed.). (1990). Special issue: Biological foundations of personality. *Journal of Personality, 58,* 1–345.

Buss, D. M. (1991). Evolutionary personality psychology. *Annual Review of Psychology, 42,* 459–491.

Buss, D. M., & Cantor, N. (Eds.). (1989). *Personality psychology: Recent trends and emerging directions.* New York: Springer-Verlag.

Buss, D. M., & Craik, K. H. (1984). Acts, dispositions, and personality. In B. A. Maher (Ed.), *Progress in experimental personality research* (Vol. 13). New York: Academic Press.

Buss, D. M., Gomes, M., Higgins, D. S., & Lauterbach, K. (1987). Tactics of manipulation. *Journal of Personality and Social Psychology, 52,* 1219–1229.

Butcher, J. N., & Keller, L. S. (1984). Objective personality assessment. In G. Goldstein & M. Hersen (Eds.), *Handbook of psychological assessment.* New York: Pergamon.

Butcher, J. N., Dahlstrom, W. G., Graham, J. R., Tellegen, A., & Kaemmer, B. (1989). *Manual for the restandardized Minnesota Multiphasic Personality Inventory: MMPI-2. An interpretive and administrative guide.* Minneapolis: University of Minnesota Press.

Byrne, D. (1961). The repression-sensitization scale: Rationale, reliability, and validity. *Journal of Personality, 29,* 334–349.

Calhoun, J. B. (1962). Population density and social pathology. *Scientific American, 206* (3), 139–148.

Campbell, D. P. (1971). *Manual for the Strong Vocational Interest Blank.* Stanford, CA: Stanford University Press.

Campbell, D. T., & Stanley, J. C. (1966). *Experimental and quasi-experimental designs for research.* Chicago: Rand McNally.

Cantor, N. (1990). From thought to behavior: "Having" and "doing" in the study of personality and cognition. *American Psychologist, 45,* 735–750.

Cantor, N., & Kihlstrom, J. F. (1987). *Personality and social intelligence.* Englewood Cliffs, NJ: Prentice-Hall.

Cantor, N., & Mischel, W. (1977). Traits as prototypes: Effects on recognition memory. *Personality and Social Psychology, 37,* 337–344.

Cantor, N., & Mischel, W. (1979). Prototypes in person perception. In L. Berkowitz (Ed.), *Advances in experimental social psychology* (Vol. 12). New York: Academic Press.

Cantril, H. (1935). Review of Lewin's *A dynamic theory of personality. Journal of Abnormal and Social Psychology, 30,* 534–537.

Carlson, R. (1971). Where is the person in personality research? *Psychological Bulletin, 75,* 203–219.

Carson, R. C. (1969). *Interaction concepts of personality.* Chicago: Aldine.

Carson, R. C. (1989). Personality. *Annual Review of Psychology, 40,* 227–248.

Carver, C. S. (1989). How should multifaceted personality constructs be tested? Issues illustrated by self-monitoring, attributional style, and hardiness. *Journal of Personality and Social Psychology, 56,* 577–585.

Carver, C. S., & Scheier, M. F. (1981). A control systems approach to behavioral self-regulation. In L. Wheeler (Ed.), *Review of personality and social psychology* (Vol. 2). Beverly Hills, CA: Sage.

Caspi, A., & Herbener, E. S. (1990). Continuity and change: Assortive marriage and the consistency of personality in adulthood. *Journal of Personality and Social Psychology, 58,* 250–258.

Cattell, J. M. (1890). Mental tests and measurements. *Mind, 15,* 373–380.

Cattell, R. B. (1950). *Personality: A systematic, theoretical, and factual study.* New York: McGraw-Hill.

Cattell, R. B. (1972). *A new morality from science: Beyondism.* New York: Pergamon.

Cattell, R. B. (1984). The voyage of a laboratory, 1928–1984. *Multivariate Behavioral Research, 19,* 121–174.

Cattell, R. B. (1990). Advances in Cattellian personality theory. In L. Pervin (Ed.), *Handbook of personality: Theory and research.* New York: Guilford.

Cattell, R. B., Blewett, D. B., & Beloff, J. R. (1955). The inheritance of personality: A multiple variance analysis determination of approximate nature-nurture ratios for primary personality ratios in Q data. *American Journal of Human Genetics, 7,* 122–146.

Cattell, R. B., & Scheier, I. H. (1961). *The meaning and measurement of neuroticism and anxiety.* New York: Ronald.

Cattell, R. B., Stice, G. F., & Kristy, N. F. (1957). A first approximation to nature-nurture ratios for eleven primary personality factors in objective tests. *Journal of Abnormal and Social Psychology, 54,* 143–159.

Chaplin, W. F., & Goldberg, L. R. (1984). A failure to replicate the Bem and Allen Study of individual differences in cross-situational consistency. *Journal of Personality and Social Psychology, 47,* 1074–1090.

Chapman, L. J., & Chapman, J. P. (1969). Illusory correlation as an obstacle to the use of valid psychodiagnostic signs. *Journal of Abnormal Psychology, 74,* 271–280.

Child, D. (1970). *The essentials of factor analysis.* London: Holt, Rinehart & Winston.

Child, I. L. (1968). Personality in culture. In E. F. Borgatta & W. W. Lambert (Eds.), *Handbook of personality theory and research.* Chicago: Rand McNally.

Christie, R., & Geis, F. L. (1970). *Studies in Machiavellianism.* New York: Academic Press.

Church, A. T., & Katigbak, M. S. (1989). Internal, external, and self-report structure of personality in a non-western culture: An investigation of cross-language and cross-cultural generalizability. *Journal of Personality and Social Psychology, 57,* 857–872.

Clarkson, P. (1989). *Gestalt counselling in action.* London: Sage.

Clayton, R. R. (1986). Multiple drug use: Epidemiology, correlates, and consequences. In M. Galanter (Ed.), *Recent developments in alcoholism* (Vol. 4). New York: Plenum.

Coates, D., & Wortman, C. B. (1980). Depression maintenance and interpersonal control. In A. Baum & J. E. Singer (Eds.), *Advances in environmental psychology: Applications of personal control* (Vol. 2). Hillsdale, NJ: Erlbaum.

Cobb, S. (1976). Social support as a moderator of life stress. *Psychosomatic Medicine, 38,* 300–314.

Cohen, J. B., & Chakravarti, D. (1990). Consumer psychology. *Annual Review of Psychology, 41,* 243–288.

Cohen, S., Evans, G. W., Krantz, D. S., & Stokots, D. (1980). Physiological, motivational, and cognitive effects of aircraft noise on children: Moving from the laboratory to the field. *American Psychologist, 35,* 231–243.

Cohen, S., Evans, G. W., Krantz, D. S., Stokots, D., & Kelly, S. (1981). Aircraft noise and children: Longitudinal and cross-sectional evidence on adaptation to noise and the effectiveness of noise abatement. *Journal of Personality and Social Psychology, 40,* 331–345.

Cohen, S., & Syme, S. L. (1985). *Social support and health.* Orlando, FL: Academic Press.

Cohen, S., & Weinstein, N. (1981). Nonauditory effects of noise on behavior and health. *Journal of Social Issues, 37*(1), 36–70.

Cohn, T. S. (1956). Relation of the F Scale to a response set to answer positively. *Journal of Social Psychology, 44,* 129–133.

Collins, W. A., & Gunnar, M. R. (1990). Social and personality development. *Annual Review of Psychology, 41,* 387–416.

Compton, M. (1984, January). Sideline computing in the NFL. *Personal Computing,* pp. 29–32.

Condiotte, M. M., & Lichtenstein, E. (1981). Self-efficacy and relapse in smoking cessation programs. *Journal of Consulting and Clinical Psychology, 49,* 648–658.

Conley, J. J (1984a). Longitudinal consistency of adult personality: Self-reported psychological characteristics across 45 years. *Journal of Personality and Social Psychology, 47,* 1325–1333.

Conley, J. J. (1984b). Relation of temporal stability and cross-situational consistency in personality: Comment on the Mischel-Epstein debate. *Psychological Review, 91,* 491–496.

Conn, J., & Kanner, L. (1940). Spontaneous erections in childhood. *Journal of Pediatrics, 16,* 337–340.

Coopersmith, S. (1967). *The antecedents of self-esteem.* San Francisco: Freeman.

Coopersmith, S. (1968). Studies in self-esteem. *Scientific American, 218*(2), 96–106.

Costa, P. T., & McCrae, R. R. (1985). *The NEO Personality Inventory Manual.* Odessa, FL: Psychological Assessment Resources.

Costa, P. T., & McCrae, R. R. (1988a). From catalog to classification: Murray's needs and the five-factor model. *Journal of Personality and Social Psychology, 55,* 258–265.

Costa, P. T., & McCrae, R. R. (1988b). Personality in adulthood: A six-year longitudinal study of self-reports and spouse ratings on the NEO Personality Inventory. *Journal of Personality and Social Psychology, 54,* 853–863.

Costos, D. (1986). Sex role identity in young adults: Its parental antecedents and relation to ego development. *Journal of Personality and Social Psychology, 50,* 602–611.

Cousins, N. (1977, May 28). Anatomy of an illness (as perceived by the patient). *Saturday Review,* pp. 4–6; 48–51.

Cousins, N. (1981a). *Human options.* New York: Norton.

Cousins, N. (1981b). *The anatomy of an illness.* New York: Norton.

Cousins, N. (1983). *The healing heart.* New York: Norton.

Cousins, N. (1989). *Head first: The biology of hope.* New York: Dutton.

Coyne, J. C. (1976). Toward an interactional description of depression. *Psychiatry, 39,* 28–40.

Coyne, J. C., & Gotlib, I. H. (1983). The role of cognition in depression: A critical appraisal. *Psychological Bulletin, 94,* 472–505.

Craik, K. H. (1986). Personality research methods: An historical perspective. *Journal of Personality, 54,* 18–51.

Cramer, P. (1987). The development of defense mechanisms. *Journal of Personality, 55,* 597–614.

Cramer, P., & Gaul, R. (1988). The effects of success and failure on children's use of defense mechanisms. *Journal of Personality, 56,* 729–742.

Crawford, C. B., & Anderson, J. L. (1989). Sociobiology: An environmentalist discipline? *American Psychologist, 44,* 1449–1459.

Cronbach, L. J. (1946). Response sets and test validity. *Educational and Psychological Measurement, 6,* 475–494.

Cronbach, L. J. (1957). The two disciplines of scientific psychology. *American Psychologist, 12,* 671–684.

Cronbach, L. J., & Meehl, P. E. (1955). Construct validity in psychological tests. *Psychological Bulletin, 52,* 281–302.

Crook, M. N. (1937). Intrafamily relationships in personality test performance. *Psychological Record, 1,* 479–502.

Crosby, F., & Crosby, T. L. (1981). Psychobiography and psychohistory. In S. Long (Ed.), *Handbook of political behavior* (Vol. 1). New York: Plenum.

Crowne, D. P., & Marlowe, D. (1964). *The approval motive: Studies in evaluative dependence.* New York: Wiley.

Csikszentmihalyi, M. (1975). *Beyond boredom and anxiety.* San Francisco: Jossey-Bass.

Csikszentmihalyi, M. (1990). *Flow: The psychology of optimal experience.* New York: Harper & Row.

Csikszentmihalyi, M., & Csikszentmihalyi, I. S. (1988). *Optimal experience: Psychological studies of flow in consciousness.* Cambridge: Cambridge University Press.

Csikszentmihalyi, M., & Larson, R. (1984). *Being adolescent: Conflict and growth in the teenage years.* New York: Basic Books.

Culver, C. M., Cohen, S. I., Silverman, A. J., & Shmavonian, B. M. (1964). Cognitive restructuring, field dependence-independence, and the psychophysiological response to perceptual isolation. In J. Wortis (Ed.), *Recent advances in biological psychiatry* (Vol. VI). New York: Plenum.

Curtis, R. C. (Ed.). (1989). *Self-defeating behaviors: Experimental research, clinical impressions, and practical implications.* New York: Plenum.

Cutrona, C. E., Russell, D., & Jones, R. D. (1985). Cross-situational consistency in causal attributions: Does attributional style exist? *Journal of Personality and Social Psychology, 47,* 1043–1058.

Daly, M., & Wilson, M. (1990). Is parent-offspring conflict sex-linked? Freudian and Darwinian models. *Journal of Personality, 58,* 163–189.

Darley, J. M., & Latané, B. (1968). Bystander intervention in emergencies: Diffusion of responsibility. *Journal of Personality and Social Psychology, 8,* 377–383.

Darwin, C. R. (1859). *The origin of species.* London: Murray.

Davis, C. M. (1928). Self-selection of diet by newly weaned infants. *American Journal of Diseases of Children, 36,* 651–679.

Davis, P. J. (1987). Repression and the inaccessibility of affective memories. *Journal of Personality and Social Psychology, 53,* 585–593.

Davis, P. J., & Schwartz, G. E. (1987). Repression and the inaccessibility of affective memories. *Journal of Personality and Social Psychology, 52,* 155–162.

Deci, E. L., & Ryan, R. M. (1980). The empirical exploration of intrinsic motivational processes. In L. Berkowitz (Ed.), *Advances in experimental social psychology* (Vol. 13). New York: Academic Press.

Derry, P. A., & Kuiper, N. A. (1981). Schematic processing and self-reference in clinical depression. *Journal of Abnormal Psychology, 90,* 286–297.

Deutsch, G. (1990, June 4). Baseball scouting now a mind game. *The Sporting News,* p. 48.

Deutsch, M. (1968). Field theory in social psychology. In G. Lindzey & E. Aronson (Eds.), *The handbook of social psychology* (2nd ed., Vol. I). Reading, MA: Addison-Wesley.

Dewey, J. (1896). The reflex arc concept in psychology. *Psychological Review, 3,* 357–370.

Diamond, S. (1957). *Personality and temperament.* New York: Harper.

Digman, J. M. (1990). Personality structure: Emergence of the five-factor model. *Annual Review of Psychology, 41,* 417–440.

Dillehay, R. C. (1978). Authoritarianism. In H. London & J. E. Exner (Eds.), *Dimensions of personality.* New York: Wiley.

Dimitrovsky, L., Singer, J., & Yinon, Y. (1989). Masculine and feminine traits: Their relation to suitedness for and success in training for traditionally masculine and feminine army functions. *Journal of Personality and Social Psychology, 57,* 839–847.

Dollard, J., Doob, L. W., Miller, N. E., Mowrer, O. H., & Sears, R. R. (1939). *Frustration and aggression.* New Haven: Yale University Press.

Dollard, J., & Miller, N. E. (1950). *Personality and psychotherapy: An analysis in terms of learning, thinking, and culture.* New York: McGraw-Hill.

Downey, J. E. (1923). *The will temperament and its testing.* New York: World Book.

Dunnette, M. D. (Ed.) (1976). *Handbook of industrial and organizational psychology.* Chicago: Rand McNally.

Dunnette, M. D., & Borman, W. C. (1979). Personnel selection and classification systems. *Annual Review of Psychology, 30,* 477–525.

Edwards, A. L. (1957). *The social desirability variable in personality assessment and research.* New York: Dryden.

Edwards, V. J., & Spence, J. T. (1987). Gender-related traits, stereotypes, and schemata. *Journal of Personality and Social Psychology, 53,* 146–154.

Egeland, J. A., et al. (1987). Bipolar affective disorders linked to DNA markers on chromosome II. *Nature, 325,* 783–787.

Ekehammar, B. (1974). Interactionism in psychology from a historical perspective. *Psychological Bulletin, 81,* 1026–1048.

Ellis, A. (1962). *Reason and emotion in psychotherapy.* New York: Stuart.

Ellis, A. (1973). *Humanistic psychotherapy: The rational-emotive approach.* New York: Julian.

Emmons, R. A. (1989). The Big Three, The Big Four, or The Big Five? *Contemporary Psychology, 34,* 644–646.

Endler, N. S., & Magnusson, D. (Eds.). (1976a). *Interactional psychology and personality.* Washington, DC: Hemisphere.

Endler, N. S., & Magnusson, D. (1976b). Toward an interactional theory of personality. *Psychological Bulletin, 83,* 956–974.

Engel, G. L. (1971). Sudden and rapid death during psychological stress. Folklore or folkwisdom? *Annals of Internal Medicine, 74,* 771–782.

Epstein, S. (1979). The stability of behavior: I. On predicting most of the people much of the time. *Journal of Personality and Social Psychology, 37,* 1097–1126.

Epstein, S. (1980). The stability of behavior: II. Implications for psychological research. *American Psychologist, 35,* 790–806.

Epstein, S. (1983a). Aggregation and beyond: Some basic issues on the prediction of behavior. *Journal of Personality, 51,* 360–392.

Epstein, S. (1983b). The stability of confusion: A reply to Mischel and Peake. *Psychological Review, 90,* 179–184.

Epstein, S. (1984). The stability of behavior across time and situations. In R. A. Zucker, J. Aronoff, & A. I. Rabin (Eds.), *Personality and the prediction of behavior.* Orlando, FL: Academic Press.

Erdelyi, M. H. (1974). A new look at the new look: Perceptual defense and vigilance. *Psychological Review, 81,* 1–25.

Erdelyi, M. H. (1985). *Psychoanalysis: Freud's cognitive psychology.* New York: Freeman.

Erikson, E. H. (1950). *Childhood and society.* New York: Norton.

Erikson, E. H. (1958). *Young man Luther.* New York: Norton.

Erikson, E. H. (1964). *Insight and responsibility.* New York: Norton.

Erikson, E. H. (1968). *Identity: Youth and crisis.* New York: Norton.

Erikson, E. H. (1969). *Ghandi's truth.* New York: Norton.

Erikson, E. H. (1974). *Dimensions of a new identity.* New York: Norton.

Ernst, C., & Angst, J. (1983). *Birth order: Its influence on personality.* Berlin: Springer-Verlag.

Evans, G. W., & Jacobs, S. V. (1981). Air pollution and human behavior. *Journal of Social Issues, 37*(1), 95–125.

Eysenck, H. J. (1947). *Dimensions of personality.* London: Routledge & Kegan Paul.

Eysenck, H. J. (1952a). The effects of psychotherapy: An evaluation. *Journal of Consulting Psychology, 16,* 319–324.

Eysenck, H. J. (1952b). *The scientific study of personality.* London: Routledge & Kegan Paul.

Eysenck, H. J. (1953). *Uses and abuses of psychology.* Harmondsworth, England: Penguin.

Eysenck, H. J. (1954). The science of psychology: Nomothetic! *Psychological Review, 61,* 339–342.

Eysenck, H. J. (1967). *The biological basis of personality.* Springfield, MA: Thomas.

Eysenck, H. J. (1971). *Readings in extraversion-introversion. II. Fields of application.* London: Staples.

Eysenck, H. J. (1973). *The inequality of man.* London: Temple Smith.

Eysenck, H. J. (1976). *Sex and personality.* Austin: University of Texas Press.

Eysenck, H. J. (1982). *Personality, genetics, and behavior.* New York: Praeger.

Eysenck, H. J. (1990). Genetic and environmental contributions to individual differences: The three major dimensions of personality. *Journal of Personality, 58,* 245–261.

Eysenck, H. J., & Wilson, G. D. (1973). *The experimental study of Freudian theories.* London: Methuen.

Fairbairn, W. R. D. (1952). *Psychoanalytic studies of the personality.* London: Routledge & Kegan Paul.

Falbo, T., & Polit, D. F. (1986). Quantitative review of the only child literature: Research evidence and theory development. *Psychological Bulletin, 100,* 176–189.

Fancher, R. E. (1973). *Psychoanalytic psychology: The development of Freud's thought.* New York: Norton.

Farrell, B. A. (1981). *The standing of psychoanalysis.* Oxford: Oxford University Press.

Feather, N. T., & Volkmer, R. E. (1988). Preference for situations involving effort, time, pressure, and feedback in relation to Type A behavior, locus of control, and test anxiety. *Journal of Personality and Social Psychology, 55,* 266–271.

Feeney, J. A., & Noller, P. (1990). Attachment style as a predictor of adult romantic relationships. *Journal of Personality and Social Psychology, 58,* 281–291.

Fernald, G. G. (1912). The defective-delinquent class differentiating tests. *American Journal of Insanity, 68,* 524–594.

Ferster, C. B., & Skinner, B. F. (1957). *Schedules of reinforcement.* New York: Appleton-Century-Crofts.

Festinger, L. (1957). *A theory of cognitive dissonance.* Evanston: Row, Peterson.

Festinger, L. (1983). *The human legacy.* New York: Columbia University Press.

Fisher, S., & Greenberg, R. P. (1977). *The scientific credibility of Freud's theories and therapy.* New York: Basic Books.

Fiske, D. W. (1971). *Measuring the concepts of personality.* Chicago: Aldine.

Fiske, D. W. (1973). Can a personality construct be validated empirically? *Psychological Bulletin, 80,* 89–92.

Fiske, S. T., & Linville, P. W. (1980). What does the schema concept buy us? *Personality and Social Psychology Bulletin, 6,* 543–557.

Fiske, S. T., & Taylor, S. E. (1984). *Social cognition.* Reading, MA: Addison-Wesley.

Fiske, S. T., & Taylor, S. E. (1991). *Social cognition* (2nd ed.). New York: McGraw-Hill.

Fiske, V., & Peterson, C. (1991). Love and depression: The nature of depressive romantic relationships. *Journal of Social and Clinical Psychology, 10,* 75–90.

Flaherty, J. E., & Dusek, J. B. (1980). An investigation of the relationship between psychological androgyny and components of self-concept. *Journal of Personality and Social Psychology, 38,* 984–992.

Forbach, G. B., Evans, R. G., & Bodine, S. M. (1986). Gender-based schematic processing of self-descriptive information. *Journal of Research in Personality, 20,* 372–384.

Forward, J. R., Wells, K., Canter, R., & Waggoner, M. (1975). Teacher control strategies and choice of educational objectives among college students. *Journal of Educational Psychology, 67,* 757–763.

Frable, D. E. S. (1989). Sex typing and gender ideology: Two facets of the individual's gender psychology that go together. *Journal of Personality and Social Psychology, 56,* 95–108.

Frankel, A., & Snyder, M. L. (1978). Poor performance following unsolvable problems: Learned helplessness or egotism? *Journal of Personality and Social Psychology, 36,* 1415–1424.

Frankl, V. E. (1963). *Man's search for meaning: An introduction to logotherapy.* New York: Washington Square Press.

Frankl, V. E. (1975). Paradoxical intention and dereflection. *Psychotherapy: Theory, Research, and Practice, 12,* 226–237.

Freedman, J. L. (1982). *Introductory psychology* (2nd ed.). Reading, MA: Addison-Wesley.

Freeman, A. (Ed.). (1983). *Cognitive therapy with couples and groups.* New York: Plenum.

Freeman, F. N. (1926). *Mental tests: Their history, principles, and applications.* Boston: Houghton Mifflin.

Freeman, F. S. (1962). *Theory and practice of psychological testing* (3rd ed.). New York: Holt, Rinehart & Winston.

Freud, A. (1937). *The ego and the mechanisms of defense.* London: Hogarth.

Freud, S. (1900). The interpretation of dreams. *Collected works* (Vol. IV). London: Hogarth.

Freud, S. (1901a). On dreams. *Collected works* (Vol. V). London: Hogarth.

Freud, S. (1901b). The psychopathology of everyday life. *Collected works* (Vol. VI). London: Hogarth.

Freud, S. (1905a). Fragment of an analysis of a case of hysteria. *Collected works* (Vol. VII). London: Hogarth.

Freud, S. (1905b). Humor and its relation to the unconscious. *Collected works* (Vol. VIII). London: Hogarth.

Freud, S. (1905c). Three essays on the theory of sexuality. *Collected works* (Vol. VII). London: Hogarth.

Freud, S. (1908a). Character and anal eroticism. *Collected works* (Vol. IX). London, Hogarth.

Freud, S. (1908b). Creative writers and day-dreaming. *Collected works* (Vol. IX). London: Hogarth.

Freud, S. (1909a). Analysis of a phobia in a five-year-old boy. *Collected works* (Vol. X). London: Hogarth.

Freud, S. (1909b). Notes upon a case of obsessional neurosis. *Collected works* (Vol. X). London: Hogarth.

Freud, S. (1910). Leonardo da Vinci and a memory of his childhood. *Collected works* (Vol. XI). London: Hogarth.

Freud, S. (1911). Psycho-analytic notes on an autobiographical account of a case of paranoia (dementia paranoides). *Collected works* (Vol. XII). London: Hogarth.

Freud, S. (1912). Papers on technique: The dynamics of transference. *Collected works* (Vol. XII). London: Hogarth.

Freud, S. (1917). Mourning and melancholia. *Collected works* (Vol. XIV). London: Hogarth.

Freud, S. (1920). Beyond the pleasure principle. *Collected works* (Vol. XVIII). London: Hogarth.

Freud, S. (1925). An autobiographical study. *Collected works* (Vol. XX). London: Hogarth.

Freud, S. (1928). Dostoevsky and parricide. *Collected works* (Vol. XXI). London: Hogarth.

Freud, S. (1930). Civilization and its discontents. *Collected works* (Vol. XXI). London: Hogarth.

Freud, S. (1939). Moses and monotheism. *Collected works* (Vol. XXIII). London: Hogarth.

Freud, S. (1950). Project for a scientific psychology. *Collected works* (Vol. I). London: Hogarth.

Friedlander, S. (1978). *History and psychoanalysis: An inquiry into the possibilities and limits of psychohistory.* New York: Holmes & Meier.

Friedman, H. S., & Booth-Kewley, S. (1987). The "disease-prone personality": A meta-analytic view of the construct. *American Psychologist, 42,* 539–555.

Friedman, H. S., & DiMatteo, M. R. (1989). *Health psychology.* Englewood Cliffs, NJ: Prentice-Hall.

Friedman, J. (1959). Weight problems and psychological factors. *Journal of Consulting Psychology, 23,* 524–527.

Friedman, S. M. (1952). An empirical study of the castration and Oedipus complexes. *Genetic Psychology Monographs, 46,* 61–130.

Fromm, E. (1941). *Escape from freedom.* New York: Rinehart.

Fromm, E. (1947). *Man for himself.* New York: Rinehart.

Fromm, E. (1955). *The sane society.* New York: Rinehart.

Fromm, E. (1968). *The revolution of hope.* New York: Harper & Row.

Fromm, E. (1973). *The anatomy of human destructiveness.* New York: Fawcett Crest.

Fromm, E., & Maccoby, M. (1970). *Social character in a Mexican village.* Englewood Cliffs, NJ: Prentice-Hall.

Fulker, D. W., Eysenck, S. B. G., & Zuckerman, M. (1980). A genetic and environmental analysis of sensation seeking. *Journal of Research in Personality, 14,* 261–281.

Funder, D. C. (1983). The "consistency" controversy and the accuracy of personality judgments. *Journal of Personality, 48,* 473–493.

Funder, D. C., & Block, J. (1989). The role of ego-control, ego-resiliency, and IQ in delay of gratification. *Journal of Personality and Social Psychology, 57,* 1041–1050.

Funder, D. C., Block, J. H., & Block, J. (1983). Delay of gratification: Some longitudinal personality correlates. *Journal of Personality and Social Psychology, 44,* 1198–1213.

Funder, D. C., & Colvin, C. R. (1988). Friends and strangers: Acquaintanceship, agreement, and the accuracy of personality judgment. *Journal of Personality and Social Psychology, 55,* 149–158.

Funder, D. C., & Dobroth, K. M. (1987). Differences between traits: Properties associated with interjudge agreement. *Journal of Personality and Social Psychology, 52,* 409–418.

Funder, D. C., & Ozer, D. J. (1983). Behavior as a function of the situation. *Journal of Personality and Social Psychology, 44,* 107–112.

Funk, S. C., & Houston, B. K. (1987). A critical analysis of the hardiness scale's validity and utility. *Journal of Personality and Social Psychology, 53,* 572–578.

Furlong, W. B. (1971, January 10). What is a punter's 'hang time'? *New York Times Magazine,* pp. 30–32+.

Gallup, G. (1972). *The sophisticated poll watcher's guide.* Princeton, NJ: Princeton Opinion Press.

Galton, F. (1869). *Hereditary genius.* London: Macmillan.

Galton, F. (1874). *English men of science: Their nature and nurture.* London: Macmillan.

Galton, F. (1876). The history of twins, as a criterion of the relative powers of nature and nurture. *Journal of the Anthropological Institute, 5,* 324–329.

Galton, F. (1888). Co-relations and their measurement. *Proceedings of the Royal Society, 45,* 135–145.

Galton, F. (1889). *Natural inheritance.* London: Macmillan.

Ganellen, R. J. (1988). Specificity of attributions and overgeneralization in depression and anxiety. *Journal of Abnormal Psychology, 97,* 83–86.

Garcia, J., & Koelling, R. A. (1966). Relation of cue to consequence in avoidance learning. *Psychonomic Science, 4,* 123–124.

Gardner, H. (1983). *Frames of mind: The theory of multiple intelligence.* New York: Basic Books.

Gardner, H. (1985). *The mind's new science: A history of the cognitive revolution.* New York: Basic Books.

Gardner, R. J. M., & Sutherland, G. R. (1989). *Chromosome abnormalities and genetic counseling.* New York: Oxford.

Gay, P. (1988). *Freud: A life for our time.* New York: Norton.

Gebhardt, D. L., & Crump, C. E. (1990). Employee fitness and wellness programs in the workplace. *American Psychologist, 45,* 262–272.

Geen, R. G. (1984). Preferred stimulation levels in introverts and extraverts: Effects on arousal and performance. *Journal of Personality and Social Psychology, 46,* 1303–1312.

Geller, E. S. (1983). Rewarding safety belt usage at an industrial setting: Tests of treatment generality and response maintenance. *Journal of Applied Behavioral Analysis, 16,* 189–202.

Genest, M., & Genest, S. (1987). *Psychology and health.* Champaign, IL: Research Press.

Gergen, K. J. (1973). Social psychology as history. *Journal of Personality and Social Psychology, 26,* 309–320.

Ghiselli, E. E. (1973). The validity of aptitude tests in personnel selection. *Personnel Psychology, 26,* 461–477.

Gibson, H. B. (1981). *Hans Eysenck: The man and his work.* London: Peter Owen.

Gifford, R., & O'Connor, B. (1987). The interpersonal circumplex as a behavior map. *Journal of Personality and Social Psychology, 52,* 1019–1026.

Gilligan, C. (1982). *In a different voice.* Cambridge, MA: Harvard University Press.

Gilligan, C., Ward, J. V., & Taylor, J. M. (Eds.). (1988). *Mapping the moral domain.* Cambridge, MA: Harvard University Press.

Gitlin, T. (1983). *Inside prime time.* New York: Pantheon.

Glantz, K., & Pearce, J. K. (1989). *Exiles from Eden: Psychotherapy from an evolutionary perspective.* New York: Norton.

Glass, D. C. (1977). *Behavior patterns, stress, and coronary disease.* Hillsdale, NJ: Erlbaum.

Glass, D. C., & Singer, J. E. (1972). *Urban stress: Experiments on noise and social stressors.* New York: Academic Press.

Glueck, S., & Glueck, E. T. (1950). *Unraveling juvenile delinquency.* Cambridge, MA: Harvard University Press.

Glueck, S., & Glueck, E. T. (1968). *Delinquents and nondelinquents in perspective.* Cambridge, MA: Harvard University Press.

Goldfried, M. R., & Kent, R. N. (1972). Traditional versus behavioral personality assessment: A comparison of methodological and theoretical assumptions. *Psychological Bulletin, 77,* 409–420.

Goldstein, K. (1939). *The organism.* New York: American Book Company.

Goldstein, K. M., & Blackman, S. (1976). Cognitive complexity, maternal child rearing, and acquiescence. *Social Behavior and Personality, 4,* 97–103.

Goldstein, K. M., & Blackman, S. (1978). *Cognitive style: Five approaches and relevant research.* New York: Wiley.

Goleman, D. (1986, December 2). Major personality study finds that traits are mostly inherited. *New York Times,* pp. 17–18.

Goodenough, D. R. (1978). Field dependence. In H. London & J. E. Exner (Eds.), *Dimensions of personality.* New York: Wiley.

Goodwin, D. W. (1971). The alcoholism of Eugene O'Neill. *JAMA, 216,* 99–104.

Gorsuch, R. L. (1974). *Factor analysis.* Philadelphia: Saunders.

Goshen, C. E. (1952). The original case material of psychoanalysis. *American Journal of Psychiatry, 108,* 829–834.

Gould, P., & White, R. (1974). *Mental maps.* New York: Penguin.

Gould, S. J. (1981). *The mismeasure of man.* New York: Norton.

Grace, W. J., & Graham, D. T. (1952). Relationship of specific attitudes and emotions to certain bodily diseases. *Psychosomatic Medicine, 14,* 243–251.

Green, R. (1987). *The "sissy boy syndrome" and the development of homosexuality.* New Haven, CT: Yale University Press.

Greenberg, J. R., & Mitchell, S. A. (1983). *Object relations in psychoanalytic theory.* Cambridge, MA: Harvard University Press.

Greenwald, A. G. (1976). An editorial. *Journal of Personality and Social Psychology, 33,* 1–7.

Greenwald, A. G. (1980). The totalitarian ego: Fabrication and revision of personal history. *American Psychologist, 35,* 603–618.

Guion, R. M., & Gibson, W. M. (1988). Personnel selection and placement. *Annual Review of Psychology, 39,* 349–374.

Guion, R. M., & Gottier, R. J. (1965). Validity of personality measures in personnel selection. *Personnel Psychology, 18,* 135–164.

Gunderson, J. G., & Singer, M. T. (1975). Defining borderline patients: An overview. *American Journal of Psychiatry, 132,* 1–10.

Guntrip, H. (1971). *Psychoanalytic theory, therapy, and the self.* New York: Basic Books.

Gur, R. C., & Sackeim, H. A. (1979). Self-deception: A concept in search of a phenomenon. *Journal of Personality and Social Psychology, 37,* 147–169.

Gurman, A. S. (1977). The patient's perception of the therapeutic relationship. In A. S. Gurman & A. M. Razin (Eds.), *Effective psychotherapy: A handbook of research.* New York: Pergamon.

Hackman, J. R., Lawler, E. E., & Porter, L. W. (Eds.). (1977). *Perspectives on behavior in organizations.* New York: McGraw-Hill.

Hall, C. S. (1963). Strangers in dreams: An empirical confirmation of the Oedipus complex. *Journal of Personality, 31,* 336–345.

Hall, C. S., & Lindzey, G. (1957). *Theories of personality.* New York: Wiley.

Hall, C. S., & Lindzey, G. (1970). *Theories of personality* (2nd ed.). New York: Wiley.

Hall, C. S., & Lindzey, G. (1978). *Theories of personality* (3rd ed.). New York: Wiley.

Hall, C. S., & Nordby, V. J. (1973). *A primer of Jungian psychology.* New York: Mentor.

Hall, J. A., & Taylor, M. C. (1985). Psychological androgyny and the masculinity × femininity interaction. *Journal of Personality and Social Psychology, 49,* 429–435.

Hall, M. H. (1968). Abraham H. Maslow. *Psychology Today, 2*(2), 35–37; 54–57.

Halverson, C. F. (1988). Remembering your parents: Reflections on the retrospective method. *Journal of Personality, 56,* 435–443.

Hamilton, E. W., & Abramson, L. Y. (1983). Cognitive patterns in major depressive disorder: A longitudinal study in a hospital setting. *Journal of Abnormal Psychology, 92,* 173–184.

Hamilton, W. D. (1964). The genetical evolution of social behaviour. *Journal of Theoretical Biology, 12,* 12–45.

Hansen, J. C. (1984). Interest inventories. In G. Goldstein & M. Hersen (Eds.), *Handbook of psychological assessment.* New York: Pergamon.

Hansen, R. D., & Hansen, C. H. (1988). Repression of emotionally tagged memories: The architecture of less complex emotions. *Journal of Personality and Social Psychology, 55,* 811–818.

Hare, R. D. (1970). *Psychopathy: Theory and research.* New York: Wiley.

Harrington, D. M., Block, J. H., & Block, J. (1987). Testing aspects of Carl Rogers's theory of creative environments: Child-rearing antecedents of creative potential in young adolescents. *Journal of Personality and Social Psychology, 52,* 851–856.

Hartmann, H. (1939). *Ego psychology and the problem of adaptation.* New York: International Universities Press.

Hartshorne, H., & May, M. A. (1928). *Studies in deceit.* New York: Macmillan.

Harvey, J. H., & Galvin, K. S. (1984). Clinical implications of attribution theory and research. *Clinical Psychology Review, 4,* 15–33.

Hathaway, S. R., & McKinley, J. C. (1943). *The Minnesota Multiphasic Personality Inventory.* Minneapolis: University of Minnesota Press.

Hazan, C., & Shaver, P. (1987). Romantic love conceptualized as an attachment process. *Journal of Personality and Social Psychology, 52,* 511–524.

Heider, F. (1944). Social perception and phenomenal causality. *Psychological Review, 51,* 358–374.

Heider, F. (1958). *The psychology of interpersonal relations.* New York: Wiley.

Heinstein, M. I. (1963). Behavioral correlates of breast-bottle regimes under varying parent-infant relationships. *Monographs of the Society for Research in Child Development, 28,* No. 88.

Hemmings, R. (1972). *Fifty years of freedom: A study of the development of the ideas of A. S. Neill.* London: George Allen & Unwin.

Hendry, L. B., & Gillies, P. (1978). Body type, body esteem, school, and leisure: A study of overweight, average, and underweight adolescents. *Journal of Youth and Adolescence, 7,* 181–194.

Henry, W. A. (1990, July 30). Did the music say "Do it"? *Time,* p. 65.

Herman, J., Perry, J. C., & van der Kolk, B. A. (1989). Childhood trauma in borderline personality disorder. *American Journal of Psychiatry, 143,* 1293–1296.

Higgins, E. T. (1987). Self-discrepancy: A theory relating self and affect. *Psychological Review, 94,* 319–340.

Higgins, E. T., & Bargh, J. A. (1987). Social cognition and social perception. *Annual Review of Psychology, 38,* 369–425.

Higgins, E. T., King, G. A., & Marin, G. H. (1982). Individual construct accessibility and subjective impressions and recall. *Journal of Personality and Social Psychology, 43,* 35–47.

Hilgard, E. R. (1987). *Psychology in America: A historical survey.* San Diego: Harcourt Brace Jovanovich.

Hirsch, J. (Ed.). (1967). *Behavior-genetic analysis.* New York: McGraw-Hill.

Hockey, G. R. J. (1972). Effects of noise on human efficiency and some individual differences. *Journal of Sound Vibrations, 20,* 299–304.

Hoffman, M. L. (1963). Childrearing practices and moral development: Generalizations from empirical research. *Child Development, 34,* 295–318.

Hogan, R., Carpenter, B. N., Briggs, S. R., & Hansson, R. O. (1984). Personality assessment and personnel selection. In H. J. Bernardin & D. A. Bownas (Eds.), *Personality assessment in organizations.* New York: Praeger.

Hogan, R., deSoto, C. N., & Solano, C. (1977). Traits, tests, and personality research. *American Psychologist, 32,* 255–264.

Hogan, R., & Nicholson, R. A. (1988). The meaning of personality test scores. *American Psychologist, 43,* 621–626.

Holland, J. L. (1966). *The psychology of vocational choice: A theory of personality types and model environments.* Waltham, MA: Blaisdell.

Holland, J. L. (1985). *Making vocational choices: A theory of vocational personalities and work environments* (2nd ed.). Englewood Cliffs, NJ: Prentice-Hall.

Hollon, S., & Beck, A. T. (1986). Cognitive and cognitive-behavioral therapies. In S. L. Garfield & A. E. Bergin (Eds.), *Handbook of psychotherapy and behavior change* (3rd ed.). New York: Wiley.

Holmes, T. H., & Rahe, R. H. (1967). The social readjustment scale. *Journal of Psychosomatic Research, 11,* 213–218.

Holt, R. R. (1970). Yet another look at clinical and statistical prediction: Or, is clinical psychology worthwhile? *American Psychologist, 25,* 337–349.

Hormuth, S. E. (1986). The sampling of experiences in situ. *Journal of Personality, 54,* 262–293.

Horney, K. (1937). *Neurotic personality of our times.* New York: Norton.

Horney, K. (1945). *Our inner conflicts.* New York: Norton.

House, J. S., Landis, K. R., & Umberson, D. (1988). Social relationships and health. *Science, 241,* 540–545.

House, J. S., Robbins, C., & Metzner, H. L. (1982). The association of social relationships and activities with mortality: Prospective evidence from the Tecumseh Community Health Study. *American Journal of Epidemiology, 116,* 123–140.

Howard, J. A., Blumstein, P., & Schwartz, P. (1987). Social or evolutionary theories? Some observations on preferences in human mate selection. *Journal of Personality and Social Psychology, 53,* 194–200.

Howes, D., & Solomon, R. L. (1950). A note on McGinnies' emotionality and perceptual defense. *Psychological Review, 57,* 229–234.

Hoyt, M. F., & Raven, B. H. (1973). Birth order and the 1971 Los Angeles earthquake. *Journal of Personality and Social Psychology, 28,* 123–128.

Hull, C. L. (1943). *Principles of behavior.* New York: Appleton-Century-Crofts.

Hull, J. G., Van Treuren, R. R., & Virnelli, S. (1987). Hardiness and health: A critique and alternative approach. *Journal of Personality and Social Psychology, 53,* 518–530.

Jaccard, J. J. (1974). Predicting social behavior from personality traits. *Journal of Research in Personality, 7,* 358–367.

Jackson, D. N., & Paunonen, S. V. (1985). Construct validity and the predictability of behavior. *Journal of Personality and Social Psychology, 49,* 554–570.

Jackson, L. A., Ialongo, N., & Stollak, G. E. (1986). Parental correlates of gender role: The relations between parents' masculinity, femininity, and child-rearing behaviors and their children's gender roles. *Journal of Social and Clinical Psychology, 4,* 204–224.

Jacoby, J. (1976). Consumer psychology: An octennium. *Annual Review of Psychology, 27,* 331–358.

James, W. (1890). *Principles of psychology* (2 vols.). New York: Holt.

Janis, I. L. (1983). Foreword. In E. J. Langer, *The psychology of control.* Beverly Hills, CA: Sage.

Jankowicz, A. D. (1987). Whatever became of George Kelly? Applications and implications. *American Psychologist, 42,* 481–487.

Janoff-Bulman, R., & Brickman, P. (1980). Expectations and what people learn from failure. In N. T. Feather (Ed.), *Expectancy, incentive, and failure.* Hillsdale, NJ: Erlbaum.

Jaret, P. (1986). Our immune systems: The wars within. *National Geographic, 169*(6), 702–735.

Jastrow, J. (1915). The antecedents of the study of character and temperament. *The Popular Science Monthly, 86,* 590–613.

Jemmott, J. B., & Locke, S. E. (1984). Psychosocial factors, immunologic mediation, and human susceptibility to infectious diseases: How much do we know? *Psychological Bulletin, 95,* 78–108.

Jenkins, C. D., Rosenman, R. H., & Zyzanski, S. J. (1974). Prediction of clinical coronary heart disease by a test for the coronary-prone behavior pattern. *The New England Journal of Medicine, 23,* 1271–1275.

Jenkins, C. D., Zyzanski, S. J., & Rosenman, R. H. (1976). Risk of new myocardial infarction in middle age men with manifest coronary heart disease. *Circulation, 53,* 342–347.

Jenkins, S. R. (1987). Need for achievement and women's careers over 14 years: Evidence for occupational structure effects. *Journal of Personality and Social Psychology, 53,* 922–932.

Johansson, C. B., & Campbell, D. P. (1971). Stability of the Strong Vocational Interest Blank for Men. *Journal of Applied Psychology, 55,* 24–26.

John, O. P. (1990). The "Big Five" factor taxonomy: Dimensions of personality in the natural language and in questionnaires. In L. A. Pervin (Ed.), *Handbook of personality: Theory and research.* New York: Guilford.

John, O. P., Goldberg, L. R., & Angleitner, A. (1984). Better than the alphabet: Taxonomies of personality-descriptive terms in English, Dutch, and German. In H. J. C. Bonarius, G. L. M. van Heck, & N. G. Smid (Eds.), *Personality psychology in Europe.* Lisse, Switzerland: Swets & Zeitlinger.

Johnson, C., & Larson, R. (1982). Bulimia: An analysis of moods and behavior. *Psychosomatic Medicine, 44,* 341–351.

Johnson, J. A., Germer, C. K., Efran, J. S., & Overton, W. F. (1988). Personality as the basis for theoretical predictions. *Journal of Personality and Social Psychology, 55,* 824–835.

Johnson, M. H., & Magaro, P. A. (1987). Effects of mood and severity on memory processes in depression and mania. *Psychological Bulletin, 101,* 28–40.

Jones, E. (1910). The Oedipus complex as an explanation of Hamlet's mystery. *American Journal of Psychiatry, 67,* 279–286.

Jones, E. (1923). *Papers on psychoanalysis.* London: Bailliere Tindall.

Jones, H. E. (1931). Order of birth in relation to the development of the child. In C. Murchinson (Ed.), *Handbook of child psychology.* Worcester, MA: Clark University Press.

Jones, R. G. (1968). *A factored measure of Ellis' irrational belief systems.* Wichita, KS: Test Systems.

Judd, C. M., Jessor, R., & Donovan, J. E. (1986). Structural equation models and personality research. *Journal of Personality, 54,* 149–198.

Jung, C. G. (1907). The psychology of dementia praecox. *Collected works* (Vol. 3). New York: Pantheon.

Jung, C. G. (1912). Symbols of transformation. Part II. *Collected works* (Vol. 5). New York: Pantheon.

Jung, C. G. (1924). *Psychological types.* New York: Random House.

Kagan, J. (1989). Temperamental contributions to social behavior. *American Psychologist, 44,* 668–674.

Kamin, L. J. (1969). Predictability, surprise, attention, and conditioning. In B. A. Campbell & R. M. Church (Eds.), *Punishment and aversive behavior.* New York: Appleton-Century-Crofts.

Kaplan, G. A., & Camacho, T. (1983). Perceived health and mortality: A nine-year follow-up of the human population laboratory cohort. *American Journal of Epidemiology, 117,* 292–304.

Kaplan, M. (1983). A woman's view of DSM-III. *American Psychologist, 38,* 786–792.

Kaplan, S., & Peterson, C. (1990). *Psychological influences on health and illness: Toward an integrated theory.* Unpublished manuscript, University of Michigan.

Kazdin, A. E. (1977). *The token economy.* New York: Plenum.

Keen, E. (1975). *A primer in phenomenological psychology.* New York: Holt, Rinehart & Winston.

Keen, S. (1986). *Faces of the enemy: Reflections of the hostile imagination.* New York: Harper & Row.

Kellogg, M. A. (1976, May 3). Updating Dr. Spock, *Newsweek,* p. 86.

Kelly, G. A. (1933). Some observations on the relation of cerebral dominance to the perception of symbols. *Psychological Bulletin, 30,* 583–584.

Kelly, G. A. (1955). *The psychology of personal constructs* (2 vols.). New York: Norton.

Kelly, J., & Worrell, L. (1976). Parent behaviors related to masculine, feminine, and androgynous sex role orientations. *Journal of Consulting and Clinical Psychology, 44,* 843–851.

Kelman, H. (Ed.). (1966). *Feminine psychology.* New York: Norton.

Kendall, P. C., & Hollon, S. D. (1979). *Cognitive-behavioral interventions: Theory research, and procedures.* New York: Academic Press.

Kendall, P. C., et al. (1979). Cognitive-behavioral and patient education interventions in cardiac catheterization procedures: The Palo Alto medical psychology project. *Journal of Consulting and Clinical Psychology, 47,* 49–58.

Kendall, P. C., & Turk, D. C. (1984). Cognitive-behavioral strategies and health enhancement. In J. D. Matarazzo et al. (Eds.), *Behavioral health: A handbook of health enhancement and disease prevention.* New York: Wiley.

Kenny, D. A. (1979). *Correlation and causality.* New York: Wiley.

Kenrick, D. T., & Funder, D. C. (1988). Profiting from controversy: Lessons from the person-situation debate. *American Psychologist, 43,* 23–34.

Kenrick, D. T., & Stringfield, D. O. (1980). Personality traits and the eye of the beholder: Crossing some traditional philosophical boundaries in the search for consistency in all of the people. *Psychological Review, 87,* 88–104.

Kernberg, O. (1975). *Borderline conditions and pathological narcissism.* New York: Jason Aronson.

Kessler, R. C., Price, R. H., & Wortman, C. B. (1985). Social factors in psychopathology: Stress, social support, and coping processes. *Annual Review of Psychology, 36,* 531–572.

Kessler, S. (Ed.). (1979). *Genetic counseling: Psychological dimensions.* New York: Academic Press.

Key, W. B. (1973). *Subliminal seduction.* Englewood Cliffs, NJ: Prentice-Hall.

Key, W. B. (1976). *Media sexploitation.* Englewood Cliffs, NJ: Prentice-Hall.

Kihlstrom, J. F. (1990). The psychological unconscious. In L. A. Pervin (Ed.), *Handbook of personality: Theory and research.* New York: Guilford.

Kihlstrom, J. F., & Harackiewicz, J. M. (1990). An evolutionary milestone in the psychology of personality. *Psychological Inquiry, 1,* 86–100.

Kimeldorf, C., & Gelwitz, P. J. (1966). Smoking and the Blacky orality factors. *Journal of Projective Techniques and Personality Assessment, 30,* 167–168.

Kinsey, A. C., Pomeroy, W. D., & Martin, C. E. (1948). *Sexual behavior in the human male.* Philadelphia: Saunders.

Kinsey, A. C., Pomeroy, W. D., Martin, C. E., & Gebhard, P. H. (1953). *Sexual behavior in the human female.* Philadelphia: Saunders.

Klein, M. (1948). *Contributions to psycho-analysis, 1921–1945.* London: Hogarth.

Kline, P. (1968). Obsessional traits, obsessional symptoms, and anal eroticism. *British Journal of Medical Psychology, 41,* 299–305.

Kline, P. (1972). *Fact and fantasy in Freudian theory.* London: Methuen.

Kline, P. (1984). *Psychology and Freudian theory.* London: Methuen.

Kobasa, S. C. (1979). Stressful life events, personality, and health: An inquiry into hardiness. *Journal of Personality and Social Psychology, 37,* 1–11.

Kobasa, S. C. (1982). Commitment and coping in stress resistance among lawyers. *Journal of Personality and Social Psychology, 42,* 707–717.

Kobasa, S. C., Maddi, S. R., & Courington, S. (1981). Personality and constitution as mediators in the stress-illness relationship. *Journal of Health and Social Behavior, 22,* 368–378.

Kobasa, S. C., Maddi, S. R., & Kahn, S. (1982). Hardiness and health: A prospective study. *Journal of Personality and Social Psychology, 42,* 168–177.

Kohlberg, L. (1963). The development of children's orientations toward a moral order: 1. Sequence in the development of human thought. *Vita Humana, 6,* 11–33.

Kohlberg, L. (1966). A cognitive-developmental analysis of children's sex-role concepts and attitudes. In E. Maccoby (Ed.), *The development of sex differences.* Stanford: Stanford University Press.

Kohlberg, L. (1981). *Essays on moral development* (Vol. 1). New York: Harper & Row.

Kohlberg, L. (1984). *Essays on moral development* (Vol. 2). New York: Harper & Row.

Kohler, W. (1924). *The mentality of apes.* London: Kegan Paul.

Kohut, H. (1966). Forms and transformations of narcissism. *Journal of the American Psychoanalytic Association, 14,* 243–272.

Kolata, G. (1980, August). Texas counselors use psychology in cancer therapy. *Smithsonian,* pp. 48–57.

Korchin, S. J. (1983). The history of clinical psychology: A personal view. In M. Hersen, A. E. Kazdin., & A. S. Bellack (Eds.), *The clinical psychology handbook.* New York: Pergamon.

Korchin, S. J., & Schuldberg, D. (1981). The future of clinical assessment. *American Psychologist, 36,* 1147–1158.

Krantz, D. S., Grunberg, N. E., & Baum, A. (1985). Health psychology. *Annual Review of Psychology, 36,* 349–383.

Kretschmer, E. (1921). *Korperbau und Charakter.* Berlin: Springer.

Kris, E. (1952). *Psychoanalytic explorations in art.* New York: International Universities Press.

Kuhl, J. (1981). Motivational and functional helplessness: The moderating effect of state versus action orientation. *Journal of Personality and Social Psychology, 40,* 155–170.

Kuhn, T. S. (1970). *The structure of scientific revolutions* (2nd ed.). Chicago: University of Chicago Press.

Kulik, J. A., Bangert-Drowns, R. L., & Kulik, C. C. (1984). Effectiveness of coaching for aptitude tests. *Psychological Bulletin, 95,* 179–188.

Kunst-Wilson, W. R., & Zajonc, R. B. (1980). Affective discrimination of stimuli that cannot be recognized. *Science, 207,* 557–558.

Kushner, H. S. (1981). *When bad things happen to good people.* New York: Avon.

Laing, R. D. (1959). *The divided self.* London: Tavistok.

Laing, R. D. (1967). *The politics of experience.* New York: Ballantine.

Laing, R. D., & Esterson, A. (1964). *Sanity, madness, and the family.* London: Tavistok.

Lamb, D. H. (1978). Anxiety. In H. London & J. E. Exner (Eds.), *Dimensions of personality.* New York: Wiley.

Lamiell, J. T. (1987). *The psychology of personality: An epistemological inquiry.* New York: Columbia University Press.

Langer, E. J., Janis, I. L., & Wolfer, J. (1975). Reduction of psychological stress in surgical patients. *Journal of Experimental Social Psychology, 11,* 155–165.

Langer, E. J., & Rodin, J. (1976). The effects of choice and enhanced personal responsibility for the aged: A field experiment in an institutional setting. *Journal of Personality and Social Psychology, 34,* 191–198.

Langston, C. A., & Cantor, N. (1989). Social anxiety and social constraint: When making friends is hard. *Journal of Personality and Social Psychology, 56,* 649–661.

Larkin, J. H., McDermott, J., Simon, D. P., & Simon, H. A. (1980). Models of competence in solving physics problems. *Science, 200,* 1335–1342.

Larsen, R. J., & Diener, E. (1987). Affect intensity as an individual difference characteristic: A review. *Journal of Research in Personality, 21,* 1–39.

Lazarus, R. S. (1966). *Psychological stress and the coping process.* New York: McGraw-Hill.

Lazarus, R. S. (1982). Thoughts on the relations between emotion and cognition. *American Psychologist, 37,* 1019–1024.

Lazarus, R. S. (1990). Theory-based stress management. *Psychological Inquiry, 1,* 3–13.

Lazarus, R. S., & Folkman, S. (1984). *Stress, appraisal, and coping.* New York: Springer.

Leary, T. (1957). *Interpersonal diagnosis of personality.* New York: Ronald Press.

Ledwidge, B. (1978). Cognitive behavior modification: A step in the wrong direction? *Psychological Bulletin, 85,* 353–375.

Lehmann, H. E. (1980). Schizophrenia: Clinical features. In H. I. Kaplan, A. M. Freedman, & B. J. Sadock (Eds.), *Comprehensive textbook of psychiatry* (3rd ed., Vol. 2). Baltimore: Williams and Wilkins.

Leo, J. (1985, October 21). Are criminals born, not made? *Time,* p. 94.

Lerner, M. J. (1971). Observers' evaluation of a victim: Justice, guilt, and veridical perception. *Journal of Personality and Social Psychology, 20,* 127–135.

Levant, R. F., & Schlien, J. M. (Eds.). (1984). *Client-centered therapy and the person-centered approach: New directions in theory, research, and practice.* New York: Praeger.

Levenkron, J. C., Cohen, J. D., Mueller, H. S., & Fisher, E. B. (1983). Modifying the Type A coronary-prone behavior pattern. *Journal of Consulting and Clinical Psychology, 51,* 192–204.

Lewin, K. (1935). *A dynamic theory of personality.* New York: McGraw-Hill.

Lewin, K. (1951). *Field theory in social science: Selected theoretical papers.* New York: Harper.

Lewinsohn, P. M. (1974). A behavioral approach to depression. In R. J. Friedman & M. M. Katz (Eds.), *The psychology of depression: Contemporary theory and research.* Washington, DC: Winston-Wiley.

Lewinsohn, P. M., Mischel, W., Chaplin, W., & Barton, R. (1980). Social competence and depression: The role of illusory self-perceptions. *Journal of Abnormal Psychology, 89,* 203–212.

Lewis, C. S. (1941). Psycho-analysis and literacy criticism. *Essays and Studies by Members of the English Association, 27,* 7–21.

Lewis, H. B. (1981). *Freud and modern psychology: The emotional basis of mental illness* (Vol. 1). New York: Plenum.

Lidz, T. (1975). *The origin and treatment of schizophrenic disorders.* London: Hutchinson.

Lin, E., & Peterson, C. (1990). Pessimistic explanatory style and response to illness. *Behaviour Research and Therapy, 28,* 243–248.

Linville, P. W. (1987). Self-complexity as a cognitive buffer against stress-related illness and depression. *Journal of Personality and Social Psychology, 52,* 663–676.

Lloyd, C. (1980). Life events and depressive disorders reviewed. I. Events as predisposing factors. II. Events as precipitating factors. *Archives of General Psychiatry, 37,* 529–548.

Locke, K. D., & Horowitz, L. M. (1990). Satisfaction in interpersonal interactions as a function of similarity in level of dysphoria. *Journal of Personality and Social Psychology, 58,* 823–831.

Loehlin, J. C. (1984). R. B. Cattell and behavior genetics. *Multivariate Behavioral Research, 19,* 310–321.

Loehlin, J. C., & Nichols, R. C. (1976). *Heredity, environment, and personality.* Austin: University of Texas Press.

Loehlin, J. C., Willerman, L., & Horn, J. M. (1987). Personality resemblance in adoptive families: A 10-year follow-up. *Journal of Personality and Social Psychology, 53,* 961–969.

Loevinger, J. (1976). *Ego development.* San Francisco: Jossey-Bass.

Loewenberg, P. (1983). *Decoding the past: The psychohistorical approach.* New York: Knopf.

Logue, A. W. (1979). Taste aversion and the generality of the laws of learning. *Psychological Bulletin, 86,* 276–296.

London, I. D. (1944). Psychologists' misuse of the auxiliary concepts of physics and mathematics. *Psychological Review, 51,* 266–291.

London, M., & Bray, D. W. (1980). Ethical issues in testing and evaluation for personnel decisions. *American Psychologist, 35,* 890–901.

Lord, C. G. (1982). Predicting behavioral consistency from an individual's perception of situational similarities. *Journal of Personality and Social Psychology, 42,* 1076–1088.

Lorenz, K. S. (1966). *On aggression.* New York: Harcourt Brace Jovanovich.

Luborsky, L. (1964). A psychoanalytic research on momentary forgetting during free association. *Bulletin of the Philadelphia Association for Psychoanalysis, 14,* 119–137.

Luborsky, L. (1970). New directions in research on neurotic and psychosomatic symptoms. *American Scientist, 58,* 661–668.

Luborsky, L. (1984). *Principles of psychoanalytic psychotherapy.* New York: Basic Books.

Luborsky, L., & Crits-Christoph, P. (1988). Measures of psychoanalytic concepts—The last decade of research from "the Penn studies." *International Journal of Psychoanalysis, 69,* 75–86.

Luborsky, L., & Crits-Christoph, P. (1989). A relationship pattern measure: The core conflictual relationship theme. *Psychiatry, 52,* 250–259.

Luborsky, L., Crits-Christoph, P., & Mellon, J. (1986). Advent of objective measures of the transference concept. *Journal of Consulting and Clinical Psychology, 54,* 39–47.

Luborsky, L., Sackeim, H., & Christoph, P. (1979). The state conducive to momentary forgetting. In J. F. Kihlstom & F. J. Evans (Eds.), *Functional disorders of memory.* Hillsdale, NJ: Erlbaum.

Lykken, D. T. (1957). A study of anxiety in the sociopathic personality. *Journal of Abnormal and Social Psychology, 55,* 6–10.

Lynn, M. (1989). Race differences in sexual behavior: A critique of Rushton and Bogaert's evolutionary hypothesis. *Journal of Research in Personality, 23,* 1–6.

MacCorquodale, K., & Meehl, P. E. (1948). On a distinction between hypothetical constructs and intervening variables. *Psychological Review, 55,* 95–107.

MacDonald, K. B. (1988). *Social and personality development: An evolutionary synthesis.* New York: Plenum.

MacFarlane, K., & Waterman, J. (1986). *Sexual abuse of young children: Evaluation and treatment.* New York: Guilford.

Maddi, S. R. (1980). *Personality theories: A comparative analysis.* Homewood, IL: Dorsey.

Maddi, S. R. (1984). Personology for the 1980's. In R. A. Zucker, J. Aronoff, & A. I. Rabin (Eds.), *Personality and the prediction of behavior.* New York: Academic Press.

Magnusson, D., & Endler, N. S. (Eds.). (1977). *Personality at the crossroads: Current issues in interactional psychology.* Hillsdale, NJ: Erlbaum.

Maher, B. A., & Maher, W. B. (1979). Psychopathology. In E. Hearst (Ed.), *The first century of experimental psychology.* Hillsdale, NJ: Erlbaum.

Mahoney, M. J. (1974). *Cognition and behavior modification.* Cambridge, MA: Ballinger.

Maier, S. F. (1970). Failure to escape traumatic shock: Incompatible skeletal motor responses or learned helplessness? *Learning and Motivation, 1,* 157–170.

Maier, S. F., Laudenslager, M., & Ryan, S. M. (1985). Stressor controllability, immune function, and endogenous opiates. In F. Bush & J. B. Overmier (Eds.), *Affect, conditioning, and cognition.* Hillsdale, NJ: Erlbaum.

Maier, S. F., & Seligman, M. E. P. (1976). Learned helplessness: Theory and evidence. *Journal of Experimental Psychology: General, 105,* 3–46.

Marcuse, H. (1962). *Eros and civilization.* New York: Vintage.

Marks, I. M. (1969). *Fears and phobias.* New York: Academic Press.

Markus, H. (1977). Self-schemas and processing information about the self. *Journal of Personality and Social Psychology, 35,* 63–78.

Markus, H. (1980). The self in thought and memory. In D. M. Wegner & R. R. Vallacher (Eds.), *The self in social psychology.* New York: Oxford.

Markus, H., Crane, M., Bernstein, S., & Siladi, M. (1982). Self-schemas and gender. *Journal of Personality and Social Psychology, 42,* 38–50.

Markus, H., & Nurius, P. (1986). Possible selves. *American Psychologist, 41,* 954–969.

Markus, H., Smith, J., & Moreland, R. L. (1985). Role of the self-concept in the perception of others. *Journal of Personality and Social Psychology, 49,* 1494–1512.

Markus, H., & Wurf, E. (1987). The dynamic self-concept: A social psychological perspective. *Annual Review of Psychology, 38,* 299–337.

Markus, H., & Zajonc, R. B. (1985). The cognitive perspective in social psychology. In G. Lindzey & E. Aronson (Eds.), *The handbook of social psychology* (3rd ed., Vol. 1). New York: Random House.

Marsh, H. W., & Parker, J. W. (1984). Determinants of student self-concept: Is it better to be a relatively large fish in a small pond even if you don't learn to swim as well? *Journal of Personality and Social Psychology, 47,* 213–231.

Marshall, W. L., Gauthier, J., & Gordon, A. (1979). The current status of flooding therapy. In M. Hersen, R. M. Eisler, & P. M. Miller (Eds.), *Progress in behavior modification* (Vol. 7). New York: Academic Press.

Martindale, A. E., & Martindale, C. (1988). Metaphorical equivalence of elements and temperaments: Empirical studies of Bachelard's theory of imagination. *Journal of Personality and Social Psychology, 55,* 836–848.

Maslow, A. H. (1966). *The psychology of science: A reconnaissance.* New York: Harper & Row.

Maslow, A. H. (1970). *Motivation and personality* (2nd ed.). New York: Harper & Row.

Masson, J. M. (1984). *The assault on truth: Freud's suppression of the seduction theory.* New York: Farrar, Straus, & Giroux.

Masson, J. M. (1988). *Against therapy: Emotional tyranny and the myth of psychological healing.* New York: Atheneum.

Masters, W. H., & Johnson, V. E. (1970). *Human sexual inadequacy.* Boston: Little, Brown.

Matarazzo, J. D. (1986). Computerized clinical psychological test interpretations: Unvalidated plus all mean and no sigma. *American Psychologist, 41,* 14–24.

Matthews, K. A. (1982). Psychological perspectives on the Type A behavior pattern. *Psychological Bulletin, 91,* 293–323.

Maule, T. (1968, January 29). Make no mistakes about it. *Sports Illustrated,* pp. 24–26.

May, R. (1950). *The meaning of anxiety.* New York: Ronald Press.

May, R. (1969). *Existential psychology* (2nd ed.). New York: Random House.

May, R. (1983). *The discovery of being: Writings in existential psychology.* New York: Norton.

May, R., Rogers, C., & Maslow, A. (1986). *Politics and innocence: A humanistic debate.* Dallas: Saybrook.

Mazur, A., & Robertson, L. S. (1972). *Biology and social behavior.* New York: Macmillan.

McAdams, D. P. (1988). Biography, narrative, and lives: An introduction. *Journal of Personality, 56,* 1–18.

McAdams, D. P. (1990). *The person: An introduction to personality psychology.* San Diego: Harcourt Brace Jovanovich.

McAdams, D. P., & Ochberg, R. L. (Eds.). (1988). Special issue: Psychobiography and life narratives. *Journal of Personality, 56,* 1–326.

McCain, G., & Segal, E. M. (1973). *The game of science* (2nd ed.). Monterey, CA: Brooks/Cole.

McCall, R. J. (1983). *Phenomenological psychology: An introduction.* Madison, WI: University of Wisconsin Press.

McClelland, D. C. (1961). *The achieving society.* Princeton, NJ: Van Nostrand.

McClelland, D. C. (1965). Toward a theory of motive acquisition. *American Psychologist, 20,* 321–333.

McClelland, D. C. (1971). *Assessing human motivation.* Morristown, NJ: General Learning Press.

McClelland, D. C. (1975). *Power: The inner experience.* New York: Wiley.

McClelland, D. C. (1980). Motive dispositions: The merits of operant and respondent measures. In L. Wheeler (Ed.), *Review of personality and social psychology* (Vol. I). Beverly Hills, CA: Sage.

McClelland, D. C. (1982). The need for power, sympathetic activation, and illness. *Motivation and Emotion, 6,* 31–41.

McClelland, D. C. (1989). Motivational factors in health and disease. *American Psychologist, 44,* 675–683.

McClelland, D. C., Atkinson, J. W., Clark, R. A., & Lowell, E. I. (1953). *The achievement motive.* New York: Appleton-Century-Crofts.

McClelland, D. C., Koestner, R., & Weinberger, J. (1989). How do self-attributed and implicit motives differ? *Psychological Review, 96,* 690–702.

McClelland, D. C., & Winter, D. G. (1969). *Motivating economic achievement.* New York: Free Press.

McCormick, E. J. (1976). *Human factors in engineering and design* (4th ed.). New York: McGraw-Hill.

McCrae, R. R., & Costa, P. T. (1987). Validation of the five-factor model of personality across instruments and observers. *Journal of Personality and Social Psychology, 52,* 81–90.

McCrae, R. R., & Costa, P. T. (1989a). Reinterpreting the Myers-Briggs Type Indicator from the perspective of the five-factor model of personality. *Journal of Personality, 57,* 16–40.

McCrae, R. R., & Costa, P. T. (1989b). The structure of interpersonal traits: Wiggins's circumplex and the five-factor model. *Journal of Personality and Social Psychology, 56,* 586–595.

McGinnies, E. (1949). Emotionality and perceptual defense. *Psychological Review, 56,* 244–251.

McGregor, D. (1960). *The human side of enterprise.* New York: McGraw-Hill.

McGuire, W. J., & McGuire, C. V. (1981). The spontaneous self-concept as affected by personal distinctiveness. In M. D. Lynch, A. A. Norem-Hebeisen, & K. J. Gergen (Eds.), *Self-concept: Advances in theory and research.* Cambridge, MA: Ballinger.

McKusick, V. A. (1986). *Mendelian inheritance in man* (8th ed.). Baltimore: Johns Hopkins University Press.

McNeal, J. U. (1982). *Consumer behavior: An integrative approach.* Boston: Little, Brown.

McQuiston, J. T. (1989, August 24). R. D. Laing, rebel and pioneer on schizophrenia, is dead at 61. *New York Times,* p. D21.

Mednick, M. T. (1989). On the politics of psychological constructs: Stop the bandwagon, I want to get off. *American Psychologist, 44,* 1118–1123.

Mednick, S. A., Gabrielli, W. F., & Hutchings, B. (1984). Genetic influences in criminal convictions: Evidence from an adoption cohort. *Science, 224,* 891–894.

Meehl, P. E. (1954). *Clinical versus statistical prediction.* Minneapolis: University of Minnesota Press.

Meehl, P. E. (1957). When shall we use our heads instead of the formula? *Journal of Counseling Psychology, 4,* 268–273.

Meer, J. (1984). The winter of schizophrenia. *Psychology Today, 18*(8), 14.

Meichenbaum, D. H. (1977). *Cognitive behavior-modification: An integrative approach.* New York: Plenum.

Meichenbaum, D. H. (1990). Paying homage: Providing challenges: *Psychological Inquiry, 1,* 96–100.

Meissner, W. W. (1980). Theories of personality and psychopathology: Classical psychoanalysis. In H. I. Kaplin, A. M. Freedman, & B. J. Sadock (Eds.), *Comprehensive textbook of psychiatry* (3rd ed., Vol. 1). Baltimore: Williams & Wilkins.

Mellsop, G., Varghese, F., Joshua, S., & Hicks, A. (1982). The reliability of Axis II of DSM-III. *American Journal of Psychiatry, 139,* 1360–1361.

Mellstrom, M., Cicala, G. A., & Zuckerman, M. (1976). General versus specific trait anxiety measures in the prediction of fear of snakes, heights, and darkness. *Journal of Consulting and Clinical Psychology, 44,* 83–91.

Mendelsohn, G. A. (1983). What should we tell students about theories of personality? *Contemporary Psychology, 28,* 435–437.

Mershon, B., & Gorsuch, R. L. (1988). Number of factors in the personality sphere: Does increase in factors increase predictability of real-life criteria? *Journal of Personality and Social Psychology, 55,* 675–680.

Messick, S., & Jungeblut, A. (1981). Time and method of coaching for the SAT. *Psychological Bulletin, 89,* 191–216.

Metzner, R. (1979). *Know your type: Maps of identity.* Garden City, NY: Anchor Press.

Milgram, S. (1963). Behavioral study of obedience. *Journal of Abnormal and Social Psychology, 67,* 371–378.

Milgram, S. (1970). The experience of living in cities. *Science, 167,* 1461–1468.

Milgram, S. (1974). *Obedience to authority.* New York: Harper & Row.

Miller, D. T., & Turnbull, W. (1986). Expectancies and interpersonal processes. *Annual Review of Psychology, 37,* 233–256.

Miller, G. A. (1969). Psychology as a means of promoting human welfare. *American Psychologist, 24,* 1063–1075.

Miller, N. E. (1969). Learning of visceral and glandular responses. *Science, 163,* 434–445.

Miller, N. E., & Dworkin, B. R. (1974). Visceral learning: Recent difficulties with curarized rats and significant problems for human research. In P. A. Obrist, A. H. Black, J. Brener, & L. V. DiCara (Eds.), *Cardiovascular psychophysiology.* Chicago: Aldine.

Miller, S. M. (1979). Controllability and human stress: Method, evidence, and theory. *Behaviour Research and Therapy, 17,* 287–304.

Miller, S. M., Brody, D. S., & Summerton, J. (1988). Styles of coping with threat: Implications for health. *Journal of Personality and Social Psychology, 54,* 142–148.

Millon, T. (1981). *Disorders of personality.* New York: Wiley.

Mineka, S., & Kihlstrom, J. F. (1978). Unpredictable and uncontrollable events: A new perspective on experimental neurosis. *Journal of Abnomral Psychology, 87,* 256–271.

Miner, J. B. (1984). The validity of usefulness of theories in an emerging organizational science. *Academy of Management Review, 9,* 296–306.

Mischel, W. (1968). *Personality and assessment.* New York: Wiley.

Mischel, W. (1971). *Introduction to personality.* New York: Holt, Rinehart & Winston.

Mischel, W. (1973). toward a cognitive social learning theory reconceptualization of personality. *Psychological Review, 80,* 252–283.

Mischel, W. (1977). On the future of personality assessment. *American Psychologist, 32,* 246–254.

Mischel, W. (1979). On the interface of cognition and personality: Beyond the person-situation debate. *American Psychologist, 34,* 740–754.

Mischel, W. (1984). On the predictability of behavior and the structure of personality. In R. A. Zucker, J. Aronoff, & A. I. Rabin (Eds.), *Personality and the prediction of behavior.* New York: Academic Press.

Mischel, W. (1986). *Introduction to personality* (4th ed.). New York: Holt, Rinehart & Winston.

Mischel, W. (1990). Personality dispositions revisited and revised: A view after three decades. In L. A. Pervin (Ed.), *Handbook of personality: Theory and research.* New York: Guilford.

Mischel, W., Ebbesen, E. B., & Zeiss, A. R. (1973). Selective attention to the self: Situational and dispositional determinants. *Journal of Personality and Social Psychology, 27,* 129–142.

Mischel, W., & Peake, P. K. (1982). Beyond deja-vu in the search for cross-situational consistency. *Psychological Review, 89,* 730–755.

Mischel, W., Shoda, Y., & Peake, P. K. (1988). The nature of adolescent competencies predicted by preschool delay of gratification. *Journal of Personality and Social Psychology, 54,* 687–696.

Mischel, W., Zeiss, R., & Zeiss, A. R. (1973). Internal-external control and persistence: Validation and implications of the Stanford Preschool Internal-External Scale. *Journal of Personality and Social Psychology, 29,* 265–278.

Mischler, E. G., & Waxler, N. (1968). *Interaction in families: An experimental study of family processes and schizophrenia.* New York: Wiley.

Mixon, D. (1971). Behavior analysis treating subjects as actors rather than organisms. *Journal for the Theory of Social Behaviour, 1,* 19–32.

Mollinger, R. N. (1981). *Psychoanalysis and literature: An introduction.* Chicago: Nelson-Hall.

Monson, T. C., Hesley, J. W., & Chernick, L. (1982). Specifying when personality traits can and cannot predict behavior: An alternative to abandoning the attempt to predict single-act criteria. *Journal of Personality and Social Psychology, 43,* 385–399.

Montag, I., & Birenbaum, M. (1986). Psychopathological factors and sensation seeking. *Journal of Research in Personality, 20,* 338–348.

Monty, R. A., & Perlmuter, L. C. (1975). Persistence of the effects of choice on paired-associate learning. *Memory & Cognition, 3,* 183–187.

Mook, D. G. (1987). *Motivation: The organization of action.* New York: Norton.

Moreno, J. L. (1946). *Psychodrama.* Boston: Beacon House.

Morgan, C. D., & Murray, H. A. (1935). A method for investigating fantasies. *Archives of Neurology and Psychiatry, 34,* 289–306.

Morgan, E., Mull, H. K., & Washburn, M. F. (1919). An attempt to test the moods or temperament of cheerfulness and depression by directed recall of emotionally toned experiences. *American Journal of Psychology, 30,* 302–304.

Mosher, D. L., & Anderson, R. D. (1986). Macho personality, sexual aggression, and reactions to guided imagery of realistic rape. *Journal of Research in Personality, 20,* 77–94.

Mosher, D. L., & Sirkin, M. (1984). Measuring a macho personality constellation. *Journal of Research in Personality, 18,* 150–163.

Moskowitz, D. S. (1988). Cross-situational generality in the laboratory: Dominance and friendliness. *Journal of Personality and Social Psychology, 54,* 829–839.

Mossey, J. M., & Shapiro, E. (1982). Self-rated health: A predictor of mortality among the elderly. *American Journal of Public Health, 72,* 800–808.

Mullin, E. (1990). *Coping with AIDS: A multiple-life-history approach.* Unpublished masters thesis, University of Michigan.

Munsterberg, H. (1913). *Psychology and industrial efficiency.* Boston: Hougton Mifflin.

Murphy, G. (1947). *Personality: A biosocial approach to origins and structure.* New York: Harper.

Murray, H. A. (1938). *Explorations in personality.* New York: Oxford.

Murray, H. A., & MacKinnon, D. W. (1946). Assessment of OSS personnel. *Journal of Consulting Psychology, 10,* 76–80.

Myers, I. B. (1962). *Manual: Myers-Briggs Type Indicator.* Palo Alto, CA: Consulting Psychologists Press.

Nash, J. M. (1990, September 17). Tracking down killer genes. *Time,* pp. 11–14.

Neale, M. C., & Stevenson, J. (1989). Rater bias in the EASI Temperament Scales: A twin study. *Journal of Personality and Social Psychology, 56,* 446–455.

Neill, A. S. (1960). *Summerhill: A radical approach to child rearing.* New York: Hart.

Neimeyer, R. A. (1985). *The development of personal construct psychology.* Lincoln: University of Nebraska Press.

Neisser, U. (1967). *Cognitive psychology.* Englewood Cliffs, NJ: Prentice-Hall.

Nelkin, D., & Tancredi, L. (1989). *Dangerous diagnostics.* New York: Basic Books.

Nemiah, J. C. (1980a). Obsessive-compulsive disorder (obsessive-compulsive neurosis). In H. I. Kaplan, A. M. Freedman, & B. J. Sadock (Eds.), *Comprehensive textbook of psychiatry* (3rd ed., Vol. 2). Baltimore: Williams & Wilkins.

Nemiah, J. C. (1980b). Phobic disorder (phobic neurosis). In H. I. Kaplan, A. M. Freedman, & B. J. Sadock (Eds.), *Comprehensive textbook of psychiatry* (3rd ed., Vol. 2). Baltimore: Williams & Wilkins.

Nemiah, J. C. (1980c). Somatoform disorders. In H. I. Kaplan, A. M. Freedman, & B. J. Sadock (Eds.), *Comprehensive textbook of psychiatry* (3rd ed., Vol. 2). Baltimore: Williams & Wilkins.

Nevill, D. (1974). Experimental manipulation of dependency motivation and its effects on eye contact and measures of field dependency. *Journal of Personality and Social Psychology, 29,* 72–79.

Newman, H. H., Freeman, F. N., & Holzinger, K. Z. (1937). *Twins.* Chicago: University of Chicago Press.

Newsweek. (1968, September 23). Talk with Dr. Spock: In praise of the younger generation (pp. 70–71).

Nezu, A. M., Nezu, C. M., & Nezu, V. A. (1986). Depression, general distress, and causal attributions among university students. *Journal of Abnormal Psychology, 95,* 184–186.

Nicholls, J. G., Licht, B. G., & Pearl, R. A. (1982). Some dangers of using personality questionnaires to study personality. *Psychological Bulletin, 92,* 572–580.

Niederland, W. **(1959).** The "miracled-up" world of Schreber's childhood. *Psychoanalytic Study of the Child, 14,* 383–413.

Nisbett, R. E., & Ross, L. **(1991).** *The person and the situation.* New York: McGraw-Hill.

Nisbett, R. E., & Wilson, T. W. **(1977).** Telling more than we can know: Verbal reports on mental processes. *Psychological Review, 84,* 231–259.

Nolen-Hoeksema, S. **(1990).** *Sex differences in depression.* Stanford, CA: Stanford University Press.

Noller, P., Law, H., & Comrey, A. L. **(1987).** Cattell, Comrey, and Eysenck personality factors compared: More evidence for the five robust factors? *Journal of Personality and Social Psychology, 53,* 775–782.

Norem, J. K., & Cantor, N. **(1986).** Defensive pessimism: "Harnessing" anxiety as motivation. *Journal of Personality and Social Psychology, 51,* 1208–1217.

Norman, W. T. **(1963).** Toward an adequate taxonomy of personality attributes: Replicated factor structure in peer nomination personality ratings. *Journal of Abnormal and Social Psychology, 66,* 574–583.

Office of Srategic Services Assessment Staff. **(1948).** *Assessment of men.* New York: Rinehart.

Ogilvie, D. M. **(1987).** The undesired self: A neglected variable in personality research. *Journal of Personality and Social Psychology, 52,* 379–385.

Ohman, A., Fredrickson, M., Hugdahl, L., & Rimmo, P. **(1976).** The premise of equipotentiality in human classical conditioning: Conditioned electrodermal responses to potentially phobic stimuli. *Journal of Experimental Psychology: General, 105,* 313–337.

O'Leary, A. **(1985).** Self-efficacy and health. *Behaviour Research and Therapy, 23,* 437–451.

Oltman, P. K., Goodenough, D. R., Witkin, H. A., Freedman, N., & Friedman, F. **(1975).** Psychological differentiation as a factor in conflict resolution. *Journal of Personality and Social Psychology, 32,* 730–736.

Orne, M. T. **(1962).** On the social psychology of the psychology experiment: With particular reference to demand characteristics and their implications. *American Psychologist, 17,* 776–783.

Ornstein, R. E. (Ed.) **(1973).** *Nature of human consciousness.* San Francisco: Freeman.

Ornstein, R. E. **(1977).** *The psychology of consciousness* (2nd ed.). New York: Harcourt Brace Jovanovich.

Ostrom, T. **(1984).** The sovereignty of social cognition. In R. S. Wyer & T. K. Srull (Eds.), *Handbook of social cognition* (Vol. 1). Hillsdale, NJ: Erlbaum.

Owen, D. **(1985).** *None of the above.* Boston: Houghton Mifflin.

Oyserman, D., & Markus, H. **(1990).** Possible selves and delinquency. *Journal of Personality and Social Psychology, 59,* 112–125.

Ozer, E. M., & Bandura, A. **(1990).** Mechanisms governing empowerment effects: A self-efficacy analysis. *Journal of Personality and Social Psychology, 58,* 472–486.

Packard, V. **(1957).** *The hidden persuaders.* New York: David McKay.

Paddock, J. R., & Nowicki, S. **(1986).** An examination of the Leary circumplex through the Interpersonal Check List. *Journal of Research in Personality, 20,* 107–144.

Parisi, T. **(1987).** Why Freud failed: Some implications for neurophysiology and sociobiology. *American Psychologist, 42,* 235–245.

Patterson, C. M., Kosson, D. S., & Newman, J. P. **(1987).** Reaction to punishment reflectivity, and passive avoidance learning in extraverts. *Journal of Personality and Social Psychology, 52,* 565–575.

Paul, G. L. (1967). Insight vs. desensitization in psychotherapy two years after termination. *Journal of Consulting Psychology, 31,* 333–348.

Payne, T. J., Connor, J. M., & Colletti, G. (1987). Gender-based schematic processing: An empirical investigation and reevaluation. *Journal of Personality and Social Psychology, 52,* 937–945.

Peabody, D., & Goldberg, L. R. (1989). Some determinants of factor structures from personality-trait descriptors. *Journal of Personality and Social Psychology, 57,* 552–567.

Pedersen, N. L, Plomin, R., McClearn, G. E., & Friberg, L. (1988). Neuroticism, extraversion, and related traits in adult twins reared apart and reared together. *Journal of Personality and Social Psychology, 55,* 950–957.

Pedhazur, E. J., & Tetenbaum, T. J. (1979). Bem Sex Role Inventory: A theoretical and methodogical critique. *Journal of Personality and Social Psychology, 37,* 996–1016.

Pennebaker, J. W., Hughes, C. F., & O'Heeron, R. C. (1987). The psychophysiology of confession: Linking inhibitory and psychosomatic processes. *Journal of Personality and Social Psychology, 52,* 781–793.

Pennebaker, J. W., & O'Heeron, R. C. (1984). Confiding in others and illness rate among spouses of suicide and accidental-death victims. *Journal of Abnormal Psychology, 93,* 473–476.

Perlmuter, L. C., & Monty, R. A. (Eds.). (1979). *Choice and perceived control.* Hillsdale, NJ: Lawrence Erlbaum.

Perls, F. S. (1969). *Gestalt therapy verbatim.* Lafayette, CA: Real People Press.

Perris, C. (1989). *Cognitive therapy with schizophrenic patients.* New York: Guilford.

Persons, J. B. (1989). *Cognitive therapy in practice: A case formulation approach.* New York: Norton.

Pervin, L. A. (1985). Personality: Current controversies, issues, and directions. *Annual Review of Psychology, 36,* 83–114.

Pervin, L. A. (1990). Personality theory and research: Prospects for the future. In L. A. Pervin (Ed.), *Handbook of personality theory and research.* New York: Guilford.

Peters, T. J., & Waterman, R. H. (1982). *In search of excellence: Lessons from America's best-run companies.* New York: Warner.

Peterson, C. (1988). Explanatory style as a risk factor for illness. *Cognitive Therapy and Research, 12,* 117–130.

Peterson, C. (1991). The meaning and measurement of explanatory style. *Psychological Inquiry, 2,* 1–10.

Peterson, C., & Barrett, L. C. (1987). Explanatory style and academic performance among university freshmen. *Journal of Personality and Social Psychology, 53,* 603–607.

Peterson, C., & Bossio, L. M. (1989). Learned helplessness. In R. C. Curtis (Ed.), *Self-defeating behaviors.* New York: Plenum.

Peterson, C., & Bossio, L. M. (1991). *Health and optimism.* New York: Free Press.

Peterson, C., Schulman, P., Castellon, C., & Seligman, M. E. P. (1991). The explanatory style scoring manual. In C. P. Smith (Ed.), *Thematic content analysis for motivation and personality research.* New York: Cambridge University Press.

Peterson, C., & Scott, W. A. (1975). Generality and topic specificity of cognitive styles. *Journal of Research in Personality, 9,* 366–374.

Peterson, C., & Seligman, M. E. P. (1984). Causal explanations as a risk factor for depression: Theory and evidence. *Psychological Review, 91,* 347–374.

Peterson, C., & Seligman, M. E. P. (1985). The learned helplessness model of depression: Current status of theory and research. In E. E. Beckham & W. R. Leber (Eds.), *Handbook of depression: Treatment, assessment, and research.* Homewood, IL: Dorsey.

Peterson, C., Seligman, M. E. P., & Vaillant, G. E. (1988). Pessimistic explanatory style is a risk factor for physical illness: A thirty-five year longitudinal study. *Journal of Personality and Social Psychology, 55,* 23–27.

Peterson, C., et al. (1982). The Attributional Style Questionnaire. *Cognitive Therapy and Research, 6,* 287–299.

Peterson, C., & Stunkard, A. J. (1989). Personal control and health promotion. *Social Science and Medicine, 28,* 819–828.

Peterson, C., & Villanova, P. (1988). An expanded Attributional Style Questionnaire. *Journal of Abnormal Psychology, 97,* 87–89.

Peterson, D. R. (1968). *The clinical study of social behavior.* New York: Appleton.

Phares, E. J. (1984). *Introduction to personality.* Columbus, OH: Merrill.

Phillips, B. N., Martin, R. P., & Meyers, J. (1972). Interventions in relation to anxiety in school. In C. D. Spielberger (Ed.), *Anxiety: Current trends in theory and research* (Vol. II). New York: Academic Press.

Pittman, T. S., & Heller, J. F. (1987). Social motivation. *Annual Review of Psychology, 38,* 461–489.

Plomin, R. (1986). Behavioral genetic methods. *Journal of Personality, 54,* 226–261.

Plomin, R., Chipuer, H. M., & Loehlin, J. C. (1990). Behavioral genetics and personality. In L. A. Pervin (Ed.), *Handbook of personality: Theory and research.* New York: Guilford.

Plomin, R., & Daniels, D. (1987). Why are children in the same family so different from each other? *Behavioral and Brain Sciences, 10,* 1–16.

Plomin, R., DeFries, J. C., & McClearn, G. E. (1980). *Behavioral genetics: A primer.* San Francisco: Freeman.

Plomin, R., & Nesselroade, J. R. (1990). Behavior genetics and personality change. *Journal of Personality, 58,* 191–220.

Popper, K. R. (1959). *The logic of discovery.* London: Hutchinson.

Porter, N., Geis, F. L., Cooper, E., & Newman, E. (1985). Androgyny and leadership in mixed-sex groups. *Journal of Personality and Social Psychology, 49,* 808–823.

Pratt, M. W., Golding, G., Hunter, W., & Sampson, R. (1988). Sex differences in adult moral orientation. *Journal of Personality, 56,* 373–391.

Premack, D. (1971). Language in the chimpanzee? *Science, 172,* 808–822.

Pressey, S. L. (1921). A group scale for investigating the emotions. *Journal of Abnormal Psychology, 16,* 55–64.

Price, R. H., & Bouffard, D. L. (1974). Behavioral appropriateness and situational constraints as dimensions of social behavior. *Journal of Personality and Social Psychology, 30,* 579–586.

Prichard, J. C. (1837). *Treatise on insanity and other disorders affecting the mind.* Philadelphia: Haswell, Barrington, & Haswell.

Prochaska, J. O. (1984). *Systems of psychotherapy: A transhistorical analysis* (2nd ed.). Homewood, IL: Dorsey.

Putnam, F. W., Guroff, J. J., Silberman, E. K., Barban, L., & Post, R. M. (1986). The clinical phenomenology of multiple personality disorder: Review of 100 recent cases. *Journal of Clinical Psychiatry, 47,* 285–293.

Quine, W. V., & Ullian, J. S. (1978). *The web of belief* (2nd ed.). New York: Random House.

Rabkin, J. G., & Struening, E. L. (1976). Life events, stress, and illness. *Science, 194,* 1013–1020.

Rachman, S. J. (1978). *Fear and courage.* New York: Freeman.

Rado, S. (1928). The problem of melancholia. *International Journal of Psychoanalysis, 9,* 420–428.

Rapaport, D. (1959). The structure of psychoanalytic theory: A systematizing attempt. In S. Koch (Ed.), *Psychology: A study of a science* (Vol. 1). New York: McGraw-Hill.

Raps, C. S., Peterson, C., Reinhard, K. E., Abramson, L. Y., & Seligman, M. E. P. (1982). Attributional style among depressed patients. *Journal of Abnormal Psychology, 91,* 102–108.

Raynor, J. O. (1970). Relationships between achievement-related motives, future orientation, and academic performance. *Journal of Personality and Social Psychology, 15,* 28–33.

Reeves, C. (1977). *The psychology of Rollo May.* San Francisco: Jossey-Bass.

Reeves, D. J., & Booth, R. F. (1979). Expressed versus inventoried interests as predictors of paramedic effectiveness. *Journal of Vocational Behavior, 15,* 155–163.

Reich, W. (1933). *Charakteranalyse.* Berlin: Selbstverlag des Verfassers.

Revusky, S. H., & Garcia, J. (1970). Learned associations over long delays. In G. H. Bower & J. T. Spence (Eds.), *Psychology of learning and motivation* (Vol. 4). New York: Academic Press.

Rhodewalt, F., & Zone, J. B. (1989). Appraisal of life change, depression, and illness in hardy and nonhardy women. *Journal of Personality and Social Psychology, 56,* 81–88.

Riddle, M., & Roberts, A. H. (1977). Delinquency, delay of gratification, recidivism, and the Porteus maze tests. *Psychological Bulletin, 84,* 417–425.

Riggio, R. E., Lippa, R., & Salinas, C. (1990). The display of personality in expressive movement. *Journal of Research in Personality, 24,* 16–31.

Roazen, P. (1975). *Freud and his followers.* New York: Knopf.

Rodin, J., & Langer, E. J. (1977). Long-term effects of a control-relevant intervention with the institutionalized aged. *Journal of Personality and Social Psychology, 35,* 897–902.

Rodin, J., & Salovey, P. (1989). Health psychology. *Annual Review of Psychology, 40,* 533–579.

Rodin, J., Solomon, S., & Metcalf, J. (1978). Role of control in mediating perceptions of density. *Journal of Personality and Social Psychology, 36,* 988–999.

Rodriguez, M. L., Mischel, W., & Shoda, Y. (1989). Cognitive personal variables in the delay of gratification of older children at risk. *Journal of Personality and Social Psychology, 57,* 358–367.

Rogers, C. R. (1942). *Counseling and psychotherapy: Newer concepts in practice.* Boston: Houghton Mifflin.

Rogers, C. R. (1951). *Client-centered therapy: Its current practices, implications, and theory.* Boston: Houghton Mifflin.

Rogers, C. R. (1961). *On becoming a person.* Boston: Houghton Mifflin.

Rogers, C. R. (1969a). *Freedom to learn.* Columbus, OH: Merrill.

Rogers, C. R. (1969b). Two divergent trends. In R. May (Ed.), *Existential psychology* (2nd ed.). New York: Random House.

Rogers, C. R. (1970). *On encounter groups.* New York: Harper & Row.

Rogers, C. R. (1972). *Becoming partners.* New York: Dell.

Rogers, C. R. (1977). *Carl Rogers on personal power: Inner strength and its revolutionary impact.* New York: Delacorte.

Rogers, C. R. (1980). *A way of being.* Boston: Houghton Mifflin.

Rogers, C. R., & Dymond, R. F. (Eds.). (1954). *Psychotherapy and personality change.* Chicago: University of Chicago Press.

Rogers, C. R., Gendlin, E. T., Kiesler, D. J., & Truax, C. B. (1967). *The therapeutic relationship and its impact: A study of psychotherapy with schizophrenics.* Madison: University of Wisconsin Press.

Rogers, C. R., & Ryback, D. (1984). One alternative to nuclear planetary suicide. In R. F. Levant & J. M. Shlien (Eds.), *Client-centered therapy and the person-centered approach: New directions in theory, research, and practice.* New York: Praeger.

Rogers, C. R., & Skinner, B. F. (1956). Some issues concerning the control of human behavior. *Science, 124,* 1057–1066.

Romney, D. M., & Bynner, J. M. (1989). Evaluation of a circumplex model of DSM-III personality disorders. *Journal of Research in Personality, 23,* 525–538.

Rorschach, H. (1942). *Psychodiagnostics: A diagnostic test based on perception.* Berne: Huber.

Rose, R. J. (1988). Genetic and environmental variance in content dimensions of the MMPI. *Journal of Personality and Social Psychology, 55,* 302–311.

Rose, R. J., Koskenvuo, M., Kaprio, J., Sarna, S., & Langinvainio, H. (1988). Shared genes, shared experiences, and similarity of personality: Data from 14,288 adult Finnish co-twins. *Journal of Personality and Social Psychology, 54,* 161–171.

Rosenbaum, M. (1984). Anna O. (Bertha Pappenheim): Her history. In M. Rosenbaum & M. Muroff (Eds.), *Anna O.: Fourteen contemporary interpretations.* New York: Free Press.

Rosenberg, M. J. (1965). When dissonance fails: On eliminating evaluation apprehension from attitude measurement. *Journal of Personality and Social Psychology, 1,* 18–42.

Rosenhan, D. J., & Seligman, M. E. P. (1989). *Abnormal psychology* (2nd ed.). New York: Norton.

Rosenthal, P. A., & Rosenthal, S. (1984). Suicidal behavior by preschool children. *American Journal of Psychiatry, 141,* 520–525.

Rosenthal, R. (1966). *Experimenter effects in behavioral research.* New York: Appleton-Century-Crofts.

Rosenthal, R. (1990). How are we doing in soft psychology? *American Psychologist, 45,* 775–777.

Rosenthal, R., & Rosnow, R. L. (Eds.). (1969). *Artifact in behavioral research.* New York: Academic Press.

Rosenthal, R., & Rubin, D. B. (1982). A simple, general purpose display of magnitude of experimental effect. *Journal of Educational Psychology, 74,* 166–169.

Rosenwald, G. C. (1988). A theory of multiple-case research. *Journal of Personality, 55,* 239–264.

Rosenzweig, S. (1954). A transvaluation of psychotherapy: A reply to Hans Eysenck. *Journal of Abnormal and Social Psychology, 49,* 298–304.

Rosenzweig, S. (1986). Idiodynamics vis-a-vis psychology. *American Psychologist, 41,* 241–245.

Rosenzweig, S. (1988). The identity and idiodynamics of the multiple personality "Sally Beauchamp": A confirmatory supplement. *American Psychologist, 43,* 45–48.

Ross, M. (1989). Relation of implicit theories to the construction of personal histories. *Psychological Review, 96,* 341–357.

Roth, D. L., Wiebe, D. J., Fillingim, R. B., & Shay, K. A. (1989). Life events, fitness, hardiness, and health: A simultaneous analysis of proposed stress-resistance effects. *Journal of Personality and Social Psychology, 57,* 136–142.

Rotter, J. B. **(1954).** *Social learning and clinical psychology.* Englewood Cliffs, NJ: Prentice-Hall.

Rotter, J. B. **(1966).** Generalized expectancies for internal versus external control of reinforcement. *Psychological Monographs, 81* (1, Whole No. 609).

Rotter, J. B. **(1967).** A new scale for the measurement of interpersonal trust. *Journal of Personality, 35,* 651–655.

Rotter, J. B. **(1971).** Generalized expectancies for interpersonal trust. *American Psychologist, 26,* 443–452.

Rotter, J. B. **(1975).** Some problems and misconceptions related to the construct of internal versus external reinforcement. *Journal of Consulting and Clinical Psychology, 43,* 56–67.

Rotter, J. B. **(1990).** Internal versus external control of reinforcement: A case history of a variable. *American Psychologist, 45,* 489–493.

Roubertoux, P. **(1985).** Genetic correlates of personality and temperament: The origins of individual differences. In J. Strelau, F. H. Farley, & A. Gale (Eds.), *The biological bases of personality and behavior: Theories, measurement techniques, and development* (Vol. 1). Washington, DC: Hemisphere.

Rowe D. C. **(1987).** Resolving the person-situation debate: Invitation to an interdisciplinary debate. *American Psychologist, 42,* 218–227.

Rozin, P., & Fallon, A. E. **(1987).** A perspective on disgust. *Psychological Review, 94,* 23–41.

Rozin, P., & Kalat, J. W. **(1971).** Specific hungers and poison avoidance as adaptive specializations of learning. *Psychological Review, 78,* 459–486.

Runyan, W. M. **(1981).** Why did Van Gogh cut off his ear? The problem of alternative explanations in psychobiography. *Journal of Personality and Social Psychology, 40,* 1070–1077.

Runyan, W. M. **(1982).** *Life histories and psychobiography: Explorations in theory and method.* New York: Oxford.

Runyan, W. M. (Ed.). **(1988).** *Psychology and historical interpretation.* New York: Oxford.

Rushton, J. P. **(1985).** Differential K theory: The sociobiology of individual and group differences. *Personality and Individual Differences, 6,* 441–452.

Rushton, J. P. **(1988).** Race differences in behaviour: A review and evolutionary analysis. *Personality and Individual Differences, 9,* 1009–1024.

Rushton, J. P. **(1989).** The evolution of racial differences: A response to Mr. Lynn. *Journal of Research in Personality, 23,* 7–20.

Rushton, J. P., & Bogaert, A. F. **(1987).** Race differences in sexual behavior: Testing an evolutionary hypothesis. *Journal of Research in Personality, 21,* 529–551.

Rushton, J. P., & Bogaert, A. F. **(1988).** Race versus social class differences in sexual behavior: A follow-up test of the r/k dimension. *Journal of Research in Personality, 22,* 259–272.

Rushton, J. P., Brainerd, C. J., & Pressley, M. **(1983).** Behavioral development and construct validity: The principle of aggregation. *Psychological Bulletin, 94,* 18–38.

Ryle, G. **(1949).** *The concept of mind.* London: Hutchinson.

Sackeim, H., Nordlie, J., & Gur, R. **(1979).** A model of hysterical and hypnotic blindness: Cognition, motivation, and awareness. *Journal of Abnormal Psychology, 88,* 474–489.

Sande, G. N., Goethals, G. R., & Radloff, C. E. **(1988).** Perceiving one's own traits and others': The multifaceted self. *Journal of Personality and Social Psychology, 54,* 13–20.

Sanford, N. **(1976).** Graduate education then and now. *American Psychologist, 31,* 756–764.

Sarason, I. G. (Ed.). (1980). *Test anxiety: Theory, research, and applications.* Hillsdale, NJ: Erlbaum.

Sartre, J.-P. (1956). *Being and nothingness: An essay on phenomenological ontology.* New York: Philosophical Library.

Scarf, M. (1980, September). Images that heal: A doubtful idea whose time has come. *Psychology Today,* pp. 32–46.

Scarr, S. (1968). Environmental bias in twin studies. *Eugenics Quarterly, 15,* 34–40.

Scarr, S. (1988). Race and gender as psychological variables: Social and ethical issues. *American Psychologist, 43,* 56–59.

Schachter, S. (1959). *The psychology of affiliation.* Stanford, CA: Stanford University Press.

Schachter, S., & Latané, B. T. (1964). Crime, cognition, and the autonomic nervous system. In D. Levine (Ed.), *Nebraska Symposium on Motivation* (Vol. 12). Lincoln: University of Nebraska Press.

Schachter, S., & Singer, J. E. (1962). Cognitive, social, and physiological determinants of emotional state. *Psychological Review, 65,* 379–399.

Schaffer, H. R., & Emerson, P. R. (1964). The development of social attachments in infancy. *Child Development Monographs, 29*(2).

Schank, R. C., & Abelson, R. P. (1977). *Scripts, plans, goals, and understanding.* Hillsdale, NJ: Erlbaum.

Schapiro, M. (1956). Leonardo and Freud: An art-historical study. *Journal of the History of Ideas, 17,* 147–178.

Schatzman, M. (1971). Madness and morals. In R. Boyers (Ed.), *R. D. Laing and anti-psychiatry.* New York: Harper & Row.

Scheier, M. F., & Carver, C. S. (1985). Optimism, coping, and health: Assessment and implications of generalized outcome expectancies. *Health Psychology, 4,* 219–247.

Scheier, M. F., Weintraub, J. K., & Carver, C. S. (1986). Coping with stress: Divergent strategies of optimists and pessimists. *Journal of Personality and Social Psychology, 51,* 1257–1264.

Scheier, M. F., et al. (1989). Dispositional optimism and recovery from coronary artery bypass surgery: The beneficial effects on physical and psychological well-being. *Journal of Personality and Social Psychology, 57,* 1024–1040.

Schill, T. (1966). Sex differences in identification of the castrating agent on the Blacky Test. *Journal of Clinical Psychology, 22,* 324–325.

Schlenker, B. R. (Ed). (1985). *The self and social life.* New York: McGraw-Hill.

Schmidt, D. E., & Keating, J. P. (1979). Human crowding and personal control: An integration of the research. *Psychological Bulletin, 86,* 680–700.

Schneider, D. J. (1973). Implicit personality theory: A review. *Psychological Bulletin, 79,* 294–309.

Schooler, C. (1972). Birth order effects: Not here, not now! *Psychological Bulletin, 78,* 161–175.

Schooler, C., Zahn, T. P., Murphy, D. L., & Buchsbaum, M. S. (1978). Psychological correlates of monoamine oxidase in normals. *Journal of Nervous and Mental Diseases, 166,* 177–186.

Schutte, N. S., Kenrick, D. T., & Sadalla, E. K. (1985). The search for predictable settings: Situational prototypes, constraint, and behavioral variation. *Journal of Personality and Social Psychology, 49,* 121–128.

Schwartz, B. (1984). *Psychology of learning and behavior* (2nd ed.). New York: Norton.

Scott, J. P., & Fuller, J. L. (1965). *Genetics and the social behavior of the dog.* Chicago: University of Chicago Press.

Scott, W. A. (1969). Structure of natural cognitions. *Journal of Personality and Social Psychology, 12,* 261–278.

Scott, W. A. (1974). Varieties of cognitive integration. *Journal of Personality and Social Psychology, 30,* 563–578.

Scott, W. A., Osgood, D. W., & Peterson, C. (1979). *Cognitive structure: Theory and measurement of individual differences.* Washington, DC: Winston.

Scott, W. A., & Peterson, C. (1975). Adjustment, Pollyannaism, and attraction to close personal relationships. *Journal of Consulting and Clinical Psychology, 43,* 872–880.

Scott, W. D. (1908). *Psychology of advertising.* Boston: Small, Maynard.

Sears, P. S. (1953). Child-rearing factors related to playing of sex-types roles. *American Psychologist, 8,* 431.

Sears, R. R. (1943). *Survey of objective studies of psychoanalytic concepts.* New York: Social Science Research Council.

Sears, R. R. (1970). Relation of early socialization experiences to self-concept and gender role in middle childhood. *Child Development, 41,* 267–289.

Sears, R. R., Rau, L., & Alpert, R. (1965). *Identification and childrearing.* Stanford, CA: Stanford University Press.

Sedgwick, P. (1971). R. D. Laing: Self, symptom, and society. In R. Boyers (Ed.), *R. D. Laing and anti-psychiatry.* New York: Harper & Row.

Sedney, M. A. (1987). Development of androgyny: Parental influences. *Psychology of Women Quarterly, 11,* 311–326.

Segal, Z. V. (1988). Appraisal of the self-schema construct in cognitive models of depression. *Psychological Bulletin, 103,* 147–162.

Seligman, M. E. P. (1970). On the generality of the laws of learning. *Psychological Review, 77,* 406–418.

Seligman, M. E. P. (1971). Phobias and preparedness. *Behavior Therapy, 2,* 307–321.

Seligman, M. E. P. (1974). Depression and learned helplessness. In R. J. Friedman & M. M. Katz (Eds.), *The psychology of depression: Contemporary theory and research.* Washington, DC: Winston.

Seligman, M. E. P. (1975). *Helplessness: On depression, development, and death.* San Francisco: Freeman.

Seligman, M. E. P. (1978). Comment and integration. *Journal of Abnormal Psychology, 87,* 165–179.

Seligman, M. E. P. (1981). A learned helplessness point of view. In L. P. Rehm (Ed.), *Behavior therapy for depression: Present status and future directions.* New York: Academic Press.

Seligman, M. E. P. (1988). *Why is there so much depression today? The waxing of the individual and the waning of the commons.* Invited lecture at the Annual Convention of the American Psychological Association, Atlanta.

Seligman, M. E. P., & Schulman, P. (1986). Explanatory style as a predictor of productivity and quitting among life insurance agents. *Journal of Personality and Social Psychology, 50,* 832–838.

Seligman, M. E. P., et al. (1988). Explanatory style change during cognitive therapy for unipolar depression. *Journal of Abnormal Psychology, 97,* 13–18.

Shaw, J. S. (1982). Psychological androgyny and stressful life events. *Journal of Personality and Social Psychology, 43,* 145–153.

Sheldon, W. H. (1940). *The varieties of human physique.* New York: Harper.

Sheldon, W. H. (1942). *The varieties of temperament.* New York: Harper.

Sherman S. J., Judd, C. M., & Park, B. (1989). Social cognition. *Annual Review of Psychology, 40,* 281–326.

Sherrod, D. R. (1974). Crowding, perceived control, and behavioral after-effects. *Journal of Applied Social Psychology, 4,* 171–186.

Shields, J. (1976). Heredity and environment. In H. J Eysenck & G. D. Wilson (Eds.), *A textbook of human psychology.* Baltimore: University Park Press.

Shostak, M. (1981). *Nisa: The life and words of a !Kung woman.* Cambridge: Harvard University Press.

Shostrom, E. L. (1964). An inventory for the measurement of self-actualization. *Educational and Psychological Measurement, 24,* 207–218.

Siegel, B. S. (1986). *Love, medicine, and miracles.* New York: Harper & Row.

Siegel, B. S. (1989). *Peace love, & healing.* New York: Harper & Row.

Signorella, M. L., & Jamison, W. (1986). Masculinity, femininity, androgyny, and cognitive performance: A meta-analysis. *Psychological Bulletin, 100,* 207–228.

Silver, R. L., & Wortman, C. B. (1980). Coping with undesirable life events. In J. Garber & M. E. P. Seligman (Eds.), *Human helplessness: Theory and applications.* New York: Academic Press.

Silverman, L. H. (1971). An experimental technique for the study of unconscious conflict. *British Journal of Medical Psychology, 44,* 17–25.

Silverman, L. H. (1976). Psychoanalytic theory: "The reports of my death are greatly exaggerated." *American Psychologist, 31,* 621–637.

Silverman, L. H., Bronstein, A., & Mendelsohn, E. (1976). The further use of the subliminal psychodynamic activation method for the experimental study of the clinical theory of psychoanalysis: On the specificity of relationships between manifest psychopathology and unconscious conflict. *Psychotherapy: Theory, Research, and Practice, 13,* 2–16.

Silverman, L. H., & Fishel, A. K. (1981). The Oedipus complex: Studies in adult male behavior. In L. Wheeler (Ed.), *Review of personality and social psychology* (Vol. 2). Beverly Hills, CA: Sage.

Silverman, M. A. (1980). A fresh look at the case of Little Hans. In M. Kanzer & J. Glenn (Eds.), *Freud and his patients.* New York: Aronson.

Silverstein, A. (1988). An Aristotelian resolution of the idiographic versus nomothetic tension. *American Psychologist, 43,* 425–430.

Simonton, O. C., Matthews-Simonton, S., & Creighton, J. (1978). *Getting well again: A step-by-step, self-help guide to overcoming cancer for patients and their families.* Los Angeles: Tarcher.

Simonton, O. C., & Simonton, S. (1975). Belief systems and management of the emotional aspects of malignancy. *Journal of Transpersonal Psychology, 7,* 29–48.

Singer, J. L. (1966). *Daydreaming.* New York: Random House.

Singer, J. L. (1975). *The inner world of daydreaming.* New York: Harper & Row.

Singer, J. L. (1984). *The human personality.* San Diego: Harcourt Brace Jovanovich.

Singer, J. L., & Kolligian, J. (1987). Personality: Developments in the study of private experience. *Annual Review of Psychology, 38,* 533–574.

Skinner, B. F. (1938). *The behavior of organisms.* New York: Appleton-Century-Crofts.

Skinner, B. F. (1950). Are theories of learning necessary? *Psychological Review, 37,* 193–216.

Skinner, B. F. (1971). *Beyond freedom and dignity.* New York: Knopf.

Skinner, B. F. (1986). What is wrong with daily life in the western world? *American Psychologist, 41,* 568–574.

Skinner, B. F. (1987). Whatever happened to psychology as the science of behavior? *American Psychologist, 42,* 780–786.

Smart, J. C. (1982). Faculty teaching goals: A test of Holland's theory. *Journal of Educational Psychology, 74,* 180–188.

Smedslund, J. (1978). Bandura's theory of self-efficacy: A set of common sense theorems. *Scandanavian Journal of Psychology, 19,* 1–14.

Smith, M. L., & Glass, G. V. (1977). The meta-analysis of psychotherapy outcome studies. *American Psychologist, 32,* 752–760.

Smith, R. E. (1989). Effects of coping skills training on generalized self-efficacy and locus of control. *Journal of Personality and Social Psychology, 56,* 228–233.

Smuts, B. (1985). *Sex and friendship in baboons.* New York: Aldine.

Snyder, C. R., & Higgins, R. L. (1988). Excuses: Their effective role in the negotiation of reality. *Psychological Bulletin, 104,* 23–35.

Snyder, M. (1983). The influence of individuals on situations: Implications for understanding the links between personality and social behavior. *Journal of Personality, 51,* 497–516.

Synderman, M., & Rothman, S. (1987). Survey of expert opinion in intelligence and aptitude testing. *American Psychologist, 42,* 137–144.

Sontag, S. (1979). *Illness as metaphor.* New York: Vintage Books.

Spence, K. W. (1960). *Behavior theory and learning.* Englewood Cliffs, NJ: Prentice-Hall.

Spielberger, C. D. (1966). *Anxiety and behavior.* New York: Academic Press.

Spock, B. (1946). *Common sense book of baby and child care.* New York: Duell, Sloane, & Pearce.

Spock, B. (1984, October). Coercion in the classroom will not work. *The Education Digest,* pp. 28–31.

Springer, S. P., & Deutsch, G. (1985). *Left brain, right brain* (Rev. ed.). New York: Freeman.

Stagner, R. (1936). *Psychology of personality.* New York: McGraw-Hill.

Stein, J. A., Newcomb, M. D., & Bentler, P. M. (1986). Stability and change in personality: A longitudinal study from early adolescence to young adulthood. *Journal of Research in Personality, 20,* 276–291.

Stelmack, R. M. (1990). Biological bases of extraversion: Psychophysiological evidence. *Journal of Personality, 58,* 293–311.

Stephenson, W. (1953). *The study of behavior: Q-technique and its methodology.* Chicago: University of Chicago Press.

Stern, G. G. (1970). *People in context: Measuring person-environment congruence in education and industry.* New York: Wiley.

Stern, W. (1904). *The psychological methods of testing intelligence.* Baltimore: Warwick & York.

Sternberg, R. J. (1985). *Beyond IQ: A triarchic theory of human intelligence.* Cambridge: Cambridge University Press.

Stewart, A. J. (1982). The course of individual adaptation to life changes. *Journal of Personality and Social Psychology, 42,* 1100–1113.

Stewart, A. J., & Healy, J. M. (1989). Linking individual development and social changes. *American Psychologist, 44,* 30–42.

Stewart, A. J., Sokol, M., Healy, J. M., & Chester, N. L. (1986). Longitudinal studies of psychological consequences of life changes in children and adults. *Journal of Personality and Social Psychology, 50,* 143–151.

Storms, M. D., & Nisbell, R. E. (1970). Insomnia and the attribution process. *Journal of Personality and Social Psychology, 16,* 319–328.

Stross, L., & Shevrin, H. (1969). Hypnosis as a method for investigating unconscious thought processes: A review of research. *Journal of the American Psychoanalytic Association, 17,* 100–135.

Suler, J. R. **(1980).** Primary process thinking and creativity. *Psychological Bulletin, 88,* 144–165.

Sullivan, H. S. **(1947).** *Conceptions of modern psychiatry.* Washington, DC: William Alanson White Psychiatric Foundation.

Sullivan, H. S. **(1953).** *The interpersonal theory of psychiatry.* New York: Norton.

Sulloway, F. J. **(1979).** *Freud: Biologist of the mind.* New York: Basic Books.

Suls, J., & Greenwald, A. G. (Eds.). **(1983).** *Psychological perspectives on the self* (Vol. 2). Hillsdale, NJ: Erlbaum.

Suls, J., & Rittenhouse, J. D. (Eds.). **(1987).** Special issue: Personality and physical health. *Journal of Personality, 55,* 155–393.

Swan, J. A. **(1972).** Public response to air pollution. In J. F. Wohlwill & D. H. Carson (Eds.), *Environment and the social sciences.* Washington, DC: American Psychological Association.

Swann, W. B., Pelham, B. W., & Krull, D. S. **(1989).** Agreeable fancy or disagreeable truth? Reconciling self-enhancement and self-verification. *Journal of Personality and Social Psychology, 57,* 782–791.

Swede, S. W., & Tetlock, P. E. **(1986).** Henry Kissinger's implicit theory of personality: A quantitative case study. *Journal of Personality, 54,* 617–646.

Sweeney, P. D., Anderson, K., & Bailey, S. **(1986).** Attributional style in depression: A meta-analytic review. *Journal of Personality and Social Psychology, 50,* 974–991.

Szasz, T. S. **(1961).** *The myth of mental illness.* New York: Hoeber.

Taylor, M. C., & Hall, J. A. **(1982).** Psychological androgyny: Theories, methods, and conclusions. *Psychological Bulletin, 92,* 347–366.

Taylor, R. B., Denham, J. R., & Ureda, J. W. **(1982).** *Health promotion: Principles and clinical applications.* Norwalk, CT: Appleton-Century-Crofts.

Taylor, S. E. **(1989).** *Positive illusions.* New York: Basic Books.

Taylor, S. E. **(1990).** Health psychology: The science and the field. *American Psychologist, 45,* 40–50.

Taylor, S. E., & Brown, J. D. **(1988).** Illusion and well-being: A social psychological perspective on mental health. *Psychological Bulletin, 103,* 193–210.

Taylor, S. E., & Fiske, S. T. **(1982).** Getting inside the head: Methodologies for process analysis in attribution and social cognition. In J. Harvey, W. Ickes, & R. Kidd (Eds.), *New directions in attribution research* (Vol. 3). Hillsdale, NJ: Erlbaum.

Tellegen, A. **(1988).** The analysis of consistency in personality assessment. *Journal of Personality, 56,* 621–663.

Tellegen, A., et al. **(1988).** Personality similarity in twins reared apart and together. *Journal of Personality and Social Psychology, 54,* 1031–1039.

The telltale gene. **(1990, July).** *Consumer Reports.* Pp. 483–488.

Tennen, H. **(1982).** A re-view of cognitive mediators of learned helplessness. *Journal of Personality, 50,* 526–541.

Terman, L. M., & Childs, H. G. **(1912).** A tentative revision and extension of the Binet-Simon measuring scale of intelligence. *Journal of Educational Psychology, 3,* 61–74, 133–143, 198–208, 277–289.

Thigpen, C. H., & Cleckley, H. **(1957).** *The three faces of Eve.* New York: McGraw-Hill

Thoits, P. A. **(1983).** Dimensions of life events that influence psychological distress: An evaluation and synthesis of the literature. In H. Kaplan (Ed.), *Psychosocial stress: Trends in theory and research.* New York: Academic Press.

Thomas, A., & Chess, S. **(1977).** *Temperament and development.* New York: Bruner/Mazel.

Thomas, A., Chess, S., Birch, H., Hertzig, M., & Korn, S. **(1963).** *Behavioral individuality in early childhood.* New York: New York University Press.

Thompson, S. (1981). Will it hurt less if I can control it? A complex answer to a simple question. *Psychological Bulletin, 90,* 89–101.

Thorndike, E. L. (1911). *Animal intelligence: Experimental studies.* New York: Macmillan.

Thorndike, E. L. (1916). Tests of aesthetic appreciation. *Journal of Educational Psychology, 7,* 509–522.

Thorne, A. (1987). The press of personality: A study of conversations between introverts and extraverts. *Journal of Personality and Social Psychology, 53,* 718–726.

Thorngate, W. (1976). Possible limits on a science of social behavior. In L. H. Strickland, F. E. Aboud, & K. J. Gergen (Eds.), *Social psychology in transition.* New York: Plenum.

Thurston, J. R., & Mussen, P. E. (1951). Infant feeding gratification and adult personality. *Journal of Personality, 19,* 449–458.

Time. (1990, September 17). Wow, that's disgusting! (p. 66).

Tolman, E. C. (1932). *Purposive behavior in animals and man.* New York: Appleton-Century-Crofts.

Tolman, E. C. (1948). Cognitive maps in rats and men. *Psychological Review, 55,* 189–208.

Tomkins, C. (1976, January 5). New paradigms. *New Yorker,* pp. 30–36+.

Tooby, J., & Cosmides, L. (1990). On the universality of human nature and the uniqueness of the individual: The role of genetics and adaptation. *Journal of Personality, 58,* 17–67.

Treffert, D. A. (1989). *Extraordinary people: Understanding "idiot savants."* New York: Harper & Row.

Tribich, D., & Messer, S. (1974). Psychoanalytic type and status of authority as determiners of suggestibility. *Journal of Consulting and Clinical Psychology, 42,* 842–848.

Trilling, L. (1977). Art and neurosis. In W. Anderson (Ed.), *Therapy and the arts.* New York: Harper & Row.

Turnbull, C. (1962). *The forest people.* New York: Simon & Schuster.

Urban, H. B. (1983). Phenomenological-humanistic approaches. In M. Hersen, A. E. Kazdin, & A. S. Bellack (Eds.), *The clinical psychology handbook.* New York: Pergamon.

Vaihinger, H. (1911). *The psychology of "as if": A system of the theoretical, practical, and religious fictions of mankind.* New York: Harcourt, Brace & World.

Vaillant, G. E. (1971). Theoretical hierarchy of adaptive ego mechanisms. *Archives of General Psychiatry, 24,* 107–118.

Vaillant, G. E. (1977). *Adaptation to life.* Boston: Little, Brown.

Vaillant, G. E. (1983). *The natural history of alcoholism.* Cambridge, MA: Harvard University Press.

Vandenberg, S. G. (1962). The hereditary abilities study: Hereditary components in a psychological test battery. *American Journal of Human Genetics, 14,* 220–227.

Van Hook, E., & Higgins, E. T. (1988). Self-related problems beyond the self-concept: Motivational consequences of discrepant self-guides. *Journal of Personality and Social Psychology, 55,* 625–633.

Vannoy, J. S. (1965). Generality of cognitive complexity-simplicity as a personality construct. *Journal of Personality and Social Psychology, 2,* 385–396.

van Rillaer, J. (1970). A therapy of set roles: The contribution of G. Kelly. *Bulletin de Psychologie, 23,* 793–798.

Vernon, P. E. (1964). *Personality assessment: A critical survey.* New York: Wiley.

Viorst, M. (1972, June 4). Meet the People's Party candidate. *New York Times Magazine,* pp. 42–58.

Wachtel, P. (1973). Psychodynamics, behavior therapy, and the implacable experimenter: An inquiry into the consistency of personality. *Journal of Abnormal Psychology, 82,* 323–334.

Wagner, M. E., & Schubert, H. J. P. (1977). Sibship variables and United States presidents. *Journal of Individual Psychology, 33,* 78–85.

Walker, J. I., & Brodie, H. K. H. (1980). Paranoid disorders. In H. I. Kaplan, A. M. Freedman, & B. J. Sadock (Eds.), *Comprehensive textbook of psychiatry* (3rd ed., Vol. 2). Baltimore: Williams & Wilkins.

Watson, D. (1989). Strangers' ratings of the five robust personality factors: Evidence of a surprising convergence with self-report. *Journal of Personality and Social Psychology, 57,* 120–128.

Watson, J. B. (1913). Psychology as the behaviorist views it. *Psychological Review, 20,* 158–177.

Watson, J. B. (1930). *Behaviorism* (Rev. ed.). New York: Norton.

Watson, J. B., & Rayner, R. (1920). Conditioned emotional reactions. *Journal of Experimental Psychology, 3,* 1–14.

Weatherall, D. J. (1985). *The new genetics and clinical practice* (2nd ed.). Oxford: Oxford University Press.

Wegner, D. M. (1989). *White bears and other unwanted thoughts.* New York: Penguin.

Wegner, D. M., Schneider, D. J., Carter, S. R., & White, T. L. (1987). Paradoxical effects of thought suppression. *Journal of Personality and Social Psychology, 53,* 5–13.

Wegner, D. M., Shortt, J. W., Blake, A. W., & Page, M. S. (1990). The suppression of exciting thoughts. *Journal of Personality and Social Psychology, 58,* 409–418.

Weinberger, D. A., Schwartz, G. E., & Davidson, R. (1979). Low anxious, high anxious, and repressive coping styles: Psychometric patterns and behavioral and physiological responses to stress. *Journal of Abnormal Psychology, 88,* 369–380.

Weinberger, J. (1989). Response to Balay and Shevrin: Constructive critique or misguided attack. *American Psychologist, 44,* 1417–1419.

Weiner, B. (1978). Achievement strivings. In H. London & J. E. Exner (Eds.), *Dimensions of personality.* New York: Wiley.

Weiner, B. (1990). Attribution in personality psychology. In L. A. Pervin (Ed.), *Handbook of personality theory and research.* New York: Guilford.

Weiner, H. (1977). *Psychobiology and human disease.* New York: Elsevier.

Weiss, A. S. (1987). Shostrom's personal orientation inventory: Arguments against its basic validity. *Personality and Individual Differences, 8,* 895–903.

Wells, B. W. P. (1983). *Body and personality.* London: Longman.

Wenzlaff, R. M., Wegner, D. R., & Roper, D. W. (1988). Depression and mental control: The resurgence of unwanted negative thoughts. *Journal of Personality and Social Psychology, 55,* 882–892.

Wertheimer, M. (1972). *Fundamental issues in psychology.* New York: Holt, Rinehart & Winston.

Wertheimer, M. (1978). Humanistic psychology and the humane but tough-minded psychologist. *American Psychologist, 33,* 739–745.

Wertheimer, M. (1979). *A brief history of psychology* (Rev. ed.). New York: Holt, Rinehart & Winston.

West, S. G. (1983). Personality and prediction: An introduction. *Journal of Personality, 51,* 275–285.

West, S. G. (Ed.). (1986). Special issue: Methodological developments in personality research. *Journal of Personality, 54,* 1–331.

West, S. G., & Graziano, W. G. (Eds.). (1989). Special issue: Long-term stability and change in personality. *Journal of Personality, 57,* 175–545.

Westen, D. (1990). Psychoanalytic approaches to personality. In L. A. Pervin (Ed.), *Handbook of personality: Theory and research.* New York: Guilford.

Westen, D. (1991). Social cognition and object relations. *Psychological Bulletin, 109,* 429–455.

White, R. W. (1959). Motivation reconsidered: The concept of competence. *Psychological Review, 66,* 297–333.

White, R. W. (1966). *Lives in progress* (2nd ed.). New York: Holt.

Whiting, J. W. M., & Child, I. L. (1953). *Child-training and personality.* New Haven: Yale University Press.

Wicklund, R. A., & Braun, O. L. (1987). Incompetence and the concern with human categories. *Journal of Personality and Social Psychology, 53,* 373–382.

Wiggins, J. S. (1979). A taxonomy of trait-descriptive terms: The interpersonal domain. *Journal of Personality and Social Psychology, 37,* 395–412.

Wiggins, J. S. (1980). Circumplex models of interpersonal behavior. In L. Wheeler (Ed.), *Review of personality and social psychology* (Vol. 1). Beverly Hills, CA: Sage.

Wiggins, J. S. (1985). Interpersonal circumplex models: 1948–1983. *Journal of Personality Assessment, 49,* 626–631.

Wiggins, J. S., Phillips, N., & Trapnell, P. (1989). Circular reasoning about interpersonal behavior: Evidence concerning some untested assumptions underlying diagnostic classification. *Journal of Personality and Social Psychology, 56,* 296–305.

Wiggins, J. S., Steiger, J. H., & Gaelick, L. (1981). Evaluating circumplexity in personality data. *Multivariate Behavior Research, 16,* 263–289.

Wilhelm, R., & Jung, C. G. (1931). *The secret of the golden flower.* New York: Harcourt, Brace & World.

Willerman, L., & Cohen, D. B. (1990). *Psychopathology.* New York: McGraw-Hill.

Williams, D. E., & Page, M. M. (1989). A multi-dimensional measure of Maslow's hierarchy of needs. *Journal of Research in Personality, 23,* 192–213.

Wilson, E. O. (1975). *Sociobiology: The new synthesis.* Cambridge, MA: Harvard University Press.

Wilson, E. O. (1978). *On human nature.* Cambridge, MA: Harvard University Press.

Wilson, G. D. (1978). Introversion/extraversion. In H. London & J. E. Exner (Eds.), *Dimensions of personality.* New York: Wiley.

Wilson, J. Q., & Herrnstein, R. J. (1985). *Crime and human nature.* New York: Simon & Schuster.

Wilson, T. D., & Linville, P. W. (1982). Improving the academic performance of college freshmen: Attribution therapy revisited. *Journal of Personality and Social Psychology, 42,* 367–376.

Wilson, T. D., & Linville, P. W. (1985). Improving the performance of college freshmen with attributional techniques. *Journal of Personality and Social Psychology, 49,* 287–293.

Wimer, R. E., & Wimer, C. C. (1985). Animal behavior genetics: A search for the biological foundations of behavior. *Annual Review of Psychology, 36,* 171–218.

Winnicott, D. W. (1971). *Playing and reality.* New York: Basic Books.

Winter, D. G. (1973). *The power motive.* New York: Free Press.

Winter, D. G. (1987). Leader appeal, leader performance, and the motive profiles of leaders and followers: A study of American Presidents and elections. *Journal of Personality and Social Psychology, 52,* 196–202.

Winter, D. G. (1988). The power motive in women—and men. *Journal of Personality and Social Psychology, 54,* 510–519.

Winter, D. G., & Stewart, A. J. (1978). The power motive. In H. London & J. E. Exner (Eds.), *Dimensions of personality.* New York: Wiley.

Witkin, H. A. (1949). Perception of body position and of the position of the visual field. *Psychological Monographs, 63,* (7, Whole No. 302).

Witkin, H. A., Lewis, H. B., Hertzman, M., Machover, K., Meissner, P. B., & Wapner, S. (1954). *Personality through perception.* New York: Harper.

Wittgenstein, L. (1953). *Philosophical investigations.* New York: Macmillan.

Wolpe, J. (1958). *Psychotherapy by reciprocal inhibition.* Stanford: Stanford University Press.

Wolpe, J., & Rachman, S. J. (1960). Psychoanalytic "evidence": A critique based on Freud's case of Little Hans. *Journal of Nervous and Mental Disease, 131,* 135–147.

Wolpert, E. A. (1980). Major affective disorders. In H. I. Kaplan, A. M. Freedman, & B. J. Sadock (Eds.), *Comprehensive textbook of psychiatry* (3rd ed., Vol. 2). Baltimore: Williams & Wilkins.

Woodruffe, C. (1984). The consistency of presented personality: Additional evidence from aggregation. *Journal of Personality, 52,* 307–317.

Woodworth, R. S. (1918). *Dynamic psychology.* New York: Columbia University Press.

Woodworth, R. S. (1919). *Personal data sheet (Psychoneurotic inventory).* Chicago: Stoelting.

Wright, J. C., & Mischel, W. (1987). A conditional approach to dispositional constructs: The local predictability of social behavior. *Journal of Personality and Social Psychology, 53,* 1159–1177.

Wright, J. C., & Mischel, W. (1988). Conditional hedges and the intuitive psychology of traits. *Journal of Personality and Social Psychology, 55,* 454–469.

Wulff, D. M. (1990). *Psychology of religion: Classic and contemporary views.* New York: Wiley.

Yalom, I. D. (1980). *Existential psychotherapy.* New York: Basic Books.

Yerkes, R. M. (1943). *Chimpanzees.* New Haven: Yale University Press.

Zajonc, R. B. (1965). Social facilitation. *Science, 149,* 269–274.

Zajonc, R. B. (1980). Feeling and thinking. *American Psychologist, 35,* 151–175.

Zajonc, R. B. (1984). On the primacy of affect. *American Psychologist, 39,* 117–123.

Zajonc, R. B. (1986). The decline and rise of Scholastic Aptitude Scores: A prediction derived from the confluence model. *American Psychologist, 41,* 862–867.

Zajonc, R. B., & Bargh, J. (1980). Birth order, family size, and decline of SAT scores. *American Psychologist, 35,* 662–668.

Zajonc, R. B., & Markus, G. B. (1975). Birth order and intellectual development. *Psychological Review, 82,* 74–88.

Zimring, C. M. (1981). Stress and the designed environment. *Journal of Social Issues, 37,* 145–171.

Zirkel, S., & Cantor, N. (1990). Personal construal of life tasks: Those who struggle for independence. *Journal of Personality and Social Psychology, 58,* 172–185.

Zucker, R. A., & Gomberg, E. S. L. (1986). Etiology of alcoholism reconsidered: The case for a biopsychosocial process. *American Psychologist, 41,* 783–805.

Zuckerman, M. (1969a). Theoretical formulations. In J. P. Zubek (Ed.), *Sensory deprivation: Fifteen years of research.* New York: Appleton-Century-Crofts.

Zuckerman, M. (1969b). Variables affecting deprivation results. In J. P. Zubek (Ed.), *Sensory deprivation: Fifteen years of research.* New York: Appleton-Century-Crofts.

Zuckerman, M. (1974). The sensation seeking motive. In B. A. Maher (Ed.), *Progress in experimental personality research* (Vol. 7). New York: Academic Press.

Zuckerman, M. (1978). Sensation seeking. In H. London & J. E. Exner (Eds.), *Dimensions of personality.* New York: Wiley.

Zuckerman, M. (1985). Biological foundations of the sensation-seeking temperament. In J. Strelau, F. H. Farley, & A. Gale (Eds.), *The biological bases of personality and behavior: Theories, measurement techniques, and development* (Vol. 1). Washington, DC: Hemisphere.

Zuckerman, M. (1988). Sensation seeking, risk taking, and health. In M. P. Janisse (Ed.), *Individual differences, stress, and health psychology.* New York: Springer-Verlag.

Zuckerman, M. (1990). The psychophysiology of sensation seeking. *Journal of Personality, 58,* 313–345.

Zuckerman, M., & Brody, N. (1988). Oysters, rabbits, and people: A critique of "Race differences in behavior" by J. P. Rushton. *Personality and Individual Differences, 9,* 1025–1033.

Zuckerman, M., Kuhlman, D. M., & Camac, C. (1988). What lies beyond E and N? Factor analyses of scales believed to measure basic dimensions of personality. *Journal of Personality and Social Psychology, 54,* 96–107.

Zukav, G. (1979). *The dancing Wu Li masters: An overview of the new physics.* New York: Morrow.

Zullow, H. M., Oettingen, G., Peterson, C., & Seligman, M. E. P. (1988). Pessimistic explanatory style in the historical record: CAVing LBJ, Presidential candidates, and East versus West Berlin. *American Psychologist, 43,* 673–682.

Zytowski, D. G. (1973). Considerations in the selection and use of interest inventories. In D. G. Zytowski (Ed.), *Interest measurement.* Minneapolis: University of Minnesota Press.

NAME INDEX

A

Abelson, R. P., 68, 463
Abraham, K., 113, 177
Abrahamsen, D., 210
Abramson, L. Y., 448, 452, 459, 481–484
Adams-Webber, J. R., 475
Addams, J., 239
Adelson, J., 178
Ades, D., 218, 220–221
Adler, A., 49, 104, 122–124, 130, 137–138, 141, 174, 176, 237, 241, 303, 446–447, 462
Adorno, T. W., 51, 78
Aesop, 119
Ahadi, S., 335
Ainsworth, M. D. S., 174
Akiskal, H. S., 191
Alda, A., 111, 319
Alexander, F., 97, 199–202, 281, 326
Allen, A., 55, 340–341, 356, 376, 455
Alloy, L. B., 459, 484
Allport, F. H., 273–274
Allport, G. W., 9–10, 23, 49–50, 55, 57, 69, 71, 79, 272–281, 287, 289, 292, 296, 311, 329, 340, 345, 347–348, 391–392, 434, 460, 510
Allport, S., 431
Allred, K. D., 253
Alpert, R., 172
Altman, I., 95
Amabile, T. M., 342

American Psychiatric Association, 188, 211, 356, 359, 361
American Psychological Association, 353
Anastasi, A., 93–94, 355
Anderson, C. A., 450
Anderson, J. L., 297
Anderson, K., 450
Anderson, R. D., 180
Anderson, T. H., 208
Andreasen, N. C., 357
Andrews, J. D. W., 285
Angell, M., 262
Angleitner, A., 330
Angst, J., 176
Annis, R. C., 323
Ansbacher, H. L., 123
Anthony, E. J., 254
Archer, J., 310
Ardrey, R., 161
Argyris, C., 95, 264
Arieti, S., 483
Atkinson, J. W., 317
Averill, J. R., 251, 447

B

Bailey, S., 450
Baker, L. A., 304
Balay, J., 165
Baldessarini, R. J., 329
Balke, W. M., 472

Bandura, A., 55, 65, 91, 161, 170, 228–229, 392–393, 424–427, 436, 447, 459, 466, 468, 492–494, 498, 510
Bangert-Drowns, R. L., 383
Bannister, D., 474–475
Barban, L., 193
Barefoot, J. D., 202
Bargh, J. A., 175, 456, 458
Barker, R. G., 396
Baron, R. A., 416, 500
Barr, R., 346
Barrett, L. C., 450–451
Bartlett, F., 454
Barton, R., 480
Bassett, A. S., 357
Bateson, G., 85
Baum, A., 495
Baumeister, R. F., 161, 248
Beck, A. T., 66, 191, 476–480, 482–483, 494–495
Becker, H., 193, 220
Beethoven, L., 208
Bellack, A. S., 488
Belmont, L., 175
Bem, D. J., 55, 340–342, 346–348, 356, 372, 376, 455
Bem, S. L., 318–319, 457
Bemporad, J., 483
Benjamin, L. S., 287
Bentler, P. M., 336
Berger, P. L., 409
Berglas, S., 451
Berkowitz, L., 161
Bernstein, D. A., 489–490
Bernstein, S., 457
Berry, J. W., 323–324
Bersoff, D. N., 353
Bevan, W., 165
Bieri, J., 413, 435
Biernat, M., 318
Biletnikoff, F., 376
Binet, A., 41, 44–45, 57, 385
Binswanger, L., 242
Birch, H., 302
Birenbaum, M., 328
Blackman, S., 77–78, 435–436
Blake, A. W., 166
Blaney, P. H., 430, 458
Blatt, S. J., 178
Bliss, E. L., 192
Bloch, E., 210

Block, Jack, 237, 336–339, 422
Block, Jean H., 237, 337
Blum, G. S., 178
Blumstein, P., 310
Bobko, P., 318
Bodine, S. M., 457
Bogaert, A. F., 367, 369
Bol, M., 301
Boldizar, J. P., 173
Bonaparte, N., 208
Booth, R. F., 370
Booth-Kewley, S., 201
Boring, E. G., 30, 42–43, 46
Borkenau, P., 339
Borman, W. C., 373
Bossio, L. M., 97, 262, 484, 496
Botwin, M. D., 330
Bouffard, D. L., 345
Bowen, E., 384
Bower, G. H., 46
Bowers, K. S., 55, 344–345
Bowlby, J., 136
Brainerd, C. J., 343
Braun, O. L., 369
Bray, D. W., 353
Breland, H. M., 175
Breton, A., 221
Breuer, J., 41, 107, 145, 186, 202
Brewin, C. R., 483
Brickman, P., 420
Briggs, S. R., 373
Brigham, J. C., 382
Brodie, H. K. H., 192
Brody, B., 144
Brody, D. S., 496
Brody, N., 368
Bromberg, W., 38, 357
Bronstein, A., 165
Bronzaft, A. L., 502
Brooks, C. V., 256
Broverman, D. M., 320
Broverman, I. K., 320
Brown, B. B., 327
Brown, James A. C., 130
Brown, Jonathon D., 459
Brown, N. O., 99
Browne, A., 193, 253
Brucke, E., 106–107
Bruner, J. S., 408
Buchsbaum, M. S., 329
Bursten, B., 38

D

Dahlstrom, W. G., 202, 355
Dali, S., 64, 218, 221–222
Daly, M., 170
Daniels, D., 304
Darley, J. M., 185, 335
Darwin, C. R., 29, 42, 56, 105, 139, 271,
  297–299, 385
Davidson, R., 164
da Vinci, L., 97, 208, 218
Davis, C. M., 232
Davis, P. J., 164
Deci, E. L., 264
Deemer, D. K., 173
DeFries, J. C., 304
Dembo, T., 396
Denham, J. R., 495, 497
Derry, P. A., 440
Descartes, R., 443
deSoto, C. N., 334, 348
Deutsch, Georg, 468
Deutsch, Glenn, 376
Deutsch, M., 32
Dewey, J., 33–34, 203, 237
Dewey, T., 377
Diamond, S., 302
Dickinson, E., 208
Diener, E., 228, 335
Digman, J. M., 329
Dillehay, R. C., 52
DiMatteo, M. R., 253
Dimitrovsky, L., 320
Dobroth, K. M., 342
Dolittle, J., 72
Dollard, J., 52, 415–419, 427
Donahue, P., 319
Donovan, J. E., 89
Doob, L. W., 415
Dostoyevski, F., 98, 208
Downey, J. E., 47
Duchamp, M., 220
Dukakis, M., 217
Dunnette, M. D., 94, 373
Dusek, J. B., 319
Dworkin, B. R., 76
Dymond, R. F., 235

E

Ebbesen, E. B., 439
Edwards, A. L., 314

Edwards, V. J., 457
Efran, J. S., 62
Egeland, J. A., 357
Einstein, A., 105
Eisenhower, D., 326
Ekehammar, B., 55, 344
Ellis, A., 482, 484–485, 487–488, 495
Emerson, P. R., 169
Emery, G., 66, 479
Emmons, R. A., 509
Endler, N. S., 55, 344–345
Engel, G. L., 201
Epstein, S., 55, 76–77, 342–343, 345
Erdelyi, M. H., 163, 392
Erikson, E. H., 52, 98, 130, 133–135,
  139, 156, 208–209, 281–282, 462
Ernst, C., 176
Esterson, A., 246
Evans, G. W., 503
Evans, R. G., 457
Eysenck, H. J., 52–53, 79, 158, 171,
  197–198, 273, 291, 294–296, 300,
  302, 306, 311, 320, 324, 329–330,
  333, 349
Eysenck, S. B. G., 328

F

Fairbairn, W. R. D., 136
Falbo, T., 176
Fallon, A. E., 216
Fancher, R. E., 117, 121
Farrell, B. A., 149, 158, 160–161
Feather, N. T., 347
Feeney, J. A., 174
Fernald, G. G., 47
Ferster, C. B., 403
Festinger, L., 309, 435
Fillingim, R. B., 253
Finkelhor, D., 193, 253
Fishel, A. K., 165
Fisher, E. B., 202
Fisher, S., 80, 87, 158, 160, 169, 177–
  179, 192–193
Fiske, D. W., 314–315
Fiske, S. T., 81, 429, 437–438, 460–461
Fiske, V., 191
Flaherty, J. E., 319
Folkman, S., 493
Forbach, G. B., 457
Ford, G., 175
Forward, J. R., 420

Green, R., 192
Greenberg, J. R., 136
Greenberg, R. P., 80, 87, 158, 160, 169, 177–179, 192, 193
Greenwald, A. G., 76, 459–460
Grunberg, N. E., 495
Guion, R. M., 374–375
Gunderson, J. G., 359
Gunnar, M. R., 302
Guntrip, H., 136
Gur, R. C., 167–168, 188
Gurman, A. S., 235
Guroff, J. J., 193

H

Hackman, J. R., 94
Haley, J., 85
Hall, C. S., 66, 124, 129–131, 170, 275, 284, 300, 396, 418
Hall, J. A., 318–319
Hall, M. H. 237
Halverson, C. F., 179
Hamilton, E. W., 452
Hamilton, W. D., 299
Hammond, K. R., 472
Hansen, C. H., 164
Hansen, J. C., 370
Hansen, R. D., 164
Hansson, R. O., 373
Harackiewicz, J. M., 393
Hare, R. D., 362
Hari, M., 278
Harrington, D. M., 237
Hartmann, H., 120
Hartshorne, H., 331–332, 334
Harvey, J. H., 486
Hathaway, S. R., 48
Hazan, C., 174
Healy, J. M., 181
Heidegger, M., 241
Heider, F., 461
Heinstein, M. I., 179
Heller, J. F., 460
Hemmings, R., 206–207
Hendry, L. B., 301
Henri, V., 44
Henry, O., 134
Henry, W. A., 215
Herbener, E. S., 338
Herman, J., 136

Herrnstein, R. J., 363–367
Hersen, M., 488
Hertzig, M., 302
Hesley, J. W., 345
Hicks, A., 362
Higgins, D. S., 347
Higgins, E. T., 235, 456, 458
Higgins, R. L., 459
Hilgard, E. R., 283
Hill, C., 376
Hippocrates, 39, 188
Hirsch, J., 299
Hitler, A., 98, 135, 209–210, 303
Hockey, G. R. J., 375
Hoffman, M. L., 171
Hogan, R., 77, 334, 336, 348, 373, 374
Holland, J. L., 371–373
Hollon, S., 480, 492, 494
Holmes, T. H., 201
Holt, R. R., 355
Holzinger, K. Z., 306
Hoover, H., 326
Homburger, T., 133
Hormuth, S. E., 249
Horn, J. M., 307
Horney, K., 130–131, 138, 257, 284
Horowitz, L. M., 236, 450
Houdini, H., 208
House, J. S., 253, 496
Houston, B. K., 253
Howard, J. A., 310
Howes, D., 163
Hoyt, M. F., 176
Hugdahl, K., 404
Hughes, C. F., 202
Hull, C. L., 50, 415, 418, 424, 427
Hull, J. G., 253
Hunt, H. F., 178
Hunter, W., 173
Husserl, E., 241
Hutchings, B., 363
Hutchinson, A., 208

I

Ialongo, N., 318

J

Jaccard, J. J., 55
Jackson, V. E. (Bo), 249, 301

Kripke, S., 387
Kris, E., 120, 218
Krull, D. S., 459
Kuhl, J., 451
Kuhlman, D. M., 296
Kuhn, T. S., 60–61, 73, 509, 511
Kuiper, N. A., 440
Kulik, C. C., 383
Kulik, J. A., 383
Kunst-Wilson, W. R., 162
Kushner, H. S., 262

L

Laing, R. D., 64, 85, 226, 245–247, 269, 475
Lamb, D. H., 320
Lamiell, J. T., 511
Landers, A., 66
Landis, K. R., 496
Langer, E. J., 251–252, 494
Langinvainio, H., 307
Langston, C. A., 464
Larkin, J. H., 462
Larsen, R. J., 228
Larson, R., 250
Latané, B. T., 19, 185, 335
Laudenslager, M., 496
Lauterbach, K., 347
Law, H., 329
Lawler, E. E., 94
Lazarus, R. S., 493
Leary, T., 272, 285–287, 289, 311
Ledwidge, B., 398
Lehmann, H. E., 192
Lennon, J., 453
Leo, J., 363, 367
Lerner, M. J., 472
Levant, R. F., 236
Levenkron, J. C., 202
Levinson, D., 51, 78
Lewin, K., 32–33, 50, 57, 94, 345, 392, 395–397, 407–408, 410, 426, 454–455, 472
Lewinsohnn, P. M., 480, 491
Lewis, C. S., 219
Lewis, H. B., 192
Licht, B. G., 332
Lichtenstein, E., 498
Lidz, T., 85
Lin, E., 262, 496
Lincoln, A., 208, 239

Lindzey, G., 66, 124, 130–131, 275, 279, 284, 300, 396, 418
Linville, P. W., 248, 460, 487
Lippa, R., 279
Lloyd, C., 144
Locke, K. D., 236
Locke, S. E., 326
Loehlin, J. C., 293, 304, 307–308, 324
Loevinger, J., 105
Loewenberg, P., 209
Logue, A. W., 399
Lohr, M. J., 327
Lombroso, C., 272, 363
London, I. D., 397
London, M., 353
Lord, C. G., 347
Lorenz, K. S., 161
Lowell, E. I., 317
Luborsky, L., 150–154, 196–198
Luckmann, T., 409
Luther, M., 98, 135, 208
Lykken, D. T., 362
Lynn, M., 368

M

Maccoby, M., 181
MacCorquodale, K., 431
MacDonald, K. B., 358
MacFarlane, K., 108
Machiavelli, N., 272
MacKinnon, D. W., 373–374
Madden, J., 188
Maddi, S. R., 163–164, 252, 348
Magaro, P. A., 458
Magnusson, D., 55, 344–345
Magritte, R., 222
Maher, B. A., 37
Maher, W. B., 37
Mahoney, M. J., 492
Maier, S. F., 448, 450, 496
Manners, Miss, 346
Manson, C., 127, 339
Marcuse, H., 99
Marks, I. M., 189
Markus, G. B., 175
Markus, H., 248, 441–442, 456–458
Marlowe, D., 164
Marolla, F. A., 175
Marsh, H. W., 327
Marshall, W. L., 490

Martin, C. E., 159
Martin, R. P., 321
Martindale, A. E., 296
Martindale, C., 296
Marx, K., 105, 131
Maslow, A. H., 64, 225–227, 237–241, 255–256, 260, 262–263, 269, 332, 345, 348, 391, 510
Masson, J. M., 108
Masters, W. H., 206, 237, 489
Matarazzo, J. D., 355
Matthews, K. A., 202
Matthews-Simonton, S., 260
Maule, T., 376
Mavin, G. H., 458
May, M. A., 331–332, 334
May, R., 225–226, 241–244, 248, 269
Mazur, A., 161
McAdams, D. P., 54–55, 212, 510
McCain, G., 60
McCall, R. J., 225
McClearn, G. E., 304, 307
McClelland, D. C., 52, 284, 316–318, 326
McCormick, E. J., 95
McCrae, R. R., 329–330, 336
McDermott, J., 462
McGillivray, B. C., 357
McGinnies, E., 163
McGregor, D., 263–265
McGuire, C. V., 24
McGuire, W. J., 24
McKinley, J. C., 48
McKinney, W. T., 191
McKusick, V. A., 308
McNeal, J. U., 380
McQuiston, J. T., 247
Mednick, M. T., 320
Mednick, S. A., 363–364
Meehl, P. E., 77, 355–356, 366, 431
Meer, J., 81
Meichenbaum, D. H., 492, 495
Meissner, W. W., 196–197
Mellon, J., 153–154
Mellsop, G., 362
Mellstrom, M., 328
Mendel, G., 298
Mendelsohn, E., 165
Mendelsohn, G. A., 510
Mershon, B., 295
Mesmer, F. A., 39–40
Messer, S., 178

Messick, S., 383
Metalsky, G. I., 484
Metcalf, J., 501
Metzner, H. L., 253
Metzner, R., 301
Meyer, G. D., 472
Meyers, J., 321
Milgram, S., 10–11, 91–92, 335, 501
Miller, D. T., 463
Miller, G. A., 93
Miller, N. E., 52, 76, 415–419, 427, 491–492
Miller, S. M., 251, 447, 496
Millon, T., 360
Mineka, S., 321
Miner, J. B., 241
Mischel, W., 10, 53–55, 57, 76–77, 141, 315, 331–334, 336, 339–344, 348–349, 352, 373, 408, 421–424, 427, 432, 436, 439, 442, 456, 480
Mischler, E. G., 86
Mitchell, S. A., 136
Mixon, D., 91
Mollinger, R. N., 218
Monroe, M., 68
Monson, T. C., 345
Montag, I., 328
Monty, R. A., 251
Mook, D. G., 161
Moreland, R. L., 442
Moreno, J. L., 256
Morgan, C. D., 48, 282
Morgan, E., 46
Moses, 98, 208
Mosher, D. L., 179–180
Moskowitz, D. S., 342
Mossey, J. M., 496
Mowrer, O. H., 415
Mozart, W. A., 387
Mueller, H. S., 202
Mull, H. K., 46
Mullin, E., 227
Munsterberg, H., 94
Murphy, D. L., 329
Murphy, G., 50
Murphy, M., 256, 258
Murray, H. A., 48–50, 55, 57, 93, 272, 281–284, 311, 316, 325, 330, 343, 345, 348, 372–375, 379, 446–447, 462, 510
Mussen, P. E., 179
Myers, I. B., 181

N

Namath, J., 376
Nash, J. M., 358
Neale, M. C., 347
Neill, A. S., 203, 205–207
Neill, Z., 207
Neimeyer, R. A., 408
Neisser, U., 455
Nelkin, D., 358
Nemiah, J. C., 188–189
Nesselroade, J. R., 306
Nevill, D., 323
Newcomb, M. D., 336
Newman, E., 320
Newman, H. H., 306
Newman, J. P., 295
Newman, O., 106
Newton, I., 29, 208
Nezu, A. M., 484
Nezu, C. M., 484
Nezu, V. A., 484
Nicholls, J. G., 332
Nichols, R. C., 304
Nicholson, R. A., 77
Niederland, W., 203
Nietzel, M. T., 489–490
Nietzsche, F., 241
Nisbett, R. E., 63, 75, 315, 438, 486
Nixon, R. M., 68, 209–211
Nolen-Hoeksema, S., 483
Noller, P., 174, 329
Nordby, V. J., 129
Nordlie, J., 188
Norem, J. K., 465–466
Norman, W. T., 329
Nowicki, S., 289
Nurius, P., 248, 458

O

O'Connor, B., 289
O'Heeron, R. C., 201–202
O'Leary, A., 498
O'Neill, E., 82–84
Ochberg, R. L., 55
Odbert, H. S., 9–10, 287, 292
Oettingen, G., 152
Office of Strategic Services Assessment
    Staff, 93, 373–374
Ogilvie, D. M., 248

Ohman, A., 404
Oltman, P. K., 323
Orne, M. T., 92
Ornstein, R. E., 248
Osgood, D. W., 77, 432, 436
Ostendorf, F., 339
Ostrom, T., 461
Overton, W. F., 62
Owen, D., 383–384
Oyserman, D., 458
Ozer, D. J., 334–335
Ozer, E. M., 494

P

Packard, V., 213–214
Paddock, J. R., 289
Page, Michelle S., 166
Page, Monte M., 240
Pantzar, J. T., 357
Pappenheim, B., 145
Parisi, T., 310
Park, B., 440
Parker, J. W., 327
Pascal, B., 188
Patterson, C. M., 295
Paul, 484
Paul, G. L., 489
Paunonen, S. V., 342
Pavlov, I., 36, 399–401
Payne, T. J., 457
Peabody, D., 329
Peake, P. K., 341–343, 422
Pearce, J. K., 358
Pearl, R. A., 332
Pedersen, N. L., 307
Pedhazur, E. J., 318
Pelham, B. W., 459
Pennebaker, J. W., 201–202
Perlmuter, L. C., 251
Perls, F. S., 256–258
Perris, C., 480
Perry, J. C., 136
Pershing, J., 47
Persons, J. B., 480
Pervin, L. A., 334, 336, 512
Peters, T. J., 265–266
Peterson, C., 77, 97, 152, 191, 262, 432,
    436–437, 447, 449–452, 468, 481–
    482, 484, 496–497
Peterson, D. R., 315

Ryback, D., 236
Ryle, G., 430

S

Sackeim, H., 152, 167–168, 188
Sadalla, E. K., 345
Salinas, C., 279
Salovey, P., 495
Sampson, R., 173
Sande, G. N., 456
Sanford, N., 50–51, 78, 510
Sarason, I. G., 322
Sarna, S., 307
Sartre, J.-P., 230, 241, 387
Sayers, G., 376
Scarf, M., 260–261
Scarr, S., 24, 304
Schachter, S., 19, 176, 485–486
Schaffer, H. R., 169
Schank, R. C., 463
Schapiro, M., 218
Schatzman, M., 247
Scheier, I. H., 293
Scheier, M. F., 463, 465, 496
Scher, S. J., 161
Schill, T., 170, 178
Schlenker, B. R., 460
Schlien, J. M., 236
Schmidt, D. E., 95
Schneider, D. J., 166, 455
Schooler, C., 176, 329
Schramm, T., 376
Schreber, D. P., 146–147, 203
Schubert, H. J. P., 175
Schuldberg, D., 354, 356
Schulman, P., 449–451
Schutte, N. S., 345
Schwartz, B., 400
Schwartz, G. E., 164
Schwartz, J. P., 318
Schwartz, P., 310
Schwarzenegger, A., 424
Schweitzer, A., 239
Scott, J. P., 302
Scott, Walter D., 96
Scott, William A., 77, 432–437, 454, 468–469
Sears, P. S., 170
Sears, R. R., 158, 160, 172, 327, 415

Sedgwick, P., 246
Sedney, M. A., 318
Segal, E. M., 60
Segal, Z. V., 441, 480
Seligman, M. E. P., 152, 191, 195, 243, 362, 404, 448–452, 466, 480–484, 486, 496
Shakespeare, W., 15, 119, 188, 217, 219
Shapiro, E., 496
Shaver, P., 174
Shaw, B. F., 66, 479
Shaw, G. B., 98, 135
Shaw, J. S., 319
Shay, K. A., 253
Sheldon, W. H., 50, 273, 300–301
Sherman, S. J., 440
Sherrod, D. R., 501
Shevrin, H., 165, 168
Shields, J., 324
Shmavonian, B. M., 323
Shoda, Y., 422
Shortt, J. W., 166
Shostak, M., 309
Shostrom, E. L., 239
Siegel, B. S., 97, 260, 262
Signorella, M. L., 320
Siladi, M., 457
Silberman, E. K., 193
Silver, R. L., 254
Silverman, A. J., 323
Silverman, L. H., 144, 165–166
Silverman, M. A., 145
Silverstein, A., 79
Simon, D. P., 462
Simon, H. A., 462
Simon, T., 44
Simonton, O. C., 260–262
Simonton, S., 260, 262
Singer, Jaffa, 320
Singer, Jerome E., 447, 485–486, 502–503
Singer, Jerome L., 218, 248–249, 327, 468
Singer, M. T., 359
Sirhan, S., 339
Sirkin, M., 179–180
Skinner, B. F., 50, 79, 231, 402–403, 407, 415, 443, 491
Smart, J. C., 352
Smedslund, J., 426
Smith, J., 442

Smith, M. L., 55
Smith, R. E., 493
Smith, T. W., 253
Smuts, B., 309
Snyder, C. R., 459
Snyder, Mark, 346
Snyder, Melvin L., 451
Snyderman, M., 308
Socrates, 208
Sokol, M., 181
Solano, C., 334, 348
Solomon, R. L., 163
Solomon, S., 501
Somers, S., 381
Sontag, S., 262
Sophocles, 217
Spearman, C., 291
Spence, J. T., 457
Spence, K. W., 321, 424
Spencer, H., 33
Spielberger, C. D., 320–321
Spock, B., 203–205, 453
Springer, S. P., 468
Stagner, R., 50
Stanley, J. C., 81, 88
Steiger, J. H., 288
Stein, J. A., 336
Stelmack, R. M., 324
Stephenson, W., 235
Stern, G. G., 287
Stern, W., 45
Sternberg, R. J., 460
Stevenson, J., 347
Stewart, A. J., 181, 326
Stollak, G. E., 318
Storms, M. D., 486
Stringfield, D. O., 341
Strong, E., 369
Stross, L., 168
Struening, E. L., 496
Stunkard, A. J., 447, 452–453, 497
Suler, J. R., 218
Sullivan, H. S., 137, 284–285, 287
Sulloway, F. J., 38, 63, 106
Suls, J., 55, 460
Summerton, J., 496
Sutherland, G. R., 358
Swan, J. A., 503
Swann, W. B., 459
Swede, S. W., 279–280
Sweeney, P. D., 450

Syme, S. L., 253
Szasz, T. S., 53

T

Taft, W., 326
Tancredi, L., 358
Taylor, J. M., 173
Taylor, M. C., 318–319
Taylor, R. B., 495, 497
Taylor, S. E., 81, 429, 437–438, 459, 461, 495
Teasdale, J. D., 448
Tellegen, A., 55, 307, 341, 355
Tennen, H., 451
Terman, L. M., 45
Tetenbaum, T. J., 318
Tetlock, P. E., 279–280
Thigpen, C. H., 84
Thoits, P. A., 484
Thomas, A., 302–303, 305
Thompson, S., 251, 447
Thorndike, E. L., 36, 47, 94, 291, 400
Thorne, A., 347
Thorngate, W., 67
Thurston, J. R., 179
Tolman, E. C., 50, 405
Tolstoy, L., 166
Tomkins, C., 256
Tooby, J., 308
Tota, M. E., 458
Trapnell, P., 289
Treffert, D. A., 387
Tribich, D., 178
Trilling, L., 218
Trotsky, L., 208
Truax, C. B., 235
Truman, H., 175, 377
Turk, D. C., 494
Turnbull, C., 309
Turnbull, W., 463
Twain, M., 498

U

Ullian, J. S., 60, 77
Umberson, D., 496
Urban, H. B., 226
Ureda, J. W., 495, 497

V

Vaihinger, H., 123
Vaillant, G. E., 120, 154–157, 187, 193–
194, 196, 337, 365, 450, 452, 496
van der Kolk, B. A., 136
Van Gogh, V., 211–212
Van Hook, E., 458
van Rillaer, J., 476
Van Treuren, R. R., 253
Vandenberg, S. G., 323
Vannoy, J. S., 435
Varghese, F., 362
Vernon, P. E., 50, 279, 315
Villanova, P., 449
Viorst, M., 204
Virnelli, S., 253
Vogel, S. R., 320
Volkmer, R. E., 347

W

Wachtel, P., 347
Waggoner, M., 420
Wagner, M. E., 175
Walker, J. I., 192
Wallace, A. R., 29
Walters, R., 424
Ward, J. V., 173
Washburn, M. F., 46
Washington, G., 175
Waterman, J., 108
Waterman, R. H., 265–266
Watson, D., 330
Watson, J. B., 35–37, 67, 75, 90, 203,
237, 397, 399, 443
Waxler, N., 86
Weakland, J., 85
Weatherall, D. J., 358
Wegner, D. M., 166–167
Weinberger, D. A., 164
Weinberger, J., 165, 318
Weiner, B., 317, 483
Weiner, H., 201
Weinstein, N., 502–503
Weintraub, J. K., 463
Weiss, A. S., 240
Wells, B. W. P., 302
Wells, K., 420
Wenzlaff, R. M., 166
Wertheimer, Max, 31–32, 237
Wertheimer, Michael, 30, 49, 70, 256

West, S. G., 54, 55, 333
Westen, D., 136, 158
White, Robert W., 81, 447
White, Rodney, 504–506
White, T. L., 166
Whiting, J. W. M., 52, 179
Wicklund, R. A., 369
Wiebe, D. J., 253
Wiggins, J. S., 272, 288–289, 311, 330
Wilhelm, R., 128
Willerman, L., 190, 307, 357
Williams, D. E., 240
Williams, R. B., 202
Wilson, E. O., 56, 299
Wilson, G. D., 158, 171, 324
Wilson, J. Q., 363–367
Wilson, K. L., 173
Wilson, M., 170
Wilson, T. W., 75, 315, 438, 487
Wilson, W., 326
Wimer, C. C., 299
Wimer, R. E., 299
Winnicott, D. W., 136
Winter, D. G., 318, 325–326
Witkin, H. A., 53, 322–323
Wittgenstein, L., 3
Wittig, B. A., 174
Wolfer, J., 494
Wolpe, J., 149, 488
Wolpert, E. A., 191
Woodruffe, C., 343
Woodward, J., 85
Woodworth, R. S., 34, 47, 93, 354, 373
Worrell, L., 318
Wortman, C. B., 254, 327, 357
Wright, J. C., 421
Wrightsman, L. S., 382
Wulff, D. M., 248
Wundt, W., 30–31, 35, 43, 56, 90, 229
Wurf, E., 248, 456

Y

Yalom, I. D., 244
Yerkes, R. M., 302
Yinon, Y., 320

Z

Zahn, T. P., 329
Zajonc, R. B., 162, 175–176, 417, 442,
468

Cognitive complexity, 413, 435
Cognitive map, 406, 503–507
Cognitive therapy, 479–480, 483
Collective unconscious, 126–129
Compulsion to repeat, 121
Confound, 78, 86–87
Consciousness, 229, 248, 274
Consistency controversy, 10–11, 20–21,
    53–54, 76–77, 276–277, 315, 331–
    336, 352, 421
    reactions to Mischel's position on, 54,
        336–348
    summary of Mischel's position on,
        332–333
Core conflictual relationship theme
    method, 152–154
Correlation (correlation coefficient),
    19–21, 43, 142, 331, 334–336
Correlational studies, 84–89, 96, 158,
    443–445, 451–452
Creativity, 97, 217–218
Criminality, 363–367
Crowding, 392, 500–502

D

Dadaism, 220–222
Daydreaming, 217, 248–249
Death instinct, 121–122, 161
Defense mechanisms, 118–120, 156–
    157
Defensive pessimism, 465–466
Delay of gratification, 422–423
Depression, 66, 190–191, 329, 430, 436,
    440, 450, 458, 474, 477–478, 480–
    484, 491
Diagnostic council, 282
Dreams, 109–110, 117, 209, 217
Drive, 34, 415

E

Effectance motivation, 447
Ego, 117–118
Ego mechanisms (*see* Defense
    mechanisms)
Ego psychology, 119–120, 133, 196–
    197
Ego-control, 337
Ego-resiliency, 337
Enlightenment effect, 185–186, 384

Environmental psychology, 95, 499–507
Essence, 228
Evolution, 18, 34, 42, 56, 71, 105, 271,
    297–300, 309–311, 385, 404, 512
Existence, 228
Existentialism, 64, 241–245
Experience sampling, 249–250
Experimental artifact, 92
Experiments, 89–93, 143, 158, 168–169
Explanatory style, 448–452, 481–482,
    496

F

Factor (factor analysis), 52, 289–296
Family resemblance, 3
    of cognitive-behavioral theories, 392–
        394
    of humanistic theories, 226–230
    of personal control theories, 452–453
    of personality, 6–8
    of psychodynamic theories, 104–105
    of trait theories, 271–272
Field dependence, 53, 322–324
Fixed-role therapy, 476
Flow, 250–251
Free association, 107, 188
Frustration-aggression hypothesis, 415–
    416
Functional autonomy of motives, 276
Functionalism, 31, 33–35, 93

G

Gender, 24, 91, 115–116, 122, 310,
    318–320, 363, 371, 457
Generality, 76–77, 84
Genetics, 55, 293, 296, 298–300, 306–
    309, 320, 323–324, 328–329, 356–
    359, 363–367, 512 (*see also*
    Evolution)
Germ model, 37–38
Gestalt, 31–32
Gestalt psychology, 31–33, 65, 97, 98,
    395–398, 455

H

Hardiness, 252–253
Health (health psychology), 55, 97, 152,
    198–202, 251–253, 258–262, 326,
    450, 452, 495–499

Helping alliance, 196–197
Hierarchy of motives, 237–241
Homosexuality, 146–148, 191–192
Human potential movement, 256–258
Humanistic paradigm, 50, 53, 59, 64, 69,
    70, 71, 72, 73, 74, 75, 77, 78, 79, 80,
    96, 97, 99, 225–231, 392, 437, 511
Humor, 109–111
Hypnosis, 39–41, 188
Hysteria, 39, 40–41, 61, 145, 148, 186,
    188

I

Id, 118
Idiographic-nomothetic issue, 50, 79–
    80, 278–280
    modified idiographic approach, 55,
    340–342
Implicit personality theory, 455
Inferiority, 122–123
Instinct, 158
Instrumental conditioning (*see*
    Learning)
Intelligence testing (*see also* Social
    intelligence), 42–46, 175–176, 271,
    313, 382–385
    multiple intelligences, 385–388
Interactionism, 55, 344–348
Interest inventory, 369–370
Interpersonal trust, 420
Intrinsic motivation, 264–265
Introspection (*see* Self-report)
Introversion-extraversion, 128, 294–295,
    307, 324, 338–339

J

Jury selection, 381–382

L

Learned helplessness, 447–452
Learning, 36–37, 52, 65, 94
    types of, 399–406
Libido, 104, 187
Life instinct, 121, 159–161
Life space, 32, 395–396, 454
Life task, 462–465
Literary criticism, 218–219
Locus of control, 53, 419–420

M

Machiavellianism, 272
Macho personality constellation, 179–
    180
Medical model, 38
Mental control, 167
Mere exposure, 162
Mesmerism (*see* Hypnosis)
Metapsychological proposition, 143–
    144, 247–248
Midrange theory, 511
Minnesota Multiphasic Personality
    Inventory (MMPI), 48, 355
Model of human nature, 70, 95
    defined, 11–12
    people as actors, 15–16
    people as animals, 13
    people as computers, 14–15
    people as energy systems, 13
    people as fields, 14
    people as machines, 13–14
    people as pilots, 16
    people as scientists, 15
    people as white rats, 13
Modeling, 66, 424–425
Moral behavior (moral development;
    moral reasoning), 118, 172–173,
    239, 299, 337–338, 422–423
Multiple personality disorder, 84, 192–
    193

N

Natural history method, 154–157
Nature versus nurture (*see* Evolution)
Need, 130–132, 282–284
NeoFreudians, 104, 105, 124, 129–135,
    437, 446
Neurosis (neurotic; neuroticism), 109,
    130 131, 218, 274, 294–295, 307
Noise, 502–503

O

Object relations (object relations
    theory), 104, 136–137
Obsessive-compulsive disorder, 146,
    189–190
Oedipus complex, 115–116, 136, 143,
    145, 169–172, 195

Regression, 119, 396, 416–417
  in the service of the ego, 218
Reliability, 21, 76–77, 84
REP (Role Constructs Repertory) Test,
    411–412, 431, 435–436
Repression, 53, 119, 164–165, 272, 416
Resistance, 196
Response set, 315
Rorschach, 48, 333, 355

S

Schema, 438–439, 441–442, 454–460
Schizophrenia, 81, 85, 126, 226, 245–
    247, 435, 474–475
Secondary process, 105–106, 193
Seduction hypothesis (*see* Childhood
    sexuality)
Self, 16, 24, 128, 233, 276–277
Self-actualization, 50, 64, 226, 228, 239,
    379
Self-deception, 167–168
Self-efficacy, 55, 425
Self-esteem, 326–327
Self-monitoring, 346
Self-report, 31, 75, 78, 81, 429–431, 438
Self-theory, 52, 231–236, 267–269
Sensation seeking, 327–329, 414
Sex role (*see* Gender)
Social desirability, 314–315
Social intelligence, 423–424, 460–466
Social learning theory, 65, 414–426,
    510–511
Social support, 253–254
Sociobiology, 56, 299–300, 310–311
Structural theory, 116–118 (*see also* Id;
    Ego; Superego)
Structuralism, 30–31
  reactions against, 31–37
Sublimation, 119
Subliminal stimulation, 165–166, 214–
    215

Summerhill, 205–207
Superego, 118, 193
Surrealism, 220–222
Symbolic interactionism, 284
Symptom-context method, 150–152

T

Teleology, 123
Television polls, 380–381
Temperament, 273, 302–306
Thema, 284
TAT (Thematic Apperception Test), 48,
    282, 316–317, 325
Theory X versus Theory Y, 262–264
Topographical theory, 108 (*see also*
    Unconscious)
Trait paradigm, 59, 64–65, 69, 70–75,
    77–81, 94, 96, 97, 99, 271–273,
    311, 313–316, 329–331, 348–349,
    351, 354, 388, 511
Traits, 8–10, 275–276 (*see also*
    Consistency controversy)
  common, 277–280
  personal, 277–280
  source, 292
  surface, 292
Trait stability, 336–338
Transference, 107, 152–154
Type (typology), 296–297 (*see also*
    Character type)
Type A coronary-prone behavior
    pattern, 97, 202

U

Unconscious, 63, 97, 108–112, 117,
    162–169, 281

V

Validity, 21–22, 77–79, 84

ILLUSTRATION CREDITS

CHAPTER 1:   Page 4: Brown Brothers; 12: (left) © Walter Chandoha; (right) AP/Wide World Photos; 15: STAR TREK. Copyright © 1966, 1991 by Paramount Pictures. All Rights Reserved.

CHAPTER 2:   Page 35: Courtesy of Professor Benjamin Harris, University of Wisconsin—Parkside. Taken from John Watson's 1919 film, *Experimental Investigation of Babies;* 40: The Bettmann Archive; 45: Signal Corps Photo/National Archives III-SC-386; 51: © Dennis Budd Gray/Stock, Boston.

CHAPTER 3:   Page 76: © Bob Daemmrich/Stock, Boston; 85: Photofest; 95: © Nancy J. Pierce/Photo Researchers, Inc.

CHAPTER 4:   Page 106: AP/Wide World Photos; 114: © James Holland/Stock, Boston; 125: AP/Wide World Photos; 129: *The Collected works of C. G. Jung,* trans. R. F. C. Hull, Bollingen Series XX, Vol. 9, I: *The Archetypes and the Collective Unconscious.* Copyright © 1959, 1969 by Princeton University Press. Figures 1 and 40 (between pp. 356 and 357) reprinted with permission of Princeton University Press; 135: © Tim Davis/Photo Researchers, Inc.

CHAPTER 5:   160: © Elizabeth Crews; 171: Photofest; 180: The Bettmann Archive.

CHAPTER 6:   Page 186: © Robert Brenner/Photo Edit; 209: AP/Wide World Photos; 212: The Bettmann Archive; 214: Photofest; 216: ©Arthur Wolff/FPG; 219: Assemblage: metal wheel, mounted on painted wood stool, overall $50\frac{1}{2}''$ x $25\frac{1}{2}''$ x $16\frac{5}{8}''$. Sidney and Harriet Janis collection. Gift to the Museum of Modern Art, New York; 220: Courtesy Alexander Iolas Gallery, New York; 221: Oil and collage on composition board, $9\frac{3}{8}''$ x $13\frac{3}{4}''$. Sidney and Harriet Janis collection. Gift to the Museum of Modern Art, New York; 222: Courtesy Robert des Charnes.

CHAPTER 7:   Page 227: © Susan Kuklin 1989/Photo Researchers, Inc.; 232: © Barbara Rios/Photo Researchers, Inc.; 233: (left) © 1990 Myrleen Ferguson/Photo Edit; (right) © 1990 David Young-Wolff/Photo Edit; 234: Courtesy of the Center for the Study of the Person; 244: © George Azar/The Image Works; 246: UPI/Bettmann; 251: © David Young-Wolff/Photo Edit; 255: The Bettmann Archive; 257: Deke Simon; 259: AP/Wide World Photos; 263: © Richard Hutchings/Photo Edit; 266: © Mary Wolf/TSW; 267: © Elizabeth Crews.

ILLUSTRATION CREDITS

COPYRIGHTS AND ACKNOWLEDGMENTS

PAGE 134:   Adapted from CHILDHOOD AND SOCIETY, Second Edition, by Erik H. Erikson, by permission of W. W. Norton & Company, Inc. Copyright 1950, © 1963 by W. W. Norton & Company, Inc. Copyright renewed 1978 by Erik H. Erikson.

PAGE 179:   Adapted from Table 1 from "Measuring a Macho Personality Constellation," by D. L. Mosher and M. Sirskin, *Journal of Research in Personality, 18,* Copyright © 1984 by Academic Press. Reprinted by permission.

PAGES 238–239:   Material adapted from MOTIVATION AND PERSONALITY, 2nd ed. by Abraham H. Maslow. Copyright 1954 by Harper & Row, Publishers, copyright © 1970 by Abraham H. Maslow. Reprinted by permission of HarperCollins Publishers.

PAGE 372:   Table 10-2: From "Faculty Teaching goals: A Test of Holland's Theory," by J. C. Smart. *Journal of Educational Psychology, 74,* pp. 180–188. Copyright 1982 by the American Psychological Association. Adapted by permission of the publisher and the author.

A   1
B   2
C   3
D   4
E   5
F   6
G   7
H   8
I   9
J   0